GAINES & COLEMAN

FLORIDA

REAL ESTATE PRINCIPLES, PRACTICES & LAW

29TH EDITION

Broker = 6mo
After Sales.
chubb. INS, source

LINDA L. CRAWFORD

Comp. Software.
"Top agent"

$1 - 6 = 45^8$ exam

Dearborn™
Real Estate Education

President: Roy Lipner
Publisher: Evan M. Butterfield
Associate Publisher: Louise Benzer
Development Editor: Tony Peregrin
Managing Editor, Production: Daniel Frey
Creative Director: Lucy Jenkins
Typesetting: Elizabeth Pitts

by Dearborn Financial Publishing, Inc.®

Published by Dearborn™ Real Estate Education
a division of Dearborn Financial Publishing, Inc.®
30 South Wacker Drive
Chicago, Illinois 60606-7481
(312) 836-4400
www.dearbornRE.com

Contents

Preface

Congratulations! Your decision to pursue a career in real estate in Florida is an exciting one. You probably have many questions about real estate as a career, requirements for becoming licensed, and real estate in general. I have made every attempt to address your questions. The material is concise, yet presented in sufficient detail to facilitate your understanding. The content conforms to the Florida Division of Real Estate's prescribed Florida Real Estate Commission (FREC) Course I Syllabus for the prelicense course for sales associates.

As with any profession, the real estate profession has an abundance of terms unique to the industry. Key terms are presented at the beginning of each Chapter. Learn what these terms mean and apply them in your real estate discussions. To aid your learning process, each term that is presented in a key term section is defined in the corresponding Chapter. The term will appear in **boldface** type immediately preceding its definition. You should master these definitions in preparation for your licensing examination.

There are literally hundreds of real estate terms that you will use and apply in your professional career. However, only a limited number of these terms appear in the key term sections. This is because a priority system has been used to help you plan your preparation. Bolded key terms are top priority terms. Throughout the Chapters you will also find italicized terms. These are important real estate terms that you should understand and be able to apply in your real estate discussions. However, it is not necessary to be able to "recite" a precise definition for italicized terms.

I have also included learning objectives for each Chapter's Overview section. The objectives have been carefully selected to coordinate with the key concepts in the Course Syllabus. Think of the learning objectives as a "road map" to help guide you into your journey toward licensure. As you complete each Chapter, be sure also to complete the Review Questions section that follows it so that you can see how well you have mastered the content presented in the Chapter.

You will note also that in the left margins, each line of the text is numbered for easy reference. In the right margins you will find scales with Florida Statute and Administrative Rule numbers below. I have cross-referenced the material in your textbook with the FREC statutes and rules. You are encouraged to read the actual laws and rules in the Handbook. They may be downloaded from the Division of Real Estate's Web site at: **http://www.myflorida.com/dbpr/re/frec_statutes_and _rules.shtml.**

Text boxes are featured in your textbook. These boxes contain valuable information. The boxes titled To Remember contain learning crutches called acronyms to help you recall certain information. Be sure to study these. Other text boxes feature excerpts of Florida statutes and rules for easy reference. The text boxes titled Formula feature arithmetic formulas that you must be able to apply. You will find all of these special features very valuable as you delve into this book. I am excited for you and wish you the very best as you embark on your new career.

I would like to acknowledge the original authors of this book, George Gaines, Jr. and David S. Coleman. George and David's dedication to real estate education set the level of excellence in Florida. They never settled for second best. They always covered each topic in your textbook in the detail necessary for the reader to understand the concept. It has been a pleasure working with them.

I would be remiss if I did not take a moment to thank the very special people who contributed to this book. Prior to developing this edition of your book, I received specific comments and suggestions that I incorporated into this edition to assure you of the very best quality textbook. Special thanks are extended to Jack Bennett, Instructor, Gold Coast School of Real Estate; Nancy Culler, Instructor, Watson School of Real Estate; Valleri Crabtree, Director of Instructor and Course Development, IFREC Real Estate Schools, Inc.; Sandi M. Kellogg, Instructor, Central Florida Community College; Dallie Moriarity, Instructor, Cooke Real Estate School; and Joe Schwartz, Instructor, Bob Hogue School of Real Estate. Valleri Crabtree provided many fresh ideas to this edition of the textbook. Her attention to detail and support are most appreciated. Sandi Kellogg has reviewed several editions of this textbook. She continues to be an important reason why this book gets better with each new edition. I am grateful to Joe Schwartz for his ideas regarding the Chapter concerning legal descriptions. Thanks to Joe's suggestions this edition features several enhanced exhibits that will assist students' understanding of legal descriptions. Nancy Culler also provided valuable suggestions to this edition of the textbook. She is a knowledgeable and enthusiastic educator. Jack Bennett and Dallie Moriarity were also valuable reviewers. Jack reviewed many of the revisions to this edition as they were developed, and Dallie gave me valuable input based on her experience with teaching the sales associate course.

This book is coordinated with additional study tools designed to assist you with mastery of the material. Many students choose the Florida Sales Associate Prelicensing Key Point Review Audio CD, which is designed to aid aspiring real estate sales associates in successfully completing the prelicensing course, end-of-course exam, and state licensing exam. If you are concerned about the real estate math associated with this course, consider the companion book *Real Estate Math: What You Need to Know.* If you are looking for a concise overview of the entire course and practice questions to help prepare you for your licensing examination, we recommend *Florida Real Estate Exam Manual.*

I wish you the very best in your endeavor and would like to hear from you. Please be sure to complete the **Feedback Sheet** located in the back of your book. It can be carefully removed without damaging your book. Please complete and send it to the addressee named. Your comments are personally read by the author. Feedback from students like you is a valuable consideration in revising future editions of this book. I welcome your input!

Linda L. Crawford
November, 2005

CHAPTER 1

The Real Estate Business

[handwritten: Lady up Front or mirror Look at Misses]

[handwritten: Get them To Listen - Like you. - Trust them.]

■ KEY TERMS

absentee owners	comparative market analysis (CMA)	property management
agricultural		real estate business
appraisal	counselors	residential
business brokers	dedication *[handwritten: Start.]*	restrictive covenants
business opportunity brokerage	farm area *[handwritten: = #50 houses]*	subdivision plat map
	follow-up	

*[handwritten: * Leave Cards every where.]*

*[handwritten boxed: * Picture on Cards + Signs Full Name]*

■ OVERVIEW

The purpose of this Chapter is to introduce the reader to the real estate business. The Chapter discusses real estate brokerage, development, and construction.

After completing this Chapter, the student should be able to:

- define *farm area;*

- identify reasons why property management has grown in importance;

- define *absentee owner;*

- define *residential* real estate;

[handwritten: Build repore.]

- describe the appraisal process;

- identify the reasons for the method of compensation for appraisal services; and

[handwritten: Follow up 6 Time a yr Min.]

- distinguish among the three categories of residential construction.

[handwritten: Buy Door Knocker.]

■ AN INTRODUCTION TO THE REAL ESTATE BUSINESS

The term **real estate business** (profession) refers to the industry or occupation whose activities involve real property transactions handled by licensed real estate professionals. The real estate business consists of many activities including real estate brokerage, development and construction, and investment. Real estate brokerage is examined in detail because the majority of licensed professionals are involved in brokerage.

Real estate brokers provide specialized service for others in return for compensation in the form of a commission, fee, or other valuable consideration. Real estate licensees work as (1) transaction brokers providing limited representation, as (2) nonrepresentatives facilitating transactions, or as (3) agents for others. Today a real estate licensee is paid to handle other people's properties because he or she is a professional who provides specialized service and expertise in at least three areas:

1. *Details of property transfer.* A competent real estate practitioner must know the economic and legal intricacies associated with transfers of title, property taxes, financing, and local zoning ordinances.

2. *Knowledge of market conditions.* No market is ever completely static. Market conditions are concerned with price changes over time. Changes in market conditions also may result from changes in income tax laws, building moratoriums, and fluctuations in supply and demand.

3. *Knowledge of how to market real estate or businesses.* To be successful, licensees must know how to market real estate and/or businesses. The sale presentation most effective when working with a physician who is relocating to a new city may be completely different from the approach used to assist the owner of an expanding gourmet coffee bar in choosing an additional location.

Marketing also includes expertise in locating prospects. For example, a real estate professional who specializes in finding homes for relocated physicians will develop contacts with the personnel in various local hospitals who work as liaisons with new hospital staff. While there may be exceptions, the bulk of evidence indicates that a property handled by a broker normally will be sold more quickly and with less reduction in the desired sale price than if an owner handles the sale without professional assistance.

■ REAL ESTATE BROKERAGE

SALES AND LEASING

Sales is the most prevalent and most well-known component of real estate brokerage. Owing to its annual dollar volume, real estate sales has been called the *lifeblood of the brokerage business.*

Some brokers prefer to specialize in residential property. Others specialize in commercial, industrial, or agricultural property, or only in business brokerage. Furthermore, a real estate professional might specialize exclusively in new residential construction, medical office space, or food service businesses. The typical real estate firm consists of three to five licensed persons, and the firm's numbers alone limit its

FIGURE 1.1   Real Estate Sale Process

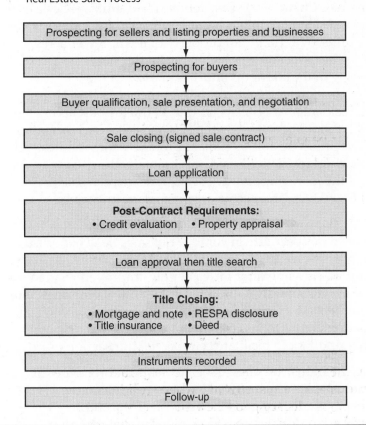

1 ability to handle all types of property. Regardless of size or type of
2 property handled, sale transactions are critical to the success of a real
3 estate firm.

4   Many brokers and sales associates prefer to select one specific portion
5 of a city and become expert in that particular portion, known as a **farm**
6 **area.** Licensees get to know almost every lot, house, and business in their
7 farm areas. *Farming* involves maintaining data on each property,
8 including when it was built, the sale history, typical marketing time,
9 assessed value, the amount of property taxes, and so forth. Real estate
10 professionals meet the people in the area and make it known that they
11 specialize in that section of town. The farm area soon begins to produce a
12 harvest in the form of listings and sales. Licensees create a reputation for
13 expertise through hard work. When residents in the farm area move or
14 decide to sell, they call on the area expert who knows what their property
15 will bring on the market.

16   The real estate sale process is complex and involves a series of ten
17 steps. These steps are outlined in Figure 1.1. The series of steps, which
18 should be completed in the proper sequence, are applicable to all types of
19 real estate sales. Unfortunately, in some cases a sales associate will obtain
20 a listing and ignore the need to market the property. As a result, the seller
21 becomes dissatisfied with the sales associate when very little sales
22 "activity" results, and the listing eventually expires.

23   Real estate sales associates involved in sales and leasing often
24 specialize in any of five major sales specialties:

comit !! (handwritten)

1. *Residential.* Most real estate professionals are involved in residential sales. Chapter 475, F.S., defines **residential** real estate as four or fewer residential units, vacant land zoned for four or fewer residential units, or agricultural property of ten or fewer acres. Residential sales associates should acquire a thorough understanding of the strengths and weaknesses of the neighborhoods in the areas in which they specialize (farm). To be successful, residential specialists need to know the best access routes and locations of schools, shopping facilities, and recreation facilities. They must be able to explain property taxes, homestead exemptions, deed restrictions, and approximate utility costs in the area. One of the more important aspects of residential sales is knowing how to help prospective buyers obtain financing.

2. *Commercial.* To provide competent service to investors, real estate professionals who specialize in commercial sales need expertise regarding income-producing properties and the various techniques for increasing after-tax cash flow. Improved residential property of more than four units, retail stores, office buildings, and shopping centers are examples of income-producing commercial properties. Contacts with institutional investors and mortgage lenders are important to facilitate commercial transactions.

* Specialize 1 or 2 areas (handwritten)

3. *Industrial.* The industrial sales associate deals in three types of properties: (1) sites in industrial parks or subdivisions; (2) redeveloped industrial parcels in central areas; and (3) industrial acreage. Sales associates of industrial real estate must have technical knowledge of the needs of different industries, such as transportation requirements, including access to railroad or airport transportation; industrial construction features, such as steel versus concrete block construction; and local land-use restrictions affecting industrial properties. With the increase in technological industries, more and more industrial brokers are finding it rewarding to develop and sell beautifully landscaped and well-conceived industrial subdivisions. Almost every large city in Florida has seen the development of industrial parks.

4. *Agricultural.* **Agricultural** property is defined in Chapter 475, F.S., to mean agricultural property of more than ten acres. Professionals who specialize in the sale of farms and agricultural land must be familiar with the operation of farms and the economic problems associated with the various types of farming. One of the licensee's most important skills is the ability to communicate with farmers. Sales associates who are effective in dealing with farm operators are knowledgeable about farm operations and the federal programs affecting farm operations.

351 A/c. (handwritten)

5. *Businesses.* Real estate licensees who engage in the sale, purchase, or lease of businesses are referred to as **business brokers.** This real estate activity is sometimes referred to as **business opportunity brokerage.** Business brokers must understand and be able to value

1 goodwill and personal property. (Refer to Chapter 17.) Individuals
2 and business entities engaged in the sale, purchase, or lease of
3 businesses must qualify and be licensed as active real estate
4 licensees.

5 Real estate licensees have a moral and ethical obligation to acquire
6 knowledge and expertise that will prove that the money paid for their
7 commissions and fees is money well spent. Furthermore, one of the best
8 ways to ensure satisfied buyers and sellers is through **follow-up.** *Follow-*
9 *up* is what a sales associate does for buyers and sellers after the sale. The
10 follow-up is important to all aspects of sales in real estate because it
11 results in a good reputation, future referrals, and word-of-mouth
12 advertising.

PROPERTY MANAGEMENT

14 **Property management** is devoted to the leasing, managing, marketing,
15 and overall maintenance of property for others. Many investors desiring
16 to participate in the growth of income-producing property have become
17 **absentee owners** who do not personally manage or reside on the
18 premises. The field of property management has experienced rapid
19 growth and specialization, primarily due to the increase in absentee
20 ownership. Absentee owners are dependent on qualified property
21 managers.

22 The scope of a *property manager's* functions goes far beyond rent
23 collection, maintenance, and repair. A property manager is the local
24 representative of the owner. His or her primary task is to produce the
25 greatest possible net income over the longest possible time. This may
26 involve development of plans for modernization, remodeling, or
27 alteration of existing properties, for which the cost must be clearly
28 justified by the benefits.

29 As agents of absentee owners, property managers are typically
30 responsible for improving tenant relations and for advertising and
31 merchandising the space. Apartment buildings, condominium
32 developments, shopping centers, and office buildings all require efficient
33 management. Corporations, banks, investment companies, and
34 individuals realize that a trained property manager can usually cope
35 with the details involved in operating income properties better than an
36 owner, whose business expertise lies in other areas. This is particularly
37 true for physicians, lawyers, and other professionals who recognize the
38 tax benefits of owning income-producing real estate. Such investors
39 normally hire qualified property managers because the investors have
40 neither the time nor the desire to become involved in the complexities of
41 property management.

42 Property managers are compensated in a number of ways. Some
43 work for a guaranteed base amount plus a small percentage of effective
44 gross income (total income collected).

80% of Appraised Value.

APPRAISING

Appraisal is the process of estimating the value of real property.
Appraising is considered to be an art, not a science, because although the
appraisal process involves mathematical calculations, appraisers also
use their own judgment when appraising real property.

475.612, F.S.

The Florida Real Estate Appraisal Board regulates state-certified,
licensed, and registered appraisers. Real estate licensees are entitled to
appraise real property for compensation, provided they do *not* represent
themselves as state-certified, registered, or licensed appraisers. When
conducting appraisals of real property, real estate licensees must abide by
the Uniform Standards of Professional Appraisal Practice (USPAP).

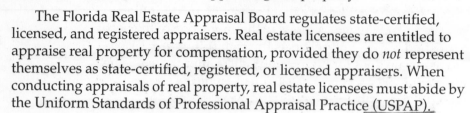

475.611, F.S.
475.25, F.S.

A real estate licensee is not allowed to prepare some appraisals.
A state-certified or licensed appraiser must prepare an appraisal that
involves a federally related transaction. A *federally related transaction* is
defined in the Financial Institutions Reform, Recovery, and Enforcement
Act (FIRREA) to mean a real estate-related transaction that requires an
appraisal and involves a federally insured financial institution. Federally
related transactions include the sale, lease, purchase, exchange,
investment, refinancing, or other use of real estate as security for a loan
or investment that has a transaction value greater than $250,000.

Sellers often ask real estate brokers and sales associates what a buyer
is likely to pay for their properties. Real estate licensees may help
potential sellers determine an asking price by preparing a **comparative
market analysis (CMA).** CMAs are developed by collecting information
concerning real estate activity in the area, including recent sales of
similar properties, properties currently offered for sale, and recently
expired listings. A CMA is a marketing tool and may *not* be referred to or
be represented as an appraisal. Licensees may charge a fee or otherwise
be compensated for preparing a CMA, either as a part of or in addition to
the normal sale commission.

An appraiser carefully analyzes past sales, computes the cost to
reproduce a structure, and determines the worth of future income that a
property might produce. These calculations are important not only to
buyers and sellers but also to mortgage lenders and insurance companies.
Various levels of government also use appraisers to arrive at a value for
properties condemned in order to build roads, highways, and expressways.
Individual investors have learned the value of obtaining an appraisal
before investing.

Appraisers are paid a fee, not a commission, to reduce the possibility
of any conflict of interest. If an appraiser were to be paid a percentage
of the appraised value, the temptation to exaggerate the value might
prove irresistible. USPAP's ethics rule states that it is unethical for an
appraiser to accept compensation that is contingent on the value of the
property. (Refer to Chapter 15.)

FINANCING

If sales are the lifeblood of real estate, financing can be regarded as the
lifeblood of real estate sales. More than 90 percent of all purchases are

financed. Knowledge of how to arrange financing and how to solve financing problems is essential to success in real estate. The licensee who can demonstrate how a prospective buyer can afford to buy has a tremendous advantage over the individual who only can show houses. Real estate licensees may not operate as mortgage brokers unless they also hold mortgage broker licenses. (Refer to Chapter 13.)

COUNSELING

Real estate **counselors** provide advice to individuals and firms regarding the purchase and use of real estate investments. A counselor is typically paid a flat fee. Because few people have the education, experience in real estate, knowledge of investing, and tested judgment required to be a qualified counselor, they are few in number. Our expanding economy, the increasing complexity of problems associated with real estate, and the need for professional counseling services (a legitimate business tax deduction) all indicate that counseling will grow as a real estate specialty. The services of counselors are already in demand by developers, investors, corporations, and large-scale buyers and sellers.

■ DEVELOPMENT AND CONSTRUCTION

Development and construction involve dividing larger parcels of land into lots, constructing roads and other off-site improvements, and then constructing buildings on the developed lots. There are three general phases of development and construction:

1. *Land acquisition.* Developers and builders acquire raw land and then prepare the site for construction. They must carefully study zoning and land-use plans to determine what type of development is permissible.

2. *Subdividing and development. Subdividing* is the process of converting parcels of land into smaller units or lots. *Development* is the process of improving raw land so that it can be put to productive use. Development of raw land may involve excavation for roads and utilities. The costs of grading and street paving and of installing curbs, storm drainage systems, and water and sewer systems often exceed the purchase price of the raw land. Site preparation includes identification of protected trees and vegetation and then the clearing of excess trees from the site.

   To protect consumers, most local governments require that developers submit a **subdivision plat map** of a new development to the applicable government planning agency. (See Figure 10.9 on page 204.) A plat is a map of the subdivision that indicates the size and location of individual lots, streets, and public utilities, including water and sewer lines. Typically the developer is responsible for improving the raw land with paved streets that then are dedicated to the local city or county. **Dedication** is the gift of land by an owner, in this case a developer, to a government body for a public use. Acceptance of the dedicated streets obligates the local government to maintain the streets once they are installed.

1   County subdivision ordinances, in effect, have combined
2   subdividing the land into individual lots with the development
3   phase to provide greater protection to the public.

4   Developers of residential subdivisions typically record in the
5   public records restrictive covenants that affect the entire
6   ✳ subdivision. **Restrictive covenants** affect how the land can be used
7   and establish criteria such as minimum square footage, type of
8   construction, architectural design, and so forth, to ensure that
9   homes built there conform to the neighborhood. Developers use
10 restrictive covenants to ensure that no homes will be built that
11 might decrease the value of neighboring properties.

12 3. *Construction.* Licensed contractors construct buildings on the
13 prepared site. There are three general categories of residential
14 construction: speculative homes (commonly referred to as *spec*
15 homes), custom homes, and tract homes.

Residential Construction	
Spec Homes	Building "on speculation" involves purchasing one or more lots and constructing a home(s) without securing a buyer in advance of construction.
Custom Homes	A custom builder constructs homes under contract with a buyer, often using building plans provided by architects or buyers.
Tract Homes	Tract homes are a type of speculative building. A new subdivision will typically feature several model homes. Buyers select a floor plan from the models and a lot on which to build in the new subdivision.

16 Effective marketing is critical to new construction. For large-scale
17 developments, the use of model homes is an important part of the
18 marketing function. While many developers employ a small sales force
19 to show their model homes, some developers rely on help from real
20 estate brokers to market their houses and lots. Normally, developers pay
21 for all advertising, and brokers agree to accept a reduction in their
22 customary sale commission to help offset this expense.

redEstate Co - Builder - Buys + Sells own Property.

23 ## ■ THE ROLE OF GOVERNMENT

24 The real estate business is regulated or influenced by the federal, state,
25 and local governments:

26 • *Local government* impacts the real estate business through property
27   taxation and regulatory activities such as occupational licensing,
28   building permits, building moratoriums, and zoning.

29 • *State government* owns and manages a large amount of property
30   and identifies coastal regions and other areas that are protected
31   from development. State documentary and intangible taxes are

required when ownership to real property is transferred or pledged as collateral for a mortgage. (Refer to Chapter 14.)

- The *federal government* impacts the real estate business through its fiscal and monetary policies. Various agencies influencing the real estate field include the Department of Housing and Urban Development (HUD), the Federal Housing Administration (FHA), the Department of Veterans Affairs (VA), the Environmental Protection Agency (EPA), and the Internal Revenue Service (IRS). Subsequent Chapters will cover in greater detail the role of the various units of government in the real estate business.

■ PROFESSIONAL ORGANIZATIONS

Professional associations and trade organizations play an important role in the real estate industry. The largest trade organization in the world is the National Association of REALTORS® (NAR). Today, in Florida, approximately two-thirds of real estate licensees belong to the NAR. The NAR promotes ethics and education in the real estate industry. Many of the state laws designed to promote professionalism and improve ethical standards begin in the NAR's REALTOR® Code of Ethics and Standards of Practice. (See Chapter 4 for more information concerning the Code of Ethics.)

The NAR's fundamental strength is the local association of REALTORS®. These local associations (or boards) are organized across the nation. To become a member of a local association, licensees must apply to and be approved by the association's membership committee. Each real estate office makes the decision regarding whether to join a local association of REALTORS®. If a particular real estate office belongs to an association, all of the associates in that office must also join the association. However, if the real estate office does not join an association, individual licensees within that office cannot join the association.

Both the National Association of REALTORS® (NAR) and the Florida Association of REALTORS® (FAR) sponsor comprehensive educational programs for members, publish trade papers, and advertise special services that their members are qualified to provide. These and other resources help to mark the true professional—an individual constantly seeking self-improvement.

■ SUMMARY

The real estate business includes real estate brokerage, development and construction, and investment. The vast majority of real estate licensees are active in real estate brokerage. All levels of government impact the real estate industry. True professionals in real estate seek out membership in organizations that offer members educational programs, trade publications, and other services designed to benefit the individual, the industry, and the public.

■ REVIEW QUESTIONS

1. Developer Bob acquires a tract of land that he divides into 25 home sites. Prior to marketing the home sites, Bob must submit the subdivision plat to the
   A. Department of Housing and Urban Development.
   B. local governmental planning agency.
   C. Florida Real Estate Commission.
   D. local building code enforcement department.

2. The term *follow-up* refers to
   A. returning calls in a timely manner.
   B. completing instructions given by one's broker.
   C. following through on listing calls made to "for sale by owners."
   D. what a sales associate does for buyers and sellers after the sale.

3. An active real estate licensee is legally entitled to appraise real property for compensation concerning a nonfederally related transaction
   A. as long as she does not represent herself as a state-certified or licensed appraiser, and complies with the USPAP.
   B. only if the appraisal is referred to as a *comparative market analysis.*
   C. provided the compensation is based on a commission agreed on before the appraisal work is done.
   D. provided a licensed or certified appraiser signs the appraisal report.

4. The field of property management has experienced growth and specialization primarily because of
   A. the deregulation of the real estate industry.
   B. the increase in the numbers of licensees specializing in property management.
   C. the increase in the number of absentee owners.
   D. higher construction costs that have caused an increase in the number of renters.

5. Appraising is considered to be
   A. an art.
   B. a science.
   C. a precise determination of value.
   D. purely mathematical with no room for personal judgment.

6. Appraisers are paid a fee because
   A. to accept compensation based on the appraised value is a conflict of interest.
   B. custom dictates the method of compensation.
   C. the fee would be too high if it were based on a percentage of property value.
   D. only brokers and sales associates are paid commissions for their services.

7. When a developer makes lots available for custom building in a newly developed subdivision, the overall purpose of restrictive covenants is to ensure that custom-built homes will
   A. not conflict with local zoning ordinances.
   B. not exceed the minimum square footage requirements.
   C. conform to standard building codes.
   D. not decrease the value of neighboring properties.

8. The real estate activity that is devoted to leasing, managing, marketing, and overall maintenance of property for others is referred to as
   A. commercial sales.
   B. property management.
   C. counseling.
   D. rental agents.

9. Which type of construction involves building for a specific buyer to his or her specifications?
   A. Tract homes
   B. Spec homes
   C. Custom homes
   D. Model homes

10. The term *dedication* as it applies to development and construction refers to
   A. a gift of land by the owner to the local government for a public use.
   B. the builder's careful attention to construction details.
   C. recording a subdivision plat map in the public records.
   D. preparing raw land for site improvements.

11. Sales associate Harry recently began working at All Action Realty. All Action is not a member of the local association of REALTORS®. Can Harry join the association?
   A. Yes, Harry can join any association of REALTORS® as an independent member.
   B. No, Harry cannot join the association unless All Action Realty joins the association.
   C. Yes, Harry may join the association. However, Harry cannot use the MLS.
   D. Yes, Harry can join the association, but he will be charged a nonmember office surcharge.

12. In which way(s) does local government affect real estate?
    A. Property taxes
    B. Documentary stamp taxes on deeds
    C. Mortgage interest rates
    D. All of the above

13. The real estate profession requires
    A. skill and experience in real estate values, specialized service, and expertise.
    B. only the ability to list property.
    C. expertise in all types of real estate.
    D. that licensees also act as mortgage brokers from time to time.

14. Selecting a limited geographical area in which a real estate professional develops special expertise is referred to as
    A. farming.
    B. follow-up.
    C. subdividing.
    D. dedicating land.

15. Broker Mike charges a prospective seller $50 for a comparative market analysis (CMA). Which statement applies?
    A. Brokers are not permitted to charge for CMAs.
    B. This is permissible, provided Mike does not represent the CMA as an appraisal.
    C. Broker Mike must be a state-certified or licensed appraiser to do this.
    D. The CMA must be signed by a state-certified or licensed appraiser.

CHAPTER 2

License Law and Qualifications for Licensure

■ KEY TERMS

broker

broker associate

caveat emptor

compensation

license

nolo contendere

owner-developer

real estate services

registration

sales associate

■ OVERVIEW

The purpose of this Chapter is to give the reader a historical perspective of real estate license law in Florida and to describe in detail the requirements for obtaining a real estate license. The Chapter discusses real estate services that require a license and exemptions from licensure.

After completing this Chapter, the student should be able to:

- define *sales associate, broker associate,* and *broker;*

- list the academic requirements for sales associate and broker licenses;

- list the application requirements for sales associate and broker licenses;

- identify services of real estate requiring licensure;

- recognize exemptions from licensure; and

- distinguish between post-licensing education and continuing education.

■ HISTORICAL PERSPECTIVE OF FLORIDA REAL ESTATE LICENSE LAW

Prior to the latter part of the nineteenth century, the real estate business was unorganized and extremely competitive. The policy of **caveat emptor,** a Latin term meaning *let the buyer beware,* prevailed. In 1923, the

475.021(1), F.S.
20.03, F.S.

1 Florida Legislature passed the Real Estate License Law, Chapter 475 of
2 the *Florida Statutes.*

3   In 1925, the Florida Legislature created the Florida Real Estate
4 Commission (also referred to as the *Commission* or as the *FREC*). The
5 Legislature granted the Commission authority to keep records, conduct
6 investigations, and the power to grant, deny, suspend, and revoke
7 registrations.

8   Today, the Division of Real Estate (DRE) provides support services to
9 the Commission. The DRE is under the Department of Business and
10 Professional Regulation (DBPR).

11   The intent of real estate regulation is to protect the health, safety, and
12 welfare of the public (consumer protection) *only when:*

455.201, F.S.

13   • the unregulated practice can harm the public, the potential harm is
14   recognizable, and the danger outweighs any anticompetitive
15   impact that might result from regulation;

16   • the public is not adequately protected by other state statutes, local
17   ordinances, or federal laws; or

18   • less restrictive means of regulation are not available.

19   An applicant is determined to be qualified for a real estate license if
20 he or she meets certain application and academic requirements and
21 demonstrates minimal competence with regard to the real estate
22 business. Prospective licensees must demonstrate knowledge of real estate
23 business practices and knowledge of the Florida real estate license law and
24 certain federal laws pertaining to real estate. To be prepared
25 for the licensure examination and to competently perform real estate
26 practices, the licensee must be familiar with the laws regulating the real
27 estate business.

Important Real Estate Statutes and Rules

Florida Statute 475	Real Estate License Law
Florida Statute 455	Regulation of Professions and Occupations
Florida Statute 120	Administrative Procedures Act
Chapter 61J2	Rules of the Florida Real Estate Commission

---

wwweb.link

The best way to access the Florida Statutes is using the official Online Sunshine Web site: **http://www.leg.state.fl.us/statutes/index.cfm.**

wwweb.link

For the most up-to-date version of the administrative rules (including the rules of the Florida Real Estate Commission), go to the Florida Administrative Code at: **http://fac.dos.state.fl.us/.** *Scroll down and click on the Chapter desired. (Chapter 61 contains the rules for the DBPR.) Note: High speed Internet access is needed to navigate this site effectively.*

1 ## ■ GENERAL LICENSING PROVISIONS

Two Types of Real Estate Licenses

Sales Associate A person who performs real estate services for compensation but who does so under the direction, control, or management of another person.

Broker A person who, for another and for compensation, performs real estate services.

Reference: Section 475.01, F.S.

---

2 An individual begins his or her real estate career in Florida as a licensed
3 **sales associate.** Applicants who have completed the required education
4 and passed the license exam are initially licensed as inactive sales
5 associates. Inactive sales associates can become active by finding an
6 employer and filing the information with the Division of Real
7 Estate (DRE).

475.01, F.S.

8 Sales associates must work under the direction of an employer. Most
9 frequently, the employer is a real estate broker. However, a sales associate
10 may also work for an owner-developer. An **owner-developer** is an
11 unlicensed entity that sells, exchanges, or leases its own property. An
12 example of an owner-developer is a real estate development company that
13 owns land that it develops into subdivisions, and then builds and sells
14 homes. An owner-developer's sales staff must hold active real estate
15 licenses in order to be paid a commission or other compensation based on
16 actual sales (that is, on a transactional basis). The sales staff is exempt from
17 real estate licensure if paid strictly on a salaried basis.

18 To become a **broker** requires additional education and passing the
19 broker license exam. While many sales associates want the prestige of a
20 broker's license, they are not interested in opening their own real estate
21 brokerage business. A **broker associate** is an individual who holds a
22 broker's license but who chooses to register and work in real estate under
23 the direction of another broker.

24 ## APPLICATION REQUIREMENTS

25 A person desiring to be licensed must submit either a notarized or
26 electronically authenticated application. The application is furnished by
27 the Division of Real Estate (DRE) and may be downloaded from the
28 Internet at the DRE's Form Center. (See Web link on the next page.)
29 Applicants may download, print, and mail the application, or they may
30 apply online.

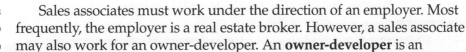

475.175, F.S.

31 Applicants are cautioned to complete the application carefully,
32 particularly with respect to past history concerning felonies,
33 misdemeanors, and traffic offenses (other than parking, speeding,
34 inspection, or traffic signal violations). When responding regarding past
35 history (background information section on application), applicants who
36 have been convicted of a crime, found guilty, or entered a plea of guilty or

1   **nolo contendere** (no contest), even if court action (*adjudication*) was
2   withheld, should attach full details of all cases with dates and outcomes,
3   including any sentence and conditions imposed. Failure to truthfully
4   disclose this information may result in denial of a real estate license. In
5   cases where a license has already been issued, it may result in revocation of
6   the license.

7   The application must be accompanied by a current FBI fingerprint
8   card, properly filled out, and the required fee. (See Table 3.1 on page 37.)
9   If applying online, the applicant should mail the fingerprint card with an
10 Attest Statement (Form DBPR-0030) and include a cover letter referencing
11 the application number. An application number is assigned when the
12 application is filed online. If an applicant responded "yes" to any of the
13 background questions, he or she should also include in the mailing any
14 additional explanation and important documentation such as copies of
15 police records. The notice of satisfactory completion of the prescribed
16 course (grade report) may either be forwarded with the application or be
17 presented at the examination site before taking the exam.

*You can access the license application online at the DRE's Form Center.
The address is:* **http://www.state.fl.us/dbpr/re/forms/ index.shtml.**
*Click on "Real Estate Sales Associate Package." As this is a multipurpose
application, review the instructions carefully and complete all
applicable sections.*

To check the status of your application, use the DBPR Online Services at:
https://www.myfloridalicense.com/Default.asp. *Under Public
Services, click on "View Application Status."*

18   A 30-day period is allowed after receipt of the application to check
19 for errors and omissions and to notify the applicant of any additional
20 information required. An applicant's failure to supply additional
21 information may not be grounds for denial of a license unless the applicant
22 was notified within the 30-day period. Any application for a license that is
23 not approved or denied within legislated time periods must be considered
24 approved. An applicant must be informed of approval or denial *within*
25 *90 days* after receipt of the last correctly submitted application. Once the
26 application has been processed, the DRE conducts a thorough
27 investigation of the applicant, including processing the applicant's
28 fingerprints.

475.181, F.S.
61J2-2.032,
F.A.C.

29 **LICENSE EXAMINATIONS**

30 When the application processing is complete and the applicant is
31 considered to be qualified, the DRE notifies the national testing vendor.
32 The vendor then sends a notice informing the candidate that he or she is
33 eligible to take the state license examination.

61J2-2.029,
F.A.C.

34   Applicants schedule examination appointments directly through the
35 testing vendor. License examinations for sales associate and broker
36 applicants are given at a minimum of 15 test sites located throughout
37 Florida. The license exam may also be taken in any state where the test
38 vendor has a test center.

1   The examination consists of multiple-choice questions and is
2 administered as a computerized test. The license exam is offered in English
3 and Spanish. Students who want the Spanish version must request the
4 Spanish language examination when making the test reservation. The
5 passing score on the license exam is a grade of 75 percent or higher.

6   Students' answers are graded at the test site. Students who pass the
7 exam are given a "pass" notification at the test site. A real estate license is
8 mailed to students who passed the exam. New sales associates must
9 change their license to *active* status before legally operating as a sales
10 associate. To do this, licensees simply notify the DRE of their employer's
11 name and address by filing form DBPR RE-2050 (Request for Change of
12 Status) with the DRE. Once the form has been filed, licensees may
13 begin working.

Regulations Pertaining to Prelicense Courses

A student may not miss more than eight hours of instruction. An instructional hour is considered to be 50 minutes. (Section 475.17, F.S.)

A student may attend makeup classes to take the end-of-course exam or a makeup exam if absences were due to student or family illness, if done within 30 days of the regularly scheduled exam time, or later with Commission approval. Makeup classes must consist of the original course material that the student missed. (61J2-3.008, F.A.C.)

The school or institution provides each student passing the end-of-course exam with a FREC-prescribed grade report of successful completion of the course. The school must submit a roster notifying the Commission of the name of each student who has satisfactorily completed the education requirements. (Section 475.175, F.S.)

The student must pass the school-administered end-of-course exam with a grade of 70 or higher. (61J2-3.008, F.A.C.)

A student failing the end-of-course exam must wait at least 30 days from the date of the original examination to retest. Within one year of the original examination, a student may retest a maximum of one time. Otherwise, a student failing the end-of-course exam must repeat the course prior to being eligible to retake the end-of-course examination. Schools must administer a different form of the end-of-course exam to a student who is retaking the exam or repeating the course. (61J2-3.008, F.A.C.)

Students may choose to complete a distance-learning course and satisfactorily complete a timed, distance learning course examination. (Section 475.17, F.S.)

The prelicense course may be taken by correspondence or other suitable means by anyone who, because of individual physical hardship, cannot attend the course where it is regularly conducted or who does not have access to distance learning courses. (Section 475.17, F.S.)

An active member in good standing with The Florida Bar who is otherwise qualified under the real estate license law is exempt from the Commission-prescribed prerequisite education course for licensure as a real estate sales associate. (61J2-3.008, F.A.C.)

An applicant for licensure who has received a four-year degree in real estate from an accredited institution of higher education is exempt from the Commission-prescribed courses for licensure. (Section 475.17, F.S.)

Students who fail the license exam are given a failure notice at the test site. The failure notice includes a breakdown of the points scored in each major subject area. The notice also includes information about reviewing the exam, retaking the exam, and requesting a hearing to challenge the exam. Appointments to review the exam must be made within two years of the test date. Review appointments are scheduled with the test vendor. Students may only review the questions they answered incorrectly.

455.217, F.S.
120.57, F.S.
120.569, F.S.
61-11.017(8),
F.A.C.

Applicants who fail the license exam at their own expense have the right to have an attorney review the exam with them. If an applicant finds any incorrectly keyed questions or questions that are poorly written or obsolete, they should write down their objections to the specific questions and turn in their comments to the test center employee (review monitor). Applicants may also request that the Validation Committee review the objections to specific exam questions. The request must be made in writing to the DRE within 30 days from the date of the examination review. If the examination review results in a corrected score, the new score will apply only to the student who challenged the examination questions.

A student also has the right to petition for a formal hearing before the Division of Administrative Hearings. A request for a hearing before an administrative law judge must be filed within 21 days from the date of the on-site grade notice, or 21 days from the date of the letter notifying the student of the DBPR evaluation decision regarding his or her challenges. The request for a hearing is filed with the Chief, Bureau of Education and Testing, DBPR.

61J2-2.030,
F.A.C.

wwweb.link

Download a copy of the Candidate Information Booklet at: **http://www.myflorida.com/dbpr/servop/testing/booklets/ real/sl_bk.pdf.** *The Booklet includes important information regarding taking the state license exam.*

wwweb.link

The Department's administrative rule regarding examinations is available on the Internet. Go to: **http://fac.dos.state.fl.us/.** *Click on "Chapter 61 Department of Business and Professional Regulation." Scroll down to "Chapter 61-11 Examinations."*

NONRESIDENT APPLICATION REQUIREMENTS

U.S. citizenship is *not* required of applicants. Furthermore, applicants do not have to be residents of Florida. If a nonresident applicant or licensee wishes to become licensed in Florida, he or she must sign the *irrevocable consent to service* section on the application form. This agreement provides that lawsuits and other legal actions may be initiated against the applicant in any county of Florida in which the person bringing suit resides. The notarized consent includes the provision that any legal service or pleading against the applicant may be made by delivery or by certified mail, return receipt requested, to the director of the DRE, with a copy to the applicant by registered mail. Nonresident applicants and licensees must comply with all other F.S. 475 requirements and FREC rules.

475.180, F.S.

Any resident licensee who becomes a nonresident must notify the Commission within 60 days of the change in residency and comply with

1 all nonresident requirements. Failure to notify the Commission subjects
2 the licensee to penalties cited in Section 475.25, F.S. Furthermore, all
3 licensees are required by rule to inform the DBPR in writing of a change in
4 mailing address within ten days after the change. (See also Current
5 Mailing Address, page 36.) Nonresident licensees must satisfactorily
6 complete the post-licensing and continuing education required of all
7 Florida real estate licensees.

Rules Pertaining to Nonresident Licensees

Any resident licensee who becomes a nonresident must notify the Commission within 60 days of the change in residency and comply with all nonresident requirements.

A Florida resident licensee who fails to notify the Commission of becoming a nonresident as prescribed in Section 475.17(7) may be issued a citation and fined $100.

Reference: Section 475.180, F.S., and 61J2-24.002, F.A.C.

---

8 **Mutual recognition agreements.** The FREC has entered into mutual
9 recognition agreements with licensing authorities in other states. The
10 intent of these agreements is to recognize the education and experience
11 that real estate licensees have acquired in another state or nation. These
12 agreements *apply exclusively to nonresidents licensed in other jurisdictions.*
13 Each licensee who applies for Florida licensure from a state or jurisdiction
14 that has a current mutual recognition agreement with Florida must
15 take and pass a written Florida-specific real estate law examination
16 (a prelicense course is not required of these candidates). The exam
17 consists of 40 questions worth 1 point each.

61J2-26.001,
F.A.C.

18   A grade of 30 points (75 percent) or higher is required to pass the
19 exam. The mutual recognition agreements also ensure that Florida
20 licensees have equal opportunity for licensure in those jurisdictions with
21 which agreements are concluded. The FREC has entered into mutual
22 recognition agreements with ten states: Alabama, Arkansas, Colorado,
23 Georgia, Indiana, Kentucky, Mississippi, Nebraska, Oklahoma, and
24 Tennessee.

[handwritten: recinite Fl.]

[handwritten: — 29# STATES,]

25 **Florida resident defined.** For application and licensing purposes, the
26 FREC rules define a *resident of Florida* as a person who has resided in
27 Florida continuously for a period of four calendar months or more within
28 the preceding year, regardless of whether the person resided in a
29 recreational vehicle, hotel, rental unit, or other temporary or permanent
30 location. Any person who presently resides in Florida in any of the
31 above-described accommodations with the intention of residing
32 continuously in Florida for four months or longer, beginning on the
33 date the person established the current period of residence, is also
34 considered a legal Florida resident.

61J2-26.002,
F.A.C.

35 ## ■ SALES ASSOCIATE QUALIFICATIONS FOR LICENSURE

475.17(2), F.S.
61J2-3.008,
F.A.C.

36 In addition to the general licensing provisions cited above, sales associate
37 candidates must meet a number of other criteria to be licensed. Their first

1   step toward licensure is to successfully complete FREC Course I or an
2   equivalent FREC-approved course. The course is based on understanding
3   and applying the fundamentals of real estate principles and practices,
4   real estate law, real estate license law, and real estate mathematics.

5   FREC Course I consists of 60 hours of instruction plus 3 hours for
6   an end-of-course examination. The end-of-course examination consists
7   of 100 questions worth 1 point each and is normally organized with
8   45 questions on principles and practices, 45 questions on real estate law,
9   and 10 math questions. Attorneys who are active members of The Florida
10 Bar are exempt from FREC Course I. Additionally, individuals who have
11 received a four-year degree in real estate from an institution of higher
12 education are exempt from the prelicense course.

61J2-3.008(8),
F.A.C.

13   The sales associate applicant *must:*

14 • be 18 years of age or older;   Age of Majority

475.17, F.S.
61J2-2.027,
F.A.C.

15 • have a high school diploma or its equivalent;

16 • be honest, truthful, trustworthy, of good character, and have a
17   reputation for fair dealing;

18 • disclose if ever convicted or found guilty of a crime or ever entered
19   a plea of *nolo contendere* (no contest); if under investigation for
20   civil or criminal prosecution; or if any judgment or decree has
21   been rendered wherein the charges involved moral turpitude or
22   fraudulent or dishonest dealing;

23 • disclose if any name or alias other than the name signed on the
24   application has ever been used, including a maiden name;

25 • disclose if he or she has ever been denied licensure or has had a
26   license suspended or revoked by the real estate licensing agency of
27   another state or nation;*

28 • disclose if he or she has ever been denied registration or a license
29   to practice any regulated profession, business, or vocation, or has
30   had his or her registration or license suspended or revoked in this
31   or any other state or nation; and

32 • disclose if he or she has been guilty of any conduct or practice that
33   would have been grounds for suspension or revocation under F.S. 475
34   had the applicant then been licensed to practice real estate in this state
35   or elsewhere. This includes acting, or attempting to act, as a real estate
36   sales associate or broker in violation of F.S. 475 during the year before
37   the applicant filed an application, or until a valid license was issued,
38   regardless of whether compensation was an issue.*

*Note: Applicants guilty of these offenses will be considered qualified for registration only if passage of
time, good behavior, or other sufficient reasons cause the Commission to believe that the interests and
welfare of the general public will not be endangered.

■ POST-LICENSING EDUCATION

2 Sales associates are required to successfully complete a prescribed post-
3 licensing education requirement *before the first renewal* of their licenses.
4 This requirement has the effect of placing all initial licenses in a
5 conditional (probationary) status because failure to complete the post-
6 licensing education requirement will cause the initial license to become
7 null and void. Sales associates who do not complete the 45-hour post-
8 licensing requirement and want to continue in the real estate business are
9 *required to requalify* for licensure by repeating the prelicense course and
10 end-of-course exam and by again passing the state licensing exam.

475.17, F.S.
61J2-3.020,
F.A.C.
61J2-3.008,
F.A.C.

$160⁰⁰

11   Post-licensure courses are offered by accredited colleges, universities,
12 and community colleges; area technical centers; real estate proprietary
13 schools; and FREC-approved sponsors. Post-licensure courses are offered
14 in live classroom format and online. Students must pass the 45-hour end-
15 of-course exam with a score of 75 percent or higher. Licensees who fail the
16 end-of-course exam must wait at least 30 days from the date of the original
17 examination to retake a different form of the end-of-course examination.
18 (Alternatively, licensees who do not want to wait 30 days may choose to
19 retake the course and, in such cases, take a different form of the end-of-
20 course exam.)

21   Students are cautioned *not* to enroll in a post-licensing course until first
22 becoming licensed. Individuals who have attained a four-year degree in
23 real estate from an institution of higher education are exempt from the
24 post-license education requirements. (Real estate attorneys are *not* exempt
25 from the post-licensing course.)

CONTINUING EDUCATION

27 After completing the post-licensing education requirement during the
28 initial license period, active and inactive licensees must complete at least
29 14 hours of continuing education during every 2-year license period after
30 that. Three of the 14 hours must consist of core law that includes updates
31 to applicable rules and statutes. A licensee who takes the 3-hour core-law
32 course in each year of the renewal period receives 6 hours of credit
33 toward the 14-hour continuing education requirement. The continuing
34 education requirement may be satisfied by attending a classroom course,
35 by completing an approved distance education course, or by attending a
36 Commission-approved education seminar or conference. A licensee can
37 earn 3 hours of specialty continuing education (not core law) by
38 attending a Commission meeting. Licensees must preregister with the
39 DRE to earn credit for attending such a meeting. Active members in good
40 standing with The Florida Bar are exempt from the continuing education
41 requirements for real estate licensees.

61J2-3.009,
F.A.C.

■ BROKER REQUIREMENTS

43 Applicants who possess a Florida sales associate's license must fulfill
44 their sales associate's post-licensing education *before* the expiration of the

initial sales associate's license or before applying for a broker's license (whichever occurs first).

Broker applicants must successfully complete FREC Course II or an equivalent FREC-approved course (unless qualifying as a broker under the mutual recognition provision). FREC Course II consists of 69 hours of instruction plus 3 hours for the end-of-course examination.

475.17(2)&(3), F.S.
61J2-3.008, F.A.C.

BROKER EXPERIENCE REQUIREMENTS

Broker applicants must fulfill an experience requirement in addition to the educational requirements. Applicants must complete at least 12 months of real estate experience during the five-year period preceding their becoming licensed as brokers. Credit, standing, or experience as an active real estate sales associate cannot be established by working for an owner-developer unless the owner-developer is a licensed broker holding a current, valid, and active license as such.

61J2-2.027, F.A.C.

Individuals who have held an active real estate license in another state may apply the experience toward a Florida broker's license if the applicant has held an active salesperson's or broker's license for at least 12 months during the preceding five years. However, an applicant who also holds a Florida real estate sales associate's license *must* fulfill the sales associate's post-licensing education requirement before the initial sales associate's license expires in order to be eligible to obtain a broker's license, even if the individual is applying real estate experience from another state.

BROKER POST-LICENSING EDUCATION

Broker licensees are required to successfully complete post-licensing education *before the first renewal* of their licenses. If a broker does not complete the 60-hour post-licensing requirement, the broker's license becomes null and void. However, the broker may request and receive a sales associate's license if he or she completes 14 hours of continuing education within the 6 months following expiration of the broker's license and has complied with all requirements for renewal.

475.17, F.S,
61J2-3.020, F.A.C.
61J2-3.008, F.A.C.

Any licensee who has received a four-year degree in real estate from an institution of higher education is exempt from the broker prelicense and post-license education requirements to become initially licensed (but not continuing education).

BROKER CONTINUING EDUCATION

Broker licensees must complete the same continuing education requirements required for sales associates. (See Continuing Education on page 21.)

■ REGISTRATION AND LICENSURE

Registration is the process of submitting information to the DRE that is entered into the Division's records. Information that is placed on record

FIGURE 2.1   Real Estate License and Application

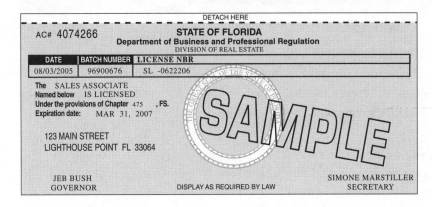

1 with the DRE includes the name and address of each licensed broker and
2 sales associate; the name and business address of each sales associate's
3 employer; the sales associate's and broker's license status (active or
4 inactive); and the person's involvement as an officer, director, or partner
5 of a real estate business. Sales associates and broker associates licensed in
6 Florida must be registered under their employing broker (or owner-
7 developer, if applicable). Sales associates and broker associates may have
8 only one registered employer. Florida licensees may also hold active
9 licenses in other states. Individuals who do not intend to engage actively
10 in the real estate business, such as a director of a real estate corporation,
11 simply register this information with the DRE so that the information can
12 be entered into the FREC's records. However, an individual who wishes
13 to actively engage in the real estate industry must be licensed and
14 registered as active with the DRE.

15   When an applicant successfully passes a state licensing examination,
16 he or she is issued a wallet-size **license** and certificate of registration. (See
17 Figure 2.1.) The license is a written document issued by the DBPR.

18   The effective date and expiration date are indicated on the face of
19 the license. The two-letter prefix before the license number indicates the
20 license type: BK signifies broker; SL, sales associate; BO, branch office;
21 CQ, corporation; and PR, partnership.

22 ■ **REAL ESTATE SERVICES**

475.01, F.S.

23 The Florida Real Estate License law identifies eight real estate-related
24 activities referred to as *real estate services* that require a Florida real estate
25 license. **Real estate services** include any real estate activity involving
26 compensation for performing the service for another.

TO REMEMBER

A BAR SALE

A	**A**dvertise real estate services
B	**B**uy
A	**A**ppraise
R	**R**ent or provide rental information or lists
S	**S**ell
A	**A**uction
L	**L**ease
E	**E**xchange

1 To remember the eight services of real estate, use the memory crutch
2 (mnemonic) acronym A BAR SALE, where the first letter of each service
3 forms the memory aid.

4   *Anyone* who performs any of the real estate services for another person
5 for compensation of any type must be licensed, unless specifically
6 exempted by law. It is a violation of license law to share a commission with
7 or to pay a fee or other compensation to an unlicensed person for the
8 referral of real estate business clients, prospects, or customers. However, a
9 Florida broker may pay a referral fee to a broker licensed in another state
10 so long as the foreign broker does not violate Florida law. **Compensation** is
11 defined as anything of value or a valuable consideration, directly or
12 indirectly paid, promised, or expected to be paid or received.

13 ## ■ INDIVIDUALS WHO ARE EXEMPT FROM LICENSURE

475.011, F.S.

14 Individual property owners do not need a license to buy, sell, exchange,
15 or lease their own real estate. Additionally, business entities such as
16 corporations, partnerships, trusts, or joint ventures may sell, exchange, or
17 lease their own real property. Salaried employees of business entities
18 who sell, exchange, or lease real property for their employer are exempt
19 from licensure, provided they are not paid a commission or compensated
20 on a transactional basis.

21   Individuals exempt from licensure also include:

22 • persons who buy or sell cemetery lots;

23 • individuals who rent lots in a mobile home park or recreational
24   travel park;

25 • radio and television announcers and persons in public relations
26   and advertising media, provided the services performed are
27   incidental to employment; individuals negotiating the sale,
28   purchase, or lease of radio, television, or cable enterprises,

provided the sale or purchase does not involve the sale or lease of land, buildings, fixtures, and all other improvements to the land;

- attorneys-at-law and certified public accountants when acting within the scope of their professional duties (*Note:* Holding a Florida Bar license does *not* entitle an attorney to compensation for performing services of real estate.);

- attorneys-in-fact (a person who has a power of attorney), for the purpose of the execution of contracts and conveyances only; (See also page 219.)

- persons who deal in personal property only, such as mortgage brokers (however, an individual in this category who attempts to negotiate a lease must be licensed);

- full-time graduate students enrolled in a Commission-approved degree program in appraising at a Florida college or university, provided they are acting under the direct supervision of a licensed broker or a licensed or certified appraiser and are engaged only in appraisal activities related to the approved degree program;

- persons acting within the limitations of their duties as designated by a will, proper court, or statutory authority to serve as personal representatives, trustees, receivers, guardians, masters in chancery, or special masters (for example, sheriffs or appraisers);

- employees who are paid a salary as managers of condominiums or cooperative apartment complexes who rent individual units, if the rentals are for periods no longer than one year;

- salaried employees of an owner (or of a registered broker for an owner) of an apartment community who work in an on-site rental office in a leasing capacity;

- salaried employees of a public utility, rural electric cooperative, railroad, or state or local government agency who act within the scope of their regular employment;

- any person or legal business entity that, for another and for compensation or valuable consideration, rents or advertises for rent for transient occupancy any public lodging establishment licensed under F.S. 509;

- owners of one or part of one or more time-share periods for their own use and occupancy who later offer one or more such periods for resale;

- any person registered, licensed, or certified by the DBPR under Part II of the Real Estate License Law as an appraiser performing appraisals in accordance with that part;

- federally regulated banks and dealers registered with the Securities and Exchange Commission (SEC) selling business enterprises to accredited investors; and

1   • owners of an apartment complex or any property management
2   firm for the purpose of paying a finder's fee of not more than $50
3   to a tenant of the apartment complex.

4   ## ■ SUMMARY

5   In the early 1900s real estate began to change from an unorganized and
6   suspect business to a semiprofession with standards. In the 1920s the
7   Florida Legislature created laws to establish a real estate commission
8   charged with the responsibility of administering and enforcing real estate
9   licensing. Today, each candidate for a real estate sales associate's or
10   broker's license must meet educational and administrative requirements.
11   Special provisions apply to initial licensees (post-licensing education)
12   and to nonresident applicants and licensees. Anyone who performs any
13   of the eight services of real estate in Florida for another for compensation
14   must be licensed, unless specifically exempted by Chapter 475, Florida
15   Statutes (the real estate license law).

Note to Readers. The same FREC rule may appear in several different forms: "Rule 61J2-1.011, Florida Administrative Code"; "Chapter 61J2-1.011, F.A.C."; "Commission Rule 61J2-1.011"; simply as "61J2-1.011"; etc. Similar variations apply to the same Florida law: "Chapter 475.01, Florida Statutes"; "Florida Statute 475.01"; "Section 475.01"; "s. 475.01"; "475.01, F.S."; etc.

■ REVIEW QUESTIONS

1. A licensed sales associate may operate
    A. for any registered broker.
    B. for the broker registered as the sales associate's employer.
    C. independently as long as he or she is registered with the FREC.
    D. as a broker associate.

2. A sales associate applicant is NOT required to comply with which requirement?
    A. Submit an application fee
    B. Be 18 years of age or older
    C. Be a bona fide Florida resident
    D. Have a high school diploma or its equivalent

3. Sarah's license status as registered with the DRE is broker associate. All of the statements apply to Sarah EXCEPT that she
    A. holds an active license.
    B. is broker-qualified.
    C. has an employer.
    D. may hold more than one Florida broker associate license.

4. Which statement does NOT describe the intent of the Florida Legislature concerning regulation of professional and licensed occupations to protect the public?
   A. When the potential for harm to the public is clear
   B. When other ordinances and laws are not sufficient to protect the public
   C. Whenever deemed appropriate by the Legislature
   D. When less-constraining measures of regulation are not available or apparent

5. A sales associate applicant is NOT required to disclose which information on the license application?
   A. Convicted of a crime
   B. Proof of U.S. citizenship
   C. Maiden name, if applicable
   D. Found guilty of conduct that would have resulted in disciplinary action if the applicant had been licensed to practice real estate

6. Sales associate Sam sells real estate for Seasonal Sales Realty. He also works as a sales associate for Two Sides Realty.
   A. Sam is in violation of F.S. 475.
   B. Sam may work for both companies as long as he registers both employers with the FREC.
   C. This is legal as long as he only works part-time for each company.
   D. Sam must be a broker associate for this to be legal.

7. What is the Latin term for a plea of "no contest"?
   A. Prima facie
   B. Caveat emptor
   C. Writ of mandamus
   D. Nolo contendere

8. Nancy helped her father sell some property he owned. Nancy is not a real estate licensee. Nancy's father was grateful for his daughter's assistance, but Nancy declined any compensation for assisting her father. Which statement is true?
   A. This was unlicensed real estate activity, and both Nancy and her dad could be prosecuted.
   B. Nancy is legally allowed to sell her father's real estate and be compensated for it because she is a family member.
   C. This was a legal arrangement because Nancy did not receive compensation for performing real estate services.
   D. Nancy can be fined by the FREC for performing real estate services without a license.

9. Which event may cause the FREC to refuse to certify an individual as qualified for licensure?
   A. Dropped out of high school and later earned a GED
   B. Was convicted of fraud in an insurance scam
   C. Changed residency to a state other than the state of Florida
   D. Lost a lot of his or her own money in a bad real estate investment

10. To receive a notice of satisfactory completion of FREC Course I or Course II, a student may not miss more than
    A. 4 instructional hours.
    B. 6 instructional hours.
    C. 8 instructional hours.
    D. 12 instructional hours.

11. Devora received her Florida sales associate's license in 2005. Which requirement must Devora complete to become a licensed real estate broker?
    A. Successfully complete the 45-hour post-licensing course
    B. Complete 14 hours of continuing education for sales associates
    C. Document at least three closed real estate transactions
    D. Complete at least two years of experience as a sales associate before taking the broker license exam

12. Vincent Black has a North Carolina broker's license, but he is not licensed in Florida. He sells a parcel of land he owns in Florida. Assuming all else is proper, this is a legal transaction because
    A. mutual recognition agreements allow this.
    B. Florida law exempts from licensure individual owners selling their own real property.
    C. Florida has honored his nonresident broker's license.
    D. he has the knowledge and qualifications necessary to handle the transaction.

13. A sales associate applicant who has submitted a correctly completed application for the state license examination and who successfully passes the state exam may legally begin to operate as a licensee when the
    A. application and proper fees are received by the state.
    B. applicant receives a return receipt acknowledging acceptance of the application.
    C. applicant receives his or her canceled check as evidence of payment followed by an assigned date for the state exam.
    D. applicant is notified of having passed the state exam and has filed the appropriate form with the DRE.

14. If the post-licensing requirement is not fulfilled before the first renewal and a sales associate licensee wishes to continue in the real estate business, the licensee
    A. must retake the state exam within one year.
    B. must requalify for licensure.
    C. is allowed a six-month grace period to meet the requirement but must hold an inactive license during that period.
    D. must retake the prelicense course within one year.

15. Services of real estate do NOT include
    A. advertising rental property lists.
    B. appraising real property.
    C. selling cemetery lots for compensation.
    D. conducting an auction of real property.

16. Which statement BEST describes who must be licensed to practice real estate in Florida?
    A. Anyone who performs any of the services of real estate
    B. Anyone who performs any of the services of real estate for another
    C. Anyone who performs any of the services of real estate for another for compensation
    D. Anyone who performs any of the services of real estate for another for compensation, unless specifically exempted by law

17. Which individual is NOT exempt from licensure under F.S. 475?
    A. Individual owner selling his or her own property
    B. Mortgage broker dealing in personal property only
    C. Individual serving as a personal representative and acting within the statutory limits of that designated role
    D. Business broker who negotiates leases of business property only

18. A salaried individual manages a condominium building and rents units for three-month to six-month periods. The manager
    A. must be licensed under F.S. 475 because leasing is one of the real estate services.
    B. must be licensed under F.S. 475 because she rents condominium units for compensation.
    C. must be licensed by the Division of Condominiums and Time Share Sales.
    D. is exempt from licensure under F.S. 475.

19. Rhoda is an on-site manager of an apartment complex. Rhoda receives a meager salary from the owner of the apartment complex. According to F.S. 475, Rhoda
    A. is exempt from licensure.
    B. must be a licensed real estate sales associate.
    C. must be a licensed real estate broker.
    D. is not exempt from licensure because she receives compensation.

20. FBI files reveal that six months ago Mr. Croft worked as a real estate broker in Georgia, where he was charged with arson related to a large insurance claim. To avoid a long court fight without pleading guilty, Mr. Croft agreed to revocation of his real estate license and entered a plea of *nolo contendere*. The FREC has just received Mr. Croft's application for licensure as a sales associate disclosing the above information. The application shows that all academic requirements have been met, and a background check reveals no incriminating information other than the facts mentioned above. The FREC will probably decide that
    A. Mr. Croft is not qualified for licensure.
    B. Mr. Croft can be licensed based on the information on the application.
    C. because Mr. Croft was never convicted of the charge in Georgia, he can be licensed in Florida.
    D. the recommendations from the references provide adequate grounds for the licensure of Mr. Croft.

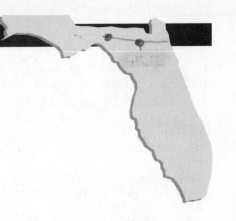

CHAPTER 3

License Law and Administration

■ KEY TERMS

canceled	involuntary inactive	quasi-judicial
current mailing address	multiple licenses	quasi-legislative
executive	prima facie evidence	void
group license	promulgate	voluntary inactive
ineffective		

1 ## ■ OVERVIEW

2 The purpose of this Chapter is to discuss in detail the Florida Real Estate
3 Commission and its composition and powers. The Chapter also explains
4 license requirements, including active and inactive status, license
5 activation, and void and ineffective licenses.

6   After completing this Chapter, the student should be able to:

7 • describe the composition and member qualifications of the Florida
8   Real Estate Commission;

9 • explain how members of the Commission are appointed;

10 • distinguish between active and inactive license status;

11 • explain the purpose of multiple and group licenses; and

12 • distinguish between void licenses and ineffective licenses.

13 ## ■ FLORIDA REAL ESTATE COMMISSION

14 The Florida Real Estate Commission (the FREC) is administratively part
15 of the Department of Business and Professional Regulation (the DBPR).
16 The FREC's purpose is to protect the general public by regulating real
17 estate brokers and brokerage firms, broker associates, sales associates,
18 and real estate schools and instructors, and to foster the education of real
19 estate licensees and permit holders. This includes the regulation of
20 proprietary real estate schools and all noncredit, FREC-approved courses
21 offered by colleges, universities, community colleges, and area technical

475.451, F.S.
475.04, F.S.
475.001, F.S.
455.201(1), F.S.

1 centers. The objective of such regulation is to protect the public
2 (consumer protection) by ensuring that real estate licensees have at least
3 a minimal degree of competence.

Purpose of Regulation

The Legislature deems it necessary in the interest of the public welfare to regulate real estate brokers, sales associates, and schools in this state.

Reference: Section 475.001, F.S.

---

4 ## COMPOSITION AND QUALIFICATIONS

5 The Florida Real Estate Commission (the FREC) consists of seven
6 members:

475.02, F.S.
455.209, F.S.
20.165, F.S.
61J2-20.040,
F.A.C.

7 • four must be licensed Florida real estate brokers who have held
8   active licenses during the five years preceding appointment;

7 Total

9 • two must be consumer members who have never been real estate
10   brokers or sales associates; and

11 • one must be either a licensed broker or sales associate who has
12   held an active license during the two years preceding
13   appointment.

14 The governor, subject to confirmation by the state Senate, appoints
15 Commission members to four-year terms. Commissioners may *not* serve
16 more than two consecutive terms.

17 Each member of the Commission is accountable to the governor, not
18 the DBPR, for proper performance. All FREC members are exempt from
19 civil liability while performing in their official capacity. At least one of the
20 seven members must be 60 years of age or older.

21 ## COMPENSATION

22 Commission members do not receive a salary. However, in lieu of salary,
23 they are paid $50 per day for each day they attend an official meeting and
24 for each day they participate in other Commission business. In addition,
25 they receive reimbursement for expenses connected with their official
26 activities. Any travel outside the state as members of the Commission
27 requires the prior approval of the DBPR Secretary.

455.207, F.S.
61J2-20.049,
F.A.C.

28 ## MEETINGS

29 The FREC meetings are held each month. There must be a quorum
30 consisting of at least 51 percent (or four Commission members) to
31 conduct official business. One of the meetings is designated the *annual*
32 *meeting* when the Commission elects from its members a chairperson and
33 vice-chairperson.

455.207, F.S.

COMMISSION GENERAL POWERS AND DUTIES

The powers and duties of the FREC fall into three general areas of responsibility:

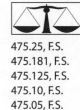

475.25, F.S.
475.181, F.S.
475.125, F.S.
475.10, F.S.
475.05, F.S.

1. **Executive** powers to regulate and enforce the license law are delegated to the Commission by the legislature.

2. **Quasi-legislative** responsibilities include the power to enact and revise administrative rules and regulations and to interpret questions regarding the practice of real estate.

3. **Quasi-judicial** responsibilities include the power to grant or deny license applications, to determine license law violations, and to administer penalties.

The FREC's powers and duties also include these specific responsibilities:

- *Adopt a seal.* The seal, when affixed to rules, regulations, or other official documents, properly signed, becomes **prima facie evidence** that the document is authentic. This means that it is good and sufficient and must be accepted on its face in all courts of the state.

- *Foster the education of applicants and licensees.* The Commission fosters the education of brokers, broker associates, sales associates, and instructors in ethical, legal, and business principles. It also prescribes post-licensing education requirements and continuing education requirements for brokers and sales associates to qualify for license renewal.

- *Make determinations of violations.* The Commission is obligated to report any criminal violation of Chapter 475, when it knows of such violations, to the state's attorney having jurisdiction. Furthermore, the FREC must inform the Division of Florida Land Sales, Condominiums, and Mobile Homes when any disciplinary action is taken by the FREC against any of its licensees.

- *Regulate professional practices.* For example, when requested and deemed appropriate, the Commission may issue an escrow disbursement order (EDO) to determine entitlement to escrowed property. The Commission also establishes rules and regulations requiring that records be maintained by brokers and the manner in which deposits of money, funds, checks, or drafts are to be made in escrow, pending disbursement.

- *Create and pass rules and regulations.* The Commission **promulgates** (enacts) rules and regulations that enforce the Florida statutory license law.

- *Establish fees.* The Commission uses the DBPR estimates of required revenue to determine the amount of licensing fees needed to implement the real estate license law and other laws and regulations relating to the regulation of real estate practitioners.

- *Grant or deny applications for licensure.* The Commission certifies an applicant as qualified before a license is issued.

- *Suspend or revoke licenses and impose administrative fines.* The Commission adopts, by rule, guidelines for the disciplinary actions that it imposes.

With the prior approval of the attorney general, the Commission may retain independent counsel to provide legal advice. However, an attorney employed to provide legal advice to the Commission may not also prosecute the same case.

475.03, F.S.

The powers of the FREC are limited to administrative matters and do not extend to criminal actions. The FREC may *not* impose imprisonment as a penalty. The primary purpose of the administrative jurisdiction granted to the Commission is to enforce duties and obligations as they apply to individuals and firms actively engaged in the real estate business. (See Chapter 6.) The Commission makes decisions and sets policies that are carried out by the Division of Real Estate (DRE).

The DRE provides all services required to administer the Florida Real Estate License Law. However, the FREC is empowered by law to delegate by majority vote any duty or duties to whichever division within DBPR the Commission feels is appropriate. The FREC can also rescind, by majority vote, any delegation of duties at any time.

■ DEPARTMENT OF BUSINESS AND PROFESSIONAL REGULATION (DBPR)

The DBPR regulates licensed professions in Florida. The chief administrator of the DBPR is the Secretary of the DBPR who is appointed by the governor. The main DBPR office is located in Tallahassee, Florida. The divisions under the Department of Business and Professional Regulation that are most relevant to real estate are presented below.

20.165, F.S.
61J2-20.048, F.A.C.

THE DIVISION OF PROFESSIONS AND REGULATION

The Division of Professions and Regulation administers numerous professional boards. Due to the magnitude of the real estate profession, it is organized as a separate division under the DBPR. The Division of Professionals and Regulation is responsible for the enforcement of the professions and related businesses regulated by the DBPR.

DIVISION OF SERVICE OPERATIONS AND LICENSURE

The Division of Service Operations and Licensure is another division under the DBPR that is of interest to real estate licensees. Several important units are under the Division of Service Operations and Licensure:

- The Bureau of Education and Testing regulates education courses and license examinations for each profession under the DBPR.

- The Customer Contact Center handles all incoming telephone, postal, and e-mail inquiries from licensees and the general public.

1 • The Central Intake Unit processes all of the license applications
2 and license fees that come into the DBPR. The Central Intake Unit
3 is also responsible for the issuance of all licenses and license
4 renewal notifications for the Department.

DIVISION OF REAL ESTATE

475.021, F.S.

6 The Division of Real Estate performs all functions related to the regulation
7 of general real estate in Florida. Administrative and ministerial services
8 performed by the DRE include but are not limited to record-keeping,
9 examination, legal, and investigative services. The DRE is funded by fees,
10 publication sales, and other charges assessed by the Commission. Money
11 generated from these sources must be used only to fund real estate
12 regulation activities. Florida statute mandates that the DRE offices and
13 the principal office of the Commission are located in Orlando. Additional
14 facts concerning the DRE are presented below:

15 • The Director of the DRE is appointed by the Secretary of the DBPR,
16 subject to approval by majority vote of the FREC. The Director is a
17 senior employee charged with the direct service assistance to the
18 Commission.

19 • The DBPR employs all DRE personnel to support FREC activities.

20 • Members of the Commission, on the other hand, are appointed by
21 the governor, subject to senate confirmation, and are *not* employees.

■ REAL ESTATE REGULATION

LICENSING EXAMINATIONS

455.217, F.S.

24 The Division of Technology, Licensure, and Testing (TLT) provides or
25 contracts for exam development services. The DBPR, acting with its
26 Division of TLT and the Division of Real Estate, must ensure that the
27 license examinations adequately and reliably measure an applicant's
28 ability to practice real estate. The FREC or the DBPR may reject any
29 question that does not reliably measure the general areas of competency
30 specified in the FREC rules.

31 Florida law requires that an accurate record of each applicant's
32 examination questions, answers, papers, grades, and grading key be stored
33 for two years. Examinees' grades and the state examination questions are
34 confidential. The theft of a DBPR license examination or unauthorized
35 copying of an examination is a third degree felony.

LICENSE FEES

37 New applicants for licensure are assessed an initial application fee and a
38 fingerprint card fee in addition to the biennial license fee. All applicants
39 for initial licensure and for subsequent license renewal also pay an
40 unlicensed activity fee and may be required to pay a Real Estate
41 Recovery Fund fee, if applicable. (See Real Estate Recovery Fund in

1 Chapter 6.) Applicants submit the license exam fee directly to the test
2 vendor. Table 3.1 presents a complete list of fees. (See page 37.)

CURRENT MAILING ADDRESS

4 Licensees are responsible for notifying the DBPR in writing of their
5 current mailing address. **Current mailing address** is the current
6 residential address a licensee uses to receive mail through the U.S. Postal
7 Service. A post office box is considered to be an acceptable mailing
8 address.

9   Licensees must notify the DBPR in writing within 10 days of a change
10 in current mailing address. Licensees who fail to timely notify the DBPR of
11 a change of address are in violation of Florida Statute 455 and are subject to
12 a citation and $100 fine. Florida licensees who move out of state must also
13 comply with all nonresident requirements. (See Nonresident Application
14 Requirements in Chapter 2.)

455.275(1), F.S.
61J2-10.038,
F.A.C.

LICENSE RENEWAL PERIODS

16 Real estate licenses expire on either March 31 or September 30. The
17 expiration date of the initial license is the date (March 31 or September
18 30) that provides at least 18 months of initial licensure but does not
19 exceed 24 months. For example, assume on July 25, 2005, an initial license
20 is issued. That license will expire on March 31, 2007 (approximately
21 20 months of licensure). Thereafter, every two years (biennially) on
22 March 31, the real estate license expires and must be renewed. Sixty days
23 before the end of the license period, the DBPR mails a renewal notice
24 to the licensee's last known address.

455.203, F.S.
475.182, F.S.

LICENSE RENEWAL

26 Sales associates and brokers must complete their post-license education
27 *before the first renewal* of their initial licenses. After the post-license
28 education is satisfied and the initial license is renewed, licensees must
29 complete 14-hours of continuing education during each renewal period.

30   To renew a real estate license, the licensee submits a renewal
31 application and the biennial license fee. Real estate licensees must
32 complete the applicable post-licensing or continuing education
33 requirement *before* renewing a license. When a licensee signs and returns
34 the renewal application the licensee is attesting to have completed the
35 education requirement. (Refer to Post-licensing Education and Continuing
36 Education in Chapter 2.)

475.182, F.S.
455.02, F.S.
61J2-3.020,
F.A.C.

37   If licensees renew after the expiration date a late fee is charged. (See
38 Table 3.1.) If a licensee does not renew his or her license by the expiration
39 date, the license reverts automatically to involuntary inactive status.
40 (Involuntary inactive status is discussed later in this Chapter.) An active
41 licensee who fails to renew his or her license following expiration has
42 24 months in which to renew the license. A real estate licensee must *not*
43 practice real estate following the expiration of his or her license. It is also
44 unlawful for a licensee holding a current *inactive* license to perform the
45 services of real estate for compensation.

TABLE 3.1   Schedule of Fees*

LICENSE	INITIAL LICENSE AND APPLICATION FEE†‡	BIENNIAL LICENSE FEE‡
Broker	$162	$90
Broker Associate	—	90
Sales Associate	152	80
Mutual Recognition Broker	162	90
Mutual Recognition Sales Associate	152	80
Branch Office (broker, corporation, partnership, limited liability company, or limited liability partnership)	80	80
Corporation, partnership, limited liability company, or limited liability partnership	90	90
Late fee for renewal		45

REISSUE	FEE
Change of address by corporation, partnership, broker, *or* school	none
Change of broker, owner, *or* school by broker associate, sales associate, *or* instructor	none
Change of individual license to Professional Association (P.A.) *or* change from P.A. to individual license	$30 each
Lost or destroyed license (all licensees) to be duplicated	$25
Change from active broker to broker associate	none

LICENSE EXAMINATION	FEE
Exam fees (paid directly to National Testing Vendor)	
Broker	$31.50
Sales Associate	$31.50
Real Estate Law Exam	$13.50

* FREC Rule 61J2-1.011. Fees subject to rule change by the FREC. License period duration subject to change by DBPR. Check with the instructor or the DRE for the latest fees.

† An administrative processing charge that includes the fingerprint card fee and the initial license fee. For example, the fee for a sales associate is: $80 license fee + $47 fingerprint card + $20 application fee + $5 unlicensed activity fee = $152.

‡ Note 1: An unlicensed activity fee of $5 also applies to all brokers, broker associates, sales associates, brokerage entities, schools, and instructors.

Note 2: When applicable, a Real Estate Recovery Fund fee for brokers ($3.50 per year) and sales associates ($1.50 per year) is collected from both active and inactive licensees for new and renewal licenses. (See also Chapter 6.)

Armed Forces exemption. A licensee in good standing who is a member of the U.S. Armed Forces is exempt from the renewal provisions during his or her active duty and for a period of six months after discharge from active duty. If the military duty is out of state, the exemption also applies to a licensed spouse. The Armed Forces exemption applies provided the licensee is not engaged in real estate brokerage activity in the private sector for profit.

455.02, FS.
61J2-1.015,
F.A.C.

Obtained a License by Fraud, Misrepresentation, or Concealment

In the case of a licensee who renews his or her license without having complied with Rule 61J2-3.009 and the licensee's act is discovered by the BPR, the usual action of the Commission shall be to impose a penalty of revocation or suspension.

Reference: 61J2-24.001(3)(n) [Note: Lesser penalties apply for a first-time offense according to Citation Authority Rule 61J2-24.002(2)(k).]

INACTIVE STATUS

Licensees who choose not to engage in the real estate business may place their licenses on inactive status. There are two types of inactive status recognized in Florida: (1) voluntary inactive and (2) involuntary inactive.

475.183, F.S.
475.182, F.S.

Voluntary inactive. A licensee who has qualified for license status but who voluntarily chooses not to engage in the real estate business during a given period and requests such a change is placed on **voluntary inactive** status. A licensee may change an active license to a voluntary inactive license status by submitting to the DRE a Request for Change of Status form. Such licensees hold a current inactive license. Before the expiration date of a license, a renewal notice is mailed to all inactive and active licensees.

Voluntary inactive licensees who subsequently wish to activate their licenses may do so at any time simply by completing the proper form requesting an active license with an active broker or owner-developer. As with an active license, a licensee may renew a current voluntary inactive license indefinitely. Voluntary inactive licensees who satisfactorily complete the prescribed continuing education courses every two years must pay the appropriate fees to qualify for renewal of a voluntary inactive license. A license that is not renewed at the end of the license period reverts automatically to involuntary inactive status, except in the case of initial licenses when post-licensing education requirements have not been completed satisfactorily.

61J2-1.014,
F.A.C.

Involuntary inactive. If a licensee fails to renew an active or voluntary inactive license before the expiration date (other than the first renewal), the license reverts automatically to **involuntary inactive** status. The licensee must complete his or her continuing education and renew the license to either active or voluntary inactive status within the next two years. A license is placed in involuntary inactive status for no more than two years. After two years the license automatically becomes null and void without further FREC or DBPR action.

	Inactive Status
Voluntary Inactive	The licensure status that results when a licensee has applied to the Department to be placed on inactive status and has paid the fee prescribed by rule
Involuntary Inactive	The licensure status that results when a license is not renewed at the end of the license period prescribed by the Department

Reference: Section 475.01, F.S.

1 Ninety days before expiration of an involuntary inactive license, the
2 DBPR notifies licensees of this upcoming deadline. Once a license becomes
3 void, the individual must reapply for licensure by retaking the 63-hour
4 prelicense course and again passing the license exam.

5 Involuntary inactive licensees may activate their licenses during the
6 two-year period following expiration of a valid current license only after
7 satisfactorily completing FREC-prescribed courses of instruction. When a
8 licensee has been involuntary inactive for:

475.183, F.S.
455.271(6), F.S.
61J2-3.010,
F.A.C.
61J2-1.014
F.A.C.

9 • 12 months or less, licensees may satisfy the education requirement
10   by completing 14 hours of FREC-approved continuing education;
11   or

12 • more than 12 months but less than 24 months, licensees are
13   required to complete two 14-hour continuing education courses.

14 There is another situation that will cause a license to be placed in
15 involuntary inactive status. If a sales associate's broker is disciplined and
16 as a result the broker's license is suspended or revoked, the sales
17 associate's license will be automatically placed in involuntary inactive
18 status. This is because a sales associate can only perform real estate
19 services for compensation under the direction of his or her employer.
20 A sales associate's license is returned to active status as soon as a new
21 broker is chosen and the information is filed with the DBPR.

22 ## VOID AND INEFFECTIVE LICENSES

23 When a license becomes **void** it no longer exists. A license becomes void
24 when the following situations occur:

475.183(2), F.S.
61J2-24.005,
F.A.C.

25 • **Expired.** When a license is involuntary inactive for more than
26   two years, the license automatically expires and it becomes null
27   and void.

28 • **Revoked.** Revocation of a license following a disciplinary
29   proceeding is *permanent*, putting the licensee out of the real estate
30   business, with two exceptions:

31   1. A licensee has filed for renewal but has not complied with the
32   continuing or post-licensing education requirements prior to
33   the expiration date.

2. An individual has filed an application for licensure that contained false or fraudulent information.

In these situations, an individual may reapply for a sales associate's license after five years have passed.

*   **Canceled.** A person who no longer wants to engage in the real estate business can voluntarily cancel being licensed. When a license is **canceled** it becomes void. Cancellation of a license is effective on the date it is approved by the Commission. Cancellation does not involve disciplinary action.

When a license is **ineffective,** the license exists but the licensee cannot use it. A license becomes ineffective when the following situations occur:

1. **Inactive.** Real estate licensees may *not* perform real estate services with an inactive license.

    *   A licensee who has met all of the requirements for licensure but chooses not to work in the real estate industry may request that his or her license status be changed to voluntary inactive status.

    *   If a licensee fails to renew his or her license prior to the expiration date (other than the first renewal), the license is automatically placed in involuntary inactive status.

    *   When a broker's license is suspended or revoked, no disciplinary action is taken against the sales associates and broker associates registered under that broker. However, the licensees registered under the disciplined broker cannot continue working because their employer's license is either void (revoked) or ineffective (suspended). The DBPR places the licenses of any sales associates and broker associates registered under the penalized broker on involuntary inactive status. The sales associates and broker associates are free to seek another employer and register as active under the new employer. Otherwise, the licensee should request a change of status to voluntary inactive status.

2. **Suspended.** If the result of a disciplinary proceeding is to suspend a license, the licensee is prevented from working for a period of time. The license is ineffective during the period of suspension.

475.31, F.S.

The Commission must be notified within ten days when either of the following actions occurs:

*   A broker or registered school changes business address.

*   A sales associate or real estate instructor changes employer.

475.23, F.S.

The license will *cease to be in force* until the Commission receives proper notification. Failure to give notification in a timely manner may result in disciplinary action.

When a broker or a real estate school changes business address, the brokerage firm or school permit holder must file with the Commission a notice of the change of address, along with the names of any sales associates or instructors who are no longer employed by the brokerage or school. Sales associates who are no longer employed with the broker of record will be placed on *involuntary inactive status*. The notification to the Commission fulfills the change of address notification requirements for sales associates who remain employed by the brokerage and instructors who remain employed by the school. The licenses of sales associates working for a broker who changes his or her business address remain in force. The same is true for instructors working for a real estate school that changes its business address.

MULTIPLE AND GROUP LICENSES

Multiple licenses are issued to brokers who qualify as the broker for more than one business entity. A broker who holds more than one Florida broker license is said to hold **multiple licenses.** Because a sales associate or broker associate may work for only one employer at a time, neither a sales associate nor a broker associate may hold multiple licenses.

475.215, F.S.

A **group license** is a term used to mean that a sales associate is registered with an owner-developer who owns properties in the name of various entities. The owner-developer may produce proof to the DRE that all of the various entities are connected, interlocked, or affiliated entities, meaning that ownership and control, for practical purposes, rest substantially in the same individual(s). In such a situation, a sales associate or broker associate employed by the owner-developer may be issued a group license. It is understood that the sales associate or broker associate may work for any of the subsidiaries but that the subsidiaries are all under the owner-developer/employer. In actual practice, the sales associate is issued a sales associate license and no distinction is made on the face of the license.

61J2-6.006, F.A.C.

REGISTRATION OF PROPRIETARY REAL ESTATE SCHOOLS

Each person, school, or institution in Florida that offers courses or training programs designed to aid applicants in becoming licensed real estate sales associates or brokers must be registered and receive a permit. This requirement does not apply to accredited colleges, universities, community colleges, or area technical centers when transferable college credit courses are involved (their noncredit courses are not exempt). However, all courses conducted by institutions exempt from obtaining a permit must meet the equivalency standards established by the FREC. This means that the Commission is not required to recognize students from exempt institutions as qualified to take a state licensing examination until and unless those courses have been approved by the FREC as equivalent to the Course I and Course II standards.

475.451, F.S.
475.04, F.S.
61J2-17.009, F.A.C.
61J2-3.008, F.A.C.

Proprietary schools of real estate are prohibited from advertising or making representations that are known to be false, inaccurate, misleading, or exaggerated. The content of advertisements must conform to specified

475.4511, F.S.

guidelines. A proprietary real estate school may not promise or guarantee employment or placement of a student or prospective student on the basis of training to be provided unless the school actually offers the student a bona fide employment contract.

A school permit may be suspended for:

- guaranteeing that students will pass a state examination;

- offering a refund to students who fail;

61J2-17.013, F.A.C.

- representing that a state agency endorses the school;

- obtaining a list of questions that appear on any state examination;

- representing that the school or an instructor has obtained questions from such an examination; or

- furnishing anyone, student or otherwise, questions purported to be from a state examination.

■ REAL ESTATE EDUCATION AND RESEARCH FOUNDATION

The 1985 Florida Legislature established the Florida Real Estate Commission Education and Research Foundation. The Foundation is administered by the Florida Real Estate Commission. The Foundation funds worthy real estate education projects and real estate research. The Foundation is required to give priority to "projects with the greatest potential for direct or indirect benefit to the public." The law lists a number of other purposes, objectives, and duties, all centered around the Foundation's overall purpose, which is "to create and promote educational projects to expand the knowledge of the public and real estate licensees in matters pertaining to Florida real estate." To carry out its duties, the Foundation may solicit advice and information from real estate licensees, universities, colleges, real estate schools, and the general public.

475.045, F.S.
215.37, F.S.
61J2-25, F.A.C.

Foundation activities and projects are funded from income derived from the real estate portion of the Professional Regulation Trust Fund. The director of the DRE is responsible for submitting to the Commission, in advance of each fiscal year, a budget for expenditure of funds to conduct proposed activities. The Commission then reviews and approves the proposed budget. A report of the Foundation's activities and accomplishments must be published annually.

■ SUMMARY

The Florida Real Estate Commission administers and enforces laws regulating real estate practices and the licensing of applicants. However, the Commission does not regulate those real estate practices that relate to appraising, as described in Chapter 475, Part II, F.S. The Division of Real Estate, Department of Business and Professional Regulation, provides

1 the Commission with all of the services necessary to administer the
2 Florida Real Estate License Law (Chapter 475, Part I, F.S.). Initial licenses,
3 active and inactive licenses, registration of private schools of real estate,
4 license renewal and activation, and license fees are described.

■ REVIEW QUESTIONS

1. The statements below are true with respect to the members of the
   Florida Real Estate Commission EXCEPT that they
   A. are a mix of real estate practitioners and consumer members.
   B. are accountable to the governor for proper performance.
   C. are DBPR employees.
   D. depend on the DRE for their administrative assistance.

2. Members of the FREC are appointed by the
   A. governor and confirmed by the cabinet.
   B. governor and confirmed by the DBPR Secretary.
   C. DBPR Secretary and confirmed by the governor.
   D. governor and confirmed by the state Senate.

3. The Commission's purpose is to regulate
   A. real estate brokers, broker associates, and sales associates.
   B. real estate schools and instructors.
   C. real estate brokerage firms.
   D. all of the above.

4. A holder of a voluntary inactive license on active duty with the
   U.S. Army is required to renew his or her license
   A. every two years.
   B. on discharge.
   C. within one year after discharge.
   D. within six months after discharge.

5. The term of office for each Commission member is
   A. two years.
   B. four years.
   C. five years.
   D. seven years.

6. The members of the Commission receive
   A. no compensation for their services.
   B. only a per-diem fee when on official business.
   C. $50 per day when on official business, plus expenses.
   D. an annual salary equal to a state legislator's annual salary.

7. Legal counsel to the Commission is provided by
    A. the DRE chief staff attorney and his or her staff.
    B. the Florida Bar Association.
    C. the Division of Administrative Hearings.
    D. independent counsel with the prior approval of the attorney general.

8. The Commission is NOT empowered to
    A. make determinations of violations.
    B. impose administrative fines.
    C. levy fines and imprisonment as penalties for certain crimes.
    D. adopt an official seal that, when used on a document, certificate, proceeding, or act of the Commission, is prima facie evidence of its authenticity in all matters of law in this state.

9. Specific responsibilities of the FREC do NOT include
    A. determining the amount of licensing fees needed to operate the Commission.
    B. reporting criminal violations to the state's attorney.
    C. informing the Division of Florida Land Sales, Condominiums, and Mobile Homes of disciplinary action against any of its licensees.
    D. providing the services necessary for the preparation and administration of licensing examinations.

10. Fees assessed by the Commission are to be used for
    A. general state revenues.
    B. overall DBPR activities.
    C. the regulation of all DBPR licensees.
    D. the regulation of real estate practitioners.

11. Sales associate Jenny recently moved from Dunedin, Florida, to High Springs, Florida.
    A. Jenny must notify the DRE of her change in current mailing address within 60 days of the change.
    B. Jenny must notify the DRE of her change in current mailing address within 10 days of the change.
    C. If Jenny does not change brokers, she is not required to notify the DRE of her change in mailing address.
    D. Jenny's license is automatically canceled until she notifies the DRE of her change in current mailing address.

12. Sales associate Sal is employed by Broker Barb. Barb's license is suspended. This action causes Sal's license to be
    A. placed in involuntary inactive status.
    B. suspended.
    C. revoked.
    D. unaffected.

13. When an active broker changes his or her business address and the broker notifies the FREC within the required ten days, the licenses of the sales associates
    A. remain in force.
    B. cease to be in force.
    C. are null and void.
    D. are temporarily ineffective.

14. If an active licensee fails to renew her third two-year license before the expiration date on the license, the license will
    A. revert automatically to involuntary inactive status at the end of the license period.
    B. be suspended automatically.
    C. be canceled, and the licensee will have to retake both the course and the licensing exams.
    D. be canceled, and the licensee will have to retake the licensing exam only.

15. An involuntary inactive license will automatically expire without further action by the FREC or the DBPR after
    A. two years.
    B. four years.
    C. five years.
    D. ten years.

16. Who may NOT reactivate a license to active status?
    A. A voluntary inactive sales associate
    B. A licensed corporate director of a real estate company
    C. An involuntary inactive broker
    D. A sales associate who did not complete his or her post-licensing education prior to the expiration of the initial license

17. An owner-developer owns several properties with different names, but all are business entities closely connected and controlled by the owner-developer. A sales associate working for that owner-developer may legally obtain
    A. a group license.
    B. multiple licenses.
    C. either a group license or multiple licenses, but not both.
    D. neither a group license nor multiple licenses.

18. Broker Vagabond moves his real estate office to a new, trendy location. He is so busy coordinating the move that he forgets to notify the DBPR. Broker Vagabond's license
    A. will cease to be in force.
    B. is null and void.
    C. is automatically suspended.
    D. is canceled.

19. The statements below are true regarding the inactive status of a real estate licensee EXCEPT that a license
    A. may be placed on voluntary inactive status at any time at the request of the licensee.
    B. that has been on involuntary inactive status for more than two years shall expire automatically.
    C. that has been on voluntary inactive status may be reactivated by making application to the DBPR and submitting proof of completing the education requirement and payment of the appropriate fees.
    D. that has been on involuntary inactive status automatically expires at the end of four years.

20. Sandi decides to relocate her real estate brokerage office. She notifies the Commission of the change in business address. Sandi also informs the Commission of the names of two sales associates who are no longer associated with her brokerage. The sales associates' licenses will be
    A. suspended until they find new employment.
    B. canceled.
    C. null and void.
    D. placed on involuntary inactive status.

CHAPTER 4

Brokerage Relationships and Ethics

■ KEY TERMS

agent	fiduciary	residential sales
customer	fraud	single agent
designated sales associate	general agent	special agent
dual agent	misrepresentation	transaction broker
	principal	universal agent

■ OVERVIEW

This Chapter begins with a general explanation of the law of agency and then details the various types of brokerage relationships practiced in Florida. The Chapter also explains the licensee's duties and obligations to principals and customers. The terms *misrepresentation* and *fraud* are defined, and fraudulent activities are discussed. The Chapter concludes with a section about professional ethics.

After completing this Chapter, the student should be able to:

- distinguish between the terms *general agent* and *special agent;*

- describe which legal provisions apply only to residential real estate transactions;

- describe the duties and disclosure requirements of a transaction broker;

- describe the duties and disclosure requirements that single agents have to their principals;

- define a *dual agent;*

- describe the purpose and requirements of the no brokerage relationship notice;

- list the no brokerage relationship duties;

- describe the process of transition from a single agent to a transaction broker;

- identify actions that will terminate an agency; and

- recognize activities that are considered to be fraudulent.

■ LAW OF AGENCY

When a person delegates authority to someone to act on his or her behalf, an agency relationship has been created. Agency relationships fall within the body of law called *law of agency.*

There are two types of law that society looks to for guidance regarding agency relationships: common law and statutory law.

775.01, F.S.

Common law derives authority from customs rooted in the common law of England prior to the American Revolution and from the judgments and decrees of the courts (case law) that have since affirmed and enforced those customs. Under the English common law, a servant owed absolute loyalty to his or her master. This absolute loyalty is one of the fundamental principles of the agency relationship as we know it today.

Statutory law includes the statutes and rules enacted by legislatures and other governing bodies. In addition to the statutory laws of agency, real estate license law and the Florida Real Estate Commission (the FREC) rules directly affect and regulate the brokerage relationships among real estate licensees, buyers and sellers, and the public.

AGENCY RELATIONSHIPS IN GENERAL BUSINESS DEALINGS

In general, a person who delegates authority to another is referred to as the *principal.* A person who accepts the authority (and responsibilities, duties, and obligations associated with that authority) is referred to as the *agent.* An **agent** is the person entrusted with another's business. An agent is authorized to represent and act for his or her principal.

The agency relationship creates a *fiduciary relationship* with the principal. A *fiduciary* acts in a position of trust or confidence for another. The fiduciary owes complete allegiance to the principal. A fiduciary relationship contrasts with the common public relationship that exists in normal trading transactions where people with adverse interests are said to be *dealing at arm's length* with one another. In such cases, the legal doctrine of *caveat emptor* (let the buyer beware) usually applies. Agency relationships exist in many business transactions such as between an attorney (agent) and client (principal). An agency relationship may exist in certain real estate transactions. (This will be explained in detail in the next section of the Chapter.)

Various degrees of authority can be given to an agent. There are three types of agents characterized by the scope of authority delegated to an agent in general business dealings: (1) universal agent, (2) general agent, and (3) special agent.

A **universal agent** is authorized by the principal to perform all acts that the principal can personally perform and that may be lawfully delegated to another. An attorney who manages the trust agreement of a mentally retarded adult is a universal agent for his or her client (the principal). Duties of the attorney-agent would include, for example, overseeing the principal's financial affairs, medical care, employment opportunities, and living arrangements.

1 A **general agent** is authorized by the principal to perform only acts
2 related to a business or to employment of a particular nature. A property
3 manager, for example, acts as a general agent if he or she is authorized to
4 show and rent apartments, collect rents, supervise maintenance and
5 upkeep of the property, handle tenant relations, and perform
6 bookkeeping duties.

7 A **special agent** is authorized by the principal to handle only a
8 specific business transaction or to perform only a specific act. If you hire
9 a certified public accountant (CPA) to prepare your tax return and, if
10 necessary, to answer any inquiries from the IRS concerning the tax
11 return, the CPA is acting as a special agent for you (the principal). A real
12 estate licensee may act as a special agent with buyers or sellers. This
13 occurs when the buyer or seller and the brokerage firm enter into a single
14 agent relationship. The broker agrees to represent the buyer or seller with
15 regard to a single business transaction. Not all real estate brokers act as
16 agents of buyers and sellers. (See Single Agent Relationship on page 52.)

17 ## ■ BROKERAGE RELATIONSHIPS IN FLORIDA

18 Historically, there has been confusion among buyers and sellers
19 regarding what role real estate licensees have in real estate negotiations.
20 The payment or promise of payment (compensation) alone to a licensee
21 does not determine whether a brokerage relationship has been created.
22 Offer and acceptance of authority to act is required. Earlier studies that
23 surveyed buyers of real estate found that the buyers typically believed
24 that the real estate licensee represented them instead of the sellers. This
25 led to a move by most state legislatures to enact agency laws. The Florida
26 legislature and the real estate industry have made several attempts to
27 define brokerage relationships and disclosure requirements as they apply
28 to real estate dealings.

475.255, F.S.
475.01, F.S.

29 Buyers and sellers have three basic options in all real estate
30 transactions concerning the role the real estate brokerage firm will
31 assume for them:

32 1. The brokerage firm may work as a *transaction broker* for the buyer
33   and/or the seller.

34 2. The brokerage firm may work as a *single agent* of either the buyer
35   or the seller (but *not* for both buyer and seller in the same
36   transaction).

37 3. The parties may agree that the brokerage firm will not represent
38   the buyer or the seller at all. This situation is referred to as *no*
39   *brokerage relationship*. The brokerage firm simply facilitates the
40   transaction.

41 In Florida, a real estate licensee may enter into a brokerage
42 relationship either as a transaction broker or as a single agent with
43 prospective buyers and sellers. Buyers and sellers are not required to
44 establish a brokerage relationship with a real estate broker. Alternatively,
45 the customer may have no brokerage relationship with the brokerage

1 firm. For example, property owners who have found buyers for their
2 own homes (for-sale-by-owners, also referred to as FSBOs) may want a
3 knowledgeable real estate firm to handle the paperwork regarding the
4 transaction. However, a FSBO seller may not need or desire the broker to
5 represent or negotiate on the seller's behalf. In such cases, FSBOs may
6 elect no brokerage relationship with the brokerage firm.

7 A real estate licensee may _not_ operate as a dual agent. The term **dual**
8 **agent** means a broker who represents as a fiduciary both the prospective
9 buyer and the prospective seller in a real estate transaction. When a
10 broker represents a buyer or a seller as a **fiduciary,** the broker is in a
11 relationship of trust and confidence between the broker as agent and the
12 seller as principal or the buyer as principal. A fiduciary relationship is
13 created when a real estate broker accepts employment as a single agent of
14 the seller or the buyer. Florida real estate license law prohibits a broker
15 from creating a fiduciary relationship with both the buyer and the seller.

475.01, F.S.

RESIDENTIAL TRANSACTIONS

17 Chapter 475 mandates certain duties and obligations in each type of
18 brokerage relationship. These duties and obligations apply to _all_ real
19 estate transactions. However, written disclosures are required only when
20 dealing in residential real estate transactions.

475.278, F.S.

21 A **residential sale** is defined as the sale of improved residential
22 property of four or fewer units, the sale of unimproved residential
23 property intended for use as four or fewer units, or the sale of
24 agricultural property of ten or fewer acres. Furthermore, the disclosure
25 requirements do _not_ apply to:

26 • nonresidential transactions;

27 • the rental or leasing of real property, unless an option to purchase
28 all or a portion of the property improved with four or fewer
29 residential units is given;

30 • auctions;

31 • appraisals; and

32 • dispositions of any interest in business enterprises or business
33 opportunities, except for property with four or fewer
34 residential units.

TRANSACTION BROKER RELATIONSHIP

36 Under Florida law, it is presumed that all licensees are operating as
37 transaction brokers unless a single agent or no brokerage relationship is
38 established, in writing, with the customer. A **transaction broker** is a
39 broker who provides limited representation to a buyer, a seller, or both in
40 a real estate transaction, but who does _not_ represent either party in a
41 fiduciary capacity or as a single agent. In this relationship, the seller
42 (or the buyer) is considered to be a customer of the real estate broker and
43 _not_ a principal. In a transaction broker relationship the buyer or seller
44 (customer) is not responsible for the acts of a licensee.

475.278, F.S.
475.01, F.S.

Chapter 475 defines **customer** to mean a member of the public who is or may be a buyer or a seller of real property and may or may not be represented by a real estate licensee in an authorized brokerage relationship. Therefore, the seller (or the buyer) is a customer if he or she chooses limited representation under the transaction broker relationship. A licensee may enter into a transaction broker relationship with both parties (buyer and seller) in a real estate transaction. The seven duties of the transaction broker in this limited form of representation are as follows:

1. **Deal honestly and fairly.** Licensees owe a duty of good faith and honesty to customers. A broker's customers are entitled to rely on any material statement related to a real estate transaction that is made by a licensee.

2. **Account for all funds.** The broker must account for all funds entrusted to him or her with regard to a real estate transaction. Such holdings are considered trust funds or escrow funds. Money and valuables entrusted to a broker must be kept separate from the broker's funds. The broker is not entitled to any trust or escrow funds until the transaction is concluded at a title closing. Brokers are required to keep complete records of all transactions and funds as well as to make available to the Department of Business and Professional Regulation (DBPR) such books, accounts, and records as will enable the DBPR to determine whether the broker is in compliance with Chapter 475.

475.5015, F.S.

3. **Use skill, care, and diligence in the transaction.** The broker, for example, must keep informed of current zoning and other developments that may affect the value of the property and must use diligence in facilitating the transaction.

4. **Disclose all known facts that materially affect the value of residential real property and are not readily observable to the buyer.** Licensees have a duty to disclose to buyers all known facts that materially affect the value of residential property. For example, a licensee is obligated to inform the buyer if a building lot is in a floodplain and requires landfill before the lot can be used. A licensee also is obligated to inform a buyer if a construction lien has been recorded against a listed property.

Questions sometimes arise regarding whether certain information concerning the seller or previous occupants of a property must be disclosed to prospective buyers. Federal fair housing law and the Florida statutes specifically mandate that the fact that an occupant of real property is infected or has been infected with human immunodeficiency virus (HIV) or diagnosed with acquired immune deficiency syndrome is *not* a material fact in a real estate transaction. This is personal medical information and must not be disclosed without prior authorization. Furthermore, Florida statute mandates the fact that a property was, or was at any time suspected to have been, the site of a homicide, suicide, or death is *not* a material fact in a real estate transaction. A cause of action will not arise against a property owner or a real estate licensee for failure to disclose any of the information or events listed above.

689.25, F.S.

5. **Present all offers and counteroffers in a timely manner.** Unless a party has previously directed the licensee otherwise in writing, the licensee must present all offers and counteroffers in a timely manner.

6. **Exercise limited confidentiality, unless waived in writing by a party.** This limited confidentiality will prevent disclosure that the seller will accept a price less than the asking or listed price; that the buyer will pay a price greater than the price submitted in a written offer; of the motivation of any party for selling or buying property; that a seller or buyer will agree to financing terms other than those offered; or of any other information requested by a party to remain confidential.

7. **Perform any additional duties that are mutually agreed to with a party.** A real estate licensee must be careful not to accept duties beyond the scope of limited representation. To do so might create an unintended fiduciary relationship with a customer. For example, a transaction broker may not promise complete allegiance to a customer because to do so could be interpreted by a court of law to have created a fiduciary relationship.

In a transaction broker relationship, the parties to a real estate transaction are giving up their rights to the undivided loyalty of a licensee. This aspect of *limited representation* allows a licensee to facilitate a real estate transaction by assisting both the buyer and the seller. However, a licensee will not work to represent one party to the detriment of the other party when acting as a transaction broker to both parties. The seven duties listed above apply to all real estate transactions (residential and otherwise) when the parties have agreed to a transaction broker relationship. (See Figure 4.1 on page 64.)

SINGLE AGENT RELATIONSHIP

A seller (or a buyer) may want to be represented by a real estate broker. In this case, the real estate broker is a single agent who represents the seller as a fiduciary in selling his or her home or the buyer in finding a home. The Florida real estate license law defines a **single agent** as a broker who represents, as a fiduciary, either the buyer or the seller, but *not both*, in the same transaction. In a single agent relationship, the seller (or the buyer) is the principal and the real estate broker is the agent. The term **principal** is used to mean the party with whom a real estate licensee has entered into a single agent relationship.

475.278, F.S.
475.01, F.S.

A *subagent* is a person whose duties as an agent are delegated by the original agent. A sales associate who works under the supervision of a broker who has a single agent relationship with a principal is a subagent of the broker. Sales associates and broker associates owe the same fiduciary obligations to the principal as does their broker. (*Note:* This is true regardless of whether the associate, for tax purposes, is an employee or an independent contractor of the broker.) The nine duties a real estate licensee owes to a buyer or seller who engage the real estate brokerage as a single agent are as follows:

1. **Deal honestly and fairly.** (See page 51, for explanation.)

2. **Loyalty.** The agent as fiduciary in a real estate transaction must be to avoid any situation that might breach the duty of undivided loyalty to the principal. The overriding rule is that a broker may not adopt an attitude that is adverse to the interests of the principal or act for himself or herself or some other person whose interests are contrary to those of the principal. Loyalty (faithfulness) requires the broker to always place the principal's interests above those of other persons with whom the broker deals. Courts have ruled (case law) that for brokers to be loyal to their principals, they cannot exercise duties in such a manner as to profit themselves or anyone else at the expense of the principal. The duty of loyalty includes, for example:

   - obtaining the most favorable price and terms for the principal;

   - acting on behalf of the agent's principal;

   - not acting for parties with adverse interest in the same transaction;

   - never concealing the identity of the purchaser to induce the principal to sell;

   - disclosing to the principal if the agent becomes interested in the principal's property; and

   - never advancing the agent's or another person's interest at the expense of the principal.

3. **Confidentiality.** Much of the information a broker gains while employed by the principal is confidential. An agent may not reveal to a third party, without the principal's permission, personal or private information that might lessen the principal's bargaining position. For example, a licensee may not tell a buyer that a seller is forced to sell owing to poor health or loss of a job without the principal's permission. Brokers may not divulge confidential information learned during the course of the single agency even after the transaction is concluded and the agent-principal relationship is ended. A broker is never free to use confidential information to the disadvantage of or reveal any harmful or unfavorable information about a former principal.

4. **Obedience.** An agent is obligated to act in good faith according to the principal's lawful instructions. The broker-agent is at all times obligated to act in conformity with the principal's instructions as long as those instructions are legal and relevant to the contractual relationship. If a broker feels that carrying out the principal's legal directions will harm the principal, then the broker must promptly inform the principal of all known facts along with the broker's opinion. However, if the principal will not change the instructions, the broker must either carry them out or withdraw from the relationship.

Brokers may not violate the law. For example, if a principal instructs a listing broker not to show the property or sell to a member of a particular minority or ethnic group, the broker may not obey the principal's instructions because doing so would violate the law. In such an instance, the broker must inform the principal that to restrict certain groups of people from seeing or purchasing a listed property is a violation of the fair housing laws.

5. **Full disclosure.** It is a broker-agent's duty to keep the principal fully informed at all times of all the facts or information that might affect the transaction or the value of the property. An agent is obligated to disclose facts regarding a property's true worth. Agents may be held responsible for material facts they should have known and communicated to their principal but did not. Also, broker-agents must inform their seller principals, for example, of the buyer's financial condition, the status of the earnest money deposit, or if a personal relationship exists between the agent and the buyer. All material facts must be revealed to the principal even if the disclosure of such facts might cause the transaction to fail.

Full, fair, and prompt disclosure also includes notifying the principal if the broker is personally interested in buying the listed property. In such an event, the broker must clearly terminate the agent-principal relationship and inform the principal of all facts regarding the property that the broker has learned while in an agent's capacity. Otherwise, the broker could buy from the principal and subsequently sell at a higher price and keep the profit ("overage," "secret profit," or "secret commission"). To do so could be construed as fraud, misrepresentation, concealment, and/or dishonest dealing and could expose the broker to liability to both seller and buyer for the full amount of the secret profit. It might further give rise to disciplinary proceedings against the licensee.

6. **Account for all funds.** (See page 51, for explanation.)

7. **Skill, care, and diligence in the transaction.** A broker's obligations extend beyond merely selling a listing or locating a suitable property for a buyer. A real estate broker holds himself or herself out to the public as specially qualified by reason of experience, ability, and knowledge. If a broker's principal is a buyer, then the broker should attempt to obtain the property at the lowest price possible. If the broker's principal is a seller, then the broker should try to get the seller the most favorable price. This includes researching a property thoroughly to advise the seller of a reasonable listing price. Brokers should discuss with their principals any anticipated tax consequences and advise them to seek expert tax advice when appropriate. The duty of using skill, care, and diligence does not end with the signing of a contract. It continues via numerous services by the agent until the transaction is closed. If an agent does not perform with the required degree of skill, care, and diligence, the agent becomes liable to the principal for the damages the principal may have sustained and may be disciplined by the FREC.

8. **Present all offers and counteroffers in a timely manner.** (See page 52, for explanation.)

9. **Disclose all known facts that materially affect the value of residential real property and are not readily observable to the buyer.** (See page 51, for explanation.)

The nine duties listed above apply to *all* real estate transactions (residential and otherwise) when the parties have agreed to a single agent relationship. (See Figure 4.2 on page 65.)

NO BROKERAGE RELATIONSHIP

The seller (or the buyer) can choose not to be represented by a real estate broker. In such a situation, the broker would simply facilitate the sale (or the purchase) of real property without entering into either a single agent relationship or transaction broker relationship. A broker working in a no brokerage relationship capacity with a seller can enter into a listing agreement with that seller and be paid a commission. Similarly, a brokerage firm working in a no brokerage relationship capacity can work with a buyer. Florida law does not require that prospective buyers and sellers be represented. A real estate licensee working in a no brokerage relationship capacity with a buyer or a seller has the following three duties:

1. **Deal honestly and fairly.**

2. **Disclose all known facts that materially affect the value of residential real property that are not readily observable to the buyer.**

3. **Account for all funds entrusted to the licensee.**

(See Figure 4.3 on page 66.)

TABLE 4.1 Brokerage Relationship Duties

Duty	No Brokerage	Transaction	Single Agent
Deal honestly and fairly	✔	✔	✔
Disclose all known facts that affect value of residential property	✔	✔	✔
Account for all funds	✔	✔	✔
Use skill, care, and diligence		✔	✔
Present all offers and counteroffers		✔	✔
Exercise limited confidentiality		✔	
Perform additional duties that are mutually agreed to		✔	
Loyalty			✔
Confidentiality			✔
Obedience			✔
Full disclosure			✔

DISCLOSURE REQUIREMENTS

The duties of the chosen relationship must be fully described and disclosed in writing to a buyer or the seller, either as a separate and distinct disclosure document or included as part of another document, such as a listing agreement or buyer broker agreement. If the disclosure document is incorporated into a listing or buyer broker agreement, a signature line must be inserted immediately following the disclosure information. (See listing agreement on page 230, for example.) It is not sufficient to only have a signature line at the bottom of the listing or buyer broker agreement. The disclosure must be made before, or at the time of, entering into a listing agreement or an agreement for representation, or before the showing of property, whichever occurs first.

When incorporated into other documents, the required disclosure notice must be of the same size as, or larger type than, other provisions of the document and must be conspicuous in its placement to advise customers (or principals in a single agent relationship) of the brokerage duties. The first sentence must be printed in uppercase and bold type. The list of duties must be presented on the disclosure in the same order as listed in the statute. The disclosure notice may include information concerning the real estate brokerage such as the company name and logo, address, phone number, e-mail address, and so forth. (Sample disclosure notices are presented at the end of this Chapter, beginning on page 64.)

Although the disclosure notice provides for the customer's (principal's) signature, the signature is *not* mandatory (except for the transition to transaction broker notice discussed later in this Chapter). If a customer or principal desires to proceed with the relationship but refuses to sign or initial the disclosure document, the licensee should include a copy of the disclosure in the file with a note indicating that the buyer or the seller refused to sign the document.

PRACTICAL APPLICATIONS—WORKING WITH BUYERS AND SELLERS

Licensees must give buyers or sellers whom they do not represent the no brokerage relationship notice before showing them property. However, there are specific exceptions to this requirement. A licensee is *not* required to give a prospective buyer or a prospective seller the no brokerage relationship notice in the following six situations:

1. When the licensee knows that a single agent or a transaction broker represents a prospective seller or a prospective buyer

2. At a bona fide "open house" or model home showing that does not involve eliciting: confidential information; the execution of a contractual offer or an agreement for representation; or negotiations concerning price, terms, or conditions of potential sale

3. During unanticipated casual encounters between a licensee and a prospective seller or a prospective buyer that do not involve eliciting: confidential information; the execution of a contractual

1. offer or an agreement for representation; or negotiations
concerning price, terms, or conditions of a potential sale

4. When responding to general factual questions from a prospective
   seller or a prospective buyer concerning properties that have been
   advertised for sale

5. Situations in which a licensee's communications with a
   prospective buyer or a prospective seller are limited to providing
   either written or oral communication that is general, factual
   information about the qualifications, background, and services
   of the licensee or the licensee's brokerage firm

6. When an owner is selling new residential units built by the owner
   and the circumstances or setting should reasonably inform the
   potential buyer that the owner's employee or single agent is acting
   on behalf of the owner, whether because of the location of the sales
   office or because of office signage or placards or identification
   badges worn by the owner's employee or single agent

For example, let's assume that a brokerage firm, Complete Real
Estate Services, has a listing agreement with Seller Chris and is
representing Seller Chris as a transaction broker.

- Sales associates of Complete Real Estate Services must give
  prospective buyers the no brokerage relationship notice before
  showing them Seller Chris' home. However, the notice would not
  have to be given to a prospective buyer if Complete Real Estate
  Services also represents the prospective buyer as a transaction
  broker. Similarly, the notice would not have to be given to the
  prospective buyer if Complete Real Estate Services has already
  entered into a no brokerage relationship with the prospective
  buyer.

- If Complete Real Estate Services holds an open house at the listed
  property, the sales associate is not required to give a disclosure
  notice to each prospective buyer who walks through the property
  unless certain events occur, such as a contractual offer results, the
  prospective buyer elicits confidential information concerning
  income, and so forth.

- If a sales associate from another brokerage firm desires to show
  Complete Real Estate Services' listing to a prospective buyer, the
  sales associate will not be required to give Seller Chris a disclosure
  notice because Seller Chris is represented by Complete Real Estate
  Services. Sales associates of other companies will need to give their
  prospective buyers the no brokerage relationship notice unless
  they are already representing the prospective buyer as either a
  transaction broker or as a single agent.

Now let's assume that Complete Real Estate Services represents
Buyer Andrew as a transaction broker.

- Sales associates of Complete Real Estate Services may show Buyer
  Andrew in-house listings provided the firm represents the sellers
  as either a transaction broker or they have entered into a no

1 brokerage relationship. If the firm represents the seller as a single
2 agent, the sales associate of Complete Real Estate Services must get
3 the written consent from the seller to transition to a transaction
4 broker before showing Buyer Andrew the listing. (This is discussed
5 in more detail in the next section of this Chapter.)

6 • If a sales associate from Complete Real Estate Services wants to
7 show Buyer Andrew properties that are listed through another
8 brokerage, the sales associate will not be required to give the
9 sellers a disclosure notice because they have already entered into
10 some form of brokerage relationship with the listing company.
11 However, if the sales associate decides to show Buyer Andrew any
12 for-sale-by-owner listings (FSBOs), the sales associate must give
13 the no brokerage relationship notice to the FSBO seller before
14 showing the property to Buyer Andrew.

TRANSITION TO ANOTHER RELATIONSHIP

16 A licensee may change from one brokerage relationship to another as
17 long as the buyer or the seller, or both, give consent before the change
18 occurs. For example, a single agent relationship may be changed to a
19 transaction broker relationship at any time during the relationship
20 between the agent and principal, provided the agent first obtains the
21 principal's written consent to the change in relationship. To gain the
22 principal's written consent to a change in relationship, the buyer or seller
23 (or both) *must* either sign or initial the consent to transition to transaction
24 broker notice set forth in Chapter 475. Note that this disclosure notice
25 requires the buyer's or seller's signature (or initials) before the licensee
26 may change from one brokerage relationship to another.

475.278, F.S.

27 Assume that a brokerage firm represents seller Rebecca as a single
28 agent. Buyer Mike enters the brokerage firm with the purpose of finding
29 a home to purchase. Buyer Mike is not working with any other real estate
30 company. Buyer Mike indicates that he wants the real estate firm to
31 represent him in the real estate negotiations and to work solely in his best
32 interest. Therefore, Buyer Mike has indicated to the licensee that he
33 desires single agency representation. The licensee must give Buyer Mike
34 the single agent notice before entering into a buyer agency agreement or
35 before showing Mike any property.

36 Because Buyer Mike has entered into a single agent relationship with
37 the brokerage firm, the sales associate may not show Seller Rebecca's
38 home to the buyer. This is because a broker may not be a single agent of
39 the buyer *and* a single agent of the seller in the same transaction. This is
40 true even if Rebecca and Mike use different sales associates with the
41 same company because the single agent agreement is with the brokerage
42 firm. If a real estate broker represents both parties in a transaction in a
43 fiduciary capacity, an illegal **dual agent** relationship is created. Because
44 the seller and the buyer have each entered into single agent relationships
45 with the brokerage firm, they must both give written consent to
46 transition (change) to transaction broker relationships in order for Buyer
47 Mike to be shown Seller Rebecca's home. This is the purpose of allowing
48 a licensee to transition from one agency status to another.

1 The consent to transition to transaction broker notice includes
2 wording regarding the principal's permission to allow the single agent to
3 transition to a transaction broker. The notice also includes a list of the
4 duties that a transaction broker owes to the customer. The consent to
5 transition to transaction broker notice can either be a separate document
6 or be included as part of another document, for example, in the listing
7 agreement. Refer to page 56 for information concerning the required
8 format of the disclosure notice. (See Figure 4.4 on page 67.)

9 A licensee may also transition from a transaction broker relationship
10 to a single agent relationship. Furthermore, a licensee may transition
11 from any one of the brokerage relationships to another relationship.
12 However, there is no specific disclosure language provided in the Florida
13 license law for these situations. The licensee will have to accomplish the
14 transition in a manner sufficient to withstand civil challenge under the
15 common law.

16 ## NONRESIDENTIAL TRANSACTIONS

17 In a real estate transaction other than a residential sale, as defined in
18 Chapter 475, and where the buyer and seller each have assets of
19 $1 million or more, the broker at the request of the buyer and seller may
20 designate two sales associates to act as single agents for the buyer and
21 seller in the same transaction. The two sales associates in such an
22 arrangement are referred to as **designated sales associates.** Note that in a
23 residential transaction this would be an illegal dual agency.

475.2755, F.S.

24 In this arrangement, the broker serves as an advisor to the designated
25 sales associates—*not* to the buyer and seller. The broker serves as a
26 neutral party helping to facilitate the process without giving guidance or
27 representation to the parties in the transaction. The designated sales
28 associates have the duties of a single agent and must give the buyer and
29 the seller a special disclosure notice. (See Disclosure Notice below.) The
30 buyer and seller *must* sign the disclosure notice stating that their assets
31 meet the threshold and requesting that the broker use the designated
32 sales associate form of representation. (*Note:* A transition notice is not
33 required.)

Disclosure Notice

Florida law prohibits a designated sales associate from disclosing, except to the broker or persons specified by the broker, information made confidential by request or at the instruction of the customer the designated sales associate is representing. However, Florida law allows a designated sales associate to disclose information allowed to be disclosed or required to be disclosed by law and also allows a designated sales associate to disclose to his or her broker, or persons specified by the broker, confidential information of a customer for the purpose of seeking advice or assistance for the benefit of the customer in regard to a transaction. Florida law requires that the broker must hold this information confidential and may not use such information to the detriment of the other party.

Reference: 475.2755, F.S.

RECORD KEEPING

Brokers must retain brokerage relationship disclosure documents for five years for all residential transactions that result in a written contract to purchase and sell real property and all nonresidential transactions that utilize designated sales associates. This requirement includes files of properties that may have failed to close. If a transaction fails to close, the licensee should retain the brokerage relationship disclosure documents with the purchase and sale contract, escrow documentation, and other documents associated with the property, and place them in the "dead" (failed to close) file. The Commission may discipline a licensee for failure to abide by any provision in Section 475.278, F.S., including the duties owed to customers and principals, disclosure requirements, and record keeping requirements set forth in law.

TERMINATING A BROKERAGE RELATIONSHIP

Generally speaking, a transaction broker relationship or a single agent relationship is terminated when the objectives have been accomplished according to the terms of the contract that created the brokerage relationship. A principal is justified in revoking a single agent relationship with the broker if the broker-agent breaches any of the fiduciary duties.

A brokerage relationship between a principal (or a customer) and a broker may be terminated for any one of the following reasons:

- Fulfillment of the brokerage relationship's purpose.

- Mutual agreement to terminate the brokerage relationship.

- Expiration of the terms of the agreement. (If no term is specified, the courts have ruled that a brokerage relationship may be terminated after a "reasonable" time.)

- Broker renounces the single agent relationship by giving notice to the principal or the broker renounces the transaction broker relationship by giving notice to the customer.

- Principal revokes a single agent relationship or the customer revokes a transaction broker relationship. (In this case, the principal or the customer may be liable for damages, such as advertising expenses, incurred by revoking the brokerage relationship prior to the termination date of the listing contract or exclusive buyer contract.)

- Death of a seller's broker or the seller before the broker finds a ready, willing, and able buyer.

- Death of the buyer's broker or the buyer before the broker finds a suitable property for the buyer.

- Destruction of the property or condemnation by eminent domain.

- Bankruptcy of the principal or the customer.

■ MISREPRESENTATION AND FRAUD

Licensees must avoid misrepresenting a property or making false promises. **Misrepresentation** is the misstatement of fact or the omission or concealment of a factual matter. Misrepresentation can lead to fraud. The elements of a cause of action for **fraud** are: (1) the licensee made a misstatement or failed to disclose a material fact, (2) the licensee either knew or should have known that the statement was not accurate or that the undisclosed information should have been disclosed, (3) the buyer relied on the misstatement, and (4) the buyer was damaged as a result.

The law prohibits deceptive practices. For example, it is fraudulent and dishonest dealing by trick, scheme, or device for a licensee or registrant to:

- knowingly sell or offer for sale any property covered by a mortgage that also covers other property sold, unless the particular property sold or offered for sale may be released from the mortgage any time before foreclosure sale on payment of an amount less than that remaining due from the purchaser after the sale;

- induce any person to buy property by promising that the licensee or the owner will resell or repurchase the property at any future time, unless there is proof that the guaranteed repurchase agreement has been approved by an agency of the State of Florida or there is evidence that the repurchase has been accomplished as promised;

- offer lotteries and schemes of sale involving the sale of chances or similar devices whereby it is represented that the purchaser is to receive property in an order to be determined by chance, whereby the price will depend on chance or the amount of sales made, or whereby the buyer may or may not receive any property; and

- invite the public to solve puzzles on the pretense of a drawing to receive property free, at a nominal price, or at cost.

■ PROFESSIONAL ETHICS

Defining *ethics* is like trying to pick up mercury with one's fingers. Even philosophers disagree on exactly how to define ethics. While there are no hard-and-fast standards that constitute ethical behavior, everyone knows what ethical conduct is.

A licensee can easily determine if a course of action is ethical by asking, "Would I want someone else to act in the same manner toward me?" Failure to apply the Golden Rule results in a double standard: how you treat others and how you expect others to treat you.

Ethics is not in conflict with enterprise or profit. Time and time again, ethical performance has proved to be good business. The most important factor influencing a real estate agent to operate ethically is his or her personal code of behavior. The most important factor influencing a real

1 estate agent to operate unethically is the behavior of his or her employer
2 and, then, other real estate agents.

3   Ethics should not have to be regulated or dictated by government. In
4 fact, all the laws in the world will not prevent unethical conduct. It is a
5 matter of personal integrity when individuals—and real estate agents as
6 a group—take care to be honest in all dealings with others. Just a few
7 unethical brokers or sales associates will reflect on the entire industry.
8 Licensees have a moral duty to behave ethically and to take action
9 against the practices of any licensees who act unethically. Real estate
10 agents have a duty to support efforts to raise the qualifications of new
11 brokers and sales associates, not to limit competition but to improve
12 professional standards within the industry.

13   Some acts may be legal but unethical. For example, a broker regularly
14 may include in all employment contracts with his or her sales associates a
15 clause stating that all rights to listing commissions cease ten days after
16 a sales associates leaves the firm for any reason. Suppose a marginal
17 employee brings in a listing for a $400,000 commercial building, the first
18 listing that sales associate has had in 12 months. The broker accepts the
19 listing, then two days later fires the marginal sales associate. The broker
20 may not have broken any laws, but the broker's actions are unethical.

21 ## PROFESSIONALISM AND A CODE OF ETHICS

22 As you no doubt have concluded, the real estate business is becoming
23 increasingly complex, with rapid changes and constant pressures. A real
24 estate brokerage firm is only as good as its reputation, and a good
25 reputation can result only from a history of ethical business practices.
26 Because just one dishonest or unethical person in a firm may destroy
27 years of honest effort by others, ethical service is the only focal point
28 around which a lasting reputation and career can be built. Licensees must
29 strive for individual ethical conduct and strive to maintain a high
30 standard of ethical professionalism within the industry.

31   Most professional and trade organizations have requirements
32 designed to raise the professional and ethical standards of their
33 members. The National Association of REALTORS® adopted its Code of
34 Ethics in 1913. The Code emphasizes fair dealings in three major areas:
35 (1) with clients, (2) with other real estate brokers, and (3) with the general
36 public. Through the years, the NAR's "Code of Ethics and Standards of
37 Practice" has been updated and has proved helpful to everyone in the
38 real estate business because it contains practical applications of business
39 ethics and statements of good practices that everyone in the business
40 should know and carefully follow.

41 ## ■ SUMMARY

42 A person who delegates authority to another is referred to as the
43 principal. A person who accepts the authority is referred to as the agent.
44 An agent is authorized to represent and act for his or her principal.

1 The agency relationship creates a fiduciary relationship with the
2 principal. A fiduciary acts in a position of trust or confidence with the
3 principal.

4 There are three types of agents in general business dealings:
5 (1) universal agent, (2) general agent, and (3) special agent. The types of
6 agents are characterized by the scope of authority that is delegated to the
7 agent. A real estate licensee may act as a special agent with buyers or
8 sellers. This occurs when the buyer or seller and the brokerage firm enter
9 into a single agent relationship.

10 Florida real estate license law defines brokerage relationships and
11 disclosure requirements as they apply to real estate dealings. Buyers and
12 sellers have three basic options in all real estate transactions concerning
13 the role the real estate brokerage firm will assume for them: (1) the
14 brokerage firm may work as a transaction broker for the buyer and/or
15 the seller; (2) the brokerage firm may work as a single agent of either the
16 buyer or the seller; or (3) the parties may agree that the brokerage firm
17 will not represent the buyer or the seller at all (no brokerage relationship).

18 Licensees may not operate as dual agents. A dual agent is a broker
19 who represents as a fiduciary both the buyer and the seller in a real estate
20 transaction. When a broker represents a buyer or a seller as a fiduciary,
21 the broker is in a relationship of trust and confidence between the broker
22 as agent and the seller as principal or the buyer as principal.

23 The duties and obligations in each type of brokerage relationship
24 apply to all real estate transactions. However, written disclosures are
25 required only when dealing in residential real estate transactions.
26 A residential sale is defined as the sale of improved residential property
27 of four or fewer units, the sale of unimproved residential property
28 intended for use as four or fewer units, or the sale of agricultural
29 property of ten or fewer acres.

30 Under Florida law it is presumed that all licensees are operating as
31 transaction brokers unless a single agent or no brokerage relationship is
32 established, in writing. A transaction broker is a broker who provides
33 limited representation to a buyer, a seller, or both in a real estate
34 transaction, but who does not represent either in a fiduciary capacity or
35 as a single agent. The duties of the transaction broker include: (1) dealing
36 honestly and fairly; (2) accounting for all funds; (3) using skill, care, and
37 diligence in the transaction; (4) disclosing all known facts that materially
38 affect the value of residential real property and are not readily observable
39 to the buyer; (5) presenting all offers and counteroffers in a timely
40 manner; (6) exercising limited confidentiality, unless waived in writing
41 by a party; and (7) performing any additional duties that are mutually
42 agreed to with a party.

43 A seller (or a buyer) may want to be represented by a real estate
44 broker. In this case, the real estate broker is a single agent who represents
45 the seller as a fiduciary in selling his or her home or the buyer in finding
46 a home. A single agent is a broker who represents, as a fiduciary, either
47 the buyer or the seller, but not both, in the same transaction. The duties of
48 a single agent include: (1) dealing honestly and fairly; (2) loyalty;

FIGURE 4.1   Transaction Broker Disclosure Form

IMPORTANT NOTICE

FLORIDA LAW REQUIRES THAT REAL ESTATE LICENSEES PROVIDE THIS NOTICE TO POTENTIAL SELLERS AND BUYERS OF REAL ESTATE.

You should not assume that any real estate broker or salesperson represents you unless you agree to engage a real estate licensee in an authorized brokerage relationship, either as a single agent or as a transaction broker. You are advised not to disclose any information you want to be held in confidence until you make a decision on representation.

TRANSACTION BROKER NOTICE

FLORIDA LAW REQUIRES THAT REAL ESTATE LICENSEES OPERATING AS TRANSACTION BROKERS DISCLOSE TO BUYERS AND SELLERS THEIR ROLES AND DUTIES IN PROVIDING A LIMITED FORM OF REPRESENTATION.

As a transaction broker, (insert name of Real Estate Firm and its Associates) provides to you a limited form of representation that includes the following duties:

1. Dealing honestly and fairly;
2. Accounting for all funds;
3. Using skill, care, and diligence in the transaction;
4. Disclosing all known facts that materially affect the value of residential real property and are not readily observable to the buyer;
5. Presenting all offers and counteroffers in a timely manner, unless a party has previously directed the licensee otherwise in writing;
6. Limited confidentiality, unless waived by a party. This limited confidentiality will prevent disclosure that the seller will accept a price less than the asking or listed price, that the buyer will pay a price greater than the price submitted in a written offer, of the motivation of any party for selling or buying property, that a seller or buyer will agree to financing terms other than those offered, or of any other information requested by a party to remain confidential; and
7. Any additional duties that are entered into by this or by separate written agreement.

Limited representation means that a buyer or seller is not responsible for the acts of the licensee. Additionally, parties are giving up their rights to the undivided loyalty of the licensee. This aspect of limited representation allows a licensee to facilitate a real estate transaction by assisting both the buyer and the seller, but a licensee will not work to represent one party to the detriment of the other party when acting as a transaction broker to both parties.

Seller or (buyer) _____   _____
Signature   Date

_____   _____
Signature   Date

FIGURE 4.2   Single Agent Disclosure Form

IMPORTANT NOTICE

FLORIDA LAW REQUIRES THAT REAL ESTATE LICENSEES PROVIDE THIS NOTICE TO POTENTIAL SELLERS AND BUYERS OF REAL ESTATE.

You should not assume that any real estate broker or salesperson represents you unless you agree to engage a real estate licensee in an authorized brokerage relationship, either as a single agent or as a transaction broker. You are advised not to disclose any information you want to be held in confidence until you make a decision on representation.

SINGLE AGENT NOTICE

FLORIDA LAW REQUIRES THAT REAL ESTATE LICENSEES OPERATING AS SINGLE AGENTS DISCLOSE TO BUYERS AND SELLERS THEIR DUTIES.

As a single agent, (insert name of Real Estate Entity and its Associates) owe to you the following duties:

1. Dealing honestly and fairly;
2. Loyalty;
3. Confidentiality;
4. Obedience;
5. Full disclosure;
6. Accounting for all funds;
7. Skill, care, and diligence in the transaction;
8. Presenting all offers and counteroffers in a timely manner, unless a party has previously directed the licensee otherwise in writing; and
9. Disclosing all known facts that materially affect the value of residential real property and are not readily observable.

Seller or (buyer) _____   _____

Signature   Date

_____   _____

Signature   Date

---

1 (3) confidentiality; (4) obedience; (5) full disclosure; (6) accounting for all
2 funds; (7) using skill, care, and diligence in the transaction; (8) presenting
3 all offers and counteroffers in a timely manner; and (9) disclosing all
4 known facts that materially affect the value of residential real property
5 and are not readily observable.

6   A broker may simply facilitate the sale or purchase of real property
7 without entering into a brokerage relationship with the buyer or the
8 seller. A real estate broker working in a no brokerage relationship
9 capacity has the following duties: (1) dealing honestly and fairly;
10 (2) disclosing all known facts that materially affect the value of
11 residential real property that are not readily observable to the buyer;
12 and (3) accounting for all funds entrusted to the licensee.

FIGURE 4.3   No Brokerage Relationship Disclosure Form

IMPORTANT NOTICE

FLORIDA LAW REQUIRES THAT REAL ESTATE LICENSEES PROVIDE THIS NOTICE TO POTENTIAL SELLERS AND BUYERS OF REAL ESTATE.

You should not assume that any real estate broker or salesperson represents you unless you agree to engage a real estate licensee in an authorized brokerage relationship, either as a single agent or as a transaction broker. You are advised not to disclose any information you want to be held in confidence until you make a decision on representation.

NO BROKERAGE RELATIONSHIP NOTICE

FLORIDA LAW REQUIRES THAT REAL ESTATE LICENSEES WHO HAVE NO BROKERAGE RELATIONSHIP WITH A POTENTIAL SELLER OR BUYER DISCLOSE THEIR DUTIES TO SELLERS AND BUYERS.

As a real estate licensee who has no brokerage relationship with you, (insert name of Real Estate Entity and its Associates) owe to you the following duties:

1. Dealing honestly and fairly;
2. Disclosing all known facts that materially affect the value of residential real property which are not readily observable to the buyer; and
3. Accounting for all funds entrusted to the licensee.

Seller or (buyer) _____   _____
Signature   Date

_____   _____
Signature   Date

---

1   The duties of a licensee who has either a brokerage relationship or no
2   brokerage relationship with the customer (or a principal) must be fully
3   disclosed in writing to a buyer or a seller. The disclosure must be made
4   before, or at the time of, entering into a listing agreement or an
5   agreement for representation, or before the showing of property,
6   whichever occurs first.

7   A single agent relationship (or any other brokerage relationship) may
8   be changed to a transaction broker relationship at any time during the
9   relationship between the agent and the principal, provided the agent
10 gives the transition notice to the principal and the principal gives written
11 consent to the transition before a change in relationship.

12 In a nonresidential transaction, and where the buyer and the seller
13 each have assets of $1 million or more, the broker at the request of the
14 buyer and the seller may designate two sales associates to act as single
15 agents for the buyer and the seller in the same transaction. The two sales
16 associates are referred to as designated sales associates.

FIGURE 4.4   Consent to Transition to Transaction Broker

FLORIDA LAW ALLOWS REAL ESTATE LICENSEES WHO REPRESENT A BUYER OR SELLER AS A SINGLE AGENT TO CHANGE FROM A SINGLE AGENT RELATIONSHIP TO A TRANSACTION BROKERAGE RELATIONSHIP IN ORDER FOR THE LICENSEE TO ASSIST BOTH PARTIES IN A REAL ESTATE TRANSACTION BY PROVIDING A LIMITED FORM OF REPRESENTATION TO BOTH THE BUYER AND THE SELLER. THIS CHANGE IN RELATIONSHIP CANNOT OCCUR WITHOUT YOUR PRIOR WRITTEN CONSENT.

As a transaction broker,:_____ (insert name of Real Estate Firm and its Associates) provides to you a limited form of representation that includes the following duties:

1. Dealing honestly and fairly;
2. Accounting for all funds;
3. Using skill, care, and diligence in the transaction;
4. Disclosing all known facts that materially affect the value of residential real property and are not readily observable to the buyer;
5. Presenting all offers and counteroffers in a timely manner, unless a party has previously directed the licensee otherwise in writing;
6. Limited confidentiality, unless waived by a party. This limited confidentiality will prevent disclosure that the seller will accept a price less than the asking or listed price, that the buyer will pay a price greater than the price submitted in a written offer, of the motivation of any party for selling or buying property, that a seller or buyer will agree to financing terms other than those offered, or of any other information requested by a party to remain confidential; and
7. Any additional duties that are entered into by this or by separate written agreement.

Limited representation means that a buyer or seller is not responsible for the acts of the licensee. Additionally, parties are giving up their rights to the undivided loyalty of the licensee. This aspect of limited representation allows a licensee to facilitate a real estate transaction by assisting both the buyer and the seller, but a licensee will not work to represent one party to the detriment of the other party when acting as a transaction broker to both parties.

_____ I agree that my agent may assume the role and duties of a transaction broker. [must be initialed or signed]

Misrepresentation is the misstatement of fact or the omission or concealment of a factual matter. The elements of a cause of action for fraud are: (1) the licensee made a misstatement or failed to disclose a material fact; (2) the licensee either knew or should have known that the statement was not accurate or that the undisclosed information should have been disclosed; (3) the buyer relied on the misstatement; and (4) the buyer was damaged as a result.

■ REVIEW QUESTIONS

1. Which disclosure notice must be given before a single agent can change to a transaction broker?
   A. No brokerage relationship
   B. Single agent
   C. Consent to transition to transaction broker
   D. Transaction broker

2. Steven is so cautious that he refuses to sign all legal documents. Your office policy is to include a note in his file indicating the time, date, place, and circumstance under which you made the disclosure that Steven refused to sign. You may NOT work with Steven under which circumstance?
   A. List Steven's home as a single agent
   B. Provide limited representation to Steven in locating a new home
   C. Provide real estate services to Steven in a no brokerage relationship
   D. Change from a single agent to a transaction broker to show Steven's home to an in-house buyer-principal

3. The brokerage relationship disclosure requirements in Chapter 475 apply to the
   A. sale of a 20-unit apartment complex.
   B. sale of a condominium unit.
   C. residential lease agreement in a duplex.
   D. sale of a book store business and real property.

4. Which statement BEST describes the duty of loyalty in a single agent relationship?
   A. The broker must act in the best interest of the principal.
   B. The broker must disclose all latent defects to prospective buyers.
   C. The broker is held to a standard of care that requires knowledge concerning the land and physical characteristics of the property.
   D. The broker must be able to account for all funds received on behalf of the principal.

5. A real estate broker who works in a limited capacity for both the buyer and the seller in the same transaction is
   A. a dual agent.
   B. a transaction broker.
   C. bound to fiduciary duties to both the buyer and the seller.
   D. a single agent of both the buyer and the seller.

6. A buyer has entered into a buyer broker agreement with a real estate company. The agreement includes the transaction broker notice. The licensee added the duties of loyalty and full disclosure to the agreement.
    A. Licensees may not modify the transaction broker notice.
    B. The licensee may add any additional duties provided both parties agree to the new duties.
    C. The duties of loyalty and full disclosure are duties associated with a single agent relationship and may subject the licensee to liability.
    D. The buyer must initial each additional duty to indicate his or her consent.

7. A licensee of ABC Realty must give the no brokerage relationship notice to
    A. a buyer who has a single agent relationship with XYZ Realty.
    B. every prospective buyer and prospective seller in all cases.
    C. a for-sale-by-owner (FSBO) seller before showing the FSBO home to a buyer customer of ABC Realty.
    D. every prospective buyer who walks through an open house listed by ABC Realty.

8. Broker Murl is an agent of the seller. The seller has disclosed to Murl that the ceramic tile is loose in the dining room because the cement did not adhere to the tile. The loose tile is not readily visible because it is covered with an area rug to protect the seller's toddler. Murl has satisfied his legal obligation if he tells the buyer
    A. that the floor appears to be in good condition.
    B. that ceramic tiles in the dining room are loose.
    C. that the buyer can order an inspection at his own expense if he is concerned about the floor.
    D. nothing unless he is asked specifically about the tile floor's condition.

9. A transaction broker has all of the duties listed below EXCEPT
    A. limited confidentiality.
    B. to use skill, care, and diligence.
    C. to disclose all known facts that materially affect the value of residential real property and are not readily observable to the buyer.
    D. obedience.

10. A brokerage relationship is terminated under which circumstance?
    A. The broker agent renounces the brokerage relationship.
    B. The purchase and sale contract is signed.
    C. At the will of either party without notice.
    D. An offer is accepted.

11. A seller lists her home for $116,900. The seller tells the sales associate that she needs to get at least $112,000 for the home. Following Sunday's open house, the sales associate receives two offers on the home. The first offer for $116,900 is contingent on the seller's financing a portion of the down payment. The second offer is for $112,000, with the buyer to secure her own financing. The sales associate should
    A. seek his broker's advice regarding which offer to present.
    B. present the full-price offer to the seller.
    C. present the second offer to the seller.
    D. present both offers, explaining the details of each to the seller.

12. In the common public relationship that exists in a typical real estate transaction, buyers and sellers are said to be dealing
    A. in a fiduciary capacity.
    B. at arm's length with each other.
    C. in an agency status with each other.
    D. under the doctrine of ethical confidentiality.

13. If a principal gives his or her broker instructions that will result in loss or harm to the principal, the broker
    A. is justified in not carrying out such instructions.
    B. should carry out such instructions without question.
    C. should carry out only that portion of the instructions that will not cause loss or harm to the principal.
    D. should inform the principal of possible harm inherent in the instructions, and then either do as instructed or withdraw from the relationship.

14. A broker's obligations to consumers with whom the brokerage firm has no brokerage relationship include the duty of
    A. full disclosure.
    B. accounting for all funds.
    C. loyalty.
    D. limited confidentiality.

15. Designated sales associates are best described as
    A. single agents for the buyer and the seller in nonresidential transactions where the buyer and the seller meet certain asset thresholds.
    B. the sales associates designated to represent the buyer and the seller in a transaction broker relationship.
    C. undisclosed dual agents.
    D. the sales associates in charge of the required brokerage disclosure forms for the brokerage office.

16. An individual who is empowered by a principal to handle a particular transaction for the principal is a
    A. third party.
    B. special agent.
    C. general agent.
    D. universal agent.

17. Jim, an ambitious, hardworking sales associate, was eager to snag a listing on a beautiful two-story home. The seller told Jim that the mortgage on the home also encumbered the adjoining vacant lot he owned. The seller plans to build a new home for his family on the vacant lot. Jim did not mention to prospects that the mortgage also included the vacant lot because he was confident that there would be enough seller proceeds to satisfy the lien at closing.
    A. This is legal as long as the lien is satisfied at closing.
    B. Jim must disclose that the lien also encumbers the vacant lot at the time an offer is reduced to writing.
    C. Jim is guilty of culpable negligence.
    D. Jim is guilty of fraudulent and dishonest dealing by trick, scheme, or devise.

18. For a buyer to prove a charge of fraud against a real estate licensee who has made a nonfactual statement about a property, the buyer must prove all EXCEPT that the
    A. misstatement was made by the licensee.
    B. misstatement made by the licensee was material to the transaction.
    C. buyer was damaged by the misstatement.
    D. information misstated could be proved to be false with due diligence.

19. A transaction broker involved in a residential sale discovered before the closing that a large recycling facility will be built approximately three-quarters of a mile from the home site. The transaction broker should
    A. disclose the information to both the buyer and the seller.
    B. inform only the buyer of this fact.
    C. inform only the seller of this fact.
    D. ignore the information to protect the transaction.

20. A real estate sales associate must disclose to a prospective buyer that
    A. a former occupant of the property committed suicide in the home.
    B. the seller has been diagnosed with HIV.
    C. the family room addition does not comply with local building codes.
    D. families of other racial groups live in the immediate area.

CHAPTER 5

Real Estate Brokerage Operations

Lots of ? on Test.

■ KEY TERMS

advance fees

arbitration

blind advertisement

commingle

conflicting demands

conversion

corporation

deposit

earnest money deposit

escrow account

escrow disbursement
order (EDO)

general partnership

good faith

interpleader

kickback

limited liability company

limited liability
partnership

limited partnership

mediation

ostensible partnership

point of contact
information

policy manual

puffing

sole proprietorship

telephone solicitation

■ OVERVIEW

This Chapter concerns the day-to-day operations of a real estate office. Statutory requirements detail principal office and branch office regulations as well as rules governing signs, advertising, record keeping, and conduct. This Chapter discusses the broker's role as an expert and the proper handling of escrow funds, advance fees, fees for rental information or rental lists, and compensation. The Chapter also describes the various forms of business entities that may be encountered and that are permitted to engage in real estate brokerage activities in Florida.

After completing this Chapter, the student should be able to:

- identify the requirements for a broker's office(s);

- explain what determines whether a temporary shelter must be registered as a branch office;

- list the requirements related to sign regulation;

- list the requirements related to the regulation of advertising by real estate licensees;

- explain the term *immediately* as it applies to earnest money deposits;

1 • describe the four settlement procedures available to a broker who
2 has received conflicting demands or who has a good-faith doubt as
3 to who is entitled to disputed funds;

4 • list the rule requirements for the handling of advance fees;

5 • explain the rule regarding the advertisement of rental property
6 information or lists or negotiation of rentals;

7 • describe the obligations placed on a sales associate who changes
8 employers; and

9 • contrast the features of the various types of business organizations.

■ BROKERAGE OFFICES

All active Florida real estate brokers are required to have an office and to
register the office with the Department of Business and Professional
Regulation (DBPR). A broker's office must consist of at least one enclosed
room in a building of stationary construction that will provide the
privacy necessary to conduct negotiations and closings of real estate
transactions. The broker's primary office is referred to as the *principal
office.* The broker's books, records, and files pertaining to the real estate
transactions of others are to be kept in the office. If local zoning permits,
the broker's office may be in his or her residence, provided the required
sign is displayed properly. A broker may have an office or offices in
another state, provided the broker agrees in writing to cooperate with
any investigation initiated under Chapter 475, F.S.

475.42, F.S.
475.22, F.S.
61J2-10.022,
F.A.C.

Sales associates are *not* permitted to open offices of their own. They
must be registered from and work out of an office maintained and
registered in the name of their employer.

BRANCH OFFICES

If a broker desires to conduct business from additional locations, the
broker must register each additional location as a branch office and pay
the appropriate registration fees.

The Florida Real Estate Commission (FREC) may insist that a licensee
open and register a branch office whenever the FREC decides that the
business conducted at a place other than the principal office is of such a
nature that the public interest requires registration of a branch office.
Further, any office will be considered a branch office if the advertising of
a broker, who has a principal office elsewhere, is such that it leads the
public to believe that the office of concern is owned or operated by
the broker in question.

475.24, F.S.
61J2-10.023,
F.A.C.

A *temporary shelter* in a subdivision being sold by a broker is not a
branch office if the shelter is intended only for the protection of customers
and sales associates. But if sales associates are assigned there, necessary
sales supplies are on hand, and sale transactions are concluded there, then
the temporary structure must be registered as a branch office. In short, the

1 permanence, use, and character of activities customarily conducted at the
2 office or shelter determine whether it must be registered.

3 Registrations issued to branch offices are *not* transferable. To illustrate,
4 suppose a broker decides to close one branch office and open a new
5 branch office at a different location. Even though these actions may take
6 place at the same time, the registration of the closed office may not be
7 transferred to another office. The new location must be registered and the
8 fee paid just as though the old branch office had not been closed. The
9 broker may, however, reopen the old branch office at any time during the
10 license period on application to the DBPR without paying an additional
11 fee. At the discretion of their employing broker, sales associates may be
12 registered from the principal office or from the branch office to which they
13 regularly report or from which they normally work.

61J2-10.023,
F.A.C.

14 OFFICE SIGNS

15 Active real estate brokers must display a sign on either the exterior or
16 interior of the entrance to their principal office and all branch offices. The
17 sign(s) must be easily observed and read by anyone entering the office.
18 The sign must contain the following information:

19 • Broker's name

20 • Trade name (if one is used)

21 • The words, "Licensed Real Estate Broker" or "Lic. Real Estate
22 Broker"

475.22, F.S.
61J2-10.024,
F.A.C.

1 in Letters on yard Signs

1/2 inch Inside

23 Refer to the first example of an office sign. The broker's name is Murl
24 H. Crawford, the registered trade name is Little Mo Realty, and the
25 required wording "Licensed Real Estate Broker" appears on the sign.

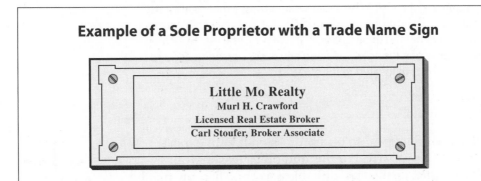

Example of a Sole Proprietor with a Trade Name Sign

Little Mo Realty
Murl H. Crawford
Licensed Real Estate Broker
Carl Stoufer, Broker Associate

26 The names of sales associates and broker associates may be placed
27 below the name of the broker(s). The associate's license status ("Sales
28 Associate" or "Broker Associate") must appear next to the name. A line or
29 observable space must separate the names of the real estate brokers from
30 the names of the sales associates or broker associates (Refer to the
31 previous example of an office sign.)

32 If the brokerage entity is a partnership, corporation, limited liability
33 company (LLC), or limited liability partnership, the sign must contain the
34 following information:

1 • Name of the firm or corporation (or trade name, if one is used)

2 • Name of at least one active broker

3 • The words, "Licensed Real Estate Broker" or "Lic. Real Estate
4   Broker"

Example of a Brokerage Corporation Sign

Kellogg Real Estate, Inc.
Sandi M. Kellogg
Licensed Real Estate Broker

5 ■ **ADVERTISING**

6 State law declares that any person who advertises or makes any oral or
7 printed representation that he or she is engaged in any real estate
8 services is acting as a real estate broker. Publication of false or misleading
9 information by means of radio, television, or written matter for the
10 purpose of inducing any other person to buy, lease, rent, or acquire an
11 interest in title to real property located in Florida is illegal.

475.01(1), F.S.

False Advertising

A person may not disseminate or cause to be disseminated by any means any false
or misleading information for the purpose of offering for sale, or for the purpose of
causing or inducing any other person to purchase, lease, or rent, real estate located
in the state or for the purpose of causing or inducing any other person to acquire
an interest in the title to real estate located in the state.

Reference: 475.42(1)(o), F.S.

---

12 A real estate licensee is deemed to be a professional with expert
13 knowledge regarding real property. For this and other reasons, all
14 advertising must be worded so that a reasonable person will know that he
15 or she is dealing with a real estate licensee or brokerage firm. Because
16 letterhead stationery and personalized business cards are a form of
17 advertising, they are included in this requirement. An advertisement that
18 provides only a post office box number, telephone number, and/or street
19 address is considered to be a **blind advertisement** and is prohibited. *Blind*
20 *advertising* is advertising that fails to disclose the licensed name of the
21 brokerage firm. When advertising on an Internet site, the name of the
22 brokerage firm must appear adjacent to or immediately above or below
23 the point of contact information. **Point of contact information** refers to
24 any means by which to contact the brokerage firm or individual licensee
25 including mailing address(es), physical street address(es), e-mail

61J2-10.025,
F.A.C.

1 address(es), telephone number(s), or facsimile (FAX) telephone
2 number(s).

3   A broker or sales associate may not advertise real estate services in
4 such a manner as to lead the public to believe that the offer was made by
5 a private individual rather than a real estate licensee. Every broker who
6 advertises must do so in a manner that clearly and unquestionably reveals
7 the licensed name of the brokerage firm as opposed to the broker's
8 personal name. When licensees include their personal name in an
9 advertisement, they must use their last name as registered with the FREC.
10 Yard signs or classified ads that differ from the registered name of a
11 licensed brokerage firm are illegal.

475.25(1)(c),
F.S.
61J2-10.025,
F.A.C.

12   If sales associates create promotional materials, such as refrigerator
13 magnets and notepads, they must include the licensed name of the
14 brokerage firm on them. Sales associates may not advertise to perform
15 any real estate service in their own names. Their ads must be supervised
16 directly by their employer, although this does not prevent sales associates'
17 names from appearing in ads in addition to their employer's name, if both
18 are properly identified. Sales associates and their brokers should review
19 advertisements for accuracy and to make sure they are canceled when
20 they are no longer valid because of sale closing of the property or listing
21 expiration.

22 TELEMARKETING

23 *Telemarketing* is the use of the telephone as a marketing tool to solicit
24 services directly to the public. Telemarketing is regulated by state and
25 federal law. The Telephone Consumer Protection Act of 1991 (TCPA) is a
26 federal law concerning telephone solicitations. A **telephone solicitation**
27 is defined as the initiation of a telephone call for the purpose of
28 encouraging the purchase of, or investment in, property, goods, or
29 services. The TCPA established a National Do-Not-Call Registry for
30 consumers who wish to avoid telemarketing calls. Consumers at no
31 charge may request to be on the list. Telemarketers must first search the
32 national registry before making telemarketing calls. Calls are restricted to
33 the hours of 8:00 A.M. to 9:00 P.M.

501.6, F.S.

34   The federal law covers both interstate (between states) and intrastate
35 (within state) telemarketing calls. The law exempts (1) political
36 solicitations; (2) telephone surveys (callers purporting to take a survey,
37 but who also offer to sell goods or services, must comply with the do-not-
38 call registry); and (3) charitable solicitations.

39   Florida's telemarketing law is administered through the Department
40 of Agriculture and Consumer Services. Florida maintains a no sales
41 solicitation calls registry for consumers at an initial charge of $10 ($5 each
42 year thereafter). Florida has made its registry part of the National Do-Not-
43 Call Registry. Violators of Florida's Telemarketing Act may be fined
44 $10,000 per call.

45   A major difference between the state and federal telemarketing laws
46 is that the Florida law exempts real estate licensees who solicit listings in
47 response to a "For Sale" yard sign. However, the federal law does not

exempt calls to for sale by owners (FSBOs). The Federal Communications Commission (FCC) recently ruled that under the federal law, real estate sales associates may *not* call for sale by owners (FSBOs) and homeowners with expired listings to solicit for listings if the owners' names are listed on the National Do-Not-Call Registry, even if the homeowner's telephone number appears on a yard sign or in a newspaper ad. The federal law provides the following exceptions:

- A sales associate representing a potential buyer may call the FSBO seller, but only if they have an actual buyer interested in the property and to negotiate a sale.

- A sales associate may contact individuals with whom he or she has had an established business relationship, even if the customer's number is on the national registry. For example, the company that previously listed a property may contact the former customer to solicit new business for up to 18 months after the business transaction has been concluded.

- Sales associates may contact a customer for three months after a business inquiry or application (such as a customer who registered at an open house or a FSBO seller who requested information from a sales associate).

If a sales associate calls a FSBO or an expired listing under the exceptions listed above and the homeowner requests not to be called, the sales associate must comply. Telemarketers must state their names, the business name, and the business telephone number. Telemarketers may not block their phone numbers. Violators of the federal law may be fined up to $11,000 for each illegal call. Sales associates beware—even though the state law exempts real estate licensees for the purposes of soliciting for listings, the federal law does not. Don't end up in a federal court—know the law *before* telemarketing for business!

 To learn more about the National Do-Not-Call Registry, visit the FCC Web site at: **http://www.fcc.gov/cgb/donotcall/.**

 To find out more regarding Florida's Do-Not-Call Registry, visit the Florida Department of Agriculture and Consumer Services at: **http://www.800helpfla.com/nosales.html.**

■ ESCROW OR TRUST ACCOUNTS

In the course of doing business, a broker will be entrusted with money, documents, and other things of value. Florida laws and FREC rules are very explicit in requiring that all such property be accounted for. The types of money that a broker may handle for others in the ordinary course of business include, for example, **earnest money deposits** (also referred to as *good-faith deposits* or *binder deposits*), rent deposits, and security deposits. All cash or cash-like property entrusted to a licensee must be placed "immediately" in an escrow (trust) account.

475.25(2)(k), F.S.
61J2-14.008, F.S.

An **escrow account** is an account for the deposit of money held by a third party (for example, the broker) in trust for another. A **deposit** is defined as a sum of money, or its equivalent, delivered to a real estate licensee as earnest money, payment, or partial payment in connection with a real estate transaction. An earnest money deposit may be in the form of cash, currency, or any medium of exchange or securities that can be converted into money.

Sales associates must *immediately* deliver earnest money deposits to their broker-employer no later than the end of the next business day. If an escrow check is made out to the sales associate personally, the best course of action is to ask the prospective buyer to write a new check payable to the broker's escrow account. However, if this is not practical, the sales associate should immediately endorse the check and include the words, "For Deposit Only to the (name of the escrow account)" and turn it over to the broker.

61J2-14.009, F.A.C.

Brokers must *immediately* place trust funds into their escrow account no later than the end of the third business day after their sales associate (or an employee of their brokerage company) has received it. The three-business-day time period coincides with the day that the sales associate must turn over the deposit to the broker.

61J2-14.008, F.A.C.

Assume a sales associate receives a deposit from a prospective buyer on a Tuesday (no legal holidays are involved).

- The sales associate has until the end of the next business day (Wednesday) to deliver the deposit to the broker

- The broker has until the end of the third business day (Friday) to deposit the funds. The three-business-day time period for the broker to deposit the funds begins on the day the sales associate is required to deliver the funds to the broker (In this example, the first day of the three-business-day period is Wednesday.)

Occasionally a licensee may be given a postdated check or a promissory note as an earnest money deposit. Although Florida statute (F.S. 673) provides for checks and other negotiable instruments to be postdated, extreme caution should be taken in handling such deposits. In all cases, the seller's approval must be obtained before accepting the postdated check. Once accepted, the broker should secure the instrument in a proper place, such as an office safe, until the date on the check becomes current, and then immediately deposit the check into his or her escrow account.

673.1131, F.S.

Brokers may maintain either an interest-bearing or noninterest-bearing escrow account in a Florida commercial bank, credit union, or savings association. Some brokers do not want the responsibility and liability of maintaining an escrow account. Instead they may choose to have a Florida-based title company that has trust powers to maintain the escrow funds, or alternatively, if designated in the sale contract, a Florida attorney may escrow the funds. (*Note:* Real estate license law governs only broker's escrow accounts. Chapter 475, F.S. has no authority over title company escrow accounts or attorney escrow accounts. However, real estate licensees are still bound to the time periods mentioned previously.)

61J2-24.002 (gg), F.A.C. 61J2-14.014, F.A.C.

1   A broker who maintains an escrow account must be a signatory on
2   the account. If the escrow account is an interest-bearing account, the
3   broker must get written permission from all parties before placing the
4   funds in this type of account. The written authorization must specify
5   who is entitled to the interest earned. The broker may receive the interest
6   earned, but only if it is specifically agreed to by all parties. A broker can
7   be disciplined by the FREC for failure to secure the written permission of
8   all interested parties prior to placing trust (escrow) funds in an interest-
9   bearing escrow account.

10   Brokers must keep business records, books, and accounts in
11   compliance with Florida law and Commission rules and make them
12   available for audit or spot checks by DBPR at any reasonable time.
13   Records must be preserved for at least five years, both for trust funds
14   following their receipt and for transactions not involving entrusted funds,
15   from the date of any executed agreement, oral or written. Records must
16   also be preserved for two years beyond the conclusion of any
17   court proceedings.

475.5017, F.S.
475.5015, F.S.
61J2-14.012,
F.A.C.

Key Concepts Regarding Escrow Accounts

- Broker may open an escrow account in a Florida bank, savings association, or credit union.

- Broker must be a signatory on his or her escrow account.

- Broker must review, sign, and date the monthly reconciliation statements.

- If the broker chooses not to open an escrow account, the funds may be held by a title company or in an attorney's trust account.

- Brokers must maintain records of real estate transactions for five years regardless of whether escrow funds were pledged (or two years after litigation if beyond the five-year period).

---

18   ## DISPOSITION OF ESCROW DEPOSITS

19   Brokers must place earnest money deposits immediately in an escrow
20   account. They may not intermingle or commingle (mix) those deposits
21   with other types of funds. To **commingle** funds is the illegal practice of
22   mixing a buyer's, seller's, tenant's, or landlord's funds with the broker's
23   own money or of mixing escrow money with the broker's personal funds
24   or brokerage funds. However, the broker is allowed to place in the sales
25   escrow account an amount up to $1,000 of personal or brokerage funds.
26   Brokers may keep up to $5,000 of their own monies in a property
27   management escrow account.

28   The escrow account must be properly reconciled each month, and the
29   broker must review, sign, and date the monthly reconciliation. All trust
30   funds deposited in an escrow account must be kept in that account until
31   the transaction is closed or other fulfillment of an escrow condition occurs
32   or until otherwise legally disposed of. Misappropriation of another's
33   property will expose the broker to charges of conversion. **Conversion,**

1 therefore, is the unauthorized control or use of another person's personal
2 property.

3 **Conflicting demands** occur when the buyer and seller make demands
4 regarding the disbursing of escrowed property that are inconsistent and
5 cannot be resolved. If a broker who maintains an escrow account receives
6 conflicting demands on escrowed property, the broker must notify the
7 FREC, in writing, within 15 business days of receiving the conflicting
8 demands unless specifically exempted (see below). Further, the broker
9 must institute one of the four settlement (or escape) procedures (listed on
10 page 82) within 30 business days from the time the broker received the
11 conflicting demands. For example, if a broker waits 10 business days to
12 report the conflicting demands, the broker has just 20 business days
13 remaining to implement one of the settlement procedures.

475.25(1)(d),
F.S.
61J2-10.032(1)
(a), F.A.C.

14 (*Note:* If a title company or an attorney is the escrow agent, the broker
15 has no obligation to report an escrow dispute to the FREC or to institute a
16 settlement procedure. Generally a title company or the attorney will not
17 disburse funds without authorization from the parties to the transaction.
18 Usually, if the parties cannot come to an agreement regarding the funds
19 the matter is submitted to a court of law for resolution.)

20 Florida license law provides three exceptions to the notice
21 requirements for sales escrow accounts:

22 1. Brokers who are entrusted with an earnest money deposit
23   concerning a residential sale contract utilized by HUD in the sale
24   of HUD-owned property are exempted from the notice and
25   settlement procedures in Chapter 475, F.S. In such cases, the broker
26   is required to follow HUD's Agreement to Abide, Broker
27   Participation Requirements.

28 2. If a buyer of a residential condominium unit timely delivers to a
29   licensee written notice of the buyer's intent to cancel the contract
30   as authorized by the Condominium Act, the licensee may return
31   the escrowed property to the purchaser without notifying the
32   Commission or initiating any of the settlement procedures.
33   (See also Chapter 8, page 159.)

34 3. If a buyer of real property in good faith fails to satisfy the terms
35   specified in the financing clause of a contract for sale and purchase,
36   the licensee may return the escrowed funds to the purchaser
37   without notifying the Commission or initiating any of the
38   settlement procedures.

39 If a broker has a *good-faith doubt* as to which party should receive the
40 escrowed property, the broker must notify the FREC, in writing, within
41 15 business days after having such doubt and institute one of the
42 settlement procedures within 30 business days after having such doubt.
43 The term **good faith** is used to describe a party's honest intent to transact
44 business, free from any intent to defraud the other party, and generally
45 speaking, each party's faithfulness to his or her duties or obligations as
46 set forth by contract. Therefore, if the broker doubts the parties' good
47 faith, the law requires that the broker abide by the notice requirement and
48 initiate one of the settlement procedures in a timely manner. Individuals

must look to case law for interpretations of what specific circumstances constitute a good-faith doubt. Situations that *may* constitute good-faith doubt by the broker include the following:

- The transaction closing date has passed, and the broker has not received conflicting or identical instructions from all parties concerning escrow disbursement.

- The transaction closing date has not passed, but one or more parties have expressed the intention not to close and the broker has not received conflicting or identical instructions from all parties concerning escrow disbursement.

- One party to a failed transaction does not respond to a broker's inquiry about escrow disbursement. In this situation, the broker may send a certified notice letter, return receipt requested, to that nonresponding party stating that a demand has been made on the escrowed funds and that failure to respond by a designated date will be regarded as authority for the broker to release the funds to the demanding party. (*Note:* Although *not* required by law, to limit the broker's potential liability, it is advisable before releasing the trust funds to secure the postal return receipt as proof the notice was delivered.)

TO REMEMBER

Four Settlement Procedures

M	**M**ediation
A	**A**rbitration
L	**L**itigation
E	**E**scrow disbursement order

The four settlement procedures are as follows:

455.2235, F.S.

1. **Mediation.** If all of the parties give written consent, the dispute may be mediated. **Mediation** is an informal, nonadversarial process intended to reach a negotiated settlement. If the nonbinding mediation process is not successfully completed within 90 days following the party's last demand for the disputed funds, the licensee must employ one of the other three settlement procedures.

2. **Arbitration. Arbitration** is a process whereby, with the consent of all parties to the dispute, the matter is submitted to a disinterested third party. Each side presents its case to a third party, who makes a binding judgment in favor of one side or the other. The parties must agree in advance to abide by the arbitrator's final decision.

3. **Litigation.** If the two parties (such as a buyer and seller) cannot reach agreement, the matter may be submitted to a court of law for resolution by interpleader or other legal remedy such as a declaratory judgment. **Interpleader** is a legal proceeding whereby the broker, having no financial interest in the disputed funds,

1 deposits with the court the disputed escrow deposit so that the
2 court can determine who is the rightful claimant. A *declaratory*
3 *judgment* is a statutory remedy to establish the rights of the party
4 when the rights are in doubt.

5 4. **Escrow disbursement order (EDO).** The broker may choose to
6 request that the Commission issue an **escrow disbursement order**
7 **(EDO),** a determination of who is entitled to the disputed funds.
8 The FREC may choose not to issue an EDO. If the broker is
9 informed in writing that the Commission will not issue an EDO,
10 the broker must utilize one of the other settlement procedures. In
11 such an instance, the broker must notify the Commission as to
12 which settlement procedure he or she will use. FREC rules require
13 a broker to notify the Commission within 10 business days if the
14 dispute is settled between the parties or if the matter goes to court
15 before the EDO is issued.

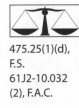

475.25(1)(d),
F.S.
61J2-10.032
(2), F.A.C.

only 25
agents
in FL.

16 If the real estate licensee promptly employs one of the four settlement
17 procedures and abides by the resulting order or judgment, a complaint
18 may not be filed against the licensee for failure to account for or deliver
19 escrowed property (the broker has immunity from disciplinary action).

Key Reporting Deadlines Regarding Escrow Accounts

- Sales associates must deliver escrow deposits to their broker by the end of the **next business day.**

- Brokers must deposit escrow funds by the end of the **third business day.**

- Brokers must notify the FREC in writing of conflicting demands or of a good faith doubt within **15 business days.**

- Brokers must institute one of the settlement procedures within **30 business days** of receiving conflicting demands or of having a good faith doubt.

- If a broker requests an EDO and the escrow dispute is either settled or goes to court before the EDO is issued, the broker must notify the FREC within **10 business days.**

---

20 ## ADVANCE FEES

21 Fees collected by a broker in advance for the listing of real property are
22 referred to as **advance fees.** For example, a broker who specializes in the
23 sale of shopping centers may obtain money from the seller in advance to
24 cover the advertising and promotional expenses of the listing.

25 Any broker who collects, receives, or contracts for an advance fee for
26 a listing to sell, rent, or lease real property must deposit, when collected,
27 at least 75 percent of the advance fee into a special account, called an
28 *advance fee trust account* or *advance fee escrow account.* The account may be
29 established in a bank or any recognized depository in Florida. The
30 advance fee escrow account may not be commingled with any other
31 escrow accounts or personal accounts. Separate and distinct accounting
32 records are required for all advance fees collected. The broker must
33 reconcile the advance fee account(s) monthly and produce the accounting

475.452, F.S.
61J2-10.029,
F.A.C.

1 records upon demand to the DBPR with prior notice. When the advance
2 fee escrow account has a zero balance or only a small balance in order to
3 keep the account open, and the account has had no activity during a given
4 reporting period, the broker must prepare a report. The report must
5 contain a copy of the bank statement. The format required for such reports
6 is specified in s. 475.452, F.S., and Rule 61J2-10.029, F.A.C.

7   Before a broker withdraws any funds from an advance fee trust
8 account, he or she is required to furnish the seller with a statement
9 itemizing how the advance fee money will be spent and the amount that
10 will be spent. A broker may withdraw funds from the account only if the
11 monies to be expended are for the direct benefit of the seller, or for special
12 advertising of the seller's interest only, or as provided by statute. A real
13 estate broker's expenses, such as office supplies, telephone, rent,
14 automobile, commissions, or controlled publications, are regarded as
15 broker overhead and may *not* be paid from the advance fee account.

16   Brokers who collect advance fees must furnish each seller with a
17 verified copy of all accounting records related to the advance funds each
18 calendar quarter. They also must provide a separate accounting when the
19 listing contract has been performed completely and at any other time
20 the FREC thinks it appropriate. Brokers are required to provide to the
21 Commission, on demand, a verified copy of any or all accounts related to
22 advance fees collected.

475.452, F.S.

23   If an advance fee has been paid in connection with a listing and the
24 property is not sold during the term of the listing contract or within a
25 period of 18 months from the contract date, whichever is shorter, the
26 broker must return all funds to the seller with a complete final accounting
27 that includes any and all money spent. The advance fee requirements do
28 not apply to a real estate broker auctioning real property if in advance of
29 the auction the broker and seller have entered into a written agreement
30 providing for anticipated expenses to be incurred and paid. However, any
31 trust funds received by the broker in advance of the auction must be
32 deposited into a trust account (but not an advance fee trust account).

775, F.S.

33   Violation of advance fee requirements is a misdemeanor of the first
34 degree and is punishable by a fine of up to $1,000 and/or imprisonment
35 for up to one year and possible license suspension or revocation. In
36 addition, violation of this section of the law allows a seller *treble* or triple
37 damages (three times the amount) for any funds misapplied, plus
38 reasonable lawyer's fees.

39 ## ■ RENTAL LISTS AND RENTAL COMPANIES

40 The routine activities of most brokerage firms often include requests
41 related to rental properties. Either property owners seek assistance in
42 renting property or prospective tenants request help in locating rental
43 property. However, very few brokerage firms sell rental lists.

475.453, F.S.
61J2-10.030,
F.A.C.

44   Rental companies or anyone who advertises rental property
45 information or lists in any manner is acting as a broker or a broker's

1 representative and is subject to the laws regulating licensed occupations.
2 Accordingly, any broker or sales associate who attempts to negotiate a
3 rental or who furnishes rental information to a prospective tenant for
4 a fee must provide the prospective tenant with a contract or receipt that
5 contains a provision for repayment under specified conditions. It must
6 state that if the prospective tenant does not obtain a rental, he or she is
7 entitled to be repaid 75 percent of the fee paid if requested within 30 days
8 of the contract/receipt date.

9   If the information provided to the prospective tenant is not current or
10 is inaccurate in any material respect, the broker must repay the full fee to
11 the prospective tenant on demand. Any demand from the prospective
12 tenant for the return of any part or all of the fee must be made within
13 30 days from the date the broker or sales associate contracted to provide
14 services. Such demands may be made orally or in writing. The contract or
15 receipt agreement must follow FREC guidelines, and the licensee must
16 send a copy to the DBPR within 30 days of the first use.

Notice

PURSUANT TO FLORIDA LAW: If the rental information provided under this contract is not current or accurate in any material aspect, you may demand within 30 days of this contract date a return of your full fee paid. If you do not obtain a rental you are entitled to receive a return of 75% of the fee paid, if you make demand within 30 days of this contract date.

Reference: 61J2-10.030, F.A.C.

---

17   Advertising rental property information or lists that are not current or
18 are materially inaccurate is illegal. Any person who violates the
19 requirements outlined above is guilty of a misdemeanor of the first
20 degree, is subject to a fine of up to $1,000 and/or imprisonment of up to
21 one year, and is subject to license suspension or revocation.

22 ## ■ BROKER'S ROLE AS AN EXPERT

95.11(4)(a), F.S.

23 Real estate brokers are held to be professionals who possess expert
24 knowledge regarding the field of real estate. The average layperson is
25 inclined to believe that all licensed brokers are experts in all areas of the
26 real estate business. Most brokers, however, specialize in one or a few
27 areas. The general public is not always aware of the special fields of
28 expertise of a broker and will tend to accept as fact most statements made
29 by a broker involving special areas of real estate or real estate values.
30 Normally, an opinion would not be a representation of fact on which
31 anyone would have the right to rely. However, when an *opinion* is given
32 by a so-called expert, such as a real estate licensee, the general public
33 should be able to rely on that opinion. Therefore, unless a real estate
34 broker is qualified or is quoting a qualified expert, he or she may be
35 guilty of negligence in giving an opinion that is not well founded in fact.
36 Licensees should exercise special care in the following areas:

- *Opinions of title.* Statements regarding title to property are an especially hazardous subject for brokers. A broker first must obtain a current opinion from an attorney before quoting an opinion that title to a property is good or marketable. When questions of title arise, all brokers are required to advise prospective buyers to have their attorneys examine the abstract or to obtain a title insurance policy. In the event a broker knows that the title to a property is not marketable or that liens exist, the broker is required to inform prospective buyers of all such conditions.

475.25(2)(j), F.S.

- *Representations of value.* The law allows real estate agents to enthusiastically describe the value of real estate and/or the potential of the property. The licensee may not, however, exaggerate, conceal, or misrepresent by making statements he or she knows to be untrue. **Puffing** is the term used to describe a licensee's boasting of a property's benefits. For example, the statement, "The apartment has a fantastic view," is puffing because the prospect can clearly assess the view for himself or herself, and the statement is the licensee's opinion. However, if the licensee had instead made the remark, "The apartment has a fantastic view of the lake," when in fact all of the windows face the street, the statement is untrue and would be illegal misrepresentation.

Any representation made by a broker may later become the basis for charges of fraud, breach of contract, or breach of trust. In general, a purchaser has only a limited right to rely on the statements of a broker. However, if a broker invites trust and then betrays that trust, the broker is guilty of breach of trust. This legal concept brings to light an important ethical principle relating to those engaged in the sale of real estate: Whenever the trust or confidence of a buyer or seller is invited, by actions or words, that trust or confidence, once given, must not be betrayed.

■ BROKER'S COMMISSION

ANTITRUST LAWS

The real estate industry is subject to state and federal antitrust laws. At the federal level, the Sherman (1890), Clayton (1914), and Federal Trade Commission (1914) acts and subsequent amendments deal with preserving competition and ensuring against restraint of trade. It is illegal for real estate brokers to conspire to fix commissions or fees for the services they perform. Local real estate boards and multiple-listing services may not fix commission rates or splits between cooperating brokers.

542, F.S.

The amount of commission to be paid is negotiable, and it is arrived at by agreement between the broker and buyer or seller. If no specific agreement exists, a judicially determined commission will apply. Neither the FREC nor Florida law establishes or regulates the amount of commission paid. The sharing of brokerage compensation by a licensee with a party to the real estate transaction, with full disclosure to all interested parties, is allowed under Chapter 475, F.S.

61J2-10.028, F.A.C.

LIENS ON REAL PROPERTY

A broker may place a lien on real property for nonpayment of commission *only* if the broker is expressly authorized to do so in a contractual agreement. Otherwise, when a buyer or seller refuses to pay a broker's commission after the commission has been earned, the broker would be required to take legal action to collect the monies due by filing a suit against the party for the amount due. The broker would have to obtain a civil judgment against the party who owed the commission. The FREC is authorized to suspend or revoke a real estate license for the unauthorized recording of an instrument that affects the title of real property or that encumbers real property.

475.42(1)(j), F.S.
61J2-24.001(3)(ee), F.A.C.

Effective October, 2005, brokers will be able to place a lien on the owner's net proceeds (lien on personal property, not the real estate) from the sale of commercial real estate only for the commission earned by the broker under a listing agreement. The broker must include specific disclosure language in the listing agreement concerning the broker's right to file a lien against the seller's net proceeds.

475, Part III, F.S.

SALES ASSOCIATE'S COMMISSION

All monies earned by a sales associate as a result of any real estate service must be paid to the sales associate by his or her employer and not directly by the buyer or seller. Sales associates are compensated by splitting commissions paid to their broker-employer. What split is retained by a broker and what split is received by a sales associate is usually agreed upon when they reach an employment agreement.

Under Florida law a sales associate may not operate as a broker, nor may he or she operate independently. Therefore, all commissions and all listings are legally the property of the broker. Sales associates are prohibited from initiating any suit or action for compensation in connection with a real estate transaction against any person *except* the person registered as their employer. A sales associate who accepts listings, deposits, or commissions from any source *must* accept them in the name of his or her broker and with the express consent of that broker.

KICKBACKS

When a broker receives money from someone other than the buyer or seller, it is usually considered to be a **kickback** or rebate. For example, assume Broker Murl refers buyers to Nifty Mini Blinds and receives $25 for each buyer who purchases window treatments from Nifty. Broker Murl may legally accept the kickback, provided he, prior to the payment and receipt of the kickback, fully advises his buyer or seller and all affected parties in the transaction of the arrangement. Licensees are prohibited from receiving, either directly or indirectly, any kickback or rebate without prior full disclosure. Laws other than the real estate license law, however, prohibit a licensee from receiving a kickback or rebate involving title insurance or property (hazard) insurance, regardless of disclosure. Furthermore, it is illegal for a licensee to pay an *unlicensed* person any sum of money for the referral of real estate

475.25(2)(h), F.S.
61J2-10.028, F.A.C.

1 business or for performing any real estate service, unless specifically
2 exempted. (See box below.)

Finder's Fee Exemption

A property management firm or an owner of an apartment complex may pay a finder's fee (or referral fee) of up to $50 to an unlicensed person who is a tenant of the apartment complex. The finder's fee may be in the form of a fee or a credit toward rent paid to the tenant for introducing or arranging an introduction between the owner/management firm and another person who becomes a tenant of an apartment unit.

Reference: Section 475.011(13), F.S.

---

3 ## ■ CHANGE OF EMPLOYER

475.23, F.S.

4 Sales associates who change employers are required to take certain
5 actions before they may legally work for the new employer. A sales
6 associate's license ceases to be in force when a sales associate changes
7 employer. The sales associate must notify the FREC within ten days after
8 the change by filing a *Request for Change of Status* (DBPR RE-2050) form,
9 disclosing the name and address of the new employer. Sales associates
10 may not perform real estate services until they are properly registered
11 with their new employer. The request of change of registration also
12 serves to notify the Commission of the termination of employment with
13 the former employer.

14 After leaving a former employer, a sales associate may not divert a
15 buyer or seller of the former employer from completion of a transaction.
16 To divert buyers or sellers or use confidential information is both
17 unethical and illegal in Florida. Additionally, a sales associate may have
18 agreed contractually to a noncompete agreement.

19 Because of the fiduciary relationship between sales associate and
20 employer, the obligations of the sales associate do not end with
21 termination of employment. The sales associate is prohibited from
22 disclosing confidential information learned as a result of employment.
23 A licensee is further prohibited from doing anything that might discredit
24 the former employer or damage the goodwill of the employer's business.

25 If a sales associate duplicates records, listings, or confidential
26 information from the office of a former employer without consent, he or
27 she is guilty of breach of trust, even though the sales associate may have
28 placed those items in his or her employer's records.

29 If a sales associate takes the original records from an employer's office,
30 as opposed to duplicating them, then the sales associate is guilty of
31 larceny (theft) and is exposed to administrative penalties by the FREC,
32 civil action in court, and criminal penalties.

33 Every real estate brokerage firm should have a procedures guide
34 and/or a policy manual for its sales associates and employees. A **policy**
35 **manual** is a collection of office rules and regulations created to inform

sales associates and employees of the standards and procedures in that
particular office. Further, a policy manual helps to eliminate the necessity
for new personnel to be constantly asking questions regarding floor time,
listing and sales quotas, vacation schedules, advertising, commissions,
and so forth.

■ MEMBERSHIP IN ORGANIZATIONS

The real estate brokerage business thrives on social contact. Membership
in various clubs and organizations is rewarding in many ways. It is a
violation of 61J2-10.027 for a real estate broker or sales associate to use
or display the insignia, emblems, or names of any association or
organization having to do with real estate unless the licensee is entitled
to use the identification or designation by means of membership,
payment of dues, and so forth. The DBPR may issue a citation and fine a
licensee for the unauthorized use of the name of an association or
organization.

61J2-24.002(2)
(aa), F.A.C.
61J2-10.027,
F.A.C.

■ TYPES OF BUSINESS ENTITIES THAT MAY REGISTER

A broker may choose from a variety of business entities. (See Figure 5.1.)
Sole proprietorships, partnerships (both general and limited), limited
liability partnerships, corporations, and limited liability companies may
be registered as real estate brokers and/or brokerage entities. (Chapter
475.01, F.S., defines the term *broker* to include any person who is a general
partner, officer, or a director of a partnership or corporation that acts as a
real estate broker.)

475.15, F.S.
475.01(1)(a),
F.S.

SOLE PROPRIETORSHIPS   *MOST BUSINESS IN U.S.*

A **sole proprietorship** is a business owned by one person. It is easy to
organize and flexible to operate. The sole proprietor may run a real estate
brokerage business if he or she has a current and valid broker's license.
The broker may use his or her own name or a fictitious name as a trade
name once it has been registered with the FREC. (See Trade Names on
page 93.)

The sole proprietor is personally liable not only for his or her own
actions but also for those of any employees acting within the scope of their
employment. A sole proprietorship may be dissolved by ceasing business
activities and notifying the Commission, or by expiration of the license,
court order, or death of the owner.

PARTNERSHIPS

A **general partnership** is an association of two or more persons for the
purpose of jointly conducting a business. Each person is responsible for
all the debts incurred in the conducting of that business; each has the
power to bind the other or others in transactions; and each is entitled to

620, F.S.
475.15, F.S.

FIGURE 5.1 Business Entities

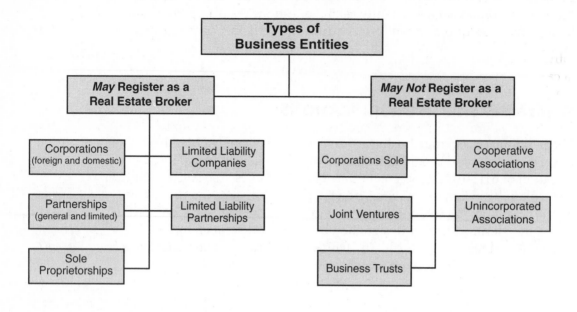

receive a share of the profits in an amount agreed on by the parties. A
general partnership is created by a contract that may be written, oral, or
implied from the conduct of the parties.

Partnerships registered as real estate brokers obtain registration in the
name of the partnership. As in the case of a corporation, the partnership
itself is registered, and at least one of its partners must be licensed as an
active broker. Each partner who expects to deal with the public as a broker
in the partnership's business must hold a valid and current active broker's
license. A sales associate or broker associate may not be a general partner
in a partnership registered as a real estate broker. All of the provisions and
prohibitions related to controlling parties of corporations apply to control
of partnerships.

Any change in the composition of a partnership must be reported to
the FREC, in order to drop the affected party from the registration record
as well as to add any new partners. If the partnership has only one active
broker (broker of record) and he or she dies, resigns, or is removed from
office, he or she must be replaced within 14 days. Failure to timely appoint
another active broker will result in the automatic cancellation of the
partnership registration, and the licenses of all the people associated with
the partnership will become involuntary inactive. The FREC also wants to
ensure that the new partner obtains the appropriate registration showing
membership in the partnership.

61J2-5.018,
F.A.C.
61J2-4.009,
F.A.C.

An **ostensible partnership** (or quasi partnership) exists where the
parties do not form a real partnership but act, or do business, in such a
manner that the public, having no knowledge of the private relations of
the parties, would reasonably be deceived into believing that a partnership
exists. The law further states that because the arrangement is fraudulent
and deceitful, for the purpose of administering the law it is deemed to be

1 a partnership. Any registrants who operate as ostensible partners shall be
2 subject to suspension of their registrations. Ostensible partners may also
3 be liable for each other's debts and torts.

4   Brokers sometimes share office space (each having at least one private
5 office) and conduct their business separately, which is permissible. In such
6 a case, they should not use joint names or operate under the same trade
7 name. They should have their telephones listed separately, use separate
8 letterheads, and clearly indicate their completely separate status by
9 maintaining individual signs as required by the license laws and
10 FREC rules.

11   A **limited partnership** is created by a written instrument filed with
12 the Florida Department of State. There must be one or more general
13 partners and one or more limited partners to qualify under the law. The
14 limited partners must make an investment of cash or of property, but not
15 of services.

16   The liability of the general partner(s) is nearly the same as in a general
17 partnership. A limited partner is *not* liable to creditors of the partnership
18 unless the limited partner's name appears in the partnership name (with
19 certain exceptions) or the limited partner takes part in the control of the
20 business. A limited partner is liable only for any unpaid part of his or her
21 pledged contribution, any assets of the partnership in his or her hands,
22 and any distribution made to him or her while the partnership is
23 insolvent.

620, F.S.
475.15, F.S.

24   A limited partnership that engages in any of the services of real estate
25 must be registered with the FREC. All general partners who expect to deal
26 with the public on behalf of the limited partnership must be licensed as
27 active brokers, with at least one of the general partners personally
28 qualified and licensed as an active broker at all times. All other general
29 partners must be registered with the DRE. Florida license law prohibits
30 sales associates and broker associates from registering as general partners
31 in a limited partnership registered as a real estate broker. Licensed sales
32 associates may be limited partners in a limited partnership. Thus, they are
33 regarded in the same light as stockholders in a corporation. Limited
34 partners need not register with the DRE.

35 ## LIMITED LIABILITY PARTNERSHIPS

36 The partners in a **limited liability partnership** enjoy protection from
37 personal liability in much the same way as limited partners in a limited
38 partnership. Limited liability partners are not liable for obligations or
39 liabilities of the partnership arising from contract, errors or omissions,
40 negligence, malpractice, or wrongful acts committed by another partner
41 or by an employee, agent, or representative of the partnership. A limited
42 liability partner is liable for any errors, omissions, negligence,
43 malpractice, or wrongful acts committed by him or her, or any person
44 under the partner's direct supervision and control in any activity in
45 which the wrongful act occurred, or for any debts for which the partner
46 agreed in writing to be liable. The partners in a limited liability
47 partnership are not subject to the limitations imposed on limited partners
48 in a traditional limited partnership. Registered limited liability

1   partnerships must file with the Florida Department of State. The name
2   of a registered limited liability partnership must include the words
3   "Registered Limited Liability Partnership" or the abbreviation "L.L.P." or
4   the designation "LLP" as the last words or letters of its name.

CORPORATIONS

6   A **corporation** is an artificial person or legal entity created by law and
7   consisting of one or more persons. A corporation may be formed for any
8   lawful business purpose. That business purpose must be carefully
9   described in the application for charter approved by the Florida
10 Department of State. Both foreign and domestic corporations may be
11 registered as brokerage entities. A *foreign corporation* is a corporation
12 organized under the laws of a state other than Florida but that conducts
13 business in Florida. Corporations for profit are managed by a board of
14 directors, acting through the officers, such as president, vice-president,
15 secretary, and treasurer.

607, F.S.
475.15, F.S.
61J2-24.002
(2)(x-y), F.A.C.
61J2-5.012-
.20, F.A.C.

16   In Florida, a corporation may be formed as a real estate brokerage firm
17 only after providing proof of legal corporate existence. At least one of the
18 officers or directors must personally be qualified and licensed as an active
19 broker (the *principal broker* or *qualifying broker*). Officers and directors who
20 deal with the public in brokerage transactions must be qualified and
21 licensed as active brokers. All other officers and directors may hold either
22 active or inactive broker licenses and, if not qualified for licensure, must
23 be registered with the FREC for identification purposes. A sales associate
24 or broker associate may *not* be an officer or director of a real estate
25 brokerage corporation. The Commission may issue a citation and fine a
26 sales associate or broker associate for serving as an officer or director of a
27 registered brokerage corporation.

28   If the only active broker of a brokerage corporation dies, resigns, or is
29 removed from office, the vacancy must be filled within 14 calendar days.
30 New brokerage business may not be performed by the corporation or by
31 a licensee registered with the corporation until a new active broker is
32 designated and registered. Failure to meet the 14-day deadline will result
33 in the automatic cancellation of the brokerage firm's registration, and the
34 licenses of all its officers, directors, and sales associates will become
35 involuntary inactive. If, on the other hand, the corporation has more than
36 one active broker and one of the brokers dies or resigns, the corporate
37 registration and the licenses of the officers, directors, and sales associates
38 are not affected by the vacancy. It is the responsibility of every active
39 corporate officer and director to see that the corporation and all officers,
40 directors, and sales associates have current and appropriate registration
41 and licenses.

61J2-5.018,
F.A.C.

42   *Nonprofit corporations* are organized in substantially the same manner
43 as corporations for profit. Chapter 475, F.S., does not make a distinction
44 between profit and nonprofit corporations. However, any broker who is
45 considering forming a nonprofit corporation for real estate brokerage
46 activity should consult the Florida Department of Revenue and the
47 Internal Revenue Service (IRS) before proceeding.

617, F.S.
61J2-5.012-
.020, F.A.C.

¹ LIMITED LIABILITY COMPANIES

² A **limited liability company** (LLC) is a form of business organization
³ that offers the best features of a corporation and a partnership. It
⁴ provides the owners protection from personal liability for business debts
⁵ in the same way a corporation does, but the IRS treats an LLC as
⁶ a partnership for tax purposes. Income is taxed only once, as in a
⁷ partnership, and an LLC has great flexibility in how it passes income and
⁸ deductions to its members. Limited liability companies are formed
⁹ under Chapter 608, F.S.

¹⁰ ■ TRADE NAMES

¹¹ A *trade name* is a fictitious name that may be any name except the actual
¹² name or trade name of another FREC licensee or registrant. An
¹³ individual broker or brokerage partnership or corporation may use a
¹⁴ trade name after that name is entered in Commission records. A
¹⁵ brokerage entity may not be registered or operate under more than one
¹⁶ trade name. Licensed real estate brokers are exempt from complying
¹⁷ with the provisions of the Florida Fictitious Name Act because they must
¹⁸ register their trade name (if one is used) directly with the Commission.
¹⁹ However, brokerage corporations, partnerships, and limited
²⁰ partnerships must comply with the registration requirements of the
²¹ Florida Department of State.

865.09, F.S.
475.42(1)(k), F.S.
61J2-10.034, F.A.C.
61J2-9.007, F.A.C.

> **Trade Names**
>
> No person shall operate as a broker under a trade name without causing the trade name to be noted in the records of the Commission and placed on his license, or so operate as a member of a partnership or as a corporation or as an officer or manager thereof, unless such partnership or corporation is the holder of a valid current registration.
>
> Reference: Section 475.42, F.S.

²² Broker associates and sales associates must have their licenses issued
²³ in their legal names. They may not be licensed or registered under a trade
²⁴ name. However, a broker associate or a sales associate is allowed by law
²⁵ to form as a limited liability company (LLC) or a professional corporation
²⁶ (PA). In this case, the DBPR issues the license in the licensee's actual
²⁷ (legal) name and includes the entity designation on the face of the license.
²⁸ A real estate sales associate or broker associate may form an LLC or a PA
²⁹ for income tax purposes only, and this is not to be confused with a
³⁰ brokerage business entity. Sales associates and broker associates must
³¹ work under a broker or an owner-developer. Sales associates and broker
³² associates are not allowed to register or be licensed as a general partner,
³³ member, manager, officer, or director of a real estate brokerage firm.

475.161, F.S.

■ BUSINESS ARRANGEMENTS AND ENTITIES THAT MAY NOT REGISTER AS BROKERS

A *corporation sole* is an ecclesiastical or church organization and should not be confused with a corporation for profit. It is normally headed by a bishop or other clerical official who has been empowered by a church to hold title to church property. However, the title descends to successors in office and not to heirs. A broker should exercise caution in dealing with a corporation sole. Before dealing with a corporation sole, a broker should obtain a written opinion from a lawyer who has experience in such titles. A corporation sole cannot be registered as a real estate broker.

A *joint venture* (or joint adventure) is a temporary form of business arrangement often encountered in the real estate business. The joint venture structure is normally used when two or more parties combine their efforts to complete a single business transaction or a fixed number of business transactions. No written agreements are required for the formation of a joint venture. The rights, duties, and obligations of joint venturers are similar to those of partners in a partnership, except that they are restricted to the transaction for which the joint venture was formed.

Real estate brokers often combine their efforts in real estate transactions to create a joint venture. A joint venture, when composed of separate real estate brokers, can broker real property. In such a case, the joint venture would not be required to register with the FREC because each of the individuals is registered and licensed.

609, F.S.
475.011(2), F.S.

A *business trust* is a form of business entity that may be formed to engage in transactions involving its own real property. A business trust is formed by any number of persons who make an investment at a stipulated amount per unit. The monies collected in this manner are then used to buy, develop, and/or sell real estate. Title to real property acquired by a business trust is taken in the name of a trustee or group of trustees. A business trust cannot be registered with the FREC as a real estate broker. However, any employee who buys or sells real property for a trust and is compensated on a transaction basis must be licensed.

A *cooperative association* is permitted to conduct commercial business and to convey, sell, or buy its own property, but it cannot be registered as a real estate broker. (See also Chapter 8.)

619, F.S.

Unincorporated associations are generally recognized as groups of people associated for some noncommercial common purpose. They are not regarded as partners and are not incorporated. An example would be a group of property owners in a subdivision who organize for such purposes as beautification, planning, maintenance, or even the performance of services such as garbage removal. Such associations can incur liabilities, and members are liable for debts to creditors in the same manner as partners. For example, each member is liable for all the debts, but as to each other, each member is liable only for his or her proportionate share. Unincorporated associations sometimes buy or sell their own real property through a trustee or board of trustees. A real estate broker or sales associate should always exercise the same caution in dealing with an unincorporated association as in dealing with a corporation sole. Unincorporated associations may not be registered as real estate brokers.

■ SUMMARY

All active real estate brokers are required to open and maintain an office. Active sales associates and broker associates must work either for a licensed broker or an owner-developer. State laws and FREC rules are explicit about the manner in which brokers advertise and hold themselves out in oral and written form to the public. Brokers may receive money, funds, checks, deposits, drafts, and advance fees during the course of doing business, but they must abide by strict state laws and Commission rules governing such monies held in trust.

Licensees possess expertise in real estate and real estate values and are compensated when they perform the terms of their employment. Sales associates are agents of their employing brokers and as such are duty-bound by all of the laws, rules, and regulations that apply to their broker.

Because real estate licensees encounter businesses organized in many different ways, it is important that they understand the types of business entities that exist and know how to deal with these various entities in real estate transactions.

■ REVIEW QUESTIONS

1. John Anderson is a licensed real estate associate. Under which name may he register and be licensed?
    A. Complete Real Estate Sales Services
    B. John Anderson Brokerage
    C. John Anderson, LLC
    D. John Anderson and Partners

2. Which statement is FALSE concerning brokerage signs?
    A. The sign must include the broker's trade name, if applicable.
    B. The broker must maintain a sign at the entrance to each branch office.
    C. A sign is not required if the broker's office is located in his or her residence.
    D. The words "Licensed Real Estate Broker" must be included on the sign.

3. Real estate brokerage trust funds may NOT be deposited into a
    A. title company in Florida that has trust powers.
    B. credit union in Florida.
    C. commercial bank in Florida.
    D. life insurance company in Florida.

4. In connection with escrow accounts, the Florida Real Estate Commission has rules and regulations that
    A. permit the depositing of personal funds into an escrow account as long as adequate records are kept.
    B. prohibit the depositing of more than $1,000 of personal funds into a sales escrow account.
    C. require deposits to be placed in an escrow account by the sales associate.
    D. require escrow disbursement orders to be prepared when making all deposits.

5. Real estate sales associates who receive checks payable to them as deposits on the purchase of real property must
    A. endorse the checks, deposit them in their employers' accounts, and maintain good records.
    B. endorse the checks and immediately turn them over to their employers.
    C. deposit the checks immediately in their own accounts and notify their employers of the transactions.
    D. deposit the checks immediately and give their employers the equivalent amounts in the form of checks or cash.

6. Broker Murl decides to use the trade name Little Mo Realty for the name of his real estate business. Murl must
    A. register the trade name with the Florida Department of State.
    B. obtain a charter from the State of Florida.
    C. register the trade name with the FREC so that it can be entered into the Commission's records.
    D. do all of the above.

7. Which statement is FALSE regarding escrow accounts?
    A. The escrow account may be either interest-bearing or noninterest-bearing.
    B. A broker may choose to have an attorney or a Florida title company maintain the escrow account.
    C. It is illegal for the broker to keep any earned interest even if the buyer and the seller give written permission.
    D. A broker must get written authorization from the buyer and the seller prior to placing escrow funds in an interest-bearing escrow account.

8. A dispute arises between the buyer and seller as to which one is entitled to escrowed property. The broker should first
    A. mediate the matter.
    B. arbitrate the matter with the consent of both parties.
    C. notify the FREC, unless exempted from the notice requirements.
    D. submit the matter to a court of law for adjudication.

9. Regarding advance fee trust accounts
    A. 100 percent of all such advance fees collected must be deposited.
    B. at least 75 percent of all such advance fees collected must be deposited, with the exception of advance fees for auctioning real property.
    C. such accounts may be combined with other escrow or trust accounts but not with personal accounts.
    D. a broker may use such funds if the expenditures are limited to general business expenses and accurate records are kept.

10. An individual who paid for rental information but did not obtain a rental is entitled to repayment of
    A. the fee.
    B. the fee if requested within 10 days of the contract/receipt date.
    C. 75 percent of the fee if requested within 10 days of the contract/receipt date.
    D. 75 percent of the fee if requested within 30 days of the contract/receipt date.

11. Rebecca purchased a rental list one week ago from a real estate broker. Rebecca inspected an apartment described in the list. The apartment manager told Rebecca that cats were not allowed. Rebecca had specifically looked at the apartment because the rental list indicated that pets were allowed. Immediately, Rebecca orally demanded and should legally receive from the broker
    A. nothing, because the demand is not in writing.
    B. 75 percent of the fee paid.
    C. 100 percent of the fee paid.
    D. nothing, because the broker may not be held accountable for the actions of the property manager.

12. If the license issued to the only active broker of a real estate corporation becomes void for any reason, another active broker must be appointed within 14 calendar days. Failure to appoint another active broker will result in what action against the corporation's registration?
    A. Automatic cancellation
    B. Denial
    C. Automatic suspension
    D. Revocation

13. Murl decides to incorporate his new real estate business, Little Mo Realty, Inc., in order to reduce his personal liability. Murl must do each requirement EXCEPT
    A. register the brokerage entity with the Commission.
    B. obtain a charter from the Florida Department of State.
    C. register all officers and directors of the company with the Commission.
    D. obtain a charter from the Secretary of the DBPR.

14. A corporation sole is a(n)
    A. commercial enterprise organized and managed by one individual.
    B. unincorporated association organized for a single common purpose other than to operate as a church.
    C. church organization registered as a real estate broker.
    D. ecclesiastical organization.

15. To form a general partnership, two or more persons must
    A. agree to share equally in the profits and losses.
    B. agree to engage in business together and share in the profits and losses.
    C. be personally qualified and licensed as real estate brokers.
    D. invest equal amounts of money in the business and each be entitled to a share of the profits.

16. One difference between a general partnership and a limited partnership is that
    A. only a general partnership may be registered as a real estate broker.
    B. limited partners must make a cash or property investment.
    C. while both have general partners, there must be two or more general partners in a limited partnership.
    D. limited partners must be licensed as either active or inactive sales associates.

17. Which business entity may be registered as a real estate broker?
    A. Corporation sole
    B. Cooperative association
    C. Limited partnership
    D. Business trust

18. A broker has conflicting demands from a buyer and a seller regarding an escrow deposit. The broker may employ all of the escape procedures listed below EXCEPT
    A. request an escrow disbursement order.
    B. provided all of the parties consent, submit the matter to arbitration.
    C. request an informal hearing before the FREC to resolve the matter.
    D. through an interpleader, submit the matter to a court proceeding for determination of the rightful claimant.

19. Broker Murl is getting prepared to open Little Mo Realty as a sole proprietorship and is placing an order to have an entrance sign made. Which wording does NOT need to be included on the sign?
    A. Little Mo Realty
    B. Murl's legal name
    C. Licensed real estate broker
    D. 1000 Sunset Blvd.

20. In answering questions pertaining to quality of title, real estate brokers are
    A. required to give opinions because of their role as experts.
    B. required to advise prospective buyers to have a lawyer render an opinion or obtain title insurance.
    C. allowed to give their opinions because of their role as experts.
    D. allowed to give their opinions only when specifically asked by the buyer.

21. A broker receives conflicting demands concerning a roof inspection report. Both the buyer and seller claim the earnest money deposit. The broker must
    A. provide written notification to the FREC within 10 business days.
    B. follow the written instructions of the broker's buyer or seller.
    C. institute one of the statutory settlement procedures within 30 business days after the last demand.
    D. request an escrow disbursement order from the DBPR.

22. The sales commission rates applicable to the various types of property sold in Florida are determined by
    A. FREC rules and regulations.
    B. agreement between each broker and buyer or seller.
    C. the local board of REALTORS®.
    D. agreement between each seller and buyer.

23. When a sales associate decides to leave the employ of her broker to work for another broker, she
    A. may take copies of all listings she personally obtained while employed by her former broker.
    B. must notify the FREC within ten days of her change in broker-employer.
    C. may telephone sellers of her former employer to encourage them to cancel their listing agreements with the former employer and then list with her new broker.
    D. must apply for a new real estate license under the name of her new broker.

24. A real estate transaction for the sale of residential property has been closed, but the seller refuses to pay the broker the commission earned as a result of the sale. The broker may
    A. collect triple damages per F.S. 475.
    B. file suit in a court of law against the seller.
    C. file an interpleader action in a court of law against the seller.
    D. request that the FREC issue an escrow disbursement order.

25. Broker Murl decides to organize Little Mo Realty as a limited partnership. What must Murl accomplish?
    A. File the limited partnership agreement with the Florida Department of State
    B. Register the limited partnership with the Commission
    C. Register all general partners with the Commission
    D. Do all of the above

26. In Florida, listings obtained and any commissions paid by the buyer or seller are
    A. legally the sales associate's property.
    B. jointly owned by the sales associate and the sales associate's employer.
    C. legally classified as the property of the employing property owner.
    D. legally the property of the sales associate's employer.

27. An active real estate sales associate signed an employment agreement with Broker Denton two days ago. Broker Denton is out of town today, and the sales associate needs to know the office rules pertaining to the advertising of listings. That information should be available in the
    A. office policy manual.
    B. office administration manual.
    C. FREC Handbook.
    D. FREC letter of guidance.

28. Broker Murl of Little Mo Realty and Broker Dan of Boyds of Naples agree to work with one another to market a prestigious marina in Naples, Florida. Murl is particularly knowledgeable regarding marinas and Dan is an expert on the Naples real estate market, so they decide to combine their expertise on this particular listing. This business arrangement is referred to as a(n)
    A. ostensible partnership.
    B. general partnership.
    C. joint venture.
    D. limited partnership.

CHAPTER 6

Complaints, Violations, and Penalties

25% of Test

Legal Affairs check Violation

Very Nit-Picky!

■ KEY TERMS

citations	legally sufficient	recommended order
complaint	notice of noncompliance	subpoena
formal complaint	probable cause	summary suspension

1 ## ■ OVERVIEW

2 This Chapter details the step-by-step procedures for investigations and
3 hearings via the complaint process. The Chapter describes many types of
4 violations of the laws and rules governing real estate activities and the
5 possible consequences that may result. Finally, the Real Estate Recovery
6 Fund is explained regarding its function when damages are suffered in a
7 real estate transaction owing to a wrongful act of a Florida licensee.

8 After completing this Chapter, the student should be able to:

9 • explain the procedures involved in the reporting of violations, the
10 investigation of complaints, and the conduct of hearings;

11 • describe the elements of a valid complaint;

12 • describe the composition of the probable-cause panel;

13 • describe events that would cause a license to be denied;

14 • recognize actions that would cause a license to be subject to
15 suspension or revocation;

16 • identify individuals who would be eligible to seek reimbursement
17 from the Real Estate Recovery Fund; and

18 • describe the monetary limits imposed by law on the Real Estate
19 Recovery Fund.

20 ## ■ PROCEDURES FOR INVESTIGATIONS AND HEARINGS

21 In Florida, the legal bases for investigations and hearings are:

22 • Chapter 120, F.S. (Administrative Procedure Act);

- Chapter 455, F.S. (Regulation of Professions and Occupations);
- Chapter 475, F.S. (Florida Real Estate License Law);
- Chapter 28, Sections 101 through 110 (Division of Administrative Hearings), Florida Administrative Code (F.A.C.); and
- Chapter 61J2 (Florida Real Estate Commission), Florida Administrative Code (F.A.C.).

The Division of Real Estate (DRE) is assigned the responsibility for investigative functions related to real estate. This includes DRE investigations to verify information provided by applicants as well as investigations of complaints against licensees. Based on its findings, the DRE prosecutes licensees before the Florida Real Estate Commission.

475.021, F.S.

The DRE investigates applications for licensure to determine whether all requirements and qualifications have been met. The investigative process also includes determining whether licensed brokers and sales associates are guilty of violating the laws of Florida or some other state or federal law. State law prohibits any process, requirement of a report, inspection, or any other investigative demand for any purpose except as authorized by statute. Any person who is asked to respond to a request or demand for an oral statement by a state agency is entitled to a copy of the transcript in the same manner as any other public record request under Chapter 119, F.S., provided the agency had the proceeding transcribed. (*Note:* State agencies are required to tape-record official proceedings, however, they are not required to transcribe official proceedings.)

455.225, F.S.
455.203(7), F.S.
120.62, F.S.

■ COMPLAINT PROCESS—SEVEN STEPS

Seven steps are involved in the process of dealing with complaints of alleged violations:

1. Filing the complaint

2. Investigation

3. Probable cause

4. Formal complaint

5. Informal hearing or formal hearing

6. Final order

7. Judicial review (appeal)

STEP 1: FILING THE COMPLAINT

The complaint process begins when a **complaint** (an alleged violation of a law or rule) is filed with the Department of Business and Professional Regulation (DBPR). Any complaint that is filed in writing and is legally sufficient will be investigated. A complaint is **legally sufficient** if it contains facts indicating that a *violation* of any of the following has occurred:

475.25, F.S.
455.225, F.S.

1   • Florida statute

2   • Federal statute

3   • Any existing, legally enacted DBPR rule

4   • Any existing, legally enacted FREC rule

5   Anyone may file a complaint against a licensee, an applicant, or an
6 unlicensed person for actions believed to be in violation of Chapter 475,
7 F.S. The alleged violation(s) need not pertain to real estate transactions
8 and need not have taken place in Florida. A "Uniform Complaint Form"
9 is available from the DBPR.

 You can download the Uniform Complaint Form at the DRE's Form Center. The address is: **http://www.state.fl.us/dbpr/re /forms/ index.shtml.** *Click on "Uniform Complaint Form Division of Real Estate RE 2200."*

 Consumers may also file a complaint online. To learn more about the DBPR's online services, visit the Online Service Center Home Page at: **https://www.myfloridalicense.com/Default.asp.**

455.225(3), F.S.
120.695, F.S.
61J2-24.003,
F.A.C.

10   In instances that involve a first-time offense of a minor violation, the
11 Department may issue a **notice of noncompliance.** The Commission has
12 established by rule minor violations that do not endanger the public
13 health, safety, and welfare and that do not demonstrate a serious inability
14 to practice the profession. If a licensee fails to correct the violation and
15 fails to comply with the statute or rule within the statutory time limit, the
16 licensee may be issued a citation. If the violation is not listed in the citation
17 rule, however, the DBPR initiates regular disciplinary proceedings.

18 ## STEP 2: INVESTIGATION

19 The DBPR may investigate an anonymous complaint or one made by a
20 confidential informant if the complaint is in writing and is legally
21 sufficient; if the alleged violation of law or rules is substantial; and if
22 the Department has reason to believe, after preliminary inquiry, that the
23 alleged violations in the complaint are true.

24   The Department may initiate an investigation on its own if it has
25 reasonable cause to believe that a licensee has violated a Florida statute,
26 Department rule, or FREC rule. Furthermore, the Department may
27 conduct an investigation without notification to anyone subject to the
28 investigation if the act under investigation is a criminal offense.

29   If the original *complainant* (person who files the complaint) withdraws
30 his or her complaint or otherwise indicates a desire not to cause it to be
31 investigated or prosecuted to completion, the Department may continue
32 with the investigation and the Commission may take the appropriate final
33 action on the complaint. When an investigation of a subject is undertaken,
34 the DBPR will forward a copy of the complaint to the subject or to the
35 subject's attorney. The subject of the investigation may submit a written
36 response to the complaint. The response must be considered by the
37 probable-cause panel. A complaint and all information obtained during
38 any resulting investigation must be treated as confidential until ten days

after probable cause has been found to exist or the subject of the
investigation waives the privilege of confidentiality, whichever
occurs first.

The DBPR is empowered to administer oaths; take depositions; and
examine respondents, witnesses, and plaintiffs. It can also issue
subpoenas to obtain records, documents, or information that is material to
the investigation. A Department investigator interviews the subject of the
allegation(s), and, if applicable, an audit is performed of any escrow
account(s). Once the investigative process is completed, and provided the
complaint is legally sufficient, the Department prepares a written
investigative report that then is submitted to the probable-cause panel.

The report consists of the investigative findings and contains
recommendations regarding the existence of **probable cause** (reasonable
grounds for prosecution) and a recommended course of action.

STEP 3: PROBABLE CAUSE

The *probable-cause panel* is composed of two members of the FREC who
are appointed by the chairperson of the Commission. A former
Commissioner may serve on a probable-cause panel. However, one of the
two panel members must be a current member. The panel must include
at least one professional member (present or former). However, in the
case of a former professional member, he or she must hold an active valid
license. If a present or former consumer member is available and willing
to serve, then one of the panelists must be a consumer member.

455.225(4), F.S.
61J2-20.009,
F.A.C.

Probable-cause proceedings are not open to the public, and the
remaining FREC members are prohibited from attending. The segregation
of the Commission members allows the probable-cause panel to serve in a
"grand jury" type of arrangement. Because the remaining commissioners
do not participate in the probable-cause proceedings, they are able to
maintain objectivity in the matter if it comes before the Commission in an
informal hearing.

455.207(4), F.S.

The probable-cause panel's sole responsibility is to determine whether
probable cause exists. (If a licensing board does not have a probable-cause
panel, the DBPR makes the determination as to whether probable cause
exists.) The probable-cause panel reviews the facts of the case and the staff
attorney's recommendations. After a complete review of the record, the
probable-cause panel makes a determination as to whether probable
cause exists. If the complaint information presented to the probable-cause
panel is not adequate in content, the panel may request, and the DBPR
must provide, any available or necessary additional information. A
request for additional information must be made within the time frame
set forth in the statute.

The probable-cause panel (or DBPR when there is no panel) must
make a decision within 30 days after receipt of the final investigative
report, unless an extension is granted by the Secretary of the Department.
If the panel fails to act within the statutory time limit (plus legal
extensions), the Department may make a determination in the case.

If the panel finds that probable cause does not exist, the DBPR is allowed ten days to override that decision and to file charges. Furthermore, if the Department finds that the panel was unwise in deciding that probable cause existed, it may choose not to prosecute a complaint. In such cases, the Department refers the matter to the FREC. The Commission may retain independent legal counsel, employ investigators, and continue the investigation if it deems necessary.

If the panel finds that probable cause does not exist, it may simply dismiss the case, or it may dismiss the case with a *letter of guidance* to the subject. Once the probable-cause proceeding has been concluded, the complainant and the subject of the investigation are sent written notification of the outcome.

STEP 4: FORMAL COMPLAINT

If probable cause is found to exist, the probable-cause panel will direct the Department to file a formal complaint against the subject of the investigation (respondent). A **formal complaint** (also referred to as an *administrative complaint*) is an outline of allegations of facts and charges against the licensee. The licensee must answer within the statutory time limit. In no response (default) cases, the license is usually revoked.

455.225, F.S.

The licensee is entitled to an informal hearing, a formal hearing, or the licensee may agree to a "stipulation." A *stipulation* is an agreement as to the penalty reached between the attorneys for the DRE and the licensee or licensee's attorney. The licensee and the licensee's legal counsel, where there is one, are encouraged to appear before the FREC. The FREC may approve or deny the stipulation. If the FREC denies the stipulation, it usually provides guidance to the DRE attorney concerning additional penalties it believes appropriate in order for it to support a revised stipulation.

20 day To Appeal.

NCCO. ADMIN LAW ATT

STEP 5: CASE IS PRESENTED IN EITHER AN INFORMAL HEARING OR A FORMAL HEARING

Counts for 2.

If the licensee-respondent's case was not resolved with a stipulation, the respondent's case will either be heard by the FREC in an informal hearing or the case may be heard before an administrative law judge in a formal hearing. The licensee-respondent must admit to the alleged facts to be entitled to an informal hearing. If the licensee-respondent disputes the alleged facts that are made in the complaint, the licensee-respondent's case must be heard by an administrative law judge in a formal hearing.

455.225(5), F.S.
120.57(2), F.S.
61J2-2.032,
F.A.C.

An informal hearing is an expedited way of resolving the disciplinary case provided the licensee does not dispute the alleged facts stated in the complaint. During an **informal hearing,** normally held at a regular Commission meeting, the licensee-respondent is given an opportunity to explain the details of his or her case with supporting evidence and/or witnesses. Any commissioners who served on the probable-cause panel for the particular complaint may not participate in this informal hearing. If any party raises an issue of disputed fact during an informal hearing,

120.575(3), F.S.
455.2273(5). F.S/
120.52, F.S.

the hearing is terminated and a formal hearing will be scheduled before an administrative law judge. The FREC will determine based on the admitted facts whether the licensee is guilty of the charges alleged in the complaint. If the licensee is found guilty of the charges, the FREC will determine which penalties are appropriate based on the details of the case, taking into consideration any mitigating circumstances (reasons to reduce the impact of the violation), and it will issue a final order. (Refer also to Step 6 below.)

If the licensee-respondent requests a **formal hearing** or if the licensee-respondent disputes the allegations, the DBPR requests that the case be prosecuted under Chapter 120, F.S. Hearings under Chapter 120 are conducted by full-time Florida administrative law judges who are employed by the Division of Administrative Hearings (DOAH). The DOAH may legally employ only those persons who have been members of The Florida Bar in good standing for the preceding five years. Administrative law judges are not subject to control, supervision, or direction by any party, commission, or department of state government. Once an administrative law judge is assigned, the DBPR may take no further action except as a litigating party.

455.225, F.S.
120.60(5), F.S.
120.57(1), F.S.

The administrative law judge has the power to swear witnesses, to take their testimony under oath, and to issue subpoenas. A **subpoena** is a command to appear at a certain time and place to give testimony. Failure to comply with a subpoena could result in a finding of contempt of court.

The administrative law judge prepares and submits to the DBPR and to all other parties a **recommended order** that includes the administrative law judge's findings and conclusions and the recommended penalty, if any, in accordance with the Commission's range of penalties as set forth in rule. Any party of record in the case may submit (within the statutory time limit) written exceptions to the administrative law judge's recommended order.

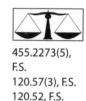

455.2273(5), F.S.
120.57(3), F.S.
120.52, F.S.

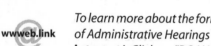

To learn more about the formal hearing process, visit the Florida Division of Administrative Hearings Web site at: **www.doah.state.fl.us/internet/.** *Click on "DOAH Rules."*

STEP 6: FINAL ORDER

The FREC (with the members who served on the probable-cause panel excused) issues the **final order** in each disciplinary case. The final order is FREC's final decision as to innocence or guilt and the determination of the appropriate penalty. The FREC issues a final order at the conclusion of an informal hearing. If the matter was heard by an administrative law judge in a formal hearing, the FREC must review and consider the administrative law judge's findings and recommended order before issuing its final order.

475.31, F.S.
455.255, F.S.
120.57, F.S.
61J2-24.001, F.A.C.

The respondent may appear in person or be represented by an attorney or both. Independent legal counsel represents the Commission in disciplinary proceedings. The Commission members who did not serve on the probable-cause panel consider the administrative law judge's report and recommended order, plus any filed exceptions to the report and the accused party's final arguments, if any. After all final arguments are heard, the Commission members make a determination and issue the final order, concluding the quasi-judicial process.

The final order must be in writing. It must include the facts established during the proceeding and state each conclusion of law separately. A copy of the final order is mailed to each party in the case. The notice must inform the recipient of the appeal process. The final order becomes effective 30 days after it has been entered. A licensee has the right to practice real estate during the complaint process and up until the final order becomes effective.

455.225(8), F.S.
120.60, F.A.C.

In some extreme circumstances, however, the DBPR or the FREC may decide that to allow the licensee to continue to practice real estate during the 30 day period and/or during the appeal process may endanger the public. In such a case, the DBPR Secretary (or a legally appointed designee) may issue a **summary suspension.** A summary suspension is an emergency or immediate suspension of a license. Summary suspensions when ordered must be followed promptly by a formal suspension or by a revocation hearing.

STEP 7: JUDICIAL REVIEW (APPEAL)

The licensee-respondent may challenge the final order within 30 days by filing a petition for judicial review. The petition for judicial review (notice of appeal) must be filed with the DBPR and with the appropriate district court of appeals. In order for a licensee to continue practicing real estate during the appeal process, the court must grant a *stay of enforcement.*)To obtain a stay (stop enforcement) of the final order, the court must issue a *writ of supersedeas* which stops enforcement of the final order (stays suspension or revocation) pending the outcome of the appeal.

475.37, F.S.
120.68, F.S.

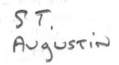

If the reviewing court finds that a material error in procedure by the FREC has affected the fairness of the hearing or the correctness of the action taken, the case will be sent back to the FREC for corrective action. Unless the court finds legitimate grounds to set aside, modify, remand for further FREC proceeding, order additional action by the FREC, or order some auxiliary relief under Florida Statute 120.68, the court is required to affirm (support) the action taken by the Commission.

The DBPR is authorized to seek judicial review of any final order issued by the Commission. If a FREC final order is affirmed, reversed, or set aside, a mandate (copy) is filed with the Commission attesting to that event. The respondent's rights and privileges as a licensee will be restored as of the date of filing, if the final order is reversed. Thereafter, the matters examined and the charges alleged cannot be reexamined in any other proceedings concerning the licensure of that person or party. When the inquiry or proceeding is in reference to an application to become licensed, the application must be approved and processed. If a court reverses or sets aside a final order, the court may award attorney's fees and costs to the aggrieved prevailing party. (See Summary of the Complaint Process on page 108.)

Summary of the Complaint Process

- Complaint is filed with DBPR; the alleged wrongdoing is reviewed.

- DBPR conducts investigation and notifies licensee-respondent.

- Investigative report is given to FREC probable-cause panel for decision and returned to DBPR.

- If probable cause is found, FREC directs the DBPR to issue a formal complaint.

- Licensee is entitled to an informal or a formal hearing.

- If there are no disputed facts, the Commission (probable-cause panel is excused) decides the case and imposes the penalty at the informal hearing.

- If there are disputed facts, the matter goes to a formal hearing.

- Once the formal hearing is concluded, the administrative law judge prepares a recommended order.

- The Commission imposes the final order (members of probable-cause panel do not participate).

- Licensee-respondent may appeal the final order.

■ VIOLATIONS AND PENALTIES

475.455, F.S.
475.42, F.S.
475.25, F.S.
61J2-24.002, F.A.C.

The FREC is authorized to deny, suspend, or revoke licenses; to issue citations; and to otherwise discipline licensees. For the purposes of the following discussion, the term *license* also includes the terms *registration*, *certification*, and *permit*. The grounds and penalties for these actions are numerous and are listed in the following sections.

GROUNDS FOR DENIAL

Denial of an applicant's request for licensure keeps him or her from becoming licensed to practice real estate in Florida. Several reasons for denial exist. Some denials result from errors made in the application process, or from failing the state licensing examination. When such instances occur, the applicant may correct or file a new application, or submit an application to retake the exam.

Examples of grounds for license denial are:

- neglecting to answer completely all questions on the application;

- neglecting to forward the proper fees with the application request;

- neglecting to correct errors or omissions on applications returned; and

- failing to complete successfully the required written examination.

475.181, F.S.
475.17, F.S.

Other grounds for denial are more serious and result in an applicant being denied licensure. Examples of cause for license denial are that the applicant:

- lacked qualifications to register;

- did not possess the character required by the provisions of Florida Statutes 455 and 475;

- did not possess the general competence to deal with the public, or complaints against him or her were received by the FREC or the DBPR;

- was guilty of acts that would have resulted in revocation or suspension of license had he or she already been licensed;

- acted in violation of any provision of F.S. 475.42 or was at the time subject to discipline under F.S. 475.25; and

- received assistance or cheated while taking a state exam.

If the FREC denies an applicant on two occasions, the applicant may appeal to the Division of Administrative Hearings (DOAH). The DOAH makes a recommendation to the FREC, which may adopt or reject the DOAH recommendation. A judicial court may only vacate the order of the FREC if it denied the applicant due process or breached a mandate of law. A court of law cannot force the FREC to issue a license because Florida statutes reserved the power to grant or deny a real estate license to the FREC.

GROUNDS FOR SUSPENSION

Suspension of an individual's license is a temporary penalty. The maximum period for which the FREC may suspend a license is ten years. Florida statutes refer to many acts that are illegal, any one of which may result in license suspension. Each illegal act constitutes grounds for suspension or revocation of licensure, depending on the seriousness attached to the offense by the Commission. A second suspension for the same or a different violation may well result in revocation of the license, registration, certification, or permit.

475.42, F.S.
475.25, F.S.

GROUNDS FOR REVOCATION

The most severe type of administrative penalty that the FREC is authorized to impose is revocation of a license. Revocation of a license is permanent. When the FREC revokes a license, that licensee is put out of the real estate business. Exceptions to "permanent" occur when a licensee has filed for renewal but has not complied with the continuing or post-licensing education requirements prior to the expiration date or when an individual filed an application for licensure that contained false or fraudulent information. In such cases, the applicant may not apply for a sales associate's license for five years unless the Commission specifies a lesser period of time in the final order based on mitigating factors presented by the licensee. At their discretion the FREC is empowered to revoke a licensee's license for any of the causes that constitute grounds for suspension or denial. Suspension or revocation plus a $1,000 fine is the minimum penalty for obtaining a license by fraud, misrepresentation, or concealment.

475.31, F.S.
475.25, F.S.
455.227, F.S.
61J2-24.005, F.A.C.

1   When a real estate broker's license is suspended or revoked, all
2   licenses issued to sales associates who work for the penalized broker are
3   placed in involuntary inactive status. If the revoked or suspended broker
4   is a partnership or corporation, affected sales associates, partners, officers,
5   and directors may request registration with a new employer or in the
6   same partnership or corporation if it reorganizes to requalify under
7   Florida statutes and FREC rules.

Revocation or Cancellation Without Prejudice

A license may be revoked or canceled if it was issued through the mistake or
inadvertence of the Commission. Such revocation or cancellation shall not
prejudice any subsequent application for licensure filed by the person against
whom such action was taken.

Reference: Section 475.25(2), F.S.

---

8   # ■ TYPES OF PENALTIES

9   There are three types of penalties that may be imposed for violations of
10 the real estate license law: administrative, civil, and criminal.

475.42, F.S.

11 ## ADMINISTRATIVE PENALTIES

12 The Commission may impose an administrative penalty for violations
13 of the law or rules and regulations. Possible administrative penalties
14 include denial of an application for a license; refusal to recertify a license
15 for renewal; revocation of a license; suspension of a license for not more
16 than ten years; a fine not to exceed $5,000 for each F.S. 455 violation or
17 $1,000 for each F.S. 475 violation or separate offense; and probation,
18 reprimand, citation, notice of noncompliance, or other penalty.

475.25, F.S.
455.227, F.S.
61J2-24.001,
F.A.C.

19 DBPR investigator-auditors have the authority to immediately issue
20 citations in the field for minor violations discovered during an
21 investigation or audit. **Citations** involve fines that can range from $100 to
22 $1,000 per offense and may include other assessments (for example,
23 require educational course attendance). Several of the more common
24 offenses cited include failure to perform and/or sign monthly
25 reconciliation of escrow account(s) or advertising in a manner in which a
26 reasonable person would not know that one is dealing with a licensee or
27 brokerage. A licensee receiving a citation has 30 days to accept or reject the
28 alleged violation(s), as specified in the citation. If the licensee does not
29 dispute the matter, the citation penalty will become effective (a final order)
30 and the case will be closed. If the licensee disputes the alleged violation(s),
31 the licensee must file a written objection. The licensee will be allowed to
32 state his or her case and, based on the merits, will have the case dismissed
33 or carried forward to a formal hearing. If the licensee fails to pay the fine
34 in a timely manner, the FREC will file an administrative complaint.

455.228, F.S
455.224, F.S.
61J2-24.002,
F.A.C.

35 The DBPR may issue a *notice of noncompliance* as a first response to a
36 minor violation by a licensee. It must identify the specific statute(s) and
37 rule(s) violated, provide information on how to comply, and state the time

to comply. Some minor violations deemed by the FREC not to endanger the health, safety, or welfare of the public include failure in an ad to include the registered name of the brokerage firm, failure to maintain an office entrance sign, or failure in an ad to use the licensee's last name as registered with the Commission. If a licensee fails to take action to correct one of the listed minor violations within 15 days after being notified, the licensee may be fined or subjected to other disciplinary penalties.

455.225(3), F.S.
120.695, F.S.
61J2-24.003, F.A.C.

The FREC may, in addition to other disciplinary penalties, place a licensee on *probation*. The Commission is empowered to set the time period and conditions of probation. Probationary conditions may include, for example, requiring the licensee to attend a prelicense or post-license course or other educational offering, to submit to and successfully complete the state-administered examination, or to be subject to periodic inspections by a DBPR investigator.

Summary of Types of Administrative Penalties

- **Denial** of license application (or refusal to renew a license).

- **Letter of reprimand** is a letter that is placed in the licensee's file describing a minor incidence of misconduct that resulted in no disciplinary action (also called a *letter of guidance*).

- **Notice of noncompliance** is a warning for a minor violation (an initial offense only) that allows a licensee 15 days to correct the minor infraction without consequence (nonresponse could result in disciplinary action).

- **Citation** concerns violations that are of no substantial threat to the public involving a fine that can range from $100 to $1,000.

- **Probation** allows the licensee to continue to practice real estate under the guidance of the FREC for a period of time while completing conditions specified by the FREC such as to complete education courses, attend FREC meetings, and satisfy all of the terms of the penalty.

- **Fine** may be up to $1,000 for each violation of Chapter 475 and up to $5,000 for each violation of Chapter 455.

- **Suspension** of a license (for up to 10 years).

- **Revocation** of a license is permanent (with continuing education exception).

CIVIL PENALTIES

Civil penalties may be enforced by the courts if a person has performed any real estate services without a license. The courts may rule that no sale commission is due, which could be a much greater penalty than an administrative fine or a criminal penalty.

CRIMINAL PENALTIES

A violation of Florida Statute 475 or any lawful order, rule, or regulation is legally a misdemeanor of the second degree (except as noted below). It may be punishable by a fine of not more than $500 and/or by imprisonment for not more than 60 days. A corporation may only be fined, because a corporation cannot be imprisoned. All imprisonment penalties or fines,

775.081-3, F.S.
455.2277, F.S.

Licensure Reissue

The Department shall reissue the license of a licensee against whom disciplinary action was taken upon certification by the Commission that the licensee has complied with all of the terms and conditions of the final order imposing discipline.

Reference: Section 475.25(3), F.S.

---

1. except administrative fines, must be obtained in a court of law because
2. the Commission lacks the authority to assess such penalties. The FREC
3. must report any criminal violation of Chapter 475, F.S., to the appropriate
4. state attorney's office.

5. **First-degree criminal penalties.**   There are two violations of real estate
6. license law that are first-degree misdemeanors:

7.   1. Unlawfully collecting an advance fee for listing real property

8.   2. Failing to provide accurate and current rental information for a fee

3 False Information.

9.   The penalty for a first-degree misdemeanor is a fine of not more than
10. $1,000 and/or up to one year in jail.

475.453(3)(a), F.S.
475.452(4), F.S.

11. **Other penalty actions.**   The assessing of one of the three types of
12. penalties (administrative, civil, or criminal) does not prevent or affect the
13. prosecution of any other proceeding. The same facts that are the basis for
14. the prosecution of violations of the real estate license law may prove to be
15. an offense committed under other state statutes. Both violations may be
16. charged, but the punishment (fine and/or sentence) cannot be greater than
17. the highest prescribed in either statute. However, the Commission may, in
18. addition to any other disciplinary action imposed, assess costs related to
19. the investigation and prosecution of a case, excluding attorney's fees.

455.227(2), F.S.

20. **Unlicensed practice of real estate.**   It is a felony of the third degree for
21. a person to perform real estate services for compensation without a real
22. estate license. The Secretary of the DBPR assigns a probable cause panel
23. and a hearing officer to hear cases of unlicensed activity. The DBPR can
24. issue fines of up to $5,000 per count to a person it finds guilty of
25. unlicensed activity.

475.42 (1)(a), F.S.
455.228, F.S.

26.   The DBPR may issue a cease and desist order to an unlicensed person
27. who has violated F.S. 475, F.S. 455, or any other statute relating to the
28. practice of real estate. The DBPR may also file a proceeding in the name of
29. the state requesting the circuit court to issue an injunction or a *writ of*
30. *mandamus* ordering the unlicensed activity to stop. If the person found
31. guilty of unlicensed activity refuses to pay a fine issued by the DBPR, it
32. may seek enforcement of the penalty through a civil court. The DBPR
33. must refer any criminal matters to the State Attorney's Office. The state
34. attorney may institute criminal prosecution against an unlicensed person.

35. # ■ FREC DISCIPLINARY GUIDELINES

36. The Commission uses guidelines that apply to each specific ground for
37. disciplinary action that it may impose. The purpose of these disciplinary

455.2273, F.S.
61J2-24.003, F.A.C.
61J2-24.002, F.A.C.
61J2-24.001, F.A.C.

guidelines is to give notice to licensees of the range of penalties that normally will be imposed for each count (offense) during a formal or informal hearing. A finding of *mitigating* (less severe) circumstances or *aggravating* (more severe) circumstances allows the Commission to impose a penalty other than those provided. The extent of a penalty, ranging from least to most severe, is reprimand to suspension and revocation or denial. Combinations of these and other penalties are permitted. Grounds and penalties are listed in Table 6.1 (see page 118) in numerical order by statute.

■ DENIAL AND RECOVERY OF COMPENSATION

There are two different methods of denying compensation or recovering compensation already paid. One is an administrative penalty, wherein the FREC will act to deny, suspend, or revoke licensure. While the FREC cannot deny payment of compensation or direct repayment of compensation already paid, the Commission can issue an order to deny, suspend, or revoke a license and include a stipulation that the compensation already received must be repaid before the order will be vacated (set aside), thereby indirectly influencing a licensee's decision.

The second, more direct method of denying or recovering compensation is through the civil courts. A plaintiff may seek a civil action wherein the court is asked to impose a denial of compensation or judicial forfeiture of monies already collected plus damages if appropriate.

Normally, the grounds for denial or recovery of compensation involve fraudulent acts by a real estate broker or sales associate or noncompliance with Chapters 455 or 475, F.S., or Commission rules.

■ REAL ESTATE RECOVERY FUND *I Mil Broker coverage.*

475.482, F.S.
215.37, F.S.

The Florida Real Estate Recovery Fund was created as a separate account in the Professional Regulation Trust Fund. Its purpose is to reimburse any person, partnership, or corporation judged by a Florida court to have suffered monetary (compensatory) damages (but not punitive damages) as a result of an act committed by a broker or sales associate who:

- was at the time the alleged act was committed, the holder of a current, valid, active real estate license issued under Chapter 475;

- was not the seller, buyer, landlord, or tenant in the transaction (except as noted below) nor an officer or director of a corporation, a member of a partnership, a member of a limited liability company, or a partner of a limited liability partnership which was the seller, buyer, landlord, or tenant in the transaction; and

- was acting solely in the capacity of a real estate licensee in the transaction.

A real estate licensee who was the buyer or seller (lessor or lessee) in a real estate transaction may also make a claim against the fund *provided*

1 the licensee did *not* act in the capacity of a real estate agent. In other
2 words, if a licensed person is the buyer or seller of real property and
3 suffers monetary damages as a result of an act committed by another
4 licensed broker or sales associate who did act in the capacity of an agent,
5 the fact that the victim is licensed will not prevent him or her from seeking
6 reimbursement from the fund.

7 If a broker who complied with an escrow disbursement order is later
8 required by a court of law to pay damages as a result of legal actions taken
9 by the buyer or seller in the transaction, the FREC is authorized to order
10 reimbursement to the broker for the amount of the judgment against the
11 broker up to $50,000. No disciplinary action will be taken against a broker
12 who had previously requested an EDO and followed its instructions. The
13 broker's license will not be suspended and no repayment to the fund is
14 required.

15 To be eligible for reimbursement, the broker must notify the FREC of the
16 court case and the broker-defendant must diligently defend in court his or
17 her actions concerning the transaction. Furthermore Florida Statute provides
18 for the Commission to pay the broker-defendant's reasonable attorney's fees
19 and court costs and, if the plaintiff prevails in court, the plaintiff's (person
20 who filed the lawsuit) reasonable attorney's fees and court costs. In cases
21 other than those regarding compliance with an EDO, court costs and
22 attorney's fees may *not* be awarded. In *all* cases, punitive damages, treble
23 (triple) damages, and interest may *not* be recovered from the fund.

24 A claim for possible recovery will not be accepted unless a civil suit
25 has been filed and a final judgment subsequently rendered against an
26 individual licensee as defendant, not merely against a real estate
27 brokerage, partnership, corporation, limited liability company, or limited
28 liability partnership. A claimant must cause a *writ of execution* to be issued
29 on the judgment, and the results (an asset search) must show that
30 insufficient funds or property are available to satisfy the judgment. The
31 claimant must also execute an affidavit showing that the final judgment is
32 not on appeal or, if it was the subject of an appeal, that the appellate
33 proceedings have concluded and show the outcome of the appeal.
34 Notice of the filing should be sent to the Commission or the Department
35 of Legal Affairs by certified mail. The filing of a bankruptcy petition by a
36 licensee does not relieve a claimant from the obligation to obtain a final
37 judgment against the licensee in order to recover from the fund. The FREC
38 may waive the requirement for a final judgment if a bankruptcy court
39 obstructs obtaining such a judgment.

40 To receive reimbursement from the recovery fund, a claimant must
41 meet all of the criteria and standards specified in 475.482 and 475.483, F.S.,
42 except in those cases for which the Commission is authorized to waive the
43 requirements for a final judgment. A claim must be made within two
44 years of either the alleged violation or discovery of the alleged violation.
45 However, in no case may a claim for recovery be made more than four
46 years after the date of the alleged violation. The State Treasurer makes all
47 payments from the fund following receipt of a voucher signed by the
48 DBPR Secretary.

Payments for claims arising out of the same transaction are limited, in total, to $50,000 or the unsatisfied portion of a judgment claim, whichever is less, regardless of the number of claimants or parcels of real estate involved in the transaction. Payments for claims based on judgments against one broker or sales associate may not exceed, in total, $150,000.

475.484, F.S.

Suspension of a licensee's license is mandatory on payment of any amount from the Real Estate Recovery Fund in settlement of a claim to satisfy a judgment against any licensee as described in 475.482(1), F.S. The license is automatically suspended on the date of payment from the recovery fund and will not be restored until the licensee has repaid the amount paid from the fund in full (plus interest).

475.484(7), F.S.

The suspension is in addition to any penalties imposed as a result of the disciplinary action associated with the judgment. Bankruptcy will not relieve a license from the penalties of Subsection 475.484, F.S., except to the extent that this subsection conflicts with Chapter 11 of the United States Code, in which case the Commission may order the license not to be suspended or otherwise discriminated against. Anyone who files a false document, makes a material misstatement of fact, or otherwise violates Subsections 475.482–486, F.S., is guilty of a misdemeanor of the second degree.

The following cannot make a claim for recovery from the fund:

475.483, F.S.

- The spouse of the judgment debtor or the spouse's personal representative.

- A licensee who acted as a single agent or transaction broker in a real estate transaction that is the subject of the claim.

- One who bases the claim on a real estate transaction in which a licensee was the owner and controlled the property under contract, and the licensee was dealing for licensee's own account. That is, the licensee was not acting as a broker or sales associate.

- One who bases the claim on a real estate transaction handled by a licensee who at the time did not hold a valid and current license.

- When the judgment is against a real estate brokerage entity only rather than against a licensed individual.

A total of $1 million is the authorized limit for the fund at any one time. Funds are accumulated by charging each active and inactive licensee a recovery fund fee when a new license is issued or an existing license is renewed. In addition, fines imposed by the FREC and collected by the DBPR are transferred into the fund under Section 475.482(4), F.S. The collection of these special fees stops when the limit is reached, and it begins again when the amount drops below $500,000. At that time, a fee of $3.50 per year for brokers and $1.50 per year for sales associates is added to the license fee for both new and renewed licenses.

■ LEGAL TERMS TO KNOW

As a final focus on license law and to assist you in learning important but often difficult-to-understand real estate terms in the legal realm, the following definitions and examples are provided to supplement those in the text, cases, and glossary:

- **Breach** (as in **breach of duty** or **breach of contract**). The breaking of a promise or obligation, either by an act of commission or omission; default; nonperformance.

- **Commingle (intermingle).** To mix the money or other personal property of a buyer or seller with a broker's own money or property; to combine escrow money with personal or business funds.

- **Concealment.** The withholding of information or a material fact. *Example:* In a fiduciary relationship, the broker has a duty to speak, unless the principal knows the information or fact.

- **Conversion.** Unauthorized control or use of another's personal property; the taking of another person's property (may be legal, as when a government unit condemns a property under eminent domain, or illegal, as when a broker misappropriates the funds of a client, employed sales associate, or cooperating broker).

- **Culpable negligence.** Guilty of failing to use the care a reasonable person would exercise. *Example:* Broker does not give ordinary, careful attention to his or her business and does not exercise reasonable control over his or her agents.

- **Failure to account for and deliver.** The act of failing to pay money to a person entitled to receive it. *Example:* Broker's failure to pay an earnest money deposit in accordance with the contract for sale and purchase.

- **Fraud.** Intentional deceit for the purpose of inducing another to rely on information to part with some valuable thing belonging to him or her or to surrender a legal right. *Example:* Seller or broker not disclosing known defects or remaining "silent" under such circumstances when the buyer could not have verified for himself or herself.

- **Material fact.** A piece of information that is relevant to a person making a decision and that affects the value of the real property. *Example:* Information about the condition of a property, such as known defects or code violations.

- **Misrepresentation.** An untrue statement of fact. An incorrect or false misrepresentation of the facts. *Example:* Failing to indicate in a newspaper that the property is advertised by a real estate licensee.

- **Moral turpitude.** Conduct contrary to honesty, good morals, justice, or accepted custom. Case law has further defined moral turpitude to mean a depravity against society. *Example:* Embezzlement and crimes of larceny, including writing bad checks, are generally considered moral turpitude.

■ SUMMARY

The DRE is assigned the responsibility for investigating information provided by license applicants and for investigating complaints filed against licensees. If a complaint appears to be legally sufficient, an investigative report is submitted to the FREC's probable-cause panel. If probable cause is found to exist, the panel asks the DBPR to file a formal complaint. An informal hearing or a formal hearing will follow. After a fact-finding hearing, the administrative law judge from the Division of Administrative Hearings submits his or her recommended order to the FREC, the DBPR, and all other parties to the complaint. The Commission (probable-cause members are excused) decides the case and the appropriate penalties. Anyone adversely affected by the final order may appeal through the courts.

Numerous grounds exist for denial, suspension, and revocation of licenses. Disciplinary guidelines spell out a range of penalties based on the severity of specific offenses. The Real Estate Recovery Fund provides a means for reimbursing an individual or organization suffering monetary damages as a result of illegal acts committed by licensees who are part of a real estate brokerage activity and that involve real estate located in Florida.

TABLE 6.1   Disciplinary Guildelines: 61J2-24.001, F.A.C.

	Statute	Violations and Usual Actions of the Commission (Current through June 2005)
(a)	475.22	Broker fails to maintain office and sign at entrance of office. *Usual action of the Commission:* Up to 90-day suspension
(b)	475.24	Failure to register a branch office. *Usual action of the Commission:* Up to 90-day suspension
(c)	475.25(1)(b)	Guilty of fraud, misrepresentation, concealment, false promises, false pretenses, dishonest dealing by trick, scheme or device, culpable negligence or breach of trust. Guilty of violating a duty imposed by law or by the terms of a listing agreement; aided, assisted or conspired with another, or formed an intent, design or scheme to engage in such misconduct and committed an overt act in furtherance of such intent, design or scheme. *Usual action of the Commission:* In the case of fraud, misrepresentation and dishonest dealing, a penalty of revocation. In the case of concealment, false promises and false pretenses, a penalty of a 3-to 5-year suspension and an administrative fine of $1,000. In the case of culpable negligence and breach of trust, a penalty from a $1,000 fine to a 1-year suspension. In the case of violating a duty imposed by law or a listing agreement; aided, assisted or conspired; or formed an intent, design or scheme to engage in such misconduct, a $1,000 fine to a 5-year suspension.
(d)	475.25(1)(c)	False, deceptive or misleading advertising. *Usual action of the Commission:* An administrative fine of $1,000 to a 1-year suspension
(e)	475.25(1)(d)	Failed to account for or deliver to any person as required by agreement or law, escrowed property. *Usual action of the Commission:* An administrative fine of $1,000 to a 5-year suspension
(f)	475.25(1)(e)	Violated any rule or order or provision under Chapters 475 and 455, F.S. *Usual action of the Commission:* From an 8-year suspension to revocation and an administrative fine of $1,000
(g)	475.25(1)(f)	Convicted or found guilty of a crime related to real estate or involves moral turpitude or fraudulent or dishonest dealing. *Usual action of the Commission:* From a 7-year suspension to revocation and an administrative fine of $1,000
(h)	475.25(1)(g)	Has license disciplined or acted against or an application denied by another jurisdiction. *Usual action of the Commission:* Imposition of discipline comparable to the discipline which would have been imposed if the substantive violation had occurred in Florida or suspension of the license until the license is unencumbered in the jurisdiction in which the disciplinary action was originally taken, and an administrative fine of $1,000
(i)	475.25(1)(h)	Has shared a commission with or paid a fee to a person not properly licensed under Chapter 475, F.S. *Usual action of the Commission:* An administrative fine of $1,000 to a 5-year suspension
(j)	475.25(1)(i)	Impairment by drunkenness, or use of drugs or temporary mental derangement. *Usual action of the Commission:* Suspension for period of incapacity
(k)	475.25(1)(j)	Rendered an opinion that the title to property sold is good or merchantable when not based on opinion of a licensed attorney or has failed to advise prospective buyer to consult an attorney on the merchantability of title or to obtain title insurance. *Usual action of the Commission:* An administrative fine of $1,000 to a 6-month suspension

TABLE 6.1   Disciplinary Guildelines: 61J2-24.001, F.A.C. (Continued)

	Statute	Violations and Usual Actions of the Commission (Current through June 2005)
(l)	475.25(1)(k)	Has failed, if a broker, to deposit any money in an escrow account immediately upon receipt until disbursement is properly authorized. Has failed, if a sales associate, to place any money to be escrowed with his registered employer. *Usual action of the Commission:* A minimum of a 90-day suspension and $1,000 fine up to revocation
(m)	475.25(1)(l)	Has made or filed a report or record which the licensee knows to be false or willfully failed to file a report or record or willfully impeded such filing as required by state or federal law *Usual action of the Commission:* An administrative fine of $1,000 to a 2-year suspension
(n)	475.25(1)(m)	Obtained a license by fraud, misrepresentation or concealment *Usual action of the Commission:* In the case of a licensee who renews the license without having complied with Rule 61J2-3.009 and the act is discovered by the DBPR, a penalty of revocation. In the case of a licensee who renews the license without having complied with Rule 61J2-3.009 and the licensee brings the matter to the attention of the DBPR, the usual action of the Commission shall be to impose a penalty of a $1,000 administrative fine. In all other cases, imposition of a penalty revocation and an administrative fine of $1,000.
(o)	475.25(1)(n)	Confined in jail, prison or mental institution; or through mental disease can no longer practice with skill and safety *Usual action of the Commission:* Revocation
(p)	475.25(1)(o)	Guilty for the second time of misconduct in the practice of real estate that demonstrates incompetent, dishonest or negligent dealings with investors *Usual action of the Commission:* An administrative fine of $500 and a 1-year suspension to revocation
(q)	475.25(1)(p)	Failed to give Commission 30-day written notice after a guilty or nolo contendere plea or convicted of any felony *Usual action of the Commission:* 5-year suspension to revocation
(r)	475.25(1)(q)	Licensee has failed to give the Transaction Broker Notice or Single Agent Notice at the requisite period of time under the provision of s. 475.278, F.S.; failed to properly secure the Consent to Transition to Transaction Broker or Designated Sales Associate forms as required in ss. 475.2755 or 475.278, F.S.; failed to act in a manner as prescribed in ss. 475.2755 or 475.278 *Usual action of the Commission:* An administrative fine of $1,000 to a 5-year suspension
(s)	475.25(1)(r)	Failed to follow the requirements of a written listing agreement *Usual action of the Commission:* An administrative fine of $1,000 to a 3-year suspension
(t)	475.25(1)(s)	Has had a registration suspended, revoked or otherwise acted against in any jurisdiction *Usual action of the Commission:* Impose a penalty from a 6-year suspension to revocation and an administrative fine of $1,000
(u)	475.25(1)(t)	Violated the Uniform Standards of Professional Appraisal Practice as defined in s. 475.611, F.S. *Usual action of the Commission:* Impose a penalty of a 5-year suspension to revocation
(z)	475.42(1)(d)	A sales associate shall not collect any money in connection with any real estate brokerage transaction except in the name of the employer *Usual action of the Commission:* An administrative fine of $1,000 to a 3-year suspension
(aa)	475.42(1)(e)	A violation of any order or rule of the Commission *Usual action of the Commission:* 8-year suspension to revocation and an administrative fine of $1,000

TABLE 6.1		Disciplinary Guildelines: 61J2-24.001, F.A.C. (Continued)

	Statute	**Violations and Usual Actions of the Commission (Current through June 2005)**
(bb)	475.42(1)(g)	Makes false affidavit or affirmation or false testimony before the Commission *Usual action of the Commission:* An administrative fine of $1,000 to a 3-year suspension
(cc)	475.42(1)(h)	Fails to comply with subpoena *Usual action of the Commission:* An administrative fine of $1,000 and a 6-month suspension to a 5-year suspension
(dd)	475.42(1)(i)	Obstructs or hinders the enforcement of Chapter 475, F.S. *Usual action of the Commission:* Revocation
(ee)	475.42(1)(j)	No broker or sales associate shall place upon the public records any false, void or unauthorized information that affects the title or encumbers any real property *Usual action of the Commission:* Up to 5-year suspension or revocation
(ff)	475.42(1)(k)	Failed to register trade name with the Commission *Usual action of the Commission:* An administrative fine of $1,000 to a 6-month suspension
(gg)	475.42(1)(l)	No person shall knowingly conceal information relating to violations of Chapter 475, F.S. *Usual action of the Commission:* An administrative fine of $1,000 to a 3-year suspension
(hh)	475.42(1)(m)	Fails to have a current license as a broker or sales associate while listing or selling one or more timeshare periods per year *Usual action of the Commission:* Revocation
(ii)	475.42(1)(n)	Licensee fails to disclose all material aspects of the resale of timeshare period or timeshare plan and the rights and obligations of both buyer and seller *Usual action of the Commission:* Revocation
(jj)	475.42(1)(o)	Publication of false or misleading information; promotion of sales, leases and rentals *Usual action of the Commission:* An administrative fine of $1,000 to a 1-year suspension
(kk)	475.451	School teaching real estate practice fails to obtain permit from the Department and does not abide by regulations of Chapter 475, F.S., and rules adopted by the Commission *Usual action of the Commission:* An administrative fine of $1,000 to a 6-month suspension
(ll)	475.452	A broker contracts for or collects an advance fee for the listing of real property and fails to properly deposit 75 percent in a trust account according to Chapter 475, F.S., and rules adopted by the Commission *Usual action of the Commission:* An administrative fine of $1,000 to a 3-year suspension
(mm)	475.453	Broker or sales associate participates in any rental information transaction that fails to follow the guidelines adopted by the Commission and Chapter 475, F.S. *Usual action of the Commission:* An administrative fine of $1,000 to a 3-year suspension

■ REVIEW QUESTIONS

1. The probable-cause panel includes
   A. a total of two members.
   B. at least one professional member.
   C. at least one current member.
   D. all of the above.

2. A person is eligible to seek recovery from the Real Estate Recovery Fund if
   A. he or she has received a final judgment against a licensee in any action wherein the cause of action was based on a real estate brokerage transaction, unless specifically precluded.
   B. he or she is a licensed broker who acted as the agent in the transaction that is the subject of the claim.
   C. his or her claim is based on a real estate transaction in which the broker did not hold a valid, current, and active license at the time of the transaction.
   D. any of the above events has occurred.

3. The decision as to whether probable cause exists is made by a majority vote of the
   A. Commission.
   B. Commission or the Department, as appropriate.
   C. administrative law judges.
   D. probable-cause panel (or the Department if there is no panel).

4. Which action would cause a license to be revoked without prejudice?
   A. A licensee accepted an earnest money deposit on a property that he knew was encumbered by an undisclosed lien.
   B. The broker obtained his license by means of fraud, misrepresentation, or concealment.
   C. A sales associate received her license as a result of an administrative error by the Division of Real Estate.
   D. For the referral of real estate business a licensee shared a commission with a person (not party to the transaction) who did not have a real estate license.

5. Which offense is a misdemeanor of the second degree?
   A. Failing to provide current and accurate rental information for a fee.
   B. Publishing false or misleading information to induce a buyer to purchase real property.
   C. Unlawfully collecting an advance fee for listing real property.
   D. All of the violations are misdemeanors of the second degree.

6. Who prepares and submits a recommended order of findings and conclusions in a complaint case?
   A. Court of law
   B. Administrative law judge
   C. Probable-cause panel
   D. The DBPR

7. Any final order issued by the DBPR Secretary or a legally appointed designee that results from circumstances that pose an immediate danger to the public's health, safety, or welfare is called a
   A. petition for review.
   B. stay of enforcement.
   C. summary or emergency suspension.
   D. license revocation.

8. Broker Jack of Farm Acres Realty listed a 15-acre farm. Jack accepted a $5,000 earnest money deposit from the buyer. However, the buyer was unable to secure financing and requested the funds be returned according to the terms of the contract. Jack was unable to reimburse the buyer because he used the money to pay his office rent and other overhead. Jack is guilty of
   A. dishonest dealing by trick, scheme, or devise.
   B. failure to account and deliver.
   C. fraud.
   D. culpable negligence.

9. The DBPR is authorized to investigate a written complaint filed against a licensee
   A. if the alleged complaint is legally sufficient.
   B. only if the claimant has been harmed by the actions of the licensee.
   C. only if the alleged violation was committed in the State of Florida.
   D. only if all of the above conditions have been met.

10. Neglecting to correct omissions or errors on a license application returned by the DBPR to the applicant for correction is considered grounds for
    A. suspension of an applicant's rights.
    B. denial of the application.
    C. revocation of the application.
    D. administrative revocation.

11. If a broker's license is suspended, the licenses of all sales associates working for that broker are
    A. placed in involuntarily inactive status.
    B. denied.
    C. suspended.
    D. revoked.

12. One of the grounds for the suspension or revocation of a licensee's license is the unauthorized use or retention of money or property, otherwise known as
    A. concealment.
    B. conversion.
    C. culpable negligence.
    D. commingling.

13. Less than careful attention to duties, one of the grounds for suspension or revocation of a licensee's license, is otherwise called
    A. concealment.
    B. conversion.
    C. culpable negligence.
    D. commingling.

14. When payment from the Real Estate Recovery Fund is made to satisfy a claim against a licensee because the licensee did not comply with an escrow disbursement order, the Commission's action against the licensee must be
    A. citation.
    B. probation.
    C. automatic suspension.
    D. emergency suspension.

15. Which type(s) of penalties may be imposed for violations of the real estate license law?
    A. Civil penalties only
    B. Administrative penalties only
    C. Civil and administrative penalties only
    D. Criminal, civil, and administrative penalties

16. The Florida Real Estate Commission may NOT impose which disciplinary penalty?
    A. Imprisonment
    B. Probation
    C. Administrative fine
    D. Denial of a license application

17. One penalty that the Commission may NOT legally levy is to
    A. deny the issuance of a license.
    B. deny the payment of compensation.
    C. suspend a license.
    D. revoke a license.

18. The collective amount to be paid from the Real Estate Recovery Fund as a result of any one real estate transaction may not exceed
    A. $25,000.
    B. $50,000.
    C. $75,000.
    D. $150,000.

CHAPTER 7

Federal and State Housing Laws

■ KEY TERMS

annual percentage
rate (APR)

blockbusting

Civil Rights Act of 1866

Fair Housing Act

good faith estimate

redlining

servicing disclosure statement

special information
booklet

steering

triggering terms

■ OVERVIEW

For many families the purchase of a home is the largest single investment they will make during their lifetimes. The federal government and all state governments have enacted laws to ensure that the public interest in real estate is adequately protected. This Chapter highlights some of the laws most important to Florida real estate practitioners. Licensees should study these laws to make certain they comply with the laws to better serve the public.

After completing this Chapter, the student should be able to:

- describe the features of the Civil Rights Acts of 1866 and 1968;

- recognize examples of steering, redlining, and blockbusting;

- describe the features of the Truth-in-Lending Act, the Equal Credit Opportunity Act, and the Real Estate Settlement Procedures Act; and

- describe the provisions of the Florida Residential Landlord and Tenant Act.

■ FEDERAL FAIR HOUSING LAW

CIVIL RIGHTS ACT OF 1866 *Based on slaves rights*

The **Civil Rights Act of 1866** prohibits any type of discrimination based on *race* in *any* real estate transaction (sale or rental) *without exception*. This law is still in force today. A suit can be filed in a federal court under the

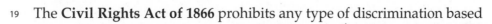

1866 Civil Rights Act. The court may award actual (monetary) damages and punitive damages for racial discrimination.

The Civil Rights Act of 1866 states that:

All citizens of the United States shall have the same right, in every
State and Territory, as is enjoyed by white citizens thereof to inherit,
purchase, lease, sell, hold, and convey real and personal property.

To learn more regarding the Civil Rights Act of 1866, go to the AFRO-American Almanac at: **http://www.toptags.com/aama/index.htm.** Click on "Historical Documents" and then choose "The Civil Rights Act of 1866."

FAIR HOUSING ACT

The **Fair Housing Act** is contained in Title VIII of the Civil Rights Act of 1968. The Fair Housing Act (as amended in 1988) created *protected classes* of people and prohibits discrimination when selling or renting residential property when based on the following:

- Race

- Color

- Religion

- Sex

- Handicap status (mental or physical)

- Familial status (families with children younger than 18 and pregnant women—certain exceptions apply for housing for older persons)

- National origin

To help recall the seven protected classes, think of how to spell "fresh corn" but without the vowels (FRSH CRN).

The Fair Housing Act covers two categories of housing:

1. Single-family houses

   - Residential property that is *not* privately owned (for example, dwellings owned or operated by the federal government)

   - Privately owned residential property if a real estate licensee is employed to sell or rent the property

   - Residential property owned by a person who owns four or more residential units in total

   - Residential property when the owner, during the immediate past two-year period, sells two or more houses in which the owner was not a resident

2. Multifamily housing

   - Multifamily dwellings of five or more units

- Multifamily dwellings of four or fewer units if the owner does not reside in any of the units

Special exemptions under the act. Housing operated by religious organizations and private clubs is exempt from the Fair Housing Act provided the housing is *not* operated for commercial purposes:

1. Religious organizations may restrict dwelling units they own or operate to members of their religion if the organization does not otherwise discriminate in accepting its membership.

2. Private clubs may restrict rental or occupancy of its units to its members.

Activities prohibited. Discrimination against any of the protected classes in the sale or rental of housing, financing of housing, or the provision of brokerage services is illegal. It is a violation of the Fair Housing Act to do any of the following activities:

Test

- Channel protected-class homeseekers away from areas that are not mixed with that class into areas that are (commonly known as **steering**) *RACE.*

- Use the entry, or rumor of the entry, of a protected class into a neighborhood to persuade owners to sell (commonly known as **blockbusting**) *SCARING PEOPLE.*

- Deny loans or insurance coverage by a lender or insurer that present different terms or conditions for homes in certain neighborhoods (commonly known as **redlining**) – *NO DENIAL DUE TO AREA.*

- Refuse to rent to, sell to, negotiate with, or deal with a member of a protected class

- Quote different terms or conditions for buying or renting

- Advertise that housing is available only to people of a certain race, color, religion, sex, national origin, handicap status, or familial status

- Deny membership in or use of any real estate service, broker's organization, or multiple-listing service

- Make false statements concerning the availability of housing for inspection, rent, or sale

Fair housing poster. The Fair Housing Act requires the use of an equal opportunity poster. The poster features the equal housing logo and a statement pledging adherence to the Fair Housing Act. The poster (Figure 7.1) is available from the Department of Housing and Urban Development (HUD). The poster must be displayed at real estate offices and other businesses involved in the housing industry. Failure to display the poster may be considered evidence of discrimination in the event a discrimination complaint is made against the broker.

EQUAL HOUSING OPPORTUNITY

Jones v. Mayer. Joseph Lee Jones filed a complaint in 1965 in District court alleging that Alfred H. Mayer Company had refused to sell him a home because he was black. The famous legal case known as *Jones v. Alfred*

FIGURE 7.1 Equal Housing Opportunity Poster

U.S. Department of Housing and Urban Development

Must Have

EQUAL HOUSING
OPPORTUNITY

We Do Business in Accordance With the Federal Fair Housing Law

(The Fair Housing Amendments Act of 1988)

It is Illegal to Discriminate Against Any Person Because of Race, Color, Religion, Sex, Handicap, Familial Status, or National Origin

- In the sale or rental of housing or residential lots
- In advertising the sale or rental of housing
- In the financing of housing

- In the provision of real estate brokerage services
- In the appraisal of housing
- Blockbusting is also illegal

Anyone who feels he or she has been discriminated against may file a complaint of housing discrimination:
   1-800-669-9777 (Toll Free)
   1-800-927-9275 (TDD)

**U.S. Department of Housing and Urban Development
Assistant Secretary for Fair Housing and Equal Opportunity
Washington, D.C. 20410**

Previous editions are obsolete

form HUD-928.1A (2/2003)

1 *H. Mayer Company* reached the Supreme Court in 1968. The court upheld the Civil Rights
2 Act of 1866. This decision was important because the Fair Housing Act covers only the sale
3 or rental of single-family and multifamily housing and provides certain exemptions to
4 private homeowners. The Civil Rights Act of 1866 prohibits *all racial discrimination without*
5 *exception.* The Supreme Court declared that the 1866 Act still applies, and that it prohibits
6 all racial discrimination (public and private) in the sale of all real property (residential and
7 commercial). Remember, when race is involved, *no exemptions apply.*

www**@**web.link

*Title VIII of the Civil Rights Act of 1968 (Fair Housing Act) is published
in the United States Code and is available on the Internet at:*
http://www4.law.cornell.edu/uscode/42/ch45.html.

Regulation. Complaints of housing discrimination under the Fair Housing Act are filed with HUD. If a discriminatory housing practice has occurred, HUD issues the parties to the complaint a *Charge of Discrimination*. A hearing is then scheduled before a HUD administrative law judge. The parties may elect instead to have the matter heard in Federal court. An injunction (court order to stop the discriminatory practice), actual (monetary) damages, and punitive damages may be awarded for discriminatory practices. Furthermore, the Florida Real Estate Commission may initiate an administrative proceeding against a licensee found guilty of a discriminatory act.

 To learn more about the Fair Housing Act, download the booklet, Fair Housing-Equal Opportunity for All *at:* **http://www.hud.gov/offices/fheo/FHLaws/FairHousingJan2002.pdf.**

AMERICANS WITH DISABILITIES ACT OF 1990

The Americans with Disabilities Act (ADA) of 1990 is a federal statute designed to remove barriers that prevent qualified individuals with disabilities from enjoying the same employment opportunities that are available to persons without disabilities. This act also addresses disabled individuals' accessibility to public accommodations, commercial facilities, and multifamily dwelling units. The ADA requires that multifamily dwellings be designed and constructed so that the public and common-use portions of the dwelling are readily accessible to and usable by all persons with disabilities. Further, the ADA mandates certain design specifications (width of doorways, height of light switches, grab bars in bathrooms, etc.) for dwelling units in multifamily housing built after the enactment of the law.

 To learn about the ADA, visit the ADA home page at the U.S. Department of Justice's Web site. The address is: **http://www.usdoj.gov/crt/ada/adahom1.htm.**

■ FEDERAL LAWS REGARDING LAND AND THE ENVIRONMENT

INTERSTATE LAND SALES FULL DISCLOSURE ACT

The Interstate Land Sales Full Disclosure Act, passed in 1968, is designed to protect consumers from misrepresentation by unscrupulous land developers. This law applies to subdivisions with lots for sale as part of a common promotional plan in interstate commerce. Developers are not permitted to sell or lease lots in subdivisions of 100 or more lots unless they have filed a Statement of Record and registered the subdivision with HUD. Information concerning the land, its physical characteristics, the condition of title, and identification of owners must be provided. In addition, each purchaser must be furnished a Property Report containing items from the Statement of Record before signing a purchase contract or lease.

OTHER LAWS REGARDING LAND AND THE ENVIRONMENT

The Coastal Zone Management Act and Environmental Control Act are two federal laws designed to protect coastal land and the environment. The Coastal Zone Management Act requires that coastal states develop and implement a management plan to protect their coastal areas. Florida's management plan places significant restrictions on oceanfront development.

■ FEDERAL LAWS REGARDING MORTGAGE LENDING

CONSUMER CREDIT PROTECTION ACT (TITLE I: TRUTH-IN-LENDING ACT)

Truth-in-lending regulations were passed via several acts in 1968 and went into effect in 1969. The overall purpose of these laws is to inform consumers of exact credit costs before they make a purchase so they may compare various credit terms and costs. The laws placed advertising of credit associated with a real estate purchase under the supervision and enforcement of the Federal Trade Commission (FTC). One immediate result was to make "bait and switch" advertising a federal offense. For example, if a subdivision developer advertises homes for sale with a down payment of $1,000, the seller must accept $1,000 as the complete down payment or be in violation of the law.

The Truth-in-Lending (TIL) Act is implemented by Federal Reserve Regulation Z. Regulation Z applies to credit associated with residential mortgage loans. The law requires that lenders disclose the annual percentage rate of interest and finance charges imposed on consumers. The **annual percentage rate (APR)** includes the interest rate and other loan costs and represents the true yearly cost of credit. Any other charges listed by some other name also must be included if such charges are a cost of obtaining the loan. It is not uncommon to see an ad that states *mortgage interest rates at 10 percent* followed by a parenthetical statement such as *(annual percentage rate 10.5 percent)* or *(APR 10.5%)*.

If creditors include in advertisements certain credit terms or specific financing information, referred to as **triggering terms,** additional information must also be included. Trigger terms include the:

- amount or percentage of any down payment;

- number of payments;

- period (term) of repayment;

- amount of any payment; and

- amount of any finance charge.

Advertisements containing any of the triggering terms must also disclose the following:

- Amount or percentage of down payment

- Terms of repayment

1   • Annual percentage rate, using that term, and if the rate may be
2   increased in the future, that fact must also be disclosed

3   The Truth-in-Lending Act allows general expressions such as
4   "owner will finance." Such expressions are too general to trigger
5   additional disclosure requirements. The law does *not* attempt to regulate
6   interest rates.

EQUAL CREDIT OPPORTUNITY ACT (ECOA)

8   The Equal Credit Opportunity Act (ECOA) of 1974 ensures that financial
9   institutions and firms engaged in extending credit will make credit
10 available with fairness and without discrimination on the basis of race,
11 color, religion, national origin, sex, marital status, age, or receipt of income
12 from public assistance programs.

REAL ESTATE SETTLEMENT PROCEDURES ACT (RESPA)

14 RESPA is a consumer protection law intended to ensure that buyers are
15 informed regarding the amount and type of charges they will pay at
16 closing. RESPA also attempts to eliminate kickbacks and referral fees that
17 increase closing costs. RESPA applies to federally-related residential
18 loans. RESPA covers loans secured with a mortgage on a one-family to
19 four-family residential property. These include most purchase loans,
20 assumptions, refinances, property improvement loans, and equity lines of
21 credit. (See also exempt transactions on page 132.)

(handwritten margin note: RESPA = STANDARDIZED REALESTATE closings)

(handwritten margin note: Test)

22 **RESPA disclosures at time of loan application or within three business**
23 **days.**   When borrowers apply for a mortgage loan, they must be given
24 the following disclosures:

25 • **Special Information Booklet,** which contains consumer
26   information regarding closing services (required for purchase
27   transactions only) the borrower may be charged for at closing

28 • **Good Faith Estimate (GFE)** of closing (settlement) costs, listing the
29   charges the buyer is likely to pay at closing

30 • **Servicing Disclosure Statement** which discloses to the borrower
31   whether the lender intends to service the loan or transfer it to
32   another lender or servicing company

33   If the borrower did not receive the disclosures at the time of loan
34 application, the lender must mail them within three business days of
35 receiving the loan application.

wwweb.link

You can download a copy of the Special Information Booklet at:
http://www.hud.gov/offices/hsg/sfh/res/stcosts.pdf.

36 **Affiliated business relationships.**   Sometimes, several businesses that
37 offer settlement (closing) services are owned or controlled by a common
38 corporate parent. These businesses are known as *affiliates.* When a lender,
39 real estate broker, or other closing participant refers a borrower to an
40 affiliate for a settlement service (for example, when a real estate broker
41 refers a buyer to a mortgage broker affiliate), RESPA requires the referring

party to give the borrower an Affiliated Business Arrangement Disclosure. This form explains to borrowers that they are not required, with certain exceptions, to use the affiliate and are free to shop for other providers. Except in cases where a lender refers a borrower to an attorney, credit reporting agency, or real estate appraiser to represent the lender's interest in the transaction, the referring party may not require the consumer to use the affiliated business.

Purchase of title insurance. RESPA prohibits a seller from requiring the home buyer to use a particular title insurance company as a condition of sale. Generally, the lender will require title insurance. The borrower can shop for and choose a company. However, if the seller is paying for the owner's title insurance policy, the law does not prohibit the seller from choosing the title company.

HUD-1 settlement statement. The closing agent must provide borrowers with the HUD-1 Settlement Statement at closing. The HUD-1 statement shows all of the charges imposed on the borrower and the seller and any credits due the borrower and the seller. It itemizes the actual closing costs of the loan transaction. Borrowers may request a copy of the HUD-1 statement one day before the actual settlement.

Kickbacks, fee-splitting, and unearned fees. It is illegal under RESPA for anyone to pay or receive a fee, kickback, or anything of value because they agree to refer settlement service business to a particular person or organization. For example, a mortgage lender may not pay a real estate broker a fee for referring a buyer to the lender. In Florida, sales associates must hold mortgage broker's licenses to legally be paid a fee for referring prospective borrowers to affiliated mortgage lenders. It is also illegal for anyone to accept a fee or part of a fee for services if that person has not actually performed settlement services for the fee. For example, a lender may not add to a third party's fee, such as an appraisal fee, and keep the difference. RESPA does not prevent title companies, mortgage brokers, appraisers, attorneys, closing agents, and others, who actually perform a service in connection with the mortgage loan or the closing, from being paid for the reasonable value of their work.

It is a crime for someone to pay or receive an illegal referral fee. The penalty can be a fine, imprisonment, or both. The borrower may also be entitled to recover three times the amount of the charge (triple damages) for any settlement service by bringing a private lawsuit.

Exempt transactions. Transactions *exempt* from RESPA include:

- loans to finance the purchase of 25 acres or more;

- loans for home improvement or to refinance or any other type of loan if its purpose is not to purchase or transfer title;

- loans to finance the purchase of a vacant lot if none of the loan proceeds will be used to place a residential structure or mobile home on the lot;

- sale or transfer of property involving only an assumption of an existing loan or sale subject to an existing loan;

- construction loans, except those intended for conversion into permanent loans;

- permanent loans to finance construction of a one-family to four-family structure when the lot is owned by the borrower; and

- loans to finance the purchase of property when the primary purpose is resale of the property.

 To learn more about RESPA, visit the RESPA home page at: **http://www.hud.gov/offices/hsg/sfh/res/respa_hm.cfm.**

■ STATE LAW REGARDING MORTGAGE LENDING

FLORIDA FAIR LENDING ACT

This law prohibits certain practices related to high-cost home loans. A *high-cost home loan* means a loan for a consumer credit transaction that is secured by the consumer's principal dwelling and features high points and or fees. What constitutes "high" is defined in the federal law. The Florida Fair Lending Act was created to prevent abusive practices regarding such loans. Abusive practices include, for example, making consumer loans based on equity in the home rather than based on the borrower's ability to pay the loan payments; and loans that finance the points and fees so that the lender receives immediate income, thereby encouraging lenders to repeatedly refinance the same property. Two of the most significant features of the Florida Fair Lending Act are:

- Prepayment penalty. A lender may include a prepayment penalty for up to the first 36 months from the creation of the loan, but only if the borrower has also been offered a choice of another product without a prepayment penalty, and the borrower has been given a written disclosure of the terms of the prepayment fee.

- No refinancing. No lender or its affiliate may refinance a loan to the same borrower within the first 18 months when doing so does not reasonably benefit the borrower.

494.0078, F.S.

■ STATE HOUSING AND LAND SALES LAWS

FLORIDA FAIR HOUSING ACT

The objective of Florida's Fair Housing Act is to provide for fair housing throughout the state. The Florida act is similar in scope to the federal Fair Housing Act. However, whenever the federal Fair Housing Act is in conflict with or broader in scope than the Florida act, the federal act prevails.

FLORIDA UNIFORM LAND SALES PRACTICES ACT

This act, Chapter 498, F.S., created the Division of Land Sales, Condominiums, and Mobile Homes, now part of the Department of Business and Professional Regulation, to investigate and regulate the sale of subdivided lands. The act identifies the elements that must be included in an application for registration of subdivided lands for sale to individuals. The term *subdivided lands* pertains to land divided into 50 or more lots, parcels, units, or interests. The contents of the public offering statement are specified and are similar to those in the statement required by the federal Interstate Land Sales Full Disclosure Act. The purpose of Florida's law is to provide prospective buyers full and fair disclosure of information concerning the property in question. The purchaser has the right to cancel the agreement within seven business days after signing it. Subdivisions with lots for sale only to builders are exempt from this requirement.

GROWTH MANAGEMENT ACT

Florida's Growth Management Act of 1985 (see also Chapter 20) requires that cities and counties prepare a comprehensive plan of land use. The act also contains a concurrency provision that requires that the infrastructure be in place before new development can begin.

■ STATE LAWS REQUIRING REAL ESTATE DISCLOSURES

DECEPTIVE AND UNFAIR TRADE PRACTICES ACT (FLORIDA'S "LITTLE FTC ACT")

Chapter 501, Part II, F.S., is titled the Deceptive and Unfair Trade Practices Act (Florida's "Little FTC Act"). This law declares that unfair methods of competition, unconscionable acts or practices, and unfair or deceptive acts or practices in the conduct of any trade or commerce are unlawful. When Chapter 501 and Chapter 475 are in conflict, real estate licensees selling real property in Florida must abide by the Florida real estate law.

RESPA and HUD require that licensees disclose in writing to buyers before the buyer signs the purchase agreement that, on closing the sale, additional costs may be required of the buyer. Brokerage firms in Florida provide prospective purchasers of real property with a list of closing items that may be costs to the buyer. However, firms do not have to list brokerage commissions, advance hazard insurance costs, or escrow items such as taxes and insurance.

FLORIDA RESIDENTIAL LANDLORD AND TENANT ACT

The intent of the Residential Landlord and Tenant Act is to place Florida landlords of residential properties and their tenants on a more equitable basis in their legal relationship. The law applies only to the rental of dwelling units (residential tenancies). It does not apply to commercial leases; medical facilities; transient accommodations (motels and hotels);

or cooperative apartments, condominiums, or mobile home parks when used as transient accommodations.

For purposes of this law the following definitions apply:

- A *dwelling unit* is a structure that is rented for use as a home, residence, or sleeping place by one person or by two or more persons who maintain a common household.

- A *landlord* is the owner or lessor of a dwelling unit.

- A *tenant* is any person entitled to occupy a dwelling unit under a rental agreement.

Under present Florida law, an 18-year-old is vested with the rights of majority and is thus entitled to enter into a rental agreement.

Section 83.45, F.S., contains a prohibition of "unconscionable rental agreement or provision" aimed at correcting instances where "fine print" binds a tenant or a landlord to unreasonable or unjust conditions. A court may refuse to enforce the unconscionable provision, the remainder of the rental agreement, or the entire rental agreement.

Deposits and advance rents.   A security deposit is typically paid to guarantee that the property will be left in good condition. Rent in advance is also often paid (typically the last month's rent). When money is given to a landlord as a security deposit or advance rent, the landlord is obligated to account for such deposits in one of three ways:

1. Hold the money in a separate noninterest-bearing Florida bank and not commingle, hypothecate, that is, pledge as security for a debt, or use any such funds until due to the tenant.

2. Hold the money in a separate interest-bearing Florida bank and pay the tenant at least 75 percent of any annualized average interest rate or 5 percent per year simple interest, and not commingle, hypothecate, or use any such funds until due to the tenant.

3. Post a surety bond with the clerk of the circuit court in the county in which the rental property is located in the total amount of the security deposits and advance rents or $50,000, whichever is less, and pay the tenant 5 percent per year simple interest. If the landlord chooses this method, the landlord is not obligated to place the funds (deposits) into a special account.

The Florida Residential Landlord and Tenant Act requires that the landlord inform tenants in writing, within 30 days from the receipt of advance rent or security deposit, of the manner in which the tenant's funds are being held. In the notice to the tenant, the landlord also must show the bank name and address, the amount deposited, the rate of interest (if any), and the date interest payments will be made to the tenant. The landlord is required to pay or credit the interest at least once each year. If the landlord is acting in the role of a licensed real estate agent, or if the landlord has hired a broker to act as agent, the real estate licensee must abide by the escrow requirements specified in Chapter 475. (See also Chapter 5.)

Landlord's obligation to maintain premises. A landlord's obligations to tenants include the following:

- Maintain the rented dwelling unit in a condition that meets all building, housing, and health codes in the community. (If no codes have been established for the area, the law requires that the premises be maintained in "good repair and capable of resisting normal forces and loads.")

- Provide exterminating service for insect and rodent control.

- Provide garbage receptacles and pickup.

- Provide working equipment for heat plus running hot water.

The landlord is allowed to charge tenants for services, provided the charges are included in the rental agreement. If the dwelling unit is either a single-family home or a duplex, the obligation of a landlord to provide insect extermination and garbage pickup may be altered or set aside by a written agreement between the tenant and the landlord.

Landlords may not be held responsible for conditions caused or created by negligent or wrongful acts of tenants or their guests. A landlord is not required to maintain a mobile home when a tenant is renting the landlord's lot.

Tenant's obligations. A tenant's obligations include the following:

- Maintain the rented premises by complying with existing building, housing, and health codes.

- Maintain the interior plumbing fixtures in a clean and sanitary condition.

- Use reasonable care in the operation of all plumbing, electrical, heating, and air-conditioning equipment.

- Conduct self and make sure guests behave so as not to disturb the peace of other tenants.

Landlord's access to premises. A tenant may not unreasonably withhold consent for a landlord to enter rented premises from time to time to:

- inspect the premises;

- make necessary or agreed-on repairs, decorations, alterations, or improvements;

- supply agreed-on services; and

- exhibit or show the premises.

In case of emergency or when necessary to protect or preserve the premises, a landlord is entitled to enter a dwelling unit at any time. However, the law prohibits a landlord from abusing this right of access to harass a tenant. Except in emergencies, landlords are obligated to enter rented premises at times reasonable and convenient for the tenant.

1   If a tenant is to be absent from the rented dwelling for a period of time
2 up to one-half the time for normal periodic rent payments, special
3 conditions apply to landlord access. If the rent is current and the tenant
4 notifies the landlord of an intended absence, the landlord may not enter
5 the premises during the period of absence except with the tenant's consent
6 or in an emergency for protection or preservation of the dwelling unit.

7 **Vacating premises.**   When a tenant vacates a rental unit at the end of a
8 lease agreement, the landlord must abide by certain time restrictions as
9 follows:

10   • The landlord has *15 days* to return the security deposit and any
11   accrued interest, if applicable, provided the landlord does *not*
12   intend to make a claim on the security deposit.

13   • The landlord has *30 days* to notify the tenant if the landlord intends
14   to impose a claim on the deposit.

15   The notification must be in writing and be sent by certified mail to the
16 tenant's last-known mailing address. The notice must include the reason
17 for the claim and contain a statement similar to the example in the box
18 below. Failure to give the required notice to the tenant within the 30-day
19 period forfeits the right to claim part of the deposit. The deposit must then
20 be returned to the tenant with any accrued interest.

Notice to Impose a Claim

This is a notice of my intention to impose a claim for damages in the amount of *(insert amount)* upon your security deposit, due to *(insert reason for claim)*. It is sent to you as required by s. 83.49(3), F.S. You are hereby notified that you must object in writing to this deduction from your security deposit within 15 days from the time you receive this notice or I will be authorized to deduct my claim from your deposit. Your objection must be sent to *(insert landlord's address)*.

Reference: Section 83.49(3)(a), F.S.

---

21   If a tenant is properly notified of the landlord's claim on the security
22 deposit, the tenant is allowed 15 days after receipt of the landlord's notice
23 to file an objection. The date established by delivery of the landlord's
24 notice begins the tenant's 15-day period. If a dispute must be settled in
25 court, the law states that the prevailing party in the litigation is entitled to
26 receive reimbursement for court costs plus reasonable attorney's fees
27 from the other party.

28   The Florida Landlord and Tenant Act relieves brokers of the duty to
29 notify the FREC of disputes regarding security deposits and advance rent.
30 Section 83.49, F.S., provides that brokers holding security deposits and
31 advance rent may *disburse* the funds from the rental escrow account
32 without complying with the Commission's escrow dispute and
33 notification procedures, provided the broker has fully complied with the
34 Florida Landlord and Tenant Act. (See Chapter 5.)

35 **Termination of rental agreements by the tenant.**   If a landlord fails
36 to maintain rented premises or fails to comply with the terms and

conditions of the rental agreement, a tenant may terminate the agreement by following this procedure:

1. The tenant first must give written notice to the landlord citing the noncompliance and stating the intent to cancel the agreement if the noncompliance is not corrected.

2. Thereafter, the landlord has seven days to correct the noncompliance and resolve the problem.

3. If the noncompliance is not corrected within seven days after delivery of the tenant's complaint to the landlord, the tenant is entitled to terminate the agreement.

In those cases in which a tenant does not desire to terminate his or her rental agreement but does want to correct a landlord's noncompliance, the law provides alternative courses of procedure:

- If the dwelling unit is habitable despite the landlord's failure to comply, the tenant may remain in occupancy of the premises, and the law states that the rent may be reduced by a court in proportion to the loss in rental value caused by the failure to comply.

- If the dwelling unit is rendered untenable (uninhabitable) owing to the landlord's failure, the tenant may not be liable for the rent during the period the premises remain untenable, if the court agrees with the tenant's assertions. This is a departure from the requirements of a nonresidential lease under which the landlord has no obligation to repair damaged premises unless the obligation is specifically contained in the lease agreement.

Termination of rental agreements by the landlord. If a tenant fails to comply with a lease or rental agreement, the landlord may terminate the agreement by following the three-step procedure previously mentioned. The same period of seven days is allowed for compliance by the tenant. However, if the tenant's noncompliance is *failure* to pay rent when due, the following procedure is required for a landlord to terminate the agreement:

1. The landlord must give the tenant written notice demanding either payment of rent within three days or possession of the premises. The written notice can be mailed, personally delivered, or if the tenant is absent from his or her place of residence, attached to the door of the dwelling. It is always advisable to be accompanied by another person to witness delivery of the notice. The three-day time limit begins from the time the notice is posted by mail or delivered at the residence, not including weekends or holidays.

2. The tenant has three days to either pay the rent or surrender the premises. If the tenant continues the default in payment of rent after the allotted days have lapsed, the landlord must resort to formal eviction to have the tenant removed.

3. If the tenant vacates the rented premises, the landlord then is required to give the tenant written notice by certified mail of any claim on the tenant's security deposit or advance rent held by the landlord, as described previously.

Eviction requirements. From time to time, a landlord has to evict tenants from rented dwelling units. In any eviction process the landlord must adhere to the following procedure:

1. The tenant must be notified in writing that the landlord is demanding possession of the premises. The notice may be mailed to or served on the tenant or posted on the door of the tenant's residence. The landlord keeps a copy of the notice and indicates the date mailed or delivered.

2. If the tenant does not surrender the premises to the landlord within three days after notification for nonpayment of rent (seven days for all other breaches of the rental agreement), the landlord must file a *complaint for eviction* in the court of the county where the dwelling is located. This complaint identifies the premises and cites the reasons that justify recovery of the property. The sheriff's department usually delivers the complaint to the tenant.

3. The tenant is allowed five days to file a reply defending himself or herself against the complaint. If the tenant decides to defend continued possession, the courts must decide the case.

4. If the tenant merely continues to occupy the premises without answering the landlord's complaint, the landlord must obtain a final judgment from the court. A landlord is entitled to have the motion for final judgment advanced on the court's calendar if the court approves the request.

5. After entry of judgment in favor of the landlord, the clerk of the court issues a writ to the sheriff to put the landlord in possession after a 24-hour notice has been posted on the premises.

6. At the time the sheriff executes (signs) the writ of possession or at any time thereafter, the landlord or the landlord's agent may remove any personal property found on the premises. Subsequent to executing the writ of possession, the landlord may request that the sheriff stand by to keep the peace while the landlord changes the locks and removes the personal property from the premises.

When a tenant refuses to vacate and defends for continued possession, it sometimes takes one month to two months to complete the entire eviction procedure. In the meantime, any unpaid rent creates a lien in favor of the landlord. That lien applies to all property of the tenant except beds, bedclothes, and wearing apparel, either on or off the rented premises. This general lien dates from the date a judgment is issued by a court in favor of the landlord. Any right or duty stated in Florida's Landlord Tenant Law is enforceable by civil action. This means that all legal remedies sought by either tenant or landlord under this statute are pursued through the civil courts.

You can learn more about Florida's Residential Landlord Tenant Act. The Florida Statutes are available on the Internet at: **http://www.leg.state.fl.us/welcome/index.cfm.** *Click on "Statutes" and then go to "Chapter 83."*

Summary of Eviction Process

The landlord serves the tenant a written notice allowing three days (excluding weekends and legal holidays) for the tenant to pay the rent or to vacate the premises.

If the tenant does not pay the rent or move, the landlord may begin legal action to evict by filing a *complaint for eviction* in county court.

If the court agrees with the landlord, the tenant is notified in writing. The tenant has five days (excluding weekends and legal holidays) to respond in writing to the court.

If the tenant does not respond or if a judgment is entered against the tenant, the clerk of the county court issues a *writ of possession* to the sheriff.

The sheriff notifies the tenant that eviction will take place after a 24-hour notice has been posted.

The Division of Consumer Services has published a consumer brochure concerning Florida's Landlord Tenant Law. You can download the brochure at: **http://www.800helpfla.com/landlord_text.html.**

The Florida Association of Residential Property Manager's Web site address is: **http://www.farpm.org/.** *Click on "Legislative Updates" to find recent changes to the Florida Landlord Tenant Law.*

■ SUMMARY

Federal and state laws affecting real property and housing represent the foundation on which real estate activity is built. One of the earliest and most important of these legal bases is the Civil Rights Act of 1866, which guarantees the rights of all citizens "to inherit, purchase, lease, sell, hold, and convey real and personal property." Subsequent federal and state laws have ensured further protection of the public.

This Chapter has addressed only a few of the most important laws with which persons new to real estate in Florida need to be familiar. The brief overview of various laws in this Chapter is intended for educational purposes only. It does not qualify a reader to render legal advice without seeking counsel from an attorney.

Note Regarding Test Anxiety

If you are concerned or even panicky about taking the end-of-chapter practice quizzes and the practice exam, as well as the state licensing examination, obtain in advance a personal copy of the author's *Florida Real Estate Exam Manual*. It contains, among other valuable sections, a section entitled "Successful Exam-Taking Strategies" and two sample exams, both designed and proven to improve your test-taking ability and scores.

■ REVIEW QUESTIONS

1. The federal statute that prohibits a private homeowner from discriminating strictly on the basis of race if selling, renting, or leasing is the
   A. 1968 Fair Housing Act.
   B. 1866 Civil Rights Act.
   C. 1934 National Housing Act.
   D. 1968 Interstate Land Sales Full Disclosure Act.

2. The law that requires that lenders disclose the annual percentage rate (APR) of interest is the
   A. Real Estate Settlement Procedures Act (RESPA).
   B. Federal Housing Act (FHA).
   C. Florida Deceptive and Unfair Trade Practices Act (Little FTC Act).
   D. Consumer Credit Protection Act (Truth-in-Lending).

3. The federal 1968 Fair Housing Act prohibits discrimination based on
   A. race, color, religion, sex, national origin, familial status, or handicap status.
   B. race or age.
   C. religion, age, race, familial status, or handicap status.
   D. race, color, religion, age, or national origin.

4. The Truth-in-Lending Act
   A. does not affect real estate financing credit.
   B. attempts to regulate maximum interest rates charged consumers.
   C. requires disclosure of finance charges as well as annual percentage rates of interest.
   D. accomplishes all of the above.

5. The Real Estate Settlement Procedures Act (RESPA) was enacted to
   A. establish a maximum cost for all closing items.
   B. ensure that sellers are informed regarding the amount and types of expenses expected at closing.
   C. ensure that buyers are informed regarding the amount and types of expenses to be expected at closing.
   D. establish a minimum cost for all closing items.

6. If requested by the borrower, and to the extent that information is available to the closing agent, the borrower must be provided with which item at least one day before closing?
   A. Uniform Settlement Statement
   B. Borrower's Special Information Booklet
   C. Guaranteed amount of settlement costs
   D. Notice of title-closing-agent selection

7. As part of the preparation for a closing, a listing broker referred a property owner to an appraiser. The appraiser completed the appraisal and charged the owner $250, which was entered on the RESPA settlement statement. The appraiser gave the listing broker $50 for the referral, which the broker accepted. According to RESPA
   A. the listing broker also must be licensed as an appraiser.
   B. the appraiser has not violated the law as long as he or she is state certified.
   C. both the broker and the appraiser have violated the law.
   D. the arrangement is entirely legal.

8. Which transaction is exempt from RESPA requirements?
   A. The sale of a house where the only financing is assumption of an existing loan
   B. A construction loan that will become a permanent loan only after the building is completed
   C. A loan to purchase a new house in a new subdivision
   D. An adjustable rate mortgage loan to purchase a five-year-old residence

9. The intent of the Florida Landlord and Tenant Act is to
   A. give the tenant a legal advantage in his or her relationship with the landlord.
   B. make the landlord-tenant relationship more equitable.
   C. provide landlords the legal assistance needed to create an advantageous relationship.
   D. regulate residential and commercial rental property.

10. When security deposits or advance rents are required by a landlord in Florida, such funds
    A. must always be kept in a separate account.
    B. may be deposited in the landlord's account if he or she posts a $50,000 surety bond.
    C. must always be placed in an interest-bearing account.
    D. must bear interest at the rate of 7 percent.

11. The sales associates in a real estate office have been instructed to send all of their Spanish-speaking prospects to a new subdivision "beautifully designed with a Spanish flavor." This is an example of
    A. steering.
    B. subordination.
    C. alienation.
    D. blockbusting.

12. A landlord who rents a duplex to two tenants is obligated to provide
    A. pest extermination service.
    B. garbage pickup service.
    C. garbage receptacles.
    D. all of the above unless waived in the rental agreement.

13. Which disclosure requirement is required to be given to tenants in multifamily buildings of five or more units?
    A. No brokerage relationship notice
    B. Notice of where deposit is held within 30 days
    C. 15-day cancellation privilege
    D. Transaction broker notice

14. If a tenant vacates rented premises promptly when a lease or tenancy expires, the landlord must
    A. inform the tenant within 45 days if the landlord claims part of the security deposit.
    B. return the tenant's security deposit within 30 days or explain any exception.
    C. inform the tenant within 25 days if part of the tenant's deposit will be claimed.
    D. inform the tenant within 30 days if part of the tenant's deposit will be claimed.

15. A tenant is obligated to
    A. ensure that his or her guests do not disturb the peace.
    B. be reasonable in operating air-conditioning equipment.
    C. maintain interior plumbing in a clean and sanitary way.
    D. do all of the above.

16. If a tenant's rent is current and he or she notifies the landlord of an intended absence, the landlord
    A. may not enter the tenant's rented premises without the tenant's consent except in an emergency.
    B. may enter only if accompanied by a second party.
    C. may enter without any restriction.
    D. may not enter the tenant's rented premises without first obtaining a sheriff's affidavit.

17. How long does a landlord have to correct a noncompliance that is brought to his or her attention by written notice from a tenant?
    A. 7 days
    B. 10 days
    C. 2 weeks
    D. 30 days

18. A landlord must follow designated procedures in evicting a tenant. The first step in a legal eviction is to
    A. personally deliver a written notice demanding possession.
    B. notify the tenant by mail of the landlord's demand for possession.
    C. attach a notice to the door of the premises that possession of the premises is demanded.
    D. do any of the above.

19. The law that requires that lenders furnish borrowers with a good-faith estimate of closing costs is the
    A. Truth-in-Lending Act.
    B. Real Estate Settlement Procedures Act.
    C. Consumer Credit Protection Act.
    D. Fair Housing and Lending Act.

20. Which phrase may legally be included in an advertisement to sell real estate?
    A. "Cute cottage home, perfect for first-time buyer"
    B. "Beautiful neighborhood rich in ethnic heritage"
    C. "Spanish-speaking community"
    D. "Quiet neighborhood, no young children please"

CHAPTER 8

Property Rights: Estates, Tenancies, and Multiple Ownership Interests

■ KEY TERMS

bylaws	joint tenancy	riparian rights
concurrent ownership	land	separate property
condominium	leasehold estate	tenancy at sufferance
cooperative	life estates	tenancy at will
declaration	littoral rights	tenancy by the entireties
elective share	marital assets	
estate for years	personal property	tenancy in common
estate in severalty	proprietary lease	tenants in common
fee simple estate	real estate	time-share
fixtures	real property	trade fixture
freehold estate	remainderman	undivided interest
homestead	right of survivorship	

■ OVERVIEW

This Chapter begins with a description of the physical components of real property. It goes on to discuss various types of estates and the rights that are included in each type of estate. It describes multiple ownership interests as well as special ownership interests, including the constitutional homestead. The Chapter concludes with a thorough presentation of cooperatives, condominiums, and time-shares.

After completing this Chapter, the student should be able to:

- define *real property* based on the definition in Chapter 475, F.S.;

- list and explain the physical components of real property;

- explain the four tests courts use to determine if an item is a fixture;

- distinguish between real and personal property;

- describe the bundle of rights associated with real property ownership;

- list the principal types of estates (tenancies) and describe their characteristics;

- describe the features associated with the Florida homestead law;

- distinguish between cooperatives, condominiums, and time-shares; and

- describe the four main documents associated with condominiums.

■ THE NATURE OF PROPERTY

In medieval times kings and lords owned the land, and the common people worked the land under the *feudal* system of ownership. In the United States today the *allodial* system, which grew out of the English feudal system, allocates full property ownership rights to private individuals.

Land refers not only to the *surface* of the earth but also to everything attached to it by nature, such as trees and lakes. Land also includes products of nature beneath the surface, such as oil and limestone. Technically, land extends downward to the center of the earth and upward into the air to infinity.

Real estate refers to the land and all *improvements* permanently attached to the land. Improvements are artificial (human-made) things attached to land, such as homes, factories, fences, streets, sewers, and other additions.

Real property includes all real estate plus the legal *bundle of rights* inherent in the ownership of real estate. (The bundle of rights is explained in detail under General Property Rights later in this Chapter.) The terms *real property* and *real estate* are often used interchangeably. (See the definition of real property in the box below.) However, some references reserve the term *real property* to include the concept of a bundle of rights associated with ownership. Real property, therefore, includes not only the real estate (land plus improvements) but also the legal interests, rights, and privileges associated with the ownership of real estate.

Definition of Real Property

Real property or real estate means any interest or estate in land and any interest in business enterprises or business opportunities, including any assignment leasehold, subleasehold, or mineral right; however, the term does not include any cemetery lot or right of burial in any cemetery, nor does the term include the renting of a mobile home lot or recreational vehicle lot in a mobile home park or travel park.

Reference: Section 475.01, F.S.

FIGURE 8.1   Physical Components of Real Property

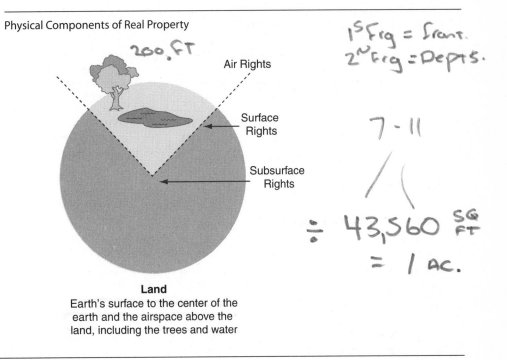

200.FT

Air Rights

Surface Rights

Subsurface Rights

Land
Earth's surface to the center of the
earth and the airspace above the
land, including the trees and water

[Handwritten margin notes:]
1ˢᵗ Frg = front.
2ᴺᵈ Frg = Depts.

7 - 11

÷ 43,560 SQ FT
= 1 AC.

PHYSICAL COMPONENTS OF REAL PROPERTY

An owner's rights to use the physical components of surface, subsurface, and air are referred to as *surface rights, subsurface rights,* and *air rights.* (See Figure 8.1.)

Surface rights.   Surface rights include land and water rights. Two types of water rights are:

1. **Riparian rights.** Associated with land abutting the banks of a river, stream, or other watercourse.   *[margin: Fresh. water]*

2. **Littoral rights.** Associated with land abutting tidal bodies of water such as an ocean, sea, or lake.   *[margin: Salt water]*

Definitions Associated with Water Rights	
Accretion	The process of land buildup from water-borne rock, sand, and soil
Alluvion	Deposits of land as a result of accretion
Erosion	Gradual loss of land due to natural forces
Reliction	Gradual receding of water, uncovering additional land

Subsurface rights.   These consist of an owner's rights to underground minerals, petroleum, natural gas, and so forth.

Air rights.   Air rights involve that space above a tract, extending up to a height established by law (e.g., building rights, easements, aerial navigation).   *[margin: = 200 FT.]*

Most real property transactions include all three physical components in the exchange of ownership rights. However, it is entirely possible for

FIGURE 8.2   Real Versus Personal Property

Real Estate	Personal Property
Land and anything permanently attached to it	Movable items not attached to real property; items severed from real property

Fixture	Trade Fixture
Item of personal property converted to real property by attaching it to the real property with the intention that it become permanently a part thereof	Item of personal property attached to real property that is owned by a tenant and is used in a business; legally removable by tenant

the seller to retain one or even two of the components if the buyer and seller agree. For example, the Met Life Building in New York City was built by purchasing the air rights over Grand Central Station. The surface and subsurface components of that parcel continue to perform the same function as before construction of the Met Life Building. Another example of the separation of components of real estate occurred near Jay, Florida. Before the oil supply there was exhausted, owners often sold or leased the subsurface component, including oil rights, while retaining the surface and air rights.

PERSONAL PROPERTY

The two basic types of assets are real property and personal property. (See Figure 8.2.) Thus, any asset that is not real property is **personal property** (also known as *chattel*). A savings account, a car, and jewelry are all personal property. Just as the term *realty* is used to denote real property, the term *personalty* is used to indicate personal property. It is important to distinguish between real property and personal property in a real estate transaction. All personal property included in the sale should be identified in the contract for sale, or the seller is entitled to remove the property.

Real property can become personal property by the *act of severance*. For example, timber is real property, but when cut it becomes personal property by the act of severance. Vice versa, personal property can become real property by *attachment*. (See Fixtures.)

FIXTURES

Fixtures are objects that were personal property but have been permanently attached to or made part of real property and thus are now real property. A bathtub, for example, was personal property in its container in a warehouse, but once permanently attached in a home, it became real property. Some items, such as drapes, rugs, and chandeliers, are more difficult to classify. In those cases where contracting parties have not had the foresight to include such items in a real estate sale contract, the

1   courts generally use the following set of *tests* to decide if
2   an item is a fixture.

3   **Intent of the parties.**   As in most points of law, intent of the party
4   placing an article on or in real property is of primary importance.
5   Statements made by an owner to witnesses may indicate the intent to
6   make an item a fixture. For example, including a washer and dryer in a
7   sale contract as part of the real property would remove any doubt about
8   the owner's intention. In disputes between buyer and seller, the terms and
9   conditions of the sale contract usually are strictly enforced unless there is
10 some indication that the buyer was misled.

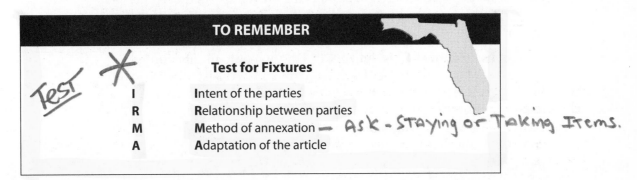

TO REMEMBER

Test for Fixtures

I   **I**ntent of the parties
R   **R**elationship between parties
M   **M**ethod of annexation — *Ask - Staying or Taking Items.*
A   **A**daptation of the article

Test ✗

11 **Relationship between the parties.**   In this test the courts seek to
12 determine the exact nature of the relationship between the parties. Is it
13 buyer and seller or landlord and tenant? Ordinarily, a residential tenant is
14 required to leave any item he or she has attached to the landlord's real
15 property. However, if a building is leased as a retail store and display
16 racks are attached to the walls and counters are attached to the floor, the
17 courts generally rule that such items are trade fixtures and may be
18 removed. A **trade fixture** is an article that is attached by a commercial
19 tenant as a necessary part of the tenant's trade or business and is personal
20 property.

21 **Method of annexation.**   The manner in which an article is attached to
22 real property generally indicates whether it is a fixture or personal
23 property. Normally, if removing the item results in damage to real
24 property, the article is classified as a fixture. A set of built-in storage
25 cabinets in the utility room would normally be considered a fixture if
26 removing it would damage the wall.

27 **Adaptation of the article.**   This test seeks to determine if an article was
28 designed for, or necessary to, the normal use of a specific property. If the
29 item is adapted or custom built to fit the property, it will likely be
30 considered a fixture. Custom-made bookshelves, storm windows, or
31 custom-made draperies that are of the same pattern as the wallpaper
32 would be classified as fixtures.

33   These tests should not be necessary if all personal property to be
34 sold with the real estate is listed in the sale contract. This eliminates
35 misunderstanding and possible litigation. Frequently, a potential buyer
36 will ask an owner who is anxious to sell, "Do the washer and dryer go
37 with the house, or are you taking them with you?" To which the owner
38 might reply, "Oh, yes!" (yes, what?), or the owner might even make a

1 forthright statement like "They go with the house." In either case the
2 buyer would be well advised to list the washer and dryer in the sale
3 contract to remove any doubt.

■ GENERAL PROPERTY RIGHTS

The practical result of the allodial system has been government
recognition and protection of private rights of ownership. Real property
ownership rights (or bundle of rights) include the:

- **right of disposition**. This right permits the owner to sell, mortgage,
  dedicate, give away, or otherwise dispose of all or any portion of the
  property.

- **right of use (control).** This right entitles the owner to uninterrupted
  use and control of his or her land in any manner consistent with
  local laws. In earlier times, this right was almost absolute. As the
  density of population increased, it became necessary to enact
  legislation to ensure that one owner's use of land did not and
  would not interfere with his neighbors' use of land.

- **right of possession.** This right allows an owner to occupy the
  premises in privacy with maximum legal control over entry and use
  of that property. An owner acquires the right of possession of a
  property on the day that owner becomes legally entitled to the rents
  or income from such property, even though the owner may not have
  set foot on the land itself.

- **right of exclusion (quiet enjoyment).** This right is formal
  recognition that "a man's home is his castle." An owner has the
  right to control entry onto his or her land without interference and
  to collect damages for certain forms of trespass. Other parties must
  have permission to enter the land of an owner with this right. This
  right has also been modified by judicial decisions and legislation.

TO REMEMBER

Tennent.

Bundle of Rights

Disposition (sell or give away)
Use (control)
Possession (occupy)
Exclusion (quiet enjoyment)

■ ESTATES AND TENANCIES

Estate refers to the degree, quantity, nature, and extent of the bundle
of rights in real property. The terms *estate* and *tenancy* are to be used
interchangeably. Estates are divided into two broad classifications:
freehold (unknown duration) and nonfreehold (known duration).
(See Figure 8.3.)

FIGURE 8.3   Estates in Real Property

[handwritten: in Fl. all Properties are reasignable.]

Freehold Estates are estates of ownership
- **Fee Simple** (Absolute) is the most comprehensive estate and it is inheritable.
- **Life Estate** is measured by a natural life span ("for the life of").
  - **Estate in Reversion** occurs when property returns to the grantor.
  - **Remainder Estate** occurs when property goes to a third party.
    - **Vested Remainderman** refers to someone whose legal name is specified.
    - **Continginent Remainderman** refers to someone whose legal name is not specified (such as, first-born child).

Nonfreehold Estates (Leasehold) are estates of possession.
- **Estate for Years** is a written lease agreement with a specific starting and ending date.
- **Tenancy at Will** is either an oral agreement or one that has no specific beginning and ending date.
- **Tenancy at Sufferance** occurs when the lease period has ended and the tenant is a holdover.

FREEHOLD ESTATES

A **freehold estate** is an ownership interest for an indefinite period. That interest can be inherited (fee simple estate) or can be measured by the lifetime of an individual (life estate).

Fee simple estate.   The most comprehensive collection of real property freehold rights is the fee simple estate. A **fee simple estate** means absolute and complete ownership, subject only to governmental restrictions (for example, taxation and police powers). Sometimes called *fee* and sometimes *fee simple absolute,* all these terms identify an ownership interest with complete power to use, to dispose of, and to allow the property to descend to heirs. It is the highest type of real property interest recognized by law.

Life estate.   Following the Norman Conquest of England, estates granted by the king (or lesser lord) to feudal tenants were for the tenant's life only. **Life estates,** which still exist today, are another type of freehold estate. The owner has considerably fewer rights than the owner of a fee simple estate. He or she owns the property for only the period of the lifetime of an individual (the owner or other designated person). During the time an owner enjoys a life estate, he or she must maintain the property and not permit *waste* (anything that reduces the value of property) to occur. The owner also must pay the taxes and property insurance and keep current any mortgage(s) or lien(s) to preserve the property.

When the life estate ends, the property reverts (returns) to the original grantor or goes to a third party, called a **remainderman.** If the life estate reverts to the original grantor, an *estate in reversion* (reversion estate) is created. If the life estate is to go to a remainderman, the remainderman owns a *remainder estate* while the life estate exists. Normally, the instrument that establishes the life estate also designates the remainderman. The remainderman acquires either a fee simple estate or some concurrent tenancy if more than one remainderman is designated.

NONFREEHOLD OR LEASEHOLD ESTATES

A **leasehold estate** (tenancy) is an interest in real property that is measured in calendar time. Leasehold estates are *not* freehold estates because they do not exist for an indefinite period of time. Leasehold estates are considered *nonfreehold* or *less-than-freehold* estates. There are three types of leasehold estates: estate for years, tenancy at will, and tenancy at sufferance. (See Figure 8.3 on previous page.)

Estate for years.   An **estate for years** (or tenancy for years) is a tenancy with a specific starting and ending date. It exists for a designated period, which may be any length of time from less than a year to a period of many years (such as a 99-year lease). An estate for years is a leasehold estate that is created by a written lease agreement. An estate for years establishes an interest in real property for the tenant (right to use, possession, and exclusion) but does not convey actual title (or ownership) or the right of disposition. (Refer also to page 150.)

Tenancy at will.   A **tenancy at will** is a leasehold in which the tenant holds possession of the premises with the owner's permission but without a fixed term. Florida statute refers to this as a *tenancy without specific term.* For example, assume that a woman executive is the mother of three young children. The children's nanny occupies a cottage apartment on the premises in addition to receiving a salary. Such an arrangement creates a tenancy at will. In Florida, property notice for termination of tenancies at will is set in statute and is based on the time interval between rent payments:

- Week to week—7 days notice

- Month to month—15 days notice

When the rent is incidental to employment, the duration is determined by the time interval between wage payments.

Tenancy at sufferance.   A **tenancy at sufferance** occurs when a tenant stays in possession of the property beyond the ending date of a legal tenancy without the consent of the landlord. The tenant has no estate or title but only "naked" possession and is not entitled to notice to terminate. The payment and acceptance of rent alone shall not be construed to be a renewal of the lease. However, if the tenant's *holding over* is continued with the written consent of the lessor, then the tenancy becomes a tenancy at will under Florida law.

83.04, F.S.

SOLE OWNERSHIP AND CONCURRENT OWNERSHIP

When title to property is held by one person, it is called an **estate in severalty** or sole ownership. (To help you remember, think of "severed" ownership.) Ownership by two or more persons at the same time is **concurrent ownership.** There are three types of estates (tenancies) with concurrent owners: tenancy in common, joint tenancy, and tenancy by the entireties. (Refer to Figure 8.4.).

Tenancy in common.   When two or more persons wish to share the ownership of a single property, they may choose to do so as **tenants in**

83.57, F.S.

FIGURE 8.4   Sole Ownership Versus Concurrent Ownership

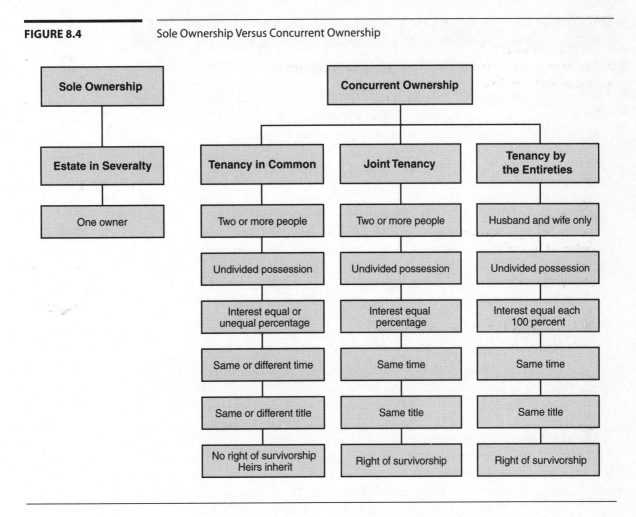

common. It is the most frequently used form of co-ownership, except for
husband-and-wife ownership. Tenants in common may acquire title at
different times or at the same time. As tenants in common, each owns an
"undivided interest" in the property. An **undivided interest** is interest in
the entire property, rather than ownership of a particular part of the
property. For example, Sally and Kathy own a house as tenants in
common. Sally holds two-thirds interest in the entire property, and Kathy
owns one-third interest in the entire property. When Sally and Kathy die,
their interest in the property will descend to their heirs. On Sally's death,
for example, her two-thirds interest in the property will descend to her
legal heirs (or as instructed in her will.)

Joint tenancy.   A major difference between a joint tenancy and a
tenancy in common is that **joint tenancy** is characterized by the right of
survivorship. **Right of survivorship** means that when one co-owner dies,
his or her share goes to the surviving co-owner(s) and not to the deceased
tenant's heirs. Joint tenants have an undivided interest in real property.
A joint tenancy can exist only when the four "unities" of *possession,
interest, title,* and *time* are present.

<table>
<tbody>
<tr><td colspan="3">**TO REMEMBER**</td></tr>
<tr><td colspan="3">**Four Unities of a Joint Tenancy**</td></tr>
<tr><td>**P**</td><td>Possession</td><td>Joint tenants have the same rights of undivided possession</td></tr>
<tr><td>**I**</td><td>Interest</td><td>Joint tenants have equal ownership interest</td></tr>
<tr><td>**T**</td><td>Title</td><td>Joint tenants acquire title on the same instrument (deed)</td></tr>
<tr><td>**T**</td><td>Time</td><td>Joint tenants acquire their interests in the property at the same time</td></tr>
</tbody>
</table>

S. Suvivership [handwritten]

1   Today a true joint tenancy cannot be created unless specific wording
2 in the deed conveying the property provides for survivorship. Under
3 present law a deed conveying an estate in joint tenancy to ensure
4 survivorship must include wording similar to "as joint tenants with right
5 of survivorship and not as tenants in common." This continues that
6 feature of joint tenancy that prevents disposition of the property by will
7 or descent to heirs. As joint tenants die, their shares are divided among
8 the surviving tenants until only one owner is left. The sole survivor then
9 has a fee simple estate in severalty. A joint tenant who wants to sell his
10 or her share of a property may do so. However, the person who buys that
11 share cannot be a joint tenant with the other original owners, but instead
12 will be a tenant in common without the right to receive any property on
13 the death of one of the original joint tenants. The tenant in common's
14 share can be disposed of by will, descent, or other arrangement.

15 **Tenancy by the entireties.**   A **tenancy by the entireties** is basically a
16 joint tenancy between husband and wife. The four unities of a joint
17 tenancy with right of survivorship must exist, and the two co-owners
18 must be married to each other at the time they take title. This estate has its
19 origin in the common-law attitude that a husband and wife are one
20 ownership entity. The deed or other instrument of conveyance does not
21 have to state expressly that a tenancy by the entireties exists. If the parties
22 are truly husband and wife, the estate is implied. While not mandatory,
23 the deed should reflect a tenancy by the entireties to serve notice to others
24 that such an estate exists.

25   When one spouse dies, that individual's ownership interest
26 automatically transfers to the surviving spouse by *right of survivorship.*
27 Neither the husband nor the wife may will any portion of his or her
28 interest in an estate by the entireties. This unique form of co-ownership
29 can be divided by annulment or by divorce. In the event of death,
30 the survivor emerges as the severalty (sole) owner of the property. In the
31 event of annulment or divorce, the tenancy by the entireties is ended, and
32 a tenancy in common results.

■ SPECIAL OWNERSHIP INTERESTS

HOMESTEAD

Homeowners (including single persons) in Florida may homestead their permanent (principal) residence. Declaring one's residence as a homestead entitles the owners to certain protections and benefits including the following:

- *Protection of the homestead.* The homesteaded property is protected from forced sale for debts owing to personal loans, credit card debt, and so forth. However, the protection does not prevent foreclosure for nonpayment of property taxes, special assessments, mortgages, vendors' liens, or construction liens secured with the homesteaded property.

- *Tax exemption.* The Florida Constitution allows a tax exemption from assessed property value. The current homestead tax exemption is $25,000 for all qualifying homesteads and is deducted from the assessed value when calculating taxable value. (See also Chapter 18.)

- *Size of homestead.* The size of homesteaded property is restricted to 160 acres outside a municipality (city) or up to ½ acre if the property is located within the city.

- *Protection of the family.* According to Florida Statute, if a married person dies and the family homestead was titled in that deceased person's name only (in severalty), by operation of law (even if a will states otherwise), the surviving spouse receives a life estate and the children (lineal descendants) receive a remainder estate. If there are no children, the surviving spouse receives a fee simple estate in the homestead. The purpose of the homestead law, therefore, is to protect the family and prevent it from being displaced from the homestead.

 wwweb.link   *To learn more about the protections provided under Florida's Homestead law, go to:* **http://www.florida.ctic.com/guide/ Guide_homestead.htm.**

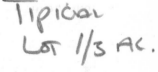
Tipical Lot 1/3 Ac.

ELECTIVE SHARE

If the surviving spouse (widow or widower) was either excluded from the deceased spouse's will entirely or was given less than the elective share (established by statute) of the estate, the surviving spouse may claim the allowed statutory share. The **elective share** has been defined as consisting of 30 percent of the decedent's net estate, except for homestead property. (Homestead property is in addition to that received by elective share because a surviving spouse is already entitled to a life estate in the homestead.) Where an estate by the entireties exists, the surviving spouse already owns 100 percent of the real property. Selection of an elective share is not mandatory.

732.207, F.S.

EXEMPT PROPERTY

Associated with the elective share rights of a surviving spouse, but completely separate and apart from such rights, is a right to property called *exempt property.* This is a category of property defined as household furniture, furnishings, and appliances in the decedent's usual place of abode up to a net value of $10,000 plus automobiles. Entitlement to this exempt property is limited by and subject to any unpaid chattel mortgages or other perfected security interests. In addition to the above-named property, the surviving spouse is entitled to the personal effects of the decedent up to a net value of $1,000, unless such effects were legally disposed of by a will. Rights to exempt property have priority over all other claims against an estate. These rights are in addition to any other benefit given or passing to the surviving spouse, unless a will of the decedent proves otherwise. If no spouse survives the decedent, minor children are jointly entitled to the same rights as would have been available to a surviving spouse.

732.402, F.S.

DISTRIBUTION OF ASSETS RESULTING FROM DIVORCE

In Florida, when a husband and wife divorce, the court generally sets apart to each spouse the spouse's nonmarital assets. Nonmarital assets are **separate property** and include any property the husband or wife owned separately prior to the marriage and property acquired during the marriage by inheritance or gift.

Florida law provides for the divorcing couple's **marital assets** to be divided equitably. Marital assets include any property acquired during the marriage individually by either spouse or jointly by them. The Florida court begins with the premise that the distribution of marital assets should be equal. The court then takes into account all relevant factors such as the economic circumstances of the parties, the duration of the marriage, any interruption of personal careers or educational opportunities of either party, the contribution of one spouse, and the personal career or educational opportunity of the other spouse, and so forth.

61.075, F.S.

■ COOPERATIVES, CONDOMINIUMS, AND TIME-SHARING

BACKGROUND

In Florida the Cooperative Act (719, F.S.), the Condominium Act (718, F.S.), and the Time-Share Act (721, F.S.) establish rights and obligations of the developer, the association, and unit owners and buyers. These statutes all require that before the sale of developer residential shared housing, purchasers be provided with certain disclosure statements. These statements include, for example, property description, form of 3title-interest, description of common areas and amenities, existence of judgments or liens, management arrangements, escrow provisions for deposits, restrictions on the sale or transfer of units, apportionment of common expenses, construction completion date, estimated operating budget, estimated closing costs, and copies of key documents.

¹   The Division of Florida Land Sales, Condominiums, and Mobile
² Homes of the Department of Business and Professional Regulation is the
³ state agency charged with ensuring compliance with the laws regulating
⁴ all three of these multiple-ownership forms. Because Florida is perhaps
⁵ the most active of the states in producing and promoting multiple-
⁶ ownership dwelling units, a complete description of cooperatives,
⁷ condominiums, and time-sharing is appropriate here.

⁸ ## COOPERATIVES

⁹   A **cooperative,** cooperative association, or co-op is normally organized as
¹⁰ a corporation. The corporation holds title to the land and improvements.
¹¹ Authority and control of the corporation may be vested in an elected
¹² board of directors or trustees. Some apartments may be more expensive
¹³ than others, depending on size and location. The owners purchase shares
¹⁴ of stock in the corporation. The important result of the stock purchase is
¹⁵ that ownership of the stock entitles the purchaser to a **proprietary lease**
¹⁶ and the right to occupy the unit for the life of the corporation.

719, F.S.

Die And It goes to The Next Person on List (handwritten annotation)

Definition of a Cooperative

Cooperative means that form of ownership of real property wherein legal title is vested in a corporation or other entity and the beneficial use is evidenced by an ownership interest in the association and a lease or other muniment of title or possession granted by the association as the owner of all the cooperative property.

Reference: Section 719.103, F.S.

---

¹⁷   Section 719.117, F.S., stipulates that ad valorem (according to
¹⁸ valuation) taxes and special assessments by taxing authorities be assessed
¹⁹ against each cooperative parcel separately. The taxes and special
²⁰ assessments levied constitute a lien on only the individual unit and not on
²¹ any other portion of the cooperative property. Owners-shareholders may
²² deduct their real estate taxes and mortgage interest from taxable income.
²³ Each individual shareholder must pay the corporation a monthly
²⁴ assessment based on a proportional share of the amount necessary for the
²⁵ payment of common expenses such as operating and maintenance
²⁶ expenses. If an owner-shareholder fails to pay the monthly assessment
²⁷ fees, the corporation may place a lien on the individual unit and
²⁸ eventually foreclose on the unit.

²⁹   The corporation, or its governing board, may stipulate that shareholders
³⁰ sell their stock to either a board-approved buyer or back to the
³¹ corporation itself. Some cooperatives require that owners-shareholders
³² sell their stock at the original purchase price, thereby depriving the
³³ unit stockholders of any profit. Most cooperatives prohibit the sale of
³⁴ stock shares to anyone until the buyer is approved by the corporation or
³⁵ association.

1 # CONDOMINIUMS

2 Florida's Condominium Act establishes procedures for the creation, sale,
3 and operation of condominiums. A buyer of a **condominium** unit
4 purchases outright in fee simple both vertical and horizontal space and
5 receives a recordable deed to prove ownership of that separate piece
6 of real estate. Buyers also own an undivided fractional share of the
7 buildings and land (or leasehold), known as *common elements.* Common
8 elements include all portions of the condominium property not included
9 in the individual units. Each owner has an undivided interest in the
10 following: land (or leasehold) within the condominium boundaries; all
11 personal property owned by the condominium; and all improvements,
12 easements, and rights intended for use in connection with the
13 condominium.

718, F.S.

14 Four main documents define the rights and obligations of
15 condominium owners:

16 1. **Declaration or master deed.** A **declaration** is the instrument by
17 which a condominium is created. The declaration describes the
18 interest that each purchaser acquires and the rights and liabilities of
19 the unit owners. It is recorded in the public records of the county
20 where the land is located, and it is executed and acknowledged
21 with the requirements of a deed.

22 2. **Bylaws.** The **bylaws** of the association govern the administration of
23 the condominium association, provide rules and regulations, and
24 specify the procedures for amending the bylaws.

25 3. **Survey.** The survey (map) includes a graphic description of the
26 improvements and a plot plan identifying common elements and
27 individual units. The legal description must also be included.

28 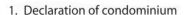 4. **Conveyance.** When the declaration or master deed is initially
29 recorded, the developer owns all of the units and all of the common
30 elements. As individual condominium units are sold, they are
31 conveyed by individual unit deeds.

Condominium Resale Disclosures

A prospective purchaser of an existing (resale) condominium unit who has entered into a contract for purchase must receive, at the seller's expense, the following five documents:

1. Declaration of condominium

2. Articles of incorporation of the association

3. Bylaws and rules of the association

4. Same year-end financial information that the condo association provided to the owners the previous year

5. The document, "Frequently Asked Questions and Answers"

718.111, F.S.

---

32 The contract for *resale* of a residential condominium unit must
33 include a clause that states that the buyer acknowledges receipt of the

above-mentioned documents and that the prospective buyer may cancel the contract within *three business days* after the date of the execution of the contract and receipt by the buyer of the condominium documents.

Developers of 20 or more new residential condominium units must prepare a prospectus and file it with the Division of Florida Land Sales, Condominiums, and Mobile Homes. A copy of the prospectus must be given to prospective purchasers. The developer must also provide buyers with a copy of a separate page entitled "Frequently Asked Questions and Answers" (FAQ). The FAQ informs prospective purchasers about their voting rights and unit use restrictions, including the following: restrictions on the leasing of a unit; information concerning assessments; and whether and in what amount the unit owners or the association are obligated to pay rent or land use fees for recreational facilities.

The Condominium Act requires that the developer include a disclosure in the contract stating that the buyer of a new residential unit may cancel the contract within *15 days* of signing the contract and of receipt by the buyer of the required documents. In addition to the prospectus, the FAQ, and the above-mentioned documents, purchasers must also receive information concerning the form of agreement for sale or lease of the units.

A real estate licensee may return the escrowed binder deposit to the prospective purchaser without first securing the seller's permission, if notified in writing that the buyer is canceling the contract during the statutory time period for cancellation. Even if the seller objects, the Real Estate License Law states that the licensee may return the deposit to the purchaser without having to notify the Commission of conflicting demands. (See also Chapter 5.)

Virtually all condominiums are administered by an association of unit owners according to the bylaws. The association will commonly be governed by a board of administration (directors) elected by the individual unit owners. The association may hire professional management. The association must obtain and keep current fire and extended coverage insurance plus liability insurance. An annual operating budget must be prepared, reflecting all anticipated operating, maintenance, personnel, and service costs. Once adopted by the general membership of the association, the budget forms the basis for the monthly assessment fees each unit owner must pay.

Real estate taxes are assessed and collected on each unit, just as if each were a detached single-family dwelling. Default in payment of taxes or mortgage by the owner of one unit may result in foreclosure of only that unit; it does not affect other unit owners.

Many condominium declaration documents stipulate that if an owner wishes to sell, the individual must first offer the unit to the association on the same terms as asked of an individual buyer. After a designated period of time (frequently 30 days), the unit owner may proceed to sell the unit if the association has not agreed to purchase it. Transfer of ownership interests may be accomplished by gift, will, or sale by the seller's granting a deed to a buyer, as in the sale of other single-family dwellings.

1 **Condominium advantages.**   Individual unit owners may deduct from
2 taxable income the amount of their real property taxes and mortgage
3 interest paid plus that portion of property taxes and mortgage interest
4 paid on the common elements assignable to their fractional ownership.
5 Building costs on a room-for-room, square-foot-by-square-foot basis
6 typically are lower in a condominium than in a single-family house.
7 A condominium's common elements can include a recreation building,
8 swimming pool, tennis court, and other amenities normally beyond the
9 budget of a single-family homeowner. Unit owners enjoy the advantages
10 of increased security and pride of ownership not available to apartment
11 dwellers. Owners may take advantage of property value increases and tax
12 benefits.

13 **Condominium disadvantages.**   Unit owners are, to a degree, controlled
14 by the association and its board of directors. Operating costs often exceed
15 projections. Limited space, noisy or objectionable neighbors, child and pet
16 limitations, and no way to enlarge a unit are all possible drawbacks to this
17 form of multiple-ownership interest. The right-of-first-refusal provision
18 reserved by many associations can slow down the sale of an owner's unit
19 unless provisions are made for a waiver.

You can learn more about Florida's Condominium Act. The Florida statutes are available on the Internet at: **http://www.leg.state.fl.us/welcome/index.cfm.** *Click on "Statutes" and then go to "Chapter 718."*

The Division of Florida Land Sales, Condominiums and Mobile Homes publishes a helpful brochure, "A Guide to Purchasing a Condominium." It can be downloaded at: **http://www.state.fl.us/dbpr/lsc/condominiums/publications/purchasing_guide.pdf.**

20 ## TIME-SHARING

21 The success of recreational condominium projects in the mountains, near
22 oceans and lakes, at golf courses and tennis facilities, or at any number of
23 other desirable locations created a demand for a new ownership format.
24 Only a few owners could afford to pay full price for a second home strictly
25 for vacation use in attractive surroundings. On the other hand, thousands
26 of buyers could afford a second home in their favorite vacation area if they
27 paid only a small, fractional part of the full price. As a result, time-sharing,
28 a spin-off of the recreational condominium concept, was born.

721, F.S.

29 Before any property may be offered to the public for time-share
30 ownership, the property must first be organized as a condominium or
31 time-share. Each unit is divided into time segments of ownership, usually
32 52 weeks. A deed or some evidence of ownership must then be prepared
33 for each ownership segment. **Time-share** ownership involves an
34 undivided interest in a living unit according to the number of weeks
35 purchased. For example, if one week is purchased, the buyer owns a
36 1/52 interest in the unit. Size, location, amenities, and time of year all
37 affect the purchase price of the time-share unit.

38 **Time-Share Act.**   Potential buyers of time-share units in Florida are
39 protected by the Condominium Act and by the Florida Real Estate Time-
40 Share Act (FRETSA), Chapter 721, F.S. FRETSA applies to all time-share

plans consisting of more than seven time-share periods over a span of at least three years and in which the facilities or accommodations are located within the State of Florida. The Time-Share Act requires a developer disclosure that purchasers may cancel the contract within *ten days* of contract signing or receipt of the public offering statement, whichever is later. Under the provisions of this act, sales personnel selling time-share plans of any type must be licensed as a real estate broker, broker associate, or sales associate except as provided in s. 475.011. If an individual is a salaried employee of an owner-developer whose primary business is the development and sale of time-share units, the salesperson is not required to hold a real estate license, provided he or she is not paid a commission or otherwise compensated on a transactional basis, such as with bonuses based on sales quotas.

721.20, F.S.
475.011, F.S.

Time-share ownership.   In actual practice, the form of time-share ownership is normally divided into two types: interval ownership and right-to-use.

1. *Interval ownership.*   Interval ownership is fee simple ownership and contains the same rights as any other property conveyed by deed. The deed must be recordable in the public records. The owner has the right to sell, rent, bequeath, or give away the property. In Florida and most other states, the original declaration of condominium must disclose the type of ownership estate that the deeds to the condominium units will convey.

2. *Right-to-use.*   Rights granted with the right-to-use forms of time-sharing are temporary in nature. A leasehold interest is long-term, usually 20 years to 40 years. After a specified period, which could be from 1 year to 99 years, such rights revert back to the developer-seller. Right-to-use time-sharing is a much greater gamble than is interval ownership, in part because of a court ruling that under some bankruptcy conditions, those rights already bought and paid for are unenforceable.

■ SUMMARY

Real property is any interest or estate in land or any interest in a business opportunity or enterprise. (See Chapter 17.) Estates are divided into types according to the degree of interest held: freehold and nonfreehold (less than freehold). A freehold estate is an ownership interest in real property; a nonfreehold estate is a leasehold interest. Sole ownership (in severalty) indicates that title is held by one person or entity; co-ownership indicates that title is held by more than one person or entity. Co-ownership may be accomplished in a number of ways. (See also Chapter 17.)

■ REVIEW QUESTIONS

1. The most comprehensive interest in real property that an individual may possess is a(n)
   A. estate for years.
   B. life estate.
   C. remainder estate.
   D. fee simple estate.

2. Physical components of real property do NOT include
   A. surface.
   B. air space.
   C. equitable rights.
   D. subsurface.

3. Fixtures are items that
   A. are fixed, or attached, to real property.
   B. were once personal property but are now real property.
   C. have been incorporated as a part of real property.
   D. are all of the above.

4. Frank and Lucille decide to get a divorce. In addition to their Florida homesteaded property, they own a vacant lot in the same subdivision acquired in both of their names during the marriage. How will the lot be distributed?
   A. The lot is considered to be separate property and will be distributed equally between Frank and Lucille.
   B. Because the real estate is community property, each spouse is entitled to a one-half interest in the lot.
   C. The interest in the lot will revert to a life estate and will be distributed to the lineal descendants.
   D. The lot is a marital asset and will be distributed equitably.

5. The bundle of rights associated with real property does NOT include
   A. use.
   B. possession.
   C. disposition.
   D. utility.

6. Mary and John were recently wed. Mary owns a residential lot that was purchased before the marriage. The lot is considered to be
   A. separate property.
   B. a marital asset.
   C. a tenancy in common.
   D. an estate by the entireties.

7. At the expiration of the lease period and before renegotiation of the lease, a tenant continued to occupy the apartment. The tenant's position is called a(n)
   A. tenancy at will.
   B. tenancy at sufferance.
   C. freehold estate.
   D. estate in reversion.

8. Lucy received a new microwave for Christmas. The microwave was installed above her range by screwing the unit to the kitchen cabinets and venting it through the attic. The microwave would be considered
   A. a fixture.
   B. a chattel.
   C. separate property.
   D. personal property.

9. The homestead tax exemption is deducted from the
   A. market value of a property.
   B. assessed value of a property.
   C. sale price of a property.
   D. total cost, including all improvements.

10. A husband and wife own a home with title in both names. The husband owns two small farms in his name only, acquired before the marriage. They have one minor child and one adult son. The husband dies. Which is most correct?
    A. The widow owns a life estate in all property.
    B. The property is split equally among the widow and the children.
    C. The widow owns all of the home and may claim 30 percent of the two farms.
    D. The widow owns 30 percent of all of the real estate.

11. The real estate protected by homestead rights is limited to
    A. 640 acres outside a city or town and one acre in town.
    B. 160 acres outside a city or town and one-half acre in town.
    C. 40 acres outside a city or town and one-half acre in town.
    D. 160 acres outside a city or town or one-half acre in town.

12. A constitutional homestead is owned by Ralph, who is head of a family consisting of himself, his wife, and their three children. Ralph dies unexpectedly. After his death, the widow
    A. owns the homestead.
    B. owns a life estate in the homestead, and the children are vested remaindermen.
    C. may claim elective share rights of 30 percent of the homestead, and the children divide the remainder.
    D. may claim all of the above.

13. Which estate features right of survivorship?
    A. Leasehold estate
    B. Estate by the entireties
    C. Tenancy at will
    D. Tenancy in common

14. Chapter 475, F.S., defines real property as any interest or estate in
    A. land, improvements, leaseholds, subleaseholds, mineral rights, cemetery lots, or any assignment thereof.
    B. land, improvements, business enterprises and business opportunities, leaseholds, subleaseholds, mineral rights, mobile homes, or any assignment thereof.
    C. land, business enterprises and business opportunities, leaseholds, subleaseholds, mineral rights, cemetery lots, mobile home lots, or any assignment thereof.
    D. land, business enterprises and business opportunities, including any assignment, leasehold, subleasehold, or mineral rights.

15. In Florida, cooperatives and time-shares are regulated by the
    A. Division of Real Estate.
    B. Division of Florida Land Sales, Condominiums, and Mobile Homes.
    C. Department of Housing and Urban Development.
    D. Florida Real Estate Commission.

16. A condominium unit buyer has how long to cancel the purchase contract following the signing of an agreement with a developer?
    A. 3 days
    B. 10 days
    C. 15 days
    D. 20 days

17. Developers of condominium projects must give buyers
    A. a copy of the prospectus.
    B. the names and business addresses of real estate sales associates assigned.
    C. the names of all current unit owners.
    D. the names of unit owners, unit numbers, and amounts due from unit owners delinquent in monthly assessment fees.

18. Which characteristic(s) is (are) unique to cooperatives as opposed to condominiums and time-share plans?
    A. The corporation holds title to land and improvements.
    B. The purchaser receives shares of stock in the corporation.
    C. A proprietary lease entitles the purchaser of a cooperative to occupy a unit.
    D. All of the characteristics listed above are unique to cooperatives.

19. All these apply to the constitutional homestead exemption EXCEPT
    A. protection from forced sale for nonpayment of certain debts.
    B. deduction of $25,000 from the assessed value of the homesteaded property, if claimed.
    C. claimants must hold title to the property and use the home as their principal residence.
    D. it automatically creates a tenancy by the entireties if the person filing for homestead is married.

20. Ms. Lee Dade paid cash for a 60-acre lemon grove in Citrus County. The estate is for an indefinite period of time. Ms. Dade does NOT own which type of estate in the property?
    A. Fee simple estate
    B. Freehold estate
    C. Leasehold estate
    D. Estate in severalty

CHAPTER 9

Titles, Deeds, and Ownership Restrictions

■ KEY TERMS

abstract of title	eminent domain	net lease
acknowledgment	encroachment	opinion of title
actual notice	escheat	owner's policy
adverse possession	further assurance	percentage lease
alienation	general lien	police power
chain of title	general warranty deed	quiet enjoyment
condemnation	grantee	quitclaim deed
construction lien	granting clause	restrictive covenants
constructive notice	grantor	seisin
deed	gross lease	specific liens
deed restriction	ground lease	testate
easement	habendum clause	title insurance
easement appurtenant	intestate	title search
easement by necessity	lender's policy	variable lease
easement by prescription	lien	warranty forever
easement in gross	lis pendens	

■ OVERVIEW

This Chapter concerns the legal instruments and methods used to transfer title to real property. The Chapter also discusses the following concepts regarding title to real property: voluntary and involuntary alienation, title insurance, the two types of notice to title, the essential elements of a valid instrument of conveyance, certain covenants found in deeds, and governmental and private restrictions on ownership.

After completing this Chapter, the student should be able to:

- differentiate between voluntary and involuntary alienation;

- explain the various methods of acquiring title to real property;

- describe the conditions necessary to acquire real property by adverse possession;

1 • list and describe the various types of governmental and private
2   restrictions on ownership of real property;

3 • distinguish between actual notice and constructive notice;

4 • distinguish between an abstract of title and a chain of title;

5 • explain the different types of title insurance;

6 • describe the essential elements of a deed; and

7 • list and describe the four types of statutory deeds.

S way to Buy Prop.

W.A.D.e.D

■ TITLE TO REAL PROPERTY

9 In 1821, Florida was purchased from King Ferdinand of Spain. This action
10 placed all of the acquired land, except for the few Spanish private land
11 grants, in the public domain. Title to most of the land in Florida can be
12 traced back to *patents* signed by various presidents transferring land to
13 private ownership. Once in the hands of private owners, title has been and
14 continues to be customarily conveyed by a legal instrument, normally a
15 deed.

16 Many authorities refer to a voluntary transfer of title from one private
17 party to another private party as a *private grant*, whether by deed, will, or
18 other legal instrument. A transfer of title from any level of government
19 to a private party is called a *public grant*, whether by patent, deed, or other
20 conveyance.

21 A person who holds vested ownership rights in property is said to
22 have *title*. The right referred to may be a limited or a full bundle of rights,
23 depending on the type of estate conveyed with the title. Therefore, title to
24 real property is a legal concept signifying ownership of the collection of
25 rights called an *estate*. The new owner receives the estate as specified in a
26 deed or other legal instrument of conveyance.

■ ACQUIRING LEGAL TITLE

28 **Alienation** is the act of transferring ownership, title, or an interest in real
29 property from one person to another. The alienation may be voluntary
30 (with the owner's control and consent) or involuntary (without control
31 and consent of the owner).

VOLUNTARY ALIENATION

33 **Deed.**   The normal real estate transaction involves the sale of property
34 under a contract and is usually consummated by delivery of a deed. A
35 *deed* is defined as a written instrument used to convey an interest in real
36 property. Thus, a deed conveys *legal title*.

37 **Will.**   A will is a legal instrument used to convey title to real and personal
38 property after the person's death. To die **testate** indicates the *decedent*
39 (deceased person) prepared a will during his or her lifetime. Conveyance

FIGURE 9.1   Involuntary Alienation

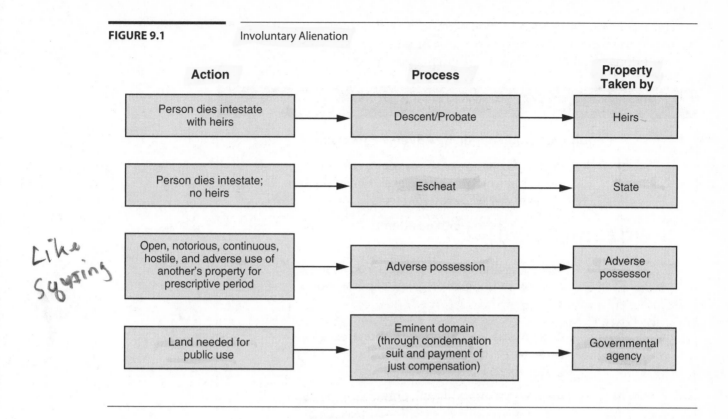

Like Squating

1 of property according to a *last will and testament* is voluntary alienation
2 because the person who left a will—the *testator* (male) or *testatrix*
3 (female)—intended to gift property to a particular individual. A gift of
4 real property is a *devise* and the recipient of the gift is the *devisee.*
5 A gift of personal property is a *bequest* and the recipient is the *beneficiary.*

6 ## INVOLUNTARY ALIENATION

7 **Descent.**   When a person dies without leaving a will **(intestate),** all the
8 property he or she owned at the time of death passes (descends) to the
9 legal descendants. The legal descendants are known as *heirs.* Priorities as
10 to their entitlement to share in the estate are fixed by Florida probate law.
11 (See Figure 9.1.)

12 **Escheat to the state.**   **Escheat** provides for a government, normally a
13 state government, to take the property of an owner who dies intestate and
14 without any known heirs entitled to receive the property. Like many U.S.
15 laws, this power has its origin in England. Under the feudal system of
16 ownership during the Middle Ages, a serf or tenant held land in what
17 could be compared today to a life estate. When the tenant died without
18 heirs, the land reverted back to the feudal lord's estate. The power of
19 escheat is a practical solution to ensure that property is always owned by
20 someone. In many states, this power extends to personal property as
21 well as to real property.

22 **Adverse possession.**   **Adverse possession** arises when the true owner
23 of record fails to maintain possession and the property is seized by
24 another. If the true owner "sleeps on his rights" and does not use the legal
25 means available to remove a hostile trespasser, the owner will lose his or her

Squating.

1 right to the property after a period of time. In Florida, the person attempting
2 to acquire property by adverse possession must comply with all of the
3 conditions listed in the following To Remember box.

TO REMEMBER

Conditions for Alienation by Adverse Possession

H   **H**ostile possession of the property (without owner's permission), to the exclusion of the true owner or any who may contest it

O   **O**pen possession with no attempt to conceal occupancy

T   **T**axes paid on the property by the adverse possessor during all the years of possession

C   **C**laim of title, even an imperfect one, exists (sometimes called color of title), thus creating a reasonable basis for the action

A   **A**dverse possession must continue for seven or more consecutive years without the consent of the owner

N   **N**otorious and flagrant public possession of the property

---

[handwritten marginalia: Squter right]
*[handwritten marginalia: * 7 yrs in FL.]*

4   Always seek competent legal advice before acquiring real property if
5 the title is based on adverse possession.

6 **Eminent domain.**   **Eminent domain** gives government the right to take
7 land from an owner through a legal process referred to as **condemnation,**
8 as long as the taking is for a public purpose. The government must pay a
9 fair price for any land taken under eminent domain. The government may
10 exercise this power (or delegate it to railroad and utility companies)
11 regardless of whether the owner wants to part with the property.
12 Therefore, it is a form of involuntary alienation.

13 **LEGAL TITLE**

14   In early English history, conveyances of freehold interests in real
15 property did not depend on written instruments. Instead, the parties
16 conducted their business on the land, and the townspeople assembled
17 around them to witness the event. The seller orally announced to the
18 townspeople that he was transferring the land to the buyer. He
19 symbolically "did the deed" by handing the buyer a twig or a clump of
20 earth to give the world *actual notice* of the transfer of ownership rights.
21 Today, there are two types of notice that have equal legal priority:

22   1. **Actual notice** is direct knowledge acquired in the course of a
23   transaction. When the townspeople witnessed the transfer of earth

FIGURE 9.2 Short Form of Acknowledgment (695.25, F.S.)

STATE OF: __Florida__

COUNTY OF: __Pinellas__

The foregoing instrument was acknowledged before me this __15th__ day of __July__, 2005, by __Martha Sammis__ who is personally known to me or has produced __a driver's license (or other type of proof)__ as identification.

Notary's Signature
Notary Public

(NOTARY SEAL)

My Commission Expires: __January 1, 2008__

---

1   or twig from one party to another, they had actual notice of the
2   transfer of ownership rights. Assume that a seller discloses orally to
3   the buyer that there is a construction lien on his home for an unpaid
4   pool repair job. The seller has given the buyer actual notice that
5   there is a lien on the property.

6   2. **Constructive notice** (or *legal notice*) is accomplished by recording
7   the information in the public records. When the pool company
8   records a construction lien on the property for the unpaid repair job,
9   it gives the world constructive notice of the lien.

10   Recording a properly executed and "acknowledged" instrument of
11   conveyance puts the world on notice regarding an owner's interests in
12   real property. All instruments affecting ownership of real property *may* be
13   recorded in the public records of the county in which the property is
14   located. (Florida law does not require documents to be recorded.) When
15   properly recorded, these instruments are considered notice to the world,
16   with precisely the same effect and authority as if the owner had given
17   actual notice. All people dealing with the real property are bound by all
18   recorded documents. Recordation of a conveyance protects both the
19   holder of the title and the public from fraud because the true ownership
20   of real property is open to verification by the public. To record a deed, it
21   must be acknowledged by the grantor and the acknowledgment must be
22   witnessed and certified by a notary public. **Acknowledgment** is the
23   formal declaration before a notary public by the grantor that his or her
24   signing is a free act. Other requirements for recording include the
25   signatures of two witnesses. In Florida, the notary public taking the
26   acknowledgment may be one of the witnesses. (See Figure 9.2.)

Lis Pendens

When litigation is initiated involving a specific parcel of real property, a **lis pendens** (notice of pending legal action) usually is filed with the clerk of the county in which the property is located. The lis pendens then becomes a form of constructive notice to anyone interested in that parcel of real property.

CONDITION OF TITLE

When in the process of obtaining title to or interest in real property, the buyer is prudent to determine the condition of the seller's title. A **chain of title** is the complete successive record of a property's ownership. Beginning with the earliest owner, title may pass to many individuals. Each owner is "linked" to the next so that a "chain" is formed. A chain of title can be traced through linking conveyances from the present owner back to the earliest recorded owner.

A **title search** is an examination of all of the public records to determine whether any defects exist in the chain of title. Recorded instruments such as deeds, divorce decrees, wills, and mortgages are included. In actual practice, the search does not go all the way back in history to the original land grant. State statute determines how far back into history the search must go. Florida's Marketable Record Titles Act limits the search to 30 years. Thus the original source of title, known as the *root of title*, goes back 30 years. The law extinguishes certain interests in real property and cures certain defects arising before the root of title. Therefore, it is necessary to search only from the current owner to the root.

712.02, F.S.

A title search establishes current ownership and claims that affect the title. If there is a gap in the chain, it may be necessary to establish ownership by a court action known as a *suit to quiet title*. All possible claimants to the property are allowed to present evidence during a court proceeding. A judgment is filed after all of the evidence is considered. Often, the procedure requires obtaining quitclaim deeds to establish ownership. (See also Quitclaim deed on page 176.)

An **abstract of title** is a summary report of what the title search found in the public record. The person who prepares this report is called an *abstractor*. The abstractor searches the public records and then prepares a condensed history of the various events and proceedings that affected the title throughout the last 30 years. All recorded liens and encumbrances are included, along with their current status. However, the abstract of title does *not* reveal such items as encroachments or forgeries, or any interests or conveyances that have not been recorded.

Some buyers will accept an **opinion of title** executed by an attorney after he or she has studied the abstract of title. The opinion will list any defects or clouds on the title, such as liens, easements, or other encumbrances, and it will include the attorney's opinion of whether the seller has a *marketable title* (merchantable title). Most attorneys do *not* guarantee the opinion of title. It is an opinion only, backed by legal training and experience. If the opinion should prove to be in error, negligence must usually be proved for the attorney's client to receive reimbursement.

No recource

The limited protection afforded buyers of real property by an opinion of title led to the need for title insurance. **Title insurance** is a contract that protects the policyholder from losses arising from defects in the title. A title search is performed to make sure that the title is good and merchantable. The title company issues a *title binder* after review of the

475.25(2)(j), F.S.
61J2-24.001, F.A.C.

CAN Sue ⁊

1 title search results. The title binder is issued prior to closing and is a
2 commitment made by the insurance company to issue a title insurance
3 policy. Florida law does not require title insurance. However, when
4 questions of title arise, real estate licensees are required to advise
5 prospective buyers to either consult an attorney regarding the condition
6 of title or to purchase title insurance.

7 The title insurance company will defend a lawsuit based on an
8 insurable defect. The title insurance company will pay claims up to the
9 face amount of the policy if the title proves to be defective. Policies do *not*
10 cover exceptions or exclusions listed in the policy such as unrecorded
11 easements, and liens arising after the issuance of the policy. There are two
12 types of title insurance:

13 1. **Owner's policy** is issued for the total purchase price of the property.
14 It helps to protect the new owner against unexpected risks such as
15 forged deed signatures and damages for any defect in the title
16 (unless listed as an exception in the policy). A one-time premium is
17 paid when the policy is issued. The policy is *not* transferable to
18 another owner.

19 2. **Lender's policy** is issued for the unpaid mortgage amount. The
20 lender policy (or *mortgagee policy*) protects the lender against title
21 defects. Unlike the owner's title insurance, the lender's title
22 insurance is transferable. If the mortgage lender sells the mortgage
23 to another investor, the title insurance is *assignable* to the new
24 mortgagee. The lender policy will protect the new owner of the
25 mortgage up to the unpaid balance of the mortgage loan. Most
26 lenders require lender's title insurance as a condition of issuing a
27 mortgage loan.

Florida uses a standardized insurance policy known as the American Land Title Association (ALTA) form. The form can be downloaded and printed at: **http://www.alta.org.** *Click on "Alta Policies and Endorsements" located under "Standard/Forms." Scroll down the list of forms and click on "Homeowner's Policy of Title Insurance for One-to-Four Family Residence." Other helpful information is available by clicking on "Questions about Title Insurance."*

28 ■ DEEDS

29 A **deed** is a written instrument that conveys title to real property. It is an
30 instrument of conveyance whereby title to real property is transferred
31 from one party to another. The two parties to a deed are the **grantor**
32 (owner giving title) and the **grantee** (new owner receiving title).
33 The deed must be signed by a *competent* (of sound mind and legal age)
34 grantor and witnessed by two people to be valid. The grantee need not be
35 competent nor sign the deed.

36 ESSENTIAL ELEMENTS OF A DEED

37 The formats of deeds may differ because the wording is immaterial, as
38 long as the intent to convey title is clearly expressed. Certain elements

1 must be present in a deed to spell out clearly the necessary intent and the
2 property to which it applies.

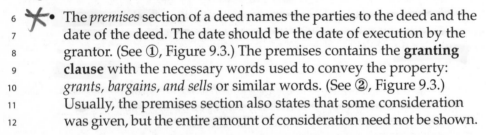

TO REMEMBER
Elements of a Deed
C   **C**onsideration (valuable or good)
E   **E**xecution (signed by a competent grantor and two witnesses)
D   **D**escription of property
D   **D**elivery and acceptance (voluntary)
I   **I**nterest or estate being conveyed (habendum clause)
N   **N**ames of a grantee and grantor
G   **G**ranting and other appropriate clauses

CLAUSES IN A DEED

4 Historically, deeds contained several formal covenants or clauses. Refer to
5 Figure 9.3 for an example of each.

6 • The *premises* section of a deed names the parties to the deed and the
7 date of the deed. The date should be the date of execution by the
8 grantor. (See ①, Figure 9.3.) The premises contains the **granting**
9 **clause** with the necessary words used to convey the property:
10 *grants, bargains, and sells* or similar words. (See ②, Figure 9.3.)
11 Usually, the premises section also states that some consideration
12 was given, but the entire amount of consideration need not be shown.

13 • The **habendum clause,** so named because in medieval times it
14 began with the Latin phrase *habendum et tenendum* ("to have and to
15 hold"), limited the estate or tenancy being conveyed. Today, the
16 habendum clause starts with the words "to have and to hold."
17 Then, usually, the word "forever" follows if the estate is fee simple
18 or the words "for the life of the grantee" if it is a life estate. (See ③,
19 Figure 9.3.)

20 • The covenant of **seisin** (also *seizin*) is a promise that the grantor owns
21 the property and has the right to convey title. (See ④, Figure 9.3.)

22 • The covenant *against encumbrances* states that the property is free
23 from liens or other encumbrances except as noted in the deed. This
24 clause gives the grantee notice of all encumbrances associated with
25 the property. (See ⑤, Figure 9.3.)

26 These covenants cannot, and do not, guarantee a marketable title. The
27 clauses are only as good as the grantor. If the grantor is insolvent or
28 unreliable, the covenants are of little or no value.

FIGURE 9.3   Example of a General Warranty Deed

SPACE ABOVE THIS LINE FOR PROCESSING DATA ——————|————— SPACE ABOVE THIS LINE FOR RECORDING DATA ———

This Warranty Deed, ①*Made the* _____ *day of* _____ , _____ , *by*

_____ ,

hereinafter called the Grantor, to _____ ,

whose post office address is _____ ,

hereinafter called the Grantee.

(Wherever used herein the terms "Grantor" and "Grantee" include all the parties to this instrument and the heirs, legal representatives, and assigns of individuals, and the successors and assigns of corporations, wherever the context so admits or requires.)

Witnesseth, *That the Grantor, for and in consideration of the sum of $ _____ and other valuable considerations, receipt whereof is hereby acknowledged, hereby grants, bargains, sells, aliens, remises, releases, conveys and confirms unto the Grantee all that certain land, situate in* _____ *County, State of* _____ , *viz:* ②

Together, *with all the tenements, hereditaments and appurtenances thereto belonging or in anywise appertaining.* **To Have and to Hold,** *the same in fee simple forever.* ③   ④

And *the Grantor hereby covenants with said grantee that the grantor is lawfully seized of said land in fee simple; that the grantor has good right and lawful authority to sell and convey said land, and hereby warrants the title to said land and will defend the same against the lawful claims of all persons whomsoever; and that said land is free of all encumbrances, except taxes accruing subsequent to December 20,   .* ⑤

In Witness Whereof, *the said Grantor has signed and sealed these presents the day and year first above written.*

Signed, sealed and delivered in the presence of:

_____	_____ **L.S.**
Witness Signature (as to first Grantor)	Grantor Signature
_____	_____
Printed Name	Printed Name
_____	_____
Witness Signature (as to first Grantor)	Post Office Address
_____	
Printed Name	
_____	_____ **L.S.**
Witness Signature (as to Co-Grantor, if any)	Co-Grantor Signature, (if any)
_____	_____
Printed Name	Printed Name
_____	_____
Witness Signature (as to Co-Grantor, if any)	Post Office Address
_____	
Printed Name	

STATE OF _____)

COUNTY OF _____)

I hereby Certify that on this day, before me, an officer duly authorized to administer oaths and take acknowledgments, personally appeared _____

known to me to be the person_____ described in and who executed the foregoing instrument, who acknowledged before me that _____ executed the same, and an oath was not taken. (Check one:) ❑ Said person(s) is/are personally known to me. ❑ Said person(s) provided the following type of identification: _____

NOTARY RUBBER STAMP SEAL

Witness my hand and official seal in the County and State last aforesaid

this _____ day of _____ , A.D. _____

_____
Notary Signature

_____
Printed Name

©Form Design, Seminole Paper & Printing Co., Inc., 1994

This form included with permission of Seminole Paper & Printing Co., Inc., 60 W. 3rd Street, Miami, Florida 33101.

STATUTORY DEEDS

There are four types of statutory deeds: (1) quitclaim deed, (2) bargain and sale deed, (3) special warranty deed, and (4) general warranty deed. These deeds are called *statutory deeds* because the law provides for a short form of deed in which the covenants or warranties mentioned are implied to exist just as if they were written out in complete and detailed form. These four deeds are described below, starting with the one that has the fewest covenants and warranties (quitclaim deed) and ending with the one that has the most covenants and warranties (general warranty deed).

Quitclaim deed.   The **quitclaim deed** is a deed by which the grantor quitclaims unto the grantee all of *his or her* rights, title, and interest to the property. The grantor makes no warranties about the quality or extent of the title being conveyed. This form of deed is useful for clearing existing or potential *clouds* on the title. A cloud might be some unreleased lien or encumbrance that may superficially impair or cast doubt on the title's validity, such as a recorded mortgage that has been paid in full, but with no satisfaction of mortgage recorded. To clear the title of these possible trouble spots, the grantor releases any claim or interest he or she may have in the property. Instead of the usual wording *grants, bargains, and sells*, the quitclaim deed uses the words *remise, release, and quitclaim*. This allows the grantor to sign a deed transferring any and all interests he or she may have, without claiming ownership of any right of title whatsoever. The grantor does not warrant to defend the title interest conveyed or to transfer a valid interest. When a quitclaim deed cannot be acquired, a *suit to quiet title* usually produces a clear title.

Bargain and sale deed.   Normally, a bargain and sale deed consists of the granting clause, habendum clause, and covenant of seisin. However, in the *bargain and sale deed*, the grantor does not covenant or warrant to defend the title against any future claims or attacks on the title. The bargain and sale deed is sufficient to convey all the title the grantor has, but it does little to protect the grantee from clouds or claims on the title.

Special warranty deed.   Another type of deed is the *special warranty deed*, a deed in which the grantor does not warrant the title (assume any responsibility for the title) in any way or manner except against acts by the grantor or the grantor's representative. In other words, the grantor guarantees that nothing has been done to encumber or cloud the title during his or her ownership. This is the type of deed that most large corporations use when selling property.

General warranty deed.   The **general warranty deed** (or sometimes the *full covenant and warranty deed*) contains all the covenants and warranties available to give the grantee every possible future guarantee to title protection. In addition to the covenant of seisin and the covenant against encumbrances, the general warranty deed contains three unique covenants:

1. **Quiet enjoyment** guarantees peaceful possession undisturbed by claims of title.

689, F.S.

2. **Further assurance** guarantees the grantor will sign and deliver any legal instrument that might be required to make the title good in the future.

3. **Warranty forever** guarantees the grantor will forever warrant and defend the grantee's title against all lawful claims. (See Figure 9.3.)

SPECIAL PURPOSE DEEDS

Legal problems may be encountered when property is being conveyed from one owner to another. Several types of deeds have evolved to provide solutions for these and other situations in which an owner cannot or refuses to sign a deed.

When an owner cannot sign a deed.   Under certain circumstances, a property owner may be unable to sign a deed. Three types of deeds used in such cases are:

1. **Personal representative's deed.** A *personal representative* is an individual either appointed by will or by order of a court to settle the estate of a deceased person. The testator typically identifies a trusted person to serve as personal representative who will be charged with carrying out the provisions of the will under the direction of the court in which the will was probated. If an owner should die without leaving a will, the probate court having jurisdiction will appoint a personal representative to settle the decedent's affairs. A personal representative's deed is used to formalize and record the transfer of title. It should show the full consideration paid for the property and contain a covenant of no encumbrances.

733.301, F.S.
475.011(1), F.S.

2. **Guardian's deed.** A *guardian* acts on behalf of a minor (or other ward) and is also a fiduciary. Normally, the permission of a court is required for a guardian to sell or convey property belonging to the minor. When authorized by the courts, a guardian's deed legally conveys the minor's property.

3. **Committee's deed.** One of the essentials of a valid deed is a competent grantor. When an owner is declared legally incompetent or is committed to an institution, a committee is often appointed by the court to administer the affairs of the incompetent. The committee functions under the direction of the court if conveying or disposing of the incompetent's estate. All members of a committee must sign the deed. A committee also must adhere to fiduciary disclosure requirements.

When an owner does not sign a deed.   All foreclosures on real property in Florida must follow prescribed legal procedures that eventually lead to a public auction of the property. The *final judgment* given to the lender that authorizes sale of the property usually requires that the sale be under the direction of the clerk of the circuit court. A *certificate of title,* prepared by the plaintiff's (lender's) attorney and given as a result of judicial foreclosure, will show ownership and any outstanding liens and encumbrances. No covenants are given, and the

1 buyer assumes all risks for title defects. Extreme caution should be taken
2 when purchasing property at a foreclosure sale.

Back Tax ect.

LEGAL REQUIREMENTS

4 If a sale contract does not specify the type of deed to be given by the seller,
5 Florida law requires that the property be conveyed by a general warranty
6 deed. A *deed* is an instrument used to convey (transfer) an estate or interest
7 in real property (it is a conveyance instrument). Transfer of title to
8 property is not effective until the conveyance instrument (usually a deed)
9 is delivered to and accepted by the grantee.

10 Placing a deed on record with the clerk of the circuit court gives the
11 world notice of true and current ownership of the property. To be
12 recorded, the deed must first be acknowledged by the grantor and
13 witnessed, and that acknowledgment must then be certified by a
14 notary public.

15 In Florida, all deeds to real property are subject to a state documentary
16 stamp tax. (See Chapter 14 for this and other state stamp tax calculations.)

■ OWNERSHIP LIMITATIONS AND RESTRICTIONS

18 The two general categories of restrictions are *public* (government) and
19 *private.* Both have several subcategories of restrictions and limitations.
20 Figure 9.4 illustrates the kinds of ownership restrictions.

PUBLIC OR GOVERNMENT RESTRICTIONS ON OWNERSHIP

22 The three most important subcategories of public or governmental
23 limitations on ownership of real property are (1) police power,
24 (2) eminent domain, and (3) right of taxation.

TO REMEMBER	
Government Restrictions	

P	Police power
E	Eminent domain
T	Taxation
E	*Escheat - Pg. 169.*

25 **Police power.**   The U.S. and state constitutions provide for the
26 government to apply any restrictions deemed necessary in the interest of
27 the general health, welfare, or safety of its citizens. Under police power,
28 the use of real property may be regulated. From these powers come the
29 many ordinances and regulations governing zoning, building codes,
30 health standards, city planning, and rent controls. State governments
31 have delegated the exercise of police powers to county, city, and local
32 governments. **Police power** represents the broadest power of the
33 government to limit or regulate the rights of property owners. The
34 owner's use and occupancy of the property can be restricted without any

FIGURE 9.4   Ownership Restrictions

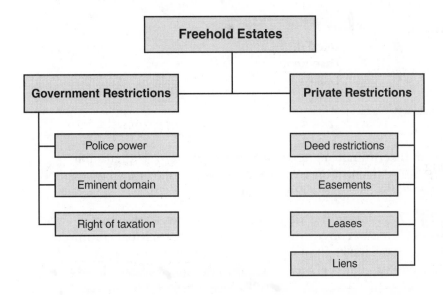

---

1 compensation to the owner whatsoever. Zoning, for example, can prevent
2 an owner from utilizing property in the most profitable manner, and the
3 owner can't recover from the government lost revenue caused
4 by the zoning.

5 **Eminent domain.**   Eminent domain is referred to as a *taking for just*
6 *compensation.* The constitutions of the U.S. government and state
7 governments grant the power (right) to take private property for a public
8 use. In Florida, if an owner believes a fair price was not offered for the
9 property taken, he or she may go to court and ask a jury, in a
10 condemnation proceeding, to settle the question of what constitutes a
11 fair price.

12 **Right of property taxation.**   This power was specifically limited to the
13 various states by the U.S. Constitution. Citizens pay for the benefits and
14 protection provided by the various levels of government. Property is
15 usually the primary basis for local taxation. Local taxing authorities can
16 foreclose on real property for nonpayment of taxes.

17 **PRIVATE RESTRICTIONS ON OWNERSHIP**

18 Private limitations on ownership of real property usually include deed
19 restrictions, easements, leases, and liens.

20 **Deed restrictions.**   Probably the most common and the broadest
21 restrictions to private property ownership are deed restrictions and
22 restrictive covenants. **Deed restrictions** are a part of the deed and affect a
23 particular property. **Restrictive covenants** are recorded along with the
24 subdivision plat and usually affect an entire subdivision. The limitations
25 may be either perpetual (continue indefinitely) or for a specified period
26 of time. While the restrictions are in effect, they restrict the use of the
27 property for the first owner and all subsequent owners. Any restriction

TO REMEMBER

Private Restrictions

D	**D**eed restrictions
E	**E**asements
L	**L**eases
L	**L**iens

that does not discriminate against race, color, religion, sex, national origin, families with children, handicap, or public policy may be included in a deed (or in the restrictive covenants).

Easements.   An **easement** is a right to use an owner's land for a specific use. Easements do not convey ownership (possession). Most commonly, an easement entails the right of a person (or the public) to use the land of another in a certain manner, such as utility easements, railroad right-of-ways, and ingress-egress easements. Easements can be terminated by agreement, abandonment, or by court order. Some easements are created by a written agreement between the parties that establishes the easement right. Two such examples are *easement appurtenant* and *easement in gross.*

- **Easement appurtenant.** This type of easement benefits an adjacent parcel of land. An easement appurtenant allows an owner the use of a neighbor's property, such as the right to cross parcel A to reach parcel B.

  Share a Driveway.

- **Easement in gross.** This type of easement benefits an individual or a business entity and is not related to a specific adjacent parcel. For example, utility easements are easements in gross. The easement allows the utility company to access the land, trim trees, and so forth to maintain utility equipment.

Certain types of easements must be created through a court of law. Two such examples are *easement by necessity* and *easement by prescription.*

- **Easement by necessity.** If a landowner subdivides land, conveying part of it in a way that causes a parcel to be landlocked, the court may authorize creation of an easement by necessity to allow property owners to enter and exit their landlocked property.

- **Easement by prescription.** This type of easement is created by longtime usage. Such easements are created and must be recognized after 20 years of open, continuous, uninterrupted use. (Note the similarity to adverse possession; however, the adverse user in an easement by prescription acquires only an easement and not title.)

  Squating for road only ect.

Unlike an easement, an **encroachment** is the unauthorized use of another's property. For example, a fence or garage located beyond a legitimate boundary without the owner's consent is an infringement or intrusion on property. When an encroachment has continued for more than seven years, it may create an *implied easement.* If encroachments are not known and a contract for sale is created before a survey reveals that one exists, the title might be unmarketable and the contract might be voidable.

Leases.   While a lease constitutes an interest in real property, it does not convey ownership. A lease is an agreement between the landlord (lessor) and a renter (lessee) that grants the lessee the right of possession and use of the property for a specified time in return for compensation. Florida law requires that a lease for more than one year be in writing and be signed to be enforceable. Any oral contract or agreement between the lessor and lessee is legally a *tenancy at will*. In fact, all oral leases and all written leases that do not fix a definite date for termination are tenancies at will. Leases for one year or less are enforceable, even when not in writing, if the terms can be verified and a termination date was agreed on. The five requirements of a valid lease are as follows: (1) names and signatures (if the lease is for more than one year) of the lessor and lessee, (2) legal capacity of the lessor and lessee to enter into a contract, (3) consideration, (4) the term of the tenancy, and (5) the property identification. A lease for real property for an indefinite term or for longer than one year must be in writing and signed by the lessor, lessee, and two witnesses.

Leases should be prepared by an attorney experienced in their preparation. Two witnesses must sign the lease as verification of its proper execution if it is for more than one year. Florida Supreme Court-approved formats for residential leases of one year or less may be completed by nonattorneys. Fill-in-the-blank lease forms approved by the court should be used by licensees. Leases of longer duration should be completed only by attorneys. Attorneys are authorized to draft leases on someone else's behalf. A property owner *may not* delegate the authority to draft a lease to a nonattorney. Long-term leases should be recorded in the public records.

Types of leases.   The major characteristics of common types of leases are described below. (See also Figure 9.5.)

- **Gross lease.** The tenant (lessee) pays a fixed (base) rent and the landlord (lessor) pays all expenses associated with the property, including taxes, insurance, and repairs. Most residential and office building leases are gross leases.

- **Net lease.** The tenant (lessee) pays fixed rent plus property costs such as maintenance and operating expenses (taxes, insurance, and utilities). Net leases are typically used on commercial property. The terms, *net, net-net,* and *triple-net* are often used in commercial real estate. The number of "nets" indicates that the tenant is assuming more and more of the expenses. In a triple-net lease, the tenant pays all operating and other expenses in addition to the fixed rent. These expenses include taxes, insurance, assessments, maintenance, utilities, and other charges associated with the property.

- **Percentage lease.** The tenant pays rent based on gross sales received by doing business on the leased property. Percentage leases are common with large retail stores, especially in shopping centers. A percentage lease can be either net or gross.

FIGURE 9.5   Types of Lease Agreements

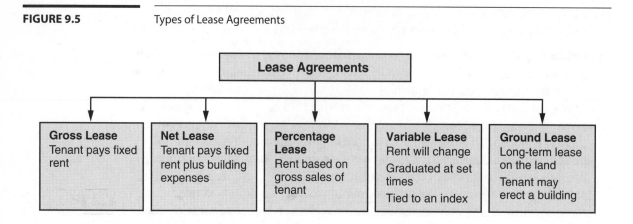

- **Variable lease.** The tenant pays specified rent increases at set future dates. A variable lease is usually tied to an index, such as the consumer price index (CPI).

- **Ground lease.** The tenant leases the land only and erects a building on the land. Ground leases (or *land leases*) are long-term leases that will run for terms up to 99 years. Ground leases are characterized by separate ownership of the land and building(s).

Assignment and sublease.   The rights of a tenant are assignable unless specifically prohibited in the lease. An *assignment* of a lease occurs when a lessee assigns to another party all of the leased property for the full remaining portion of the lease. A *sublease* is used when the lessee assigns less than the entire property or assigns all of the property for less than the full remaining period. When subleasing (also called *subrogation* and *subordination* of space), the original tenant remains obligated for contracted responsibilities.

Sale or transfer of title of rental property.   When a leased property is sold, the lease is binding on the new owner. The Florida Residential Landlord and Tenant Act provides that when a residential rental property is sold or the title of the rental property is otherwise transferred from one owner to another, the tenants' security deposits and advance rents must be transferred to the new owner. If the property owner changes the designated rental agent, all security deposits or advance rents being held by the former rental agent must be transferred to the new agent with an accounting showing the amounts to be credited on each tenant's behalf.

Liens.   A **lien** is a right given to a creditor or a unit of government to have a debt satisfied out of some specific property belonging to a debtor. (See Figure 9.6.) Liens can entitle the holder (lienor) to have property sold, regardless of the desires of the owner (lienee). As a debtor, the property owner has no choice but to pay the lienor or have the property disposed of by the courts in order to satisfy the lien. A lien is an encumbrance on the title to real property. However, not all encumbrances on property are

FIGURE 9.6   Liens

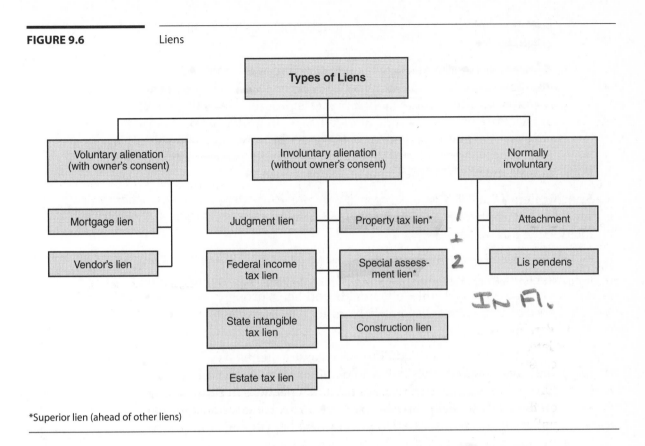

*Superior lien (ahead of other liens)

1 liens. Encumbrances can also be easements, covenants, deed restrictions,
2 encroachments, and governmental regulations.

GENERAL AND SPECIFIC LIENS

4 Liens are broadly classified as voluntary or involuntary. *Voluntary liens*
5 are ones the owner places against the property to secure payment of a
6 long-term debt, such as a mortgage lien. *Involuntary liens* are created by
7 law to protect interests of persons who have valid monetary claims
8 against the owner of real property. Liens are further divided into two
9 major classifications: general liens and specific liens.

10 **General lien.**   A **general lien** is not restricted to one property but may
11 affect all properties of a debtor. General liens include judgment liens,
12 income tax liens, and estate tax liens.

13 • *Judgment lien.* A judgment lien is an involuntary lien attaching to
14   real property when a judgment is obtained against the owner. A
15   judgment lien is a general lien on all property of the debtor (unless
16   specifically exempt by law) in the county where the judgment was
17   recorded into the public records. In Florida, a judgment lien
18   remains a lien on real property until it has been paid or expires by
19   passage of time.

20 • *Income tax lien.* Florida does not have a state income tax. However,
21   failure to pay federal income taxes can result in a lien on property
22   of the delinquent taxpayer. A federal tax lien, once filed, becomes a
23   lien on all property owned by the taxpayer at the time of filing as

well as on all future property acquired by the taxpayer until the lien is satisfied.

- *Estate tax lien.* Federal estate tax liens are imposed against a decedent's taxable assets automatically upon death. They do not require recording or filing. The tax rate is progressive as the worth of the estate increases. While Florida has no inheritance tax, it does have an estate tax designed to collect up to the maximum allowable federal estate tax credit for state death taxes paid. If Florida did not receive this tax, the federal government would.

Specific lien.   Liens classified as specific do not affect all of the debtor's property but apply only to certain specified property. **Specific liens** include the following:

- *Property tax and special assessment lien.* Municipal governments have been delegated the authority to levy real property taxes and special tax assessments. Unlike other debts and liens, property taxes and special assessments become liens as soon as the assessment is complete.

  The courts have ruled that special assessments may be levied only against properties that are benefited by an increase in value. Special assessment liens are ahead of private liens in priority and second only to real property tax liens. (Property taxes and special assessments are discussed in greater detail in Chapter 18.)

- *Mortgage lien.* This is a lien voluntarily placed on real property by a borrower (mortgagor) who pledges his or her property as security to the lender (mortgagee). The date the mortgage is filed and recorded with the clerk of the circuit court establishes the priority of the lien against other claims on the property. If the mortgagor defaults, the mortgagee can proceed to force sale of the property to satisfy the debt.

- *Vendor's lien.* If a buyer of property (vendee) is unable to make the full down payment required, a seller (vendor) frequently will allow a *purchase-money mortgage* to make up the amount of money the buyer is unable to produce. Actually, any portion of the sale price remaining unpaid to the vendor creates a vendor's lien. This is an equitable lien of the grantor (seller) on the land conveyed in the amount of the unpaid purchase price. A vendor's lien is enforceable only against the party obtaining title from the vendor. It does not apply against later purchasers unless a written mortgage has been executed and placed in the public records. A valid vendor's lien is enforceable by foreclosure. Priority is established by the recording date of the purchase-money mortgage.

- *Construction lien.* This lien is based on the principle of law called *unjust enrichment.* Unjust enrichment means that property owners may not use the labor or material of another party to add value to their property without reimbursement to that party. A **construction lien** (or *mechanic's, materialman's,* or *laborer's lien*) is a statutory right of material suppliers or laborers to place a lien on property that has been improved by their supplies and/or labor.

1 This lien must be filed with the clerk of the circuit court not later
2 than 90 days after the last supplies are delivered or the last labor is
3 performed in order to assume priority over any mortgage liens
4 created after the first material/work appeared on the property
5 affected. This, in effect, allows a construction lien filed after work is
6 completed to become retroactive to the first delivery of material or
7 first day of work. If a mortgage is placed on the property during the
8 period when construction is in progress, a lien filed after
9 construction is completed will precede the mortgage in priority.
10 Once filed, a construction lien is effective for one year. The party
11 who places the lien on the property must initiate court action to
12 collect the debt during the lien's one-year life or forfeit the
13 privilege. This lien may be discharged or canceled by expiration of
14 time, payment of the debt, or court action through a suit.

15 ## ■ SUMMARY

16 Title to real property represents ownership of that collection of rights called
17 an estate. A deed is the written instrument used to transfer title to real
18 property. A variety of deeds can be used to meet specific circumstances and
19 conditions. Real property ownership, like the ownership of all things, has
20 limitations placed upon it. The two general categories of restrictions to
21 ownership are public and private. While a real estate broker or sales
22 associate is allowed by Florida Statute to draw listing and sale contracts,
23 he or she is not allowed to draw up a deed, unless conveying property in
24 which he or she owns an interest.

Note to Readers

A real estate broker or sales associate is allowed by Florida statutes to draw listing and sale contracts, but not deeds, unless conveying property in which he or she owns an interest. In addition, only residential lease forms previously discussed may legally be completed by licensees. The drawing of any other lease or of a deed may be construed as the unlawful practice of law.

■ REVIEW QUESTIONS

1. Which type of easement gives an electric company the authority to install and maintain electric power lines?
   A. In gross
   B. Prescription
   C. Appurtenant
   D. Implied

2. Title to real property legally transfers from grantor to grantee when the
   A. deed is signed.
   B. deed is recorded.
   C. deed is voluntarily delivered and accepted.
   D. proper amount of tax is paid on the deed.

3. Courts at various levels have ruled that
   A. constructive notice is superior to actual notice.
   B. actual notice is superior to constructive notice.
   C. neither constructive notice nor actual notice is required.
   D. constructive notice and actual notice have equal legal priority.

4. A 92-year-old man is being forced from his home because of a governmental taking. The home has been in his family for four generations. What recourse, if any, does he have?
   A. He can file an injunction to stop the taking.
   B. He can pay the delinquent property taxes to prevent the foreclosure.
   C. He may request a condemnation proceeding to protest the amount of compensation being offered by the governmental body.
   D. He may do all of the above.

5. For a deed to be valid, a competent
   A. grantor, grantee, and two witnesses must sign the instrument.
   B. grantor and two witnesses must sign the instrument.
   C. grantee and two witnesses must sign the instrument.
   D. grantee only must sign the instrument.

6. The type or form of deed most commonly used to clear clouds on the title of real property is the
   A. general warranty deed.
   B. special warranty deed.
   C. bargain and sale deed.
   D. quitclaim deed.

7. If the sale contract does not specify the type of deed to be delivered, the seller is required to provide a
   A. general warranty deed.
   B. special warranty deed.
   C. bargain and sale deed.
   D. quitclaim deed.

8. The process of taking property under the power of eminent domain is called
   A. escheat
   B. foreclosure.
   C. condemnation.
   D. voluntary alienation.

9. The type of deed in which the grantor does not warrant the title in any manner except against his or her acts or the acts of his or her representatives is called a
    A. general warranty deed.
    B. special warranty deed.
    C. bargain and sale deed.
    D. quitclaim deed.

10. The covenant against encumbrances in a deed is designed to guarantee that the
    A. grantor has not encumbered the property in any manner except as noted on the deed.
    B. grantee is responsible for any unpaid encumbrances.
    C. grantee has not encumbered the property.
    D. grantor will not encumber the property.

Public records

11. The purpose of recording a deed is to
    A. comply with real estate license law.
    B. effect the transfer of ownership.
    C. give actual notice of ownership.
    D. give constructive notice of ownership.

12. A valid instrument of conveyance of real property must be
    A. recorded.
    B. signed by a competent grantor.
    C. signed by a competent grantee.
    D. notarized.

13. The seisin clause in a deed specifies
    A. the type of estate being conveyed.
    B. the improvements being transferred with the land.
    C. the rights reserved by the grantor.
    D. that the grantor actually owns the property and has the right to sell it.

14. The deed that contains the covenant in which the grantor guarantees that he or she will forever be responsible for warranting title and will defend the title and possession is a
    A. general warranty deed.
    B. special warranty deed.
    C. public patent deed.
    D. bargain and sale deed.

15. The provision in a deed that names the parties and contains the granting clause is the
    A. premises.
    B. encumbrance clause.
    C. habendum clause.
    D. seisin clause.

16. An owner placed a condition in the deed that stipulated that a commercial building could not be erected on the property until at least the year 2010. This is an example of
    A. police power.
    B. a deed restriction.
    C. involuntary alienation.
    D. governmental restriction on ownership.

17. An example of an encumbrance on title to real property is
    A. an easement.
    B. a deed restriction.
    C. a lien.
    D. All of the above are encumbrances.

18. When a lis pendens is filed properly with the county clerk, it becomes a type of
    A. attachment on the subject property.
    B. vendor's lien.
    C. constructive notice.
    D. easement by prescription.

19. Which lien is first in priority?
    A. A property tax lien effective on January 1, 2005
    B. A special assessment lien certified on December 31, 2004
    C. A first mortgage lien filed on July 15, 2005
    D. A construction lien filed on November 30, 2004

20. The complete successive history of a parcel, from the time it was conveyed from a government to a private owner to today, is referred to as
    A. an abstract of title.
    B. title insurance.
    C. warranty forever.
    D. a chain of title.

21. Mr. and Mrs. Lee signed a contract to purchase a home in a residential subdivision. When the Lees had the lot surveyed before closing, they discovered that the contractor had built the neighbor's garage three inches inside the west boundary of their lot. The garage in its present location is an example of a(n)
    A. deed restriction.
    B. easement by prescription.
    C. implied easement.
    D. encroachment.

22. When a pathway to a property has been used continuously and without interruption for more than 20 years, it creates an
    A. implied easement.
    B. encroachment.
    C. alienation by adverse possession.
    D. easement by prescription.

23. Soon after Michael's death a deed was discovered behind a brick in the basement wall of his home. The deed is for Michael's home and it deeded the property to a charitable organization. Michael is survived by his son Andrew, who discovered the deed. Michael died intestate. Based on this information, the house belongs to the

Heirs

 A. state because Michael died intestate.
 B. charitable organization because the deed conveyed ownership to it.
 C. legal heir because the deed was never delivered and accepted.
 D. legal heir because the deed was not signed by the grantee.

24. The owner's title insurance policy is
 A. issued for an amount no greater than the purchase price of the property and is transferable.
 B. issued for an amount no greater than the purchase price of the property and is not transferable.
 C. a separate policy for the amount of the unpaid balance of the mortgage and is transferable.
 D. a separate policy for the amount of the unpaid balance of the mortgage and is not transferable.

25. Which statement concerning easements is FALSE?
 A. An easement is a right to use an owner's property for a specific use.
 B. An easement is a nonpossessory interest.
 C. An easement is unauthorized use of an owner's property.
 D. An easement is a type of encumbrance.

CHAPTER 10

Legal Descriptions

■ KEY TERMS

base lines

government survey
   system

legal description

lot and block

metes-and-bounds
   description

monument

patent

point of beginning (POB)

principal meridians

range

section

township

■ OVERVIEW

This Chapter introduces the various methods used to locate and describe real property. Basic to the real estate business is a working knowledge of legal land descriptions. Unless property can be located accurately, the best of contracts and the combined efforts of the most knowledgeable brokers in the world will be defeated. Purchasers (and title companies and lenders, if applicable) want to be certain of the exact location, size, and shape of the property to be conveyed. In addition, once a property has been located accurately, that particular parcel must then be described to prepare deeds, mortgages, and other instruments affecting transfer of ownership.

After completing this Chapter, the student should be able to:

- explain the necessity for legal land descriptions;

- list and explain the various methods of describing real property;

- calculate the number of acres in a parcel described by the government survey system;

- identify the location of a township by township and range number; and

- number the sections of a township.

■ PURPOSES OF LEGAL DESCRIPTIONS

The primary purpose of a **legal description** is to describe a particular piece of property in a way that uniquely identifies that parcel from any other parcel. A legal description is so specific that given only the legal description, a surveyor can locate and identify a given parcel.

Before land could be conveyed it had to be surveyed to establish the parcel's boundaries and to create the legal description. A **survey** is a drawing of a parcel of land showing its boundary lines and includes the legal description of the property. (See Figure 10.1.) Surveys have been around since the beginning of land ownership.

There are four additional purposes of surveying property and developing legal descriptions for each parcel:

1. Current and accurate boundary information required to write a legal description is obtained.

2. The exact quantity of area within a described tract, whether it is described in square miles, acres, or square feet, is established.

3. Boundaries that may have become lost or obliterated are reestablished.

4. Data required to divide a large tract into smaller units for development and sale are obtained.

■ THE EVOLUTION OF LEGAL DESCRIPTIONS

The first private land ownership began when the government conveyed land to private individuals. A **patent** (the original deed) is a certificate issued by the federal or a state government that transfers land to a private individual. In colonial times, if settlers wanted to purchase land they would apply for a patent to the land, pay the purchase price, and hire a surveyor to mark the boundaries and create the legal description of the land. In those days the metes-and-bounds method of legal description was used throughout the 13 colonies. The settlers would take the survey and patent to the county courthouse and record their purchases.

Following the Revolutionary War, the new federal government became the owner of all the land previously claimed by England. The government wanted an efficient way to survey all of the newly acquired land. The government chose a massive undertaking known as the Government Survey System which was based on a large grid of parallel lines.

■ TYPES OF LEGAL DESCRIPTIONS

There are three types of legal descriptions used today: (1) *metes-and-bounds*, (2) *government survey system,* and (3) *lot and block descriptions.*

FIGURE 10.1   Boundary Survey

BOUNDARY SURVEY
–IN–
SECTION 10, TOWNSHIP 9 SOUTH, RANGE 19 EAST
ALACHUA COUNTY, FLORIDA

LEGEND:

F.M. = FIELD MEASUREMENT
( ) = PLAT MEASUREMENT
O = FOUND REBAR & CAP SIZE & NO. SHOWN ON PLAN
● = FOUND NAIL & DISK LS#4788 P.C.P.
◉ = DRAINAGE MANHOLE
P.C.P. = PERMANENT CONTROL POINT
P.T. = POINT OF TANGENCY
P.C. = POINT OF CURVATURE
P.S.I. = POINT OF STREET INTERSECTION
Ⓔ = ELECTRIC TRANSFORMER
Ⓒ = CABLE TELEVISION PEDESTAL
⊠ = WATER METER
C/S = CONCRETE SLAB
T.B.M. = TEMPORARY BENCH MARK
⊠ = GAS METER
⊠ = ELECTRIC METER
A/C = AIR CONDITIONER
R/W = RIGHT OF WAY
PLS = PROFESSIONAL LICENSED SURVEYOR
LB = LICENSED BUSINESS
R.P. = RADIUS POINT

LEGAL DESCRIPTION:

LOT 26, BLUES CREEK UNIT – 4, A PORTION OF A PLANNED
UNIT DEVELOPMENT AS RECORDED IN PLAT BOOK "S". PAGE 3,
OF THE PUBLIC RECORDS OF ALACHUA COUNTY, FLORIDA.

SURVEYOR'S NOTES:

1. THIS SURVEY WAS BASED FROM FOUND MONUMENTATION
WHICH, IN THIS SURVEYOR'S OPINION BEST REPRESENTS
THE ORIGINAL SURVEY FOR THIS TRACT OF LAND.

2. BEARINGS AS SHOWN HEREON HAVE BEEN BASED FROM A BEARING
OF N15° 40' 45"E, AS SHOWN FOR THE CENTER LINE OF N. W. 53RD. WAY
ON THE RECORD PLAT OF BLUES CREEK UNIT – 4.

3. THE MEASUREMENTS FOR THIS SURVEY WERE MADE IN ACCORDANCE
WITH THE UNITED STATES STANDARD.

4. THIS SURVEYOR HAS REVIEWED THE MAPS ISSUED BY THE FEDERAL
EMERGENCY MANAGEMENT AGENCY FOR THE NATIONAL FLOOD INSURANCE
PROGRAM; AND IT HAS BEEN DETERMINED FROM THESE MAPS THAT THIS
PARCEL LIES IN ZONE C – AREAS OF MINIMAL FLOODING. COMMUNITY
PANEL NO. 120001 0275 A DATED SEPTEMBER 28, 1984.

Monument. No good in FL.

DESCRIPTION BY METES-AND-BOUNDS

The **metes-and-bounds description** is the oldest type of survey method. Today, surveyors use computer software and laser equipment to create the most accurate surveys possible. The metes-and-bounds method is used for both regular and irregular shaped parcels. Metes refers to *distance* and bounds refers to *direction*.

A metes-and-bounds description begins at an exact starting point, called a **point of beginning (POB).** The POB must be accurate; otherwise the entire description is in error. A reader who understands the metes-and-bounds method can draw the boundaries of the parcel from the description. Starting at the POB, the first boundary is determined from the legal description that indicates the direction and the distance to the first corner of the parcel, followed by another direction and distance to a second corner, and so on, eventually returning to the POB so that the parcel is enclosed within its boundaries. The surveyor identifies each corner of the parcel with a visible marker called a **monument.** Surveyors in colonial times often used objects found on the site as monuments, such as "the large oak tree." Today monuments are made of concrete, iron, or brass, and they are carefully placed by the U.S. Army Corps of Engineers or trained private land surveyors.

The direction of a boundary line is expressed using compass directions. Distances are measured in feet, usually to the nearest one-hundredth of a foot. Plotting a metes-and-bounds description is not as difficult as it might appear. The POB and *all* turning points (corners of the parcel) should be regarded as being the exact center of a circle.

A compass has four primary directions: north, south, east, and west. If we draw a straight line connecting north and south, and a second line connecting east and west, the circle is divided into four quarters or *quadrants.* (See Drawing A in Figure 10.2.) The line running north and south is the *primary reference line.* Metes-and-bounds descriptions will always begin with either north or south followed by a certain number of degrees, up to a maximum of 90 degrees. The direction that follows the number of degrees indicates whether the direction is east or west of due north or south.

Let's begin by plotting *North 45 degrees East.* Using Drawing B in Figure 10.2, place your pencil in a vertical (north-south) position over the circle. The first word in the description "North" indicates that we will begin with north as our primary direction so our pencil lead should face upward (north). The second direction is "East" so rotate your pencil in an easterly direction (to the right on the drawing). How far is 45 degrees? It is half way between zero degrees (due north) and 90 degrees (due east). (Refer to Line A on Drawing B in Figure 10.2.)

The reason why the number of degrees cannot exceed 90 is that one would pass the point midway between north and south and begin to move toward the other primary reference direction. For example, let's plot *South 85 degrees West.* Begin with your pencil in a vertical (north-south) direction with the pencil lead facing south (downward). Move 85 degrees to the west (to the left on the drawing). Because 85 degrees approaches 90, we can draw a line very close to due west. (See line C on Drawing B in Figure 10.2.)

60 mi/60 Sec

FIGURE 10.2   Compass Directions

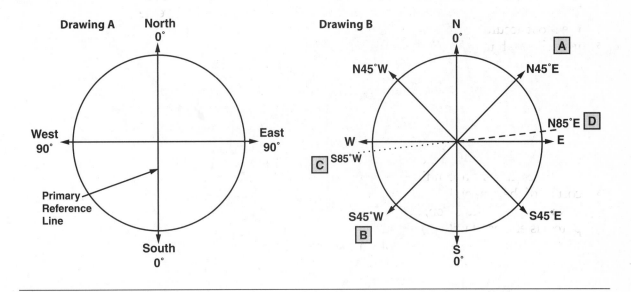

1   What would happen if you were to plot *North 95 degrees West?* (I
2 know—I just told you descriptions don't exceed 90 degrees, but let's see
3 why.) Again place your pencil in a vertical position, this time with the
4 pencil lead facing upward (north). If you rotate the pencil 95 degrees to
5 the west, notice that you pass due west (90°) and end up five degrees
6 into the lower half of the circle. Therefore, the description should have
7 begun with the primary reference direction of south. Let's rewrite the
8 description properly as *South 85 degrees West.* Place your pencil in the
9 vertical position with the pencil lead facing south. Rotate your pencil to
10 the west 85 degrees which is just five degrees shy of 90 degrees. We have
11 confirmed that the line is correctly labeled as *South 85 degrees West.*
12 (Refer to Line C on Drawing B in Figure 10.2.)

13   Notice that the opposite of S45°W (Line B in Figure 10.2) is N45°E
14 (Line A in Figure 10.2). The number of degrees does not change, only the
15 compass directions. What is the opposite of S85°W? It is N85°E. (Refer to
16 Line D in Figure 10.2.)

17   To be more accurate, directions are actually given in degrees, minutes,
18 and seconds. Minutes and seconds are more precise measurements
19 smaller than one degree. Each degree is divided into 60 minutes.
20 Therefore, half way between one degree and two degrees is one degree,
21 30 minutes. Each minute is then divided into 60 seconds. The symbols
22 for degrees (°), minutes ('), and seconds (") are used so that, for example,
23 fifteen degrees 25 minutes 20 seconds would be written 15°25'20".

DESCRIPTION BY GOVERNMENT SURVEY

25 Following the Revolutionary War, when the federal government decided
26 to open an area for settlement, it first commissioned a survey for that
27 entire area. The intent of the **Government Survey System (GSS)** (also
28 known as the *U.S. System of Rectangular Surveys,* and the *Public Domain
29 Survey*) was to create a large grid with every square of the grid uniquely

FIGURE 10.3   Government Survey System

13 colonies Do Not use Rectangle.

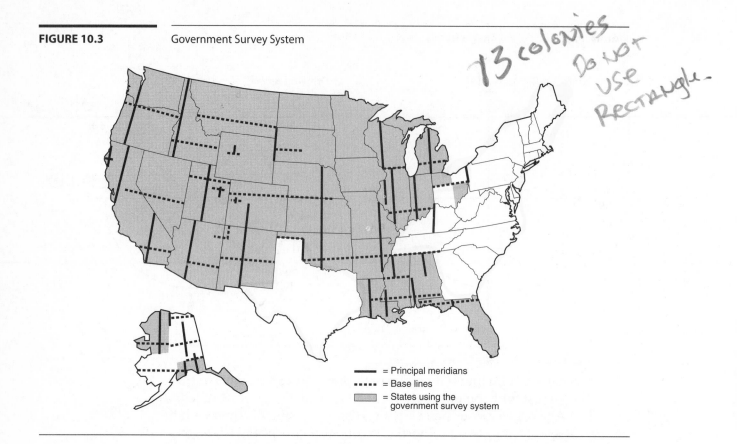

- = Principal meridians
- ⋯ = Base lines
- ▨ = States using the
  government survey system

1   identified. Over time, the government commissioned the GSS in 30 states
2   (other than the original 13 colonies and a few other states). The GSS is
3   based on intersecting lines. Once understood, the GSS is simple and
4   accurate and describes property in concise symbols and words, resulting
5   in a kind of land description shorthand.

6   **Principle meridian and base line.**   A beginning reference was
7   established in the center of the territory to be surveyed. The beginning
8   reference is the intersection of a north/south line called a **principal**
9   **meridian** and an east/west line called a **base line.** In all, 36 principal
10 meridians and base lines were established and named in the United
11 States. (See Figure 10.3 on page 198.)

12   The Tallahassee Principal Meridian and Base Line are the reference
13 lines that govern surveys in Florida. The Tallahassee Principal Meridian
14 was established in the early 1800s, and it intersects with the base line
15 in the city of Tallahassee, Florida. (See Figure 10.4.)

16 **Range.**   To create the grid system, surveyors established vertical (north/
17 south) *range lines* parallel to the principal meridian (PM) every six miles.
18 This resulted in a series of lines six miles apart on either side of the PM.
19 Each resulting six-mile-wide vertical (north/south) strip of land on either
20 side of the PM is called a **range.** (See Figure 10.5.)

21   Each range is numbered beginning at the PM. The first vertical
22 (north/south) strip of land to the east of the PM is numbered Range 1 East
23 or more concisely, R1E. (Refer to the shaded column labeled R1E in Figure
24 10.6.) The range numbers increase by one moving farther from the PM.
25 For example, the next range east of the PM is R2E, then R3E, and so on.

FIGURE 10.4   Map of Florida Showing Principal Meridian and Baseline

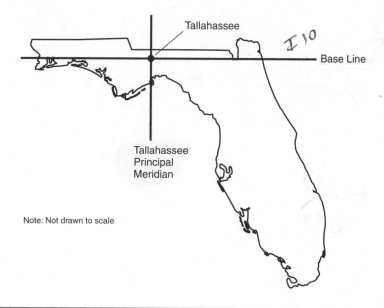

1   The numbering also begins with 1 to the west of the PM. The first range
2   west of the PM is R1W, then R2W, and so on.

3   **Township.**   The surveyors also established horizontal (east/west)
4   *township lines* parallel to the base line (BL) every six miles. This resulted in
5   a series of lines six miles apart on either side of the BL. Each resulting
6   six-mile-wide horizontal (east/west) strip of land on either side of the
7   BL is called a **township tier** or simply township. (To help remember that
8   township tiers are horizontal strips, think of tiers of a wedding cake.)
9   (See Figure 10.5.)

10   Each township tier is numbered beginning at the BL. The first
11   horizontal (east/west) strip of land above (north of) the base line is
12   numbered Township 1 North, or more concisely, T1N. The township line
13   numbers increase by one moving farther from the BL. For example, the
14   next township tier north of the BL is T2N, then T3N, and so on. The
15   numbering also begins with one below (south of) the base line. The first
16   township tier south of the BL is T1S (the shaded row in Figure 10.6), then
17   T2S, and so on.

TO REMEMBER

The directions of township lines and range lines may be
easily remembered by thinking of the words this way:

Township lines

Range lines

FIGURE 10.5 Map of Florida Showing Selected Range and Township Lines

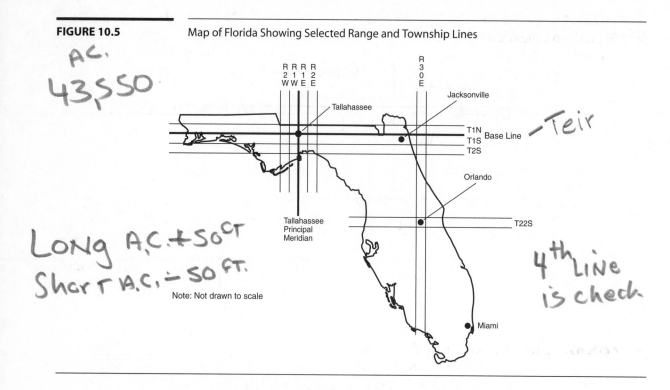

Note: Not drawn to scale

Handwritten annotations:
A.C. 43,550
Long A.C. ÷ 50 CT
Short A.C. ÷ 50 FT.
—Teir
4th Line is check

1   The resulting grid pattern formed by the crossing (or intersection) of
2 range lines and township lines produced a series of squares six miles
3 square known as **townships.** A township contains 36 square miles.

4   Note that the term *township* has two meanings: In addition to an (east/
5 west) strip of land north or south of a base line, the term also refers to the
6 square formed by the intersection of two range lines and two township
7 lines. Each 36-square-mile township (six miles on each side) is identified
8 by the strip of townships (the township tier) and the range in which it is
9 located. For example, T2S, R3E is located in the second tier of townships
10 south of the base line and the third range east of the principal meridian.
11 (Refer to the shaded township in Figure 10.6.)

FIGURE 10.6 T2S, R3E

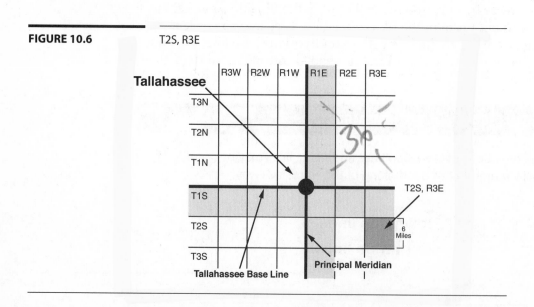

1 **Practice 1.**   Locate and shade in the townships numbered T2N, R2E and
2 T3S, R1W on the drawing below. (The solutions are at the end of this
3 Chapter.)

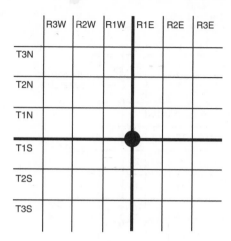

4 **Sections.**   Each township is further divided into 36 **sections.** Each
5 section is one square mile or 640 acres. Sections are numbered in an
6 S-pattern, beginning in the northeast (upper right) corner of the township
7 with section number 1. The sections are numbered from one in the
8 northeast corner and then consecutively to the west through section 6. The
9 section numbers then wrap around in an S-pattern. The second horizontal
10 row begins directly under section 6 and progresses west to east (left to
11 right) from 7 to 12. Section 13 is directly under section 12, and one moves
12 west (to the left) with section 18 last in that row. This method of
13 numbering is repeated until section number 36 is reached in the southeast,
14 or lower right, corner of every township. The numbering pattern of
15 sections repeats itself inside each township.

16 At first, this may seem odd to number sections this way, however, in the
17 1800s surveyors measured the one mile distances with metal chains and
18 walked the sections on foot. (To help remember the number system, think
19 of the pattern people usually walk when doing their weekly grocery
20 shopping at the supermarket as they go down one aisle and up another.)
21 (See Figure 10.7.)

22 In writing a legal description of a section, it is customary to show the
23 section number first, then the township tier number and direction, and
24 last the range number and direction. For example, *Section 36, Township 1*
25 *South, Range 1 West of the Tallahassee Principal Meridian and Base Line*
26 identifies Section 36 within the township that is located immediately
27 southwest of the intersection of the principal meridian and base line. It is
28 abbreviated to *Sec 36, T1S, R1W.* (Refer to the shaded Section 36 in
29 Figure 10.7.)

30 The survey of Lot 26 presented in Figure 10.1 is also identified as in
31 Section 10, Township 9 South, Range 19 East of Alachua County, Florida.

FIGURE 10.7   Sections in a Township

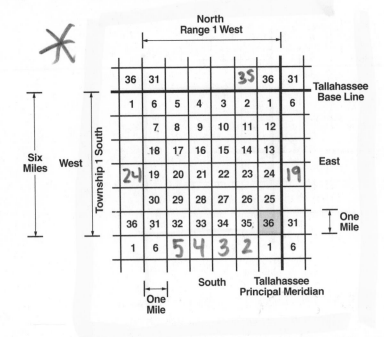

Homestead=
160 Ac.

1   **Practice 2.**   Complete numbering the sections in the township below.
2   Some of the section numbers have been provided. Fill in the missing
3   section numbers. (The solutions are at the end of this Chapter.)

After the war
Blacks got
40 Ac. + Mule.

4   **HOW TO USE THE GOVERNMENT SURVEY SYSTEM**

5   **Locating sections.**   Suppose you want to locate a section of land in
6   Florida, and this is the legal description given to you: "All of Section 36,
7   Township 1 South, Range 1 West, Tallahassee Principal Meridian and Base
8   Line." The numbers assigned to the township tier and range tell you
9   immediately that you are dealing with property very near Tallahassee
10 because the range (1 West) is the first six-mile segment immediately west
11 of the principal meridian. The tier of townships (1 South) must be the first
12 six-mile strip immediately south of the horizontal base line. Considering

1 how sections are numbered, Section 36 cannot be anywhere except in the
2 lower right corner of the township numbered T1S, R1W. Therefore, the
3 section you seek begins five miles south of the intersection of the
4 Tallahassee Principal Meridian and Base Line and immediately west of
5 the Tallahassee Principal Meridian.

Measures and Terms Associated with the Government Survey System

Check	A square 24 miles on each side created by intersecting guide meridians and correction lines; used to adjust the grid pattern of squares because of the curvature of the earth.
Township	A square 6 miles on each side (6 miles square) containing 36 square miles (36 sections); also an (east-west) strip of land north and south of a baseline (tier).
Section	A square 1 mile on each side (1 mile square) containing 1 square mile (640 acres).
Quarter section	160 acres, measuring 2,640 feet by 2,640 feet. Historically, it was the area of land originally granted to a homesteader. Today, the 160 acres is still used to establish the limits of homesteaded property outside the boundaries of municipality. (See also page 155.)
Government lot	Fractional pieces of land less than a full quarter section located along the banks of lakes and streams. Government lots were identified by a specific lot number, which became the legal description for that parcel.

Free land from gov. Patten.

---

6 **Subdividing sections.**   Each section is theoretically a square with all
7 sides measuring one mile and contains 640 acres within its boundaries.
8 It is important to remember the exact number of acres in a section because
9 the 640 figure is used for many purposes. One reason is that the section is
10 the basic reference when writing a legal description of land. It is also the
11 reference when calculating acreage in subdivided tracts. Each section can
12 easily be divided into halves, or into quarters, and so on, down into
13 smaller divisions until the particular property one wants to locate or
14 describe has been pinpointed.

15   Suppose you are interested in only a quarter section, 160 acres, of
16 Section 36. First, divide the entire section into fourths by drawing a
17 straight vertical line through the center of the section and a straight
18 horizontal line through the center of the section. The two lines are
19 perpendicular to each other and cross in the exact center of the section.
20 The quarter section now situated in the upper right corner of the section
21 is called the *Northeast Quarter,* the one in the lower right corner is the
22 *Southeast Quarter,* and so on around the section. (See Figure 10.8.)
23 Directions are always given in terms of the direction from the center
24 of the section where the two dividing lines intersect.

25   Quarter sections contain 160 acres. Suppose you are interested in a
26 tract smaller than 160 acres. You can divide any quarter just as you did the
27 section. Furthermore, you can keep on dividing the results until you find
28 the tract in which you are interested.

FIGURE 10.8   Section 36

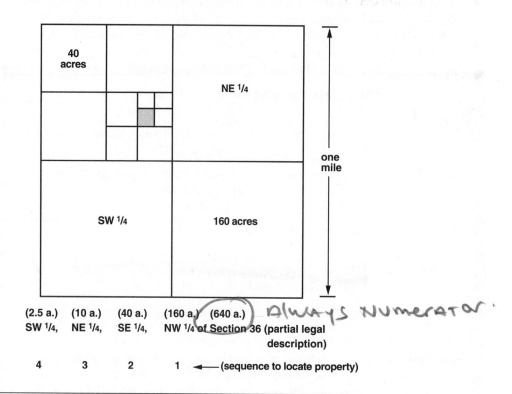

(2.5 a.)   (10 a.)   (40 a.)   (160 a.)   (640 a.)   _Always Numerator._
SW ¼,   NE ¼,   SE ¼,   NW ¼ of Section 36 (partial legal
                                                     description)

   4   3   2   1 ◀——(sequence to locate property)

Assume you need to find a 2½-acre tract located somewhere near the center of Section 36. The legal description given you is "SW¼ of the NE¼ of the SE¼ of the NW¼ of Section 36." Beginning with the section, divide it into quarters to start locating the property. In locating property from a legal description, it is necessary to start with the last part of the description and read from right to left. So, because you have located Section 36, move to the last fraction in the description (NW¼) and separate that quarter section from the whole. Move to the next fraction (SE¼), divide the previously located quarter section (NW¼) into four parts, and focus your attention on the resulting southeast quarter. Move to the next fraction (NE¼), divide the SE¼ of the NW¼ into four parts, and locate the northeast quarter of that division. You still have one more fraction (SW¼) remaining, so divide the last located parcel (NE¼) into fourths once more. When you find the southwest quarter of that division, you have located the tract described.

Calculating size.   To find the number of acres in a tract, two approaches are possible:

1. Calculate the number of acres by working backward from the 640-acre section. To do this, divide 640 by the denominator of each fraction (the bottom portion of a fraction) calculating the number of acres resulting from each division:

Example: The SW¼, NE¼, SE¼, NW¼ of a certain section contains how many acres?

$$640 \div 4 = 160; \ 160 \div 4 = 40; \ 40 \div 4 = 10; \ 10 \div 4 = 2.5; \text{ or}$$
$$640 \div 4 \div 4 \div 4 \div 4 = 2.5 \text{ acres}$$

2. Multiply the denominators of each fraction together and then divide 640 by the result.

Example: The SW¼, NE¼, SE¼, NW¼ of a certain section contains how many acres?

$$4 \times 4 \times 4 \times 4 = 256$$
$$640 \div 256 = 2.5 \text{ acres}$$

[handwritten note: Can't answer Math ? = C]

The previous exercise to determine the size of a given tract demonstrates, among other things, that generally, the longer a legal description, the smaller the number of acres contained in the parcel described. With practice, one becomes familiar with the fact that a description containing four one-fourths will always result in a 2½-acre tract. A description with only three one-fourths will result in a 10-acre parcel. If fractions other than fourths are used, the method for calculating acreage is the same.

***And* in a legal description.**   What will you do if you are required to find the total acreage of a tract with a legal description that contains the word *and* within the description? For example:

SE¼ of the NW¼ *and* NE¼ of the SW¼

You should multiply the denominators as previously mentioned. First, however, multiply only the denominators that immediately precede the *and*. Next, multiply the denominators that follow the *and*. Then, find the acreage for each. Finally, add the two answers to find the total acreage in the legal description. Now, how many acres are there in the above example? You can find the answer at the end of this Chapter on page 205.

DESCRIPTION BY LOT AND BLOCK NUMBERS

Probably the most common type of legal description used for single-family dwellings located in developed subdivisions is the **lot and block** method of land description. The lot and block method can be used only where *plat maps* have been recorded in the public records (also called *plat method, description by recorded plat,* or *description by recorded map*). The platted subdivision is divided into large areas called *blocks,* and each block is subdivided into smaller areas called *lots.* The lots are usually numbered for convenience in identifying them. If the lots are numbered, the blocks may be assigned letters to eliminate confusing block numbers with lot numbers. For example, the shaded lot in Figure 10.9 is Lot 5, Block B of Glendale Estates Subdivision.

A plat map is an engineer's plan for land use superimposed on a map of the land in question. The plat map shows the lot divisions and street locations, and it may provide for dedication of streets, parks, and school sites to the county or community. It shows actual dimensions for lots, streets, and other planned improvements. The plat map must show the location of the fixed monuments established and placed in the ground and the survey data needed to locate each lot, block, and street with reference to the permanent monuments. The entire tract is probably referenced to the government survey system. The subdivision is given a name. The plat map is recorded in the county courthouse under the subdivision name by

FIGURE 10.9   Subdivision Plat Map

Don't copy 1st Line?
whole Subdivision

Say:
See
attached

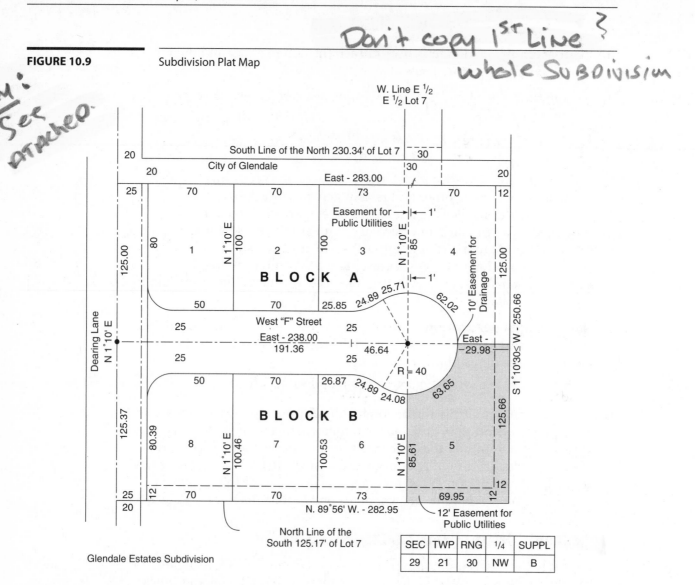

Glendale Estates Subdivision

SEC	TWP	RNG	1/4	SUPPL
29	21	30	NW	B

1   book and page number. This makes the plat map a part of the public
2   records, and it makes any further legal description of the lots a
3   simple matter.

4   The various methods of legal description are *not* mutually exclusive.
5   A lot and block description in a plat, for example, located in Florida is
6   created within section(s) of land in the Government Survey System. The
7   location of Lot 26 (see Figure 10.1) is described using the Government
8   Survey System as in Section 10, Township 9 South, Range 19 East of
9   Alachua County, Florida. A developer hired a surveyor to stake out
10 parcels using the metes-and-bounds method. The Boundary Survey
11 (Figure 10.1) indicates the surveyor's metes-and-bounds description of
12 Lot 26. And the lot and block description of Lot 26 (see Figure 10.1) is
13 worded, "Lot 26, Blues Creek Unit— 4, a portion of a planned unit
14 development as recorded in Plat Book 'S', page 3, of the public records
15 of Alachua County, Florida."

16 **Tax maps.** Every parcel of land within a tax district is assessed for tax
17 purposes. To accomplish this task, each parcel is assigned a Parcel ID

number (or *assessor's parcel number*) by the county property appraiser's office. The Parcel ID numbers are used to prepare *tax maps*. They are scaled drawings based on recorded plat maps of all the parcels within a tax district showing the exact location of the property, dimensions, and the amount of the assessed value of each parcel. The information is used each year to prepare the tax roll. Parcel ID numbers are sometimes used to identify a particular parcel.

Additional Survey Measures and Terminology	
Acre	43,560 square feet (approximately 208.71 ft. × 208.71 feet)
Bench mark	A permanent reference mark (PRM) affixed to an iron post or brass marker that is embedded in the sidewalk or street, used to establish elevations and altitudes above sea level on surveyed parcels.
Mile	5,280 feet in length

■ SUMMARY

Florida law requires that a precise description of real property set out the boundaries of each parcel of land being conveyed. A legal description of land, therefore, is an exact means of describing real property in a sale contract, deed, mortgage, or other document.

The methods for describing the location of land are metes-and-bounds, government survey system, and lot and block numbers. The various methods of legal description are not mutually exclusive. A lot and block description in a plat, for example, is created within section(s) of land in the Government Survey System, and the developer will hire a surveyor to stake out individual lots using the metes-and-bounds method of description. The rectangular system is usually used first, to identify the location of the POB within the system. For example, a legal description might read, "Starting at a concrete monument located 175 feet south of the SE corner of the SW¼, NE¼, Section 22, T5N, R3W, Tallahassee Principal Meridian; thence, 35.75 feet east to the point of beginning," and so on, back to the POB.

The answer to the acreage problem on page 203 is 80 acres.

Practice 1 Solution

	R3W	R2W	R1W	R1E	R2E	R3E
T3N						
T2N						
T1N						
T1S						
T2S						
T3S						

Practice 2 Solution

N

6	5	4	3	2	1
7	8	9	10	11	12
18	17	16	15	14	13
19	20	21	22	23	24
30	29	28	27	26	25
31	32	33	34	35	36

W   E

S

■ REVIEW QUESTIONS

1. The NW¼ of the NE¼ of the SW¼, Section 20, Township 4 South, Range 2 East, describes a tract of
   A. .125 acre.
   B. .5 acre.
   C. 10 acres.
   D. 64 acres.

2. Calculate the number of acres contained in the following legal description: NE¼ of the SE¼ and the SE¼ of the NE¼ and the N½ of the NE¼.
   A. 30 acres
   B. 80 acres
   C. 120 acres
   D. 160 acres

3. In the metes-and-bounds method of description
   A. *metes* refers to direction, and *bounds* refers to distance.
   B. *metes* refers to distance, and *bounds* refers to direction.
   C. *metes* refers to distance, and *bounds* refers to measurement.
   D. *metes* refers to metric, and *bounds* refers to boundaries.

4. The government survey system is especially adapted to describing
   A. lots in platted subdivisions.
   B. odd-shaped tracts of land carved out of former land grants.
   C. land in concise symbols and words.
   D. parcels with human-made or natural physical features.

5. What is the designation of a township located three township tiers south of the base line and five ranges east of the principal meridian?
   A. R3S, T5E
   B. T3S, R5E
   C. R7E, T2S
   D. T3N, R5E

6. Correction lines or parallels are located on each side of the base line every
   A. 1 mile.
   B. 6 miles.
   C. 24 miles.
   D. 36 miles.

7. The tract of land located inside a square formed by intersecting range lines and township lines is called a(n)
   A. acre.
   B. check.
   C. section.
   D. township.

8. The vertical strip of land six miles wide beginning at the principal meridian and extending six miles east along the length of the principal meridian is called
   A. Range 1 East.
   B. Township 1 East.
   C. Tier 1 East.
   D. Section 6.

9. If you have located a township designated as T1N, R1E, the township due north of that township is
   A. T1N, R2E.
   B. T1S, R1E.
   C. T2N, R1E.
   D. T2N, R2E.

10. Which statement is FALSE concerning townships?
    A. A township contains 36 sections.
    B. A township contains 36 square miles.
    C. A township is 6 miles square.
    D. A township contains 36 acres.

11. In writing the legal description of a section, which is the standard sequence?
    A. Range number, township number, section number
    B. Section number, township number, range number
    C. Township number, range number, section number
    D. Section number, range number, township number

12. The north boundary of Section 36, Township 1 South, Range 1 West is located
    A. 6 miles south of the principal meridian.
    B. 35 miles west of the base line.
    C. 25 miles west of the principal meridian.
    D. 5 miles south of the base line.

13. A legal description that reads, in part, "the North one-half of the Northeast one-quarter of the Northwest one-quarter Section 12, Township 42 South, Range 12 East" describes a tract of
    A. 20 acres.
    B. 10 acres.
    C. 5 acres.
    D. 2½ acres.

14. Dean owned the NW¼ of a section. He sold the W½ of that NW¼. How many acres does Dean still own?
    A. 40 acres.
    B. 80 acres.
    C. 160 acres.
    D. 640 acres.

15. Plat maps used in the lot and block method of legal description show
    A. the grid system of government squares.
    B. dimensions of streets and improvements.
    C. the numerical street address for each lot.
    D. distance and direction from the point of beginning.

CHAPTER 11

Real Estate Contracts

Like + Trust. [handwritten]

■ KEY TERMS

assignment

bilateral contract

buyer brokerage
  agreement

competent

contract

exclusive-agency listing

exclusive-right-of-sale
  listing

good consideration

liquidated damages

meeting of the minds

mutual assent

net listing

novation

open listing

option contract

parol contract — 4 yrs oral. [handwritten]

statute of frauds

statute of limitations

unenforceable

unilateral contract

valid

valuable consideration

vendee

vendor

void

voidable

■ OVERVIEW

Nearly every business transaction is based on a contract. Key to every
contract is the *promise.* In a real estate contract, the seller promises to
convey title to the real estate, and the buyer promises to pay the purchase
price. Contract promises are *enforceable* by law, provided the contract
meets certain requirements. A contract defines the parties' legal
relationship and spells out their rights and duties.

After completing this Chapter, the student should be able to:

- list and describe the essentials of a real estate contract;

- describe the differences between formal contracts and parol
  contracts;

- distinguish among bilateral, unilateral, implied, express,
  executory, and executed contracts;

- describe the various ways in which an offer is terminated;

- describe the various methods of terminating a contract;

- explain the remedies for breach of a contract;

- describe the effect of the statute of frauds and the statute of
  limitations;

- describe the elements of an option; and

- differentiate among the various types of listings.

■ PREPARATION OF CONTRACTS

To draft the wording of legal documents or legal instruments for others is considered practicing law. Because very few real estate licensees are attorneys, real estate brokers and sales associates must *not* prepare deeds, mortgages, promissory notes, or most other legal documents. Licensees who prepare such instruments could lose their licenses, regardless of whether they receive compensation. Real estate licensees may *not* draw lease agreements. However, licensees may fill in the blanks on Florida Supreme Court preapproved lease instruments for lease periods that do not exceed one year. Real estate licensees are allowed to assist buyers and sellers with the drawing of four types of contracts:

1. **Listing agreement.** A listing agreement is a broker's employment contract with a seller and, indirectly, it is the sales associate's authorization to operate.

2. **Buyer brokerage agreement.** A buyer brokerage agreement is an employment contract with a buyer.

3. **Sale and purchase contract.** A sale and purchase contract is a contract between a buyer and seller. The licensee acts as agent or facilitator for one or both of the contracting parties.

4. **Option contract.** An option contract is an agreement to keep open for a specified period of time an offer to sell or lease real property. In order to reduce liability it is strongly advised that licensees recommend to the buyer or the seller to have a real estate attorney draw option contracts (see page 222).

Real estate brokerages offices typically use standardized listing agreements, buyer brokerage agreements, sale and purchase contracts, and option contracts. The Florida Association of REALTORS® and other professional groups have developed standardized contracts for use by their members. This is desirable because the use of standardized contracts improves efficiency and greatly reduces liability. Each of these contracts is explained in this Chapter, followed by an exercise for completing a listing agreement and a sale and purchase contract. A sample Exclusive Buyer Brokerage Agreement is also provided at the end of this Chapter.

■ STATUTE OF FRAUDS

Contracts that *convey an interest* in real property must be in writing and signed to be enforceable. The **statute of frauds** applies to many types of contracts, including the following:

- Purchase and sale contracts

- Option contracts

- Lease agreements for more than one year

- Listing agreements for more than one year

Historically the statute of frauds was adopted to prevent, in particular, a person from claiming to have entered into a contract that was fictitious or that differed in its terms from those alleged. Before adoption of the statute of frauds, title to real property was transferred by delivery of possession without evidence by a writing. Laws today specify that real estate contracts must be in writing and signed to be enforceable, *except* in two specific instances:

1. When an oral contract has been formed and the buyer has paid part of the purchase price and then has either taken possession of the property or made some improvements of the property

2. If both parties have fully performed as promised

In these two situations, the resulting legal relationships are precisely the same as those that would have existed had the contract been in writing. In either instance, neither party could later rescind or recover what he or she had before contract with the other by claiming the oral contract was not valid. Failure to comply with the statutes of frauds may *not* be illegal, but it usually would make a real estate purchase and sale contract **unenforceable** (it would not stand up in a court of law).

■ STATUTE OF LIMITATIONS

The **statute of limitations** designates the period of time during which the terms of a contract may be enforced. It protects people from being compelled to perform or otherwise be sued after a period of time has expired. The times vary, depending on whether it is an oral contract or a written contract:

- Written contracts—five years Formal.

- Oral contracts—four years – Parol

- Partly written and partly oral—five years for the written portion and four years for the oral portion

■ ESSENTIALS OF A CONTRACT

A **contract** is an agreement between two or more parties to do or not to do certain things, supported by a sufficient consideration. A **valid** (enforceable) contract has four essentials:

1. Contractual capacity of the parties (competent parties)

2. Offer and acceptance (mutual assent)

3. Legality of object

4. Consideration

5. STATUE of FRAUDS.

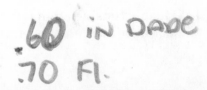
.60 in DADE
.70 FL.

Contracts may be in writing or oral with the exception of real estate contracts. Contracts that involve a transfer of real property *must be in writing*. (See Transfer of Real Property on page 213.)

CONTRACTUAL CAPACITY OF THE PARTIES

Not all persons have the ability or capacity to make a valid contract. If a person is insane, intoxicated, or legally a minor, he or she may have only limited contractual capacity. A minor's contract (a contract by an individual under the legal age to contract), for example, is **voidable** at his or her option. The minor may choose to void the contract. However, an adult is bound to honor the contract if the minor chooses to go through with the deal.

The parties to a contract are **competent** if they have the *legal capacity to contract*, meaning they have no mental defects or insanity and are both of legal age to contract. A sane person contracting with an insane person or an adult contracting with a minor produces a voidable contract.

OFFER AND ACCEPTANCE

Mutual assent refers to the making and acceptance of an offer. The parties must come to a **meeting of the minds,** meaning they must reach an agreement on all terms in the contract. One party (the *offeror*) makes an offer, and the other party (the *offeree*) accepts that offer. A complete and mutual understanding must exist to produce a meeting of the minds. The contract is formed at the instant that acceptance of the offer is communicated to the offeror. Therefore, a contract is formed on the acceptance of an offer and communication of the acceptance.

LEGALITY OF OBJECT

The provisions spelled out in a contract must not be prohibited by law. For example, a sale and purchase contract (or sale contract) that provides for payment of commission to an unlicensed person is a contract with an illegal purpose. The contract would not be enforceable in a court of law.

CONSIDERATION

Consideration is whatever is given in exchange for something else. People often think of consideration as the money exchanged by the parties. Legally, however, consideration is the *obligation* that each party makes to the other to make the contract enforceable. Each party to the contract must obligate himself or herself by placing some consideration in the agreement. A promise undertaken by one party must be supported by a promise undertaken by the other party. Mutual promises to do or not to do some specific act are sufficient consideration, even though the benefit or sacrifice may not be equal. In real estate sale contracts, the seller normally promises to sell and convey, and the purchaser promises to pay for the property. There are two types of consideration:

1. **Valuable consideration** is the money or a promise of something that can be measured in terms of money.

1   2. **Good consideration** is a promise that cannot be measured in terms
2   of money, such as love and affection.

3   Either type of consideration is sufficient to enforce a contract. The law
4 generally does not concern itself with the fairness of consideration. What
5 is exchanged need not have the same measurable value. The law will
6 accept that the parties thought the consideration to be fair because they
7 freely agreed to the exchange.

8 ## TRANSFER OF REAL PROPERTY

9   In addition to the four essential elements required in any contract, to be
10 enforceable in court, real estate contracts must be in writing and signed
11 by all parties who are bound by the agreement. Real estate contracts are
12 *not* required to be witnessed or notarized.

TO REMEMBER

Elements of a Valid Real Estate Contract

C	**C**ontractual capacity (competent parties)
O	**O**ffer and acceptance (meeting of the minds)
L	**L**egality of object
I	**I**n writing and signed (statute of frauds)
C	**C**onsideration (valuable or good)

---

13   A contract does not have to be in any particular format to be valid, as
14 long as it contains all of the essential elements. The contract should have
15 an unambiguous property identification. Because a contract is an
16 agreement designed to spell out clearly the meeting of the minds between
17 parties on a particular subject, it creates certain enforceable rights. It also
18 provides remedies for the affected parties if the contract is breached.

Void, Voidable, and Unenforceable Contracts

Void	A **void** contract does not meet all of the required elements of a valid contract and, therefore, has no legal effect.
Voidable	A **voidable** contract is a contract, but because of the manner or method in which it was brought about, one of the parties is permitted to avoid his or her contractual duties. A minor's contract is voidable because the minor can choose to void the contract.
Unenforceable	A contract may be **unenforceable** for failure to satisfy the requirements of the statute of frauds, for running beyond the statute of limitations, or because the property is destroyed.

---

19 ## ■ CONTRACT CATEGORIES

20 Contracts can be classified by their method of formation, their content, or
21 their legal effect. The first classification is *formal* and *informal* contracts.

FORMAL AND INFORMAL CONTRACTS

Formal contract.   Historically, a formal contract was in written form and under seal. The seal has evolved from the old wax impression on a document to the word *seal* or the letters *L.S.* (*locus sigilli,* Latin for "the place of the seal") that appear after the signatures of parties signing the contract. The term *formal contract* also refers to a contract that depends on a particular form. For example, a negotiable instrument such as a promissory note is referred to as a formal contract. Today, the seal is *not* required to make contracts valid.

Parol (informal) contract.   An oral agreement is a **parol contract.** Some oral real estate contracts are recognized by law as enforceable. (See Statute of Frauds on page 210.)

OTHER CONTRACT CLASSIFICATIONS

The very name of the contract classification often indicates the way in which the contract was arranged, the requirements for its performance, or even the type of parties bound by the contract. Contracts can be either *bilateral* or *unilateral.*

Bilateral and unilateral contracts.   A **bilateral contract** obligates both parties to perform in accordance with the terms of the contract. A sale contract is an example of a bilateral contract because *both* the seller and the buyer are obligated to perform.

A **unilateral contract** obligates only one party to an agreement. There is no obligation on the part of the other party involved. An example of a unilateral contract is the ordinary *option.*

If the person asking for an option (the *optionee*) pays a consideration to the person granting the option (the *optionor*), the optionor is obligated not to sell to anyone other than the optionee during the life of the option. The optionee, however, is not obligated to buy. If the optionee chooses to exercise the option, he or she may do so. The optionor then is bound to honor the option on notification of the optionee's intent to exercise it. The option (unilateral contract) becomes a bilateral contract when the optionee has promised to exercise the option specified in the contract.

Express or implied contracts.   Contracts may be classified as either *express* or *implied.*

An *express contract* exists when all the terms and conditions have been spelled out and a meeting of the minds is reached in words of agreement and mutual understanding. An express contract may be either written or parol; that is, it may be in writing or oral or be a combination of the two. The primary requirements in an express contract are mutual understanding and agreement.

An *implied contract* is one in which some or all of the obligations or conditions of a contract are not stated expressly (in words) but may be reasonably implied by the acts of the parties or by the nature of the transaction. For example, if a real estate broker identifies herself as such and states that she knows of a buyer for the property who is willing to pay

1   a good price, the courts will require that the owner pay the broker
2   compensation in the form of a commission or fee if the sale occurs.

3   The various categories of contracts are *not* mutually exclusive. For
4   example, a particular contract may be described as *parol, bilateral,*
5   and *express.*

6   **Executory or executed contracts.**   Contracts also may be referred to as
7   *executory* or *executed* contracts.

8   Assume a contract has been formed between parties, but something
9   remains to be done by one or both parties to fulfill the conditions of the
10   contract. It is an *executory contract* because it is not yet a fully performed
11   contract. A real estate sale contract, between the time of signing the
12   contract and the time of closing the transaction, is an executory contract.

13   When all parties to a contract have completely performed all the
14   obligations and promises contained in the contract, it is an *executed*
15   *contract.* For instance, a real estate sale contract becomes an executed
16   contract after the title closing and all the promises of both buyer
17   and seller have been fulfilled.

■ CONTRACT NEGOTIATION

19   In the normal sequence of forming a contract, one party begins by
20   making an *offer.* Assume that Rebecca is selling a parcel of land that she
21   owns. Ken makes an *offer* to purchase the lot from Rebecca for $34,000.
22   Ken is the *offeror* (the person making the offer) and Rebecca is the *offeree*
23   (the person who receives the offer).

24   Frequently, the offeree will make a *counteroffer* by altering the terms of
25   the original offer. For example, if Rebecca decides to make a counteroffer
26   of $35,500 and asks Ken to pay all of the closing costs, Rebecca has
27   replaced Ken's original offer with a counteroffer. When a counteroffer is
28   made, it kills the original offer and substitutes a new offer in its place.

29   When a counteroffer is made, the role of both parties also changes.
30   Because Rebecca's counteroffer is based on new terms and conditions, she
31   has "changed hats" and is now the offeror. Likewise, Ken is receiving the
32   new terms and conditions, so he has become the offeree. It is not
33   uncommon for a series of offers and counteroffers to take place before a
34   meeting of the minds is accomplished. Once a meeting of the minds is
35   reached, that is, when one party accepts the offer of the other party and
36   communicates such acceptance, a contract has been formed. Both parties
37   then are obligated to perform according to the contract.

38   An offer is terminated when any of the following happens:

39   • *Counteroffer.* A counteroffer indicates a willingness to contract,
40   but on terms or conditions different from those contained in the
41   original offer. It is *not* an acceptance because it indicates an
42   unwillingness to agree to the terms of the original offer. The
43   original offer is dead forever and cannot be later accepted.

TO REMEMBER

Ways an Offer Is Terminated

W   **W**ithdrawal by offeror
I   **I**nsanity
L   **L**apse of time
D   **D**eath

C   **C**ounteroffer
A   **A**cceptance
R   **R**ejection
D   **D**estruction of the property

1   • *Acceptance.* Acceptance of an offer is essential to the creation of a
2   contract. An acceptance must comply strictly with the terms of the
3   offer. Otherwise, an offeror who attempts to withdraw the offer
4   may be told by the offeree that he or she just signed the contract
5   and the offer is accepted. It would then become a judicial issue as
6   to whether a contract exists. This is why the FAR/BAR Contract for
7   Sale and Purchase (see sample contract on pages 233–236) states
8   that acceptance must be communicated in writing. Letters and
9   telegraphic communication can be part of a valid sale contract. If
10   Rebecca had accepted Ken's offer of $34,000 for her property
11   instead of making a counteroffer, the offer would have become a
12   contract on that acceptance and its communication.

475.5018, F.S.

24 hrs

13   • *Rejection.* To effectively terminate an offer, a rejection must be
14   communicated by the offeree to the offeror. If Rebecca had chosen
15   to reject Ken's offer, the offer would have terminated when
16   Rebecca communicated the rejection to Ken.

17   • *Withdrawal by offeror.* An offeror may withdraw (or *revoke*) the offer
18   at any time until notice of the offeree's acceptance is received by
19   the offeror or his or her designated agent. Suppose, for example,
20   that Rebecca decides to withdraw her counteroffer of $35,500. She
21   may do so as long as this is communicated to Ken before he accepts
22   her counteroffer.

23   • *Lapse of time.* Ordinarily, when an offer is made, a time limit for
24   acceptance of the offer is specified. The offer terminates after
25   expiration of that time. If no time limit for acceptance is specified,
26   the offeree is considered to have a *reasonable length of time.* This
27   time period is based on such considerations as the method of
28   communication used, the location of the parties involved, and the
29   terminology and nature of the offer.

6 mo /long enough.

30   • *Death or insanity.* The death or insanity of either the offeror or the
31   offeree terminates the offer. An offer is not assignable (transferable);
32   it may be accepted only by the person to whom it is made.

- *Destruction of the property.* Destruction of the subject matter terminates the offer.

■ TERMINATION OF CONTRACTS

A contract is terminated when any of the following happens:

- *Performance.* When both parties have fully performed the terms and conditions of a contract, the purpose of the contract has been accomplished and the contract is terminated. The emphasis is on full performance of each and every contract term or condition. This is, of course, the desired outcome of any contract. However, sometimes contracts are terminated for other reasons.

- *Mutual rescission.* A *rescission* is an agreement between the contracting parties to terminate their respective duties under the contract. Both parties must mutually agree to discontinue the contract.

- *Impossibility of performance.* Performance may be impossible and beyond the control of the parties. For example, destruction of the physical improvements is a good excuse for impossibility of performance. The death of the buyer or the seller will usually be considered a reason for impossibility of performance, unless the real estate contract provides otherwise.

- *Operation of law.* Certain circumstances, such as lapse of time, will cause a contract to be terminated by operation of law. For example, a contract may be terminated as a result of the expiration of the statute of limitations or because the contract is for an illegal purpose.

- *Bankruptcy.* The bankruptcy of one of the parties will not in itself discharge the contract. If the bankrupted party is the seller, however, control of the asset will come under the control of the courts. A court-appointed trustee will be charged with liquidating the asset.

- *Breach.* A contract is breached when one of the parties fails to perform and the law does not recognize the reason for failure to perform as valid. The aggrieved party may sue over a breach of contract.

REMEDIES FOR BREACH

The Florida Real Estate Commission ordinarily has no authority or jurisdiction over breach of contract actions. There are four legal remedies for breach of a contract:

1. **Specific performance.** If awards of money damages do not afford sufficient relief, the wronged party may sue for specific performance to have the courts force the other party to perform as the contract specifically states. This action is termed a *relief in equity* because such judgments are awarded in a court of equity.

[handwritten margin note: Good for 1 yr. or void]

2. **Liquidated damages.** Frequently the parties will stipulate an amount of money in the contract (usually the earnest money deposit) to be paid in the case of default by the buyer. This amount is referred to as **liquidated damages** to the seller.

3. **Rescission on breach of contract.** A wronged party may sue for rescission, that is, cancellation, of the contract. If the injured party is the buyer, he or she is entitled to the return of any earnest money, and the seller is obligated to return any earnest money or payment received.

4. **Compensatory damages.** Another remedy for breach of contract is a suit for damages. Usually the party bringing suit seeks an amount of money equal to the extent of loss suffered (*compensatory damages*). A wronged party may find that a certain property was misrepresented but decide to accept the property and, in addition, sue for damages. On the other hand, the buyer may decide to refuse the property and still sue for damages.

ASSIGNMENT AND NOVATION

Assignment refers to a transfer of rights and duties under a contract. Except where the terms and conditions of the contract provide otherwise, or where specifically prohibited by law, a contract is assignable (transferable). A person who assigns or transfers legal rights in a contract to another party or person is called the *assignor*. The person to whom legal rights in a contract are transferred or assigned is called the *assignee*.

An assignor does not escape the obligation to perform the terms and conditions of the contract or to see that they are performed by the person to whom it was assigned, unless given a release from the other party to the original contract. If an assignor either accidentally or intentionally assigns the same thing(s) to two or more assignees, the first assignee to notify the other party to the contract prevails over all other assignees.

The parties to a contract may agree to substitute another person's obligation to perform. **Novation** is the substitution of a new party for the original one. The effect is to discharge the original party from the obligation. For example, when a purchaser assumes the seller's existing mortgage, the lender may agree to release the seller and substitute the buyer as the party primarily liable for the mortgage debt. In a novation, the original mortgagor (borrower) is discharged and the old debt is extinguished.

■ CONTRACTS IMPORTANT TO REAL ESTATE

Four types of contracts are important to real estate brokers and sales associates because they are parties to negotiation of these contracts: (1) listing agreements, (2) buyer brokerage agreements, (3) sale and purchase contracts, and (4) option contracts.

475.25(l)(r), F.S.

ONE: LISTING CONTRACTS

In Florida, a listing contract may be written, oral, or implied. Written listing contracts must include the following:

- A definite expiration date
- Identification of the property
- Price and terms
- Fee or commission
- Signature(s) of the owner(s)

Florida law requires that a copy of the contract must be given to the owner(s) within 24 hours of execution. Furthermore, Chapter 475, F.S. forbids including an automatic renewal clause in a listing.

475.25(l)(r), F.S.

Even though Florida law recognizes oral listing contracts, all listings should be in writing because the listing contract is a broker's employment contract. If litigation should result from some misunderstanding, default, or breach, it is easier to find a remedy by showing the written terms and conditions rather than trying to prove the terms or conditions of an oral listing. However, listing contracts are not covered by the statute of frauds (*unless* they are for more than one year). Therefore, oral listing contracts are enforceable with the proper amount of evidence and testimony.

Power to bind the seller or buyer.   A broker does not have the authority or power to sign a contract for the buyer or the seller or to bind the buyer or the seller to a contract unless the power to do so is specifically granted.

Power of attorney is a written legal document designating some other person as an *attorney-in-fact.* The attorney-in-fact then may bargain and sign for the person who granted the power of attorney, provided that power is specifically granted. A real estate licensee occasionally may come in contact with either a general power of attorney or a special power of attorney. The *general power of attorney* authorizes the attorney-in-fact to act generally for the principal in all matters. The *special power of attorney* limits the attorney-in-fact to one specified area of activity or one special act, such as signing a contract for sale or purchasing a designated property. When power of attorney is granted for acts related to title to real property, the instrument must be witnessed, acknowledged, and recorded in the public records.

Usually with listing agreements, you can assume that the seller has not given power of attorney to the broker. The signatures of both parties (seller and agent) on the listing contract may create some special situations.

Conditions created by listing contract.   Exclusive-right-of-sale listings and exclusive-agency listings are usually bilateral contracts because both parties are obligated to perform. Open listing agreements are usually unilateral contracts because the only promise made is that the seller promises to pay a commission if the broker causes a transaction to be consummated.

The licensee is to find a purchaser or effect a sale. If required to *find a purchaser,* the licensee must (1) produce a buyer who is ready, willing, and able to buy at the terms specified by the seller or (2) take to the seller a buyer's offer that subsequently becomes a contract. When the licensee has performed either of the above actions, he or she is entitled to a commission, even if the buyer and seller finally negotiate a sale on different terms.

If required to *effect a sale,* the licensee must not only find a buyer ready, willing, and able to buy on the terms specified or other terms accepted by the seller, but the licensee must also ensure that the transaction actually closes.

TYPES OF LISTINGS

Listings commonly used in the real estate business are *open listings, exclusive-agency listings,* and *exclusive-right-of-sale listings.* Any of these listings, under certain conditions, also may be *net listings.*

Open listing.   A seller gives an **open listing** to any number of brokers who can work simultaneously to sell the owner's property. The seller reserves the right to sell the property and to list it with other brokers. The first broker to secure a buyer who is ready, willing, and able to purchase at the terms of the listing earns the commission. If the owner sells the property, no broker is entitled to a commission. In the event of a sale, the seller is not obligated to notify any of the brokers that the property has been sold. Open listings benefit only the seller. Therefore, few brokers accept them.

Exclusive-agency listing.   A seller gives an **exclusive-agency listing** to one broker who handles the transaction. The seller reserves the right to sell the property without paying a commission, unless the buyer was introduced to the property by the broker or others acting under the broker. If the broker or another person acting under the broker's authority sells the property before the seller is able to do so, the broker is entitled to a commission.

Exclusive-right-of-sale listing.   The **exclusive-right-of-sale** (or *exclusive-right-to-sell*) **listing** is the most advantageous listing from the broker's viewpoint. The seller gives the listing to a selected broker, who then becomes the exclusive real estate agent of the owner for the sale of the property during the time the listing contract is in effect. The broker therefore is assured of a commission regardless of who sells the property. Even if the owner sells the property during the contract period, the broker is entitled to a commission.

	Comparison of Listings	
Type of Listing	**Agent**	**Commission**
Open	Many brokers	Only to broker who sells property
Exclusive-agency	One broker	To listing broker if not sold by owner
Exclusive-right-of-sale	One broker	To listing broker no matter who sells

1   Exclusive-right-of-sale and exclusive-agency listings may be
2 submitted to a multiple-listing service (MLS) by the listing broker.
3 An MLS serves as a clearinghouse for listings obtained by REALTOR®
4 member brokers and then shared with other MLS member brokers
5 through a published list of properties for sale. Any members of MLSs,
6 regardless of the brokerage company they work for, can show their buyers
7 the listings of other MLS members and receive compensation (part of the
8 commission) if the buyer purchases the property.

9 **Net listing.** An open, exclusive-right-of-sale, or exclusive-agency listing
10 can also be a net listing. A **net listing** is created when a seller agrees to sell
11 a property for a stated acceptable minimum amount. The broker and
12 seller jointly arrive at a listing price. The broker then retains, as
13 commission, all proceeds of the sale after the costs of sale are paid and the
14 seller receives the agreed-on net amount.

15   In the strict sense of the word *net*, any amount over the agreed upon
16 net to the seller goes to the broker. However, any "remaining amount"
17 could be interpreted as "unjust enrichment." Because of the potential
18 for abuse and fraud, net listings should not be used. They are illegal in
19 nearly all states and are discouraged by the regulatory authorities
20 in Florida.

21 **BROKER'S COMPENSATION**

22 Generally, the broker's compensation is specified in the listing or buyer
23 brokerage agreement. (Buyer brokerage agreements are discussed later in
24 this Chapter.) The compensation can be in the form of a commission or
25 a brokerage fee. The compensation is computed as a percentage of the
26 total sale price, a flat fee, or an hourly rate. The amount of a broker's
27 commission is negotiable.

28   The broker earns the commission. The broker then splits the
29 commission with a cooperating broker (if applicable). The broker splits his
30 or her commission with the sales associate involved with the sale. The
31 sales associate must receive compensation from his or her employing
32 broker and not directly from the seller, buyer, or other brokers. Some
33 brokers have adopted a 100 percent commission plan. Sales associates
34 in these offices pay the broker a monthly service fee for the use of the
35 office space, telephones, and clerical support. In return associates receive
36 100 percent of the commissions from the sales transactions they negotiate
37 for the broker.

38   To be paid a commission, the broker must:

39 1. hold a current, active real estate license;

40 2. be employed by the seller or buyer through a listing agreement or
41   buyer broker agreement; and

42 3. be the procuring cause. (*Note:* Payment could also result from a
43   referral.)

44   To be a **procuring cause,** the broker must have started the chain of
45 events that resulted in a sale. The facts dictate who is the procuring cause.
46 The person whose efforts cause the parties to enter into a contract is

generally considered to be the procuring cause. The broker who has a current listing agreement with the seller is not necessarily the procuring cause. That broker may be entitled to a fee when another broker sells the property, but procuring cause goes to the broker that brings the buyer.

Procuring cause disputes between licensees are usually settled through an arbitration hearing. Disputes between a broker and a buyer or seller may be litigated in court.

TWO: BUYER BROKERAGE AGREEMENT

Less com/More Sales

A **buyer brokerage agreement** is an employment contract with the buyer. The broker is employed as the buyer's transaction broker, single agent, or as a nonrepresentative of the buyer. Buyer broker agreements typically include the following:

- The parties to and term of the agreement (beginning and ending dates)

- General characteristics of the property being sought by the buyer, including type of property, price range, and location

- Broker's obligations

- Buyer's obligations

- Retainer and compensation (either as a dollar amount or a percentage of purchase price)

- Protection period

- Early termination of the agreement and dispute resolution (buyer and broker agree to mediate first)

- Authorized brokerage relationship

Refer to the Florida Association of REALTORS® Exclusive Buyer Brokerage Agreement on pages 237–239 for a more complete description of each section of the agreement.

 The Real Estate Buyer's Agent Council of the NAR® maintains a Web site at: **http://www.rebac.net/.**

 To learn more about buyer brokers, visit the National Association of Exclusive Buyer Agents' Web site at: **http://www.naeba.org/.**

THREE: OPTION CONTRACTS

An **option contract** is an agreement to keep open for a specified period of time an offer to sell or lease real property. The property owner (*optionor*) grants a prospective buyer (*optionee*) the right to buy the property within a specified period for a specified price and terms. Option contracts must be in writing and signed because they fall under the statute of frauds. Option contracts can easily be turned into sale contracts by simply notifying the optionor in writing that the option is being exercised.

*Min Deposit
1%*

Unilateral contract.   One major difference exists between an option and a sale contract. In an option contract, the owner (optionor) is bound to perform the terms of the option if required to do so by the optionee. The optionee, however, may elect to walk away from the deal because the option contract grants the optionee a right, *not* an obligation to buy the property. This makes the option a *unilateral* contract. In the normal bilateral sale contract, if either party does not perform all of the terms, the other party may sue for breach of contract.

Consideration.   The optionee pays a fee (valuable consideration) for the right to purchase the property within a specified period of time. The option contract may provide that the money paid to purchase the option be applied as a part of the purchase price in the event the option is exercised.

Information required.   Options must contain all of the terms and provisions required for a valid contract. The option must clearly specify the length of time the option is effective, the names of the contracting parties, the price of the property, a complete legal description, and the terms of the fee paid.

Options assignable.   Unless prohibited in the terms of the agreement, an option contract is assignable (transferable).

Licensee requirements.   Real estate licensees may *draw* option contracts. There is no case law indicating otherwise and the legal counsel for the DBPR has indicated that licensees may draw options. However, because there isn't any case law that specifically addresses licensees and option contracts (only sale contracts) some attorneys disagree with this position. Licensees are encouraged to either fill in the blanks on standardized option contract forms or recommend to the buyer or to the seller to have option contracts drawn by real estate attorneys. After all, you don't want to make your mark in real estate by being the subject of precedent setting case law!

Licensees who are really interested in obtaining an option on a property as a true optionee must first divest themselves of their role as licensees. The licensee must give a valuable consideration (substantial and not nominal) for the option contract. They must inform the property owners that they are not functioning as real estate brokers or sales associates but are personally interested in acquiring an option on the property.

475.43, F.S.

FOUR: SALE AND PURCHASE CONTRACTS

The parties to a sale and purchase contract (sale contract) are the **vendor** (or seller) and the **vendee** (or buyer). Unlike the option contract, a real estate sale contract (also a *purchase agreement* or *contract for sale and purchase*) is a *bilateral* contract because it contains promises to perform by both parties.

Information contained in sale contracts.   Sale contracts must be in writing and signed and contain all of the terms and provisions required for a valid contract. Although the Florida statute of frauds requires that sale contracts be in writing, courts have required that oral sale contracts be honored in some instances (see Statute of Frauds on page 210).

1   Also, letters and telegraphic communications can be part of a valid
2 sale contract. Information spelled out in the contract includes the
3 following:

4   • Names of the vendor and vendee (or their legal representatives)

5   • Legal description (preferred) or street address of the property

6   • Consideration

7   • Purchase price

8   • Financing or cash terms

9   • Type of deed the seller will deliver (general warranty deed unless
10   agreed otherwise)

11   • Title evidence required and type of estate (fee simple estate unless
12   agreed otherwise)

13   • Terms of expenses and any prorations to paid

14   • Personal property to be left with the real property

15   • Date, time, and place of closing

16   • When possession of the property will occur

17   The consideration in a sale contract is the promises that the buyer and
18 seller make to one another. However, it is also a good idea to include a
19 provision for an earnest money (binder) deposit and when it is to be paid.
20 Earnest money is *not* required to make the contract valid. However, it
21 shows the buyer's intent to go through with the deal. The contract usually
22 states that the seller may retain the earnest money deposit as liquidated
23 damages if the buyer breaches the contract.

24   Unless otherwise stated in the contract, the seller must convey a clear
25 and merchantable title. Licensees may be guilty of fraud and subject to
26 disciplinary action if they are aware of any title problem and do not inform
27 the buyer before a contract is entered into or any part of the purchase price is
28 paid. Most sale contracts require that the seller provide the buyer with an
29 up-to-date abstract or a title insurance policy. If no such requirement is
30 included in the sale contract, then the seller need not deliver either.

31   When the property is co-owned by a married couple, or if it is the
32 homestead and one of the spouses owns the home in only his or her
33 name (*in severalty*), both spouses must sign the real estate sale contract.
34 If the seller's spouse signs the sale contract, he or she indicates a
35 willingness to convey ownership rights and to relinquish homestead
36 interest when the time comes to sign the deed that transfers title. If the
37 buyer's spouse signs the sale contract, he or she also becomes bound to
38 purchase the property. Then, in the event of failure to perform, either
39 party can be sued. If only one spouse signs a contract to purchase, only
40 that spouse is accountable.

*Seller Must Disclose Any Defect
Baby Lemon Law.*

41 ## DISCLOSURES

42 Florida has enacted mandatory disclosure laws. These laws help
43 consumers make informed decisions regarding real estate transactions.

1 Most real estate contracts refer to the disclosures in the real estate
2 contract (see Figure 11.3, Part XI. Disclosures, on page 234) or the
3 disclosures may be a separate form.

[handwritten: M.O.1. More or Less.]

4 **Material defects disclosure.** Sellers of residential real property must
5 disclose material defects concerning the property. The use of an "as is"
6 provision in a contract for the sale of real property does not circumvent
7 the duty to disclose material defects.

8 *Johnson v. Davis,* a well-known legal case in Florida, set legal
9 precedence concerning material defects. Mr. and Mrs. Davis entered into
10 a contract to purchase a home from Mr. and Mrs. Johnson. Before the
11 closing, Mrs. Davis inquired regarding peeling plaster around the corner
12 of a window frame and stains on the ceilings. The sellers indicated that a
13 minor problem with the window had been corrected a long time ago and
14 that the stains on the ceiling resulted from wallpaper glue and ceiling
15 beams being removed. Prior to closing the buyers entered the then vacant
16 home following a downpour to find water "gushing" in from around the
17 window frame and the ceiling of the family room. The Davises ordered a
18 roof inspection and were informed that the roof was defective and it
19 would need to be replaced. The Davises sued to rescind the contract and
20 to get a refund of their deposit. The Florida Supreme Court found in favor
21 of the Davises and stated that:

22 "We hold that where the seller of a home knows of facts materially
23 affecting the value of the property which are not readily observable
24 and are not known to the buyer, the seller is under a duty to disclose
25 them to the buyer."

26 The case is considered important because prior to the *Johnson v. Davis*
27 decision the courts had favored the seller under the philosophy of *caveat*
28 *emptor* (buyer beware). This Supreme Court decision makes sellers
29 accountable to truthfully disclose the condition of the property. A later
30 case (*Rayner v. Wise Realty Co of Tallahassee*) extended the duty to disclose
31 material defects to real estate licensees. Although *Johnson v. Davis*
32 concerned residential property, licensees are cautioned to always use
33 sound ethical standards when dealing in all types of real property.

34 **Radon gas disclosure.**   A radon disclosure statement on real estate sale
35 and lease contracts is required on at least one document before or at the
36 time of executing a sale contract or a rental agreement. At present, the
37 disclosure consists only of what radon is; it does not require testing to
38 disclose radon gas levels before a sale or lease. Refer to the FAR/BAR sale
39 and purchase contract on pages 233–236. The required radon disclosure is
40 included in the contract under XI. (b) Disclosures.

404.056, F.S.

[handwritten: Leave Pamphlet.]

www@.link

Download the EPA publication Consumer's Guide to Radon Reduction
at: **http://www.epa.gov/radon/pubs/consguid.html.** *The EPA has
developed a video concerning radon in real estate. The video,
"Breathing Easy: What Home Buyers and Sellers Should Know About
Radon," is intended for consumers and real estate professionals. Single
copies are available at no charge by calling 800-438-4318.*

41 **Lead-based paint disclosure.**   Because of the danger associated with
42 exposure to lead-based paint, prospective buyers of homes built prior to
43 1978 are now required to sign a "Lead Disclosure" form before signing the

---

Radon Gas Disclosure

Notification shall be provided on at least one document, form, or application executed at the time to, or prior to, contract for sale and purchase of any building or execution of a rental agreement for any building. Such notification shall contain the following language:

RADON GAS: "Radon is a naturally occurring radioactive gas that, when it has accumulated in a building in sufficient quantities, may present health risks to persons who are exposed to it over time. Levels of radon that exceed federal and state guidelines have been found in buildings in Florida. Additional information regarding radon and radon testing may be obtained from your county health department."

Reference: Section 404.056(5), F.S.

No 2# killer

sale contract. The disclosure format is presented in Figure 11.1 on page 227. Sellers are required to disclose the presence of any known lead-based paint in the home, and buyers and renters must be given an EPA pamphlet regarding lead-based paint.

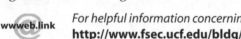 **wwweb.link** *Visit the EPA's Office of Pollution Prevention and Toxics Web site at:* **http://www.epa.gov/lead/.** *Click on "Education & Outreach" and then choose "Brochures and Posters" to download the EPA pamphlet,* Protect Your Family From Lead in Your Home *(PDF format).*

Imp¹

Energy efficiency brochure.   The Florida Building Energy-Efficiency Rating Act requires that buyers, before signing the sale contract, receive an information brochure notifying the purchaser of the option for an energy-efficiency rating on the building. The brochure contains a notice to residential purchasers that the energy-efficiency rating may qualify the purchaser for an energy-efficient mortgage from a lending institution. The act also created a uniform, statewide energy-efficiency rating system for rating new and existing residential, commercial, and public buildings.

553.996, F.S.

Winter + Summer.

 wwweb.link *For helpful information concerning energy, visit:* **http://www.fsec.ucf.edu/bldg/fyh/ratings/how.htm.**

Homeowner association disclosure.   Florida law requires sellers of property subject to a homeowners' association to provide buyers with a disclosure summary regarding the association, the existence of restrictive covenants, and any assessments that the association imposes. The real estate contract must include a statement that prospective buyers should not sign the contract until they have received and read the homeowners' disclosure summary. The sale contract must contain in conspicuous type the information contained in the text box below. If the disclosure summary is not given to the buyer prior to executing the sale contract, the buyer may void the contract for sale and purchase.

720.401, F.S.

If the disclosure summary required by section 702.401, Florida statutes, has not been provided to the prospective purchaser before executing this contract for sale, this contract is voidable by buyer by delivering to seller or seller's agent written notice of the buyer's intention to cancel within 3 days after receipt of the disclosure summary or prior to closing, whichever occurs first. Any purported waiver of this voidability right has no effect. Buyer's right to void this contract shall terminate at closing.

FIGURE 11.1   Disclosure of Information on Lead-Based Paint and/or Lead-Based Paint Hazards

---

Disclosure of Information on Lead-Based Paint and/or Lead-Based Paint Hazards

Lead Warning Statement

Every purchaser of any interest in residential real property on which a residential dwelling was built prior to 1978 is notified that such property may present exposure to lead from lead-based paint that may place young children at risk of developing lead poisoning. Lead poisoning in young children may produce permanent neurological damage, including learning disabilities, reduced intelligence quotient, behavioral problems, and impaired memory. Lead poisoning also poses a particular risk to pregnant women. The seller of any interest in residential real property is required to provide the buyer with any information on lead-based paint hazards from risk assessments or inspections in the seller's possession and notify the buyer of any known lead-based paint hazards. A risk assessment or inspection for possible lead-based paint hazards is recommended prior to purchase.

Seller's Disclosure

(a) Presence of lead-based paint and/or lead-based paint hazards (check (i) or (ii) below):

　　(i)＿ Known lead-based paint and/or lead-based paint hazards are present in the housing (explain).

　　(ii)＿ Seller has no knowledge of lead-based paint and/or lead-based paint hazards in the housing.

(b) Records and reports available to the seller (check (i) or (ii) below):

　　(i)＿Seller has provided the purchaser with all available records and reports pertaining to lead-based paint
　　　　and/or lead-based paint hazards in the housing (list documents below).

　　(ii)＿Seller has no reports or records pertaining to lead-based paint and/or lead-based paint hazards in
　　　　the housing.

Purchaser's Acknowledgment (initial)

(c)＿ Purchaser has received copies of all information listed above.

(d)＿ Purchaser has received the pamphlet Protect Your Family from Lead in Your Home.

(e)＿ Purchaser has (check (i) or (ii) below):

　　(i)＿ received a 10-day opportunity (or mutually agreed upon period) to conduct a risk assessment
　　　　or inspection for the presence of lead-based paint and/or lead-based paint hazards; or

　　(ii)＿ waived the opportunity to conduct a risk assessment or inspection for the presence of lead-
　　　　based paint and/or lead-based paint hazards.

Agent's Acknowledgment (initial)

(f)＿ Agent has informed the seller of the seller's obligations under 42 U.S.C. 4852d and is aware of his/
　　her responsibility to ensure compliance.

Certification of Accuracy

The following parties have reviewed the information above and certify, to the best of their knowledge, that the information they have provided is true and accurate.

Seller _____	Date _____	Seller _____	Date
Purchaser _____	Date _____	Purchaser _____	Date
Agent _____	Date _____	Agent _____	Date

Source: Federal Register/Vol. 61, No. 45/Wednesday, March 6, 1996/Rules and Regulations.

You can download the homeowner disclosure summary contained in the Florida statute. The Florida statutes are available on the Internet at: **http://www.leg.state.fl.us/welcome/index.cfm.** *Click on "Statutes" and then go to "Chapter 689." The summary is in section 689.261, F.S.*

Property tax disclosure.   Effective January 1, 2005, prospective buyers of residential property must be presented a disclosure summary concerning ad valorem taxes before or at the time of execution of the contract for sale. The purpose of the disclosure summary is to caution prospective buyers that they cannot rely on the amount of the seller's property taxes as an indication of the taxes purchasers will be required to pay in the year following purchase of the property.

689.261, F.S.

The disclosure may be either attached to the contact for sale or the wording may be inserted into the contract. If the disclosure is not inserted into the contract, the contract must refer to and incorporate by reference the disclosure summary. The reference to the disclosure must include, in prominent language, a statement that the potential purchaser should not execute the contract until he or she has read the required disclosure summary. The wording of the disclosure summary is presented below.

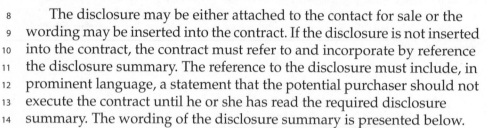

Property Tax Disclosure Summary

Buyer should not rely on the seller's current property taxes as the amount of property taxes that the buyer may be obligated to pay in the year subsequent to purchase. A change of ownership or property improvements triggers reassessments of the property that could result in higher property taxes. If you have questions concerning valuation, contact the county property appraiser's office for information.

Building code violation disclosure.   A seller who has been cited for a building code violation and is the subject of a pending enforcement proceeding must disclose in writing to the buyer the following information prior to title closing:

125.69, F.S.

- The existence and nature of the violation and proceedings

- A copy of the pleadings, notice, and other applicable documents received by the seller

- Notice that the buyer will be responsible for compliance with the applicable code and with the orders issued in the county court proceeding

The statute does not address the liability of the seller regarding the costs associated with the code violation. Liability costs should be addressed and negotiated in the contract for sale and purchase. The seller must forward to the code enforcement agency the name and address of the new owner and a copy of the disclosures given to the buyer within five days after the title transfer. A seller who violates this provision creates a rebuttable (i.e., disputable with evidence) presumption of fraud, and he or she may become the subject of a civil case.

FIGURE 11.2   Exclusive-Right-of-Sale Listing Agreement

Exclusive Right of Sale Listing Agreement
FLORIDA ASSOCIATION OF REALTORS®

This Exclusive Right of Sale Listing Agreement ("Agreement") is between

_____ ("**Seller**") and

_____ ("**Broker**").

1. AUTHORITY TO SELL PROPERTY: Seller gives **Broker** the EXCLUSIVE RIGHT TO SELL the real and personal property (collectively "Property") described below, at the price and terms described below, beginning the _____ day of _____, _____, and terminating at 11:59 p.m. the _____ day of _____, _____ ("Termination Date"). Upon full execution of a contract for sale and purchase of the Property, all rights and obligations of this Agreement will automatically extend through the date of the actual closing of the sales contract. **Seller** and **Broker** acknowledge that this Agreement does not guarantee a sale. This Property will be offered to any person without regard to race, color, religion, sex, handicap, familial status, national origin or any other factor protected by federal, state or local law. **Seller** certifies and represents that he/she/it is legally entitled to convey the Property and all improvements.

2. DESCRIPTION OF PROPERTY:
   (a) Real Property Street Address: _____

   Legal Description:_____
   _____ ❑ See Attachment _____
   (b) Personal Property, including appliances:_____
   _____
   _____ ❑ See Attachment _____
   (c) Occupancy: Property ❑ is ❑ is not currently occupied by a tenant. If occupied, the lease term expires _____.

3. PRICE AND TERMS: The property is offered for sale on the following terms, or on other terms acceptable to **Seller**:
   (a) Price: $_____
   (b) Financing Terms: ❑ Cash ❑ Conventional ❑ VA ❑ FHA ❑ Other _____
   ❑ **Seller** Financing: **Seller** will hold a purchase money mortgage in the amount of $_____ with the following terms: _____
   ❑ Assumption of Existing Mortgage: **Buyer** may assume existing mortgage for $_____ plus an assumption fee of $_____. The mortgage is for a term of _____ years beginning in _____, at an interest rate of _____% ❑ fixed ❑ variable (describe) _____
   Lender approval of assumption ❑ is required ❑ is not required ❑ unknown. Notice to **Seller**: You may remain liable for an assumed mortgage for a number of years after the Property is sold. Check with your lender to determine the extent of your liability. **Seller** will ensure that all mortgage payments and required escrow deposits are current at the time of closing and will convey the escrow deposit to the buyer at closing.
   (c) Seller Expenses: Seller will pay mortgage discount or other closing costs not to exceed _____% of the purchase price; and any other expenses **Seller** agrees to pay in connection with a transaction.

4. BROKER OBLIGATIONS AND AUTHORITY: Broker agrees to make diligent and continued efforts to sell the Property until a sales contract is pending on the Property. **Seller** authorizes **Broker** to:
   (a) Advertise the Property as **Broker** deems advisable in newspapers, publications, computer networks including the Internet and other media; place appropriate transaction signs on the Property, including "For Sale" signs and "Sold" signs (once **Seller** signs a sales contract); and use **Seller's** name in connection with marketing or advertising the Property;
   (b) Obtain information relating to the present mortgage(s) on the Property.
   (c) Place the property in a multiple listing service(s) (MLS). **Seller** authorizes **Broker** to report to the MLS/Association of Realtors® this listing information and price, terms and financing information on any resulting sale. **Seller** authorizes **Broker**, the MLS and/or Association of Realtors® to use, license or sell the active listing and sold data.
   (d) Provide objective comparative market analysis information to potential buyers; and
   (e) (Check if applicable) ❑ Use a lock box system to show and access the Property. A lock box does not ensure the Property's security; **Seller** is advised to secure or remove valuables. **Seller** agrees that the lock box is for **Seller's** benefit and releases **Broker**, persons working through **Broker** and **Broker's** local Realtor Board / Association from all liability and responsibility in connection with any loss that occurs. ❑ Withhold verbal offers. ❑ Withhold all offers once **Seller** accepts a sales contract for the Property.
   (f) Act as a single agent of **Seller** with consent to transition to transaction broker.

5. SELLER OBLIGATIONS: In consideration of **Broker's** obligations, **Seller** agrees to:
   (a) Cooperate with **Broker** in carrying out the purpose of this Agreement, including referring immediately to **Broker** all inquiries regarding the Property's transfer, whether by purchase or any other means of transfer.
   (b) Provide **Broker** with keys to the Property and make the Property available for **Broker** to show during reasonable times.
   (c) Inform **Broker** prior to leasing, mortgaging or otherwise encumbering the Property.
   (d) Indemnify **Broker** and hold **Broker** harmless from losses, damages, costs and expenses of any nature, including attorney's

ERS-10tn   Rev. 7/03   © 2003   Florida Association of REALTORS®   All Rights Reserved   Page 1 of 5

FIGURE 11.2   Exclusive-Right-of-Sale Listing Agreement (continued)

fees, and from liability to any person, that **Broker** incurs because of (1) **Seller's** negligence, representations, misrepresentations, actions or inactions, (2) the use of a lock box, (3) the existence of undisclosed material facts about the Property, or (4) a court or arbitration decision that a broker who was not compensated in connection with a transaction is entitled to compensation from **Broker**. This clause will survive **Broker's** performance and the transfer of title.

(e) To perform any act reasonably necessary to comply with FIRPTA (Internal Revenue Code Section 1445).

(f) Make all legally required disclosures, including all facts that materially affect the Property's value and are not readily observable or known by the buyer. **Seller** represents there are no material facts (building code violations, pending code citations, unobservable defects, etc.) other than the following:_____

Seller will immediately inform **Broker** of any material facts that arise after signing this Agreement.

(g) Consult appropriate professionals for related legal, tax, property condition, environmental, foreign reporting requirements and other specialized advice.

6. COMPENSATION: Seller will compensate **Broker** as specified below for procuring a buyer who is ready, willing and able to purchase the Property or any interest in the Property on the terms of this Agreement or on any other terms acceptable to **Seller**. **Seller** will pay **Broker** as follows (plus applicable sales tax):

(a) _____% of the total purchase price OR $_____, no later than the date of closing specified in the sales contract. However, closing is not a prerequisite for **Broker's** fee being earned.

(b) _____ ($ or %) of the consideration paid for an option, at the time an option is created. If the option is exercised, **Seller** will pay **Broker** the paragraph 6(a) fee, less the amount **Broker** received under this subparagraph.

(c) _____ ($ or %) of gross lease value as a leasing fee, on the date **Seller** enters into a lease or agreement to lease, whichever is soonest. This fee is not due if the Property is or becomes the subject of a contract granting an exclusive right to lease the Property.

(d) **Broker's** fee is due in the following circumstances: (1) If any interest in the Property is transferred, whether by sale, lease, exchange, governmental action, bankruptcy or any other means of transfer, regardless of whether the buyer is secured by **Broker**, **Seller** or any other person. (2) If **Seller** refuses or fails to sign an offer at the price and terms stated in this Agreement, defaults on an executed sales contract or agrees with a buyer to cancel an executed sales contract. (3) If, within _____ days after Termination Date ("Protection Period"), **Seller** transfers or contracts to transfer the Property or any interest in the Property to any prospects with whom **Seller**, **Broker** or any real estate licensee communicated regarding the Property prior to Termination Date. However, no fee will be due **Broker** if the Property is relisted after Termination Date and sold through another broker.

(e) Retained Deposits: As consideration for **Broker's** services, **Broker** is entitled to receive _____% of all deposits that **Seller** retains as liquidated damages for a buyer's default in a transaction, not to exceed the paragraph 6(a) fee.

7. COOPERATION AND COMPENSATION WITH OTHER BROKERS: **Broker's** office policy is to cooperate with all other brokers except when not in **Seller's** best interest: ❏ and to offer compensation in the amount of _____% of the purchase price or $_____ to **Buyer's** agents, who represent the interest of the buyers, and not the interest of **Seller** in a transaction; ❏ and to offer compensation in the amount of _____% of the purchase price or $_____ to a broker who has no brokerage relationship with the **Buyer** or **Seller**; ❏ and to offer compensation in the amount of _____% of the purchase price or $_____ to Transaction brokers for the **Buyer**; ❏ None of the above (if this is checked, the Property cannot be placed in the MLS.)

8. BROKERAGE RELATIONSHIP:

IMPORTANT NOTICE

FLORIDA LAW REQUIRES THAT REAL ESTATE LICENSEES PROVIDE THIS NOTICE TO POTENTIAL SELLERS AND BUYERS OF REAL ESTATE.

You should not assume that any real estate broker or salesperson represents you unless you agree to engage a real estate licensee in an authorized brokerage relationship, either as a single agent or as a transaction broker. You are advised not to disclose any information you want to be held in confidence until you make a decision on representation.

SINGLE AGENT NOTICE

FLORIDA LAW REQUIRES THAT REAL ESTATE LICENSEES OPERATING AS SINGLE AGENTS DISCLOSE TO BUYERS AND SELLERS THEIR DUTIES.

As a single agent, _____ and its associates owe to you the following duties:

1. Dealing honestly and fairly;
2. Loyalty;
3. Confidentiality;

FIGURE 11.2   Exclusive-Right-of-Sale Listing Agreement (continued)

---

4. Obedience;
5. Full disclosure;
6. Accounting for all funds;
7. Skill, care, and diligence in the transaction;
8. Presenting all offers and counteroffers in a timely manner, unless a party has previously directed the licensee otherwise in writing; and
9. Disclosing all known facts that materially affect the value of residential real property and are not readily observable.

Date	Signature

CONSENT TO TRANSITION TO TRANSACTION BROKER

FLORIDA LAW ALLOWS REAL ESTATE LICENSEES WHO REPRESENT A BUYER OR SELLER AS A SINGLE AGENT TO CHANGE FROM A SINGLE AGENT RELATIONSHIP TO A TRANSACTION BROKERAGE RELATIONSHIP IN ORDER FOR THE LICENSEE TO ASSIST BOTH PARTIES IN A REAL ESTATE TRANSACTION BY PROVIDING A LIMITED FORM OF REPRESENTATION TO BOTH THE BUYER AND THE SELLER. THIS CHANGE IN RELATIONSHIP CANNOT OCCUR WITHOUT YOUR PRIOR WRITTEN CONSENT.

As a transaction broker, _____ and its associates, provides to you a limited form of representation that includes the following duties:

1. Dealing honestly and fairly;
2. Accounting for all funds;
3. Using skill, care, and diligence in the transaction;
4. Disclosing all known facts that materially affect the value of residential real property and are not readily observable to the buyer;
5. Presenting all offers and counteroffers in a timely manner, unless a party has previously directed the licensee otherwise in writing;
6. Limited confidentiality, unless waived in writing by a party. This limited confidentiality will prevent disclosure that the seller will accept a price less than the asking or listed price, that the buyer will pay a price greater than the price submitted in a written offer, of the motivation of any party for selling or buying property, that a seller or buyer will agree to financing terms other than those offered, or of any other information requested by a party to remain confidential; and
7. Any additional duties that are entered into by this or by separate written agreement.

Limited representation means that a buyer or seller is not responsible for the acts of the licensee. Additionally, parties are giving up their rights to the undivided loyalty of the licensee. This aspect of limited representation allows a licensee to facilitate a real estate transaction by assisting both the buyer and the seller, but a licensee will not work to represent one party to the detriment of the other party when acting as a transaction broker to both parties.

_____ I agree that my agent may assume the role and duties of a transaction broker. (must be initialed or signed)

Date	Signature	Signature

IMPORTANT NOTICE

FLORIDA LAW REQUIRES THAT REAL ESTATE LICENSEES PROVIDE THIS NOTICE TO POTENTIAL SELLERS AND BUYERS OF REAL ESTATE.

You should not assume that any real estate broker or salesperson represents you unless you agree to engage a real estate licensee in an authorized brokerage relationship, either as a single agent or as a transaction broker. You are advised not to disclose any information you want to be held in confidence until you make a decision on representation.

TRANSACTION BROKER NOTICE

FLORIDA LAW REQUIRES THAT REAL ESTATE LICENSEES OPERATING AS TRANSACTION BROKERS DISCLOSE TO BUYERS AND SELLERS THEIR ROLE AND DUTIES IN PROVIDING A LIMITED FORM OF REPRESENTATION.

As a transaction broker, _____ and its associates, provides to you a limited form of representation that includes the following duties:

1. Dealing honestly and fairly;
2. Accounting for all funds;
3. Using skill, care, and diligence in the transaction;
4. Disclosing all known facts that materially affect the value of residential real property and are not readily observable to the buyer;

FIGURE 11.2   Exclusive-Right-of-Sale Listing Agreement (continued)

5. Presenting all offers and counteroffers in a timely manner, unless a party has previously directed the licensee otherwise in writing;

6. Limited confidentiality, unless waived in writing by a party. This limited confidentiality will prevent disclosure that the seller will accept a price less than the asking or listed price, that the buyer will pay a price greater than the price submitted in a written offer, of the motivation of any party for selling or buying property, that a seller or buyer will agree to financing terms other than those offered, or of any other information requested by a party to remain confidential; and

7. Any additional duties that are entered into by this or by separate written agreement.

Limited representation means that a buyer or seller is not responsible for the acts of the licensee. Additionally, parties are giving up their rights to the undivided loyalty of the licensee. This aspect of limited representation allows a licensee to facilitate a real estate transaction by assisting both the buyer and the seller, but a licensee will not work to represent one party to the detriment of the other party when acting as a transaction broker to both parties.

_____   _____   _____
Date   **Signature**   **Signature**

9. CONDITIONAL TERMINATION: At **Seller's** request, **Broker** may agree to conditionally terminate this Agreement. If **Broker** agrees to conditional termination, **Seller** must sign a withdrawal agreement, reimburse **Broker** for all direct expenses incurred in marketing the Property and pay a cancellation fee of $_____ plus applicable sales tax. **Broker** may void the conditional termination and **Seller** will pay the fee stated in paragraph 6(a) less the cancellation fee if **Seller** transfers or contracts to transfer the Property or any interest in the Property during the time period from the date of conditional termination to Termination Date and Protection Period, if applicable.

10. DISPUTE RESOLUTION: This Agreement will be construed under Florida law. All controversies, claims and other matters in question between the parties arising out of or relating to this Agreement or the breach thereof will be settled by first attempting mediation under the rules of the American Arbitration Association or other mediator agreed upon by the parties. If litigation arises out of this Agreement, the prevailing party will be entitled to recover reasonable attorney's fees and costs, unless the parties agree that disputes will be settled by arbitration as follows: **Arbitration:** By initialing in the space provided, **Seller** (_____) (_____), Listing Associate (_____) and Listing Broker (_____) agree that disputes not resolved by mediation will be settled by neutral binding arbitration in the county in which the Property is located in accordance with the rules of the American Arbitration Association or other arbitrator agreed upon by the parties. Each party to any arbitration or litigation (including appeals and interpleaders) will pay its own fees, costs and expenses, including attorney's fees, and will equally split the arbitrators' fees and administrative fees of arbitration.

11. MISCELLANEOUS: This Agreement is binding on **Broker's** and **Seller's** heirs, personal representatives, administrators, successors and assigns. **Broker** may assign this Agreement to another listing office. Signatures, initials and modifications communicated by facsimile will be considered as originals. The term "buyer" as used in this Agreement includes buyers, tenants, exchangors, optionees and other categories of potential or actual transferees.

12. ADDITIONAL TERMS: _____

_____
_____
_____
_____
_____
_____
_____
_____
_____
_____
_____
_____
_____
_____
_____
_____
_____
_____
_____
_____
_____

ERS-10tn   Rev. 7/03   © 2003 · Florida Association of REALTORS®   All Rights Reserved   Page 4 of 5

FIGURE 11.3   Contract for Sale and Purchase

THIS FORM HAS BEEN APPROVED BY THE FLORIDA ASSOCIATION OF REALTORS AND THE FLORIDA BAR

Contract For Sale And Purchase
FLORIDA ASSOCIATION OF REALTORS AND THE FLORIDA BAR

1* **PARTIES:** _____ ("Seller"),
2* and _____ ("Buyer"),
3 hereby agree that Seller shall sell and Buyer shall buy the following described Real Property and Personal Property (collectively "Property")
4 pursuant to the terms and conditions of this Contract for Sale and Purchase and any riders and addenda ("Contract"):
5 **I.   DESCRIPTION:**
6*   (a) Legal description of the Real Property located in _____ County, Florida: _____
7* _____
8* _____
9*   (b) Street address, city, zip, of the Property: _____
10   (c) Personal Property includes existing range(s), refrigerator(s), dishwasher(s), ceiling fan(s), light fixture(s), and window treatment(s) unless
11   specifically excluded below.
12*   Other items included are: _____
13* _____
14*   Items of Personal Property (and leased items, if any) excluded are: _____
15* _____

16* **II.   PURCHASE PRICE** (U.S. currency): . . . . $ _____
17   **PAYMENT:**
18*   (a) Deposit held in escrow by _____ (Escrow Agent) in the amount of (checks subject to clearance) $ _____
19*   (b) Additional escrow deposit to be made to Escrow Agent within _____ days after Effective Date
20*   (see Paragraph III) in the amount of . . . . $ _____
21*   (c) Financing (see Paragraph IV) in the amount of . . . . $ _____
22*   (d) Other . . . . $ _____
23   (e) Balance to close by cash, wire transfer or LOCALLY DRAWN cashier's or official bank check(s), subject
24*   to adjustments or prorations . . . . $ _____
25 **III.   TIME FOR ACCEPTANCE OF OFFER AND COUNTEROFFERS; EFFECTIVE DATE:**
26   (a) If this offer is not executed by and delivered to all parties OR FACT OF EXECUTION communicated in writing between the parties on or
27*   before _____, the deposit(s) will, at Buyer's option, be returned and this offer withdrawn. **UNLESS OTH-**
28   **ERWISE STATED, THE TIME FOR ACCEPTANCE OF ANY COUNTEROFFERS SHALL BE 2 DAYS FROM THE DATE THE COUN-**
29   **TEROFFER IS DELIVERED.**
30   (b) The date of Contract ("Effective Date") will be the date when the last one of the Buyer and Seller has signed or initialed this offer or the
31   final counteroffer. If such date is not otherwise set forth in this Contract, then the "Effective Date" shall be the date deter mined above for
32   acceptance of this offer or, if applicable, the final counteroffer.
33 **IV.   FINANCING:**
34*   ❏ (a) This is a cash transaction with no contingencies for financing;
35*   ❏ (b) This Contract is contingent on Buyer obtaining approval of a loan ("Loan Approval") within _____ days (if blank, then 30 days) after
36*   Effective Date ("Loan Approval Date") for (CHECK ONLY ONE): ❏ a fixed; ❏ an adjustable; or ❏ a fixed or adjustable rate loan, in the prin-
37*   cipal amount of $ _____, at an initial interest rate not to exceed _____%, discount and origination fees not to exceed
38*   _____% of principal amount, and for a term of _____ years. Buyer will make application within _____ days (if blank, then 5 days) after
39   Effective Date. Buyer shall use reasonable diligence to: obtain Loan Approval **and notify Seller in writing of Loan Approval by Loan**
40   **Approval Date**; satisfy terms and conditions of the Loan Approval; and close the loan. Loan Approval which requires a condition related to
41   the sale of other property shall not be deemed Loan Approval for purposes of this subparagraph. Buyer shall pay all loan expenses. If Buyer
42   does not deliver written notice to Seller by Loan Approval Date stating Buyer has either obtained Loan Approval or waived this financing con-
43   tingency, then either party may cancel this Contract by delivering written notice ("Cancellation Notice") to the other, not later than seven (7)
44   days prior to Closing. Seller's Cancellation Notice must state that Buyer has three (3) days to deliver to Seller written notice waiving this
45   financing contingency. If Buyer has used due diligence and has not obtained Loan Approval before cancellation as provided above, Buyer
46   shall be refunded the deposit(s). Unless this financing contingency has been waived, this Contract shall remain subject to the satisfaction,
47   by Closing, of those conditions of Loan Approval related to the Property.
48*   ❏ (c) Assumption of existing mortgage (see rider for terms); or
49*   ❏ (d) Purchase money note and mortgage to Seller (see Standards B and K and riders; addenda; or special clauses for terms).
50* **V.   TITLE EVIDENCE:** At least _____ days (if blank, then 5 days) before Closing a title insurance commitment with legible copies of instruments
51   listed as exceptions attached thereto ("Title Commitment") and, after Closing, an owner's policy of title insurance (see Standard A for terms) shall
52   be obtained by:
53*   **(CHECK ONLY ONE):** ❏ (1) Seller, at Seller's expense and delivered to Buyer or Buyer's attorney; or
54*   ❏ (2) Buyer at Buyer's expense.
55*   **(CHECK HERE):** ❏ If an abstract of title is to be furnished instead of title insurance, and attach rider for terms.
56* **VI.   CLOSING DATE:** This transaction shall be closed and the closing documents delivered on _____ ("Closing"), unless
57   modified by other provisions of this Contract. If Buyer is unable to obtain Hazard, Wind, Flood, or Homeowners' insurance at a reasonable rate
58   due to extreme weather conditions, Buyer may delay Closing for up to 5 days after such coverage becomes available.
59 **VII.   RESTRICTIONS; EASEMENTS; LIMITATIONS:** Seller shall convey marketable title subject to: comprehensive land use plans, zoning,
60   restrictions, prohibitions and other requirements imposed by governmental authority; restrictions and matters appearing on the plat or otherwise

FAR/BAR-7s   Rev. 7/04   © 2004   Florida Association of REALTORS and The Florida Bar   All Rights Reserved   **Page 1 of 4**

FIGURE 11.3   Contract for Sale and Purchase (continued)

61   common to the subdivision; outstanding oil, gas and mineral rights of record without right of entry; unplatted public utility easements of record
62   (located contiguous to real property lines and not more than 10 feet in width as to the rear or front lines and 7 1/2 feet in width as to the side
63   lines); taxes for year of Closing and subsequent years; and assumed mortgages and purchase money mortgages, if any (if additional items, see
64   addendum); provided, that there exists at Closing no violation of the foregoing and none prevent use of the Property for
65* _____ purpose(s).
66   **VIII. OCCUPANCY:** Seller shall deliver occupancy of Property to Buyer at time of Closing unless otherwise stated herein. If Property is intended
67   to be rented or occupied beyond Closing, the fact and terms thereof and the tenant(s) or occupants shall be disclosed pursuant to Standard F.
68   If occupancy is to be delivered before Closing, Buyer assumes all risks of loss to Property from date of occupancy, shall be responsible and liable
69   for maintenance from that date, and shall be deemed to have accepted Property in its existing condition as of time of taking occupancy.
70   **IX. TYPEWRITTEN OR HANDWRITTEN PROVISIONS:** Typewritten or handwritten provisions, riders and addenda shall control all printed pro-
71   visions of this Contract in conflict with them.
72* **X.   ASSIGNABILITY:** (CHECK ONLY ONE): Buyer ❏ may assign and thereby be released from any further liability under this Contract; ❏ may
73* assign but not be released from liability under this Contract; or ❏ may not assign this Contract.
74   **XI. DISCLOSURES:**
75*   (a) ❏ CHECK HERE if the Property is subject to a special assessment lien imposed by a public body payable in installments which
76*   continue beyond Closing and, if so, specify who shall pay amounts due after Closing: ❏ Seller ❏ Buyer ❏ Other (see addendum).
77   (b) Radon is a naturally occurring radioactive gas that when accumulated in a building in sufficient quantities may present health risks to per-
78   sons who are exposed to it over time. Levels of radon that exceed federal and state guidelines have been found in buildings in Florida.
79   Additional information regarding radon or radon testing may be obtained from your County Public Health unit.
80   (c) Mold is naturally occurring and may cause health risks or damage to property. If Buyer is concerned or desires additional information
81   regarding mold, Buyer should contact an appropriate professional.
82   (d) Buyer acknowledges receipt of the Florida Energy-Efficiency Rating Information Brochure required by Section 553.996, F.S.
83   (e) If the real property includes pre-1978 residential housing then a lead-based paint rider is mandatory.
84   (f) If Seller is a "foreign person" as defined by the Foreign Investment in Real Property Tax Act, the parties shall comply with that Act.
85   (g) **BUYER SHOULD NOT EXECUTE THIS CONTRACT UNTIL BUYER HAS RECEIVED AND READ THE HOMEOWNERS' ASSOCIA-**
86   **TION/COMMUNITY DISCLOSURE.**
87   (h) PROPERTY TAX DISCLOSURE SUMMARY: BUYER SHOULD NOT RELY ON THE SELLER'S CURRENT PROPERTY TAXES AS THE AMOUNT
88   OF PROPERTY TAXES THAT THE BUYER MAY BE OBLIGATED TO PAY IN THE YEAR SUBSEQUENT TO PURCHASE. A CHANGE OF OWNER-
89   SHIP OR PROPERTY IMPROVEMENTS TRIGGERS REASSESSMENTS OF THE PROPERTY THAT COULD RESULT IN HIGHER PROPERTY TAXES.
90   IF YOU HAVE ANY QUESTIONS CONCERNING VALUATION, CONTACT THE COUNTY PROPERTY APPRAISER'S OFFICE FOR INFORMATION.
91   **XII. MAXIMUM REPAIR COSTS:** Seller shall not be responsible for payments in excess of:
92*   (a) $_____ for treatment and repair under Standard D (if blank, then 1.5% of the Purchase Price).
93*   (b) $_____ for repair and replacement under Standard N not caused by Wood Destroying Organisms (if blank, then 1.5%
94   of the Purchase Price).
95* **XIII. HOME WARRANTY:** ❏ Seller ❏ Buyer ❏ N/A will pay for a home warranty plan issued by _____
96* at a cost not to exceed $_____.
97   **XIV. RIDERS; ADDENDA; SPECIAL CLAUSES: CHECK** those riders which are applicable AND are attached to and made part of this Contract:
98*   ❏ CONDOMINIUM ❏ VA/FHA ❏ HOMEOWNERS' ASSN. ❏ LEAD-BASED PAINT ❏ COASTAL CONSTRUCTION CONTROL LINE
99*   ❏ INSULATION ❏ "AS IS" ❏ Other Comprehensive Rider Provisions ❏ Addenda
100*   Special Clause(s): _____
101* _____
102* _____
103* _____

104 **XV. STANDARDS FOR REAL ESTATE TRANSACTIONS ("Standards"):** Buyer and Seller acknowledge receipt of a copy of Standards A
105 through Y on the reverse side or attached, which are incorporated as part of this Contract.
106   **THIS IS INTENDED TO BE A LEGALLY BINDING CONTRACT. IF NOT FULLY UNDERSTOOD,**
107   **SEEK THE ADVICE OF AN ATTORNEY PRIOR TO SIGNING.**
108   THIS FORM HAS BEEN APPROVED BY THE FLORIDA ASSOCIATION OF REALTORS AND THE FLORIDA BAR.
109   Approval does not constitute an opinion that any of the terms and conditions in this Contract should be accepted by the parties in a
110   particular transaction. Terms and conditions should be negotiated based upon the respective interests, objectives and bargaining
111   positions of all interested persons.
112   AN ASTERISK(*) FOLLOWING A LINE NUMBER IN THE MARGIN INDICATES THE LINE CONTAINS A BLANK TO BE COMPLETED.

113* _____   _____   _____   _____
114 (BUYER)   (DATE)   (SELLER)   (DATE)

115* _____   _____   _____   _____
116 (BUYER)   (DATE)   (SELLER)   (DATE)

117* Buyers' address for purposes of notice _____   Sellers' address for purposes of notice _____
118* _____   _____
119* _____ Phone   _____ Phone
120 **BROKERS:** The brokers (including cooperating brokers, if any) named below are the only brokers entitled to compensation in connection with
121 this Contract:
122* Name: _____   _____
123   **Cooperating Brokers, if any**   **Listing Broker**

FAR/BAR-7s   Rev. 7/04   © 2004   Florida Association of REALTORS and The Florida Bar   All Rights Reserved   **Page 2 of 4**

FIGURE 11.3   Contract for Sale and Purchase (continued)

STANDARDS FOR REAL ESTATE TRANSACTIONS

124
125 **A. TITLE INSURANCE:** The Title Commitment shall be issued by a Florida licensed title insurer agreeing to issue Buyer, upon recording of the deed to Buyer, an
126 owner's policy of title insurance in the amount of the purchase price, insuring Buyer's marketable title to the Real Property, subject only to matters contained in
127 Paragraph VII and those to be discharged by Seller at or before Closing. Marketable title shall be determined according to applicable Title Standards adopted by
128 authority of The Florida Bar and in accordance with law. Buyer shall have 5 days from date of receiving the Title Commitment to examine it, and if title is found defec-
129 tive, notify Seller in writing specifying defect(s) which render title unmarketable. Seller shall have 30 days from receipt of notice to remove the defects, failing which
130 Buyer shall, within 5 days after expiration of the 30 day period, deliver written notice to Seller either: (1) extending the time for a reasonable period not to exceed 120
131 days within which Seller shall use diligent effort to remove the defects; or (2) requesting a refund of deposit(s) paid which shall be returned to Buyer. If Buyer fails to
132 so notify Seller, Buyer shall be deemed to have accepted the title as it then is. Seller shall, if title is found unmarketable, use diligent effort to correct defect(s) within
133 the time provided. If, after diligent effort, Seller is unable to timely correct the defects, Buyer shall either waive the defects, or receive a refund of deposit(s), thereby
134 releasing Buyer and Seller from all further obligations under this Contract. If Seller is to provide the Title Commitment and it is delivered to Buyer less than 5 days prior
135 to Closing, Buyer may extend Closing so that Buyer shall have up to 5 days from date of receipt to examine same in accordance with this Standard.
136 **B. PURCHASE MONEY MORTGAGE; SECURITY AGREEMENT TO SELLER:** A purchase money mortgage and mortgage note to Seller shall provide for a
137 30 day grace period in the event of default if a first mortgage and a 15 day grace period if a second or lesser mortgage; shall provide for right of prepayment
138 in whole or in part without penalty; shall permit acceleration in event of transfer of the Real Property; shall require all prior liens and encumbrances to be kept
139 in good standing; shall forbid modifications of, or future advances under, prior mortgage(s); shall require Buyer to maintain policies of insurance containing a
140 standard mortgagee clause covering all improvements located on the Real Property against fire and all perils included within the term "extended coverage
141 endorsements" and such other risks and perils as Seller may reasonably require, in an amount equal to their highest insurable value; and the mortgage, note
142 and security agreement shall be otherwise in form and content required by Seller, but Seller may only require clauses and coverage customarily found in mort-
143 gages, mortgage notes and security agreements generally utilized by savings and loan institutions or state or national banks located in the county wherein the
144 Real Property is located. All Personal Property and leases being conveyed or assigned will, at Seller's option, be subject to the lien of a security agreement evi-
145 denced by recorded or filed financing statements or certificates of title. If a balloon mortgage, the final payment will exceed the periodic payments thereon.
146 **C. SURVEY:** Buyer, at Buyer's expense, within time allowed to deliver evidence of title and to examine same, may have the Real Property surveyed and certified
147 by a registered Florida surveyor. If the survey discloses encroachments on the Real Property or that improvements located thereon encroach on setback lines, ease-
148 ments, lands of others or violate any restrictions, Contract covenants or applicable governmental regulations, the same shall constitute a title defect.
149 **D. WOOD DESTROYING ORGANISMS:** "Wood Destroying Organisms" (WDO) shall be deemed to include all wood destroying organisms required to be report-
150 ed under the Florida Structural Pest Control Act, as amended. Buyer, at Buyer's expense, may have the Property inspected by a Florida Certified Pest Control Operator
151 ("Operator") within 20 days after the Effective Date to determine if there is any visible active WDO infestation or visible damage from WDO infestation, excluding fences.
152 If either or both are found, Buyer may within said 20 days (1) have cost of treatment of active infestation estimated by the Operator; (2) have all damage inspected
153 and cost of repair estimated by an appropriately licensed contractor; and (3) report such cost(s) to Seller in writing. Seller shall cause the treatment and repair of all
154 WDO damage to be made and pay the costs thereof up to the amount provided in Paragraph XII(a). If estimated costs exceed that amount, Buyer shall have the
155 option of canceling this Contract by giving written notice to Seller within 20 days after the Effective Date, or Buyer may elect to proceed with the transaction and
156 receive a credit at Closing equal to the amount provided in Paragraph XII(a). If Buyer's lender requires an updated WDO report, then Buyer shall, at Buyer's expense,
157 have the opportunity to have the Property re-inspected for WDO infestation and have the cost of active infestation or new damage estimated and reported to Seller
158 in writing at least 10 days prior to Closing, and thereafter, Seller shall cause such treatment and repair to be made and pay the cost thereof; provided, Seller's total
159 obligation for treatment and repair costs required under both the first and second inspection shall not exceed the amount provided in Paragraph XII (a).
160 **E. INGRESS AND EGRESS:** Seller warrants and represents that there is ingress and egress to the Real Property sufficient for its intended use as described
161 in Paragraph VII hereof and title to the Real Property is insurable in accordance with Standard A without exception for lack of legal right of access.
162 **F. LEASES:** Seller shall, at least 10 days before Closing, furnish to Buyer copies of all written leases and estoppel letters from each tenant specifying the nature
163 and duration of the tenant's occupancy, rental rates, advanced rent and security deposits paid by tenant. If Seller is unable to obtain such letter from each ten-
164 ant, the same information shall be furnished by Seller to Buyer within that time period in the form of a Seller's affidavit, and Buyer may thereafter contact ten-
165 ant to confirm such information. If the terms of the leases differ materially from Seller's representations, Buyer may terminate this Contract by delivering written
166 notice to Seller at least 5 days prior to Closing. Seller shall, at Closing, deliver and assign all original leases to Buyer.
167 **G. LIENS:** Seller shall furnish to Buyer at time of Closing an affidavit attesting to the absence, unless otherwise provided for herein, of any financing statement,
168 claims of lien or potential lienors known to Seller and further attesting that there have been no improvements or repairs to the Real Property for 90 days imme-
169 diately preceding date of Closing. If the Real Property has been improved or repaired within that time, Seller shall deliver releases or waivers of construction
170 liens executed by all general contractors, subcontractors, suppliers and materialmen in addition to Seller's lien affidavit setting forth the names of all such gen-
171 eral contractors, subcontractors, suppliers and materialmen, further affirming that all charges for improvements or repairs which could serve as a basis for a
172 construction lien or a claim for damages have been paid or will be paid at the Closing of this Contract.
173 **H. PLACE OF CLOSING:** Closing shall be held in the county wherein the Real Property is located at the office of the attorney or other closing agent ("Closing
174 Agent") designated by the party paying for title insurance, or, if no title insurance, designated by Seller.
175 **I. TIME:** In computing time periods of less than six (6) days, Saturdays, Sundays and state or national legal holidays shall be excluded. Any time periods provided
176 for herein which shall end on a Saturday, Sunday, or a legal holiday shall extend to 5:00 p.m. of the next business day. **Time is of the essence in this Contract.**
177 **J. CLOSING DOCUMENTS:** Seller shall furnish the deed, bill of sale, certificate of title, construction lien affidavit, owner's possession affidavit, assignments of leases,
178 tenant and mortgagee estoppel letters and corrective instruments. Buyer shall furnish mortgage, mortgage note, security agreement and financing statements.
179 **K. EXPENSES:** Documentary stamps on the deed and recording of corrective instruments shall be paid by Seller. All costs of Buyer's loan (whether obtained
180 from Seller or third party), including, but not limited to, documentary stamps and intangible tax on the purchase money mortgage and any mortgage assumed,
181 mortgagee title insurance commitment with related fees, and recording of purchase money mortgage to Seller, deed and financing statements shall be paid by
182 Buyer. Unless otherwise provided by law or rider to this Contract, charges for the following related title services, namely title evidence, title examination, and
183 closing fee (including preparation of closing statement), shall be paid by the party responsible for furnishing the title evidence in accordance with Paragraph V.
184 **L. PRORATIONS; CREDITS:** Taxes, assessments, rent, interest, insurance and other expenses of the Property shall be prorated through the day before Closing.
185 Buyer shall have the option of taking over existing policies of insurance, if assumable, in which event premiums shall be prorated. Cash at Closing shall be
186 increased or decreased as may be required by prorations to be made through day prior to Closing, or occupancy, if occupancy occurs before Closing. Advance
187 rent and security deposits will be credited to Buyer. Escrow deposits held by mortgagee will be credited to Seller. Taxes shall be prorated based on the current
188 year's tax with due allowance made for maximum allowable discount, homestead and other exemptions. If Closing occurs at a date when the current year's mill-
189 age is not fixed and current year's assessment is available, taxes will be prorated based upon such assessment and prior year's millage. If current year's assess-
190 ment is not available, then taxes will be prorated on prior year's tax. If there are completed improvements on the Real Property by January 1st of year of Closing,
191 which improvements were not in existence on January 1st of prior year, then taxes shall be prorated based upon prior year's millage and at an equitable assess-
192 ment to be agreed upon between the parties; failing which, request shall be made to the County Property Appraiser for an informal assessment taking into
193 account available exemptions. A tax proration based on an estimate shall, at request of either party, be readjusted upon receipt of current year's tax bill.
194 **M. SPECIAL ASSESSMENT LIENS:** Except as set forth in Paragraph XI(a), certified, confirmed and ratified special assessment liens imposed by public bod-
195 ies as of Closing are to be paid by Seller. Pending liens as of Closing shall be assumed by Buyer. If the improvement has been substantially completed as of
196 Effective Date, any pending lien shall be considered certified, confirmed or ratified and Seller shall, at Closing, be charged an amount equal to the last estimate
197 or assessment for the improvement by the public body.

FIGURE 11.3 Contract for Sale and Purchase (continued)

198
STANDARDS FOR REAL ESTATE TRANSACTIONS (CONTINUED)
199 **N. INSPECTION AND REPAIR:** Seller warrants that the ceiling, roof (including the fascia and soffits), exterior and interior walls, foundation, and dockage of
200 the Property do not have any visible evidence of leaks, water damage, or structural damage and that the septic tank, pool, all appliances, mechanical items,
201 heating, cooling, electrical, plumbing systems, and machinery are in Working Condition. The foregoing warranty shall be limited to the items specified unless
202 otherwise provided in an addendum. Buyer may inspect, or, at Buyer's expense, have a firm or individual specializing in home inspections and holding an occu-
203 pational license for such purpose (if required), or by an appropriately licensed Florida contractor, make inspections of, those items within 20 days after the
204 Effective Date. Buyer shall, prior to Buyer's occupancy but not more than 20 days after Effective Date, report in writing to Seller such items that do not meet
205 the above standards as to defects. Unless Buyer timely reports such defects, Buyer shall be deemed to have waived Seller's warranties as to defects not report-
206 ed. If repairs or replacements are required to comply with this Standard, Seller shall cause them to be made and shall pay up to the amount provided in
207 Paragraph XII (b). Seller is not required to make repairs or replacements of a Cosmetic Condition unless caused by a defect Seller is responsible to repair or
208 replace. If the cost for such repair or replacement exceeds the amount provided in Paragraph XII (b), Buyer or Seller may elect to pay such excess, failing which
209 either party may cancel this Contract. If Seller is unable to correct the defects prior to Closing, the cost thereof shall be paid into escrow at Closing. For pur-
210 poses of this Contract: (1) "Working Condition" means operating in the manner in which the item was designed to operate; (2) "Cosmetic Condition" means
211 aesthetic imperfections that do not affect the Working Condition of the item, including, but not limited to: pitted marcite or other pool finishes; missing or torn
212 screens; fogged windows; tears, worn spots, or discoloration of floor coverings, wallpaper, or window treatments; nail holes, scratches, dents, scrapes, chips
213 or caulking in ceilings, walls, flooring, fixtures, or mirrors; and minor cracks in floors, tiles, windows, driveways, sidewalks, or pool decks; and (3) cracked roof
214 tiles, curling or worn shingles, or limited roof life shall not be considered defects Seller must repair or replace, so long as there is no evidence of actual leaks
215 or leakage or structural damage, but missing tiles will be Seller's responsibility to replace or repair.
216 **O. RISK OF LOSS:** If the Property is damaged by fire or other casualty before Closing and cost of restoration does not exceed 1.5% of the Purchase Price, cost
217 of restoration shall be an obligation of Seller and Closing shall proceed pursuant to the terms of this Contract with restoration costs escrowed at Closing. If the
218 cost of restoration exceeds 1.5% of the Purchase Price, Buyer shall either take the Property as is, together with either the 1.5% or any insurance proceeds
219 payable by virtue of such loss or damage, or receive a refund of deposit(s), thereby releasing Buyer and Seller from all further obligations under this Contract.
220 **P. CLOSING PROCEDURE:** The deed shall be recorded upon clearance of funds. If the title agent insures adverse matters pursuant to Section 627.7841, F.S.,
221 as amended, the escrow and closing procedure required by this Standard shall be waived. Unless waived as set forth above the following closing procedures
222 shall apply: (1) all closing proceeds shall be held in escrow by the Closing Agent for a period of not more than 5 days after Closing; (2) if Seller's title is rendered
223 unmarketable, through no fault of Buyer, Buyer shall, within the 5 day period, notify Seller in writing of the defect and Seller shall have 30 days from date of receipt
224 of such notification to cure the defect; (3) if Seller fails to timely cure the defect, all deposits and closing funds shall, upon written demand by Buyer and within 5
225 days after demand, be returned to Buyer and, simultaneously with such repayment, Buyer shall return the Personal Property, vacate the Real Property and recon-
226 vey the Property to Seller by special warranty deed and bill of sale; and (4) if Buyer fails to make timely demand for refund, Buyer shall take title as is, waiving all
227 rights against Seller as to any intervening defect except as may be available to Buyer by virtue of warranties contained in the deed or bill of sale.
228 **Q. ESCROW:** Any Closing Agent or escrow agent (collectively "Agent") receiving funds or equivalent is authorized and agrees by acceptance of them to deposit
229 them promptly, hold same in escrow and, subject to clearance, disburse them in accordance with terms and conditions of this Contract. Failure of funds to clear shall
230 not excuse Buyer's performance. If in doubt as to Agent's duties or liabilities under the provisions of this Contract, Agent may, at Agent's option, continue to hold the
231 subject matter of the escrow until the parties hereto agree to its disbursement or until a judgment of a court of competent jurisdiction shall determine the rights of the
232 parties, or Agent may deposit same with the clerk of the circuit court having jurisdiction of the dispute. An attorney who represents a party and also acts as Agent
233 may represent such party in such action. Upon notifying all parties concerned of such action, all liability on the part of Agent shall fully terminate, except to the extent
234 of accounting for any items previously delivered out of escrow. If a licensed real estate broker, Agent will comply with provisions of Chapter 475, F.S., as amended.
235 Any suit between Buyer and Seller wherein Agent is made a party because of acting as Agent hereunder, or in any suit wherein Agent interpleads the subject matter
236 of the escrow, Agent shall recover reasonable attorney's fees and costs incurred with these amounts to be paid from and out of the escrowed funds or equivalent
237 and charged and awarded as court costs in favor of the prevailing party. The Agent shall not be liable to any party or person for misdelivery to Buyer or Seller of items
238 subject to the escrow, unless such misdelivery is due to willful breach of the provisions of this Contract or gross negligence of Agent.
239 **R. ATTORNEY'S FEES; COSTS:** In any litigation, including breach, enforcement or interpretation, arising out of this Contract, the prevailing party in such liti-
240 gation, which, for purposes of this Standard, shall include Seller, Buyer and any brokers acting in agency or nonagency relationships authorized by Chapter
241 475, F.S., as amended, shall be entitled to recover from the non-prevailing party reasonable attorney's fees, costs and expenses.
242 **S. FAILURE OF PERFORMANCE:** If Buyer fails to perform this Contract within the time specified, including payment of all deposits, the deposit(s) paid by
243 Buyer and deposit(s) agreed to be paid, may be recovered and retained by and for the account of Seller as agreed upon liquidated damages, consideration for
244 the execution of this Contract and in full settlement of any claims; whereupon, Buyer and Seller shall be relieved of all obligations under this Contract; or Seller,
245 at Seller's option, may proceed in equity to enforce Seller's rights under this Contract. If for any reason other than failure of Seller to make Seller's title mar-
246 ketable after diligent effort, Seller fails, neglects or refuses to perform this Contract, Buyer may seek specific performance or elect to receive the return of Buyer's
247 deposit(s) without thereby waiving any action for damages resulting from Seller's breach.
248 **T. CONTRACT NOT RECORDABLE; PERSONS BOUND; NOTICE; FACSIMILE:** Neither this Contract nor any notice of it shall be recorded in any public
249 records. This Contract shall bind and inure to the benefit of the parties and their successors in interest. Whenever the context permits, singular shall include
250 plural and one gender shall include all. Notice and delivery given by or to the attorney or broker representing any party shall be as effective as if given by or to
251 that party. All notices must be in writing and may be made by mail, personal delivery or electronic media. A legible facsimile copy of this Contract and any sig-
252 natures hereon shall be considered for all purposes as an original.
253 **U. CONVEYANCE:** Seller shall convey marketable title to the Real Property by statutory warranty, trustee's, personal representative's, or guardian's deed, as
254 appropriate to the status of Seller, subject only to matters contained in Paragraph VII and those otherwise accepted by Buyer. Personal Property shall, at the
255 request of Buyer, be transferred by an absolute bill of sale with warranty of title, subject only to such matters as may be otherwise provided for herein.
256 **V. OTHER AGREEMENTS:** No prior or present agreements or representations shall be binding upon Buyer or Seller unless included in this Contract. No mod-
257 ification to or change in this Contract shall be valid or binding upon the parties unless in writing and executed by the parties intended to be bound by it.
258 **W. SELLER DISCLOSURE:** There are no facts known to Seller materially affecting the value of the Property which are not readily observable by Buyer or which
259 have not been disclosed to Buyer.
260 **X. PROPERTY MAINTENANCE; PROPERTY ACCESS; REPAIR STANDARDS; ASSIGNMENT OF CONTRACTS AND WARRANTIES**: Seller shall main-
261 tain the Property, including, but not limited to lawn, shrubbery, and pool in the condition existing as of Effective Date, ordinary wear and tear excepted. Seller
262 shall, upon reasonable notice, provide utilities service and access to the Property for appraisal and inspections, including a walk-through prior to Closing, to
263 confirm that all items of Personal Property are on the Real Property and, subject to the foregoing, that all required repairs and replacements have been made,
264 and that the Property has been maintained as required by this Standard. All repairs and replacements shall be completed in a good and workmanlike manner,
265 in accordance with all requirements of law, and shall consist of materials or items of quality, value, capacity and performance comparable to, or better than,
266 that existing as of the Effective Date. Seller will assign all assignable repair and treatment contracts and warranties to Buyer at Closing.
267 **Y. 1031 EXCHANGE:** If either Seller or Buyer wish to enter into a like-kind exchange (either simultaneous with Closing or deferred) with respect to the Property
268 under Section 1031 of the Internal Revenue Code ("Exchange"), the other party shall cooperate in all reasonable respects to effectuate the Exchange, includ-
269 ing the execution of documents; provided (1) the cooperating party shall incur no liability or expense related to the Exchange and (2) the Closing shall not be
270 contingent upon, nor extended or delayed by, such Exchange.

FAR/BAR-7s   Rev. 7/04   © 2004   Florida Association of REALTORS® and The Florida Bar   All Rights Reserved   **Page 4 of 4**

FIGURE 11.4   Exclusive Buyer Brokerage Agreement

Exclusive Buyer Brokerage Agreement
FLORIDA ASSOCIATION OF REALTORS®

1.   PARTIES: _____ ("**Buyer**") grants

_____ ("**Broker**")
Real Estate Broker   /   Office
the exclusive right to work with and assist **Buyer** in locating and negotiating the acquisition of suitable real property as described below. The term "acquire" or "acquisition" includes any purchase, option, exchange, lease or other acquisition of an ownership or equity interest in real property.

2.   TERM: This Agreement will begin on the _____ day of _____, _____ and will terminate at 11:59 p.m. on the _____ day of _____, _____ ("Termination Date"). However, if **Buyer** enters into an agreement to acquire property that is pending on the Termination Date, this Agreement will continue in effect until that transaction has closed or otherwise terminated.

3.   PROPERTY: Buyer is interested in acquiring real property as follows or as otherwise acceptable to **Buyer** ("Property"):

   (a) Type of property: _____

   (b) Location: _____

   (c) Price range: $_____ to $_____ .

   ❏ **Buyer** has been ❏ pre-qualified ❏ pre-approved by _____

   for (amount and terms, if any) _____

   (d) Preferred terms and conditions: _____

   _____

   _____

   _____

4. BROKER'S OBLIGATIONS:
   (a) Broker Assistance. Broker will
      * use **Broker's** professional knowledge and skills;
      * assist **Buyer** in determining **Buyer's** financial capability and financing options;
      * discuss property requirements and assist **Buyer** in locating and viewing suitable properties;
      * assist **Buyer** to contract for property, monitor deadlines and close any resulting transaction;
      * cooperate with real estate licensees working with the seller, if any, to effect a transaction. **Buyer** understands that even if **Broker** is compensated by a seller or a real estate licensee who is working with a seller, such compensation does not compromise **Broker's** duties to **Buyer**.
   (b) Other Buyers. Buyer understands that **Broker** may work with other prospective buyers who want to acquire the same property as **Buyer**. If **Broker** submits offers by competing buyers, **Broker** will notify **Buyer** that a competing offer has been made, but will not disclose any of the offer's material terms or conditions. **Buyer** agrees that **Broker** may make competing buyers aware of the existence of any offer **Buyer** makes, so long as **Broker** does not reveal any material terms or conditions of the offer without **Buyer's** prior written consent.
   (c) Fair Housing. Broker adheres to the principles expressed in the Fair Housing Act and will not participate in any act that unlawfully discriminates on the basis of race, color, religion, sex, handicap, familial status, country of national origin or any other category protected under federal, state or local law.
   (d) Service Providers. Broker does not warrant or guarantee products or services provided by any third party whom **Broker**, at **Buyer's** request, refers or recommends to **Buyer** in connection with property acquisition.

FIGURE 11.4   Exclusive Buyer Brokerage Agreement (continued)

5. BUYER'S OBLIGATIONS: Buyer agrees to cooperate with **Broker** in accomplishing the objectives of this Agreement, including:
(a) Conducting all negotiations and efforts to locate suitable property only through **Broker** and referring to **Broker** all inquiries of any kind from real estate licensees, property owners or any other source. If **Buyer** contacts or is contacted by a seller or a real estate licensee who is working with a seller or views a property unaccompanied by **Broker**, **Buyer** will, at first opportunity, advise the seller or real estate licensee that **Buyer** is working with and represented exclusively by **Broker**.
(b) Providing **Broker** with accurate personal and financial information requested by **Broker** in connection with ensuring **Buyer's** ability to acquire property. **Buyer** authorizes **Broker** to run a credit check to verify **Buyer's** credit information.
(c) Being available to meet with **Broker** at reasonable times for consultations and to view properties.
(d) Indemnifying and holding **Broker** harmless from and against all losses, damages, costs and expenses of any kind, including attorney's fees, and from liability to any person, that **Broker** incurs because of acting on **Buyer's** behalf.
(e) Not asking or expecting to restrict the acquisition of a property according to race, color, religion, sex, handicap, familial status, country of national origin or any other category protected under federal, state or local law.
(f) Consulting an appropriate professional for legal, tax, environmental, engineering, foreign reporting requirements and other specialized advice.

6. RETAINER: Upon final execution of this Agreement, **Buyer** will pay to **Broker** a non-refundable retainer fee of $_____ for **Broker's** services ("Retainer"). This fee is not refundable and ❑ will ❑ will not be credited to **Buyer** if compensation is earned by **Broker** as specified in this Agreement.

7. COMPENSATION: Broker's compensation is earned when, during the term of this Agreement or any renewal or extension, **Buyer** or any person acting for or on behalf of **Buyer** contracts to acquire real property as specified in this Agreement. **Buyer** will be responsible for paying **Broker** the amount specified below plus any applicable taxes but will be credited with any amount which **Broker** receives from a seller or a real estate licensee who is working with a seller.
(a) Purchase or exchange: $_____ or _____% (select only one) of the total purchase price or other consideration for the acquired property, to be paid at closing.
(b) Lease: $_____ or _____% (select only one) of the gross lease value, to be paid when **Buyer** enters into the lease. If **Buyer** enters into a lease-purchase agreement, the amount of the leasing fee which **Broker** receives will be credited toward the amount due **Broker** for the purchase.
(c) Option: Broker will be paid $_____ or _____% of the option amount (select only one), to be paid when **Buyer** enters into the option agreement. If **Buyer** enters into a lease with option to purchase, **Broker** will be compensated for both the lease and the option. If **Buyer** subsequently exercises the option, the amounts received by **Broker** for the lease and option will be credited toward the amount due **Broker** for the purchase.
(d) Other: Broker will be compensated for all other types of acquisitions as if such acquisition were a purchase or exchange.
(e) Buyer Default: Buyer will pay **Broker's** compensation immediately upon **Buyer's** default on any contract to acquire property.

8. PROTECTION PERIOD: Buyer will pay **Broker's** compensation if, within _____ days after Termination Date, **Buyer** contracts to acquire any property which was called to **Buyer's** attention by **Broker** or any other person or found by **Buyer** during the term of this Agreement. **Buyer's** obligation to pay **Broker's** fee ceases upon **Buyer** entering into a good faith exclusive buyer brokerage agreement with another broker after Termination Date.

9. EARLY TERMINATION: Buyer may terminate this Agreement at any time by written notice to **Broker** but will remain responsible for paying **Broker's** compensation if, from the early termination date to Termination Date plus Protection Period, if applicable, **Buyer** contracts to acquire any property which, prior to the early termination date, was found by **Buyer** or called to **Buyer's** attention by **Broker** or any other person. **Broker** may terminate this Agreement at any time by written notice to **Buyer**, in which event **Buyer** will be released from all further obligations under this Agreement.

10. DISPUTE RESOLUTION: Any unresolveable dispute between **Buyer** and **Broker** will be mediated. If a settlement is not reached in mediation, the matter will be submitted to binding arbitration in accordance with the rules of the American Arbitration Association or other mutually agreeable arbitrator.

11. ASSIGNMENT; PERSONS BOUND: Broker may assign this Agreement to another broker. This Agreement will bind and inure to **Broker's** and **Buyer's** heirs, personal representatives, successors and assigns.

FIGURE 11.4   Exclusive Buyer Brokerage Agreement (continued)

12. BROKERAGE RELATIONSHIP: Buyer authorizes **Broker** to operate as (check which is applicable):
❑ single agent of **Buyer.**
❑ transaction broker.
❑ single agent of **Buyer** with consent to transition into a transaction broker.
❑ nonrepresentative of **Buyer.**

13. SPECIAL CLAUSES: _____

_____

_____

_____

_____

_____

14. ACKNOWLEDGMENT; MODIFICATIONS: Buyer has read this Agreement and understands its contents. This Agreement cannot be changed except by written agreement signed by both parties.

Date: _____   **Buyer:** _____   Tax ID No: __ __ __ - __ __ - __ __ __ __

                      Address: _____

                      Zip: _____   Telephone: _____   Facsimile: _____

Date: _____   **Buyer:** _____   Tax ID No: __ __ __ - __ __ - __ __ __ __

                      Address: _____

                      Zip: _____   Telephone: _____   Facsimile: _____

Date: _____   **Real Estate Associate:** _____

Date: _____   **Real Estate Broker:** _____

■ SUMMARY

Real estate licensees are allowed to draw four types of contracts: listing agreements, buyer brokerage agreements, sale and purchase contracts, and option contracts. Licensees may not draw lease agreements. However, licensees may fill in the blanks on Florida Supreme Court preapproved lease instruments for lease periods that do not exceed one year.

Under the statute of frauds, contracts that convey an interest in real property must be in writing and signed to be enforceable. The statute of limitations designates the period of time during which the terms of a contract may be enforced. The statute of limitations for written contracts is five years. For oral contracts, the statute of limitations is four years.

All valid contracts have four essentials: competent parties, mutual assent, legality of object, and consideration. If the contract is a real estate contract it must be in writing and signed (statute of frauds). Contracts can be classified by their method of formation, their content, or their legal effect. There are four legal remedies for breach of contract: specific performance, liquidated damages, rescission on breach of contract, and compensatory damages.

The parties to a sale and purchase contract are the vendor (seller) and the vendee (buyer). Certain disclosures are required to be given to prospective buyers of residential property, including: radon gas disclosure, lead-based paint disclosure (homes built prior to 1978 only), energy efficiency brochure, homeowner association disclosure, and a building code violation disclosure.

■ PRACTICE IN PREPARING CONTRACTS

Listing and sale contract formats vary. However, all that is required in a valid contract is that all the essential elements be present. Once familiarity is gained with how and where to record required information, variations among forms should pose no difficulty. To succeed in the real estate business, prospective licensees must learn how to complete listing and sale contracts.

For practice, carefully read the following narrative situations before you fill out each form. Usually it is best to complete all arithmetic calculations, such as taxes and commission, before you enter the narrative information on the appropriate contract form. (See also Chapter 14.)

Although the listing contract should be completed before the sale contract, there is no specific sequence for entering the items onto each contract. What is important is that all required information be recognized, extracted, and placed on each form. It is helpful to draw a line through each piece of information in the narrative once it is added to the contract.

LISTING CONTRACT (EXCLUSIVE-RIGHT-OF-SALE)

On December 13, 20XX, Mr. and Mrs. Hy R. Saturn signed a contractual agreement with Broker Will B. Dunn, of Neat Realty, resulting in a 90-day exclusive-right-to-sell listing of their home.

The property has been granted homestead tax exemption and is owned as an estate by the entireties.

The Saturns have decided that $94,500 is a fair selling price. The lot has been assessed at $30,000, and the dwelling has been assessed at $60,600. The property is located at 4200 Colegain Circle, Sun City, and is legally described as Lot 14, Block C, Cake Lake Subdivision, as recorded in Plat Book 19, Page 641, Shine County, Florida.

The house is a three-bedroom, two-bath, single-story, ranch-style structure. The house consists of a great room, a master bedroom, a den, a second bedroom, and a third bedroom. There is a dining area between the kitchen and the great room. A utility room, foyer, pantry, hall, and four large closets bring the total air-conditioned/heated living area to 1,776 square feet. A large garage of 720 square feet brings the total square footage under roof to 2,496.

All floors, except the kitchen, have custom carpets, and the windows have custom-made draperies or curtains. Kitchen appliances include a large, beverage-center-type refrigerator, a built-in food processor, a microwave oven, an electric oven and range, a disposal, a dishwasher, and a trash compactor. All appliances stay with the house.

The Saturns have just refinanced and now hold a 10.5 percent, 30-year, $60,000 conventional mortgage with Mutual Profit Savings Association. Their monthly payment for principal and interest is $548.85. A homeowner's insurance policy cost $264 for one year and will expire at midnight, October 18, 20BB.

The sellers have paid the property taxes for 20AA. Because Mr. Saturn must report to his new job in another state by March 1, 20BB, the 20BB taxes will be paid by the buyers and prorated. The city, county, and school board tax rate for the subdivision is 29 mills, including all bond and tax levies.

Your employer, Neat Realty (255-7597), and the Saturns have agreed on a 7 percent sale commission on the purchase price and to the use of co-brokers and/or buyers' agents. The Saturns also have agreed to give possession on the date of closing. Neat Realty has agreed to waive any contract cancellation fee if timely notice of ten days is given.

Now prepare the listing contract.   (The form appears on pages 229–232.) *Note:* Only the "narrative" portion of the listing contract is provided for the purposes of this course. In actual practice, a "profile sheet" with descriptive "features" would have to be completed.

SALE CONTRACT (OFFER TO PURCHASE)

After you have shown the house to Mr. and Mrs. Ben B. Beamer, the Beamers have decided to make an offer. On January 7, 20BB, the Beamers

1 sign an offer for $90,000. The offer is contingent on the Beamers'
2 obtaining a new, conventional mortgage for 80 percent of the total
3 purchase price at 10 percent interest, or less, for 30 years and with
4 possession before February 15, 20BB. A cashier's check for $3,000 is
5 tendered as an earnest money deposit. You present this offer to the
6 Saturns on January 7, and they make a counteroffer the same day.

7   They offer to accept $92,500 with $10,000 down and a second
8 mortgage at 12 percent for 10 years to cover the balance of the Saturns'
9 equity. The closing is to take place on February 12, 20BB, with possession
10 guaranteed the Beamers on that date. The Beamers accept the
11 counteroffer.

12 **Now prepare the sale contract.**   (The form is on pages 233–236.) *Note:*
13 Printed on the back of the FAR/BAR "Contract for Sale and Purchase" is
14 a comprehensive list of "Standards for Real Estate Transactions." A copy
15 of those standards follows the contract form. Carefully study all of the
16 standards; they are an invaluable aid to learning and understanding the
17 contents of the contract.

■ REVIEW QUESTIONS

1. Which group of legal instruments may legally be prepared by a
   licensed real estate broker?
   - A. Listing contracts, buyer brokerage agreements, commercial
     leases, and deeds
   - B. Leases, option contracts, promissory notes, and buyer
     brokerage agreements
   - C. Listing agreements, buyer brokerage agreements, sale
     contracts, and option contracts
   - D. Mortgages, promissory notes, commercial leases, and option
     contracts

2. Failure to comply with the statute of frauds
   - A. may not constitute an illegal act but would always invalidate a
     sale contract.
   - B. would have to do with whether a contract is in writing.
   - C. concerns adherence to prescribed time frames of enforcement.
   - D. is prima facie evidence that there is intent to commit fraud.

3. Which contract does NOT come under the jurisdiction of the statute
   of frauds?
   - A. Lease agreements for less than one year
   - B. Option contract
   - C. Sale contract
   - D. Listing agreement for more than one year

✱ You CAN Drop Comistin to Make Sale.

4. A valid real estate sale contract is one that
   A. contains all of the essential elements and is in writing.
   B. has been acknowledged.
   C. requires witnessing.
   D. transfers title to real property.

5. An adult contracting with a minor is an example of failure to meet which essential of a real estate contract?
   A. Legality of the object
   B. Offer and acceptance
   C. Meeting of the minds
   D. Competent parties

6. Canceling a daughter's property indebtedness in a contract due to love and affection is an example of
   A. good consideration.
   B. valuable consideration.
   C. insufficient consideration.
   D. inadequate consideration.

7. A contract that is NOT in writing is referred to as a(n)
   A. formal contract.
   B. parol contract.
   C. unilateral contract.
   D. executory contract.

8. When a contract has been formed but an undertaking remains to be performed by one or both parties, it is an example of a(n)
   A. implied contract.
   B. express contract.
   C. executory contract.
   D. unilateral contract.

9. Which statement is FALSE regarding counteroffers?
   A. The original offer is terminated by the counteroffer.
   B. The original offeree becomes the offeror.
   C. A contract is created when the new offeree accepts the counteroffer and communicates the acceptance to the new offeror.
   D. The offeror and offeree remain the same even though the terms are modified.

10. An offer is terminated by any one of the following EXCEPT a(n)
   A. counteroffer.
   B. acceptance.
   C. rejection.
   D. extension.

11. A contract may be terminated for which reason(s)?
    A. Mutual rescission
    B. Performance
    C. Breach
    D. All of the above

12. Rebecca gave an exclusive-right-of-sale listing to Broker Sammis of Sammis Realty to find a buyer for her residential lot. While Rebecca was vacationing with her family, Buyer Ken signed an offer to purchase Rebecca's lot at the full price and terms of the listing agreement.
    A. Because this is an exclusive-right-of-sale listing, Broker Sammis is authorized to accept the offer on Rebecca's behalf.
    B. Broker Sammis may accept the offer on Rebecca's behalf, as long as she gets Rebecca's signature on the contract immediately upon Rebecca's return.
    C. The exclusive-right-of-sale listing does not give Broker Sammis the authority to accept the offer on Rebecca's behalf.
    D. Broker Sammis may accept the offer because it is a full-price offer.

13. When a contract is assignable and is assigned without the consent of the other contracting party, the assignor
    A. is free of the obligation to perform the contract terms and conditions.
    B. is not free of the obligation to perform the contract terms and conditions.
    C. has legally transferred and assigned all responsibility for performance.
    D. may not legally assign any right to compensation.

14. Which applies to exclusive-right-of-sale listings?
    A. The broker is due a commission regardless of who finds the buyer.
    B. The listing may be submitted to the MLS by the listing broker.
    C. The seller must consent to the terms of the listing agreement.
    D. All of the above apply.

15. Which disclosure regarding radon is required when purchasing or leasing real property in Florida?
    A. A disclosure statement in the contract indicating that the house has been tested for radon and that the test indicated a safe level of radon.
    B. An estimate of the cost for a required radon test.
    C. A disclosure statement in the contract indicating that the seller is required to have the property tested for radon at the seller's expense if requested by the buyer.
    D. A disclosure statement in the contract explaining radon gas.

16. Joshua (aged 15) entered into a contract with Ken, who is of legal age to contract.
    A. Joshua is obligated to honor the terms of the contract.
    B. Ken may divest himself of his obligations under the contract because the contract is invalid.
    C. Joshua may choose to divest himself of his obligations under the contract.
    D. This contract is a void contract.

Can you enter into a contract with a Minor

17. Normally, a sale contract involving real property contains a provision that in case of breach by the buyer, the earnest money deposit will be regarded as
    A. compensatory damages to the seller.
    B. liquidated damages to the seller.
    C. compensatory damages to the broker.
    D. liquidated damages to be divided between seller and buyer.

18. The most advantageous type of listing from the broker's point of view is a(n)
    A. open listing.
    B. exclusive-agency listing.
    C. exclusive-right-of-sale listing.
    D. net listing.

19. Which statement is FALSE concerning Florida's building code violation disclosure?
    A. The seller is responsible for the costs associated with the code violation.
    B. The seller must inform the code enforcement agency regarding the name and address of the buyer within five days of the title closing.
    C. Copies of the pleadings and other documents concerning the code violation must be given to the buyer.
    D. The disclosure requires a statement that the buyer is responsible for compliance with the building code.

20. Kathy and Bob have decided to make a written offer to purchase a quaint little home built in the 1950s. Which task is NOT required prior to signing the sale contract?
    A. Kathy and Bob must be given a copy of the EPA pamphlet concerning lead-based paint hazards in the home.
    B. The seller must disclose any known presence of lead-based paint.
    C. Kathy and Bob must have the home inspected for lead-based paint.
    D. The buyer must sign a disclosure form regarding lead-based paint prior to signing the sale contract.

CHAPTER 12

Real Estate Finance

Eat Lunch w/ Chief Loan Officer

Know all the Banks.

■ KEY TERMS

acceleration clause

adjustable-rate mortgage (ARM)

amortized mortgage

assignment of mortgage

balloon payment

blanket mortgages

contract for deed

deed in lieu of foreclosure

defeasance clause

due-on-sale clause

equity of redemption

estoppel certificate

home equity loan

hypothecation

loan-to-value (LTV) ratio

mortgage

mortgagee

mortgage insurance premium (MIP)

mortgagor

note

novation

package mortgage

partial release clause

prepayment clause

prepayment penalty

purchase-money mortgage (PMM)

receivership clause

satisfaction of mortgage

subordination clause

wraparound mortgage

1 ## ■ OVERVIEW

2 Because almost every real property transaction involves some type of
3 financing, real estate licensees must understand this aspect of the
4 business. Fluctuating interest rates, deregulation of financial institutions,
5 and varying rates of inflation have in the past created shock waves
6 among institutional lenders and mortgage specialists. As a result, new
7 practices and variations of former lending procedures evolved. Licensees
8 must keep current in the real estate finance area.

9 After completing this Chapter, the student should be able to:

10 • distinguish between title theory and lien theory doctrines;

11 • distinguish between the mortgage instrument and the note;

12 • explain the provisions of the various mortgage clauses;

13 • differentiate among FHA, VA, and conventional mortgages;

14 • describe the features of amortized, adjustable, package, and
15   purchase-money mortgages;

- explain the purpose of an estoppel certificate;

- calculate the loan-to-value (LTV) ratio, given the purchase price and down payment amounts; and

- calculate the down payment, given the purchase price and LTV ratio.

■ LEGAL THEORIES OF MORTGAGES

Under the common law of England, the mortgage was an outright conveyance of real property by the borrower to the lender. The borrower could repossess his property only on repayment of the entire debt on a certain due date. If the borrower failed to make the full payment on the exact due date, the lender had unconditional title to the property. From this common-law practice, the *title theory* of mortgages evolved.

TITLE THEORY

In some states today, including Georgia, the doctrine that a mortgage is a conveyance of the legal title to property still prevails. Title to the mortgaged property is conveyed to the *lender* through a mortgage deed, or, in some states, to a trustee through a deed of trust. If the borrower defaults, the lender may take possession of the property.

LIEN THEORY

In most states today, including Florida, the *borrower* retains title to the property. The lender is protected with a lien on the real property to secure the payment of the mortgage debt.

■ LOAN INSTRUMENTS

Two instruments are involved in a mortgage loan: (1) the *promissory note,* which is the actual promise to repay, and (2) the *mortgage,* which creates the lien interest.

PROMISSORY NOTE

A promissory note (or *mortgage note,* or sometimes a *bond*) must accompany all mortgages in Florida. The **note** is the legal instrument that represents the evidence of a debt. A note is a promise to repay that makes the borrower personally liable for the obligation. It represents the borrower's promise to pay the lender according to the agreed-upon terms of the loan.

The note is usually a separate legal instrument and must be signed by the borrower. The note states the amount of indebtedness, interest rate, repayment method, and term or time period to repay. The mortgage note lists the penalties that will be assessed if the borrower doesn't make the monthly mortgage payments. It also warns the borrower that the lender

FIGURE 12.1   Mortgage Financing

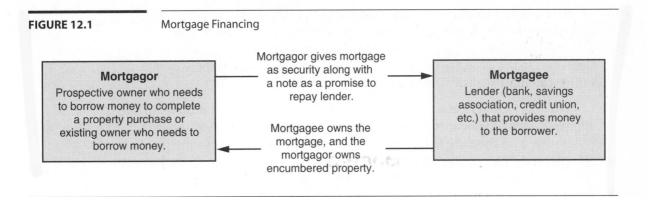

1 can *call* the loan (demand repayment of the entire loan before the end
2 of the term) if the borrower violates the terms of the mortgage. The note
3 is usually *not* recorded.

 wwweb.link

Download the Fannie Mae/Freddie Mac Uniform Florida fixed rate note
for single family property at:
http://www.efanniemae.com/sf/formsdocs/documents/notes/doc/
3210w.doc.

4 MORTGAGE

5 A **mortgage** is an instrument that pledges the property as security
6 (collateral) for a debt. It is the legal document that represents the lien on
7 the real estate that secures the debt. For the lender, the property becomes
8 security, legally sufficient to ensure recovery of the loan. **Hypothecation**
9 refers to the pledging of property as security for payment of a loan
10 without surrendering possession of the property. Mortgages identify the
11 property being used to secure a loan and contain the borrower's
12 promises to fulfill certain other obligations to the lender. A mortgage
13 instrument must be in writing to be enforceable. The mortgage is
14 recorded to establish constructive notice of the lien and to establish
15 priority ahead of subsequent liens.

16 **Parties to a mortgage.**   There are two parties to a mortgage: (1) the
17 **mortgagor,** or borrower (debtor), and (2) the **mortgagee,** or lender
18 (creditor). The mortgagor owns the property, and the mortgagee owns the
19 mortgage. A mortgage is regarded as an investment or *chattel* (personal
20 property) by the mortgagee and, like other such investments, may be sold
21 to another investor if desired. (See Figure 12.1.)

22 ASSIGNMENT OF MORTGAGE

23 When a homebuyer borrows money to purchase a home, the borrower
24 (mortgagor) signs a promissory note and mortgage instrument. The
25 mortgage and promissory note are property of the mortgagee (lender).
26 The mortgagee may choose to sell the negotiable instruments rather than
27 continue to receive the monthly payments from the mortgagor.

28   When ownership of a mortgage is transferred from one company
29 or individual to another, it is called an *assignment*. This process is
30 accomplished by executing an **assignment of mortgage.** The assignment

701.01, F.S.

of mortgage is a legal instrument that states that the mortgagee assigns (transfers) the mortgage and promissory note to the purchaser. The assignment of mortgage is signed by the assignor (mortgagee) and delivered to the assignee (investor). The assignee becomes the new owner of the debt and security instrument.

The individual or company purchasing the mortgage will receive an **estoppel certificate** verifying the amount of the unpaid balance, the rate of interest, and the date to which interest has been paid prior to the assignment. The purpose of an estoppel certificate is to stop a claim that the amount owed is different from the actual unpaid balance, or that the interest rate is an amount other than the contracted rate.

 Download the Fannie Mae Multistate Mortgage Assignment at: **http://www.efanniemae.com/sf/formsdocs/documents/ specialpurpose/pdf/3742.pdf.** *Note that this instrument indicates that the purchaser (assignee) is Fannie Mae.*

SATISFACTION OF MORTGAGE

Chapter 701, F.S., requires that lenders provide the mortgagor payoff information. The mortgagee must provide an estoppel certificate stating the unpaid principal balance, interest due, and the per diem rate. On that joyous occasion when the mortgagor pays the debt in full, the mortgagee executes a **satisfaction of mortgage** (or a *release of mortgage*). Florida statute requires that the mortgagee cancel the mortgage and send the recorded satisfaction to the mortgagor within 60 days. This document returns to the mortgagor all interest in the real property that had been conveyed to the mortgagee. Filing the satisfaction of mortgage in the public records shows that the mortgage lien has been removed.

FORECLOSURE

In Florida, foreclosure requires a judicial process. Typically, foreclosure is caused by the mortgagor's failure to pay the mortgage payments. However, the mortgagor's failure (default) to perform any requirements stipulated in the mortgage may also cause foreclosure (for example, the mortgagor's failure to pay the property taxes).

If default on the mortgage occurs, the mortgagee has two remedies:

1. *Initiate a suit on the promissory note.* The mortgagee may choose to sue on the note, obtain a judgment, then execute the judgment against any real or personal property of the mortgagor. This judgment may be levied against any of the mortgagor's property except property that is specifically exempted (such as homestead property, unless it is the property on which the default is based).

2. *Initiate a foreclosure proceeding.* The mortgagee may foreclose on the property that is subject to the mortgage lien. The foreclosure process begins with the mortgagee accelerating the due date of all remaining payments and then filing a lawsuit to foreclose. On receiving final judgment, the sale is advertised (public notice of the sale), and the property is sold at public auction to the highest bidder. Once the sale has taken place, the Clerk of the Court files a Certificate of Sale with the court. The court then reviews the sale

1 to ensure a fair price has been paid. If the court is in agreement, the
2 sale is confirmed; if not, another sale is ordered.

3 On confirmation of the sale, the clerk files a Certificate of Title and title
4 passes to the purchaser. The clerk then disburses the sale proceeds in
5 accordance with the final decree. Any excess proceeds are paid to
6 the mortgagor. If, however, the proceeds are not sufficient to satisfy the
7 outstanding debt, the mortgagee may request that the court issue a
8 *deficiency judgment* against the person(s) who signed the note. When
9 granted, a deficiency decree can extend to include all real and personal
10 property belonging to the maker of the note, except a homestead. The
11 doctrine of *caveat emptor* applies in foreclosure sales; that is, the purchaser
12 is presumed to know that he or she is purchasing subject to any prior
13 liens of record or interests for which there is constructive notice. The
14 mortgagee may undertake foreclosure procedures and a suit based on
15 the note as two separate actions. However, they are usually undertaken
16 simultaneously.

17 Sometimes the parties will agree to settle the matter without going to
18 court. This can be accomplished with a **deed in lieu of foreclosure.** The
19 process is sometimes referred to as a *friendly foreclosure* because it is a
20 *nonjudicial* procedure (it does not involve a law suit). The defaulting
21 borrower gives title (the deed) to the lender to avoid judicial foreclosure.
22 The lender takes title to the property subject to existing liens.

Tipical AC in Town is 1/3.

23 EQUITY OF REDEMPTION

24 The severity of the consequences under English common law of failing to
25 pay the mortgage debt on the specific due date caused the courts of
26 equity to provide some relief for mortgagors by permitting them to
27 recover their real property upon payment of their debt even after the due
28 date. This relief evolved into what is referred to today as the **equity of**
29 **redemption.** Equitable redemption, available in all states today, allows
30 the mortgagor to prevent foreclosure from occurring by paying the
31 mortgagee the principal and interest due plus any expenses the
32 mortgagee has incurred in attempting to collect the debt and initiating
33 foreclosure proceedings. The courts have generally ruled that an
34 equitable right of redemption is automatically a part of every mortgage
35 and cannot be contractually modified by the parties. In Florida, the right
36 of equity of redemption (or *equitable right of redemption*) ends once the
37 property has been sold at a foreclosure sale.

38 ■ MORTGAGE CLAUSES

Wrap around. Morg - I Pay 200 I rent for 600.00.

39 BORROWER'S COVENANTS AND AGREEMENTS

40 A mortgage is a contract between mortgagor and mortgagee and,
41 therefore, must contain the essential elements of a contract to be valid.
42 (Refer to Chapter 11.) Mortgage lenders in Florida commonly use the
43 Fannie Mae-Freddie Mac Single Family Uniform Mortgage Instrument.
44 This standard mortgage instrument contains certain uniform covenants

(warranties). An explanation of the most important clauses in the uniform mortgage instrument follows.

 It may be helpful to download a copy of the Fannie Mae/Freddie Mac Uniform Mortgage Instrument. Refer to the mortgage when reviewing the covenants and agreements to a mortgage described below. To download a copy of the mortgage instrument, go to: **http://www.efanniemae.com/sf/formsdocs/documents/ secinstruments/pdf/3010.pdf.**

Promise to repay. The borrower (mortgagor) promises to pay principal and interest according to the terms of the note. The mortgagor also agrees to pay escrowed items, prepayment charges, and late fees, if applicable.

Taxes; liens. The borrower agrees to pay all taxes, assessments, and fines that could create a lien with superior priority over the mortgage (security) instrument. This clause also stipulates that the mortgagor will pay community association dues, if applicable.

Property insurance. The mortgagor promises to keep the property insured against loss by fire and hazards included in an *extended coverage* policy. The lender may require the mortgagor to pay a one-time charge for flood zone determination and, if applicable, flood insurance coverage. If the borrower fails to maintain hazard insurance, the lender may obtain insurance coverage, at the lender's option, and charge the borrower for the expense.

Most lenders require that the mortgagor pay in advance monthly installments for property taxes and insurance. The monthly escrow payment is 1/12 of the anticipated taxes and insurance premium for the year. These payments are held in an *escrow* account for the mortgagor. The borrower makes payments before the taxes and insurance are due. When the taxes and insurance premiums are due, the lender pays the expenses out of the escrowed funds. The insurance must cover at least the unpaid balance of the mortgage. If a loss occurs, the insurance pays the mortgagee up to the unpaid balance of the mortgage.

Occupancy. The borrowers agree to use the property as their principal residence for at least one year, unless the lender otherwise agrees in writing.

Maintenance and covenant of good repair. The mortgagor promises to keep the property in good condition, maintain the property, and prevent waste. The lender is authorized to make reasonable inspections of the property.

Due-on-sale clause. If all or any part of the property or any interest in the property is sold or transferred without the lender's prior written consent, the lender may require immediate payment in full. The **due-on-sale clause** allows the mortgagee to call due the outstanding loan balance plus accrued interest. In effect, this clause prevents another party from assuming the mortgage and requires that the mortgage debt be paid in full when the property is sold.

Acceleration clause. The **acceleration clause** authorizes the mortgagee to accelerate or advance the due date of the entire unpaid balance if the mortgagor fails to fulfill any promises stated in the mortgage instrument. The acceleration clause gives the lender the power to declare the entire unpaid mortgage loan due and payable and to foreclose on the property if the mortgagor does not remedy the default. The foreclosure process cannot begin unless the entire debt is delinquent. Without the acceleration clause, the mortgagee could sue a delinquent mortgagor for only the monthly payments that are in arrears. The borrower is given 30 days from the date of the *notice of acceleration* to pay all sums secured by the mortgage instrument. If the borrower fails to pay the debt within the specified time period, the borrower is considered to be in default. The Fannie Mae-Freddie Mac Uniform Single Family Mortgage Instrument includes in the acceleration clause the remedies for curing defaults.

Right to reinstate. This clause is based on the equity of redemption. It deals with the mortgagor's right to reinstate the original repayment terms in the note *after* the mortgagee has initiated the acceleration clause. It gives the mortgagor the right to have foreclosure proceedings stopped before the foreclosure sale, provided that the mortgagor pays all sums that would be due if no acceleration had occurred plus all expenses incurred by the mortgagee in enforcing the mortgage.

Release. The **defeasance** clause requires the lender to release the security (mortgage) instrument upon payment of all sums secured by the security instrument. The mortgage is *defeated* and the real property is no longer pledged as collateral. To accomplish this, the lender executes a satisfaction of mortgage when the note has been full repaid. (See Satisfaction of Mortgage, page 250.)

OTHER MORTGAGE PROVISIONS

Prepayment clause. A **prepayment clause** allows the borrower to pay off part or all of the debt, without penalty or other fees, prior to maturity. In Florida, a borrower has the right to prepay his or her mortgage loan unless the mortgage instrument states otherwise. A prepayment clause is normally included in FHA and VA mortgages on real property. A prepayment clause typically stipulates conditions and terms under which the mortgage loan may be prepaid.

Prepayment penalty clause. The lender may choose to charge a **prepayment penalty** for early payment, if provided for in the mortgage instrument.

SPECIAL MORTGAGE PROVISIONS

Escalator clause. This clause permits the lender to increase the interest rate. The action is usually tied to an event or a contingency, such as the transition of a property from owner-occupied to investment property during the initial year of the mortgage.

Exculpatory clause. This clause requires that the lender waive the right to a deficiency judgment against the borrower. It relieves the borrower of personal liability to repay the loan.

Open-end clause. This allows the borrower to increase the loan amount as long as the total debt does not exceed the original amount of the loan. It's also called a *mortgage for future advances* and amounts to an expandable loan. The lender often reserves the right to adjust the interest rate to current market rates.

LAND DEVELOPMENT LOANS

Developers commonly purchase land for development by securing seller financing. The developer usually requests that the seller agree to a **subordination clause.** This clause provides that the lender (usually the seller) voluntarily will permit a subsequent mortgage to take priority over the lender's otherwise superior mortgage (the act of yielding priority). This arrangement allows the developer to secure a construction loan from a traditional lending institution.

Another clause associated with land development is the **partial release clause.** Release clauses usually occur in what are called **blanket mortgages** that cover a number of parcels, usually building lots. The developer-mortgagor is the owner of record, who normally wishes to sell the lots but wants to pay off the blanket mortgage gradually as individual lots are sold. The developer typically uses the money from the sale of each lot to pay off part of the mortgage. A *partial release clause* stipulates the conditions under which the mortgagee will grant a release of lots, free and clear of the mortgage.

INCOME PROPERTY

A **receivership clause** is included in most mortgages for income-producing property. It requires that income from the property be used to make mortgage payments in the event of default. If it becomes necessary for the mortgagee to foreclose, the legal proceedings could take several months. The receivership clause permits the mortgagee to appeal to the courts to appoint a *receiver* to take over management of the property and to collect the rents or other income. The receiver pays the bills and carrying charges until the foreclosure action is concluded by the sale of the property. Any net profits at the conclusion of the receivership may be used by the mortgagee to satisfy the mortgage debt, if need be.

■ TYPES OF MORTGAGES

Today, mortgages fall into one of three descriptive categories—FHA, VA, and conventional. FHA does *not* make loans; it *insures* loans made by private lenders. VA has a limited direct-loan program but is involved chiefly in *guaranteeing* (not insuring) loans made by private lenders. Conventional loans are those that are neither FHA nor VA and receive no government insurance or guarantee.

Important Mortgage Clauses

Acceleration—upon default, accelerates the entire debt due and payable

Defeasance—upon mortgage satisfaction, defeats conveyance to the lender

Due-on-sale—upon sale (alienation) loan is due and payable

Escalator— tied to an event or a contingency, it allows the lender to increase the interest rate

Exculpatory—lender agrees not to hold borrower personally liable for the debt

Open-end—may borrow additional funds secured by the same mortgage

Prepayment—conditions to repay debt in advance of due date

Prepayment penalty—allows extra charge if any amount of the loan is paid off early

Receivership—appointment of a receiver for income-producing property

Subordination—lender agrees to step down in priority of lien

FEDERAL HOUSING ADMINISTRATION MORTGAGE (FHA GOVERNMENT-INSURED LOAN)

The National Housing Act of 1934 created the FHA and the Mutual Mortgage Insurance Fund to encourage reluctant lenders to invest their money in the mortgage market, thereby stimulating the depressed construction industry. Subsequent legislative acts have caused and continue to cause significant changes in FHA-insured programs.

The FHA is a government agency within the Department of Housing and Urban Development (HUD). FHA regulates participating lenders, borrowers, and the real property offered as security for their mortgages. The agency functions as an insurance company, insuring mortgage loans made by approved lenders. FHA does *not* make loans to borrowers, nor does the agency process loans or build houses.

FHA does *not* regulate interest rates. Lenders set their own interest rates for FHA-insured loans to reflect money market conditions. Lenders may charge FHA borrowers *points,* a charge by a lender designed to increase the lender's yield (see Chapter 13) and payable by any party.

Mortgage insurance premium.   Borrowers are required to pay an *up-front mortgage insurance premium* (UFMIP). The percentage of the UFMIP is based on the term of the mortgage. On a typical 30-year mortgage, the UFMIP is 1.50 percent.

The borrower is also charged an annual **mortgage insurance premium (MIP),** added to the monthly mortgage payment. The FHA's annual MIP on a 30-year residential loan is automatically canceled when the loan-to-value ratio reaches 78 percent, *provided* the mortgagor has paid the annual mortgage insurance premiums for at least five years. The annual MIP is .50 percent of the base loan amount divided by 12, paid monthly. However, the annual MIP for condominium loans is based on the term of the loan and the interest rate. Because an UFMIP is not charged

1 on a condominium loan, the monthly premium is paid for the life of the
2 mortgage. The MIP must be included in the proposed monthly expense
3 when calculating the buyer's qualifying ratios.

4 MIP payments are periodically forwarded to FHA's Mortgage
5 Insurance Fund. This fund is used to reimburse private lenders when an
6 FHA-insured loan is uncollectible. FHA does *not* protect the borrower
7 against loss of any kind.

8 The FHA is authorized to insure a number of different types of
9 mortgages, as defined in the National Housing Act of 1934 (and later
10 amendments). Some of the more commonly used FHA-insured mortgage
11 programs are:

12 • Title I: home improvement loans;

13 • Title II, Section 203(b): homeownership (one-family to four-family
14   residences), fixed-rate loans;

15 • Title II, Section 234: condominium unit loans;

16 • Title II, Section 245: five basic graduated-payment loan plans,
17   which vary the rate of monthly payment increases and the number
18   of years over which the payments increase; and

19 • Title II, Section 251: homeownership, adjustable-rate loans.

20 **FHA 203(b) loan limits.**   FHA approval of a loan application indicates
21 that it will insure the loan, thus preventing a future loss by the lender.
22 Maximum loan amounts insurable for FHA vary from area to area,
23 reflecting the agency's perception of regional differences in the cost of
24 housing. Lenders must use FHA forms and comply with FHA policies
25 and procedures to qualify for FHA mortgage insurance.

wwweb.link   *A schedule of FHA mortgage limits by area is available through the Internet at:* **http://entp.hud.gov/idapp/html/hicostlook.cfm.**

26 **FHA loan and down payment amounts.**   The maximum FHA mortgage
27 amount for an FHA residential loan is based on a fixed percentage of sale
28 price or the appraised value whichever is less. The FHA has developed two
29 sets of percentages—one for low closing cost states and the other for high
30 closing cost states. Florida is considered to be a high closing cost state. The
31 percentages for calculating the maximum loan amount in Florida are
32 presented in the text box below.

FHA Percentages for High Closing Cost States	
98.75%:	Equal to or less than $50,000 sale price (or appraised value)
97.75%:	More than $50,000

33 For example, assume the sale price and appraised value of a home is
34 $44,000. The maximum FHA loan amount would be $43,450 ($44,000 ×
35 .9875 = $43,450). The $43,450 figure is the maximum that FHA will insure
36 *provided* the borrower (mortgagor) makes a minimum *cash investment* of at

1 least 3 percent. The 3 percent cash requirement is calculated on the
2 purchase price (or appraised amount). In this example, the buyer's
3 minimum cash investment is $1,320 ($44,000 × .03 = $1,320).

4   If the buyer is paying closing costs, they may be applied toward
5 satisfying the 3 percent requirement. For example, assume the buyer has
6 closing costs totaling $700. Because the buyer is paying $700 in closing
7 costs, the total acquisition cost of the property is $44,700 ($44,000 + $700 =
8 $44,700). The maximum FHA loan amount calculated earlier was $43,450
9 leaving a difference of $1,250 ($44,700 total acquisition cost – $43,450
10 maximum loan amount = $1,250). However, the minimum cash
11 investment calculated earlier was $1,320. Therefore, the loan amount must
12 be reduced by $70 to ensure that the buyer invests at least 3 percent
13 ($1,320) into the property. The required investment must be from the
14 borrower's own funds, a bona fide gift, a loan from a family member, or
15 from a governmental agency. The money may not come from premium
16 pricing, loans from other sources, the seller, or the builder.

17   Consider a second example. Assume the property sold for and is
18 appraised at $100,000. The homebuyer is paying $1,000 in closing costs.

19 **Step One:**   Calculate the maximum FHA loan amount:

20              $100,000 × .9775 = $97,750

21 **Step Two:**   Calculate the minimum cash investment:

22              $100,000 × .03 = $3,000

23 **Step Three:** Compare:

24              $101,000 acquisition cost – $97,750 maximum loan
25   amount = $3,250
26   Because the $3,250 represents at least 3 percent (greater
27   than or equal to $3,000) of the sale price, no further
28   mortgage calculation is required. The FHA will insure up
29   to $97,750, and the buyer's closing costs will total $3,250.

30   Lenders always make FHA-insured loans in even $50 increments. For
31 example, if a loan calculates to $77,212, the lender is required to round the
32 loan amount down to the next lower even $50 increment (in this case,
33 $77,200). Rounding down increases the buyer's down payment by the
34 amount dropped in rounding down (in this example, $12).

The FHA Down Payment Simplification Act of 2002 amended the National Housing Act to permanently simplify the down payment requirements for FHA-insured mortgages for single-family homebuyers. To learn more about FHA loan amounts and down payments, refer to the FHA Mortgagee Letters on the Internet at: **http://www.hudclips.org/sub_nonhud/cgi/ hudclips_run.cgi?hudclips_run.** *Click on "Down Payment Simplification Update." (Document 03-1)*

Assuming an FHA-insured loan. The FHA has strict criteria requiring mandatory verification of creditworthiness for anyone attempting to assume an FHA-insured loan. However, the lender must release the original mortgagor from liability if the assuming mortgagor is found creditworthy and executes an agreement to assume and pay the mortgage debt. The assuming mortgagor thereby becomes the substitute mortgagor. (For a detailed explanation of current FHA rules, check with your local HUD/FHA office, mortgage broker, loan officer, or the HUD Web site.)

FHA 203(b) loans are written for a period of up to 30 years or 75 percent of the remaining economic life of an existing property, whichever is less. Some FHA loans not related to Section 203(b) residential properties have terms of up to 40 years. Buyers can use these extended mortgage terms for housing for the elderly, cooperative housing, and slum clearance. Also, *high-cost-of-living areas* have special maximums and standards. It is a good idea for real estate students to obtain and read a current FHA contract form.

FHA 203(b) Loan Assumption Criteria

Loans made prior to December 1, 1986, are assumable with no qualification of the buyer (can be owner-occupied or an investor).

Loans made between December 1, 1986, and December 14, 1989, require credit approval of the buyer assuming the loan (can be owner-occupied or an investor).

Loans made after December 14, 1989, require complete qualification of the buyer who assumes the loan. All assumed loans (and new loans) are for owner-occupied use only (no investor loans).

VETERANS AFFAIRS MORTGAGE (VA OR GI LOAN)

In 1944, the Servicemen's Readjustment Act (GI Bill of Rights) was passed to aid returning World War II veterans. This act and subsequent acts gave the Department of Veterans Affairs (VA) the authority to *partially guarantee* mortgage loans made to veterans by private lenders. The partial guarantee covers the top portion of the loan.

Eligibility requirements. Only veterans, surviving spouses of veterans, and active military personnel may apply for a VA loan. Local lenders issue VA loans. However, the VA does have the power to make direct loans to veterans in areas where VA loans are not available. Specific eligibility requirements based on minimum days of active duty are presented in the text box on page 259.

VA loans may be used to purchase, refinance, or construct a home, including farm residences, condominiums, and manufactured homes. VA loans for alterations, repairs, and improvements to an existing home are also available. Up to four units of multifamily property may be financed by a VA loan provided the veteran resides in one of the units.

VA Loan Eligibility

90 days of active duty during any one of five wartime periods (WWII, Korea, Vietnam, Persian Gulf, and Iraq)

181 days of active duty during the time periods between the four war periods

24 months of active duty on or after September 8, 1980 (except during the Persian Gulf War)

6 years of service in the Reserves or National Guard

VA loan guarantee.   The VA establishes loan guarantee limits referred to as the *VA loan guarantee* or the *maximum entitlement.* Currently, the maximum entitlement (guarantee) is $89,912.

A veteran begins by applying to the VA for a certificate of eligibility. The *certificate of eligibility* states the amount of entitlement available to the veteran borrower. The VA loan guarantee program uses a scale that establishes each veteran's entitlement based on the loan amount. (Refer to text box below.) If a veteran used his or her entitlement in the past, it is possible that the veteran is now eligible for only a portion of the entitlement. The unused portion is available to the veteran borrower up to the maximum guarantee. When a VA loan is paid off, the veteran's maximum entitlement is reinstated.

VA Home Loan Guarantee Entitlement

Loan Amount	Guaranteed Amount
0 to $45,000	50 percent of the loan amount
$45,001 to $144,000	Minimum guaranty is $22,500, with a maximum guaranty of up to 40 percent of the loan up to $36,000
More than $144,000	Up to $89,912 or 25 percent of the loan amount

---

Loan amount.   The VA does *not* set loan limits. The amount that a veteran may borrow is dependent on the value of the real estate. The loan may not exceed the amount stated in the Certificate of Reasonable Value (CRV). The CRV is based on the property value estimated by a VA approved appraiser. The other limiting factor is the veteran's income and ability to make the monthly mortgage payments. The veteran borrower's total monthly obligations may not exceed 41 percent of total monthly gross income. (See also page 270.)

Because the maximum VA guarantee is $89,912 or 25 percent of the loan amount, most lenders observe a maximum loan amount of $359,650 ($89,912 ÷ .25 = $359,650), or alternatively, four times the veteran's guarantee. If a veteran has sufficient income to qualify for a higher loan amount, the $89,912 maximum guarantee still would apply, and the veteran would make a down payment of 25 percent of the amount over $359,650.

VA funding fee. The VA requires a *funding fee* or *user's fee* to help the government defray the cost of foreclosures. Currently the funding fee is 2 percent of the loan amount for first time users. Funding fee expenses may be added to the maximum loan amount and financed over the life of the loan. If a veteran has a service-connected disability, the funding fee is waived.

Closing costs. The lender may charge reasonable closing costs. However, these costs may *not* be included in the VA loan. Closing costs vary among lenders. The veteran borrower or the seller may pay the following closing costs or the closing costs may be shared:

- VA appraisal

- Credit report

- Loan origination fee (usually 1 percent of the loan)

- Discount points

- Title search and title insurance

- Recording fees

- State transfer fees

- Survey

Assumability of VA loans. Because they do not have due-on-sale clauses, VA loans are assumable (even by nonveterans). VA loans made prior to March 1, 1988, are assumable without a credit check of the new mortgagor. However, both seller and buyer will be liable in case of default, unless the buyer qualifies and completes all substitution documents. For VA loans made on or after March 1, 1988, the buyer must qualify. The buyer must pay an assumption or transfer fee to the lender plus an assumption fee to the VA. The seller is then released from liability for the VA loan.

Other loan features. Additional features of the VA loan are listed below:

- The interest rate varies based on market conditions and is negotiated between the borrower and the lender.

- Down payments are *not* required on VA loans (except as noted above and for the purchase of manufactured homes).

- Borrowers pay 1/12 of estimated annual property taxes and hazard insurance with each month's principal and interest mortgage payment (PITI).

- The maximum loan term is 30 years.

- Veterans may prepay all or a portion of the mortgage loan ahead of schedule without penalty (no prepayment penalty).

- The VA loan *guarantee* differs from the FHA program that *insures* loans.

- VA loans do *not* require mortgage insurance premiums (MIP).

Visit the U.S. Department of Veterans Affairs Loan Guaranty Service Homepage at: **http://www.homeloans.va.gov/** *for additional information.*

CONVENTIONAL MORTGAGE

Private lenders make conventional loans. Conventional loans usually have a lower LTV ratio than either FHA or VA loans. Conventional lenders require higher down payments unless borrowers buy private mortgage insurance (PMI). This characteristically higher down payment has caused many borrowers to prefer financing by FHA or VA mortgage loans, despite their slower administrative processing.

Conventional lenders are regulated by the government agency that issued their charter and by the Federal Deposit Insurance Corporation (FDIC), if they are members. (See also Chapter 13.) Most conventional lenders are restricted to LTV ratios of no more than 80 percent of appraised value (80 percent loan and 20 percent down payment), unless the loan is insured for any increased loan amount over 80 percent of such value. If a buyer wanted to purchase a house selling for $92,000, the restriction on lending no more than 80 percent of value would require a down payment of $18,400 plus closing costs. The same house could be purchased with FHA financing for about $14,000 less in upfront cash, depending on closing costs.

Conventional lenders may lend up to 95 percent of appraised value (or up to 100 percent on special affordable housing loans) if the borrower agrees to pay for private mortgage insurance (PMI). PMI insures that portion of the mortgage loan that exceeds the 80 percent of value. Many potential buyers will pay for PMI to obtain more liberal financing. Using the previous example, with PMI a buyer might finance the $92,000 by use of a 95 percent loan and 5 percent down ($4,600). PMI makes conventional loans more competitive with FHA and VA loans. However, lenders in recent years have seen considerable increases in defaulted loans and foreclosures, resulting in substantially increased PMI costs and reluctance to make 95 percent loans.

SUBCATEGORIES OF MORTGAGES

Before 1930 buyers commonly used so-called *term mortgages* to purchase real property. With a term mortgage (or *straight-term mortgage*) they paid interest only until the full term of the mortgage expired. Then they paid all the principal or refinanced the loan. It is a *nonamortizing loan.* Term mortgages are used today, but generally for short-term financing, such as construction loans.

Partially amortized mortgage.   With a *partially amortized mortgage* the buyer makes regular payments smaller than are required to completely pay off the loan by its date of termination. In other words, the payments do not fully amortize the loan. A single large final payment, including accrued interest and all unpaid principal, then becomes due on the loan maturity date (referred to as a **balloon payment**). In Florida, a partially amortized mortgage must be clearly identified as such on the face of the mortgage, with the amount of the final balloon payment disclosed.

FIGURE 12.2 Allocation of Payments to Interest and Principal

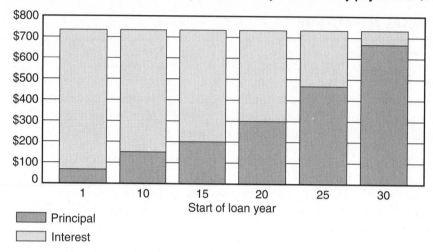

Payments on a $100,000 loan at 8 percent for 30 years. Monthly payment is $734.

Start of loan year

☐ Principal
☐ Interest

Used with permission from *Mastering Real Estate Principals,* 3rd Edition, by Gerald R. Cortesi © 2001 by Dearborn Financial Publishing, Inc., by Dearborn™ Real Estate Education, a division of Dearborn Financial Publishing, Inc., Chicago. All rights reserved.

Amortized mortgage. Today, the most popular loan payment plan is the fully amortized, level-payment plan mortgage. *Webster's* defines the word *amortize* as meaning to extinguish or deaden. An **amortized mortgage** is gradually and systematically killed or extinguished by equal regular periodic payments.

When the various components of a mortgage loan are known (the amount borrowed, the rate of interest, and the term or number of years), the level or constant monthly payment can be calculated by using a financial calculator (or compound interest tables). Each monthly payment includes both interest and principal. Although the buyer pays the same amount each month, on a fixed-rate mortgage, the portion used to pay interest decreases each month, while the portion used to repay principal increases each month. Payments during the first few years are used almost entirely to pay interest; payments during the last few years are almost entirely principal repayment. (See Figure 12.2.)

Biweekly mortgage. A **biweekly mortgage loan** is amortized the same way as other loans with monthly payments, except the borrower makes a payment every two weeks. The amount paid is equal to one-half the normal monthly payment. Because there are 52 weeks in the year, the borrower makes 26 biweekly payments. Therefore, the borrower makes the equivalent of an extra month's payment each year (26 half-size payments equal 13 full-month payments instead of 12). This saves the borrower considerable interest and the loan is paid off sooner.

Package mortgage. A **package mortgage** loan includes both real and personal property as security for the debt. A buyer uses a package mortgage, for example, when purchasing a restaurant complete with cooking equipment and other personal property that serve as a part of the collateral for the debt.

1 **Purchase-money mortgage.**   A purchase-money mortgage (PMM) is a
2 mortgage given as part of the buyer's consideration for the purchase of
3 real property. The PPM is delivered when the deed is transferred as a
4 simultaneous part of the transaction. It is usually a mortgage taken back by
5 a seller from a buyer in lieu of purchase money. A purchase-money
6 mortgage is used to fill a gap between the buyer's down payment and a
7 new first mortgage or an assumed mortgage. Title passes to the buyer, and
8 the seller retains a vendor's lien right as security for the debt.

9 ## ■ METHODS OF PURCHASING MORTGAGED PROPERTY

10 A buyer may purchase mortgaged property in at least four ways:

11 1. *Cash.* The mortgage may be paid in full from the sale proceeds, a
12   satisfaction of mortgage recorded, and the property delivered free
13   and clear of the mortgage lien at the time of closing.

14 2. *Subject to the mortgage.* If the existing mortgage does not contain a
15   due-on-sale clause, the mortgaged property may be purchased
16   *subject to* the mortgage. Here both the existing mortgage and note
17   remain the obligation of the seller. The buyer is responsible for
18   regular payments on the mortgage to retain possession. If the buyer
19   fails to make payments or defaults, the mortgagee can proceed to
20   foreclose. If the foreclosure sale does not satisfy the mortgage debt,
21   a deficiency judgment can be sought against the *original* mortgagor,
22   the seller, who has remained responsible for the mortgage although
23   the property was sold. A *subject to* buyer does not become
24   personally responsible for paying the seller's debt.

25 3. *Assumption of an existing mortgage.* An assumption of the mortgage
26   obligates the buyer to assume liability for the debt. Both buyer and
27   seller are equally liable in the event of default.

28 4. *Novation.* **Novation** is the exchange or substitution of a new debt
29   for an existing debt by mutual agreement. If mortgaged property is
30   sold, a lender may release the seller and create a new note with the
31   buyer, who becomes the individual solely responsible for the debt.
32   Unless there is a novation, the selling mortgagor will remain liable.
33   A novation provides for the discharge of the original contract and
34   creates a new agreement.

Four Ways to Purchase Mortgaged Property

1. Cash
2. Subject to the mortgage
3. Assumption of an existing mortgage
4. Novation

CONTRACT FOR DEED

Also called a *land contract, agreement for deed,* or *installment sale contract,* the **contract for deed** is another way to buy real property, usually with very little cash investment. The seller accepts a down payment from the buyer and finances the rest of the purchase price. The significant feature of a contract for deed is that the title to the real property remains with the seller until the loan is repaid. The buyer has an equitable (legal) interest in the property. *Equitable title* qualifies the buyer for homestead tax exemption.

The parties enter into a binding contract in which the seller contracts to deliver a deed at some future date, after a designated amount has been paid. The seller allows the buyer to take possession while paying the agreed-on payments. The buyer agrees to delay receiving title in his or her name until the required amount is paid to the seller. When the agreed amount is fully paid, the seller is obligated to transfer title to the buyer. At that time the buyer will assume the existing first mortgage (if any) or secure new financing, if needed.

Only an attorney should prepare a contract for deed. In case of buyer default, regular foreclosure proceedings are required, just as if it were a seller-held mortgage.

For example, a $60,000 home is for sale with an assumable mortgage of $40,500 at 8 percent. However, a willing buyer with good credit and income-earning ability who really wants the house has only $4,000 for a down payment. Using a contract for deed, the seller can retain title to the property until the buyer pays the entire $15,500 ($60,000 − $40,500 = $19,500 − $4,000 = $15,500) remaining from the desired down payment. In addition, the seller collects interest on the unpaid balance of the down payment, usually at a higher rate of return than if he or she had received the entire down payment at closing and placed the money in a savings account or certificate of deposit. Some years ago, prior to more restrictive laws, sellers found this type of financing arrangement advantageous because it was easier to reacquire possession and full title in the event of default.

WRAPAROUND MORTGAGE

A **wraparound mortgage** envelops an existing mortgage and is subordinate (junior) to it. The existing mortgage stays on the property and the new mortgage "wraps" around it. A wraparound mortgage is commonly taken by a seller who continues to be responsible for payments on a first mortgage. The seller takes a mortgage from the buyer for an amount that includes the existing mortgage balance. Wraparounds are not limited to seller financing. If the seller does not want to finance the sale, a third-party lender could take a wraparound mortgage.

Certain conditions must be present to make a wraparound mortgage economically feasible. First, a property must have an existing mortgage that does *not* have a due-on-sale clause. Second, the interest rate on the existing mortgage should be less than that on the wraparound mortgage.

And third, the owner must have sufficient equity in the property to make the wraparound economically worthwhile.

Take the example in the contract-for-deed discussion. Assume that the buyer is unwilling to enter into a contract for deed but is willing to enter into a wraparound mortgage. The seller would take back from the buyer a wraparound mortgage at perhaps 10 percent interest and would receive 10 percent interest on the combined sums of the old $40,500 mortgage and the new $15,500 mortgage. The buyer would have a $56,000 mortgage at 10 percent and make payments to the seller on that basis. If the underlying mortgage is at 8 percent, the seller would receive 2 percent interest on the $40,500 mortgage and 10 percent on the $15,500 he or she had loaned in the wraparound. ($810 + $1,550 = $2,360) That's a net return of 15 percent on the $15,500. ($2,360 ÷ $15,500 = .1523) The seller keeps the old mortgage in his or her name and makes payments just as if the property had not been sold.

■ OTHER TYPES OF FINANCING

Record-setting high interest rates in the early 1980s caused mortgage lenders to seek new and "creative" financing techniques that were more affordable to potential homebuyers. At the present time, lenders have more or less settled down to two choices: (1) fixed-rate mortgages (discussed previously) and (2) adjustable-rate mortgages. Several lesser-used financing techniques will also be covered here briefly.

Adjustable-rate mortgage.   The **adjustable-rate mortgage (ARM)** has become the most widely accepted alternative to the traditional 30-year fixed-rate level-payment mortgage. The ARM is an attempt to create a happy compromise between the needs of lenders and borrowers. FHA recognizes and approves ARMs that contain adequate consumer protection provisions. (Currently there are still old VA ARMs in existence. However, the VA ARM program itself has been discontinued.)

When ARMs were first introduced, some were offered with low-down-payment requirements and artificially low initial interest rates ("teasers"). When that first "adjustment" to the interest rate was made, it was so large in some situations that it exceeded the maximum allowable increase (cap), resulting in negative amortization. *Negative amortization* occurs when the monthly mortgage payment amounts are less than needed to pay the monthly interest costs, causing the unpaid amount to be added to the loan balance. Consumer protection measures are now an integral part of all ARMs sponsored or accepted by FHA, Fannie Mae, and Freddie Mac.

Components of adjustable-rate mortgages.   From a borrower's standpoint, the primary ingredients in evaluating an ARM are the index, lender's margin, calculated interest rate, initial interest rate, and interest rate caps.

Lending institutions legally are permitted to link the interest rate of an ARM with any recognized *index* (for example, the three-year treasury security). The primary requirements are that the index must not be controlled by the lender and it must be verifiable by the borrower. The *margin,* also called the *spread,* is a percentage added to the index and is intended to represent the amount required to cover all lender costs plus profit earned (estimated overhead costs + profit = margin). The margin percentage usually remains constant over the life of the loan, while the selected index may move up or down with fluctuations in the nation's economy. The calculated interest rate is arrived at by adding the selected index to the lender's margin **(calculated interest rate = index + margin).** This *calculated interest rate* is usually the rate to which all future adjustments and caps apply. It is frequently discounted during the initial payment period to be competitive and create a lower initial interest rate. This helps to qualify potential buyers at artificially low interest rates and establishes the amount of the monthly loan payment during the first time period of the loan. (Note that in the long run borrowers may not benefit from artificially low initial interest rates.)

The main appeal of ARMs is the lower initial rates offered as an inducement. But without some sort of protection from unacceptable increases in the interest rate, borrowers would be in danger of not being able to make future mortgage payments. To prevent this, many lenders and all federal housing agencies have established standards calling for *ceilings* on increases. Three types of ceilings *(caps)* are used to limit increases in the real interest rates of ARMs:

1. The amount of increase applied at the first adjustment (for example, caps of 1 percent or 2 percent for the first adjustment period)

2. The amount of increase applied during any other adjustment interval (for example, no more than 2 percent during any one-year period)

3. The total amount increased over the life of the loan (for example, no more than 6 percent)

Occasionally, ARMs are written with caps applied to the amount that monthly payments may be increased, for example, no more than a 7.5 percent increase in monthly payments in any given year, which is slightly less than a 1 percent increase in the interest rate.

SHARED-APPRECIATION MORTGAGE

The *shared-appreciation mortgage* (SAM) is also called an *equity-participation loan.* The lender gives the borrower a lower interest rate in exchange for a share of the future increase in the property's value. The mortgagor and mortgagee agree to the percentage split and the term of the loan. At maturity (or when the property is sold before maturity) the property is appraised to determine the amount due the lender.

REVERSE-ANNUITY MORTGAGE

The *reverse-annuity mortgage* (RAM) is designed to aid elderly homeowners. They exchange the equity they have acquired in their

1 homes over a period of years for monthly income. The lender pays the
2 borrower a fixed amount each month, based on the mortgagor's life
3 expectancy and property value.

The American Association of Retired Persons (AARP) maintains a comprehensive Web page concerning reverse mortgages. To download a fact sheet on reverse mortgages, go to: **http://www.aarp.org/revmort/.** *Click on "Basics" and then go to "Basic Loan Features."*

4 GROWING-EQUITY MORTGAGE

5 The *growing-equity mortgage* (GEM) rapidly increases the equity in a
6 property by increasing the monthly payments by a certain percentage
7 each year and applying these increases to the principal. Lenders like the
8 shorter maturity date. Borrowers see their equity grow more quickly and
9 see savings in interest as a result of their quicker payoff.

10 HOME EQUITY LOANS

11 Homeowners use **home equity loans** to finance consumer purchases;
12 consolidate existing credit card debt; and pay for college tuition, medical
13 expenses, or home improvements. Because the interest on most home
14 equity loans is tax deductible, they are more popular than other types of
15 consumer credit.

16   Home equity loans are secured by the borrower's residence. The
17 original mortgage remains in place. The home equity is usually a second
18 mortgage (junior to the original mortgage). The dollar amount of a home
19 equity loan is based on the amount of equity. The borrower may take a
20 lump sum amount or access a *line of credit.* The interest rate usually is
21 adjustable and is based on the lender's prime rate. The total LTV ratio
22 is typically limited to 80 percent of the property's value.

23 BUYDOWNS

24 A *buydown* occurs when a party (such as the seller or developer) pays an
25 upfront fee to the lender. In exchange for the fee, the mortgagor's loan
26 interest rate is reduced, generally for the first one year to three years. A
27 builder, for example, might buy down the interest rate for the first three
28 years from 7 percent to 5 percent, so that a buyer-borrower can qualify
29 for a larger loan. A builder would rather make an additional cash
30 payment to the lender than reduce the price on a home in a new
31 development.

32 ■ QUALIFYING THE BUYER

33 The constantly changing real estate financing market requires that
34 licensees keep up with the various mortgage types and formats available
35 in their local areas. Before attempting to qualify a buyer, licensees should
36 make sure that required written brokerage relationship disclosures have
37 been made. Brokerage relationship disclosure is important because

licensees need to obtain confidential information to help determine appropriate loan amounts, financing plans, and affordable income-expense ratios. Qualifying a buyer involves two separate but important processes:

1. Determining the potential buyer's real property needs (housing objectives)

2. Determining the potential buyer's economic capability to satisfy those needs (financial abilities)

Discussions of the following subjects and procedures are designed to assist licensees in reaching decisions in these two areas.

DETERMINING POTENTIAL BUYERS' REAL PROPERTY NEEDS

Licensees must listen carefully to potential buyers to separate wishes from actual needs. Then licensees must help buyers set goals and priorities regarding housing features, neighborhoods, and prices. Licensees should encourage buyers to focus on needs first and then to add wants as economic conditions permit.

A licensee should spend the time necessary to learn a potential buyer's family size, hobbies, ages of family members, distances family members are willing to drive to and from work, plus anything else that might contribute to understanding the potential buyer's needs. If breadwinners regularly bring work home from the office, they may need a quiet, controllable home workspace. Only after housing objectives have been discussed is a licensee prepared to examine financial ability.

DETERMINING POTENTIAL BUYERS' ECONOMIC CAPABILITIES

For some licensees, gauging economic capability is the more difficult part of the qualifying process. It need not be. Recognize that this is a sensitive area, one that is regarded as private information and no one else's business. However, if licensees are up to date on the financial options currently available to buyers, they find it easier to begin this portion of the qualifying process by reviewing the options available to buyers. Talking about loan options, demonstrates professionalism, introduces buyers to consideration of a down payment and monthly payments, and helps to develop confidence in the licensee.

One proven technique for economic qualification is the *explain-and-request technique*. After a brief summary of available financial options, a licensee explains the need to ask the prospective buyer some general questions and then requests permission to ask the questions. Work with reasonably general questions: "Have you a fairly good idea of how much you plan to invest as a down payment?" "Have you thought about the approximate amount you would feel comfortable with as a monthly mortgage payment?" Amounts the buyer provides may or may not be realistic. But the buyer responses will confirm such information or bring to the surface any misconceptions about the market value of real estate and how much home the buyer can afford.

WHY QUALIFY POTENTIAL BUYERS?

Many real estate licensees fail to recognize the importance of taking time to qualify potential buyers. This may be one of the reasons that 20 percent of the sales associates close 80 percent of the sales! The reasons for qualifying potential buyers fall into four areas:

1. *Saves time.* Adequate qualification of potential buyers saves time for everyone.

2. *Increases confidence.* Potential buyers gain confidence in themselves as more specifics are discussed and uncovered, and they gain confidence in the sales associate, who obviously has a plan for meeting their needs.

3. *Fits buyers to properties.* By visiting with each potential buyer and controlling the qualification interview, the sales associate learns the preferred location, size, style, price range, and special features needed to meet the buyer's housing requirements. This more precise information and the obvious interest in the buyer's needs serve to better fit properties to buyers as well as to establish a good relationship between the sales associate and the potential buyer.

4. *Retains buyers.* If licensees rush to start selling by showing listed properties without taking the time to qualify buyers and ascertain their needs, they are inviting disaster. After a long day's experience of looking at house after house, buyers become tired and discouraged. "He or she didn't show us a decent house all day!" The next day, they will go to a different real estate firm, which may well have people trained to qualify their buyers first rather than showing properties at random.

The above suggestions are intended only as a starting point. Some items may be inappropriate to a given office or situation, and the arrangement is subject to change to fit the personality and requirements of a firm or sales associate. One principle should not be ignored or violated: Always begin to qualify buyers with questions related to general information (name, address, etc.), then gradually work into items of a more specific, personal nature (income, expenses, etc.).

QUALIFYING FOR MORTGAGE LOANS

Buyers should be informed of the importance of ratios in qualifying prospective borrowers for mortgage loans. Lenders use economic ratios to analyze mortgage loan applications. For a lender to be able to sell mortgages in the secondary market (described in the next Chapter), the mortgages must meet designated expense/income ratio requirements. FHA, VA, and conventional lenders all use gross monthly income to calculate qualifying ratios for borrowers. Lenders also want to know what percentage of total monthly income is already obligated to pay other debt.

FHA-insured mortgage loans.   Applicants are subject to FHA's own formula for calculating income, monthly payments, and the money available for house payments. FHA uses a *housing expense ratio* (HER) and

1 a *total obligations ratio* (TOR) to determine borrower qualification and to
2 approach conventional loan qualifying. FHA requirements currently
3 allow up to 29 percent for the HER (monthly housing expenses/monthly
4 gross income) and up to 41 percent for the TOR (total monthly
5 obligations/monthly gross income).

FHA Qualifying Guidelines

Credit:
Late payments, judgments, or collections must be paid in full and satisfactorily explained. Bankruptcy—two years from discharge, reestablished credit, excellent reason for bankruptcy. No presently delinquent Federal debt. Qualify with all current debts; if installment debt has less than ten months remaining, the debt does not have to be included unless the amount is significant.

Income:
Must document 24 months of employment and income history. Verification of employment, paystub or alternate (W-2) documentation for two years, and paystubs for last 30 days. Certain criteria apply for other types of income such as self-employed, bonuses, etc.

Assets:
Two months' bank statements and verification of deposits. Gift funds require a gift letter and verified gift monies transferred to borrow. Rent credit—only the portion above fair market rent may be credited to borrower toward closing.

(The above FHA qualifying guidelines is a partial list only. Real estate licensees should consult a mortgage lender for current FHA qualifying guidelines.)

---

6 **VA-guaranteed mortgage loans.**   Loans guaranteed by the VA (GI Bill
7 of Rights loans) usually have more lenient standards than their FHA
8 counterparts. However, applicants for a VA loan not only must qualify as
9 veterans but also are subject to the VA's own formula for calculating
10 income, payments, and the money available for house payments. To
11 qualify loan applicants, the VA currently uses a total monthly obligations
12 ratio (currently 41 percent) and a Table of Residual Incomes calculated for
13 different regions in the United States. The VA total monthly obligations
14 ratio is determined by dividing total PITI (principal, interest, taxes, and
15 insurance) and other monthly payments by the total monthly gross
16 income.

17 **Conventional mortgage loans.**   Conventional mortgage lenders
18 typically use Fannie Mae or the Freddie Mac benchmark ratios. Until
19 recently, Fannie Mae employed two benchmark ratios: (1) a housing
20 expense ratio (HER) and (2) a total obligations ratio (TOR). However,
21 Fannie Mae recently determined from its research that there was no
22 significant relationship between the incidence of mortgage default and
23 the borrower's monthly housing expense to income ratio. Therefore,
24 FNMA now emphasizes the total debt (or total obligations) to income
25 ratio only. FNMA's benchmark ratio for total debt to income is
26 36 percent. Because this ratio is based on the overall risk of a mortgage,
27 higher ratios may be justified in individual cases. The formulas for
28 calculating both ratios are shown on the following page.

Formula:	Qualifying Ratios
Housing expense ratio: (HER)	Monthly housing expenses (PITI) ÷ Monthly gross income
Example:	$486 monthly housing expenses ÷ $1,950 monthly gross income = .25 or 25%
Total obligation ratio: (TOR)	Total monthly obligations ÷ Monthly gross income
Example:	$684 total monthly obligations ÷ $1,950 monthly gross income = .35 or 35%

MORTGAGE LOAN UNDERWRITING

Property purchased with any type of mortgage first must be qualified by the lender. After the property has been appraised, surveyed, and the title searched, the loan underwriter will make a decision about the property. The purchaser also must be qualified. Lenders generally use four major qualifying guidelines in borrower qualification and risk analysis:

1. The quantity and quality of the borrower's income (Does the borrower have the ability to repay the debt?)

2. Other assets of value (What is the proposed mortgagor's net worth, and what is the ratio of total liabilities to total assets?)

3. Past credit history (Is the borrower willing to repay the debt?)

4. Loan-to-value ratio (How much equity is the borrower investing?)

Loan underwriting (borrower qualification and property qualification) should not be confused with *buyer qualification,* which has to do with what the buyer wants and can afford. The loan underwriting process begins with the FNMA/FHLMC Uniform Residential Loan Application for all one-family to four-family homes.

Quantity and quality of income (ability to pay debt).   Prospective borrowers must provide information to lenders about their present employment, financial history, and present obligations. In addition, federal regulations require lenders to obtain documented proof, such as tax returns and financial statements. Lenders use this information to make a decision about loan approval or rejection. The lender is interested in the borrower's debt-paying ability and the risk involved. The quantity of the borrower's income is the *amount* earned. However, amount alone is not sufficient because the *probable duration* of income is also important when the debt obligation may extend up to 30 years. So the *quality* of the income is also evaluated—how long the applicant has worked in his or her present employment and the probable continuation. Lenders also evaluate demands on a prospective borrower's income, that is, income taxes, installment credit amounts, proposed mortgage payments, and property taxes.

Other assets of value (sufficient security for debt).   The second area of concern in analyzing a loan application is the total value of the mortgaged

1 property plus other assets belonging to the applicant. Other real estate,
2 savings accounts, stocks, bonds, and equity in personal property are
3 examples of assets that could act as sources of funds for mortgage
4 payments if the applicant's income is interrupted.

5 **Credit history (willingness to repay debt).**   The third area of concern is
6 the applicant's willingness to repay debts, based on his or her credit
7 history, obtainable from a local credit bureau. The existing national
8 network of credit bureaus permits a comparatively rapid check of buyers,
9 even of new residents from other states.

10 **Loan-to-value ratio.**   The **loan-to-value (LTV) ratio** is the relationship
11 between the amount borrowed and the appraised value (or purchase
12 price) of a property. Lenders use this ratio as the measure of financial risk
13 associated with lending and borrowing money. The higher the LTV ratio,
14 the lower the lender's safety cushion, should the borrower default.
15 Normally ranging between 60 percent and 90 percent, it however, can fall
16 outside these limits.

Formula:	**Loan-to-Value Ratio**
	Loan Amount
divided by	Price (or value)
equals	LTV ratio

17 *Example:* A home was purchased with a down payment of $36,000
18 and a loan of $200,000 at 10.5 percent for 30 years. Monthly payments
19 are $1,829.50. What is the LTV ratio?

20 $200,000 loan ÷ $236,000 purchase price
21 = .84745 or 85% LTV ratio

22 **Automated underwriting.**   Many mortgage lenders now use *automated*
23 *underwriting,* a service that enables lenders to obtain a credit risk
24 classification using applications software in the loan underwriting
25 process. The advantage of using automated underwriting is that the
26 risk determination is made by Fannie Mae or Freddie Mac. Once the
27 secondary market entity has approved the loan for purchase, a mortgage
28 broker can secure a lender to provide the primary financing. Fannie Mae
29 uses Desktop Underwriter® (DU) and Freddie Mac has a comparable
30 Loan Prospector® (LP). (Fannie Mae and Freddie Mac are discussed in
31 detail in Chapter 13.)

32   Both software applications use appropriate financial data to predict
33 loan performance. Credit report factors such as credit history, delinquent
34 accounts, credit card accounts, public records, foreclosures, collection
35 accounts, and credit inquiries are analyzed. The software also considers
36 the amount of equity (down payment), the LTV ratio, and how much the
37 prospective borrower has in liquid reserves. The software evaluates all of
38 the criteria in terms of the amount of risk. The same criteria are applied to
39 each loan application, ensuring an objective evaluation of the data. The
40 programs are able to consider all of the information in a way that

1 recognizes that a borrower's strengths in one area can offset risk factors in
2 another area. Automated underwriting shortens the time for the closing
3 process and reduces closing costs.

4   The majority of loan applications are classified as acceptable risks,
5 making the loans eligible for sale to Fannie Mae or Freddie Mac. When the
6 automated underwriter determines that a loan application does not
7 appear to meet its credit risk criteria, it refers the loan back to the lender
8 for further review and provides guidance on areas for improvement.
9 LP uses three risk categories: *accept* (lowest level of risk), *refer* (may be
10 acceptable with more information), and *caution* (carries substantial risk).

11   Loan Prospector® uses credit bureau scores called FICO® scores
12 in its risk assessment. FICO® scores were developed by Fair, Isaac
13 and Company, Inc. The scores range in value from approximately
14 400 (highest risk) to 900 (lowest risk). After analyzing the relationship
15 between credit scores and mortgage performance, economists concluded
16 that borrowers with low scores have substantially higher delinquency
17 rates than those with medium or high scores. Freddie Mac advises lenders
18 that applicants with FICO® scores above 660 are likely to have acceptable
19 credit reputations. Those borrowers with FICO® scores below 620 are high
20 risk and need a thorough review of their loan application.

21   Desktop Underwriter® does not use FICO® credit scores in its
22 analysis. Instead, DU analyzes the data directly from a borrower's credit
23 report. The credit report factors considered by DU include credit history,
24 delinquent accounts, credit card accounts, public records, foreclosures,
25 collection accounts, and inquiries. DU weighs each characteristic based on
26 the amount of risk and its significance to the underwriting
27 recommendation. Most public record and foreclosure information is
28 retained on credit reports for seven years (ten years for bankruptcies).

wwweb.link   *Go to:* **http://www.fanniemae.com/singlefamily/**
takingthemysteryout.jhtml *to download a copy of the consumer*
booklet, Taking the Mystery Out of Your Mortgage Loan. *This booklet*
explains Desktop Underwriter®.

29 ■ SUMMARY

30 Real property mortgages continue to be popular investment vehicles. A
31 mortgage is the instrument in which real property is pledged as security
32 for a debt. It is the contract between the lender and the borrower that
33 contains a number of provisions (clauses) specifying the terms and
34 conditions of the agreement. The note is a promise to pay the lender for
35 the debt incurred, and it exposes both personal and real property to risk
36 if the debt is not paid.

37   Mortgages are grouped into three general categories: FHA, VA, and
38 conventional. A number of other mortgage instruments exist to serve
39 specialized needs of lenders and borrowers. A process called buyer
40 qualification is used before the selection of any financing qualification to
41 determine in advance a prospective buyer's housing needs and financial
42 capabilities. Borrowers must qualify for the type of mortgage they seek by
43 meeting loan underwriting standards.

■ REVIEW QUESTIONS

1. In a fully amortized, level-payment plan mortgage, the portion of the monthly payment that goes to reducing the principal
    A. remains constant throughout the loan term.
    B. gradually increases with each payment throughout the duration of the loan term.
    C. gradually decreases with each payment throughout the duration of the loan term.
    D. fluctuates based on the prevailing interest rates.

2. A term mortgage differs from a level-payment, fully amortized mortgage because of the
    A. index chosen.
    B. number of points that may be charged.
    C. method of repayment.
    D. criteria used to qualify the borrower.

3. In a mortgage transaction in Florida, the legal evidence of the personal debt is the
    A. property (collateral).
    B. note.
    C. mortgage instrument.
    D. borrower's credit history.

4. A financing vehicle in which the vendor holds title to the property until the buyer has met the stated obligations is a
    A. balloon mortgage.
    B. purchase-money mortgage.
    C. contract for deed.
    D. term mortgage.

5. In title theory states, the mortgage clause that provides that the conveyance of title to the lender is defeated when all of the terms of the agreement have been fulfilled is the
    A. penalty clause.
    B. release clause.
    C. defeasance clause.
    D. insurance clause.

6. If a foreclosed property fails to bring sufficient proceeds at the foreclosure sale to pay the debt, the lender
    A. must absorb the loss as a bad investment.
    B. may seek recovery of the loss from the Real Estate Recovery Fund.
    C. may obtain an interpleader judgment for the amount of deficit.
    D. may obtain a deficiency judgment for the amount of deficit.

7. Which statement is true regarding discount points?
   A. Discount points are negotiable.
   B. Points are charged by a mortgagee to increase the loan's yield.
   C. FHA, VA, and conventional loans can include points.
   D. All of the above are true.

8. Which is considered an advantage of home equity loans?
   A. The interest rate is typically lower than the prevailing home mortgage rate.
   B. Home equity loans do not create a lien against the borrower's residence.
   C. The interest on most home equity loans is tax deductible.
   D. All of the above are considered home equity loan advantages.

9. The current maximum FHA loan available for a single-family dwelling is
   A. dependent on the location.
   B. $67,500.
   C. $108,000.
   D. $203,000.

10. Rebecca and Tony purchased their first home in January. The interest rate was based on the property being owner-occupied. In May of the same year, Rebecca and Tony decided to live on their sailboat and make a two-year trip around the world. Tony and Rebecca rented their home to Tony's best friend, Brad. The lender soon notified the couple in writing of the mortgagee's intent to increase the interest rate on their loan to the investor rate of interest. The lender was proceeding under which of the following clauses?
    A. Acceleration clause
    B. Escalator clause
    C. Defeasance clause
    D. Release clause

11. The maximum amount of a VA loan is
    A. $359,650.
    B. $89,912.
    C. $60,000.
    D. not a legislated limit for qualified borrowers.

12. Tony wants to buy a small restaurant and is considering financing the restaurant equipment in addition to the real estate. If Tony pledges the personal property in addition to the real estate as collateral for the mortgage, Tony's mortgage is a(n)
    A. equipment mortgage.
    B. package mortgage.
    C. all-inclusive mortgage.
    D. chattel mortgage.

13. A borrower who is in default on his or her mortgage is allowed to prevent the lender from foreclosing on the property by paying the mortgagee the delinquent principal and interest, plus any expenses the mortgagee has incurred in attempting to collect the payments. This right is referred to as
    A. novation.
    B. a satisfaction of mortgage.
    C. the equity of redemption.
    D. an acceleration clause.

14. A lender declares all the unpaid balance due and payable as a result of default. The lender is exercising the
    A. acceleration clause.
    B. due-on-sale clause.
    C. defeasance clause.
    D. escalator clause.

15. The person who borrows money to help pay for the purchase of real property is called at various times the
    A. lender.
    B. mortgagee.
    C. lienor.
    D. mortgagor.

16. The mortgage provision that relieves the mortgagor from any personal liability for the debt so that the mortgagee can look only to the mortgaged property for reimbursement in the event of default is the
    A. novation.
    B. estoppel certificate.
    C. exculpatory clause.
    D. subordination clause.

17. A mortgage
    A. creates a lien.
    B. is a contract.
    C. must be in writing.
    D. has all the above characteristics.

18. When a vendee buys "subject to the mortgage," the
    A. vendee becomes responsible for the note.
    B. original obligation is substituted with a new note by novation.
    C. vendor is relieved of the obligation for the promissory note.
    D. vendor remains responsible for the note.

19. Blanket mortgages
    A. are illegal.
    B. typically include a partial release clause.
    C. include equipment and other personal property.
    D. have all the above traits.

20. Bob and Stella have just made the final mortgage payment on their home. What document should they request the mortgagee to file on their behalf?
    A. Lis pendens
    B. Novation
    C. Satisfaction of mortgage
    D. Estoppel certificate

21. A new mortgage accepted by the seller as part of the purchase price is a(n)
    A. wraparound mortgage.
    B. shared-appreciation mortgage.
    C. assumption of the mortgage.
    D. purchase-money mortgage.

22. If a mortgagee does not want the mortgage to be paid ahead of schedule, the mortgage will normally contain a(n)
    A. prepayment penalty clause.
    B. redemption clause.
    C. defeasance clause.
    D. acceleration clause.

23. A mortgagor defaulted on a mortgage encumbering an apartment complex. Once the foreclosure proceedings were filed, the lender appealed to the courts to appoint a(n)
    A. receiver.
    B. on-site manager.
    C. attorney to handle the case.
    D. arbitrator.

24. Which statement is true regarding the mortgagor's minimum cash investment on an FHA loan?
    A. Closing costs paid by the buyer may be applied toward satisfying the cash requirement.
    B. Seller-paid closing costs may be included when calculating the cash investment amount.
    C. A loan from the seller may be used to satisfy the cash requirement.
    D. Each statement above is true.

25. An FHA loan is a
    A. government-insured loan.
    B. government-guaranteed loan.
    C. private loan that is insured with mortgage insurance.
    D. loan in which the mortgagor is protected against financial loss in the event of default.

26. Which applies to FHA 203(b) loans?
    - A. The loan program applies to loans for one-family to four-family residences.
    - B. The maximum insurable loan limit varies from area to area.
    - C. Borrowers are required to pay a one-time upfront mortgage insurance premium.
    - D. Each of the above applies to 203(b) loans.

27. A potential borrower's monthly housing expense is $504, the total monthly gross income is $1,800, and the total monthly obligations are $648. With a conventional loan, what is the monthly housing expense ratio for the borrower?
    - A. 28 percent
    - B. 38 percent
    - C. 50 percent
    - D. 54 percent

28. The loan-to-value ratio is 80 percent. A buyer wants to acquire a property with a purchase price of $116,000. Calculate the required down payment.
    - A. $20,000
    - B. $23,200
    - C. $32,800
    - D. $92,800

29. The primary purpose of an estoppel certificate is to
    - A. prevent foreclosure.
    - B. relieve the mortgagor of personal liability for the debt.
    - C. verify the loan balance.
    - D. prevent transfer of title to the mortgagee.

30. Who may pay the discount points on a VA loan?
    - A. The buyer
    - B. The seller
    - C. A third party, such as a relative
    - D. Any of the above

CHAPTER 13

The Mortgage Market

under Atlanta Bank,

■ KEY TERMS

conforming loans

demand deposits

discount points

discount rate

disintermediation

intermediation

monetary policy

mortgage bankers

mortgage broker

mortgage company

Office of Thrift
   Supervision (OTS)

open market
   operations

primary market

reserve requirements

secondary mortgage
   market

■ OVERVIEW

This Chapter discusses the money supply; primary and secondary markets; the Financial Institutions Reform, Recovery, and Enforcement Act of 1989 (FIRREA); and potential borrowers. The very strong thread that connects all of these individuals, institutions, and agencies is money, in the form of mortgage loans. The total amount of existing mortgages is estimated to be more than $5.8 trillion! If you compare this amount with the federal debt of nearly $7 trillion, you begin to appreciate the amount of money invested in mortgages! The professional real estate person must be familiar with the institutional lending picture to advise and assist potential borrowers in their search for a loan.

After completing this Chapter, the student should be able to:

- describe the factors that influence the supply and demand for mortgage funds;

- distinguish between the primary and secondary markets;

- understand the mortgage practices of commercial banks, savings associations, mutual savings banks, and life insurance companies;

- distinguish between a mortgage banker and mortgage broker;

- describe the three methods the Fed uses to control the supply of money in circulation;

- describe the function of Fannie Mae, Ginnie Mae, and Freddie Mac; and

- calculate the cost of discount points and the approximate yield resulting from discounts.

■ THE MORTGAGE MARKET AND MONEY SUPPLY

Like other markets, the mortgage market is tied irrevocably to the *law of supply and demand.* An economic fact of life is the inverse relationship between available mortgage money and mortgage interest rates. When the amount of mortgage money goes down, mortgage interest rates go up, and vice versa. The supply of mortgage money available at any given time depends (1) on the continuous and orderly flow of money into various types of financial institutions and (2) on the amount borrowed by the federal government.

All lenders in the mortgage market are tied together by long-term credit lending with real property as security. Also, despite their different locations and operating policies, all lenders are mutually dependent on the overall supply of money existing in the nation. For this reason, price movements of money in different areas are related. When a corporation in San Francisco borrows $50 million from a mutual savings bank in Boston, the money available in the mortgage market is depleted by that amount. The result could be higher interest rates for loans made in Orlando, for example.

Thus, each geographical area is a component of the entire mortgage market. The entire mortgage market is, in turn, only one component of the vast financial system called the *overall capital market.* As interrelated parts, each is responsive to changes affecting the whole system. In fact, it is the total demand for money interacting with the total available supply of money that determines the interest rate, or cost, of mortgages.

At any given time, a number of businesses or institutions are renting mortgage money to other businesses or individuals. The rent paid for the use of money is called *interest.* When money is plentiful and available from many sources, the supply of money exceeds the demand, creating an *easy money market* situation. The interest charged for money loaned during an easy money market is less than in a *tight money market.* A tight money market exists when demand for funds exceeds the available supply, resulting in an increase in the interest charged for money.

The *demand* for mortgage money is increased or decreased by the following six major influences:

1. Changes in the number and size of households

2. Shifts in geographic preference for households

3. Existing inventory of structures

4. Changes in employment rates and income

5. Changes in costs of real property services, taxes, and maintenance

6. Changes in construction costs

Influences on the *supply side* of the mortgage money market also are varied. Because they are considered long-term loans, mortgages do not compete directly with the short-term demand for funds. Mortgages must compete directly with other long-term claims for money. The long-term claims are corporate stocks and bonds and long-term bonds issued by the various federal, state, and local governments. As a consequence, the mortgage, stock, and bond markets are all in competition for the overall supply of funds in what is called the *nation's capital market*.

[handwritten: T. Bills ect.]

Another important influence on the mortgage market is the refinancing of the national debt. The U.S. government owes the owners of short-term and long-term securities trillions of dollars. At the present time, this debt is refinanced periodically by the sale of new securities on the open market. When the U.S. Treasury sells enough securities to pay interest on $500 billion, for example, it drains a large amount of money from the capital market. This drainage results in less funds available for the mortgage market and higher interest rates.

■ FEDERAL REGULATORY BODIES

FEDERAL RESERVE SYSTEM

The Federal Reserve (commonly called *the Fed*) is the central bank of the United States. It was founded by Congress to provide the nation with a safer and more stable monetary system. The Federal Reserve System (FRS) consists of a 7 member Board of Governors and 12 Reserve Banks located in major cities across the nation. The members of the Board of Governors are appointed by the President and confirmed by the U.S. Senate.

Today, the Federal Reserve's duties include: (1) conducting the nation's monetary policy; (2) supervising and regulating banking institutions and protecting the credit rights of consumers; and (3) maintaining the stability of the financial system. **Monetary policy** refers to the actions undertaken by the Fed to influence the availability and cost of money and credit to promote national economic goals. The Federal Reserve is charged with the responsibility for setting monetary policy.

The Federal Reserve also has regulatory and supervisory responsibilities over banks that are members of the FRS. Additionally, the Board is responsible for the development and administration of regulations that implement major federal laws governing consumer credit such as the Truth-in-Lending Act and the Equal Credit Opportunity Act.

The Fed uses three economic tools (or methods) of monetary policy, listed below in the order most often used:

1. **Open-market operations.** The Fed's principal tool and most effective tool for implementing monetary policy is open market operations. The Federal Open Market Committee (FOMC) consists of the seven members of the Board of Governors and five other Reserve Bank presidents. **Open-market operations** involve the purchase and sale of U.S. Treasury and federal agency securities.

[handwritten: Most effective in controling]

1 The purchase or sale of these securities results in an increase or
2 decrease of money in circulation. For example, when the Fed
3 decides to *sell* securities through open-market bulk trading, the
4 FRS holds the funds received from the sale. This reduces the
5 supply of money in circulation, which, in turn, causes a drop in
6 loanable funds and causes interest rates to rise. Higher interest
7 rates cause some business and individuals to postpone borrowing.
8 As borrowing drops off, the economy slows down and inflation
9 (if any) is reduced. When an increase in economic activity seems
10 needed, the Fed *buys* securities, thereby releasing money back into
11 normal circulation and increasing loanable funds.

12 **2. Discount rate.** The second most commonly used method of
13 controlling the supply of money is changing the discount rate.
14 The **discount rate** is the interest rate charged member banks for
15 borrowing money from the Fed. (Do not confuse *discount rate* with
16 *discount points* discussed later in this Chapter.) If the discount rate
17 is increased, member banks have to pay a higher interest rate for
18 money borrowed from their District Bank. The higher interest rate
19 is passed on in the form of higher interest to consumers. This
20 reduces the number of loans made because consumers become
21 reluctant to borrow. Because increasing or decreasing the discount
22 rate has the greatest impact on the cost of short-term credit, the
23 discount rate is considered to be the least effective economic tool
24 for influencing the interest rates of long-term real estate loans.

25 **3. Reserve requirements.** The third method the Fed uses to influence
26 the supply of money is the change in reserve requirements. The
27 **reserve requirements** are the amount of funds that an institution
28 must hold in reserve against deposit liabilities. Institutions must
29 hold reserves in the form of vault cash or deposits with Federal
30 Reserve Banks. Changing the reserve requirement is regarded as
31 perhaps the most abrupt or drastic way to influence the supply of
32 money. Because most member banks have large amounts of time
33 deposits and demand deposits, a very small increase in percentage
34 of reserve requirements has an immediate impact on the amount
35 of funds taken out of circulation.

 To learn more about the Federal Reserve, visit:
http://www.federalreserve.gov/.

FEDERAL HOME LOAN BANK SYSTEM

37 The Federal Home Loan Bank System (FHLBS) was created to provide
38 the same regulatory and administrative services for the nation's savings
39 associations that the FRS provides for commercial banks. Patterned after
40 the Fed, the FHLBS includes 12 district Federal Home Loan Banks
41 (FHLBs). They constitute a permanent pool of reserve credit for savings
42 association member institutions and ensure a source of mortgage funds
43 when local funds are insufficient. The Financial Institutions Reform,
44 Recovery, and Enforcement Act of 1989 (FIRREA) created the **Office of**
45 **Thrift Supervision (OTS)** to charter and regulate member federal

savings associations. FIRREA also created the Federal Housing Finance Board (FHFB) to supervise mortgage lending by the 12 regional FHLBs.

All federally chartered savings associations are required to be members of their district FHLB. While membership is optional for state-chartered savings associations, mutual savings banks, and insurance companies, many of these—that meet federal standards and can qualify—elect to join because only member institutions are allowed to borrow from their district FHLB for up to one year without collateral. Longer term loans, such as real estate loans, must be secured by collateral. Eligibility for membership also is dependent on the financial stability and management policies of each applicant institution. Also, membership is required to qualify for Savings Association Insurance Fund coverage.

FEDERAL DEPOSIT INSURANCE CORPORATION

The Federal Deposit Insurance Corporation (FDIC) insures individual accounts up to $100,000 per account in member institutions. The FDIC is administered by a board of governors and exercises its powers through the Deposit Insurance Fund (DIF) and its two subsidiaries:

1. Bank Insurance Fund (BIF), which insures federally chartered banks

2. Savings Association Insurance Fund (SAIF), which insures federally chartered savings associations

■ PRIMARY MORTGAGE MARKET

The primary mortgage market is made up of primary lenders that *originate* new mortgage loans for borrowers. A **primary market** is the market where securities or goods are actually created. For example, if a commercial bank lends a homebuyer the money to buy a house via the use of a mortgage loan, that would be a primary market activity. The dominant primary lenders are commercial banks, savings associations (SAs), mutual savings banks, selected credit unions, and mortgage bankers. Together, these lenders originate more than 95 percent of all residential mortgage loans.

Sometimes lenders use two types of specialists to arrange loans for the financing of real estate purchases: mortgage brokers and mortgage bankers. Both are called *middlemen* because they act as agents, bringing together a borrower and a lender. The primary differences between the two are responsibility and scope.

The role of the **mortgage broker** is limited to acting as an agent. Mortgage brokers do not have the authority to approve or reject a loan on behalf of a lender. They normally work with one or more mortgage bankers. A mortgage broker submits loan applications from prospective borrowers to various mortgage bankers and other lenders until the loans are approved or abandoned. If a loan application is approved, the mortgage broker has earned a negotiated finder's fee or commission and drops out of the loan transaction.

The role of the mortgage banker, on the other hand, is more extensive. **Mortgage bankers** (mortgage companies) originate loans with either their own funds or with money borrowed from financial institutions. They approve or reject FHA, VA, and conventional loan applications submitted to them by mortgage brokers or prospective borrowers. In addition, they sell these mortgages at a discount to large investors. They also function as middlemen by acting as *loan correspondents* (local representatives) for life insurance companies, mutual savings banks, and other lenders located in distant places. The mortgage banker often is authorized to make loans for and on behalf of one or more institutional lenders located elsewhere. After making a loan for a lender, the mortgage banker frequently services the loan by maintaining contact with the borrower, sending monthly payment notices, collecting escrow funds for taxes, and, in general, acting as a branch office of the lender. Mortgage bankers acting in the capacity of correspondents have enabled lenders located in stable and no-growth (capital-surplus) areas to invest in distant, rapidly growing (capital-deficit) areas.

[handwritten margin note: More Power Than Broker]

INTERMEDIATION AND DISINTERMEDIATION

Intermediation is a process practiced by financial institutions that serve as *intermediaries* between depositors and borrowers. Savers deposit funds into commercial banks, savings associations, and mutual savings banks, which then lend the funds to homebuyers and other borrowers. The financial institutions act as financial intermediaries (middlemen) for depositors and borrowers.

[handwritten margin note: Insured.]

Disintermediation is the removal of intermediaries. Buyers (and investors) bypass the middlemen in order to buy (or invest) directly. Dell Computers practices disintermediation because it sells many of its products directly to the consumer bypassing traditional retail chains. In finance, disintermediation is the process of bypassing the intermediary financial institutions (or middleman). For example, because recent yields on traditional savings accounts were at historical lows, many people purchased bonds on the Internet directly from the federal government.

[handwritten margin note: NOT INSURED.]

COMMERCIAL BANKS

Commercial banks are the primary reservoirs of commercial credit in this country and the largest group of financial institutions in both assets and numbers. The amount invested in real property mortgages by CBs has been increasing over the past few years. CBs hold **demand deposits** (checking accounts), as do federally chartered SAs and credit unions.

[handwritten margin note: Leading source for Constr. Loans]

CBs are chartered by either a state or the federal government (referred to as *national banks*). National banks are supervised by the Comptroller of the Currency and are members of the FRS. The chartering agency prescribes the rules and regulations that govern the business operations of a bank. If chartered by the federal government, a CB must display the word *National* or the initials *NA* (National Association) somewhere in their name. State-chartered CBs are regulated by state agencies, and membership in the FRS is optional; however, as a practical matter, almost all state banks are members of the FRS.

1   Commercial banks make conventional, FHA, and VA mortgage loans,
2 and they have long been recognized as specialists in construction loans
3 for both residential and commercial projects. Most banks also have
4 concentrated on equity loans (lines of credit); that is, loans to homeowners
5 based on the amount of equity in their homes.

6 SAVINGS ASSOCIATIONS

[handwritten: Main Sorce of $ for res. LOANS]

7 Modern savings associations (SAs), formerly called *savings and loan*
8 *associations* (S&Ls), evolved from the early building societies in Europe.
9 In 1831, the first building society in the United States was formed in
10 Pennsylvania. Early American building societies had a single objective:
11 to enable members to purchase or build a house. The added goal of thrift
12 (saving as well as borrowing) came later.

[handwritten: 1st F.O.]

13   The 1989 FIRREA legislation not only changed the name *savings and*
14 *loan association* to *savings association* but also imposed new restrictions. To
15 avoid the bad name some people associate with the financial crisis of the
16 1980s and the failed S&Ls, some SAs have changed their names to *savings*
17 *banks.* Today, most SAs invest the bulk of their assets in residential
18 mortgages and home equity loans. They adhere to strict underwriting
19 guidelines established by the secondary mortgage market (see below).

20   SAs are chartered by either the state or the federal government. If a
21 savings association is federally chartered, either *Federal* or *FA* (Federal
22 Association) must appear in the name of the association. SAs' experience
23 with residential mortgages makes them expert in underwriting and
24 making mortgage loans on single-family houses. Practically all SAs prefer
25 to make conventional mortgage loans, although they may make both
26 FHA and VA loans.

27 MUTUAL SAVINGS BANKS

28 The first mutual savings bank (MSB) was organized in 1816, some
29 15 years before the first S&L was formed. MSBs are state chartered and
30 are similar to SAs. They are mutually owned (no stockholders). While
31 CBs are located in all 50 states, most of the approximately 470 MSBs are
32 concentrated in the Northeast. MSBs are active investors in FHA and
33 VA loans all over the nation. By using mortgage bankers and other
34 representation in fast-growing capital-deficit areas, MSBs are able
35 to extend their lending activities into such areas whenever they
36 choose to do so.

[handwritten: old money No stockholders]

37 MORTGAGE COMPANIES

38 Since the 1980s, the volume of loan originations has shifted from savings
39 associations to mortgage companies. **Mortgage companies** originate
40 loans with either their own funds or borrowed capital. They package the
41 loans and sell them to institutional investors and secondary market
42 participants.

[handwritten: Dime ect.]

43   Mortgage companies, also known as *mortgage bankers,* are not financial
44 intermediaries because they do not accept savings deposits. The principal
45 activity of mortgage companies is to originate and service loans on

FIGURE 13.1   Primary and Secondaray Mortgage Markets

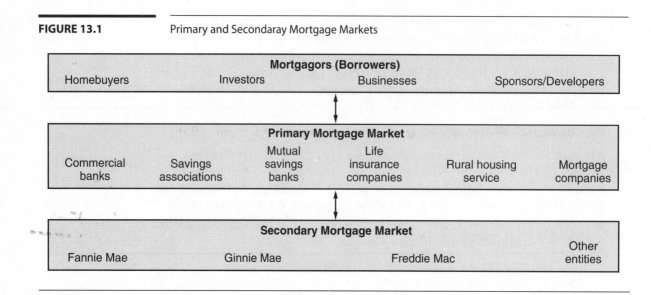

residential and income properties. Mortgage companies charge interest
and earn fees on the loans that they originate. From these fees, mortgage
companies pay interest on any interim funds borrowed, cover operating
expenses, and earn a profit. Today, mortgage companies account for more
than half of all single-family loan originations.

LIFE INSURANCE COMPANIES

Life insurance companies (LICs) are regulated by the laws of the
states in which they operate. LICs are *not* thrift institutions, nor are
they organized for the primary purpose of financing real property. As
insurance companies, they generate enormous amounts of funds that
represent huge amounts of the public's savings, mostly in the form of
policyholders' reserves. LICs, through mortgage bankers or other loan
correspondents, invest in loans secured by large-scale commercial and
industrial real estate. LICs also contribute to the availability of residential
mortgage funds by buying residential mortgages in bulk as a part of the
secondary mortgage market. The approximately 2,200 LICs in the United
States have invested billions of dollars in mortgage loans.

Comercial +Industial Loans

RURAL HOUSING SERVICE

The Rural Housing Service (formerly called the Farmer's Home
Administration) is an agency of the U.S. Department of Agriculture. It
offers direct loans and other services to farmers, rural residents, and rural
communities, enabling them to purchase and operate farms, homes,
and businesses. Loan programs fall into three categories:

1. Originate new loans

2. Insure loans (in much the same way as FHA)

3. Guarantee loans (in much the same way as VA)

Actions and interactions of the primary and secondary mortgage markets are illustrated in Figure 13.1.

■ SECONDARY MORTGAGE MARKET

Lenders can hold and service the loans they create or they can sell the loans in the secondary mortgage market. The **secondary mortgage market** is an investor market that buys and sells existing mortgages. The existence of a secondary mortgage market makes the primary mortgage market more efficient because mortgage originators are able to sell their loans more quickly and obtain funds to originate additional loans. The secondary market is the principal source of mortgage capital in the United States.

Lenders sell some of the loans on the secondary market to private mortgage investors. Private investors include banks, life insurance companies, and pension funds. However, most of the loans are sold to government-sponsored enterprises (GSEs). Fannie Mae and Freddie Mac are the two major GSEs that purchase mortgages on the secondary market.

Mortgage originators package loans they make with other loans and either sell the package as a whole or keep the package and sell securities that are backed by the loans in the package. Ginnie Mae provides liquidity to the mortgage market by guaranteeing mortgage-backed securities. Approximately two-thirds of all residential mortgage loans originated in the United States are now sold in the secondary mortgage market and used as collateral for the issuance of mortgage-backed securities.

Fannie Mae.   Fannie Mae (formerly called the Federal National Mortgage Association or FNMA) was established by Congress in 1938. Fannie Mae's initial goal was to stimulate the housing industry following the Great Depression. Fannie Mae also created the first secondary market for mortgage loans.

In 1968 Fannie Mae became a private, stockholder-owned government-regulated corporation. Its shares are traded on the New York Stock Exchange (NYSE) under the ticker symbol FNM.

Fannie Mae keeps low-cost capital flowing to mortgage lenders across the nation. Fannie Mae does *not* lend money directly to homebuyers. Instead it works with lenders to make sure they don't run out of mortgage funds. Fannie Mae provides large builders and real estate companies *master commitments* in amounts of $25 million and more for funds for up to 12 months in advance. In this way, Fannie Mae assures the mortgage lenders of available funds.

Fannie Mae operates exclusively in the secondary mortgage market by providing two important functions:

1. Fannie Mae purchases FHA, VA, and conventional mortgages from lenders and holds the mortgages in its portfolio. For loans to be sold to Fannie Mae, they must be written in accordance with

Fannie Mae's requirements (guidelines). For example, the mortgages must be Fannie Mae-Freddie Mac approved uniform mortgage instruments. Fannie Mae also sets limitations on the size and kind of loans they will buy. Loans that meet Fannie Mae guidelines are referred to as **conforming loans.**

2. Fannie Mae issues Mortgage-Backed Securities (MBSs) in exchange for pools of mortgages from lenders. MBSs are securities guaranteed by pools of mortgages. By pledging large blocks of mortgage loans as collateral, Fannie Mae can issue mortgage-backed securities that are sold to a broad market of investors. The MBSs provide the lenders with a more liquid asset to hold or sell. Fannie Mae MBSs are highly liquid investments and are traded through securities dealers and brokers.

Freddie Mac. Freddie Mac (formerly called the Federal Home Loan Mortgage Corporation, or FHLMC) was created by Congress in 1970. Freddie Mac was made a private stockholder-owned company in 1989; its shares are traded on the NYSE under the ticker symbol FRE. Freddie Mac is subject to regulatory oversight by both the Secretary of HUD and the Secretary of the Treasury Department. Freddie Mac provides a secondary market for loans originated by SAs. Most of the loans Freddie Mac handles are conventional loans. Savings associations can sell qualified mortgages to Freddie Mac for cash, then use the cash to make new mortgage loans.

[handwritten: Frees up Cash to make more loans.]

Ginnie Mae. Ginnie Mae (formerly the Government National Mortgage Association or GNMA) is a government-owned and financed corporation. Ginnie Mae is part of the Department of Housing and Urban Development (HUD).

Ginnie Mae's mission statement is "To expand affordable housing in America by linking global capital markets to the nation's markets." Ginnie Mae accomplishes its mission by guaranteeing securities that are backed by pools of mortgages. The mortgages in the MBSs are mostly FHA and VA mortgages (and some mortgages originated through the Rural Housing Service). Ginnie Mae's guaranty allows mortgage lenders to obtain a better price for their mortgage loans in the secondary market.

[handwritten: G = Government. Projects Slums Affordable Housing Never Made Any $]

Ginnie Mae serves as a *guarantor* of mortgage-backed securities (MBSs). Ginnie Mae MBSs are often referred to as Ginnie Mae pass-through securities. A *pass-through security* refers to the payments of the underlying mortgages (principal and interest) that are passed through to the investor. MBSs are created by pooling a group of similar (same interest rate and maturity date) mortgages. The mortgage pool is then used as collateral for the issuance of the MBS. Ginnie Mae does not issue, sell, or buy mortgage-backed securities, or purchase mortgage loans. Ginnie Mae-approved private institutions issue the MBSs. In exchange for a fee, Ginnie Mae guarantees the timely payment of principal and interest to the investors. Ginnie Mae mortgage-backed securities are the only MBSs to carry the *full faith and credit guarantee* of the United States government.

[handwritten: Sally Mae = Student Loan.]

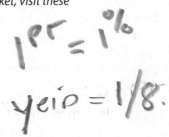

To learn more about the secondary mortgage market, visit these Web sites:
wwweb.link
Fannie Mae: **http://www.fanniemae.com/**
Ginnie Mae: **http://www.ginniemae.gov/**
Freddie Mac: **http://freddiemac.com**

■ LENDER CHARGES

MORTGAGE DISCOUNTING

Years ago, a system of discounting was created to make FHA and VA mortgage loans competitive with conventional mortgage loans. Lenders are allowed to charge **discount points** for FHA and VA loans. This extra, upfront fee increased the real yield, or annual percentage rate (APR), to the lender. With the discount points added on, the interest rate earned on FHA and VA loans then approximated the yield from conventional loans made at higher interest rates. Subsequently, FHA and VA mortgage interest rates have been allowed to float freely in the mortgage market, thereby following prevailing market rates in the same way as conventional mortgage rates. Today, lenders charge points as an interest rate adjustment factor. In other words, an up-front charge is imposed to increase the actual yield from a mortgage without showing an increase in the interest rate on the mortgage.

Discount points are based on the loan amount, not on the selling price. When calculating the actual cost in dollars added by the discount points, each point is equal to 1 percent of the loan amount (1 point = 1%).

Example: On a $40,000 loan for which the lender is charging 6 points, find the dollar cost of the points. Take 6 percent of $40,000.

$$\$40,000 \times .06 = \$2,400$$

When the lender receives the $2,400, only $37,600 is needed from the lender's funds to make up the total $40,000 that is loaned to the borrower. However, the lender will receive interest based on the entire $40,000 during the full term of the loan. The real yield to a lender includes not only this interest but also the $2,400 paid as a mortgage discount.

Lenders use computers or prepared tables to determine the number of discount points that must be paid. However, as a general rule of thumb, each discount point paid to the lender will increase the lender's yield (return) by approximately ⅛ of 1 percent (.00125). In using the rule of thumb, for each discount point charged by a lender, add ⅛ percent to the stated (contract) mortgage interest rate to estimate the lender's yield (and cost to the borrower) from the loan.

Example: A buyer wants to obtain a mortgage of $80,000, and a lender agrees to make the loan at 8½ percent interest plus 6 points up front. What will the approximate yield be to the lender?

To the quoted interest rate of 8½ percent, add ⅛, of one percent for each point, or ⁶⁄₈, which reduces to ¾:

$$\tfrac{1}{8} \times 6 = \tfrac{6}{8} = \tfrac{3}{4}$$

Add the ¾ to the mortgage interest rate of 8½ percent, and the lender's real yield is approximately 9¼ percent on the money actually loaned:

$$\text{¾\% + 8½\% = 9¼\% approximate yield}$$

Frequently, a lender will state that mortgages are "going at" 96 or 94, for example. This is a different way of quoting discount points. It means that the lender is willing to lend only 96 percent or 94 percent of the face value of a mortgage loan. If the seller, the buyer, or a third party is willing to come up with the remaining 4 percent or 6 percent, then the lender will make the loan. It means exactly the same thing as quoting 4 points or 6 points. Regardless of the method used, the real interest rate earned for the lender will be increased approximately ⅛ of 1 percent for each point charged up front.

Discounting interacts with the previously discussed FRS control of the money supply. Suppose the national economy is booming and inflation threatens to get out of hand. The Fed decides to decrease the amount of money in circulation as an inflation control effort. Securities are sold to absorb part of the money in circulation, and the discount rate at which banks are permitted to borrow is raised. The money supply drops and interest rates rise. Mortgage rates go to 10½ percent, but some lenders raise their interest rates to only 9½ percent. To offset the apparent 1 percent loss in yield, most lenders would make their mortgage loans at 9½ percent plus an 8-point discount. This means the lender actually would be lending only 92 percent of the amount needed; the additional 8 percent of the loan would come from the person(s) attempting to obtain the loan.

OTHER SOURCES OF INCOME TO LENDERS

In addition to discount points charged for making a loan, lenders frequently levy other charges. Normally, a lender charges the borrower a *loan origination fee*. Amounts vary, but the fee typically includes a 1 percent or 2 percent commission plus the total of all expenses encountered by the lender in obtaining credit reports, preparing loan documents, and processing a mortgage loan application.

Another source of income to lenders takes the form of *commitment fees*. The developer of a subdivision, a shopping center, or an apartment complex often needs to obtain a written commitment from a financial institution certifying that permanent financing will be provided when the project is completed. The point here is that the financial institution is willing to become the permanent lender in the future, but first the developer must find a lender of construction money. With the written commitment of the future permanent lender, called a *takeout commitment*, it is much easier to find a construction money lender. When the project is built, the permanent lender advances the amount committed, and the developer repays the construction lender. Most lenders that issue a takeout commitment charge a nonrefundable fee for making the commitment. The borrower, in this case the developer, is required to pay the fee at the time the commitment is made.

1   Some lenders "service" (handle the loan payment collecting and
2   record keeping) the mortgages they originate and then sell them to large
3   financial institutions or other secondary market institutions. This is an
4   additional source of income for such lenders. Today, *servicing fees*
5   typically range from ⅜ to ¾ of 1 percent of the unpaid balance of loans
6   serviced. Fannie Mae and Freddie Mac have traditionally paid a
7   ⅜ of 1 percent (.375) servicing fee, and Ginnie Mae has normally paid
8   .44 percent to lenders that continue to service mortgages sold to those
9   agencies. If a lender averages a ⅜ of 1 percent service fee for several blocks
10 of mortgages totaling $100 million, it earns a gross income of $375,000 per
11 year from that source alone. As might be expected, lenders are generally
12 eager to retain servicing of any loans sold to institutional investors.

13 ## ■ SUMMARY

14 The mortgage market, like all other markets, is linked irrevocably to the
15 principles of supply and demand. Mortgages, or more properly mortgage
16 loans, are the chief source of funds for financing real property. Mortgage
17 loans involve a borrower (mortgagor) and a lender (mortgagee).

18   Primary mortgage market activity generally involves lenders that
19 originate loans and thus supply funds directly to borrowers. Secondary
20 mortgage market activity generally involves lenders that buy mortgages
21 as investments or that make loans by using intermediaries; thus, they are
22 secondary lenders. Secondary lenders should not be confused with
23 individuals involved in secondary financing, the latter being those that
24 make second mortgage loans directly to borrowers.

25   Three basic types of mortgage loans exist: conventional, FHA-insured,
26 and VA-guaranteed. Interest is charged for the use of money loaned,
27 and discounting provides the lender a higher yield without raising the
28 interest rate.

■ REVIEW QUESTIONS

1. Rebecca and Tony purchased their home for $125,000. They financed
    the purchase with an 80 percent conventional loan. The mortgagee
    charged 2½ points. Calculate the actual cost in dollars of the points.
    A. $1,600
    B. $2,000
    C. $2,500
    D. $3,125

2. Each entity or individual below functions as a primary lender EXCEPT
    A. commercial banks.
    B. mortgage bankers.
    C. mortgage brokers.
    D. savings associations.

3. When the Fed increases the reserve requirement
   A. the supply of money increases.
   B. the supply of money decreases.
   C. inflation usually immediately follows.
   D. mortgage interest rates decline immediately.

4. A commercial bank sold a group of 2,000 mortgages directly to Fannie Mae. This is an example of
   A. primary market activity.
   B. secondary market activity.
   C. loan correspondence.
   D. intermediation.

5. Fannie Mae currently buys and sells
   A. FHA mortgages.
   B. VA mortgages.
   C. conventional mortgages.
   D. all three types of mortgages.

6. Which statement does NOT apply to Fannie Mae?
   A. Loans that meet Fannie Mae guidelines are called conforming loans.
   B. Fannie Mae provides master commitments for large real estate projects.
   C. Fannie Mae created the first secondary market for mortgage loans.
   D. Fannie Mae deals directly with homebuyers.

7. Which entity originates loans and typically services the loans, but is NOT a financial intermediary?
   A. Mortgage company
   B. Mortgage broker
   C. Life insurance company
   D. Fannie Mae

8. When the Fed purchases securities, which results?
   A. The supply of money in circulation is reduced.
   B. Interest rates begin to rise.
   C. Loanable funds are released into circulation.
   D. Pressure is applied to increase the discount rate.

9. Which competes for the available supply of funds?
   A. Corporate stock
   B. Long-term bonds issued by governmental entities
   C. Financing the national debt
   D. All of the above

10. The market where mortgage loans are created, supplying funds to finance real estate purchases directly to borrowers, is referred to as the
    A. primary market.
    B. secondary market.
    C. capital market.
    D. real estate market.

11. The primary purpose of Fannie Mae is to
    A. reduce and stabilize mortgage interest rates.
    B. purchase real estate loans to replenish the supply of mortgage money.
    C. make loans to low-income families.
    D. do all of the above.

12. The demand for residential real estate mortgage money is influenced by
    A. household formations.
    B. shifts in geographic preference for housing.
    C. household income.
    D. any of the above.

13. The Office of Thrift Supervision regulates
    A. savings associations.
    B. commercial banks.
    C. credit unions.
    D. the Rural Housing Service.

14. The discount rate is
    A. 1 percent of the loan amount.
    B. a rate adjustment factor used to increase the lender's yield on a loan.
    C. the interest rate charged member banks for borrowing funds from the Federal Reserve Bank.
    D. approximately ⅛ of 1 percent for each point charged.

15. The primary purpose of Freddie Mac is to
    A. purchase conventional loans from savings associations.
    B. regulate savings associations.
    C. insure mortgage loans.
    D. regulate conventional mortgage loan interest rates.

16. When investors bypass thrift institutions for direct investment elsewhere, the process is called
    A. loan correspondence.
    B. intermediation.
    C. disintermediation.
    D. capital-deficit area support.

17. Which provides a source of income to lenders?
    - A. Discount points
    - B. Origination fees
    - C. Servicing fees
    - D. All of the above

18. The rule of thumb used to convert discount points to annual percentage rate is that each discount point increases the yield by approximately
    - A. ⅛ of 1 percent.
    - B. ¼ of 1 percent.
    - C. ½ of 1 percent.
    - D. 1 percent.

19. A lender charged 7 percent plus 3 points. What is the approximate yield on this loan?
    - A. 7¼ percent
    - B. 7⅜ percent
    - C. 7½ percent
    - D. 7¾ percent

20. The most commonly used method of controlling the national money supply is for the Fed to
    - A. engage in open-market activities.
    - B. change the discount rate.
    - C. change the reserve requirement.
    - D. issue new currency.

CHAPTER 14

Computations and Title Closing

■ KEY TERMS

arrears	level-payment plan	profit
credit	principal	prorate
debit	pre-closing inspection	

■ OVERVIEW

Real estate brokers and sales associates must understand closing
statements and should be capable of computing the various simple
arithmetic problems to be solved in arriving at the figures entered on the
closing statements provided to the contracting parties. Many adults have
had little or no occasion to work with fractions, decimals, percentages,
and the like for years. The first section of this Chapter assumes little or no
prior knowledge about these subjects and their application.

After completing this Chapter, the student should be able to:

- compute a sale commission;

- calculate the percent of profit or loss, given the original cost of the
  investment, the sale price, and the dollar amount of profit or loss;

- amortize a level-payment plan mortgage when given the principal
  amount, the interest rate, and the monthly payment amount;

- prorate the buyer's and seller's expenses using either the
  30-day-month method or the 365-day method;

- calculate the dollar amount of transfer taxes on deeds, mortgages,
  and notes; and

- allocate taxes and fees to the proper parties and compute
  individual costs.

■ COMPUTATIONS

FRACTIONS, DECIMALS, AND PERCENTAGES

When a whole unit or number is divided into equal parts, each of the parts is a fraction (and a percent) of the whole unit. For example, if a city block is divided into two equal parts, each of the parts is ½ (or 50 percent) of a city block.

Parts of a fraction.   When dealing with fractions, the number *below* the line is called the *denominator.* The denominator always indicates the total equal parts in a whole unit. In the example of the city block above, each part was ½. The lower number indicates the total number of equal parts (two) in the entire city block. If the fraction ¼ had been used, the denominator would have indicated that the city block was divided into four equal parts.

The number in a fraction that appears *above* the line dividing the numbers is called the *numerator.* The numerator indicates how many of the equal parts of the whole unit are being counted. For example, in the fraction ¾, the top number indicates three equal parts are being counted, and the bottom number shows a total of four equal parts, so you are talking about all but one equal part of something (all but ¼).

Changing fractions to decimals.   The line separating the numerator from the denominator means division (the top number is divided by the bottom number). If you are dividing a fraction using a calculator, enter the numerator first, then the division key, followed by the denominator. For example, in the fraction ½: press 1, followed by the division key, then press 2. Press the equal sign key (=) and the answer displayed is 0.5. You have now converted (changed) a fraction (½) into a decimal number (.5).

Changing decimals to percentages.   To change a decimal to a percent, move the decimal point two places to the right and add the percent sign (%). (This is the same as multiplying the decimal number by 100.) If only one decimal number is involved, add a zero to the right of the number.

Examples: .5 = .50 = 50%   1.5 = 1.50 = 150%

Changing percentages to decimals.   To change any percentage to an equivalent decimal, simply place a decimal point two places to the left of the number and drop the percent sign. (This is the same as dividing the percentage figure by 100.)

Examples: 34% = .34
          150% = 1.50

If only one number is involved, add a zero to the left to permit moving the decimal point two places to the left.

Example: You want to calculate in dollars the 7½ percent commission on a house sale price.

Convert the fractional part of the decimal number:

$$½\% = 1 \div 2 = .5$$

FIGURE 14.1   Decimal Place Values

1   Next, convert the entire commission percentage to a decimal number.

2   7½% = 7.5% = .075

3   Thus, the decimal number .075 is used to calculate the sale commission.

4   Assume the sale price is $130,000. Calculate the commission.

5                    $130,000 × .075 = $9,750

6   **Decimal place values.**   A great deal of the basic arithmetic required to
7   compute routine real estate problems involves decimal numbers. This
8   review of decimals will be more meaningful if you refresh your memory
9   on the decimal system of place values and the importance of the decimal
10   point in separating whole numbers from fractional parts of whole
11   numbers. The chart of decimal place values shown as Figure 14.1 should
12   be memorized if you do not already know the place values. Notice that the
13   *whole numbers* are to the *left* of the decimal point. The *decimal fractions* of a
14   whole number are to the *right* of the decimal point.

Equivalent Units		
Percent	**Fraction**	**Decimal**
100%	100/100	1.00
50%	50/100	.50
6%	6/100	.06
½%	.5/100	.005
¼%	.25/100	.0025

15   **Working with decimals.**   To divide a whole number by a decimal, for
16   example, 41,500 divided by 1.85: first, enter 41500 into your calculator,
17   press the division key, then enter 1.85. When you press the equal sign key,
18   the answer will appear in the display, as demonstrated in the calculator
19   method on page 298.

20   ## SALE COMMISSIONS

21   If the broker has been hired to list and sell the property for the seller, the
22   seller is normally responsible for paying the commission. If a buyer
23   brokerage agreement exists, the buyer may be responsible for the
24   commission. The commission is agreed to in the listing contract and/or
25   the buyer brokerage agreement.

Calculator Method:

41,500 ÷ 1.85 =

Press	Display
4 then 1 then 5 then 0 then 0	41500
÷ (the division key)	41500
1 then . then 8 then 5	1.85
= (equal sign)	22432.432

---

1   Let's begin with an example of a commission calculation. In this
2 example the property is listed and sold by the same sales associate.

3 *Example:* Suppose a broker's listing agreement specifies that 6½
4 percent commission is to be paid on the sale price. A sales associate for
5 the firm lists and sells the property and is to receive 55 percent of the
6 6½ percent sale commission. How much will the sales associate earn if
7 he or she sells the property for $62,000?

8 **Step 1:** Find the total sale commission.
9          $62,000 sale price × .065 rate = $4,030 total commission

10 **Step 2:** Find the sales associate's commission.
11          $4,030 total commission × .55 split = $2,216.50 sales
12   associate's commission

13   More frequently, a property is listed with one brokerage company and
14 sold by another brokerage through the MLS system. Members of the MLS
15 (who are also members of their local REALTOR® association) make an offer
16 of cooperation ("co-broke" or "co-op") when they place their listings in
17 the MLS. When another brokerage sells the listing, it will receive the
18 portion of the total commission that was specified by the listing
19 brokerage.

20 *Example:* A broker's listing agreement specifies a 7 percent
21 commission is to be paid on the sale price. The MLS agreement
22 specifies a 50-50 split between the listing and selling offices. If the
23 property sells for $100,000, how much commission is earned by the
24 listing and the selling offices?

25 **Step 1:** Find the total sale commission.
26          $100,000 sale price × .07 rate = $7,000 total commission

27 **Step 2:** Find the selling and listing office's split.
28          $7,000 total commission × .50 split = $3,500 selling/listing
29   office commission

30   The selling commission is typically shared between the broker of the
31 selling office and the sales associate who works for the selling office that
32 found a buyer for the property. The same is true for the listing office and
33 the sales associate who listed the property for the brokerage company. The
34 percentage that sales associates earn is negotiated between each sales
35 associate and his or her broker taking into consideration the sales
36 associate's experience and production.

1 *Example:* Let's assume that the sales associate receives 60 percent of
2 the total selling office commission. How much commission did the
3 sales associate earn on the previous example? How much did the
4 broker receive for the same transaction?

5 **Step 1:** Calculate the sales associate's split of the selling office
6 commission.
7 $3,500 selling office commission × .60 split = $2,100 sales
8 associate's commission

9 **Step 2:** Calculate the broker's split of the selling office commission.
10 $3,500 selling office commission × .40 split = $1,400 broker's
11 commission

12 Today 100 percent commission arrangements are popular. A sales
13 associate in a 100 percent commission office receives the entire
14 commission due his or her respective brokerage office. Instead of splitting
15 the commission with the broker, the sales associate pays a specified share
16 of office expenses plus a fixed monthly fee.

17 A broker who lists a property with higher-than-normal value may
18 agree to a graduated sale commission. This provides an incentive for the
19 broker to get the seller the very best price possible.

20 *Example:* The broker has a listing with a seller and the parties agree to
21 a graduated commission structure. The commission is 5 percent on the
22 first $200,000 of sale price 6½ percent on the next $100,000 of sale
23 price, and 8 percent on the amount over $300,000. What is the total
24 commission if the property sells for $325,000?

25 **Step 1:** Calculate the first increment of commission.
26 $200,000 × .05 rate = $10,000 first increment commission

27 **Step 2:** Calculate the second increment of commission.
28 $100,000 × .065 rate = $6,500 second increment commission

29 **Step 3:** Calculate the third increment of commission.
30 $25,000 remaining portion of sale price × .08 rate = $2,000
31 third increment commission

32 **Step 4:** Add the commission increments to determine the total
33 commission.
34 $10,000 + $6,500 + $2,000 = $18,500 total commission

35 **Percentage applied to selling price, cost, and profit.**   Profit is how
36 much you make over and above your cost. It may be expressed as an
37 amount or as a percent of your cost.

Formula:	**Profit (or Loss)**
	Amount made (lost) on sale
divided by	Total cost
equals	Percent profit (or loss)

1   *Example:* A lot cost $8,000 and sold for $10,000, yielding a $2,000 profit.
2   What is the percentage of profit?

3   $$\$2,000 \div \$8,000 = .25 \text{ or } 25\% \text{ profit}$$

4   *Example:* A lot cost $10,000 and sold for $8,000, resulting in a $2,000
5   loss. What is the percentage of loss?

6   $$\$2,000 \div \$10,000 = .20 \text{ or } 20\% \text{ loss}$$

7   *Example:* A lot sold for $6,000, making a 25 percent profit. What was
8   the cost of the lot?

9   $$100\% \text{ cost} + 25\% \text{ profit} = \$6,000$$
10 $$125\% = \$6,000 \text{ selling price}$$
11 $$\$6,000 \text{ selling price} \div 1.25 = \$4,800 \text{ cost}$$

12 *Example:* A lot sold for $10,000, representing a 20 percent loss. What
13 was the cost of the lot?

14 $$100\% - 20\% = \$10,000$$
15 $$80\% = \$10,000$$
16 $$\$10,000 \text{ selling price} \div .80 = \$12,500 \text{ cost}$$

17 MORTGAGE AMORTIZATION

18 Mortgages used to purchase residential property usually call for regular,
19 equal payments that include both interest payments and payments on
20 the unpaid balance of the debt **(principal).** This type of mortgage is
21 called the **level-payment plan** or, more commonly, a fixed-rate *amortized*
22 *mortgage,* because the regular, periodic payments remain the same.
23 However, the amount of the payment that goes for interest gradually
24 decreases, and the amount assigned to amortizing the debt (principal)
25 gradually increases.

26   To calculate how much money is to be regarded as interest and how
27 much is to be paid on the principal, three facts are needed:

28   1. The outstanding amount of the debt (principal)

29   2. The rate of interest

30   3. The amount of the payment per period (usually monthly)

31   Interest rates for mortgages are expressed as annual interest rates.
32 Thus, a $60,000 mortgage at 10 percent simply means that the interest rate
33 is 10 percent per year. To find the monthly interest actually paid, first
34 determine what 10 percent of $60,000 will amount to for the entire year.
35 Dividing this amount by 12 (the number of months) gives the amount
36 of interest for one month. When the principal amount changes, the
37 calculation must be done over again, based on the new principal balance.
38 The new balance must be treated as if it were to be applied to the entire
39 12 months.

40   *Example:* A home for sale has a mortgage of $30,000 at 8 percent
41 interest. Your buyer wants to know how much of the $220.13 monthly
42 payment will go for interest and how much for principal during the
43 first three months.

> **Amortizing a Mortgage**
>
> **Step 1:** Principal balance × Annual interest ÷ 12 =
> First month's interest
>
> **Step 2:** Monthly mortgage payment – First month's
> interest = Payment on principal
>
> **Step 3:** Beginning principal balance – Principal
> payment = New principal balance

1 **Step 1:** $30,000 unpaid balance × .08 rate = $2,400 interest ÷
2 12 months = $200 first month's interest

3 **Step 2:** $220.13 monthly payment – $200 interest =
4 $20.13 payment on principal

5 So the first month's interest was $200, and the principal reduction in
6 month one was $20.13.

7 But the buyer wanted to know about the first three months. So take
8 credit for the $20.13 paid on the principal by subtracting that amount from
9 the $30,000.

10 **Step 3:** $30,000 – $20.13 principal paid first month =
11 $29,979.87 new principal balance

12 Now repeat the steps above to determine the answers for the second
13 and third months, beginning with:

14 **Step 4:** $29,979.87 new principal balance × .08 rate =
15 $2,398.3896 ÷ 12 months = $199.87 interest

16 Repeat steps 2 and 3 to determine the unpaid balance remaining after
17 payment of the second month's principal. Begin with this new principal
18 balance at the end of the second month and repeat steps 1, 2, and 3 to find
19 the amount paid for interest and principal during the third month. Thus,
20 the answer to your buyer's question is:

21 First month: Principal = $20.13; Interest = $200.00
22 Second month: Principal = $20.26; Interest = $199.87
23 Third month: Principal = $20.40; Interest = $199.73

24 If the amount paid for interest from the first month's mortgage
25 payment is given along with the interest rate and loan-to-value (LTV)
26 ratio, the sale price of the property for which payment was made
27 can be found.

28 *Example:* The interest portion of the first month's mortgage payment
29 is $770, the interest rate is 10.5 percent, and the LTV ratio is 80 percent.
30 Calculate the sale price of the property.

31 $770 × 12 months = $9,240 interest per annum
32 $9,240 ÷ 10.5% = $9,240 ÷ .105 = $88,000 mortgage amount
33 $88,000 ÷ 80% or .80 LTV ratio = $110,000 sale price

■ PRE-CLOSING STEPS

All real property sales or exchanges eventually conclude with a transfer of title. This occurs at the *title closing,* when the seller delivers title to the buyer in exchange for the purchase price. The date and place of title closing should be specified in the sale contract. There are usually several things to accomplish between the time of signing the sale contract and the title closing. For example some of the pre-closing steps include the following:

1. **Mortgage application.** If the buyers intend to finance the purchase, they will complete a mortgage application. The contract for sale and purchase specifies the number of days within which the buyer must submit a loan application. The real estate contract typically contains a financing contingency clause that provides for cancellation of the sale contract and return of the buyer's escrow deposit if the buyer is unable to secure financing.

   [handwritten: Letter of $ Aproval.]

2. **Survey.** The buyer should have the property surveyed to determine the exact location and size of the property and to make sure there are no encroachments, such as a neighbor's fence across the property line.

   [handwritten: Seller $ Pays]

3. **Appraisal.** Because the property is pledged as collateral for the mortgage loan, the lender will order an appraisal to determine whether the property's value is sufficient to ensure recovery of the loan amount should a default occur. In a cash transaction the buyer may want the property appraised to verify the property's value for tax or investment reasons.

   [handwritten: Buyer Pays Closing Fee.]

4. **Title insurance.** A search is made of the public records for condition of the title and existing liens, judgments, or other encumbrances. The seller is responsible for removing any encumbrances on the title. Typically there is a simultaneous issue of the owner's policy and the lender's policy. (See also page 173.)

   [handwritten: Seller Pays.]

5. **Closing documents.** The closing agent, usually a title company or an attorney, prepares the closing documents.

   [handwritten: Seller Pays.]

6. **Property inspections.** It is advisable for the buyer to have a certified property inspector check the condition of the structure and mechanical parts. An inspection for wood destroying organisms (WDO) including termites and wood rot is also recommended and may be required by the lender.

   [handwritten: Buyer Pays.]

7. **Pre-closing inspection.** Before the closing date, the buyer makes a final **pre-closing inspection** of the property (a *walk-through*) with the sales associate. The purpose of the pre-closing inspection is to verify that repairs have been completed and that the property has been left in good condition.

■ CLOSING STATEMENTS

The Florida real estate license law places the responsibility on the broker for an accurate accounting and delivery of all monies, deposits, drafts,

475.25(1)(d), F.S.

mortgages, conveyances, leases, or other documents entrusted to him or her by the parties to the transaction. The customary method of discharging this responsibility is to have the closing agent prepare and deliver complete and accurate closing statements to the buyer and the seller, plus a summary that reconciles all of the debits (charges) and credits involved.

■ CLOSING STATEMENT ITEMS

It is important for sales associates to have an understanding of the closing documents. The sales associates usually attend the title closing along with the buyer and seller. Licensees should be able to explain and verify the entries on the closing documents.

PRORATED EXPENSES

To **prorate** means to divide various charges and credits between buyer and seller. Every sale contract should specify a date and time for prorating items. It is customary when transferring title to have all prorated items determined as of the midnight before the date of closing. This means that (1) the buyer is charged for property taxes on the day of closing; (2) the buyer is charged for interest on an assumed mortgage on the day of closing; and (3) the buyer is credited for any rental income earned on the day of closing. In some areas or by negotiation, it is possible that the day of closing will be charged to the seller. In that case, the seller is charged with an additional day.

Prorating is usually required when rents are paid in advance; property taxes are paid in **arrears** (that is, at the end of the period for which payment is due); and interest on mortgages is paid in arrears (the usual practice). Therefore, all items that are to become a **credit** (reimbursed) or **debit** (charged) to either buyer or seller are *prorated* because the item applies to both the buyer and the seller.

To prorate costs, two methods may be used: 30-day-month method and 365-day method. The 365-day method is preferred and more accurate.

30-day-month method. This method is also called the *statutory month* method. In this method, all months are considered to have 30 days (even February). To use a *statutory year* (360-day year), determine the yearly cost of the item; next divide by 12 to find the cost per month; then divide by 30 to find the cost per day.

Example: Closing date is July 23. The annual property taxes are $3,400 and have not yet been paid. How much is the seller to pay the buyer for the days the seller owned the property? (The day of closing is charged to the buyer.)

$$\$3,400 \div 12 \text{ months} = \$283.333 \text{ per month}$$

$$\$283.333 \div 30 \text{ days} = \$9.444 \text{ per day}$$

The seller will credit the buyer for 6 months (January through June) and 22 days in July:

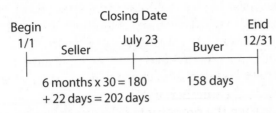

$283.333 per month × 6 months = $1,699.998
22 days in July × $9.444 per day = $207.768
$1,699.998 + $207.768 = $1,907.766 rounded to $1,907.77
(debit seller; credit buyer)

365-day method. This method calculates the proration using the actual number of days in the proration period. To use this method, first divide 365 into the annual cost of the item to find the exact daily rate, then multiply the number of days involved by the daily rate.

Example: Using the same information as in the previous example:

$3,400 ÷ 365 days = $9.315 per day

The exact number of days owed by the seller are:

January 31 + February 28 + March 31 + April 30 +
May 31 + June 30 + July 22 = 203 days

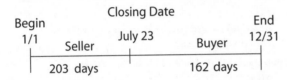

$9.315 per day × 203 days = $1,890.945, rounded to $1,890.95
(debit seller; credit buyer)

Prepaid rent. Normally, any rental income collected in advance belongs to the new owner as of the date of closing; therefore, the unused portion of advance rent belongs to the buyer. The total rent amount should be divided by the number of days involved in the rental period and allocated on a daily basis.

Example: Assume that a property rents for $260 per month. The closing date is on the 21st day of a 30-day month. The method of prorating is as follows:

$260 ÷ 30 days = $8.6666667 per day
$8.6666667 × 10 days = $86.67 (due buyer)
$260 – $86.67 = $173.33 (earned by seller)

Closing Date
1   21   30
Seller   Buyer
20 days   10 days

On the closing statements, *credit* the buyer with $86.67 and *debit* the seller $86.67. The $173.33 was earned by the seller before closing and is not mentioned on either closing statement.

County and/or city property taxes. (See also Chapter 18.) Property taxes are paid in arrears (at the end of the tax year). The seller will have had possession and use of the property for some portion of the year, unless the transfer of title is effective on January 1. To apportion the property taxes fairly, they are prorated on the basis of a 365-day year. The total tax assessment is divided by the number of days in a year to determine the tax cost per day. Then the property tax chargeable to the seller, on departure from the property, is calculated by multiplying the tax cost per day by the number of calendar days before title is conveyed. The resulting amount is entered on the seller's closing statement as a debit. It is also shown on the buyer's closing statement, but as a credit. The buyer's share of property taxes is not reflected on either closing statement because he or she will not be required to settle the tax bill at closing. The buyer pays the entire year's property tax after November 1, which includes the amount paid to the buyer by the seller.

Mortgage interest on assumed mortgages. Because mortgage payments are normally made each month, one month is usually the period used to calculate interest owed. Interest is paid at the end of the period (in arrears or, in other words, after having the use of the money). It is therefore charged to the seller up to the date of closing. This item is prorated in the same manner as property taxes. Interest is figured from the last date for which interest was paid. The exact number of days in each month is used, and interest is figured on a daily basis.

$$\text{Mortgage balance} \times \text{Annual interest rate} \div 12 \text{ months} =$$
$$\text{Month's interest}$$
$$\text{Month's interest} \div \text{Days in month} = \text{Daily rate}$$
$$\text{Daily rate} \times \text{Days interest is owed} = \text{Prorated interest}$$

STATE TRANSFER TAXES

Just as buying most things in life involves paying state taxes, so real estate transactions involve the payment of state taxes at closing. Florida has three types of state taxes that apply to deeds, notes, and mortgages associated with the transfer of ownership of real property.

State documentary stamp tax on deeds. First, the state requires the payment of a tax on deeds and other conveyances. This state *documentary stamp tax on deeds* is assessed at the rate of $.70 ($.60 in Dade County) for each $100 of the full purchase price (or any fraction of $100). It makes no difference whether the purchase is all cash, all financed, or some combination of cash and financing, because this tax is based on purchase price. This is a one-time tax and is *not* paid annually.

201.02, F.S.

Example: If a home sells for $71,200, the documentary stamp tax on the deed will be:

$$\$71,200 \div \$100 = 712 \text{ taxable increments}$$
$$712 \times \$.70 = \$498.40 \text{ documentary stamp tax on deed}$$

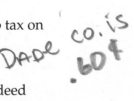

If any portion or fraction of $100 remains after dividing the purchase price by $100, a full $.70 tax is charged for the fractional part. For example, if the purchase price in the above example had been $71,250, the state "doc stamp" tax on the deed would be increased by $.70 (to $499.10) because the purchase price was $50 more than an even increment of $100.

The law requires that the seller deliver a recordable deed. Because a deed may not be recorded until the stamp tax has been paid, the seller is obligated to either deliver a deed having paid the stamp tax or negotiate with the buyer to assume the obligation. If the buyer does not agree to pay the stamp tax on the deed, the tax remains the seller's responsibility.

On normal sales or exchanges, the doc stamp tax is shown as a *debit* to the seller on the closing statement. (See Seller's Closing Statement, Figure 14.4 on page 313, for an example.)

State documentary stamp tax on notes. Second, the state requires the payment of a documentary stamp tax on notes for all executed notes and written promises to pay money. The tax rate is $.35 per $100, or fraction thereof, on the face value of the promissory note. This tax is paid on all new and assumed mortgage notes. In an assumption, the borrower pays the tax on the unpaid balance of the note. This tax is due when the note is executed.

201.08, F.S.

Example: A home sold for $90,000. The buyer paid $10,000 cash, assumed a recorded mortgage of $55,000, and created a new second mortgage in the amount of $25,000. The documentary stamp tax on notes resulting from this transaction would be:

$$\$55,000 \div \$100 = 550 \text{ taxable increments} \times \$.35 = \$192.50 \text{ (assumed)}$$
$$\$25,000 \div \$100 = 250 \text{ taxable increments} \times \$.35 = \$87.50 \text{ (new note)}$$
$$\$192.50 + \$87.50 = \$280 \text{ (tax on notes)}$$

The tax on notes is shown as a *debit* to the buyer on the closing statement.

State intangible tax on new mortgages. Third, the state requires the payment of an *intangible tax* before a mortgage is recorded, regardless of when the mortgage was executed (signed). An assumed mortgage recorded previously should not be taxed again, provided the deed or assumption document clearly identifies the county record book and page number where the assumed mortgage was recorded. (Some counties, — *why.* however, are taxing an already recorded mortgage a second time.) The tax rate for this state intangible tax on new mortgages is two mills ($.002 or two-tenths of one cent) per dollar of debt. Because this is supposed to be a one-time tax, examples throughout this book will not show a second intangible tax on previously recorded mortgages. When a mortgage is recorded, it signifies that the intangible tax has been paid to the clerk of the circuit court or to the county comptroller.

Example: Use the figures from the previous example. The intangible tax on the new second mortgage would be:

$$\$25,000 \times \$.002 = \$50 \text{ tax on second mortgage}$$

The law expects this tax to be paid by the mortgage owner (lender). However, the mortgagor (buyer-borrower) usually agrees to pay the tax to obtain the loan. Thus, this tax is normally shown as a *debit* to the buyer on the closing statement.

	TO REMEMBER	
	State Transfer Taxes	
S	**S**tamps on deed	$.70 per $100
N	**N**ote, stamps on notes	$.35 per $100
I	**I**ntangible on new mortgages	$.002 per $1 of debt

— Total Sale Price (handwritten)

1 *Example:* To illustrate the application of all three of the previous state
2 taxes, suppose a property sold for $79,950. The buyer paid $15,000
3 cash down and arranged for a $64,950 mortgage loan. The state taxes
4 on this transaction would be:

5 Deed: $79,950 ÷ $100 = 799.5,
6   rounded up to 800 taxable increments
7   800 taxable increments × $.70 = $560 tax on deed

8 Mortgage: $64,950 × $.002 = $129.90 tax on mortgage

9 Note: $64,950 ÷ $100 = 649.5,
10   rounded up to 650 taxable increments
11   650 taxable increments × $.35 = $227.50 tax on note

12 Total: $560 + $129.90 + $227.50 = $917.40

(handwritten margin notes:)
SALE
MP 215,000
DP - 100,000   NOTE
115,
1505 - Deed
NOTE 402.50
INT 230
2137.50

13 ## OTHER CHARGES

14 In addition to the various mandatory taxes, several other charges are
15 associated with a title closing.

16 **Preparation of documents.** The customary method of handling charges
17 for preparation of documents is to require the person who must sign the
18 document to pay the fee for its preparation. Therefore, the seller (grantor)
19 pays for preparation of the deed, and the buyer (mortgagor) pays for
20 preparation of the mortgage and note. The charges that result are shown
21 as a *debit* on the closing statement of the person required to pay. Such fees
22 shown on the seller's statement are not shown on the buyer's statement,
23 and vice versa.

(handwritten margin notes:)
closing cost.
Who ever signs - Pays.

24 **Recording fees.** Several of the legal instruments signed at closing should
25 be recorded to give constructive notice of new ownership and debt status.
26 Charges associated with recording these documents are usually paid by
27 the person who wants a particular document recorded. For example, the
28 grantee (buyer) wants the deed recorded and pays for this service, even
29 though the grantor (seller) paid for its preparation by an attorney. The
30 various recording fees are shown on only the appropriate party's closing
31 statement.

32 **Broker's commission.** Normally, the person who employed the broker
33 is required to pay the commission. The broker's commission is listed on
34 the employer's closing statement as a charge but, of course, does not
35 appear on the other party's closing statement.

Abstract continuation or title insurance. Legally, the seller of a property is not required to provide an abstract of title, title insurance, or an opinion of title unless he or she agrees to do so. However, title insurances are used to protect the lender and the buyer. Lenders usually will not accept abstracts of title but do demand up-to-date *lender's title insurance.* A buyer's representative should recommend that the buyer protect his or her interests by obtaining *owner's title insurance.* Actually, these charges, like many, are negotiable regarding who pays what. (See also Chapter 9.)

Liens. The seller is responsible for all existing liens of record. (See also Chapter 9.) At the time of closing, the seller must have satisfied all liens, or the buyer and the seller must reach an agreement about disposition of the liens.

CASH RECONCILIATION STATEMENT

When the closing statements for both the seller and the buyer have been completed, the broker or closing agent is prepared to summarize the entire transaction in a cash reconciliation statement (Figure 14.7 on page 316). This clearly and accurately shows the amount of money deposited by the buyer plus the balance due from the buyer at closing. It also shows the expenses chargeable to each party, including the brokerage commission and the amount due the seller at closing. Normally, the person making out the closing statements will have prepared the checks to be disbursed. After the seller and the buyer examine the closing statements, each should be requested to sign his or her copy.

RULES OF THUMB

The following five general rules of thumb may help the person who is not familiar with the proper preparation of these instruments:

1. On the *seller's closing statement,* the only entries in the *credit* column are the overall purchase price and any prepaid items.

2. On the *buyer's closing statement,* the total purchase price plus all charges and expenses are entered in the *debit* column. The resulting total is the key to the buyer's statement. When all entries in the credit column are totaled, the *difference* between total credits and total debits is the amount the buyer must pay at closing.

3. All entries from the total purchase price down through the prorated items, with the exception of (1) the buyer's deposit, (2) an existing mortgage being paid off, or (3) a new mortgage obtained from a financial institution, are "double entry" items and appear on the closing statements of both parties. *Double entry items* are shown as a credit to one party and as a debit to the other.

4. All *expenses* (attorney's fees, documentary stamps, etc.) are shown on the statement of the appropriate person and are *not* double entry items. *[handwritten: who ever Pays Them]*

5. All items are subject to negotiation between contracting parties. In the absence of a negotiated agreement, Florida statutes normally regard the parties responsible as follows:

- Items *credited to seller*
  - Total purchase price
  - Other prepaid items

- Items *debited to seller*
  - Mortgages assumed or paid off
  - Mortgages newly created—held by seller (purchase-money mortgage)
  - Prorated taxes, interest, advance rent
  - Security deposits
  - State documentary stamps on the deed
  - Broker's commission
  - Title insurance (owner's policy)
  - Preparation of deed
  - Seller's attorney's fees (if any)

- Items *credited to buyer*
  - Earnest money deposit
  - Mortgages assumed
  - Mortgages newly created
  - Prorated property taxes (city and county)
  - Prorated unpaid interest
  - Prorated advance rent
  - Security deposits

- Items *debited to buyer*
  - Purchase price
  - Title insurance (mortgagee's policy)
  - State intangible tax on the mortgage
  - State documentary stamp tax on the note
  - Recording of the deed
  - Recording of the mortgage
  - Buyer's attorney's fees (if any)
  - Preparation of mortgage and note

Key Concepts Regarding Closing Statements

- Total purchase price is entered as a credit to the seller and as a debit to the buyer.

- A (new) purchase money mortgage and assumed mortgage loans are entered as a credit to the buyer and as a debit to the seller (entries are made for both the buyer and the seller because both are involved in the financing).

- New mortgages from nonseller sources (loans from banks) and the binder deposit (earnest money or good faith deposit) are entered as a credit to the buyer (there is no entry on the seller's side). *Single entry.*

- Unpaid property taxes appear as a credit to the buyer and as a debit to the seller (prorations have the same dollar amount in each entry).

- When a prorated item is paid in arrears (such as interest on an assumed loan and property taxes for closings between January 1 and October 31) "seller days" are used to calculate the proration.

- When the prorated item is paid in advance (prepaid rent) "buyer days" are used to calculate the proration.

- Expenses are always a debit to the party paying for the expense (single entries).

1   A copy of the author's "Work Organizer for Closing Statements" and
2 completed samples of the work organizer, closing statements, and a
3 reconciliation statement appear in Figure 14.2 through Figure 14.7,
4 beginning on page 311. The author has chosen these formats with the
5 knowledge that many versions exist.

■ SUMMARY

7   All of a licensee's work effort points to one goal: successfully concluding
8 the real estate transaction. This final step in the sale process is called
9 the *title closing*. The seller delivers title to the buyer in exchange for the
10 purchase price.

11   The Florida Real Estate License Law places responsibility on the
12 broker for an accurate accounting and delivery of all monies, deposits,
13 mortgages, conveyances, and other documents entrusted to the broker by
14 the parties to the transaction. A closing statement for both buyer and
15 seller must be prepared along with a summary of the transaction in the
16 form of a broker's closing statement.

17   At the state level, three taxes may apply when real property changes
18 hands. First, the documentary stamp tax on deeds is based on the entire
19 purchase price paid for real property. Second, the documentary stamp tax
20 on notes becomes due when the written obligation to pay money is
21 executed or assumed. Third, the intangible tax on new mortgages applies
22 when a mortgage is recorded.

23   The new practitioner must be able to calculate all of the prorated and
24 full-value items to be credited and debited to the appropriate parties.
25 Because the broker or sales associate must explain the approximate costs
26 of such items to both buyer and seller before the sale contract is signed,
27 licensees themselves must first understand every aspect of income and
28 expense allocation. This Chapter has focused on and provided practice
29 opportunities on the details, mathematical and otherwise, that are a part
30 of every real estate closing.

■ SAMPLE CLOSING STATEMENT PROBLEM

32 Mr. and Mrs. Bravo have decided to buy Lot 14, Block C, Page 641, public
33 records of Foam County, Florida. They have given the sellers, Mr. and
34 Mrs. Sierra, a $7,500 binder deposit, to be held in escrow until the
35 transaction is closed. The contract stipulates that the Bravos will pay a
36 total purchase price of $72,500. They are to assume a recorded VA first
37 mortgage of $59,760, give the Sierras a new $3,640 second mortgage, and
38 pay all taxes related to the financing arrangements.

FIGURE 14.2   Work Organizer for Closing Statements

DEBIT BUYER	CREDIT BUYER	DEBIT SELLER	CREDIT SELLER
Purchase Price _____	Deposit _____	1st Mortgage _____	Purchase Price _____
	1st Mortgage _____	2nd Mortgage _____	
1st Mortgage _____	2nd Mortgage _____	Doc. Stamps	1st Mortgage _____
2nd Mortgage _____	Prorated:	on Deed _____	
Doc. Stamps	City Taxes _____	Title Ins. _____	2nd Mortgage _____
1st Note _____	County Taxes _____	Intang. Tax	
2nd Note _____	Rent _____	on Mortgage _____	TOTAL
Intang. Tax	Mort. Int. _____	Prorated:	CREDITS _____
on Mortgage _____	Security	City Taxes _____	
Atty. Fees _____	Deposit _____	County Taxes _____	
Record Deed _____		Rent _____	Total Credits _____
Record Mort. _____	TOTAL	Mort. Int. _____	
Title Ins. _____	CREDITS _____	Atty. Fees _____	less
		Commission _____	Total Debits _____
TOTAL BUYER		Miscellaneous _____	
DEBITS _____	Total Debits _____		BALANCE
		TOTAL SELLER	DUE SELLER _____
	less	DEBITS _____	
	Total Credits _____		
	DUE FROM		
	BUYER _____		

CITY TAXES	COUNTY TAXES	PREPAID RENT
Annual taxes ÷ 365 = daily cost	Annual taxes ÷ 365 = daily cost	Amount / period ÷ days in period
Daily cost × no. of days used by seller	Daily cost × no. of days used by seller	Days owned by Buyer _____
(DEBIT SELLER; CREDIT BUYER)	(DEBIT SELLER; CREDIT BUYER)	× amount per day _____
		(DEBIT SELLER; CREDIT BUYER)

1ST MORTGAGE INTEREST	2ND MORTGAGE INTEREST	COMMISSION
Balance due × % = annual interest	Balance due × % = annual interest	Purchase price
Annual interest ÷ 365 = daily interest	Annual interest ÷ 365 = daily interest	_____ × _____ %
Daily interest × no. of days used	Daily interest × no. of days used	

DOC. STAMPS DEED	DOC. STAMPS NOTE	INTANG. TAX MORT.	MISCELLANEOUS
$.70 × $100 on purchase price	$.35 × $100 on note face value	.002 (mills) × $1 mortgage face value	

Note: the debiting/crediting of all items may vary and is negotiable.

FIGURE 14.3   Work Organizer for Closing Statements

DEBIT BUYER		CREDIT BUYER		DEBIT SELLER		CREDIT SELLER	
Purchase Price	$72,500.00	Deposit	$ 7,500.00	1st Mortgage	$59,760.00	Purchase Price	$72,500.00
		1st Mortgage	59,760.00	2nd Mortgage	3,640.00		
1st Mortgage		2nd Mortgage	3,640.00	Doc. Stamps		1st Mortgage	
2nd Mortgage		Prorated:		on Deed	507.50		
Doc. Stamps		City Taxes	212.74	Title Ins.	300.00	2nd Mortgage	
1st Note	209.30	County Taxes	339.19	Intang. Tax			
2nd Note	12.95	Rent		on Mortgage		TOTAL	
Intang. Tax		Mort. Int.		Prorated:		CREDITS	$72,500.00
on Mortgage	7.28	Security		City Taxes	212.74		
Atty. Fees	175.00	Deposit		County Taxes	339.19		
Record Deed	6.00			Rent		Total Credits	$72,500.00
Record Mort.	10.00	TOTAL		Mort. Int.			
Title Ins.	300.00	CREDITS	$71,451.93	Atty. Fees	150.00	less	
				Commission	5,075.00	Total Debits	69,984.43
TOTAL BUYER				Miscellaneous			
DEBITS	$73,220.53	Total Debits	$73,220.53			BALANCE	
				TOTAL SELLER		DUE SELLER	$ 2,515.57
		less		DEBITS	$69,984.43		
		Total Credits	71,451.93				
		DUE FROM					
		BUYER	$ 1,768.60				

CITY TAXES	COUNTY TAXES	PREPAID RENT
Annual taxes ÷ 365 = daily cost	Annual taxes ÷ 365 = daily cost	Amount/period ÷ days in period
Daily cost × no. of days used by seller	Daily cost × no. of days used by seller	Days owned by Buyer _____
(DEBIT SELLER; CREDIT BUYER)	(DEBIT SELLER; CREDIT BUYER)	× amount per day _____
$429 ÷ 365 days =	$684 ÷ 365 days =	(DEBIT SELLER; CREDIT BUYER)
$1.17534 × 181 days =	$1.8797 × 181 days =	
$212.73654	$339.18857	
Round to: $212.74	Round to: $339.19	

1ST MORTGAGE INTEREST	2ND MORTGAGE INTEREST	COMMISSION
Balance due × % = annual interest	Balance due × % = annual interest	Purchase price
Annual interest ÷ 365 = daily interest	Annual interest ÷ 365 = daily interest	$72,500 × _____7_____ %
Daily interest × no. of days used	Daily interest × no. of days used	$5,075.00

DOC. STAMPS DEED	DOC. STAMPS NOTE	INTANG. TAX MORT.	MISCELLANEOUS
$.70 × $100 on	$.35 × $100 on	.002 (mills) × $1	
purchase price	note face value	mortgage face value	
$72,500.00 ÷ $100 =	$59,760 ÷ $100 = 597.6	$3,640 × .002 = $7.28	
725 × $.70 = $507.50	598 × $.35 = $209.30		
	$3,640 ÷ $100 = 36.4		
	37 × $.35 = $12.95		

Note: the debiting/crediting of all items may vary and is negotiable.

FIGURE 14.4 Seller's Closing Statement

	Debits	Credits
Date of Closing: July 1, 20AA		
Purchase Price		$72,500.00
First Mortgage—Balance	$59,760.00	
Second Mortgage	3,640.00	
Binder Deposit		
Prorations:		
Rent		
Interest: 1st Mortgage		
2nd Mortgage		
Taxes:		
City	212.74	
County	339.19	
Expenses:		
Title Insurance	300.00	
Attorney's Fee	150.00	
Documentary Stamps		
Mortgage-Note		
State on Deed	507.50	
Intangible Tax–Mortgage		
Recording:		
Mortgage		
Deed		
Brokerage Commission	5,075.00	
Miscellaneous		
Total Debits and Credits	$69,984.43	$72,500.00
Balance Due Seller	2,515.57	
Grand Total	$72,500.00	$72,500.00

FIGURE 14.5   Buyer's Closing Statement

Date of Closing: July 1, 20AA	Debits	Credits
Purchase Price	$72,500.00	
First Mortgage—Balance		$59,760.00
Second Mortgage		3,640.00
Binder Deposit		7,500.00
Prorations:		
Rent		
Interest: 1st Mortgage		
2nd Mortgage		
Taxes:		
City		212.74
County		339.19
Expenses:		
Title Insurance	300.00	
Attorney's Fee	175.00	
Documentary Stamps		
Mortgage-Note	209.30	
2nd Mortgage-Note	12.95	
Intangible Tax–Mortgage	7.28	
Recording:		
Mortgage	10.00	
Deed	6.00	
Brokerage Commission		
Miscellaneous		
Total Debits and Credits	$73,220.53	$71,451.93
Balance Due Seller		1,768.60
Grand Total	$73,220.53	$73,220.53

FIGURE 14.6   Composite Closing Statement

Seller's Statement		Item	Buyer's Statement	
Debit	**Credit**		**Debit**	**Credit**
		Purchase Terms		
	72,500.00	Total Purchase Price	72,500.00	
		Binder Deposit		7,500.00
59,760.00		First Mortgage Balance		59,760.00
3,640.00		Second Mortgage		3,640.00
		Prorations & Prepayments		
		Rent		
		Interest: First Mortgage		
		Interest: Second Mortgage		
		Prepaid: First Mortgage		
		Prepaid: Second Mortgage		
212.74		Taxes: City		212.74
339.19		Taxes: County		339.19
		Other:		
		Expenses		
300.00		Title Insurance	300.00	
150.00		Attorney's Fees	175.00	
5,075.00		Brokerage Commission		
		Documentary Stamps		
507.50		State Tax on Deed		
		State Tax on Note (209.30 + 12.95)	222.25	
		State Intangible Tax on Mortgage	7.28	
		Recording		
		Mortgage	10.00	
		Deed	6.00	
		Miscellaneous_____		
		Totals		
69,984.43	72,500.00		73,220.53	71,451.93
To		**Balance Due**	**From**	
2,515.57				1,768.60
		Grand Totals		
72,500.00	72,500.00		73,220.53	73,220.53

FIGURE 14.7   Broker's Closing Statements Cash Reconciliation Statement*

	Receipts	Disbursements
Deposit	$7,500.00	$
Check from buyer at closing	1,768.60	
Brokerage commission		5,075.00
Check to seller at closing		2,515.57
Seller's expense (less brokerage commission)		957.50
Buyer's expense		720.53
Totals	$9,268.60	$9,268.60

*It is assumed that the broker handles the recording of all instruments and the payment of the title insurance, attorney's fees, stamps, recording fees, etc.

1 The closing is scheduled for July 1, 20AA, with the proration time
2 midnight, June 30, 20AA. The sale contract specifies that the property
3 taxes will be prorated on the basis of the previous year's taxes, which
4 were $429 for the city and $684 for the county. The sellers have agreed
5 to pay the broker a 7 percent commission and to pay half of the title
6 insurance costs of $600. Title will be conveyed with a general warranty
7 deed, and the Sierras will pay the taxes on the deed.

8   Attorneys for the sellers and buyers have agreed to charge $150 for
9 preparation of the deed and $175 for the mortgage instrument and note.
10 Recording fees will be $10 for the mortgage and $6 for the deed. The
11 various applicable items from above are computed and listed on the
12 "Work Organizer for Closing Statements" in Figure 14.3. In Figure 14.4
13 through Figure 14.6, the Seller's, Buyer's, and Composite Closing
14 Statements are also completed to show their use. The 365-day method
15 of prorating is used throughout.

Note: Do not try to make the Seller's and Buyer's Closing Statement balance with each other—they are not supposed to balance. The closing statements for both seller and buyer are supposed to balance with the Cash Reconciliation Statement in Figure 14.7.

■ REVIEW QUESTIONS

(This quiz is intended not only to help you review this Chapter but also
to assist with the various computations in other Chapters.)

1. Change the percentages to decimals.
   A. 39½% *.395*
   B.   2% *.02*
   C. 75% *.75*
   D. 145% *1..45*

2. Change the percentages to fractions.
   A. 50% *1/2*
   B. 20% *1/5*
   C. 25% *1/4*
   D. 40% *2/5*

   whole
   100 ÷ %

3. Change the fractions to decimals.
   A. ⅛ *.125*
   B. ⅗ *.6*
   C. ¹⁄₁₆ *.0625*
   D. ¹⁄₂₀ *.05*

4. Divide the numbers below.
   A. 44,032 ÷ 1.72 *25,600*
   B.   493.8 ÷ 0.60 *823*
   C. 18,768 ÷ 25.5 *736*
   D.   7,735 ÷ 0.17 *45,500.*

5. A senior sales associate receives 55 percent of all sale commissions
   earned. His broker has listed a motel for $1,450,000. The listing
   contract specifies a 6½ percent sale commission for the first $600,000
   of selling price, 7 percent for the next $800,000, and 8 percent
   commission on all of the actual sale price exceeding $1.4 million.
   What will the sales associate's commission be if he sells the motel for
   the listed sale price?
   A. $44,550
   B. $54,450
   C. $95,000
   D. $99,000

   1,450,000
   1ST – 600,000 × .065 = 39,000 × 55% = 21,450
   800,000 × .07 = 56,000 × 55% = 30,800.
   50,000 × .08 = 40000 × 55% = 2200
   + 13,5000
   54,450

6. The interest portion of Mr. Highland's first monthly payment on a
   30-year, 12 percent mortgage amounts to $550. If the loan-to-value
   ratio for Mr. Highland's house is 80 percent, how much did he
   pay for the house?
   A. $44,000
   B. $68,750
   C. $110,000
   D. $171,875

   $550 INT. Per mo.
   × 12 mo
   $6600 Per yr. INT.
   ÷ .12 rate
   55,000
   ÷ .80 (80% LTV)
   68,750

7. You bought a house for $120,000. You gave a deposit of $10,000, assumed a recorded mortgage of $90,000, and signed a new second mortgage and note for $20,000. What are the total state taxes due as a result of this transfer of property?
   A. $1,445
   B. $1,405
   C. $1,265
   D. $950

8. A broker lists a property, a 7 percent commission is agreed to, and the listing is placed in the MLS. The sale commission is to be split as follows: 45 percent to the listing broker and 55 percent to the selling broker. A sales associate who works for a cooperating broker sells the property for $160,000. The sales associate's agreement with her employer calls for a 60 percent share of all commissions she brings to the company. How much is due the sales associate?
   A. $2,016
   B. $2,464
   C. $3,024
   D. $3,696

9. Ms. Judy owned ⅜ of a property. She was paid $45,000 as her share of the proceeds from the sale of the property. What was the total selling price of the property?
   A. $120,000
   B. $90,000
   C. $72,000
   D. $61,875

10. To get a mortgage loan of $31,000, a buyer has agreed to pay all state tax costs incurred by creation of the new mortgage. What is the total cost?
    A. $62.00
    B. $108.50
    C. $170.50
    D. $217.00

11. You have a VA mortgage of $48,000 at 9 percent with a 30-year term. The monthly principal and interest payment is $386.21. What portion of the second month's payment will apply to amortization of the mortgage?
    A. $26.21
    B. $26.41
    C. $359.80
    D. $360.00

12. In the mortgage cited in question 11, what would the monthly payments amount to if your property taxes were $840 and your annual insurance $176?
    A. $400.88
    B. $407.88
    C. $456.21
    D. $470.88

13. Barbara bought three 200-foot lots on a lake for $500 per front foot each. Barbara then subdivided these lots into six lakefront lots, which she then sold for $62,500 each. What was her percentage of profit on the sales?
    A. 20%
    B. 25%
    C. 75%
    D. 80%

14. A warehouse measures 720 feet by 500 feet and rents for $118,000 a month. What is the rent per square foot per month?
    A. $0.25
    B. $0.33
    C. $3.05
    D. $3.96

15. Mr. Jones incurred a 20 percent loss when he sold a 10-acre parcel (Tract A) for $100,000. He also owns a 25-acre parcel (Tract B) for which he paid $200,000. How much must he sell Tract B for if he wishes not only to recover his loss from Tract A but also to realize a 20 percent profit on his investment in Tract B?
    A. $260,000
    B. $265,000
    C. $270,000
    D. $275,000

16. Mr. and Mrs. Greer are purchasing the Hogue's apartment building. Each of the five apartments rents for $315 per month. The closing is scheduled for September 16, and the rents were collected on September 1. What is the rent proration for this transaction and to whom will the amount be credited? (Day of closing belongs to the buyer.)
    A. $157.50, credit buyer
    B. $735.00, credit seller
    C. $787.50, credit buyer
    D. $812.90, credit seller

17. A 28.5-acre parcel of land in Orange County sells for $4,100 per acre. What is the documentary stamp tax on the deed?
    A. $818.30
    B. $817.95
    C. $642.85
    D. $409.15

18. How is the buyer's binder deposit entered on the closing statement?
    A. Debit to buyer only
    B. Credit to buyer only
    C. Debit to seller and credit to buyer
    D. Debit to buyer and credit to seller

19. How is the purchase price entered on the closing statement?
    A. Credit to seller only
    B. Credit to buyer only
    C. Credit to seller and debit to buyer
    D. Credit to buyer and debit to seller

20. How are unpaid property taxes entered on the closing statement?
    A. Debit to seller only
    B. Debit to buyer only
    C. Credit to seller and debit to buyer
    D. Credit to buyer and debit to seller

Note to readers: If you need to learn and practice more than this Chapter offers about math as it relates specifically to real estate, obtain the self-study guide written by the author, *Real Estate Math: What You Need to Know*, Chicago: Dearborn™ Real Estate Education, 6th edition. It covers the basics of arithmetic and provides practice opportunities in all areas. An answer key and step-by-step solutions are included.

CHAPTER 15

Estimating Real Property Value

[handwritten notes: "Safe Loan. Bank can get. 80% do Appraisen Value"]

■ KEY TERMS

appraisal	highest and best use	principle of substitution
assemblage	income capitalization approach	progression
cost-depreciation approach	incurable	reconciliation
curable	investment value	regression
depreciation	market value	replacement cost
economic life	net operating income (NOI)	reproduction cost
effective age	overimprovement	sales comparison approach
effective gross income (EGI)	plottage	situs
gross income multiplier (GIM)	potential gross income (PGI)	subject property
gross rent multiplier (GRM)		vacancy and collection losses

■ OVERVIEW

To *appraise* real property means to estimate its value. Appraising is considered to be an art, not a science, because although the appraisal process involves mathematical calculations, appraisers also use their own judgment when appraising real property. There are many reasons for appraising real property. Local communities hire appraisers to estimate the value of property for assessment of property taxes (Chapter 18) and to determine the amount of compensation in a condemnation proceeding that involves a taking by eminent domain. However, the most prevalent use of an appraisal is to establish the value of real property that will be used as collateral to finance its purchase.

This Chapter will help students learn the basics of appraising required to develop and complete a comparative market analysis. It also will help to improve licensees' communications with professional appraisers.

After completing this Chapter, the student should be able to:

• differentiate among the terms *price, cost,* and *value;*

• describe the four characteristics of value;

[handwritten notes: "75 hr class for Appraisers"]

1 • differentiate among the three approaches to estimating the value of
2 real property;

3 • describe the three types of depreciation and recognize examples of
4 each type; and

5 • apply the steps in the various approaches to estimating value
6 when given an appropriate scenario.

7 ## ■ APPRAISAL REGULATION

8 Active real estate licensees are allowed to perform a comparative market
9 analysis (CMA) for the purpose of obtaining a listing or a prospective
10 sale. However, Section 475.612, F.S., prohibits referring to a CMA as an
11 appraisal. Real estate licensees who do conduct actual real estate
12 appraisals are required to comply with the Uniform Standards of
13 Professional Appraisal Practice (USPAP) and may charge a fee for
14 performing an appraisal. Section 475.25, F.S., empowers the Commission
15 to discipline brokers and sales associates who violate any of the
16 standards or any other provisions of USPAP. (CMAs are exempted.)
17 The Uniform Standards are developed by the Appraisal Standards
18 Board (ASB) of the Appraisal Foundation.

19 The Appraiser Qualifications Board (AQB) of the Appraisal
20 Foundation establishes the qualifications for state-certified and licensed
21 appraisers. Qualification criteria include appraiser education and
22 appraisal experience. Appraisal reports involving a federally related
23 transaction must be prepared by a state-certified or licensed appraiser,
24 *unless* the real estate licensee *also* holds such certification or license. A
25 *federally related transaction* is a real estate-related transaction that requires
26 an appraisal and involves a federally insured financial institution.
27 Federally related transactions include the sale, lease, purchase, exchange,
28 investment, refinancing, or other use of real estate as security for a loan or
29 investment that has a transaction value greater than $250,000. Fannie Mae,
30 Freddie Mac, HUD, and the VA require the use of state-certified and
31 licensed appraisers regardless of whether the loan value is greater than
32 the minimum valuation threshold of $250,000.

To view a current edition of the standards on the Internet or
to learn more about appraiser qualifications and licensure, visit:
http://www.appraisalfoundation.org.

33 ## ■ TYPES OF VALUE

34 There are many types of value that an appraiser may be hired to estimate.
35 The type of value of most importance to real estate licensees is *market*
36 *value.* (Market value will be discussed separately later in this Chapter.) A
37 brief explanation of the different types of value follows:

38 • *Assessed value* is the value used as a basis for property taxation.
39 (For additional information concerning assessed value, refer to
40 Chapter 18.)

Just Value.

1 • *Insurance value* is an estimate of the amount of money required to
2 replace a structure in the event of some catastrophic event such as fire.

3 • *Investment value* is the price an investor would pay, given his or her
4 own financing requirements and income tax situation. This type of
5 value is personal to a particular investor. (For a more detailed
6 discussion of investment value, refer to Chapter 17.)

7 • *Liquidation value* is the value associated with a rapid sale. The
8 amount of dollars a property should bring in a foreclosure sale is
9 an example of liquidation value. (See also Chapter 17.)

Quick Money.

10 • *Going-concern value* is the value of an income-producing property
11 characterized by a significant operating history. (See also Chapter 17.)

12 • *Salvage value* is the estimated amount for which improvements can
13 be sold at the end of a structure's useful life.

After Depreciation

■ MARKET VALUE

*Lowest Price to Seller will Take
Highest to Buyer will Pay.*

15 While the word *value* has many different meanings, *market value* is of
16 special interest to the field of real estate. The concept of market value is
17 based on a theory that in any open market there will be a number of
18 buyers and sellers. (See also Chapter 19.) If hundreds of transactions are
19 concluded over time, some parties will pay too much and some will pay
20 too little. But the vast majority of value decisions by both buyers and
21 sellers will tend to converge in a fairly small range. That range represents
22 a range of market value, whether the market is dealing in houses,
23 oranges, cattle, or something else.

24 Many definitions of market value, or *fair market value* as it is sometimes
25 called, can be found. Fannie Mae and Freddie Mac require the following
26 definition of **market value** for the appraisal of all real property securing a
27 mortgage intended for sale to either of those major secondary market
28 agencies:

29 The *most probable price* that a property should bring in a
30 competitive and open market under all conditions requisite to
31 a fair sale, the buyer and seller each acting prudently and
32 knowledgeably, and assuming the price is not affected by
33 undue stimulus.

34 Inherent in this definition are the assumptions that:

35 • market value applies to a specified date and may change with the
36 passage of time;

37 • the seller is able to convey a marketable title;

38 • buyer and seller are typically motivated, and neither buyer nor
39 seller is under any compulsion or pressure to conclude a sale;

40 • both buyer and seller are well informed and acting in their
41 individual best interest;

42 • the property is exposed for sale on the open market for a
43 reasonable time;

Arm Lenth = everything is Normal

1 • the terms of sale are in cash in U.S. dollars or in terms of financial
2 arrangements comparable thereto; and

3 • the price represents a normal consideration for the property,
4 unaffected by creative financing or sales concessions such as seller
5 contributions or buydowns.

VALUE, PRICE, COST = *Never the same.*

7 The *value* of something is determined by its ability to command other
8 goods in exchange. Adam Smith, the famous eighteenth century
9 economist, referred to this as *value in exchange*. Today, we regard value in
10 exchange as market value, which is a consensus of the interactions of
11 many buyers and sellers in the market.

12 *Price* refers to the amount of money (or its equivalent) for which a
13 good is actually sold. Price and value are not necessarily equal. For
14 example, you might purchase a computer for $2,000. Its *price* was $2,000.
15 However, it may actually command less (or more) than $2,000 in exchange
16 if you were to attempt to sell the computer. In real estate, *price* is
17 synonymous with *contract price*.

18 *Cost* is the total expenditure required to bring a new improvement into
19 existence plus the cost of the land. A contractor will install site
20 improvements (water, sewer, and so forth); acquire the necessary permits;
21 secure the services of architects, engineers, surveyors, and other
22 professionals; construct the building; landscape the site; market the
23 property; and so forth. The total of these expenditures is referred to as *cost*.
24 A contractor wants the *cost* to be less than the *price* a consumer will pay—
25 and the consumer will pay more than the cost only if he or she perceives
26 the property's *value* to exceed its cost.

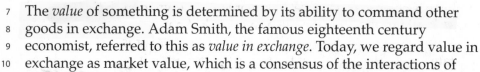

Value, Price, and Cost	*Never the same.*
Value	Exchange between buyers and sellers (many market participants)
	The amount paid in a particular transaction; contract price
	Expenditure to create an improvement; labor, materials, and land

CONSUMER PRICE INDEX

28 The concept of value in exchange is important because time and other
29 influences cause changes in value, price, and cost that do not always
30 change at the same time or to the same degree. Professionals in the real
31 estate business need to be capable of calculating the effects of inflation
32 and time on real property values. The fact that one paid $56,500 for a
33 house in 1983 and sold it for $82,700 in 1993 does not mean that the
34 exchange value of the property increased. Perhaps $82,700 in 1993
35 bought the same amount of gold, bread, or steak that $56,500 bought in
36 1983; perhaps not. The Bureau of Labor Statistics in the U.S. Department
37 of Labor provides a method for measuring fluctuations in real or
38 exchange value: the *Consumer Price Index* (CPI).

1   The CPI measures the average change in prices over time for a fixed
2 "market basket" of goods and services. Each of the thousands of items in
3 the market basket is assigned a weight, according to its current relative
4 importance to a consumer's budget. Costs of housing, food, clothing,
5 transportation, medical care, entertainment, and other goods and services
6 are obtained to determine price movements. The results then provide a
7 reliable indicator of inflation.

8   Historically, real estate prices have increased faster than the CPI. If a
9 parcel of real property is acquired at market value or less, an owner will
10 normally find that the sale price increases faster than other "market
11 basket" prices. This ability to maintain or increase purchasing power is
12 one reason real estate is regarded as one of the best protections against
13 inflation.

OVERIMPROVEMENT

15 An owner can pour more money into a property than good judgment
16 would indicate might be recaptured (recovered). For example, if the
17 owner of a $60,000 house in a neighborhood of similar homes adds a
18 $12,000 swimming pool or a $20,000 addition to the house, it is doubtful
19 that the total cost will be recaptured when the property is sold. The two
20 additions are examples of overimprovement. An **overimprovement**
21 occurs when an owner invests more money in a structure than he or she
22 may reasonably expect to recapture.

23   A $125,000 home in a neighborhood of $50,000 homes is an
24 overimprovement. Buyers who can afford to pay $125,000 for a home
25 usually will prefer a $125,000 neighborhood. So the owner of the
26 overimprovement finds few buyers willing to pay a price approaching his
27 or her investment. This is another example of the point that cost and value
28 are not the same thing. Value, then, is a concept. Price equals
29 value only when the requirements of a so-called perfect market are
30 approximated. Some "perfect market" requirements are: many buyers
31 and sellers; a homogeneous product; and easy and free entry into the
32 marketplace. Due to the unique nature of each parcel of real estate, this
33 market can only *approach* perfection.

CHARACTERISTICS OF VALUE

35 To have value, goods or services must possess the following four traits:

36   1. Demand

37   2. Utility

38   3. Scarcity

39   4. Transferability

40 **Demand.**   In economics, demand is more than a desire or need. Demand
41 also implies the available means to obtain what is desired. Herders and
42 farmers who live in the infertile desert lands of the world desire more
43 fertile land, but they do not have the financial means to obtain other, more
44 expensive land. Consequently, their desires alone have no economic

1 impact on the supply of fertile land or on the price of such lands. In
2 contrast, look at Miami Beach, where people desire to live and have the
3 money to acquire the use of part of the available supply. The need or
4 desire combined with the economic means creates effective demand.

5 **Utility.**   To be valuable, goods or services must be useful and able to fill
6 a need. In real estate, *utility* means the ability to provide useful services
7 and benefits to an owner or tenant.

8 **Scarcity.**   The availability of goods or services in relation to present or
9 anticipated demand determines *scarcity*. If the supply exceeds demand,
10 there is less scarcity, and the value falls. If demand exceeds supply, more
11 scarcity is created, and value increases. When the number of available
12 apartment units in an area exceeds the demand, apartment units are
13 relatively less scarce, and landlords must reduce rents or lose tenants.
14 When apartments are scarce, landlords can increase rents, and the excess
15 demand will fill any resulting vacancies.

16 **Transferability.**   The legal ability to convey title and possession of goods
17 creates *transferability*. This is an unusually important factor in real estate.
18 Value cannot exist in cases where rights in land and the use of property
19 cannot be transferred.

TO REMEMBER

Characteristics of Value

D	**D**emand
U	**U**tility
S	**S**carcity
T	**T**ransferability

---

20 **HIGHEST AND BEST USE**    *All Property has oNly 1* ✳

21 The most profitable use to which a property may be put is the property's
22 **highest and best use.** The use must be:

23   1. legally permissible (zoning);

24   2. physically possible (soil type, the site's shape, size, and slope); and

25   3. financially feasible (income generated considering cost of
26   improvements).

27 The use that meets these three criteria and that yields the highest return
28 to the land is the highest and best use. An appraiser estimates two types
29 of highest and best use, which are described below.

30 **Highest and best use of the land as though vacant.**   The appraiser
31 considers what use would yield the highest return to the land taking into
32 account the three elements previously described. If the site has existing
33 improvements, the appraiser considers what type of use should be placed
34 on the site if it were vacant.

Suppose there are three potential buyers for a site. The first buyer estimates the property would yield a net income of $6,000 per year. The second buyer estimates the property would yield $8,000 net income, and the third buyer estimates the property would yield $12,000 per year after expenses. Which buyer will offer the most for the land? Assume a 10 percent rate of return in all three cases. The use that produces $12,000 annually has a value of $120,000 compared to just $60,000 for the use that produces $6,000 annual net income. Therefore, assuming the three criteria (listed above) have been met, the use that yields a net income of $12,000 per year is the site's highest and best use.

Highest and best use of a property as improved.   The highest and best use of a property as improved pertains to how a property that already has improvements erected on the site can be best utilized. The appraiser considers whether (1) the improvements should continue as is, or (2) the improvements should be renovated, or (3) the improvements should be demolished and new improvements erected. In each case, the appraiser must consider the costs associated with each option in relation to the income that will be generated. Therefore, highest and best use is a *residual* concept because it is concerned with value after expenses are deducted. Demolishing an existing structure and building a new apartment building may generate more monthly income compared with remodeling the existing apartment building. But the highest and best use will be the use with the greatest yield after deducting the costs of renovation or the costs of demolition and new construction.

■ APPROACHES TO ESTIMATING REAL PROPERTY VALUE

There are three approaches to estimating real property value:

1. Sales comparison approach (comparable sales method)

2. Cost-depreciation approach (cost method)

3. Income capitalization approach (income method)

In theory, an **appraisal** report uses all three approaches to estimate the value of a property. If all the information used to prepare the appraisal were perfectly accurate, and if the real estate appraiser were perfect in his or her judgment of the information, the results from each of the three approaches theoretically would be the same.

However, in this imperfect world, most appraisers must *reconcile* the usually different results from each of the three approaches. In a **reconciliation** any detected errors are corrected and, based on the type of property, a degree of priority (importance) is assigned to each approach used. For example, if the property being appraised is a vacant lot in an established neighborhood, the sales comparison approach is considered the most relevant approach to value. If the property is an income-producing property, the income capitalization approach usually is given the most importance. The cost-depreciation approach usually is most significant for newly constructed homes and to cross-check the other two approaches. It is also considered to be the most relevant approach when appraising special-purpose properties such as hospitals, schools, or government buildings.

The **principle of substitution** is the basis for all three approaches to market value. It means that a prudent buyer or investor will pay no more for a property than the cost of acquiring, through purchase or construction, an equally desirable alternative property. This economic concept thus sets an upper limit of value for a property by establishing the cost of acquiring an equally desirable substitute property on the open market, provided no additional problems are encountered.

The remainder of this Chapter provides insight into basic appraising functions. Correct application of the information discussed should help licensees produce reasonably accurate opinions of value and comparative market analyses.

SALES COMPARISON APPROACH

The **sales comparison approach** to value is based on the theory that a knowledgeable purchaser will pay no more for a property than the cost of acquiring an equally acceptable substitute property. The sales comparison approach (also called the *comparable sales approach* or *market approach*) is based on the premise that the value of a property can be estimated accurately by reviewing recent sales of properties (*comparables* or *comps*) similar to the property being appraised (**subject property**) and comparing those properties with the subject property. Because time can affect property values, the sales used for comparison purposes must meet two qualifications:

1. They must have occurred recently in the same market area where the subject property is located.

2. The comparable properties selected must be similar to the subject property.

Because no two properties are exactly alike, adjustments must be made for any differences between the subject property and each of the comparable sale properties.

Adjustments are made for transactional differences (changes in market conditions since date of sale, for example) and property differences (size, location, etc.). All adjustments necessary to achieve the maximum degree of similarity must be made to each comparable property, *not* to the subject property. The intent is to adjust the comparable property to make it as similar to the subject property as possible. If a comparable property is *inferior* to the subject property on a given feature, an *upward* adjustment is made to that comparable property (add the value of the difference). If a comparable is *superior* on a given feature, a *downward* adjustment is made to the comparable property (subtract the value of the difference).

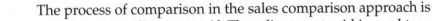

TO REMEMBER

CBS Versus CIA

Comp. **B**etter = **S**ubtract
Comp. **I**nferior = **A**dd

1 The process of comparison in the sales comparison approach is
2 organized into an *adjustment grid.* The adjustment grid is used to ensure
3 that no adjustment factor important to a value conclusion is overlooked.
4 Table 15.1 is an abbreviated adjustment grid example. The example
5 illustrates the procedure for adjusting the sale prices of selected
6 comparable properties to arrive at an approximate market value for the
7 subject property.

8 **Adjustment process.**   The appraiser prepares the adjustment grid
9 by first entering the street address and sale price for each selected
10 comparable. Adjustments for transactional differences such as conditions
11 of sale, financing terms, and changes in market conditions since the
12 date of sale are made first, followed by adjustments for property
13 characteristics. Those adjustments include the following:

ADJUST. The COMP. NOT SUBJECT.

14 • *Financing terms.* Appraisers must confirm the financing associated
15   with each sale because the sale price could reflect special financing
16   terms, such as seller financing or seller-paid points. For purposes
17   of the example presented in Table 15.1, assume the financing
18   associated with each of the sales was conventional financing and
19   that it was typical financing for the market area.

TABLE 15.1   Adjustment Grid: Sales Comparison Approach   *Pros Apprailese 1mi*

	Comparable 1	Comparable 2	Comparable 3
Address	3752 Shamrock Dr.	3748 Shamrock Dr.	3619 Shamrock Dr.
Date of sale	(6 months ago)	(3 months ago)	(0 months ago)
Sale price	$141,500	$136,000	$140,000
Financing	Conventional	Conventional	Conventional
Conditions of sale	Normal	Normal	Normal
Market conditions	+ $2,830	+ $1,360	Same as subject
Square footage	– $9,600	+ $1,200	Same as subject
Landscaping	Same as subject	Same as subject	– $1,000
Total Adjustments	– $ 6,770	+ $ 2,560	– $ 1,000
Adjusted Sale Price	$134,730	$138,560	$139,000
Reconciliation:	Comp 1: = $134,730 × .20	$ 26,946	
	Comp 2: = $138,560 × .30	$ 41,568	
	Comp 3: = $139,000 × .50	$ 69,500	
Indicated Value:		$138,014 or	
		$138,000 (rounded)	

- *Conditions of sale.* Appraisers must research the conditions of sale to determine if the buyer or seller was under abnormal pressure to buy or sell or if there was a special relationship between the parties to the transaction, such as between family members or business associates. In the example in Table 15.1, the appraiser verified the conditions of sale for each of the sales and found them to be normal.

- *Market conditions.* A property that sold last month or last year may sell for more, or for less, today, even though the property itself has not physically changed. The criterion for making an adjustment for market conditions is whether the price paid for a comparable property, if that property were sold on today's market, would differ from the price paid during some other period of time. Referring to Table 15.1, we see that the appraiser adjusted Comparable (Comp) 1 *plus* $2,830. Assume that Comp 1 sold six months ago and the appraiser has estimated a market conditions adjustment of 4 percent annually (or 2 percent for six months). The appraiser is adjusting the sale price of the comparable to estimate what the comp would have sold for under today's market conditions. Similarly, Comp 2 sold 3 months ago so the appraiser has entered a *plus* $1,360 adjustment (or 1 percent). Comp 3 sold very recently, so a market conditions adjustment was not needed.

- *Square footage.* Assume Comp 1 is 160 square feet larger than the subject property. Because Comp 1 is superior to the subject property with respect to square footage, a downward adjustment is needed. The appraiser has estimated $60 per square foot as an appropriate unit of comparison and has entered an adjustment of *minus* $9,600 (or 160 square feet x $60). Because Comp 2 is 20 square feet smaller than the subject, the appropriate upward adjustment is needed.

- *Landscaping.* Because Comp 3 has nicer landscaping, compared with the subject property, a downward adjustment is made to Comp 3.

Reconciliation. Note the method of reconciling the three adjusted sale prices. If the comparables are all equally suitable, the appraiser may simply average the adjusted sale prices. On the other hand, if the appraiser considers one comparable to be a better indicator of the subject property's value than the others, he or she may "weigh" that comparable more heavily. This is entirely a matter of judgment. In this instance, because Comp 3 was considered most similar to the property being appraised, it received a reconciliation weight of 50 percent. This means that 50 percent of whatever the appraised value of the subject property is going to be should be based on the adjusted sale price of Comp 3. Comp 2 was next in similarity and therefore was awarded a reconciliation weight of 30 percent. In each case, the adjusted sale price is multiplied by the reconciliation weight assigned, producing a part of the eventual reconciled value, which will be the estimated market value.

The comparable sales approach is the real estate market "speaking" through past sales. By using only sales already transacted, the market tells us about that particular type of property. Regardless of what one might wish for a sale price, the market indicates what value buyers and sellers have already established for properties similar to the subject property.

The same technique is employed for vacant lots. Select eight to ten recent lot sales, and from those pick the four to six lots most similar to the subject lot. Differences in size or shape are neutralized by using a common unit of comparison such as front feet or square feet. Using the recent four to six sales selected as market indicators, one can find the price paid per square foot or front foot for each lot. The reconciled average of all comparable sales gives the approximate value per square foot or front foot of the subject lot. To calculate the average cost per square foot of any property, always divide dollars by square feet.

Example: What is the estimated market value of a subject lot that is 110' × 120' (13,200 sq. ft.)?

Adjustment Analysis

Comparable Sales:

Sale 1:   A lot 100' × 120' located across the street from the subject lot sold recently for $36,800.

Sale 2:   A lot 110' × 120' in the same neighborhood as the subject lot sold recently for $37,000.

Sale 3:   A lot 100' × 100' in a different but similar-quality neighborhood sold recently for $36,000.

Sale 4:   A lot 130' × 150' located in a different but similar neighborhood but near a railroad sold recently for $39,800.

Solution:

Sale 1: $36,800 ÷ 12,000 sq. ft. = $3.067 per sq. ft.

Sale 2: $37,000 ÷ 13,200 sq. ft. = $2.803 per sq. ft.

Sale 3: $36,000 ÷ 10,000 sq. ft. = $3.600 per sq. ft.

Sale 4: $39,800 ÷ 19,500 sq. ft. = $2.041 per sq. ft.

Reconciliation:

Sale 1: $3.067 × .35 = $1.073

Sale 2: $2.803 × .30 = $ .841

Sale 3: $3.600 × .20 = $ .720

Sale 4: $2.041 × .15 = $ .306

$\overline{\qquad\qquad\qquad}$

100% = $2.940 = $2.94 per sq. ft.

Total square footage of subject lot	13,200
Reconciled value per sq. ft.	× $2.94
Estimated market value of subject lot	$38,808 (round to $38,800)

Note that in the reconciliation process, Sale 3 was given less weight in the final analysis because it was in a different neighborhood, and Sale 4 was given the least weight because of its proximity to a railroad track and its location in a different neighborhood. If the appraiser had considered all of the comparables to be good representations of the subject property,

1   he or she would have given all four comparables equal weight and simply
2   averaged them to arrive at a value per square foot.

3   ## COST-DEPRECIATION APPROACH   15yrs old only!

4   The **cost-depreciation approach** to value is based on the theory that a
5   knowledgeable purchaser will pay no more for a property than the cost
6   of acquiring a similar site and constructing an acceptable substitute
7   structure. The maximum value of a property can be measured by
8   determining the cost to acquire an equivalent site and to reproduce a
9   structure as if new, and then subtracting accrued depreciation. There are
10 four steps in the cost-depreciation approach:

11 **Step one.**   Estimate the current reproduction (or replacement) cost of the
12 improvements as of the appraisal date. **Reproduction cost** is the amount
13 of money required to build an exact duplicate of the structure.
14 **Replacement cost** is the amount of money required to replace a structure
15 having the same use and functional utility as the subject property, but using
16 modern, available, or updated materials. Consider an historic Florida
17 bungalow home. The cost to duplicate the home in exact detail, including
18 the hand carved trim on the porch, is reproduction cost. However, if the
19 home were to be reconstructed in the same bungalow style but with
20 modern materials and techniques, this cost is replacement cost.

21   Several methods are available to help in estimating building
22 reproduction costs. Three cost estimating methods are described here,
23 with the most technical and precise method first:

24 1. *Quantity survey method.* This method involves a detailed
25   inventory of all labor, materials, products, and indirect costs, plus
26   the builder's profit, required to reproduce a building. The number
27   of items is then multiplied by the cost per item. For example, in a
28   single-family dwelling with three baths, multiply the cost of one
29   commode by 3, the cost of one bathtub by 3, etc. If 1,000 lineal feet of
30   2 × 6s are required at a cost of $.50 per foot, the cost would be $500.

Big Buildings
schools-Hosp ect.

31   The man-hours for each type of labor involved are estimated and
32   multiplied by the cost per hour. All costs are totaled, then added to
33   overhead and indirect costs. The builder's profit then is added. The
34   aggregate of all costs is the reproduction cost of a new building.

Formula:	Cost-Depreciation Approach
	Reproduction cost of the building
less	Accrued depreciation
equals	Indicated value of the building
plus	Estimated value of the site
equals	Indicated value of the property

up to 15yrs only.

TABLE 15.2   Comparative Square-Foot Method

Estimated reproduction cost new:		
Main dwelling:	1,241 sq. ft. @ $50 per =	$62,050
Utility room:	117 sq. ft. @ $32 per =	3,744
Entrance porch:	75 sq. ft. @ $12 per =	900
Carport:	412 sq. ft. @ $15 per =	+ 6,180
Total estimated reproduction cost new		$72,874
Less accrued depreciation		− 4,802
Total depreciation reproduction cost		$68,072
Add value of land (by comparison)		+16,000
Add value of improvements:		
Landscaping	$2,128	
Driveway: 300 sq. ft. @ $4 per =	+1,200	
		+ 3,328
Total value of property via cost depreciation		$87,400

2. ***Unit-in-place method.*** This method is more practical for appraisers and requires less technical ability. The cost of materials plus the cost of labor to install them is calculated for each component of a structure, such as the driveway, parking area, roof, foundation, walls, and floors. For example, the unit-in-place cost for a square of roofing (100 square feet) can be obtained. The unit cost is then multiplied by the number of units in the entire roof. Each separate component is treated in the same manner. Adding the costs of installed equipment and fixtures and builder's profit results in the total reproduction cost of the structure.

3. ***Comparative square-foot or cubic-foot method.*** This method is sometimes called the *comparative unit method* or the *unit comparison method*. The cost of reproducing a recently built property similar in size and function to the subject property is often used as a basis for estimating the reproduction cost. To reduce errors in this method, square-foot or cubic-foot costs are obtained for a standard (or *benchmark*) house of average size for the locality. Exterior walls are used for measurements. Adjustments are then made for quality, shape, and extra features.

This method is relatively fast and easy. It is probably the predominant costing method used for appraisal purposes. However, its use is limited to relatively small, uncomplicated structures such as single-family homes and small office buildings. Many less cost-calculation publications are available to assist appraisers determining standard square-foot costs in different geographic regions. (Two widely used cost-information publications are the *Dodge Building Cost Calculator and Valuation Guide,* published by McGraw-Hill, and the *Boeckh Building Valuation Manual,* published by the American Appraisal Company.) An abbreviated version of the comparative square-foot method is provided in Table 15.2 to illustrate its use.

Step two.   Estimate the amount of depreciation from all causes (physical deterioration, functional obsolescence, and external obsolescence) and deduct it from the reproduction (or replacement) cost.

The appraiser begins with the reproduction cost of the new structure. Value must be deducted from this cost for depreciation. **Depreciation** is loss in value for any reason. *Accrued depreciation* is the total depreciation that has accumulated over the years a building has been standing. Accrued depreciation is the difference (loss) in value between an existing building and an exact replica in new condition. In applying the cost-depreciation approach, the item that often causes the greatest variations in value is the amount of estimated accrued (accumulated) depreciation. For this reason, the older the subject property, the less reliable the cost-depreciation approach.

Following are the three main types (causes) of depreciation.

1. **Physical deterioration.** Physical deterioration includes ordinary wear and tear caused by use, lack of maintenance, exposure to the elements, and physical damage. Brittle roof shingles or a worn out central air-conditioning compressor are examples of physical deterioration. If correction of a defect would result in as much added value as the cost to correct, the defect is said to be **curable.** An **incurable** defect is one in which the cost of curing the defect is greater than the value added by the cure.

2. **Functional obsolescence.** Anything that is inferior due to operational inadequacies, poor design, or changing tastes and preferences (for example, a poor traffic pattern, an outmoded design, too few bathrooms, lack of closet space) is classified as functional obsolescence and may be either *curable* or *incurable.* An overimprovement is also considered to be functional obsolescence.

3. **External obsolescence.** Any loss of value due to influences originating outside the boundaries of the property (for example, an expressway adjacent to a residential subdivision, an industrial area next door, deterioration of the neighborhood) is normally beyond the control of the property owner and therefore is considered to be *incurable*.

Land is not depreciated in the cost-depreciation approach. Only the buildings or other improvements to land are subject to these three types of depreciation because the *site value* is estimated separately, typically using the sales comparison approach. Any adjustments to the site for size, location, and nonstructural improvements were already made when the appraiser applied the sales comparison approach to estimate the site value. When the cost to reproduce the improvements is determined, depreciation is applied only to that portion of the property.

Straight-line depreciation.   A simplistic approach to estimating depreciation is the straight-line method. This means that an equal amount of building value is lost each year until the economic life of the building is exhausted. **Economic life** (useful life) is the total estimated time in years that an improvement can be profitably useful.

1 *Example:* Suppose you are appraising a five-year-old building with a
2 reproduction cost of $100,000 and an estimated economic life of 25
3 years (when new). Then 25 years is equal to 100 percent of economic
4 life. To find the amount of depreciation to deduct each year:

5 *Solution:* 100% of economic life ÷ 25 years of economic life =

6 4% loss per year

7 Reproduction cost new $100,000
8 Depreciation per year   × .04
9 Depreciation in dollars per year $4,000

10 (or $100,000 ÷ 25 = $4,000 per year)

11 Annual depreciation $4,000
12 Age of building in years   × 5
13 Total accumulated depreciation $20,000

14 Reproduction cost new $100,000
15 Total accumulated depreciation   − 20,000
16 Depreciated reproduction cost $80,000

17   The cost of labor and materials in today's market demands an
18 investment of $100,000 to construct the same building new. This cost is the
19 amount to be depreciated. It makes no difference what the original cost of
20 the building was. Therefore, as the preceding calculations show, the five-
21 year-old building being appraised has a value of $80,000 today. (Other,
22 more involved methods of depreciating real property are used by those
23 specializing in appraising.)

24 **Age-life method.**   The majority of appraisers take into account the
25 observed condition of the subject structure when estimating depreciation.
26 Appraisers often use the *age-life* method (also referred to as *observed*
27 *condition breakdown* method) to estimate depreciation of residential
28 structures. The age-life method is based on a ratio of a property's *effective*
29 *age* to its *economic life*. **Effective age** is the age indicated by a structure's
30 condition and utility. Chronologically, a home may be five years old.
31 However, if the structure has been well maintained, its effective age may
32 be only two years.

33   There is no precise method for estimating effective age. The appraiser
34 estimates a structure's effective age by observing the structure's current
35 condition. The appraiser divides the effective age of the structure by the
36 total economic (useful) life of the structure. Refer to the formula in
37 the text box below.

Formula:	**Accrued Depreciation**
	Effective age
divided by	Total economic life
multiplied by	Reproduction cost new
equals	Estimated total accrued depreciation

1 **Step three.** Estimate the value of the site and nonstructural site
2 improvements, assuming the site is vacant and will be put to its highest
3 and best use. The value of land is normally determined by the sales
4 comparison approach, explained earlier.

5 **Step four.** To derive the property's estimated value, add the estimated
6 value of the site, including site improvements, to the depreciated cost of
7 the structural improvements. Thus, if neighboring comparable properties
8 are selling for $2 per square foot and the lot on which this building stands
9 has an area of 11,000 square feet, the lot value must be $22,000. Adding the
10 land value of $22,000 to the depreciated reproduction value of $80,000
11 gives a total property value of $102,000.

Best Sur.
Comercial.

12 ## INCOME CAPITALIZATION APPROACH

13 The object of the income capitalization approach is to measure a flow of
14 income projected into the future. This method is a complete departure
15 from the sales comparison and cost-depreciation approaches. The
16 **income capitalization approach** develops an estimated market value
17 based on the present worth of future income from the subject property. It
18 is the primary approach for appraising income-producing property and
19 for comparing possible investments.

20 Let's begin with an explanation of the various types of income.

21 **Potential gross income.** The total annual income a property would
22 produce if it were fully rented and no collection losses were incurred is
23 called **potential gross income (PGI).**

20,000.

24 **Effective gross income.** When vacancy and collection losses are
25 *deducted* from annual PGI and any income from other sources (e.g.,
26 laundry, vending machines, parking) is *added*, the result is annual
27 **effective gross income (EGI). Vacancy and collection losses** consist of
28 the expected income loss that will result from occasional turnover of
29 renters and periodic vacancies as well as the likelihood that not all rental
30 income will be collected. Even when a property is 100 percent occupied,
31 the probability of *continuous* total occupancy is unlikely. Therefore, some
32 vacancy and collection losses always should be deducted from PGI.

Always.
-5% (1000)
=19000
-9000

33 **Net operating income.** **Net operating income (NOI)** is the income
34 remaining after subtracting all relevant operating expenses from EGI.
35 *Operating expenses* are grouped into three separate categories: (1) *fixed*
36 *expenses* (e.g., property taxes, hazard insurance); (2) *variable expenses*
37 (e.g., utilities, maintenance, management, supplies, janitorial, garbage
38 collection); and (3) *reserve for replacements.* The term *reserve for*
39 *replacements* refers to a reserve allowance that provides for the periodic
40 replacement of building components such as roof coverings and heating
41 and air-conditioning equipment that wear out at a faster rate than
42 structural components.

10060
NET
operating

43 All costs of financing, income taxes, personal expenses, and
44 business-related expenses (such as payroll and advertising) that do not
45 contribute to actual operation of the property are *business expenses,*
46 not operating expenses. Depreciation is not an operating or a business

Rental = 1% of Purchase

Formula:	**To Find Net Operating Income (NOI)**
	Potential Gross Income (PGI)
minus	Vacancy and collection losses
plus	Other income
equals	Effective Gross Income (EGI)
	EGI
minus	Operating expenses
equals	NOI

$$\frac{I}{RV} \quad \text{Divide} \atop \text{Multiply}$$

1 expense (it does not involve an outlay of cash) and is not used to
2 calculate NOI.

3   NOI is thus the annual income (before mortgage or income tax
4 payments) that may be expected to occur over the remaining economic
5 life of a property. It is this income (NOI) that is capitalized into *present*
6 *value*. To use the income capitalization approach, an appraiser must
7 know the annual NOI produced by the property, or an appraiser must be
8 able to forecast the annual NOI based on reasonable estimates.

9   Licensees may have access to the accounts; may be provided the
10 information required; or, in the case of a vacant lot on which a business
11 building will be constructed, may project a pro forma NOI statement
12 from several existing similar properties (see below).

13 *Example:* Suppose your client is considering construction of a 10-unit
14 apartment building. You are estimating the value of the vacant
15 property zoned for apartments. Your survey of other apartment
16 projects of similar size and quality in the market area reveals that each
17 of the proposed new apartments could be competitive if rented at
18 $665 per month. The survey also discloses that an annual vacancy and
19 collection loss rate of 10 percent is typical for the area. By using normal
20 costs of operation, a pro forma statement can be developed to indicate
21 the probable annual NOI. (Note: Begin by estimating the potential
22 gross income [$665 rent × 10 units × 12 months = PGI].)

23 *Solution:*

10 UNITS

24	Potential annual gross income	$79,800 — PGI
25	Vacancy and collection losses (10%)	− 7,980 —
26	Effective annual gross income	$71,820 = EGI

27	Expenses (per year):	
28	Taxes	$5,494
29	Insurance	996
30	Management	24,600
31	Repairs and maintenance	4,100
32	Reserve for replacements	+ 1,800
33	Total annual operating expenses	$36,990

34	Effective annual gross income	$71,820
35	Total annual operating expenses	− 36,990
36	NOI	$34,830

IMPORTANT

1 Once known or estimated, the NOI is usually divided by an *overall*
2 *capitalization rate* (OAR). The OAR normally is determined by using the
3 sale prices and NOIs of similar properties in the market area. Dividing
4 the NOI of a property by its current value or sale price produces an OAR.

5 Income (NOI) ÷ Value (Sale price) = Rate (OAR)

6 The components of this formula are said to be *market-driven*, that is,
7 income figures and recorded sale prices represent the market in action.
8 That is the reason most licensees, appraisers, and others prefer the OAR
9 as a capitalization rate.

10 *Example:* Sales data, income records, and expense records indicate:

Comparable Garden Apartment Complex	Annual NOI	÷ Sale Price	= Indicated OAR
A	$ 31,400	$ 325,000	.097
B	$ 48,230	$ 450,000	.107
C	$ 39,600	$ 400,000	.099
D	$ 37,400	$ 395,000	.095
E	$ 44,700	$ 440,000	.102
	$201,330	$2,010,000	.500 ÷ 5 = .100

(handwritten: NET; 5 DIF APTS.)

19 $201,330 ÷ $2,010,000 = .100 or 10% OAR

20 The same procedure could be used to determine the OAR for other
21 types of income-producing properties. Once an appropriate
22 capitalization rate and NOI are determined, the IRV formula is used to
23 estimate the present value of income-producing properties:

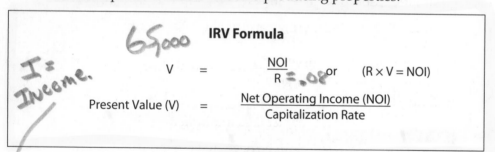

IRV Formula

$$V = \frac{NOI}{R} \quad \text{or} \quad (R \times V = NOI)$$

Present Value (V) = $\dfrac{\text{Net Operating Income (NOI)}}{\text{Capitalization Rate}}$

(handwritten: 65,000; I = Income; R = .08)

24 For example, using the results of the pro forma statement in the
25 earlier problem and the market area OAR of 10 percent, the estimated
26 value of the property is estimated.

27 $34,830 (NOI) ÷ .10 rate = $348,300 estimated value

28 Investors, on the other hand, often prefer to specify a capitalization
29 rate because each investor is free to choose the acceptable rate of return
30 he or she desires. When the type of estimated value is investor-driven,
31 the minimum rate of return acceptable to the investor is frequently used
32 as the capitalization rate. Net annual income is then divided by the
33 specified capitalization rate to obtain the investment value of the property.
34 It is important to mention, however, that this is not *market value*, but
35 rather *investment value*. **Investment value** is the value of property to a
36 particular investor based on his or her desired rate of return, risk tolerance,
37 and so forth. Market value is objective and impersonal; investment value
38 is subjective and based on personal criteria.

(handwritten margin notes:
OAR = Capitazativ rate.
R = rate.
V = Value.
NOI ÷ cap rate = Value.)

1   *Example:* A small income property produces an annual net income of
2    $8,000. Your client wants you to tell her the amount of money that she
3   may invest in the property to provide a return of 10 percent per year
4   from the investment.

5    $$V = I \div R = \$8,000 \div .10 = \$80,000$$

6   So the investment value to this investor is $80,000 if a 10 percent rate of
7   return is required from the subject property.

8   Sound income and expense data are critical in the use of the income
9   capitalization approach. It is also important to realize that a definite
10   relationship exists between present value, net income, and capitalization
11   rate. If, for example, the capitalization rate (R) is increased and the net
12   income (I) remains constant, the present value (V) will be less. Or if the
13   net income (I) goes up and the capitalization rate (R) remains constant,
14   the present value (V) will be greater.

15   **Gross rent multiplier (GRM).**   A **gross rent multiplier (GRM)** is the
16   ratio between a property's gross monthly rent and its selling price. The
17   GRM applies to rental income only. The **gross income multiplier (GIM)**
18   is based on gross annual income and can include income from sources
19   other than rent. GIMs and GRMs convert gross income into a market
20   value. Multipliers are local in nature and must be determined for each
21   local area at the time a transaction is being considered. To be useful, the
22   subject property must be in a market area where multipliers are accepted
23   and used. Also, vacancy and collection losses of the subject property
24   should be reasonably close to those of comparable properties. Use of the
25   GRM (or GIM) to find market value requires the following three steps:

26   1. Estimate (or obtain) the gross rent (or income) for the subject
27   property.

28   2. Calculate a GRM (or GIM) by using transactions of comparable
29   properties. The sale price of each property divided by its gross rent
30   (or income) will produce a GRM (or GIM) for each property. Then
31   average the multipliers to obtain a market area multiplier.

32   3. Market value equals the gross rent of the subject property
33   multiplied by the GRM for the market area.

34   *Example:*

Sale	Sale Price	÷	Monthly Rental	=	GRM
1	$98,000		$575		170.4
2	96,600		550		175.6
3	99,900		595		167.9
4	92,500		550		168.2
5	98,000		560		175.0
					857.1

42   857.1 ÷ 5 comparables = 171.4 market area GRM
43   Subject property rent $560 × GRM 171.4 = $95,984
44   Market value of subject property = $96,000 (rounded)

■ DATA SOURCES

Licensees and appraisers depend on information from many different sources. To ensure that the information needed is available and current, appraisers and some licensees maintain libraries of up-to-date statistical data and business publications. The following are a few of the more commonly used data sources:

- National statistical publications from the Departments of Labor and Commerce or the Bureau of the Census

- City and county maps (including recorded subdivisions)

- Land-use studies with zoning maps

- Economic studies

- Growth projections (usually information published by city or county planning bodies is added to and modified by appraisers using their own observations and experience)

- Services and utilities data (existing and planned networks of water, sewer, gas, electric, telephone, etc.)

- Sales data (recording of property transfer information, prices, location, etc.)

In spite of the numerous aids and resources available, the most accurate and reliable value estimates are generally produced by qualified individuals of character and integrity who are thoroughly familiar with the local area. However, the best estimate possible is not intended to represent exact market value. The best estimate is an estimate that falls within the upper and lower limits of value for the appraised property.

■ COMPARATIVE MARKET ANALYSIS

In the normal course of business, licensees typically prepare a comparative market analysis (CMA) for sellers or buyers as a means to help them make informed decisions on pricing a property. Although CMAs are a variation of the sales comparison approach, they are *not* appraisal reports. Appraisals employ all three approaches to value and must conform to the Uniform Standards of Professional Appraisal Practice (USPAP).

PREPARATION OF A COMPARATIVE MARKET ANALYSIS

Categories of comparables.   A CMA typically presents information concerning three major categories of properties: (1) sold within the previous 12 months, (2) currently on the market, and (3) listings that expired during the previous 12 months.

- *Sold within the previous 12 months.* Studying the sale prices of similar properties in the same market area that have sold within the previous 12 months provides information concerning what buyers have been willing to pay for similar properties. The amount of sale activity during the preceding 12-month period and the average days on the market are also valuable information.

- *Currently on the market.* Studying the asking prices of properties in the market area provides important information concerning what the sellers of similar properties are asking in today's market. When properties with equally desirable characteristics are available, buyers normally choose the property with the lowest price. Therefore, the seller should price the property taking into consideration the average asking price of competing properties.

- *Expired during the previous 12 months.* Properties that were listed but failed to sell during the previous 12 months often were priced too high. This information helps to explain to sellers the consequences of overpricing listings.

Common elements of comparison. It is important that all properties used in the CMA be similar to the subject property in size, age, amenities, and location. Adjustments should be made for important differences compared with the subject property, such as swimming pools, condition, style, and so forth. Examples of features that must be considered include location, size, and shape of the lot; landscaping; construction quality; style, design, and age of the structure; square feet; and number of rooms. Adjustments are made to the comps (comparables) using the same procedure as discussed in the sales comparison approach.

Computer-generated CMAs. Software programs are available that will organize the data sales associates gather into attractive presentations. Many MLS service providers offer software for REALTOR® members to download the comparable information directly into a listing presentation package.

■ COMPARATIVE MARKET ANALYSIS: CASE SITUATION

This exercise involves hypothetical properties. A Comparative Market Analysis form is provided (Figure 15.1), followed by the completed form (Figure 15.2). To prepare a CMA, the sales associate must first gather information concerning recent sales, listed properties, and expired listings. The information is entered in the appropriate sections of the CMA form. Adjustments are then made to each comp's sale price for differences, compared with the subject property.

SUBJECT PROPERTY INFORMATION

- Owners of record as listed on the deed: Donald Knight and Geneva Knight, a married couple

- Street address: 1810 Mayfair Road, St. Petersburg, Florida

- Owner's home and work phone numbers: 727-555-1212; 727-555-1806

FIGURE 15.1 Comparative Market Analysis Problem

Comparative Market Analysis Solution

Prepared for:	Donald Knight and Geneva Knight
Property address:	1810 Mayfair Road, St. Petersburg, FL
Date:	June 8, 20___
Description:	Your property has 1,420 square feet with a two-car garage. Similar properties are shown below.

Properties sold within the previous 12 months

Property Address	Sale Price	List Price	Days on Market	Living Area	Features	Estimated Adjustment	Adjusted Sale Price	Comments
1806 Mayfair Road	$78,300	$81,500	145	1,520	Pool, larger			
1831 Mayfair Road	74,200	77,000	130	1,520	Larger			
1830 Wales Drive	70,000	71,000	103	1,420	Same			
2513 Doric Drive	71,500	73,000	113	1,420	Fireplace			
2489 Salmon Drive	67,500	71,000	93	1,420	1-car garage			
2517 Doric Drive	70,500	70,500	113	1,420	Same			
1845 Mayfair Road	71,500	?	?	1,520	Larger			

Percentage sale price/list price 97%   * = most comparable   Median $___

Properties currently on the market

Property Address	List Price	Days on Market	Living Area	Features	Estimated Adjustment	As Adjusted	Comments
2505 Colleen Drive	$80,000	60 est.	1,520	Pool, larger			
2410 Ionic Drive	73,000	30 est.	1,420	Same			
2402 Gothic Drive	70,500	60 est.	1,320	Fireplace, 1-car garage, smaller			
1800 Salmon Drive	72,500	140 est.	1,420	Same			

* = most comparable   Median $___

Properties that were listed, but failed to sell during the previous 12 months

Property Address	List Price	Days on Market	Living Area	Features			
1705 Salmon Drive	$75,000	180	1,420				
2512 Colleen Drive	84,500	270	1,520	Pool, larger			
1818 Doric Drive	74,000	120	1,420	1-car garage			

* = most comparable   Median $___

The suggested marketing range is $___ to $___

This information is believed to be accurate, but is not warranted.

FIGURE 15.2   Comparative Market Analysis Solution

Comparative Market Analysis Solution

Prepared for:	Donald Knight and Geneva Knight
Property address:	1810 Mayfair Road, St. Petersburg, FL
Date:	June 8, 20____
Description:	Your property has 1,420 square feet with a two-car garage. Similar properties are shown below.

Properties sold within the previous 12 months

Property Address	Sale Price	List Price	Days on Market	Living Area	Features	Estimated Adjustment	Adjusted Sale Price	Comments
1806 Mayfair Road	$78,300	$81,500	145	1,520	Pool, larger	–8,000	$70,300	
1831 Mayfair Road	74,200	77,000	130	1,520	Larger	–4,000	70,200	
1830 Wales Drive	70,000	71,000	103	1,420	Same		70,000*	
2513 Doric Drive	71,500	73,000	113	1,420	Fireplace	–1,000	70,500	
2489 Salmon Drive	67,500	71,000	93	1,420	1-car garage	+2,000	69,500	
2517 Doric Drive	70,500	70,500	113	1,420	Same		70,500*	
1845 Mayfair Road	71,500	?	?	1,520	Larger	–4,000	67,500	
						Median	$70,200	

Percentage sale price/list price 97%

* = **most comparable**

Properties currently on the market

Property Address	List Price	Days on Market	Living Area	Features	Estimated Adjustment	As Adjusted	Comments
2505 Colleen Drive	$80,000	60 est.	1,520	Pool, larger	–8,000	$72,000	
2410 Ionic Drive	73,000	30 est.	1,420	Same		73,000	
2402 Gothic Drive	70,500	60 est.	1,320	Fireplace, 1-car garage, smaller	+5,000	75,500	
1800 Salmon Drive	72,500	140 est.	1,420	Same		72,500	
					Median	$72,750	

* = **most comparable**

Properties that were listed, but failed to sell during the previous 12 months

Property Address	List Price	Days on Market	Living Area	Features	Estimated Adjustment	As Adjusted	Comments
1705 Salmon Drive	$75,000	180	1,420			$75,000	
2512 Colleen Drive	84,500	270	1,520	Pool, larger	– 8,000	76,500	
1818 Doric Drive	74,000	120	1,420	1-car garage	+ 2,000	76,000	
					Median	$76,000	

* = **most comparable**

The suggested marketing range for your home is $70,000 to $72,500.

This information is believed to be accurate, but is not warranted.

Used with permission from *Florida Real Estate Broker's Guide* by Linda L. Crawford and Edward J. O'Donnell. ©1999 by Dearborn Financial Publishing, Inc. Published by Dearborn™ Real Estate Education, a division of Dearborn Financial Publishing, Inc., Chicago. All rights reserved.

- Number of bedrooms and baths in the home: four bedrooms, two baths

- Extra home features: two-car garage, screened-in porch

Information from online tax rolls available through the MLS system.

- Legal description: Lot 26, Block A, Otter Creek, Unit 4, Pinellas County

- Property tax appraisal: $65,300

- Annual taxes (including homestead exemption): $877

- Year built: 1977

- Base area: 1,420 square feet (later verified by actual measurement)

- Total area: 1,985 square feet (including garage)

- Date of last sale: 1977

- Last sale price: $37,100

- Mortgage: Reliant Mortgage Company

A search of the tax records shows seven sales in the subdivision within the previous year, ranging from $68,000 to $78,000. Six of the seven sales were reported in the MLS, which provides additional information. The sales are entered in the first section of the CMA. (See Figure 15.1.)

For purposes of this CMA, assume that properties sold in the neighborhood show the following value contributions (based on market data):

- The value contribution of a pool is $4,000.

- The value contribution of a fireplace is $1,000.

- The value contribution of an additional garage stall is $2,000.

- The value contribution of additional square footage is $40 per square foot.

For maximum learning benefit, first enter the appropriate figures on the Comparative Market Analysis Form (Figure 15.1) without referring to the completed form (Figure 15.2).

■ SUMMARY

There are many reasons to appraise real property. Real estate licensees and appraisers are primarily interested in estimating the market value of real property. There are three approaches to estimating value: the comparable sales approach, the cost-depreciation approach, and the income capitalization approach. The principle of substitution is the basic economic concept underlying all three approaches. Each method is usually given more weight for particular types of real property, although a thorough appraisal will utilize all three approaches, if applicable. The basis for the comparable sales and cost-depreciation approaches is the principle of substitution; the basis for the income capitalization approach is the present worth of a future income stream. Comparative market analysis is a tool used by real estate licensees to help sellers list their properties at an appropriate price.

Additional Appraisal Terms

Assemblage	The combining of two or more adjoining properties into one tract; the *process* of consolidating properties. This is usually done to increase the usability and value of the resulting consolidation.
Plottage	The added *value* as a result of assembling (combining) two or more properties into one large parcel.
Progression	The principle that the value of an inferior property is enhanced by its association with superior properties of the same type.
Regression	The principle that the value of a superior property is adversely affected by its association with an inferior property of the same type.
Situs	Refers to people's preferences, both physical and economic, for a certain area owing to factors such as weather, job opportunities, and transportation facilities.

Note: The examples of comparable sales used in this Chapter are hypothetical and offered for educational purposes only.

■ REVIEW QUESTIONS

1. Valuation of real property is an
   A. estimate of cost.
   B. estimate of value.
   C. exact value.
   D. assessment of cost.

2. The total expenditure required to bring a new improvement into existence is referred to as
   A. cost.
   B. price.
   C. market price.
   D. market value.

3. Which assumption does NOT apply to definition of market value?
   A. Payment is made in cash or its equivalent.
   B. Neither the buyer or the seller is under any compulsion to act quickly.
   C. Market value is the median price a property will bring.
   D. Both buyer and seller are fully informed.

4. The approach to estimating value that is referred to as *the real estate market speaking through past sales* because it utilizes actual sales transactions is the
   A. transactional comparison method.
   B. economic indicator method.
   C. sales comparison method.
   D. sales transaction method.

5. When more money is invested in a building than can reasonably be expected to be recaptured, it is referred to as
   A. economic lack of utility.
   B. overimprovement.
   C. underimprovement.
   D. depreciation.

6. The most probable price in terms of money that a property will bring in an open market is called the
   A. highest and best use.
   B. sale price.
   C. market value.
   D. exchange value.

7. Loss of value for any reason is called
   A. transferability.
   B. substitution.
   C. depreciation.
   D. economic obsolescence.

8. All below are characteristics required to create value EXCEPT
   A. demand.
   B. supply.
   C. utility.
   D. transferability.

9. The approach to value most likely to be relevant for appraising a community college is the
   A. comparable sales approach.
   B. cost-depreciation approach.
   C. income capitalization approach.
   D. straight-line approach.

10. In the income capitalization approach, value equals
    A. net operating income divided by an appropriate capitalization rate.
    B. net operating income multiplied by an appropriate capitalization rate.
    C. an appropriate capitalization rate multiplied by value.
    D. an appropriate capitalization rate divided by net operating income.

11. The most relevant approach to estimate the value of a vacant lot in a residential neighborhood usually is the
    A. square-foot approach.
    B. cost-depreciation approach.
    C. unit-in-place method.
    D. sales comparison approach.

12. In the comparable sales approach
    A. adjustments are made to the subject properties.
    B. adjustments are made to the comparable properties.
    C. the subject property must have sold recently in the same market area as the comparable property.
    D. the result is considered to be the median value.

13. The basis of all three approaches to market value is the principle of
    A. situs.
    B. substitution.
    C. overimprovement.
    D. economic potential.

14. When applying the cost-depreciation approach which item is NOT subject to depreciation?
    A. A poor traffic pattern in a home
    B. New solid oak wood cabinets and marble tile floors in a neighborhood of $80,000 homes
    C. Older site improvements
    D. Land

15. Which would be considered to be external obsolescence?
    A. Peeling exterior paint
    B. One bathroom in a three-bedroom home
    C. Metal utility shed that is in poor condition located just inside the property line
    D. A residential property's proximity to an industrial area

16. Loss in value due to operational inadequacies, poor design, or changing tastes is referred to as
    A. physical deterioration.
    B. functional obsolescence.
    C. external obsolescence.
    D. underimprovement.

17. A small income-producing property has a projected effective gross income of $48,000. Expenses are estimated at 20 percent of effective gross income. An appraiser has determined that an appropriate capitalization rate, based on property type and competing properties, is 9 percent. The estimated market value of this property (rounded to the nearest dollar) is
    A. $106,667.
    B. $311,111.
    C. $426,667.
    D. $533,333.

18. The economic characteristic that refers to the preference for a certain location owing to various factors such as climate, employment outlook, and so forth, is called
    A. highest and best use.
    B. plottage.
    C. economic preference.
    D. situs.

19. The total estimated time in years that an improvement can be profitably useful is referred to as
    A. effective age.
    B. economic life.
    C. accrued depreciation.
    D. chronological age of the improvement.

20. In the income capitalization approach, if the capitalization rate is increased and the net income is unchanged, the
    A. present value will be less.
    B. future value will be less.
    C. present value will be more.
    D. future value will be more.

21. A home has 1,800 square feet of living area and 200 square feet of garage. The reproduction cost new is $48 per square foot for living area and $28 per square foot for finished garage area. The site measures 75 feet wide by 110 feet deep and is valued at $3 per square foot. The economic life of the home is estimated to be 50 years. The house is 10 years old. The value of the property using the cost-depreciation approach is
    A. $73,600.
    B. $86,400.
    C. $92,000.
    D. $98,350.

22. L & D, a limited partnership, wishes to purchase an apartment building that has a monthly net income of $4,000 and monthly expenses of $1,000. If the L & D partnership is to get a 12 percent return on its investment, what should it pay for the property?
    A. $25,000
    B. $33,000
    C. $300,000
    D. $400,000

23. An income-producing property has a potential annual gross income of $81,420. Vacancy and collection losses are estimated at 10 percent of potential gross income. Expenses are estimated at $40,000. The estimated value of the property is $250,000. The capitalization rate for this property is
    A. 13.31%.
    B. 14.91%.
    C. 16.57%.
    D. 17.5%.

24. The Gigis' home recently sold for $58,500. The rent on the home is $450 per month. The GRM for the home is
    A. 130.
    B. 108.
    C. .09.
    D. .01.

25. An appraiser is calculating the reproduction cost new of a home, using the comparative square-foot method. The appraiser measures the exterior dimensions of the home, which are 27 feet by 52 feet, plus a detached garage measuring 22 feet by 24 feet. The appraiser consults an accepted cost manual and estimates the reproduction cost for heated and air-conditioned living area to be $52.50 per square foot and the finished free-standing garage to be $32.50 per square foot. The reproduction cost new of the improvements is
    A. $62,790.
    B. $73,710.
    C. $90,870.
    D. $101,430.

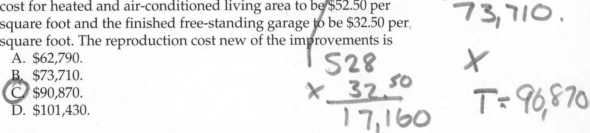

26. Effective gross income is
    A. net operating income divided by an appropriate capitalization rate.
    B. potential gross income minus vacancy and collection losses.
    C. net operating income minus annual mortgage expense.
    D. before-tax cash flow divided by equity invested.

27. Analyzing the sale price and income of comparable investment properties (NOI ÷ sale price) is a common way of determining the
    A. overall capitalization rate.
    B. gross income multiplier.
    C. dollar amount of profit.
    D. market value.

28. A building is valued at $150,000 when NOI is capitalized at a rate of 8 percent. NOI is 40 percent of effective gross income. The effective gross income is
    A. $12,000.
    B. $22,000.
    C. $30,000.
    D. $32,000.

29. A commercial property has a potential gross income of $40,000. Vacancy and collection losses are 5 percent of PGI. Additional operating expenses total $12,920. The property has a first mortgage requiring payments of $1,070.75 per month. Using a capitalization rate of 12 percent, which amount is an accurate estimate of the property's value?
    A. $101,333
    B. $107,667
    C. $209,000
    D. $316,667

30. The annual income earned on a commercial property is $85,000 and the sale price is $722,500. What is the GIM?
    A. 6.5
    B. 7.5
    C. 8.5
    D. 9.5

CHAPTER 16

Product Knowledge

[Handwritten annotations in upper right: "NOT MANY ?'s", "why", "V.A. -FHA. WANT DE-Tached Garage", "Over $150K DE-Tached"]

■ KEY TERMS

corner	flag	key
cul-de-sac	gable	r-value
dormer	hip	single-hung
double-hung	interior	t-intersection

■ OVERVIEW

Real estate professionals should have general product knowledge. Understanding basic construction methods and familiarity with common building materials and techniques are invaluable when working with customers.

After completing this Chapter, the student should be able to:

- contrast pier and slab-on-grade foundations;

- distinguish among the various lot types;

- distinguish among the three types of frame construction;

- identify various roof styles;

- explain how a basic electrical system works;

- describe basic residential plumbing and mechanical systems; and

- identify the various window types.

■ LOT TYPES

A property is characterized by many elements such as the structure's architectural design, its roof style, and so forth. The shape of the lot is also an important feature of a property.

Corner lots are bounded with streets on two sides. Commercial corner lots are generally worth more than interior lots. Residential corner lots are often desirable because of their "curb appeal." (See lot 1 in Figure 16.1.)

FIGURE 16.1   Lot Types

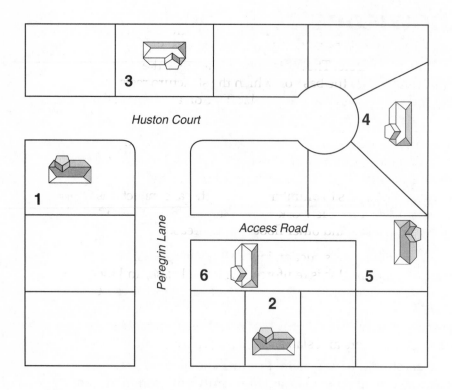

1   **Interior** lots are bounded on each side by another lot. (See lot 2 in
2   Figure 16.1.)

3   **T-intersection** lots are interior lots that suffer from their location at the
4   end of a T intersection. They are usually less desirable because of the
5   inconvenience of car headlights shining into the home and a possible
6   danger from speeding "runaway" cars. (See lot 3 in Figure 16.1.)

7   **Cul-de-sac** lots occur when a street is open at one end only and it has
8   a circular turnaround at the other end. Lots located on the cul-de-sac are
9   desirable because they usually are more spacious providing ample room
10 for backyard features such as swimming pools. Residential cul-de-sac lots
11 also tend to have less vehicular traffic. (See lot 4 in Figure 16.1.)

12 **Flag** lots are characterized by a long access road or driveway back to
13 the main part of the lot. The access road suggests the staff of a flag.
14 Typically flag lots occur as a result of residential development in what
15 once was a large homestead. The long access road usually increases the
16 cost of bringing utilities to the lot. (See lot 5 in Figure 16.1.)

17 **Key** lots are generally long skinny lots similar to the shaft of a key that
18 are often bounded by as many as five or six lots. (See lot 6 in Figure 16.1.)
19 *Note:* The term *key lot* is also used to indicate a lot that has added value
20 because of its strategic location.

■ STRUCTURAL ELEMENTS

FOOTER AND FOUNDATION

The footers and foundation provide support for the structure. The footer is usually strengthened with two ⅝-inch rods, called *rebar,* resting on metal *chairs* imbedded in concrete. The footer extends around the perimeter of the building and is the base on which the structure rests. Two basic styles of residential foundations used in Florida are the pier and slab-on-grade foundations.

Pier.   A *pier* is a column of masonry. Four or more piers are used to support a structure. Piers lift the structure above ground level to allow a *crawl space* below the structure. This type of foundation has the advantage of allowing easy access to plumbing and electrical connections as well as providing space to run ductwork. Piers can raise the structure even higher if needed in coastal and other flood-prone areas.

Slab-on-grade.   *Slab-on-grade* construction involves pouring a concrete slab directly on the ground. The slab is reinforced with steel *mesh,* and the ground is covered with a plastic, waterproof *vapor barrier.* If the footers are poured with the slab, it is a *monolithic slab.* A monolithic slab is both a foundation and a first-floor slab. This type of construction is suitable for nearly flat lots only. If the footers and slab are poured separately, the slab is referred to as *floating.*

FRAMING

The most common type of residential construction is wood frame. The vertical framing members are called *studs,* which are either 2 × 4 inch or 2 × 6 inch lumber. The top and bottom horizontal members are called *plates.* Anchor bolts and metal straps are used to connect the studs to the top and bottom plates. Pressure-treated wood must be used for the bottom (sole) plate because it comes in contact with the concrete slab. *Pressure-treated* lumber is treated with chemicals to make it resistant to wood rot and termites. A vapor barrier is attached to the exterior face of the studs, and sheathing is then installed. Various types of siding, stucco, or brick or stone veneer are applied to finish the exterior.

There are three methods of wood-frame construction: platform, balloon, and post-and-beam. Platform framing is the most common construction method today. However, balloon framing is common in older homes. Post-and-beam construction is popular in contemporary architecture.

Platform.   Each floor is built separately, with the first floor providing a work platform for the structure above. This method of construction is safer for the framers because a flat surface is provided on which to work. The subfloor extends to the outside edges of the structure and provides a platform on which exterior walls are erected. Typically, the wall framing is assembled on the concrete slab and then hoisted into place and anchored. If the house has more than one story, additional layers of floor platforms and walls are stacked on top of the first floor walls. The structure is completed with ceiling and roof framing. (See Figure 16.2.)

FIGURE 16.2   Framing

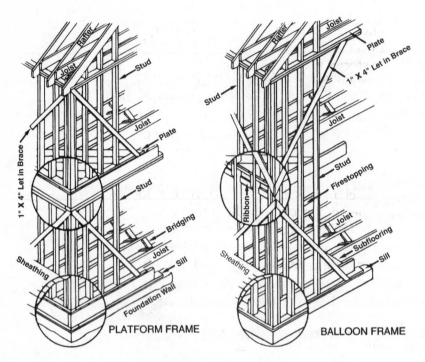

PLATFORM FRAME

BALLOON FRAME

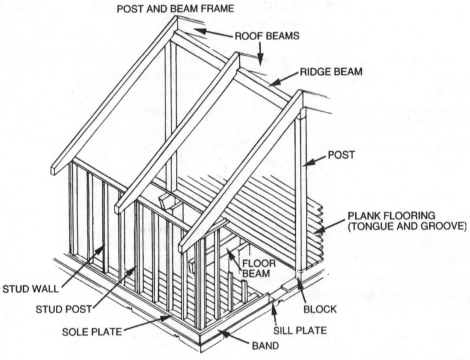

POST AND BEAM FRAME

1 **Balloon.**   Balloon construction was common until the 1930s, but it is still
2 used today for some two-story construction, especially if the structure has
3 a masonry exterior. With balloon frame construction the studs extend
4 continuously to the ceiling of the second floor, providing a smooth
5 unbroken wall surface at each floor level. For example, in two-story
6 construction, the load-bearing wall studs extend in one piece from the
7 foundation to the top plate two stories above. The continuous
8 construction reduces uneven settling that can cause cracking of brick,
9 stucco, and stone veneer finishes. Balloon framing is a more expensive
10 type of construction compared with platform construction because of
11 the cost of quality 18-foot to 20-foot studs and higher labor costs.
12 (See Figure 16.2.)

13 **Post-and-beam.**   Sturdy posts support beams that are spaced up to
14 8 feet apart and covered with 2-inch planks that serve to form the floor,
15 ceiling, and roof deck. Because the posts provide some of the ceiling
16 support, rooms can be constructed with larger spans between the
17 supporting side walls. This type of framing is popular in contemporary
18 architecture where exposed beam ceilings are desired. (See Figure 16.2.)

19 ## ROOF STRUCTURES

20 Most roof structures today use preengineered, factory-built *trusses.*
21 Trusses are lifted into place with a crane and then secured to the walls
22 with metal fasteners. Trusses are constructed with triangular-shaped
23 internal structural members that transfer the stress load of the roof away
24 from the center of the span outward to the load-bearing walls.

25   The *pitch* of a roof is its slope. All roofs have some pitch. Even
26 so-called flat roofs have a small indiscernible pitch to provide for water
27 runoff. A roof's pitch is measured as the vertical distance or height in
28 inches (referred to as the *rise*) divided by the horizontal distance in feet
29 (referred to as the *span* or *run*). A roof that rises four inches in height
30 over a one-foot horizontal distance has a pitch of 4/12. Homes are
31 characterized by the style and pitch of the roof. Roof styles include gable,
32 hip, saltbox, shed, flat, gambrel, and mansard. (See Figure 16.3.)

33 **Gable.**   **Gable** roofs are cost effective because they use a single truss
34 design. Gable roofs peak at the center ridge and extend downward on two
35 opposite sides. Gable roofs do not provide protection from the sun on the
36 two gable ends. Sometimes dormers are incorporated into gable and hip
37 (see Figure 16.3) roofs. A **dormer** is a projection that extends out of the roof
38 to provide additional light and ventilation.

39 **Hip.**   **Hip** roofs peak at the center ridge but extend downward on four
40 opposite sides. Hip roofs provide overhang protection on all four sides of
41 the structure and are architecturally pleasing. Trusses for a hip roof are
42 more expensive to manufacture because of the special engineering
43 required.

44 **Saltbox.**   Saltbox roofs are characterized by what appears to be a gable
45 roof that then slopes steeply on one side. It gets its name from the old
46 Morton saltbox of the early 1900s.

FIGURE 16.3   Roof Designs

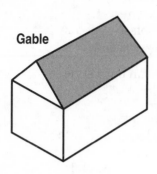

Gable

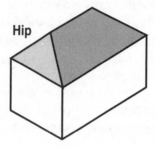

Hip

Gable with Dormers
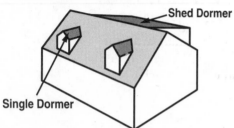
Shed Dormer
Single Dormer

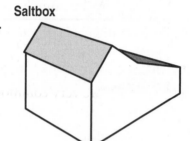

Saltbox

Flat
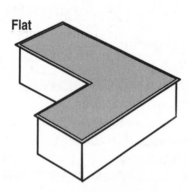

Shed
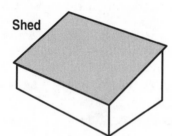

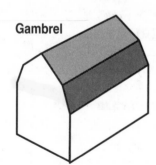

Gambrel

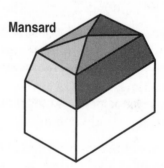

Mansard

Shed.   Shed roofs consist of a single steep plane. They are often used in contemporary architecture.

Flat.   Flat roofs are commonly referred to as *built-up* roofs because of the way they are constructed in layers of tar and gravel. Flat roofs are used in contemporary residential structures as well as commercial structures.

Gambrel.   Gambrel roofs are characterized by the American barn style of roof. They provide ample headroom in two-story construction.

Mansard.   This style of roof is named after a French architect who is credited with first using the style in Paris, France. Paris had a zoning code that prevented multistory structures because structures were being built higher than the fire equipment could reach. The zoning code defined the number of stories of a structure by the number of feet from ground level to where the roofing material began. Mansard cleverly brought the shingles down the walls of the top floor, thereby increasing the number of buildable stories without violating the zoning code. The mansard roof became very common in France and is used in French-style architecture in the United States. Mansard roofs are very common in the French Quarter district of New Orleans, for example.

ELECTRICAL SYSTEM

Electrical power is produced by large power plants. From these plants electricity enters large "step-up" transformers that increase voltage to half a million volts or more. Electricity flows easily at high voltages through transmission lines to communities miles away. "Step-down" transformers located at substations reduce the voltage for distribution along street lines. Smaller transformers placed atop utility poles or on concrete pads at ground level further reduce the voltage to 120-volt current for household use.

Years ago, voltage entering houses was rated at 110 and 220 volts. Today it has been increased to 120 and 240 volts. Lines carrying current to the house enter through wires strung overhead and attached to a post called a *weather head* or through an underground conduit. In new construction, even in those subdivisions that are serviced by overhead power lines, the electric service lines from the transformer to the house run underground. In older homes, electric service lines may go from a transformer attached to a power pole to the weather head. The energy is directed through a meter and then to the service panel inside the house.

Because electricity travels in a *circuit* (or a closed loop), there must be at least two wires entering the house; one hot wire (power is always present) and one neutral wire (the return path). Older homes with only two wires can deliver only 120-volt current. Most homes built after 1950 have three wires running to the weather head; two lines each carrying 120 volts of current and a third grounded neutral wire. One hot wire and the neutral wire provide 120 volts for circuits suitable for lights and wall outlets. Both hot wires and the neutral wire provide 240 volts for large appliances such as air conditioners, electric ranges, and electric clothes dryers.

FIGURE 16.4   Electric Service Entrance

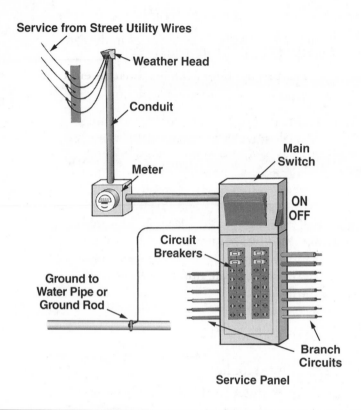

Service from Street Utility Wires

Weather Head

Conduit

Main Switch

Meter

ON
OFF

Circuit Breakers

Ground to Water Pipe or Ground Rod

Branch Circuits

Service Panel

1   The utility company connects the incoming wires to a weatherproof
2   box that holds the meter. The *meter* measures how much electricity the
3   home uses. The wires are then fed to the *service panel*. The two hot wires
4   are connected to the main circuit breaker, and the neutral wire is
5   grounded to a cold water pipe or grounding rod. The electricity is then
6   divided into branch circuits. The *branch circuits* supply power to the
7   different rooms in the house. Each circuit is protected by its own circuit
8   breaker. (See Figure 16.4.) **Circuit breakers** are used to protect an electric
9   circuit from damage caused by too much current. A breaker will *trip* (shut
10 off) if the circuit is forced to carry more current than the wire can handle.
11 Inside the breaker is a tripping mechanism that will not allow the breaker
12 to be reset until the wire has cooled. The circuit breaker, once tripped,
13 must be reset by hand. In areas of the house where there is a greater
14 danger of electrical shock (in kitchens and bathrooms), *ground-fault-*
15 *interrupters* (GFIs) are required.

16 Electricity is distributed in a three-wire system; the hot, neutral, and
17 ground wires. The hot wire carries the current to the switches, the neutral
18 wire carries the current away (completes the loop), and the ground wire
19 routes the excess electricity to the ground. The size of the wire used in
20 a circuit is based on how much current it will carry. According to the
21 American Wire Gauge (AWG) rating system, the smaller the number, the
22 larger the wire. The larger the load, the larger the wire needed. For
23 example, wire supplying power to wall switches may require #12-gauge

wire, whereas wire used to supply a clothes dryer may use #8-gauge or #6-gauge wire. Nonmetallic sheathed cable used in residential wiring is identified by the number of wires in the cable. For example, a cable stamped with the words *12/2 with ground* indicates that the cable contains two #12-gauge wires and a ground wire. The individual wires in the cable are color coded. The hot wire is normally black. If the cable has two hot wires, one is black and the other is typically red. The neutral wire is either white or gray. The ground wire can be green, but is usually a noninsulated bare copper wire. The black wire delivers power to the electrical switch and the white is the return path to complete the circuit.

Electric current moving along a wire is measured in units called *amperes,* or *amps.* Amperage describes the amount of electricity or current flowing in a particular circuit. The force that moves the current is measured in *volts.* Voltage represents the "force" in the circuit, which can be compared to water pressure; it is a measure of electricity in terms of pressure. The work performed by the voltage and current is measured in *watts.* Wattage indicates how much energy a device consumes. The electric company charges its customers according to the number of kilowatt-hours (kWh) used. A *kilowatt* is equivalent to 1,000 watts.

You can calculate the wattage or power available in a circuit by first determining the amp rating, which is indicated on the circuit breaker for the particular circuit. Most room circuits have 15-amp or 20-amp service, and 30-amp or 50-amp service is needed for heavy-duty circuits. Voltage times amperes equals watts. In the case of a device designed to operate on 120 volts and a 15-amp circuit, 120 volts × 15 amps = 1,800 watts.

PLUMBING SYSTEM

Residential plumbing systems are composed of two basic systems. The *high-pressure system* delivers *potable* water (suitable for drinking) to the various parts of a home, and the *low-pressure system* carries wastewater away from the home. Potable water typically enters the house through the water meter on the street side of the house. The potable water is delivered under pressure. Forty pounds of pressure per square inch is typical in many localities and is higher in some large cities. The *supply pipe* has a main shutoff valve near the meter. Opening and closing the *main shutoff valve* controls the water supply to the entire home. The supply pipe carries water to the house from the municipal supply and then branches out into pipes of smaller diameter to deliver water throughout the home. A *cold water main* carries water to the water heater and to all cold-water-using fixtures. *Hose bibs* (exterior water faucets) run from the cold water line to locations on the exterior of the house.

A *hot water main* starts at the water heater and runs parallel to the cold water main, providing hot water to all hot-water-using fixtures. The water heater is normally located in the garage area and has a pressure valve at the top of the tank that releases if the pressure inside the tank becomes too great, preventing a potential explosion. The hot and cold water mains are usually ¾-inch pipe and feed into smaller ½-inch pipes that supply the various fixtures throughout the home. Except for the shutoff valve, these pipes are buried in the ground or hidden in the walls or attic until they

FIGURE 16.5   Plumbing System

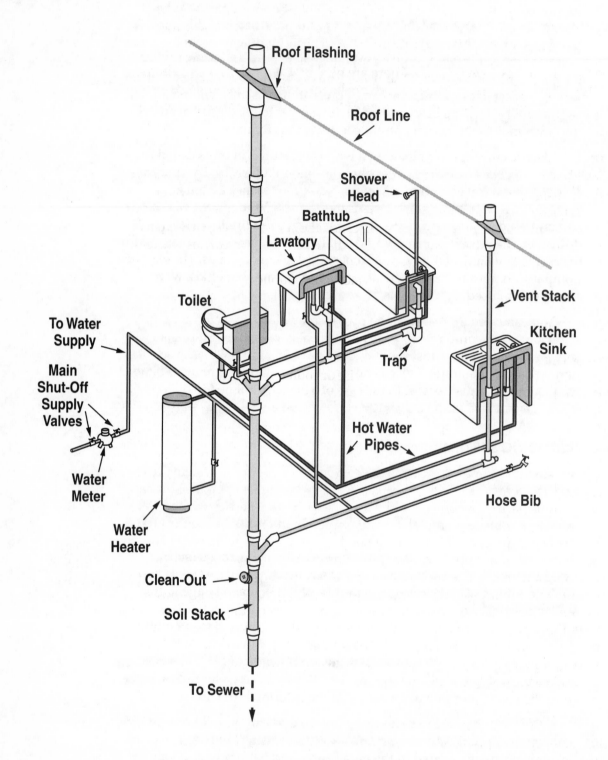

1   arrive at the various fixtures. There, a shutoff valve is normally installed
2   and the pipe diameter is reduced again. Hot water controls on all
3   plumbing fixtures are normally located on the
4   left-hand side.

5   Waste water, under normal atmospheric pressure, is drained off by
6   gravity to main sewer lines. There are two important components of the
7   low-pressure system. *Traps,* which are beneath sinks, tubs, and showers,
8   are U-shaped pipes that stay full of water. The water forms a seal in the
9   waste line and prevents odors and combustible gases from entering the
10 home. *Vent stacks* are pipes that protrude through the roof from the waste
11 lines. The vent stacks equalize the air pressure in the drain system and
12 prevent suction generated by flowing water from siphoning the water out
13 of the traps. Drain pipes slant slightly downward so that wastewater
14 flows by the force of gravity. Fixtures empty into slanting branch drains
15 that connect to a large vertical drain called the *main soil stack.* The *soil stack*
16 is a vertical 3-inch-diameter to 4-inch-diameter pipe that carries waste
17 away from toilets and other fixtures. The soil stack empties into a slanting
18 main drain that carries the waste water to the public sewer system. (See
19 Figure 16.5.)

20   There are two general types of water meter faces. The direct-read
21 meter has numerical readings and looks like an automobile odometer. The
22 other type is a cumulative-reading meter that typically has five or six
23 dials. The dials are numbered clockwise or counterclockwise and look like
24 single-hand clock faces. The six-dial meter is labeled 1, 10, 100, 1,000,
25 10,000, and 100,000 for the number of cubic feet of water they record per
26 revolution. Each dial turns the opposite direction from the one next to it.
27 Read the dials from left to right, recording the number each pointer has
28 just passed. When the pointer lies between two numbers, record the *lower*
29 number. To read a six-dial meter, begin with the 100,000 dial, noting the
30 smaller of the two numbers nearest the needle. Then read the dial labeled
31 10,000, and so on. Contact your local utility company for instructions
32 regarding how to read the type of meter in your local area.

33   You can keep track of water used for a particular purpose (such as
34 filling a swimming pool) by simply subtracting the "before" reading from
35 the "after" reading on the meter, assuming no other water usage is going
36 on at the same time. To help determine if a water stain is caused by a leak
37 in the plumbing (as opposed to a roof leak, for example), turn off all the
38 water outlets in the house and note the position of the one-cubic-foot dial
39 on the meter. After 30 minutes, check the dial. If the dial has moved, it
40 indicates a leak in the plumbing.

41 **MECHANICAL SYSTEMS**

42 Mechanical components include air cooling and heating systems. The
43 most common type of heat distribution system is a *ducted* system that
44 distributes warm air through ducts to each room of the house. There are
45 two sets of ducts. The *supply air ducts* carry the hot air from the furnace to
46 the distribution registers throughout the house. The return air intake
47 collects the cooled air through *return ducts* to a filter located in the
48 furnace, where it is reheated and recycled throughout the home. Older

1 homes may have a gravity system that distributes heat and returns air
2 throughout the system. Today, ducted systems are equipped with a
3 blower to force the flow of air throughout the home. Heating cycles are
4 rated by a Heating Seasonal Performance Factor (HSPF). The higher the
5 rating, the more energy-efficient the heater.

6   Air-conditioning systems are rated either in BTUs or in tons. Twelve
7 thousand BTUs are equivalent to a one-ton capacity. The efficiency of
8 electric air-conditioning systems is measured by a Seasonal Energy
9 Efficiency Ratio (SEER). National minimum standards for central air
10 conditioners require a SEER of 12. The higher the rating, the more energy-
11 efficient the equipment. Increasing the SEER from 12 to 14 means that you
12 are increasing the equipment's efficiency by about 20 percent.

13   A *heat pump* is equipped with a reversing valve that allows it to collect
14 heat from cold outside air or from well water. This reversing mechanism
15 allows a heat pump to heat the home in the winter and cool it in the
16 summer. Heat pumps are very efficient in Florida, where winter
17 temperatures are mild. In the event of a cold snap, electric heating coils are
18 activated when the outside temperature drops to about 25 degrees.

To learn more about energy efficient homes, visit the U.S. Department of
wwweb.link *Energy's Office of Energy Efficiency and Renewable Energy at:*
http://www.eere.energy.gov/.

19 ## INSULATION AND WINDOWS

20 The measure of the effectiveness of insulation is its resistance to heat
21 flow, or **R-value**. The higher the R-value, the better the energy efficiency.
22 Insulation materials include batt and blanket insulation (typically
23 fiberglass); loose fill (blown cellulose); foam insulation (polyurethane
24 and urea formaldehyde); and rigid board insulation. The U.S.
25 Department of Energy (DOE) has established minimum recommended
26 R-values specific to ZIP code areas.

27   Many existing homes have *single pane* or *single glazed* glass windows.
28 In an average building, windows cover about 20 percent of the total wall
29 area. As a result, in well-insulated structure, 20 percent to 50 percent of the
30 total energy loss typically occurs through and around the windows.
31 *Thermal pane* or *storm windows* are an energy-efficient alternative to single
32 pane windows.

33   Thermal pane windows consist of two panes of glass in one frame
34 with an air space in between. Thermal pane windows provide better
35 insulation than regular glass and will help to keep your home warmer in
36 the winter and cooler in the summer. Thermal windows reduce heating
37 and cooling costs. It's the layer of air between the glass that acts as the
38 insulation.

39   The width of the space between the panes is important because air
40 spaces that are too wide or too narrow generally permit too much heat to
41 be transferred. The best R-values are achieved when the spacing is
42 between about ½ inch and ⅝ inch.

FIGURE 16.6   Window Types

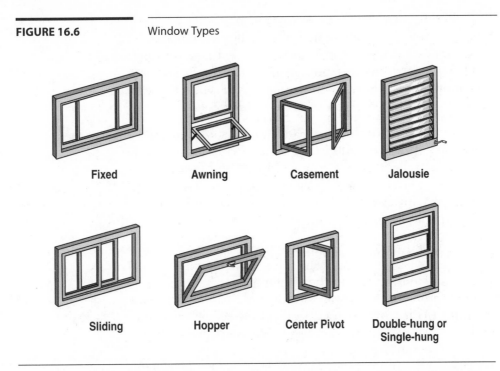

Fixed   Awning   Casement   Jalousie

Sliding   Hopper   Center Pivot   Double-hung or
Single-hung

1   Although air is a good insulator, other gases work even better in
2   preventing heat to move from one pane to the next. Today, most thermal
3   window manufactures use argon gas, which is very stable, and thus has a
4   low reaction rate to changing temperature. However, the windows need
5   to be properly sealed so that the argon can't escape. If the seal becomes
6   defective, the window can cloud up. This is a result of water vapor's
7   building up and condensing when the weather turns colder. Today, a
8   special moisture-absorbing material is used to catch any water vapor
9   trying to sneak through the window seal.

10   Window styles include the following: fixed, awning, casement,
11   jalousie, sliding, hopper, center pivot, and double or single-hung.
12   (See Figure 16.5.)

13   **Fixed.**   Fixed pane windows are also called *picture* windows. They do not
14   open, which means they do not permit ventilation or easy cleaning. Fixed
15   pane windows have sealed edges to protect against air filtration. Fixed
16   pane windows come in almost any size or shape and with various degrees
17   of glazing. In Florida, double-glazing or triple-glazing should be
18   considered for fixed pane windows, especially if they are large.

19   **Awning.**   Awning windows typically are fixed at the top and tilt out with
20   the aid of a crank to provide ventilation but have a limited open space.
21   Because they are easy to clean and provide more security than other types
22   of window, they are common in schools and in multifamily housing.

23   **Casement.**   Casement windows consist of one or more sashes hinged at
24   the side like a door, swinging horizontally out or in, usually with the aid
25   of a crank. Older casements swing on hinges while newer ones have pivot
26   mechanisms. Most swing outward, but models that swing inward are
27   available.

Casements provide excellent ventilation because both halves of the window open. Because they seal tightly when closed, they are considered energy efficient. Another advantage of casements is they are easier to clean than most other windows because both inside and outside surfaces are accessible from indoors. However, for safety reasons, it is best to locate a casement window away from traffic areas such as sidewalks.

Jalousie. Jalousie (or louver) windows are common in south Florida because they allow maximum ventilation. Glass louvers that overlap one another form the panes of a jalousie window. Operated with a crank or turn-screw, the glass louvers tilt to open, permitting airflow. A major disadvantage of jalousie windows is that they are almost impossible to seal. When closed, each glass louver rests against the one below it, rarely if ever making an airtight seal, and the hinges along the sides are almost impossible to seal without covering the entire window. They are not energy efficient and may be a security risk.

Sliding. Horizontal sliding windows move back and forth on tracks. Usually only one of the sashes moves and the other is fixed. Because only half of the window area can be opened, sliding windows provide less ventilation area than casement windows. An advantage is they are inexpensive, especially if the frame is aluminum, and easy to clean if the moveable sash is removed.

Hopper. A hopper window is hinged at the bottom and opens into the room. A major disadvantage is that it does open into the room and thus interferes with window coverings.

Center pivot. This window pivots from a point at the center of the frame. It can be hazardous if located in an area where people walk, such as near a sidewalk.

Double-hung. Double-hung windows are probably the most common type of window. They open by sliding the bottom half of the window up or sliding the top half down. Because only half of the window area can be open at one time, they provide less ventilation than casement style windows. An advantage of double-hung windows is they can be used to create air movement in the home by opening the top portion of the windows on the coolest side of the house. Air will naturally rise out of the higher opening, pulling cooler air in the lower opening.

Older double-hung windows have weight-and-pulley systems to make them easier to open. However, the weight-and-pulley system tends to stick or rattle and it is hard to stop air from leaking around the pulley openings. Newer models have spring-tension devices that work more efficiently.

Single-hung. Single hung windows are similar to the double-hung window, but only the lower sash is movable.

An informative fact sheet about insulation is available on the Internet from the Department of Energy at:
http://www.ornl.gov/sci/roofs+walls/insulation/ins_01.html.

wwweb.link   *To view the Department of Energy's recommended R-values for existing homes by region, go to:* **http://www.eere.energy.gov/consumerinfo/ energy_savers/r-value_map.html.**

■ SUMMARY

The two basic styles of residential foundations used in Florida are pier and slab-on-grade foundations. Pier foundations are used in coastal and flood-prone areas. Slab-on-grade foundations may be monolithic slabs or floating slabs. Frame construction comprises platform, balloon, and post-and-beam construction. Platform is the most common of the three types of frame construction. A prominent feature of a residential structure is the roof, which may be of gable, hip, saltbox, shed, flat, gambrel, or mansard design. Window types include fixed, double-hung or single-hung, awning, center pivot, sliding, casement, hopper, and jalousie windows.

■ REVIEW QUESTIONS

1. A type of foundation that is used in low-lying coastal areas is called
   A. slab-on-grade.
   B. floating foundation.
   C. pier foundation.
   D. monolithic slab foundation.

2. A type of frame construction that allows for large spans between supporting side walls is
   A. balloon frame.
   B. post-and-beam construction.
   C. platform construction.
   D. pier frame.

3. If you were to build a commercial structure and because of limited ground space wanted to install the mechanical equipment on the roof, which roof design would be most appropriate?
   A. Flat
   B. Gambrel
   C. Mansard
   D. Saltbox

4. In areas near water in kitchens and bathrooms, building codes require special electrical outlets referred to as
   A. circuit breakers.
   B. grounded outlets.
   C. ground-fault-interrupters.
   D. step-down outlets.

5. You want to replace a ceiling fan and have removed the old fixture. The wiring to the old fixture consists of three wires: a black wire, a white wire, and a green wire. Which wire is the ground wire?
   A. Black
   B. White
   C. Green
   D. There is no ground wire.

6. The pipe that carries water to the hot water heater is referred to as a
   A. hot water main.
   B. cold water main.
   C. soil stack.
   D. supply pipe.

7. The purpose of a U-shaped trap under a kitchen sink is to
   A. prevent food debris from traveling through the plumbing pipes.
   B. catch a small object such as a wedding ring before it enters the soil stack.
   C. equalize the air pressure in the drain system.
   D. prevent combustible gases from entering the home.

8. An electrical cable stamped with the words *6/2 with ground* is most appropriate for wiring to a
   A. ceiling fan.
   B. table lamp.
   C. window air conditioner.
   D. home fax machine.

9. You are interested in adding roof insulation to your home to reduce your monthly electrical bill. Which government agency establishes minimum recommended R-values specific to your local area?
   A. Department of Energy
   B. Department of Housing and Urban Development
   C. Fannie Mae
   D. Environmental Protection Agency

10. You are walking through a seller's contemporary-design home. There are windows set high into a loft area, that are not designed to be opened. They function simply to bring light into the loft. What window type does this describe?
    A. Jalousie
    B. Casement
    C. Fixed
    D. Hopper

11. Which type of lot provides an open view down the street but may also suffer from vehicular headlights shining into the windows?
    A. Flag
    B. Key
    C. T intersection
    D. Interior

12. Which type of lot is bounded by five or six other lots?
    A. Flag
    B. Key
    C. T intersection
    D. Interior

Cake!

CHAPTER 17

Real Estate Investment Analysis and Business Opportunity Brokerage

3? on Test.

■ KEY TERMS

appreciation	going concern value	liquidity
asset	goodwill	REIT
balance sheet	income statement	replacement cost
cash flow	investment	reproduction cost
dynamic risk	investment value	risk
equity	leverage	static risk

■ OVERVIEW

Investors consider different factors in their attempt to achieve various investment objectives according to their individual financial status, income tax bracket, motives for investing, and access to credit. Different types of real estate offer various abilities to meet investor objectives. Experience indicates that investors are motivated by one or a combination of objectives: (1) safety of principal, (2) protection against inflation, (3) liquidity, (4) increased income (current and/or future), and (5) tax advantages.

This Chapter compares business brokerage with real estate brokerage. It emphasizes the importance of special knowledge when practicing business brokerage. This Chapter also defines basic accounting terms, and discusses the methods of appraising businesses.

After completing this Chapter, the student should be able to:

- identify the advantages and disadvantages of investing in real estate;

- distinguish among the various types of risk;

- explain the concepts of liquidity and leverage;

- describe the similarities and differences between real estate brokerage and business brokerage;

- describe the types of expertise required in business brokerage;

- distinguish among the methods of appraising businesses; and

- describe the steps in the sale of a business.

■ NEED FOR REAL ESTATE INVESTMENT ANALYSIS

A knowledge of real estate investment analysis is important to a licensee in Florida because a real estate licensee is allowed to sell investment property. The public regards a real estate broker or sales associate as an expert in all types of properties. While the rewards of negotiating the purchase or sale of investment property are often greater than they are for other types of real estate, so are the liabilities for untrained or unknowledgeable people. Cases have gone to court because real estate licensees either gave bad advice or did not properly analyze an investment before recommending a course of action that could have been avoided by a knowledgeable professional.

Potential investors go to real estate professionals for help and guidance. Licensees must be qualified to provide the needed expertise when they accept the trust and confidence of a client. At the beginning of this book, the point was made that real estate licensees have one major commodity to offer the public—expertise. But part of being a professional also includes knowing when to consult a specialist (e.g., an attorney or an accountant) and when to have one's seller or buyer consult a specialist. The purpose of this Chapter, therefore, is familiarization, a first step toward developing expertise in real estate investment matters.

NATURE OF REAL ESTATE INVESTMENT ANALYSIS

An **investment** is the outlay of an investor's money in anticipation of income or profit. An investor uses some of his or her own money called **equity** and borrowed funds. *Real estate investment analysis* is the process of determining the extent to which real estate investments will achieve an investor's objectives.

■ REAL ESTATE AS AN INVESTMENT

Investors may choose to invest in real estate through a limited partnership. Another alternative is to invest in real estate through a *real estate investment trust* (REIT). A **REIT** offers investors the opportunity to invest in income-producing real estate properties. Individual REITs generally specialize in a particular type of property, such as multifamily communities, retail malls and shopping centers, office properties, and so forth. They provide a means for individuals to pool resources for investment in a professionally managed portfolio of real property and/or mortgages secured by real property. REITs are attractive because they offer diversification and liquidity, they are similar to mutual funds, and they offer the advantages of skilled centralized management and continuity of operation. REITs may be purchased through a stockbroker.

TYPES OF REAL ESTATE INVESTMENTS

Investors interested in real estate can choose from several general types: residential, commercial, industrial, agricultural, and business opportunities.

Residential.   Investments in residential properties include single-family homes, condominiums, apartments, and other multifamily complexes. Most experts agree that investing in an apartment project (or other income-producing property) is economically feasible when the projected future net income over a predetermined period will permit return of the investment (recover invested capital) and allow the investor an appropriate rate of return over the investment period.

In assessing the desirability of an apartment complex, several criteria should be considered, including the following: location, effective gross income, operating expenses, and property taxes. Existing properties should be inspected carefully, and repair and maintenance records should be studied to ensure that the property has been well maintained. A lack of proper maintenance is referred to as *deferred maintenance.*

Commercial.   This category includes retail and office properties. Retail properties include downtown commercial properties, shopping centers, and regional malls. A shopping center's economic characteristics depend on the nature of existing leases and on operating expenses. An investor should study all leases carefully to find out how much of the original term remains, whether investors participate in tenant income from sales, and whether the leases provide for appropriate costs to be shifted to tenants. Long-term leases and a tendency on the part of tenants to renew their leases are among the main attractions of investing in office properties.

Industrial.   Industrial uses of real estate in urban areas generally involve manufacturing, assembly, and/or distribution. To be suitable for industrial use, a site should be located near transportation facilities such as railroad stations, expressways, and airports because of the need to receive and ship by rail, truck, and air.

Agricultural.   Agricultural properties are often purchased by farsighted investors-developers looking for large tracts of land that lie in the path of foreseeable urban growth. However, the holding period to realize such development potential may be many years.

Business opportunities.   One of the categories that Chapter 475, F.S., defines as real estate is "any interest in business enterprises or business opportunities." This category includes the sale or lease of a business and goodwill of an existing business, including business assets such as the stock of a corporation.

ADVANTAGES OF REAL ESTATE AS AN INVESTMENT

Real estate investments have the following advantages:

- *Good rate of return.* Historically, real estate has produced a high rate of return for the owner-investor, compared with other types of investments.

- *Tax advantages.* Although the Tax Reform Act of 1986 eliminated or seriously reduced some of the tax advantages, real estate investments still receive some tax benefits.

- *Hedge against inflation.* Historically, as measured by the Consumer Price Index (CPI), real estate values have increased (property **appreciation**) at a faster pace than inflation.

- *Leverage.* Real estate is typically highly leveraged. An investor can usually borrow 70 percent to 75 percent of the appraised value to finance a real estate investment. The goal of leveraging is to increase one's yield (return) on equity (investor's own capital) by using borrowed funds.

- *Equity buildup.* As a property appreciates in value and the mortgage debt is reduced, the investor's equity grows.

DISADVANTAGES OF INVESTING IN REAL ESTATE

Following are some of the disadvantages of investing in real estate:

- *Illiquidity.* The term **liquidity** refers to the ability to sell an investment very quickly without loss of one's capital. Real estate is *not* considered to be a liquid investment. Therefore, it is said to be illiquid. Recall that two of the critical assumptions associated with the definition of market value (Chapter 15) were that (1) neither the buyer nor the seller is under any compulsion to buy or sell and (2) the property is exposed on the market for a reasonable period of time.

- *Market is local in nature.* The real estate market is very local in nature. An investor usually is interested in a particular property type and geographic area. Other types of investments, such as stocks, are bought and sold in an international marketplace.

- *Need for expert help.* Many expenses are associated with investing in real estate, including the need for property managers, financial consultants, and legal experts.

- *Management.* Real estate is a labor-intensive investment. Properties must be cared for, rents collected, and so forth.

- *Risk.* An investor must weigh the chance of losing his or her invested capital. Tenant turnover, increasing property taxes, and increased costs associated with operations are a few examples of the types of risk to which a real estate investor is exposed.

■ ANALYZING INVESTMENT PROPERTIES

A number of factors (influences or forces) affect supply and demand, and thus the value, of investment real estate. Each of the various types of investment properties has a particular set of considerations that real estate licensees need to recognize. These value-creating influences affect a property, depending on its relationship to the economy, location, physical characteristics, and legal characteristics.

RELATIONSHIP TO THE ECONOMY

One of the external forces affecting a property is the economy or, more appropriately, the econom*ies*. Both the local and the national economies must be considered.

Local economy.   Local economic considerations include the existing stock of available units and new development of competing properties. Supply and demand factors are important considerations. An investor would be ill-advised to begin construction of a new apartment complex in a community already experiencing a surplus of new apartment units. The productivity of the property would be impaired to the extent that the investor could not hope to achieve maximum return on the investment.

National economy.   The national debt, employment levels, interest rates, availability of credit, and construction costs are some of the factors that influence the national economy and also the real estate market.

LOCATION

The importance of *location* is undisputed as it applies to real property. No two parcels of real property are exactly alike because location alone creates a difference. Each property is unique and in a fixed location. Investor preferences for location vary. The economic characteristic referred to as *situs* (the preference by people for a certain location) indicates the influences on value created by location. Because real property is fixed in its location, it is affected greatly by its immediate surroundings. A change in land use of surrounding properties, for example, can have a positive or a negative impact on a particular property.

Destination properties.   Because the land is immobile, investors must find ways to direct an income stream to the property. Destination properties include *service industries* that support the needs of a local community, such as local repair shops, barbershops, local real estate agencies, and financial institutions.

Origin properties.   *Origin properties* are just as immobile and fixed as destination properties, but often they are not as attractive or as well situated on access routes. As a result, they must originate something (a product) to seek out an income stream. Assembly plants, manufacturing facilities, and distribution centers represent origin properties. These properties are regarded as *export activities* in any analysis of a community's economic base.

PHYSICAL CHARACTERISTICS

If one site and building's size, shape, and form were the same as all others, an investor could make investment decisions based on location alone. Seldom, if ever, are two properties found with identical physical characteristics.

Site.   In evaluating properties, investors are faced with the same problems as appraisers are. One of the more common ways of neutralizing variables of a site is through the use of *units of comparison.* Usually, both appraisers and investors use square feet, front feet, or acres as units of comparison. These methods of comparing sites are practical because they permit direct comparison of competing sites, regardless of differences in size or shape. For residential properties, the square-foot method is usually used. For commercial properties, either the front-foot or the square-foot unit of comparison may be used. For farms or large tracts of undeveloped land, the acre normally is used.

Other physical characteristics of a site that deserve an investor's consideration are related to topography. A site's surface, subsoil structure, drainage, orientation and view, and exposure to or protection from possible noxious environmental influences are all elements for consideration in a thorough site analysis.

Building.   Potential real estate investors will normally have at least one alternative to buying an existing property: They could buy a vacant site and construct a new building. Even when this course of action is not a serious consideration, the cost of this alternative approach tends to set the maximum price they will pay for an existing property. If the existing building has deficiencies, the value of these deficiencies subtracted from the cost of a new building indicates a reasonable market value for the building. Notice the use of the term *market value*, rather than the term *investment value*. Investment value is *not* market value. **Investment value** is the worth of a building or property to an individual investor based on that investor's individual standards for achieving a goal. It is not established by market activity, although that may be a major influence. The value of investment property should be based on the return and appreciation it will yield, not only on the cost to build. The following are three considerations that influence a building's investment value:

1. *Exterior considerations.* The first impression a building makes on both tenants and customers is its exterior and its environment. The visual image (*curb appeal*) is of great importance: building age and design, landscaping, walkways, and parking areas. Is it well maintained? What is lacking? What needs repairing? Is each repair major or minor? Is each deterioration *curable* (correction adds value) or *incurable* (correction costs more than the value added)?

2. *Interior considerations.* Investors need to make a deliberate and thorough inspection of the premises and make a record as the inspection progresses. All of the following should be noted: the number and condition of each individual office or apartment (the size, layout, number of rooms and baths, and the views from each location); the overall physical quality of the building from the inside; the condition of the plumbing, hardware, carpeting, walls, appliances, and electrical fixtures; and the condition of halls, foyers, entrances, laundry rooms, storage rooms, and recreation facilities.

3. *Building operating expenses.* While the cost of property taxes and insurance are beyond the control of investors, these costs should be verified. All other operating expenses should be examined carefully before investing. Have previous owners allocated annual amounts to a reserve for replacement of short-lived items (e.g., appliances, carpets, drapes)? Do recorded expenditures for repairs and maintenance reflect the approximate condition of the building? Will the investor be required to spend more in the future for maintenance and repairs?

In many instances, the exterior and interior features of a building at first may satisfy a potential investor. Analysis of operating expenses, however, may eliminate the property from further consideration because of unusual expenses attributable to building location, orientation, or design. For example, there may be an abnormally high expenditure for electricity owing to faulty design or an exceptionally high expense for cooling and heating because of glass walls or inadequate insulation.

LEGAL CHARACTERISTICS

Investors in real estate are investing in more than land, buildings, and equipment. They are investing in a bundle of legal rights and protected interests. The value of their investment is influenced by the degree to which these rights and ownership interests are present.

Rights.   Before investing, investors must determine what type of legal entity will be best to accomplish their investment objectives. A variety of legal ownership forms are available, and each has its own legal and tax consequences. The most commonly used forms of investment ownership are sole proprietorships, tenancies in common, joint tenancies, limited partnerships, corporations, business trusts, and REITs.

Whether a property is expected to show a tax loss or profit frequently determines the type of ownership form to use. The desirability of having the survivorship feature of joint tenancy sometimes determines whether to use tenancy in common. Both a limited partnership and a corporation provide liability protection. While the corporate form is more complex, the ability to raise capital by selling stock might influence investors to use the corporate form. Each of the forms of ownership offers advantages and disadvantages. Investors should seek professional advice in determining the greatest net advantage.

Limitations.   Many authorities believe that a type of risk termed *legal risk* is associated with real estate investments: Risk is inherent in acquiring title to real property. Warranty deeds and title insurance serve to minimize such risk but do not entirely eliminate it. Additionally, litigation against real property owners because of alleged noncompliance with ordinances, tenant suits, or liability for accidents occurring on the property is a potential problem that is part of the legal risk.

An important consideration for all investors should be to determine if the use of a site represents its highest and best use. In most situations, the legal use of land is prescribed by zoning ordinances and represents the highest use of a site. It is up to the potential investor to decide which of the alternative types of available improvements and uses might represent the best use, in accordance with the concept of highest and best use. Fortunately, procedures have been developed by appraisers to assist in making such decisions. (See Chapter 15.)

■ ASSESSMENT OF RISKS

Risk is the chance of losing all or part of an investment. Some degree of risk is always associated with an investment. **Static risk** is risk that can be transferred to an insurer such as the risk of vandalism, fire, and so forth. **Dynamic risk** is risk that arises from the continual change in the business environment and therefore dynamic risk cannot be transferred to an insurer.

RISKS ASSOCIATED WITH GENERAL BUSINESS CONDITIONS

Business risk.   Sometimes referred to as *operating business risk,* this category of risk is associated with the degree of variance between budgeted (projected) income and expenses and actual income and expenses.

Financial risk.   Sometimes referred to as *operating financial risk,* this category of risk is associated with the ability of a property to pay operating expenses from funds provided from operations, borrowing, and equity sources.

Purchasing-power risk.   This category of risk is related to inflation. In an inflationary period, the ability of a property to produce a good yield may be offset by a corresponding loss of purchasing power due to inflation. After paying all expenses, including income taxes, a loss may result from what first appeared to be a profitable investment. The reason is that the income tax is based on total taxable income, not on net gain adjusted for inflation.

Interest-rate risk.   Remember the IRV formula in Chapter 15? To find the value of a property using this formula, the net operating income (NOI) is divided by the rate of capitalization (required rate of return). While debt service (financing cost) is not deducted from gross income to arrive at net income, an investor nevertheless has to pay that debt service, which effectively reduces the real yield.

Assume, for the moment, that the only change in a real estate investment is that the interest rate is raised by the lender. The property remains unchanged, the owners remain the same, management does not change. However, with the increase in interest rates, the value of the property as an investment goes down. That is interest-rate risk at work.

RISKS THAT AFFECT RETURN

Historically, businesses and individuals have put money in investments that offer the highest return commensurate with the liquidity and safety of the money.

1 **Liquidity risk.**   Real estate investments are particularly susceptible to
2 liquidity risk (illiquidity). *Liquidity risk* is the possible loss that may be
3 incurred if the investment has to be converted quickly into cash. There is
4 no highly organized market for real estate investments, and their resale
5 usually requires time and considerable expense.

6 **Safety risk.**   *Safety risk* is the possible loss of invested capital (return of
7 investment) and/or expected earnings (return on investment). Safety risk
8 is composed of market risk (possible loss of invested capital) and risk of
9 default (possible loss of earnings).

10 • *Market risk* is the type of risk associated with a decrease in the
11 market value of an investment as a result of increased interest rates
12 (the interest-rate risk at work). Often, market risk is magnified by
13 long periods of time. Leaving the money invested exposed to the
14 cyclical gyrations of the money markets over extended periods
15 increases the risk of loss. For example, savings associations can
16 lose money by holding long-term investments in low-yielding
17 mortgages.

18 • *Risk of default* is the risk that promised earnings will be lost by the
19 investor because of the failure of the investment to earn as expected.

20 If everything were equal, an investor would prefer a liquid, short-term
21 investment because less risk would be involved. However, the possibility
22 of a higher yield will induce some investors to commit funds to a less-
23 liquid, long-term investment. It is a basic economic premise that risk and
24 the desired rate of return are directly related (e.g., high risk, high return).

25 ## ■ LEVERAGE

26 **Leverage** is the use of borrowed funds to finance the purchase of an
27 asset. Leverage is the use of other people's money to make more money.
28 Most investors use leverage to increase their purchasing power. For
29 example, an investor purchases a property for $1 million and 10 percent
30 down. The investor has increased purchasing power by using borrowed
31 funds to purchase a property costing ten times his or her cash
32 investment.

O.P.M.

33 An investor's goal is not only to increase purchasing power but also
34 to earn a higher return on equity. The investor wants an investment
35 property that can produce cash flow in excess of the cost of borrowing the
36 funds. If the benefits from borrowing exceed the costs of borrowing, it is
37 called *positive leverage.* If the borrowed funds cost more than they are
38 producing, it is called *negative leverage.*

39 To understand the impact of leveraging, consider a property that costs
40 $100,000 and produces net income of $10,000 per year. If purchased for
41 cash, the investor's annual rate of return on the equity invested is
42 10 percent ($10,000 income ÷ $100,000 equity). Assume instead that this
43 investor leverages the purchase by borrowing $75,000 at 8 percent ($6,000
44 interest) annually and makes a down payment of $25,000. The $10,000
45 income earned from the investment in the previous example is reduced by

WRAPAROUND.

the cost of financing to $4,000. The resulting *return on equity* invested is an attractive 16 percent ($4,000 income taking into account financing cost ÷ $25,000 equity = .16 or 16% rate of return on equity). This is positive leverage at work!

The higher the interest rate and the higher the loan-to-value ratio, the more cash flow from operations required to pay the principal and interest payments. If cash flow is reduced by increasing vacancy rates or an overzealous earnings forecast, the risk is greater because the larger the loan amount, the greater the chances that the investor will either have to invest more out-of-pocket funds or default on the mortgage. This increased risk is the price an investor pays for the higher potential benefits of leverage.

◼ BUSINESS BROKERAGE

Nearly 25 percent of the 14 million businesses in this country change hands each year! Business brokers and business entities engaged in the sale, purchase, or lease of businesses must qualify and hold real estate licenses. Business brokerages may be classified into business enterprise brokerages and business opportunity brokerages.

Business enterprise brokers normally deal in corporate transactions involving the sale and purchase of businesses that provide goods and/or services. Ordinarily, business enterprises are large transactions usually involving the purchase or exchange of corporate stock and the purchase of corporate assets (an **asset** is anything of value).

Business opportunity brokers typically deal in the sale and purchase of smaller businesses, such as sole proprietorships. These businesses have limited amounts of fixed assets (e.g., real property, equipment). Sometimes the real estate owned by the business is the primary component of value. Other times the real estate involved is in the form of a lease that will be assigned to the new owner.

SIMILARITIES TO REAL ESTATE BROKERAGE

A real estate relationship is established every time the sale of real property or the assignment of a lease is an integral part of a business brokerage transaction. The transfer of some interest in real property is often involved in business brokerage activities.

475.01, F.S.

DIFFERENCES FROM REAL ESTATE BROKERAGE

Business brokerage differs from real estate brokerage in at least five ways. (See Figure 17.1.)

1. Business brokerage usually involves assets other than real estate, such as *personal property* and *goodwill*. **Goodwill is** the intangible asset attributed to a business's reputation and the expectation of continued customer loyalty. The value of goodwill may be approximated by subtracting the value of tangible assets from the

FIGURE 17.1   Brokerage Comparisons

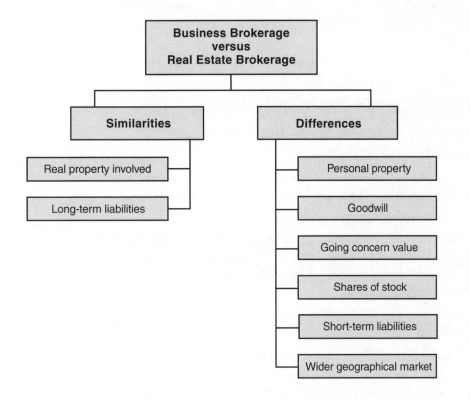

1   value of the business. Other intangible assets that add value
2   include licenses, franchises, copyrights, and patents.

3   2. The value of an established business may differ from the value of
4   the real estate. This means that the total value, called the *going*
5   *concern value,* may be different from the real estate value. **Going**
6   **concern value** is the value of an established business property
7   compared with the value of just the physical assets of a business
8   that is not yet established.

9   3. Unlike real estate, the value of a business may be allocated among
10   shares of corporate *stock,* which may be either traded publicly or
11   privately held.

12   4. Business brokerage transactions frequently involve the assumption
13   by the purchaser of short-term liabilities as well as long-term
14   liabilities such as a mortgage. Examples of short-term liabilities
15   include accounts payable and sales taxes collected by the seller but
16   not remitted to the state.

17   5. As noted in Chapter 19, the real estate market is local in nature. On
18   the other hand, the business brokerage market is much wider in
19   geographic scope, perhaps nationwide or even international.

■ EXPERTISE REQUIRED IN BUSINESS BROKERAGE

Business brokerage brings the broker or sales associate into contact with many problems not normally encountered in real estate brokerage. For example:

- What is the value of a business opportunity that consists solely of an intangible interest in a going concern?

- What is the impact on existing clientele if the business is sold?

- What of a purchaser's concern that the seller might go into competition with the purchaser?

- If the business is to be acquired by another corporation, would the seller be well advised to take stock in the other corporation?

These few questions illustrate that licensees need expertise in areas other than real estate for business brokerage. Some of the more important areas in which business brokers should be knowledgeable are corporate finance, business accounting, valuation of businesses, and the applicable laws that govern business dealings.

CORPORATE FINANCE

Business brokers know that efficient financial management is as important to profitability as good production know-how. This fact dictates that business brokers have a working knowledge of the following:

- *The classes and characteristics of corporate stock.* There are two basic types of stock: *preferred* and *common*. Some firms do not issue preferred stock, but all corporations must have common stock because it represents ownership.

- *Securities analysis and valuation.* Just as real estate brokers advise their principals, business brokers must be capable of providing advice and assistance to their principals, especially in areas of securities analysis and valuation. New owners often feel a need to raise additional funds or to refinance the capital structure. Then the question of selecting the proper type of security, or securities, must be decided. Among the factors involved in selecting sources of funds are market conditions, debt or equity funds, tax impact, voting control, stability of profits, and rate of earnings.

- *The management of working capital. Working capital* is defined as the difference between total current assets and total current liabilities. Management of this working capital is of paramount importance to the success of a business. Efficiency is lost if funds kept on hand are in excess of foreseeable needs. Conversely, it is dangerous not to have adequate funds for payment of outstanding bills, wages, and salaries. Keeping excessive inventory on hand is unnecessarily expensive, yet an inadequate inventory can cause lost sales or production time. Business brokers engaged to buy or sell a business need to be knowledgeable about how a firm's working capital is being managed.

- *Budgeting.* The generic term *budgeting* refers to an estimate of anticipated income and expenditures over a definite future period. Budget information can be used for planning and also to control borrowing, spending, and purchasing. If all aspects of a business are budgeted properly, an estimated income statement can be prepared showing not only estimated income and expenses but also estimated net income for the budget period.

BUSINESS ACCOUNTING

Accounting has been called the language of business. A business broker who is to deal in the sale and purchase of businesses must know how to speak the language. Following are some of the areas important to business accounting:

- *Income statement analysis.* The **income statement** is a concise summary of all income and expenses of a business for a *stated period of time.* It is designed to show the results of business operations over a specific period and to provide the basic data for analyzing the reasons for a firm's profits or losses. Other names sometimes given to the income statement are *profit and loss statement, operating statement, statement of income,* and *statement of net earnings.*

- *Balance sheet analysis.* The **balance sheet** shows the company's financial position at a stated *moment in time,* the close of business on the date of the balance sheet. It is customary to prepare an income statement and a balance sheet at the same time. This allows the net income or loss shown on the income statement for the prior period to be reflected on the balance sheet as of that particular moment.

- *Cash flow analysis.* **Cash flow** is the total amount of money generated from an investment after expenses have been paid. Operating expenses include reserves for replacement and payment of mortgage principal and interest. Cash flow disregards depreciation because depreciation does not involve an outlay of cash. A business broker is usually more interested in cash flow and the extent to which cash flow is sheltered from taxes than in whether the business produces a taxable income.

- *Asset depreciation.* Business brokers must be able to separate the depreciable assets of a business into real property and personal property.

- *Taxation.* Anyone interested in buying or selling a business knows the critical role taxes play in the success or failure of that business. Also known is that tax laws are forever changing. Thus, business brokers must be alert to the client's need for expert tax advice. (See also Chapter 18.)

<table>
<tr><td colspan="2" align="center">**Accounting Terminology**</td></tr>
<tr><td>**Assets**</td><td>The entire resources of a business, including tangibles and intangibles such as accounts and notes receivable, cash, inventory, equipment, real estate, and goodwill</td></tr>
<tr><td>**Liabilities**</td><td>All of the debts of a business, including accounts and notes payable, incurred but not yet paid obligations, and long-term debentures</td></tr>
<tr><td>**Capital**</td><td>The net worth of a business; the amount by which the assets exceed the liabilities</td></tr>
<tr><td>**Equity**</td><td>Current market value minus mortgage debt equals equity</td></tr>
<tr><td>**Cash flow**</td><td>The total amount of money generated from an investment after expenses have been paid</td></tr>
</table>

■ VALUATION OF BUSINESSES

In addition to being knowledgeable in the above areas, business brokers who specialize in business valuation may be called on to appraise businesses. Some of the more frequently encountered situations in which businesses need to be appraised include:

- the contemplated sale, purchase, or exchange of businesses;

- allocation of the assets of a business for tax depreciation purposes;

- obtaining of a loan or insurance coverage;

- the exercise of eminent domain by a governmental entity;

- drafting buy-sell agreements;

- in the event of partial or complete destruction or when businesses voluntarily go out of business;

- estate settlements; and

- assigning reasonable values to the business and its assets for businesses with stock option plans.

Methods of appraising businesses. The methods used to estimate a business's value are similar to those used in appraising real property. (See Chapter 15.)

- *Comparable sales analysis.* Where records reveal previous sale prices for businesses with a high degree of similarity, the appraiser can use professional judgment to account for existing differences and to arrive at a close approximation of the market value of a business.

- *Reproduction or replacement cost less depreciation analysis.* This method is appropriate for estimating the value of improvements of any type. When **reproduction** cost is used as a basis, the appraiser calculates the amount required to duplicate exactly the business or building being appraised. When **replacement cost** is used, the appraiser calculates the cost that would result in a business's (or building's) having the same use and capabilities as the one being appraised, even though the new business/building might differ physically.

- *Income capitalization analysis.* Most income-producing properties derive a large portion of their value from their ability to produce an income stream. This method of appraising attempts to estimate accurately the present value of expected future benefits (earnings and appreciation of assets) by converting the anticipated income stream into a present value through the use of a capitalization rate.

- *Liquidation analysis.* The liquidation of a business may become necessary because of the following: failure of a business, the death of a sole proprietor, the dissolution of a partnership, a court order, or any number of other reasons. In this analysis, business brokers and financial experts must consider such factors as the ability of the firm to pay off short-term obligations, the value of the inventory on hand, and the liquidation value of preferred stock.

KEY APPLICABLE LAWS

In addition to all of the activities mentioned above, a business broker is required to observe the many regulatory provisions, including Chapter 475, F.S., and state and federal securities laws.

■ STEPS IN THE SALE OF A BUSINESS

The sale of a business generally can be described as a series of steps. In the case of an outright purchase (and sale), the following nine-step sequence normally occurs:

1. List the business for sale.

2. Identify all assets belonging to the business.

3. Establish a value for the business, using the various methods of appraisal previously mentioned.

4. Subtract the value of all short-term and long-term liabilities (including the value of preferred stock) from the value of the business.

5. If organized as a corporation, divide the net value of the business by the number of common shares of stock outstanding. The value per share resulting then can be multiplied by the number of shares to be transferred.

6. Check and recheck to ensure compliance with all pertinent laws.

7. Market (advertise) the business.

8. Find a buyer and execute a purchase agreement.

9. Coordinate with all parties involved to schedule a date for closing the transaction.

■ **SUMMARY**

Real estate finance and appraisal are necessary foundations to an understanding of real estate investment analysis. Real estate licensees should be able to analyze various properties to help their clients choose investments that best meet an investor's individual objectives. Among the five general types of investment properties (residential, commercial, industrial, agricultural, and business opportunities), each has its own distinguishing characteristics as an investment.

Real estate investment analysis is necessary to evaluate the influence of external and internal forces on the value of each property. An analysis of real estate investments involves a thorough examination of the various risks and the impact of these risks on both the investor and the lender. While financial leverage can enhance an investor's return, it also increases the investor's risk of loss.

Business brokers deal primarily with the purchase and sale of small businesses. There are a number of differences between a business brokerage and a real estate brokerage. The analysis of a small business opportunity can be as difficult as the analysis of a large enterprise. The business broker needs to be knowledgeable in many areas, including business valuation, to be successful. But all of the steps involved in an outright sale or an exchange of stock require that a business broker be knowledgeable, be organized, stay current, and strive continuously to fine-tune the skills required in successful business brokerage operations.

■ **REVIEW QUESTIONS**

1. Investors who want to invest in office buildings and apartment complexes but want the advantages of liquidity and diversification often consider investing in
   A. a real estate investment trust.
   B. a large property management company.
   C. a mutual fund that invests in the broad stock market.
   D. none of the above.

2. A case in which the interest paid for borrowed funds is less than the overall rate of return to an investor is an example of
   A. loan-to-value ratio.
   B. positive leverage.
   C. negative leverage.
   D. yield.

3. Business risk (operating business risk) is chance of loss associated with the
   A. variance between projected and actual income and expenses.
   B. ability to pay all operating expenses from proceeds generated by the investment.
   C. increase in interest rates during the period of investment.
   D. effect of inflation on purchasing power.

4. Investment value is
    A. market value.
    B. effective gross income capitalized by an appropriate rate of capitalization.
    C. the worth of an investment property offered on the open market with no time constraints.
    D. the worth of an investment property to an individual investor based on the investor's standards.

5. What should an investor consider in evaluating a real estate investment?
    A. Liquidity
    B. Tax considerations
    C. Stability of income
    D. All of the above

6. A phosphate mining facility would be regarded as a(n)
    A. destination property.
    B. origin property.
    C. secondary industry.
    D. commercial property.

7. For investment purposes, the value of an investment property should be based on the
    A. property's return and the appreciation it will yield.
    B. cost to reproduce the property.
    C. prestige and appreciation the investment will afford.
    D. net income of the property capitalized by current market capitalization rates.

8. Intangible assets of a business do NOT include
    A. goodwill.
    B. customer loyalty.
    C. trademarks.
    D. improvements.

9. Which class of stock must all corporations have?
    A. Debenture bonds
    B. Preferred stock
    C. Convertible bonds
    D. Common stock

10. A firm's working capital is customarily defined as the difference between the firm's total
    A. current assets and total current liabilities.
    B. current liabilities and total cash on hand.
    C. short-term liabilities and total cash on hand.
    D. long-term liabilities and total accounts receivable.

11. How does business brokerage differ from real estate brokerage?
    A. There is usually the need for an appraisal.
    B. An interest in real property is involved.
    C. Intangible assets must be considered.
    D. Chattels may be included.

12. The financial report that indicates a firm's financial position at a stated moment in time is the
    A. operating statement.
    B. balance sheet.
    C. working capital statement.
    D. statement of net earnings.

13. The value of an established business property, compared with the value of just the physical assets of a business that is not yet established, is referred to as
    A. going concern value.
    B. goodwill.
    C. business enterprise.
    D. tangible assets.

14. All of the following are reasons for appraising a business and its assets EXCEPT
    A. to obtain financing.
    B. when a governmental unit intends to exercise its power of eminent domain over a business location.
    C. when a business has been destroyed by known or unknown causes.
    D. to ensure compliance with all pertinent state and federal securities laws.

15. A concise summary of all income and expenses of a business for a stated period of time is the
    A. balance sheet.
    B. income statement.
    C. cash flow statement.
    D. asset sheet.

16. All of the resources of a business, including tangibles and intangibles, are referred to as the
    A. net worth.
    B. capital.
    C. gross income.
    D. assets.

17. The cost to duplicate exactly the business or building being appraised is the
    A. replacement cost.
    B. benchmark.
    C. reproduction cost.
    D. liquidation analysis.

18. Investment in an apartment building is regarded as economically feasible if it
    A. shows an appropriate return on the investment.
    B. shows an appropriate return on the investment and recovers the invested capital.
    C. does not show a negative cash flow.
    D. does not show a negative after-tax cash flow.

19. Rent is $1,800 per month plus 3 percent of gross sales. The total rent for last month was $2,400. The gross sales for the same month were
    A. $20,000.
    B. $24,000.
    C. $30,000.
    D. $60,000.

20. The market value of an apartment building is $350,000. The investor has leveraged $300,000. What is the investor's equity in the property?
    A. $50,000
    B. $300,000
    C. $350,000
    D. $650,000

CHAPTER 18

Taxes Affecting Real Estate

■ KEY TERMS

adjusted basis	depreciation	mill
ad valorem	exempt	partially exempt
assessed value	Green Belt Law	special assessments
boot	immune	taxable value
capital gain	just value	tax shelter

■ OVERVIEW

City, county, school board, and numerous special tax districts are empowered to impose taxes directly on real property in Florida as part of the powers delegated to them by the state government. The U.S. Constitution prohibits the federal government from taxing real property, passing that right on to the state and local governments. Florida is one of the states, however, that does not tax real estate at the state level.

After completing this Chapter, the student should be able to:

- distinguish between immune and exempt or partially exempt properties;

- calculate the total tax exemptions on a property, given a scenario;

- describe the various personal exemptions available to qualified owners of homestead property;

- compute the property tax on a specific parcel, given the current tax rates, assessed value, and eligible exemptions;

- list the steps involved in the tax appeal procedure;

- describe the purpose of Florida's Green Belt Law;

- calculate the cost of a special assessment, given the conditions and amounts involved; and

- list tax advantages resulting from home ownership.

FIGURE 18.1 Property Tax Schedule

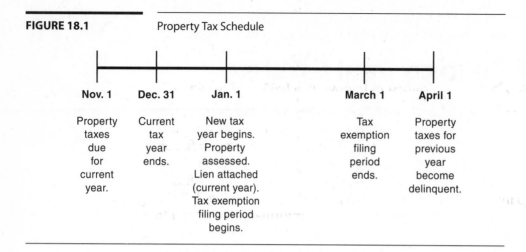

Nov. 1	Dec. 31	Jan. 1	March 1	April 1
Property taxes due for current year.	Current tax year ends.	New tax year begins. Property assessed. Lien attached (current year). Tax exemption filing period begins.	Tax exemption filing period ends.	Property taxes for previous year become delinquent.

■ CITY AND COUNTY PROPERTY TAXES

Property taxes provide the bulk of local government revenues in Florida. They account for a large portion of the revenue needed to provide law enforcement, fire protection, and other services.

193, F.S.

THE REAL PROPERTY TAXATION PROCESS

Real estate taxes (commonly called *property taxes*) are based on the value of real property, hence the term **ad valorem** tax, which means *according to value*. Florida law requires that the county property appraiser assess real property for all levels of government, thus avoiding duplication and possible controversy. All real property assessments must be updated annually.

197.122, F.S.
193.023(2), F.S.

Property taxes in Florida are levied on a calendar-year basis. Taxes are paid *in arrears* (at the end of the tax year) for the period January 1 through December 31 each year. (See Figure 18.1.) Property taxes become a lien on all real estate in Florida on January 1 each year. This lien is legally superior to any other lien, regardless of date. Taxes are payable to the county tax collector on or after November 1 each year. Property owners may pay property taxes in four installments or in a single payment. A discount system permits property owners to realize a discount through prompt payment of taxes. All payments made on or after March 1 must be for the full amount of taxes levied. Property taxes for the previous year become delinquent on April 1.

DETERMINING "JUST VALUE"

Property taxes are levied against land and all improvements to the land. The assessed values of the land and improvements are arrived at separately and then combined to reflect a single assessed value. The state supreme court has interpreted Florida statutes as requiring that all real property be assessed at **just value.** Just value is the fair and reasonable value based on objective valuation methods. In arriving at a just valuation, county property appraisers take into consideration property characteristics such as location, size, and condition of the property. The county property appraiser also considers the highest and best use of the property and, if income producing, the income generated from the property. Just value, for ad valorem purposes, may not conform to market value, but it is calculated in relation to a market value base.

Property appraisers apply three approaches to value: the sales comparison, cost-depreciation, and income approaches. (See Chapter 15.) If the property is sold during the year, the sale price becomes a factor for consideration in assessing the value of the property, but it is not the controlling factor. Representatives of the property appraiser's office typically go into the community to assess property, collecting data using specific forms and recording procedures. The information obtained from field trips is then processed through a computer, using appropriate valuation formulas to render an objective estimate of assessed value. **Assessed value** is the value of a property established for property tax purposes.

Once an assessment has been placed on a property, the owner must be informed. This requirement is considered to have been carried out when a value notice is mailed to the property owner at the last address of record. It is the responsibility of each property owner to see that a current mailing address is on file for all properties owned. Current addresses are needed to ensure that owners receive a notice of change in assessment before the time allowed for protest has expired.

Any property owner is entitled to protest a property assessment, but not every protest will be successful. For example, an owner of a home on a *standard lot* in a large, completely developed subdivision who complains that the lot was assessed too high will have little hope of getting the assessment changed. If the assessed value of the lot were changed, all of the owners of similar lots could protest their assessments.

The same homeowner might have a better chance of obtaining a lowered assessment if the evidence indicates the *house* was assessed at a value greater than justified. The county property appraiser has fairly complete details on the square footage, construction materials, year built, and amount of estimated depreciation since the date of construction, as well as records showing the assessed values of similar structures in the neighborhood.

PROTEST PROCEDURE

When a Florida property owner feels the assessed value is inaccurate or does not reflect fair market value, the owner can use the following three-step protest procedure:

Step one. The first step is to seek an adjustment by contacting the county property appraiser or a representative of that office. A property owner is allowed 25 days after the assessment notice is mailed to protest the assessment to the county property appraiser. If the arguments of the property owner are valid and have a basis in fact, the county property appraiser is authorized to make a change and to lower the assessed value.

3 County Com. + 2 School Board.

FIGURE 18.2   Protest Procedure: Property Owner Disagrees with Assessed Value

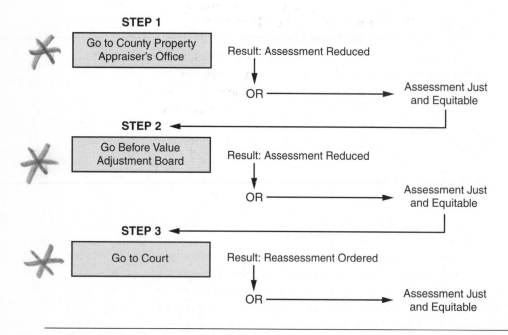

1   **Step two.**   If the property owner's request for an adjustment is rejected,
2   the owner may file an appeal (petition) with the Value Adjustment Board.
3   This board is made up of five members: three county commissioners
4   (appointed by the chair of the county commission) and two county school
5   board members (appointed by the chair of the county school board).
6   Because the purpose of the Value Adjustment Board is to act as a review
7   board and thereby ensure that all property owners receive a fair hearing,
8   the law requires that all members be elected officials. If the board agrees
9   with the taxpayer that the assessed value of the property is too high, the
10 board has the authority to change the assessment. If the board decides that
11 the county property appraiser assigned the correct assessment value, the
12 board will reject the taxpayer's request.

13 **Step three.**   The final step available to a property owner seeking a
14 change in assessed value is litigation in the courts. The taxpayer may pay
15 the taxes under protest and file a suit (a *certiorari proceeding,* meaning a
16 review of the matter by the courts) against the county property appraiser
17 and the county tax collector. The property owner's petition must be filed
18 within the statutory period (Chapter 194, F.S.). The court may not
19 arbitrarily assign an assessment value to a property. It may, however,
20 specify the methods and procedures that the county property appraiser
21 should use in reassessing the subject property. If the court judges the
22 original assessed value to be fair and equitable, the property owner has
23 used all the steps available under the protest process, other than to
24 appeal to a higher court. Figure 18.2 illustrates this protest procedure in
25 chart form.

TAX DISTRICTS: BUDGETS AND TAX RATE LEVY

Every fiscal year, each tax district (city, county, school board, or special tax district) prepares an operating budget for the next fiscal year. The operating budget prepared by each tax district is actually a summary of several departmental budgets. For example, the police department submits a budget that reflects the estimated cost of operating every phase of that department's activities during the coming fiscal year. The same process is followed by public works, health, welfare, finance, fire, and all other departments or agencies. When consolidated, all of the individual department budgets makeup the total city or county budget for the next fiscal year.

With the budget in hand, the tax district knows just about what expenses to expect for the next year. The next issue is obtaining sufficient revenue (income) to pay the expenses. No elected official is eager to levy higher property taxes than are absolutely necessary to operate the tax district. So before a general real estate tax is calculated, an attempt is made to estimate the revenue that can reasonably be expected from all sources other than real property taxes. Each tax district may have different or unique sources of income, ranging from outright federal grants to profits resulting from municipally owned utilities. Fines paid in courts, parking meter income, fees from occupational licenses, and tax funds returned by the state government are a few of the other sources of income. Estimating the amount of income from these nonproperty tax sources is made easier by records of preceding years, which indicate a predictable trend.

With a reasonable estimate in hand of the revenue expected from all nonproperty tax sources, the tax district is able to predict the amount of money needed from property taxes. The amount of property taxes paid to a tax district must come from its *tax base*. The tax base is the total assessed value of all taxable property in the tax district. The next component needed to compute a tax rate is the number and type of property tax exemptions granted.

EXEMPTIONS FROM PROPERTY TAXES

The owners of certain properties are relieved of the obligation to pay property taxes. Others are partially exempted.

Immune properties are city, county, state, and federal government properties. Examples of immune properties include county courthouses and military facilities. Immune properties also include special properties, such as municipal airports, that have been made immune by statute or ordinance. Immune properties are not assessed and are not subject to taxation.

Exempt properties include property belonging to churches and nonprofit organizations. Exempt properties are subject to taxation, but the owner is released from the obligation.

Partially exempt property is subject to taxation, but the owner is partially relieved of the burden. For example, all owners of homesteaded property are granted a partial tax exemption. For this reason, one cannot always regard the assessed value of a property as the taxable value of that

1 property. The *taxable value* of a property is not known until existing
2 exemptions are subtracted from the *assessed value*. **Taxable value**
3 (nonexempt assessed value) is determined by beginning with assessed
4 value and subtracting appropriate exemptions.

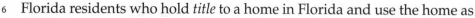

Head of Family / Filed Application

5 **HOMESTEAD TAX EXEMPTION**

6 Florida residents who hold *title* to a home in Florida and use the home as
7 their *permanent residence* may establish their residence as a homestead.
8 Doing so entitles the homeowner to a $25,000 homestead tax exemption
9 from the assessed value of the home for city, county, and school board
10 taxes. A person may hold title to more than one residence in the state of
11 Florida, but a person may homestead only one residence.

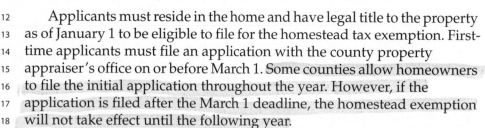

196, F.S.

12   Applicants must reside in the home and have legal title to the property
13 as of January 1 to be eligible to file for the homestead tax exemption. First-
14 time applicants must file an application with the county property
15 appraiser's office on or before March 1. Some counties allow homeowners
16 to file the initial application throughout the year. However, if the
17 application is filed after the March 1 deadline, the homestead exemption
18 will not take effect until the following year.

19   The procedure for renewing the homestead exemption varies from
20 county to county. In most counties the property appraiser mails a renewal
21 card on or before February 1 of each year. A county may choose to waive
22 the requirement to renew the exemption each year once the initial
23 application is made and the exemption is granted. However, if an
24 individual no longer qualifies for the homestead exemption and fails to
25 notify the county, the law provides for payment of penalties and interest
26 on unpaid property taxes.

40% Pay All Taxes

27   The property tax exemption for a homestead is deducted from the
28 assessed value of the property before property taxes are calculated.

Formula:	Taxable Value
	Assessed value
minus	Homestead exemptions
equals	Taxable value

29   *Example:* Suppose you bought a home that is assessed at $80,000.
30   Assuming that you have qualified for the homestead tax exemption,
31   what is your taxable property value?

32          $80,000 assessed value – $25,000 homestead exemption
33   = $55,000 taxable value

34 **Additional $500 exemptions.**   The following individuals qualify for an
35 additional $500 exemption from the assessed value of their homesteaded
36 property:

1   • Widows and widowers (surviving spouse who has not remarried)

2   • Legally blind persons

3   • Nonveterans who are totally and permanently disabled

4   A Florida physician, the Division of Blind Services, or the Social
5   Security Administration must certify the disability.

196.202, F.S.

6   **Disabled veteran exemption.**   Veterans who are at least 10 percent
7   disabled by military service-connected misfortune are entitled to an
8   additional $5,000 exemption on their homesteaded property. If the veteran
9   is totally and permanently disabled due to a service-connected injury, he
10   or she is entitled to a *total* exemption from property taxes on homesteaded
11   property. In some cases, this may carry over after the veteran's death to
12   the widow or widower.

196.24, F.S.
196.081, F.S.

13   **Age 65 and older exemption.**   Florida law authorizes counties and
14   municipalities to grant, by ordinance, an additional homestead exemption
15   of up to $25,000 for persons aged 65 and older. Household income is
16   restricted to no more than $20,000 (adjusted annually for inflation) to
17   qualify. If a county or a municipality chooses to pass this ordinance,
18   they can grant the person who is 65 and older a tax exemption. Counties
19   and municipalities, however, are *not* required to pass this ordinance.

196.075, F.S.

20   **Special exemption for quadriplegics.**   A homestead owned by a
21   quadriplegic is exempt from taxation. Also, low-income individuals with
22   total and permanent disabilities may be eligible for a total tax exemption
23   on their homesteaded property (statutory restrictions apply).

196.101, F.S.

24   **Cumulative homestead tax exemptions.**   The taxable value of a
25   homesteaded property is calculated by adding up all of the tax
26   exemptions that apply to a particular owner. For example, a widower
27   could qualify for a total tax exemption of $25,500, and a legally blind
28   widow would qualify for a total tax exemption of $26,000 on her
29   homesteaded property.

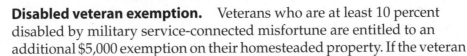

The Florida Department of Revenue has information concerning
Florida property tax exemptions posted on its Web site at:
http://www.myflorida.com/dor/. From the home page click on
"exemptions" located under the property icon.

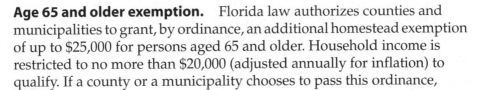

Download and print the Department of Revenue's official
application for filing Homestead Exemption at:
http://www.myflorida.com/dor/forms/2003/dr501s.pdf.

30   ## FLORIDA'S GREEN BELT LAW

31   Florida law authorizes county property appraisers to assess agricultural
32   land by a more favorable method than that used for other properties.
33   If a taxpayer's land is so classified for assessment purposes, the county
34   property appraiser must base the property tax assessment solely on the
35   basis of the land's current character and use. The highest and best use of
36   such land (such as commercial development) is not a factor in arriving at
37   just value for agricultural purposes.

193.461, F.S.

Florida's **Green Belt Law** was designed to protect farmers from having taxes increased just because the land might be in the path of urban growth and therefore well suited for development. An agricultural land classification results in a lower property assessment. Without such protection, a farmer's taxes could be raised to the point where it no longer would be economically feasible for that farmer to continue the agricultural use. Because of lower taxes on agricultural land, speculators often have been attracted to such properties when they are located in the path of urban growth. In many instances the law, which was intended to protect the farmer, has been used as a tax protection by speculators. To stop this practice, the Florida Green Belt Law was changed to require that all county property appraisers annually classify all lands within the county. Property owners desiring that their land be classified differently must request and rejustify such classification before March 1 each year. If the request is denied, these property owners may appeal the denial through the regular protest procedure used by other property owners.

210⁰⁰/Per Acre. (handwritten margin note)

SAVE OUR HOME

The *Save Our Home* amendment of the Florida Constitution (also known as *Amendment 10*) caps how much the assessed value of homesteaded property may increase in a given year. According to Chapter 193, F.S., the just value of homesteaded property may be increased either:

193.155, F.S.

- 3 percent annually (based on the assessed value for the prior year); or

- the percentage change of the Consumer Price Index (CPI) for the preceding year, whichever is less.

The statute also provides that when homesteaded property is sold, it will be assessed at just value as of January 1 of the year following a change in ownership. The assessed value of a homesteaded property may significantly increase after a change in ownership if the current owners have lived in the home for a number of years and the property in the area has experienced strong property appreciation.

689.261, F.S.

Licensees should avoid estimating a buyer's property tax liability by referring to a seller's current taxes because the purchaser may be liable for substantially higher property taxes than the previous owner of the home. Effective January 1, 2005, prospective purchasers of residential property must be given a disclosure summary regarding property taxes. The disclosure summary informs purchasers that they cannot rely on the seller's current property taxes as the amount of property taxes the purchaser may be obligated to pay in the year following purchase of the property. The disclosure further explains that the sale of the property triggers a reassessment of the property's value. A copy of the required property tax disclosure is presented in Chapter 11 on page 223. Buyers who have questions concerning the amount of property taxes they can expect to pay on the homes they are considering buying should be referred to the county property appraiser's office.

TAX RATES

To calculate the dollar amount of property taxes owed, the taxable value of the property is multiplied by the appropriate tax rate. The *tax rate* is expressed in mills. A **mill** is one one-thousandth of a dollar (or one-tenth of a cent). There are 1,000 mills in a dollar. Thus, a tax rate of .010 is expressed as 10 mills. Florida has legislated a "cap" (ceiling) that limits cities, counties, and school boards to a basic real property tax rate of no more than 10 mills each.

The following simple formula is commonly used for determining the tax rate of cities and counties:

$$\frac{\text{Approved budget } - \text{ Nonproperty tax revenue}}{\text{Total assessed value} - \text{Exemptions}} = \text{Tax rate}$$

Example: Assume that a county has an approved operating budget for the next fiscal year with expected expenditures of $10,500,000. A review of past and present experience indicates a reasonable expectation of $500,000 in revenue from sources other than property taxes. The county property appraiser reports a total assessed valuation of all taxable properties in the amount of $1,050,000,000 less $50,000,000 in exemptions. Apply the previously cited formula to these figures.

$$\frac{\$10,500,000 - \$500,000}{\$1,050,000,000 - \$50,000,000} = \frac{\$10,000,000}{\$1,000,000,000} = .010, \text{ or 10 mills}$$

Thus, the tax rate to be applied to all taxable real property in the county will be 10 mills (.010) per dollar of taxable value.

One mill is properly written in decimals as .001. When the decimal .010 is used, it means one cent, or 10 mills. To convert the tax rate from a decimal form to mills, simply move the decimal point three places to the *right*. Add zeros, if necessary. Always use three digits when expressing tax rates to prevent confusion. For example, .009 = 9 mills and .010 = 10 mills. To convert millage to its decimal form, move the decimal point three places to the *left* of the written or unwritten decimal point. For example, 20 mills = .020 and 25.9 mills = .0259.

Formula:	Annual Property Taxes Due
	Taxable value
multiplied by	Tax rate
equals	Annual property taxes due

Example: Using the tax rate of .010 for a home assessed at $80,000 that has qualified for homestead tax exemption, the calculation of the county property taxes is as follows:

$80,000 assessed value – $25,000 homestead exemption = $55,000 taxable value × .010 tax rate = $550 property taxes due

1   Note that two separate types of value are involved in determining the
2   actual property tax. The tax rate, in mills, is always applied to the taxable
3   value. Any exemption must be deducted from the assessed value to find
4   the taxable value. Where no exemptions apply, the taxable value and the
5   assessed value are the same. The taxable value is always multiplied by the
6   tax rate to find the amount of tax. The tax rate usually changes each year
7   owing to differences in operating budget costs and revenues.

8   Not all property owners are subject to the same tax rates. A
9   homeowner living in a city pays city, county, and school board taxes.
10 Perhaps additional taxes will be required as a result of bonds or other
11 obligations approved by the voters. Usually a homeowner living in the
12 county but outside the city limits pays only county and school board
13 taxes. Often, additional taxes are required of county residents who are
14 located in special tax districts. In almost all cases, special tax districts may
15 not levy more than three mills per district.

16 *Example:* Mr. Pasco owns a home in Whipsaw, Florida, in Brevard
17 County. The city tax rate is 8.7 mills, the county tax rate is 9.2 mills,
18 and the school board tax rate is 6 mills. Mr. Pasco is legally blind. He
19 has qualified for homestead exemption. His home has been assessed at
20 $65,000. What must Mr. Pasco pay in property taxes?

21 $65,000 assessed value – $25,500 total exemptions =
22 $39,500 taxable value
23 8.7 mills + 9.2 mills + 6 mills = 23.9 mills, or .0239
24 $39,500 × .0239 tax rate = $944.05 total property taxes due

25 *Example:* Mr. Pasco is interested in finding the amount of savings in
26 property taxes realized by tax exemptions.

27 $25,500 exemptions × .0239 tax rate = $609.45 savings

Formula:	Tax Savings
	Tax exemption
multiplied by	Tax rate
equals	Tax savings

28 *Example:* What if Mr. Pasco lived outside the city limits in the same
29 county? How would this affect his property taxes? The solution is
30 exactly the same as the previous example, except the city tax rate of
31 8.7 mills is omitted.

32 $65,000 assessed value – $25,500 exemptions = $39,500 taxable value
33 9.2 mills + 6 mills = 15.2 mills, or .0152
34 $39,500 × .0152 = $600.40

SPECIAL ASSESSMENTS

Special assessments are one-time taxes levied on properties to help pay
for some public improvement that benefits the property. When city
sewers are extended to neighborhoods previously dependent on septic
tanks or when unpaved streets are paved, it is assumed that the
properties affected receive an increase in value owing to the
improvement. Sometimes the municipal authority that levies the special
assessment considers affected properties to have benefited in value when
the improvement actually may have caused a decrease in value. A quiet
residential street that is widened into a four-lane boulevard to relieve
congested access routes might be an example. The increased traffic, with
its resultant noise, pollution, and danger to children, could cause
property values to drop instead of increase. In such cases, the property
owners can look for relief from the courts.

Laws that allow the levying of special assessments specifically require
that all improvements *benefit* any property against which a special
assessment is levied. Court records are abundant with instances where
courts at all levels, up to and including the U.S. Supreme Court, have
ruled in favor of property owners when improvements did not enhance
the value of affected properties.

Special assessments are *not* ad valorem taxes—they are not levied
according to the value of a property. Usually, special assessments are
levied on a front-foot basis for items such as sidewalks and street paving.
They are often levied on a per hookup basis for utility and sewer
improvements.

Example: You live on an unpaved street. The city is petitioned to pave
the street and agrees to do so. The paving cost is $24 per foot, and the
city is to pay 30 percent of the cost. If your lot frontage on the street is
100 feet, what will your special assessment be for street paving? (Don't
forget that your street has two sides and the property across the street
must bear its fair share.)

100 front feet × $24 per foot	= $2,400
$2,400 × .70 (owner's share of cost is 100% – 30%)	= $1,680
$1,680 ÷ 2 (one-half of the street paving cost)	= $ 840

? 1 Time Tax.

NONPAYMENT OF REAL PROPERTY TAXES

Property taxes constitute a lien superior to all other liens on real
property. Special assessments are next in priority. When a property
owner fails to pay property taxes, the taxing authority must take steps to
obtain the tax money needed to help pay for the cost of government.

START 18% go down.

In Florida, unpaid property taxes are considered a debt, just as if the
property owner had signed a promissory note for the amount of the taxes.
Further, the property is security for the debt and can eventually be sold to
satisfy the obligation.

The city or county government is responsible for the cost of its day-to-
day operation and must collect delinquent taxes in some manner. To do
this, a property *tax certificate* in the amount of taxes owed is issued for each

Tax Cert — 7 yr only.

1   delinquent property. A list of all delinquent properties is published in a
2   newspaper having general circulation throughout the county. This
3   publication gives all delinquent owners notice that tax certificates on their
4   properties will be sold if the taxes are not paid before the date
5   of sale.

6   The published list of properties, including the amount of taxes in
7   arrears, specifies a date, time, and place for public auction of tax
8   certificates on each property listed. At the auction, any qualified person is
9   entitled to bid for the tax certificate on any property. Instead of bidding in
10 dollars, investors bid interest rates at the auction, starting at 18 percent
11 and going down. The bidder who is willing to accept the lowest interest
12 rate is issued the tax certificate. Once the certificate is sold, the bidder
13 must pay the face amount of the certificate to the county (taxes, interest,
14 and advertising cost). For a certificate to be redeemed by the owner of the
15 property, the tax collector must collect the face amount of the certificate
16 plus all accrued interest. The certificate holder is then paid the face
17 amount of the certificate plus accrued interest.

18   The holder of the tax certificate can force a public auction of the
19 property after two years (but no later than seven years) by requesting a tax
20 deed. Anyone can bid at the foreclosure sale and the property will be sold
21 to the highest bidder. The holder of the tax certificate then will be paid the
22 amount invested plus interest if he or she is not the successful bidder on
23 the property. If there are no bidders, the holder of the certificate is issued
24 a tax deed. Once the property is transferred by tax deed, all other liens
25 against the property—including mortgages—are wiped out, with the
26 exception of any government liens.

27 ## ■ FEDERAL INCOME TAXES

28 Current federal tax laws greatly affect the benefits that may be obtained
29 from the purchase, ownership, and disposition of real property. The tax
30 considerations of owning personal or investment property are important,
31 but they are also complex. Let's begin with a discussion of a principal
32 residence.

33 ### PRINCIPAL RESIDENCE

34 Tax laws are designed to encourage homeownership and give preferred
35 treatment to taxpayers who own their residences. The owner-occupied
36 residence may be a house, condominium, mobile home, or houseboat.
37 Regardless, the homeowner has certain tax advantages. If homeowners-
38 taxpayers itemize deductions rather than claiming the standard
39 deduction on their annual federal income tax returns, they may deduct
40 the following:

41 • **Mortgage interest.** Interest paid on a mortgage loan on a principal
42   and second home is deductible. (Certain limitations apply.)

43 • **Property taxes.** The annual property taxes paid on principal and
44   second homes are deductible.

- **Interest on a home equity loan.** The interest paid is deductible if the loan does not exceed $100,000.

- **Mortgage origination fees (points).** Points are deductible in the year they are paid, unless they are paid when refinancing a loan—in such cases, the points must be deducted over the life of the loan.

Formula:	**Federal Income Tax Savings**
	Deductible expenses
multiplied by	Tax rate
equals	Tax savings

Example: Assume that a homeowner in the 28 percent tax bracket paid $5,400 in mortgage interest and $2,300 in real estate taxes. How much was the tax savings from deductions?

$$\$5,400 + \$2,300 = \$7,700 \text{ deductible expenses}$$

$$\$7,700 \times .28 \text{ tax rate} = \$2,156 \text{ tax savings}$$

(Note: The true tax savings would take into acount the IRS standard deduction.)

Additional tax advantages of homeownership include the following:

- **First-time homebuyers.** First-time homebuyers may make penalty-free (but not tax-free) withdrawals up to $10,000 from their tax-deferred individual retirement funds (IRAs) for a down payment.

- **Exclusion of gain from the sale of a principal residence.** An exclusion of up to $250,000 of gain ($500,000 for married couples filing a joint return) realized on the sale or exchange of a principal residence.

Sale of real property. Federal tax laws classify real property as a *capital asset.* **Capital gain** income is profit from the sale of a principal residence, an investment property, a property used in a trade or business, or an income-producing property, and it must be reported for tax purposes. The taxable gain on real estate is determined by two factors: the amount realized from the sale and the adjusted basis. The gain is the amount realized from the sale less the adjusted basis.

Formula:	**Amount Realized from Sale**
	Sale price
minus	Expense of the sale
equals	Amount realized

Example: Assume a homeowner sells her home for $165,000 and pays the broker $8,250, and state transfer taxes of $1,155. What is the *amount realized?*

$$\$165,000 \text{ sale price} - \$9,405 = \$155,595 \text{ amount realized from sale}$$

1   The **adjusted basis** is the owner's original cost plus buying expenses
2   plus capital improvements (less certain deductions, if applicable).

Formula:	**Adjusted Basis**
	Original purchase price
plus	Purchase expenses, and capital improvements
equals	Adjusted basis

3   *Example:* If the homeowner's original cost was $80,000 and there were
4   purchase costs of $800 and capital improvements totaling $5,200, how
5   much is the adjusted basis?

6   $80,000 price + $800 costs + $5,200 improvements =
7   $86,000 adjusted basis

Formula:	**Capital Gain (or Loss)**
	Amount realized
minus	Adjusted basis
equals	Capital gain (loss)

8   A taxpayer-seller's capital gain (loss) is the amount realized from the
9   sale less the adjusted basis.

10   Using the example above, how much *capital gain* must be reported?

11   $155,595 amount realized − $86,000 adjusted basis =
12   $69,595 capital gain

13   While profit from the sale of a principal residence (if not excluded) is
14   included as a capital gain, a loss from such a sale is not allowed as a capital
15   loss and thus may not be deducted.

16   The Taxpayer Relief Act of 1997 allows homeowners to exclude up to
17   $250,000 of gain ($500,000 for married couples filing a joint return)
18   realized on the sale or exchange of a principal residence. The exclusion is
19   allowed each time taxpayers sell or exchange a principal residence, as
20   long as the homeowners have occupied the property as their residence for
21   at least two years during the five-year period ending on the date of the
22   sale. The taxpayer is not required to reinvest the sale proceeds in a new
23   residence to claim the exclusion. The exclusion of gain is generally
24   allowed only once every two years. However, homeowners who do not
25   meet the two-year requirement due to a change in health or place of
26   employment may be eligible for a prorated exclusion of gain.

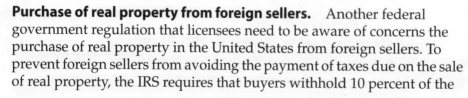

27   **Purchase of real property from foreign sellers.**   Another federal
28   government regulation that licensees need to be aware of concerns the
29   purchase of real property in the United States from foreign sellers. To
30   prevent foreign sellers from avoiding the payment of taxes due on the sale
31   of real property, the IRS requires that buyers withhold 10 percent of the

gross sale price (including cash paid and any debt assumed by the buyer). The buyer must report the purchase and pay the IRS the amount withheld. There are a few exceptions to this rule. All licensees should encourage their buyers and sellers to consult the IRS or a tax specialist regarding the application of this rule. (See also the Contract for Sale and Purchase, Figure 11.3 on page 234. Refer to Disclosures, Section XI (f).)

Tax laws are constantly changing, and they are also very complex. For example, the home equity loan as a source of funds on which the interest is tax deductible may either benefit careful homeowners or result in disaster for homeowners who mishandle their finances. For these and other reasons, it is always wise to retain professional counsel regarding tax situations.

INVESTMENT PROPERTY

Federal income tax laws encourage real estate investment. Tax benefits include the following: allowable deductions from income, tax deferral and exemptions on resale, installment sale treatment, and like-kind exchanges. Each of the tax benefits is discussed later in the Chapter. Buyers and sellers should always seek competent tax advice to ensure the most favorable tax treatment in a real estate transaction. Advance planning is necessary if an investor's after-tax return on investment is to be maximized.

Income classification.   For tax purposes, *ordinary income* consists of three types:

1. *Active income* includes wages, tips, commission, and so forth.

2. *Portfolio income* includes income from interest, stock dividends, capital gains, royalties, and annuity income.

3. *Passive income* includes income from activities in which the taxpayer does not participate. Most income from rental or leased real property is classified as passive income.

Capital gains and capital losses.   Real estate, stocks, bonds, and so forth that are owned for investment purposes are capital assets. When you sell a capital asset, the difference between the amount that you sell it for and your basis, which is usually what you paid for it, is a capital gain or a capital loss. You have a capital gain if you sell the asset for more than your basis (for profit). You have a capital loss if you sell the asset for less than your basis.

A capital gain from the sale of real estate investment property can be used to offset a capital loss from the sale of other investment property. Furthermore if an investor's capital loss exceeds capital gains, the investor may deduct up to $3,000 in losses in a given year. Assume, for example, an investor has two investment properties. One earns a capital gain of $10,000 and the other has a capital loss of $15,000. The investor can offset the $10,000 gain with $10,000 of the loss. This leaves a net $5,000 loss of which the investor can deduct $3,000. The investor must carry forward the remaining $2,000 loss to the next year. (Remember, as previously discussed, a loss from the sale of your personal residence is *not* deductible.)

Deductions from gross income. Three types of deductions from gross income are allowed when calculating the taxable income from investment real property:

1. **Operating expenses.** Operating expenses are those cash outlays necessary for running and maintaining the property, and they are deductible in the year paid. Property taxes are considered operating expenses and are deductible. While reserve for replacements is deducted when determining NOI (see Chapter 15), it is not a cash expense and is not deductible when computing taxable income. Replacement *expenses* (not capital improvements), however, are deductible in the year paid.

2. **Financing expenses.** Financing expenses include the interest paid as well as the costs of obtaining borrowed money. While mortgage interest is deductible, principal payments are not. Costs associated with obtaining borrowed funds, such as commissions, mortgage brokerage fees, and points, must be amortized over the life of the loan.

3. **Depreciation.** Depreciation is a means of deducting the costs of improvements to land over a specified period of time. The land itself is *not* depreciable. Depreciation (or cost recovery) allows taxpayers to recover the cost of depreciable property by paying less tax than they would otherwise have to pay. Under present tax law the depreciation deduction usually bears little relationship to actual changes in property value. Depreciation is used to stimulate economic expansion by making certain types of real property more attractive to investors. Depreciation is allowed only for business property and income-producing property (which includes investment property). It is not allowed for inventory property or for a personal residence.

As it relates to annual income from a property, depreciation provides favorable tax relief as an allowable deduction that requires no current outlay of cash, as is necessary to deduct other expenses (such as property taxes and mortgage interest). In addition, depreciation is based on the total cost of property, including that portion paid for with borrowed funds (the leveraged portion).

Depreciation components. The *depreciable basis* of the property is the amount that may be depreciated. For real property, it is generally the initial cost of the asset plus acquisition costs minus the value of the land. Acquisition costs generally include such items as the buyer's attorney's fees, appraisal fees, survey fees, and title insurance costs. Because land is not depreciable, this basis (total cost) must be allocated between the improvements (buildings, etc.) and the land, based on the respective values of each.

Straight-line method. Depreciation is calculated using the straight-line method. An equal amount of depreciation is taken annually over the useful life of the asset. The Internal Revenue Service (IRS) has currently established useful asset life as 27.5 years for residential rental property and 39 years for nonresidential income-producing property.

Formula:	**Straight-Line Method Depreciation**
	Depreciable basis
divided by	27.5 years (or 39 years)
equals	Annual depreciation

Example: Assume that in 2002, a residential real estate investment property is purchased for $250,000, with a land value of $50,000. The depreciable basis is $200,000 ($250,000 sale price less the land value). What is the amount of the yearly depreciation deduction?

$$\$200{,}000 \text{ depreciable basis} \div 27.5 \text{ years} =$$
$$\$7{,}273 \text{ annual depreciation deduction}$$

Tax on gain at time of sale. In general, when income property is sold for cash, all gain or loss must be recognized (reported) immediately for income tax purposes. The total realized gain is the difference between the net sale price (selling price less selling expenses) and the depreciated basis of the property. The seller pays tax on the gain from the sale of real estate in the year the gain is collected. Because of the tax consequences of the immediate recognition of gain, the installment sale method or a like-kind exchange may provide beneficial tax results.

Installment sale method. Under the *installment sale method*, the gain is received over a number of years and the seller recognizes the gain for tax purposes over the same period. The installment sale method relieves the seller of paying tax on gain not yet collected. Generally, it calls for the gain to be reported only as payments are actually received, with each payment treated as part profit and part recovery of investment in the property sold. If an installment sale results in a loss, however, the seller may not use the installment sale method to report the loss over a period of years for tax purposes. A qualified loss must be recognized (reported) in the year of sale. Because the IRS requirements regarding the installment sale method are complex, early tax counsel is mandatory.

Like-kind exchange. Real estate investors can defer paying taxes by exchanging real property. The income tax is *deferred, not eliminated.* A *like-kind exchange* enables a taxpayer-investor to realize the benefits of investment and property appreciation immediately while paying taxes later. When the investor sells the property, the capital gain will be taxed.

To qualify as a tax-deferred exchange under Section 1031 of the Internal Revenue Code, real property must be exchanged for other real property (hence the term "like-kind"). However, it may be a different type of real property. For example, a multifamily complex can be exchanged for an office complex. Any additional capital or personal property included with the transaction to even out the value of the exchange is called **boot.** The IRS requires tax on the boot to be paid at the time of the exchange by the party who receives it. Because exchanges are subject to a number of IRS rules that must be strictly adhered to, the transactions must be carefully structured, with early tax counsel mandatory. Personal residences and foreign property do not qualify.

Tax shelter. **Tax shelter** is a term that describes some of the advantages of owning real estate (or other investments). An investment is a tax shelter when it shields income or gain from payment of income taxes. One of the features of a tax-sheltered real estate investment is depreciation. **Depreciation** is a key deduction because it reduces taxable income without involving a cash outlay. Depreciation protects at least a portion of income from tax and also may produce a tax loss, thus possibly creating additional tax sheltering of other income. Under the tax code, sheltering of income is restricted.

Sound real estate investments depend primarily on the inherent productivity of a property, not on its tax aspects. A good real estate investment always combines positive cash flow (if income-producing property) with appreciation of property value. If a property declines in value in an amount equal to or greater than the depreciation deduction allowable for tax purposes, that property is *not* a tax shelter.

■ SUMMARY

Local, state, and federal government tax considerations affect the purchase, ownership, and disposition of real property. Local taxing authorities levy real property taxes annually. Taxable value is obtained when tax exemptions are subtracted from the assessed value of a property. Payment of property taxes is required before stated dates, after which penalties accrue.

Real property owners may follow a three-step procedure for protesting assessed property value. Properties not included in the taxable property tax base are either immune or exempt properties. Each city, county, and school board uses the same general procedure for establishing a real estate tax rate. Special assessments are a one-time tax, theoretically based on added value. Tax certificates constitute a lien on real property and are sold to provide money not received due to unpaid taxes.

At the national level, federal tax law classifies real property as a capital asset. Capital gains are profit from the sale of a principal residence, an investment property, or an income-producing property. Property taxes are one of the federal income tax deductions that make home ownership advantageous. Additional tax advantages are the deductibility of home mortgage interest and property taxes and the exclusion of profit from the sale of a principal residence.

Federal income taxes play an important role in the selection and productivity of investment real estate. Depreciation is a key tax shelter feature because it reduces taxable income from the investment with no effect on cash flow. Well-chosen real estate continues to be a good investment. However, the amount of immediate tax relief may be reduced owing to limitations placed on the current investment interest deduction, the classification of rental real estate as a passive activity, and, to a limited extent, the application of the at-risk rule to real estate.

■ REVIEW QUESTIONS

1. In Florida, real property taxes are levied on a
   A. county fiscal-year basis.
   B. calendar-year basis.
   C. fiscal-year basis.
   D. quarterly basis.

2. Each year in Florida, property taxes for the previous year become delinquent on
   A. January 1.
   B. April 1.
   C. November 1.
   D. December 31.

3. The first step in protesting the assessed value of real property is to
   A. contact the county property appraiser or a representative.
   B. contact the county tax collector or a representative.
   C. contact the Value Adjustment Board.
   D. file suit against the Value Adjustment Board.

4. The Value Adjustment Board is composed of
   A. the city manager, property appraiser, and three other elected officials.
   B. three school board members and two county commissioners.
   C. two school board members and three county commissioners.
   D. five school board members and two county commissioners.

5. You have been granted homestead tax exemption. Your assessed property value is $65,000. What is your taxable property value for county taxes?
   A. $65,000
   B. $60,000
   C. $40,000
   D. $25,000

6. What would be your city and county property taxes if the property assessment is $38,000, you are a Florida resident receiving homestead tax exemption, and the total tax rate is 28 mills?
   A. $364
   B. $380
   C. $429
   D. $924

7. A 25 percent service-disabled veteran, who is 75 years of age, has been granted homestead tax exemption. What will his total property tax exemption be?
   A. $25,000
   B. $25,500
   C. $30,000
   D. Totally tax-exempt

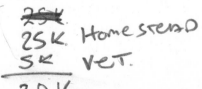

8. In arriving at a just value for agricultural property, the highest and best use
   A. is not a factor.
   B. of the property must be for agricultural purposes only.
   C. discourages speculative investing in agricultural land.
   D. encourages speculative investing in agricultural land.

9. Which statement is FALSE concerning Florida's Green Belt Law?
   A. The law is intended to protect owners of agricultural property.
   B. Farmers' lands are shielded from excessive taxation.
   C. The law has been strengthened by qualifying agricultural land annually.
   D. The law intended to promote open green spaces along our nation's interstates.

10. If a lot frontage is 100 feet, street paving costs are $40 per running foot, and the city will pay 25 percent of paving costs, what will be the assessment to the property owner?
    A. $1,000
    B. $1,500
    C. $3,000
    D. $4,000

11. Mary is a widow who owns a home in Gainesville, Florida, in Alachua County. The city tax rate is 9.3 mills, the county rate is 9.7 mills, and the school board tax rate is 6 mills. She has homesteaded her principal residence. The amount of savings in property taxes realized by all allowable tax exemptions is
    A. $625.00.
    B. $637.50.
    C. $697.50.
    D. $700.00.

12. Current state law allows the buyer of property tax certificates to collect interest up to a maximum of
    A. 12 percent.
    B. 18 percent.
    C. the tax rate in each county.
    D. allowable interest voted by the residents of each county.

13. A county or city millage rate is determined by
    A. taking into account the operating budgets of the various government departments within the city or county.
    B. majority vote of the registered voters.
    C. the mayor or county commissioners after the period for filing a protest has expired.
    D. the State Legislature.

14. In 2004, taxpayer Cary Ohver had a $20,000 gain from the sale of investment property A, a $19,000 loss from the sale of investment property B, and a $5,000 loss from the sale of his principal residence. All three properties were owned for more than 12 months. Cary's only other income was his $50,000 salary. What is his 2004 total income for tax purposes, using just this information?
    A. $46,000
    B. $47,000
    C. $50,400
    D. $51,000

15. If a married couple who files jointly realizes a profit from the sale of their home that exceeds $500,000, what is the result?
    A. The homeowners will not pay capital gains tax if at least one of them is older than 55.
    B. Up to $125,000 of the excess profit will be taxed as a capital gain.
    C. The excess gain will be taxed at the current applicable capital gains rate.
    D. The excess gain will be taxed at the homeowner's income tax rate.

16. The maximum amount of profit that may be excluded from taxation on the sale of a home for a qualifying couple, filing separately, is
    A. 0 because profit may be only deferred.
    B. $125,000.
    C. $150,000.
    D. $250,000.

17. Tax advantages of homeownership do NOT include
    A. a tax deduction of property taxes paid.
    B. penalty-free withdrawal from an IRA if used as a down payment on a personal residence for first-time homebuyers.
    C. exclusion of gain from the sale of a principal residence up to $500,000 for married couples filing a joint return.
    D. a tax deduction of homeowners hazard insurance.   *Home owner yea!*
    Flood No.

18. For tax purposes, when the installment sale method is used
    A. gain is reported as payments are received.
    B. gain or loss is reported as payments are received.
    C. gain must be deferred.
    D. gain or loss must be deferred.

19. Which item is NOT a deductible expense for an income-producing property?
    A. Depreciation
    B. Reserve for replacement
    C. Hazard insurance
    D. Mortgage interest

20. A good tax-sheltering real estate investment is one in which
    A. debt service is greater than net operating income.
    B. the secondary purpose is the productivity of the property.
    C. the primary purpose is reduction of personal taxable income.
    D. the amount of depreciation taken for tax purposes is greater than the actual depreciation of the property.

CHAPTER 19

The Real Estate Market

■ KEY TERMS

buyer's market	household	supply
demand	seller's market	vacancy rate

1 ## ■ OVERVIEW

2 The word *market* has many meanings, depending on usage. It can mean a
3 place where farmers and tradespeople display their produce and products
4 for buyers. It can mean a place where securities are exchanged, such as
5 the commodities market or the stock market. Regardless of difference in
6 form, the basic principles of market operation hold true for all. A market
7 can function only when sellers and buyers interact. Many markets use
8 intermediaries to facilitate activity between seller and buyer, and the real
9 estate market is one such market.

10 After completing this Chapter, the student should be able to:

11 • list factors that influence supply and demand for real estate;

12 • describe the five characteristics unique to the real estate
13 market; and

14 • distinguish between buyer's and seller's markets.

15 ## ■ THREE KEY QUESTIONS

16 Every economy in every land in the world has to deal with the following
17 three basic questions:

18   1. **What will be produced?** Any producer can place a product or
19   service in the marketplace, where it competes with similar
20   products or services offered by other producers. Consumers
21   evaluate the worth, quality, and price of the competing products
22   and services. The products or services sold and the profitability of
23   the producers' efforts tell them which products or services are
24   preferred by consumers. Those products or services that do not

" Millionare Next Door." Book
Get it

generate a profit will no longer be produced. So *the consumer actually decides what will be produced.* Products not desired by consumers will produce little or no profit and will be replaced by new products for consumers to evaluate.

2. **Who will do the producing?** Imagine you are a producer of canned grapefruit sections. You are competing in the marketplace against four other producers of canned grapefruit sections of similar quality and price. After a thorough analysis of your production methods, you conclude that a change in procedure will permit you to reduce your price slightly below that of your competitors, while retaining the quality and quantity of the product. Gradually thereafter, consumers begin to select your product more and more frequently. You decide to expand your factory and increase the amount of grapefruit sections produced. In time, other producers obviously must either become more efficient, as you have, or face being forced out of business because of a decrease in their sales and profits. So the *most efficient* producer of a comparable-quality product will go on doing the producing.

3. **Who will get what is produced?** If more than one person wants the same article, the one willing to spend the most money usually gets the item. Therefore, *those people who have money and are willing to spend it in the marketplace will get what is produced.* We do not worry about whether there will be enough television sets or cars for us to be allowed the privilege of buying one. We know that television sets and cars will be available. Our problem is in selecting between products and services within the limits of our income. So it is with real estate. The marketplace determines sale prices, *not* sellers and *not* real estate agents.

The consumer is the individual who exercises freedom of choice in the marketplace and, therefore, is the real decision maker. Thus, one of the characteristics of the free enterprise system is that individual consumer desires and decisions are the primary determinants in the system. In a controlled economy, the government makes those decisions.

Another characteristic of a relatively free enterprise system is the "automatic" working of the system. No committee from the Department of Commerce or any other agency has to survey the national market to determine which goods and services are selling well and which ones should be removed from the marketplace. Better results are accomplished automatically by the millions of individual consumer choices exercised every minute of every day. Those products that sell well will be replaced with more of the same. Those products that do not sell well will be removed and replaced by other products.

■ CHARACTERISTICS OF THE REAL ESTATE MARKET

Test

There are five characteristics of the real estate market that set it apart from other markets. (See Figure 19.1.)

FIGURE 19.1   Real Estate Market

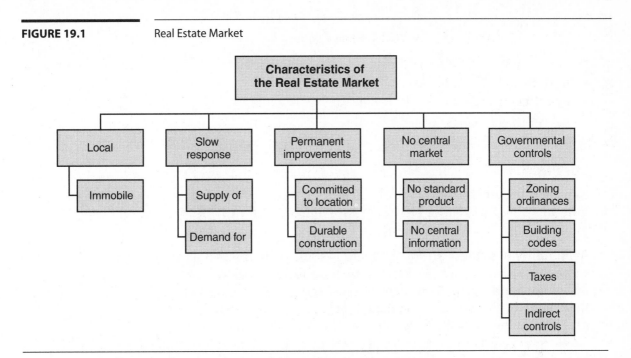

1. ***Immobility of real estate.*** The geographic location of real estate is
    fixed. The land and the improvements on the land are immovable.
    Because of the immobility of real estate, the surrounding area
    largely influences the value of a particular parcel.

2. ***The market is slow to respond to change in supply and demand.***
    Design, land acquisition, site preparation, and construction phases
    of real estate are time-consuming. For this reason, when the
    equilibrium between supply and demand is upset, it can be years
    before the imbalance is corrected.

3. ***Land is indestructible.*** Land is permanent. The physical structures
    (improvements) on the land are durable, however, they deteriorate
    and become obsolete over time.

4. ***Real estate is unique.*** No two tracts of land are identical. There is
    no standard product. Even two lots side by side have different
    geographic locations. The uniqueness of land is also referred to as
    heterogeneity.

5. ***Government controls influence the market through zoning,***
    building codes, taxes, and so forth. Government controls play an
    important role when compared with other markets. Zoning,
    building codes, and health ordinances that govern septic tank use
    and other health-related matters are examples of *direct* controls.
    The government also uses *indirect* controls such as the monetary
    policies of the federal government.

■ SUPPLY AND DEMAND FACTORS

A study of markets and their operations reveals several factors that
influence supply and demand.

[handwritten: 6 mo to get ready for a new manufactur.]

Variables That Influence Supply

- Availability of skilled labor
- Availability of construction loans and financing
- Availability of land
- Availability of materials

SUPPLY

Supply is the amount and type of real estate available for sale or rent at differing price levels in a given real estate market. The variables that influence supply are listed in the text box above.

Availability of skilled labor.   Numerous skilled laborers, such as carpenters, roofers, and electricians, are required for construction. The availability and cost of labor depend on such things as unemployment rates, skill levels required, and the influence of foreign labor. When an area is growing rapidly, the growth usually is characterized by much construction with resulting high employment in the construction industry. These conditions cause competition for labor and its cost increases.

Availability of construction loans and financing.   New construction is directly related to the availability of construction loans and short-term financing. As money becomes more available and less expensive, more speculative homes will be built, increasing the available supply of housing. The same is true for commercial development.

Availability of land.   Although land seems physically plentiful, the supply of the type and location of land most in demand is always scarce. Two factors influence the availability of land: (1) the scarcity of readily usable land and (2) regulations affecting its use and cost of development.

Availability of materials.   The availability of construction materials influences the supply of new housing. In the late 1970s and early 1980s the construction industry nationwide was severely crippled by a shortage of drywall. Drywall couldn't be found anywhere. New construction was stalled, and construction costs spiraled.

DEMAND

Demand has to do with the desire and ability to purchase or rent goods and services. In real estate, demand is the amount and type of real estate desired for purchase or rent in a given market at a given period of time. The variables that influence demand are listed in the text box on the following page.

Price of real estate.   There is an *inverse* relationship between price and the demand for real estate. When prices rise, demand goes down. When prices decrease, demand goes up.

Population numbers and household composition.   Other important variables related to demand are population numbers and household composition. Most of the transactions in the real estate market are residential property transactions. Shelter is a basic need and cannot be

Variables That Influence Demand

- Price of real estate
- Population numbers and household composition
- Income of consumers
- Availability of mortgage credit
- Consumer taste or preferences

Test!

long ignored. However, the demand for dwelling space depends on both numbers of the population and composition of households in every market area. An increase in population creates demand for additional shopping centers, office buildings, and so forth.

Mere population size does not provide sufficient information for accurately estimating the demand for dwelling space, nor does a *count* of households. Modern lifestyles, changes in economic conditions, and reduced family size have caused the household to become the basis for most population analysis. A **household**, as defined by the Bureau of the Census, U.S. Department of Commerce, is any person or group of persons occupying a separate housing space. Thus, a household may be a single person living in a rented apartment, a husband and wife with four children living in their own home in the suburbs, or two unmarried adults living in a condominium near the city center. Each constitutes a household.

It is only when Bureau of the Census data are analyzed that the benefits of *demand trend forecasting* are realized. Just before the end of the nineteenth century, 100 dwelling units housed 490 people, due to the average size of households at that time (4.9 persons). The 2000 census revealed that the decreased size of the average household (about 2.5 people per household) required approximately 196 dwelling units to house 490 people. The change in average household size alone had therefore caused an increase of 96 percent in demand. Demographers and others who study population trends state that a further reduction in average household size is anticipated. This again will change the demand for housing, not only in numbers of units but also in size of dwellings.

Demand for new dwellings every year does not mean that each of the 50 states and the District of Columbia will share this growth on a proportional basis. Natural increase in population (that is, the number of births exceeding the number of deaths) and *immigration*—new residents moving to a location from other places—are two important components of the population factor. Increased longevity of the elderly contributes to the natural increase of population by increasing the number of births over deaths, even if the birth rate remains static. As a result, Florida, along with a few other states, such as California and Arizona, has experienced exceptional population gains. This has been reflected in increased demand for housing.

1   The most important cause of population increase for Florida as a
2   whole has been *immigration*. Every reason exists to suppose that this trend
3   will continue.

The U.S. Census for year 2000 is available on the Internet at:
http://www.census.gov/. *For valuable information click on "Latest Economic Indicators." Data concerning construction spending, new home sales, and housing starts are updated monthly.*

4   **Income of consumers.**   Whereas change in price is inversely related to
5   change in demand, income is directly related to demand. As individual
6   income increases, so does demand for dwelling space. Any change
7   in local employment numbers or salary-wage levels causes a change in
8   demand for dwelling space and related loan considerations.

9   **Availability of mortgage credit.**   The availability and cost of mortgage
10 credit has been called the barometer of the real estate market. Because the
11 typical purchase of residential property involves two or three times the
12 buyer's annual net income, it is easy to understand why more than
13 90 percent of homebuyers use credit to arrange the purchase. If a potential
14 homebuyer can afford the monthly mortgage payments (principal and
15 interest), plus property taxes and hazard insurance, the total cost of the
16 house is of secondary importance.

17 The amortized (principal) portion of a monthly payment can be
18 increased or decreased by (1) the amount of the down payment made on
19 the property and (2) the term of the loan. Both of these have a direct
20 bearing on demand for housing.

21 When a *tight money market* develops and interest rates rise, a
22 corresponding drop is reflected in housing demand because the amount
23 of money needed to make monthly mortgage payments increases. For
24 example, a $90,000 mortgage loan at 7 percent interest for a period of
25 30 years requires a monthly payment of $598.77, not including taxes and
26 insurance. The same amount of money for the same period of time but at
27 9 percent interest requires a monthly payment of $724.16, an additional
28 $125.39 per month. An increase in mortgage interest rates of even
29 1 percent causes a definite drop in demand for housing.

30 **Consumer tastes or preferences.**   Another factor related to demand
31 concerns changing consumer tastes or preferences. Different architectural
32 designs are sometimes introduced into the residential market and may
33 enjoy brief periods of popularity. Generally speaking, however, enduring
34 changes in consumer tastes occur slowly, over extended time periods.
35 Outside elevations or exterior appearances may be subject to change in
36 consumer taste. For example, today there is more and more preference for
37 what are loosely termed modern contemporary exteriors. Whatever style
38 and type of house the buying public prefers at a given time is the type of
39 dwelling that will be built more often, until a new demand creates a new
40 style preference.

41 Changes in demand for condominiums or second homes for vacation
42 purposes also reflect changes in consumer preferences. For years, *empty
43 nesters* (those parents whose children are grown and have moved away)
44 continued to live in the same house where they had reared their children,

1 although it was then entirely too large for their needs as a couple. The
2 numerous chores of the homeowner related to maintenance, repairs, and
3 grounds upkeep were often a joy but sometimes too physically
4 demanding. The advent of condominiums and other forms of smaller,
5 maintenance-free housing units offered a solution to these empty nesters
6 and other small families.

INTERPRETING MARKET CONDITIONS

8 Whenever the supply and demand equilibrium of a market is upset by
9 excess supply, a **buyer's market** develops. The number of excess units in
10 that particular market allows a potential buyer to shop among anxious
11 owner-sellers to obtain better prices and terms. When this condition
12 exists, more intelligent builders may stop building because the excess
13 supply results in a lack of profit. On the other hand, whenever the supply
14 and demand equilibrium is upset by excess demand, a **seller's market**
15 develops. This allows sellers to demand higher prices from buyers, who
16 are forced to compete for available space. More building again takes
17 place until oversupply occurs once more.

More than 500 Buyers Market

- Less than 5% Sellers Market

18 What the average real estate sales associate and broker would like is
19 some sort of dependable reference guide to help interpret market conditions.
20 Fortunately, several indicators help to clarify what the market is doing.
21 Market indicators include:

22 • price levels,

23 • vacancy rates, and

24 • sales volume.

25 **Price levels.** The changes in price levels of home sales and the number
26 of building permits issued for a given period of time are indicators of new
27 housing supply and demand for certain price ranges.

28 **Vacancy rates.** A **vacancy rate** is the percentage of rental units that are
29 not occupied. Vacancy rates are one indicator of the need and demand for
30 housing in a certain market area. An increase in vacancy rates in rental
31 housing indicates a surplus of housing space. A 5 percent vacancy rate
32 (95 percent occupancy rate) is usually considered indicative of a healthy
33 housing market. As the occupancy rate increases, rental rates tend to
34 increase, and apartment dwellers who have been waiting to buy homes of
35 their own are given impetus to start looking for houses for sale and to
36 move out of apartments. This causes increased apartment vacancies and
37 eventually a drop in rents as well as a halt in construction of new
38 apartments.

39 One of the first indications of a revived real estate market has always
40 been an increase in rental occupancies that cannot be attributed
41 to reduced rents or giveaway programs. High occupancy rates lead to
42 increased rents. Increased rents lead to new construction and a revived
43 real estate market.

44 **Sales volume.** There are many ways to collect information on the
45 number and prices of homes sold during the recent past. One can go to the
46 public records, either in person or via the Internet, and extract the number

1 of houses sold. Then, from the state documentary stamp tax on deeds, the
2 approximate sale price of each can be calculated. Tax laws require that the
3 price of each real estate sale be reported. This requirement reduces the
4 problem of collecting housing data.

5 Most towns and cities have newspaper publication of sales during the
6 previous week or previous month. From these published accounts one can
7 extract information on how many sales occurred, the approximate sale
8 prices, where the properties sold were located, and sometimes, the types
9 of houses involved. Licensees in towns and cities that have multiple-
10 listing services find the job a great deal easier.

11 No market indicator is of any value unless one learns how to use it.
12 A database system arranged by subdivision, by streets, or alphabetically
13 can be of great value in building a current sales data file. A large-scale
14 map of a town or those areas of a city where interest is high can become a
15 valuable tool to pinpoint areas of greatest activity and to forecast direction
16 of growth. When a sale is reported in a publication, a color-coded pin can
17 be placed on the map to indicate price range and location of property. A
18 glance at such a map shows where most sales are occurring and the
19 general price ranges. Direction and rate of growth also can be estimated
20 from a sales data map.

Good Idea

Need Maps + Pins

21 ■ SUMMARY

22 A market permits products and services to be bought and sold. Goods
23 and services have no value in and of themselves. Only when they are
24 desired by consumers who can afford them do they have value. The
25 function of every market is to facilitate exchange between buyers
26 and sellers.

27 While the real estate market differs in a number of distinctive ways
28 from other markets, it acts much like all markets with respect to changes
29 in supply and demand, but with a slower response time. Major factors
30 influencing the real estate market are supply, demand, and price of the
31 various types of real estate. If a new industry moves to a small town, the
32 demand for housing will increase, resulting immediately in higher
33 housing costs until the supply of new units can reach equilibrium with the
34 demand for housing units.

■ REVIEW QUESTIONS

1. Any economy in any nation must find answers for three questions: what will be produced, who will do the producing, and
   A. when will production cease?
   B. what will production cost?
   C. who will get what is produced?
   D. which producers will produce what?

2. The company who will do the producing is the
   A. biggest producer of a given product.
   B. company that budgets the most for product promotion.
   C. company that uses only part-time help to avoid expensive employee benefits.
   D. most efficient producer of a comparable-quality product.

3. The ultimate decision makers in the marketplace are
   A. salespersons.
   B. producers.
   C. manufacturers.
   D. consumers.

4. Which characteristic does NOT describe the real estate market?
   A. Land is indestructible.
   B. The market is quick to respond to changes in supply and demand.
   C. Real estate is heterogeneous.
   D. Real estate is immobile.

5. Which statement is FALSE regarding the relationship between price and demand?
   A. An increase in price causes a decrease in demand.
   B. A decrease in price causes an increase in demand.
   C. There is an inverse relationship between price and demand.
   D. An increase in price causes an increase in demand.

6. Government controls influence the real estate market both directly and indirectly. An example of an indirect control is
   A. zoning ordinances.
   B. building moratoriums.
   C. monetary policy.
   D. building codes.

7. Which statement is NOT associated with the economic concept of demand?
    A. Demand is the desire and ability to purchase or lease goods and services.
    B. Changes in price cause an inverse change in demand.
    C. Consumer preferences influence demand.
    D. The availability of building materials influences demand.

8. Variables that influence demand include
    A. consumer tastes and preferences.
    B. population size and household composition.
    C. consumer income.
    D. all of the above.

9. IRS tax statutes regulating depreciation of income-producing property
    A. encourage real estate ownership.
    B. directly affect the supply and demand equilibrium.
    C. affect the available supply of income-producing property.
    D. bring about all of the above.

10. When the equilibrium of the real estate market is upset by an excess supply
    A. builder activity increases in response to the need.
    B. a seller's market exists.
    C. a buyer's market exists.
    D. demand decreases.

11. One person or a group of persons occupying a separate housing space is technically defined as a
    A. unit.
    B. household.
    C. family.
    D. multiple ownership unit.

12. The most important cause of population increase in Florida has been the
    A. increase in consumer income.
    B. number of births exceeding deaths.
    C. in-migration of new residents.
    D. expansion of mortgage credit.

13. The barometer of the real estate market is considered to be the
    A. change in consumer income.
    B. cost and availability of credit.
    C. number of housing starts.
    D. change in consumer tastes.

14. The typical homebuyer today is concerned primarily with the
    A. style of the house being current.
    B. total cost of the house.
    C. amount of the monthly mortgage payment.
    D. occupancy and vacancy ratios.

15. Factors affecting the supply side of the real estate market are related to
    A. availability of land.
    B. availability of skilled labor.
    C. availability of material.
    D. all of the above.

+100!

CHAPTER 20

Planning and Zoning

■ KEY TERMS

base industries

buffer zone

building codes

certificate of occupancy

concurrency

economic base studies

health ordinances

nonconforming use

planned unit develop-
ment (PUD)

service industries

special exception

variance

zoning ordinances

■ OVERVIEW

In a residential community located in a fashionable area, homes are meticulously landscaped with rose bushes and beautiful fountains. It is a neighborhood of executives and their families. Across the street from one of the fashionable homes is a small candy factory, and farther down the street is a soft-drink bottling company. This is just one example of what happens when community planning and land-use control are absent.

After completing this Chapter, the student should be able to:

- distinguish among the six types of land-use planning background studies;

- distinguish among zoning ordinances, building codes, and health ordinances;

- explain the purpose of a variance, a special exception, and a nonconforming use;

- calculate the number of lots available for development, given the total number of acres contained in a parcel, the percentage of land reserved for streets and other facilities, and the minimum number of square feet per lot; and

- describe the characteristics of a planned unit development.

■ HISTORY OF PLANNING AND ZONING

Planning and land-use control have been practiced in this country to varying degrees since the first European settlers arrived. During the colonial period, the British colonies enacted ordinances restricting slaughterhouses and gunpowder mills to the outskirts of the community. Later in the 1800s, cities established fire districts and building height restrictions.

Some early planners attempted to combine the worthy features of several European cities into a single, planned city in the New World. Philadelphia, planned in 1682; Savannah, Georgia, 1733; Washington, D.C., 1791; and New York City, 1811, are notable examples. City planning in the United States experienced highs and lows in popular acceptance. An attitude of on-again, off-again was probably the most discernible characteristic of city planning until the early 1900s.

In the 1800s, industrialization brought a decreased interest in planning and land use regulations. The philosophy of *laissez-faire* (French for "let alone") prevailed among business and political leaders. Laissez-faire, a philosophy of noninterference by the government in private business affairs, advocated letting the owners of land and business fix the rules of competition. Planning and growth management were largely ignored. Property owners used their land to produce the greatest private gain without regard to the impact on the community. As industrialization expanded, people left the farms for city jobs. Unorganized growth resulted.

In 1916 the first serious efforts were made to create and enforce zoning ordinances. The garment industry in New York City was about to expand into the exclusive Fifth Avenue district. A zoning ordinance was enacted to protect Fifth Avenue property values by prohibiting all but specified property uses in that district. Other cities began to adopt zoning ordinances to create or protect local property values. Many property owners objected to the introduction of zoning laws. Most of the objections were raised because of zoning ordinances that prohibited owners from using their land to generate profit or income without compensating them for the rights lost. In 1926 the U.S. Supreme Court ruled that legally enacted zoning laws were constitutional. This ruling gave powers of enforcement to municipalities that had enacted zoning laws for the purpose of regulating future growth. These controls gave rise to city planning and growth management all across the nation.

PLANNING GOALS

As part of the *growth management* process, *city planning* attempts to regulate city growth as required to achieve four basic goals:

1. To plan future land uses that allow the highest and best use of the maximum number of properties

2. To reduce the possibility that a particular type of land use may cause loss of value to neighboring properties

3. To reduce present and future growth costs that must be borne by taxpayers

4. To create an optimal social and economic environment as a result of community growth

Florida's growth management laws require that all local governments discourage urban sprawl and inadequate infrastructure in their comprehensive plans. *Urban sprawl* is the unplanned expansion of a municipality over a large geographic area. Typical urban sprawl patterns of leapfrog development, ribbon or strip development, and low-density residential uses over large land areas increase the cost of public *infrastructure* services (for example, bridges, sewers, utilities, and roads). Growth management planning by a city or county increases the likelihood of goal accomplishment.

■ LOCAL PLANNING AGENCY

Hartford, Connecticut, organized the first official land-use planning agency in the United States, in 1907. Today there are planning agencies at all levels of government. Planning commissions in Florida are primarily at the city and county level. The **concurrency** provision in Florida's Growth Management Act of 1985 mandates that the infrastructure, such as roads and water and waste treatment facilities needed to support additional population, be in place before new development is allowed. Many communities have experienced complete curtailment of new construction because of a building moratorium until a new sewage treatment plant, for example, was completed.

Cities and counties compete with each other to attract new residents and industries. To plan efficiently beyond local community boundaries, a *comprehensive plan* (or master plan) is thought necessary. The process of developing such plans often uncovers unexpected obstacles. Chapter 163, F.S., charged the Department of Community Affairs (DCA) with the regulation and standardization of regional, county, and city comprehensive plans and required that all levels of government within the state develop comprehensive plans to guide and control future growth.

COMPOSITION

Planning commissions are most effective when composed of members who represent all walks of life. Members most often are not trained professional planners. The overriding goal is to have representatives from a cross section of interests. A planning commission composed entirely of developers, for example, could not possibly speak for all the people. The homes, desires, and goals of all residents should be considered.

Members of the planning commission usually are appointed (not elected) and serve in a voluntary, unpaid capacity. The primary legislative body of the city or county is the appointing authority, normally a city

1 council or a county commission. Planning commissions vary in size, and
2 the terms for which planning commissioners are appointed may vary
3 from the terms of their colleagues. This ensures a staggered rate of
4 replacement and is designed to prevent any one appointing authority
5 from selecting an entire planning commission. Planning commissioners
6 are usually appointed for terms longer than the term of the appointing
7 authority to reduce the commissioners' obligation to any single political
8 body. This minimizes political influence within the planning body.

9   The planning commission or board serves as an advisory body to
10 the elected city or county government. As important as the planning
11 function may be to the future welfare of a community, the commission is
12 not the final authority in matters related to planning. The commission
13 is responsible for planning, just as the police department is responsible for
14 law enforcement, but the elected government must make the final
15 decisions based on recommendations from subordinate agencies.

AUTHORITY

17 Three areas of responsibility for which city planning commissions are
18 commonly delegated final authority are: (1) subdivision plat approval,
19 (2) site plan approval, and (3) sign control.

20 **Subdivision plat approval.**   A developer planning to create a
21 subdivision must submit a *subdivision plat* to the planning commission for
22 approval. (See also Chapter 1.) A developer is not issued a building permit
23 until final approval is granted by the planning commission. When
24 approval is received, the developer may proceed to record the plat in the
25 public records and receive a building permit.

26 **Site plan approval.**   The *site plan* serves the same function that a
27 subdivision plat serves for a subdivision. It is a detailed plan of how the
28 project is to be developed, how traffic and parking will be dealt with, and
29 what impact on neighboring properties may be expected. This is an area
30 in which the expertise of the planning commission's support staff can be
31 of great assistance. Reviewing and checking site plan proposals requires
32 painstaking attention to detail and a well-rounded background of
33 information. This ensures compliance with all physical, economic, and
34 environmental requirements.

35 **Sign control.**   More and more cities are exercising control over signs.
36 The primary aims of sign control are to minimize distraction to motorists
37 and to eliminate actual safety hazards created by signs at blind corners,
38 lighted signs that glare into the eyes of drivers at night, and the like.
39 Any aesthetic improvement resulting from sign control is a welcomed
40 by-product.

SUPPORT STAFF

42 While each appointed member of the commission may be expert in his or
43 her own field, he or she is often not an urban planning expert. The
44 planning commission's function is to make policy recommendations
45 regarding the type of city it feels that citizens want in the future. It sets

FIGURE 20.1   Comprehensive Plan

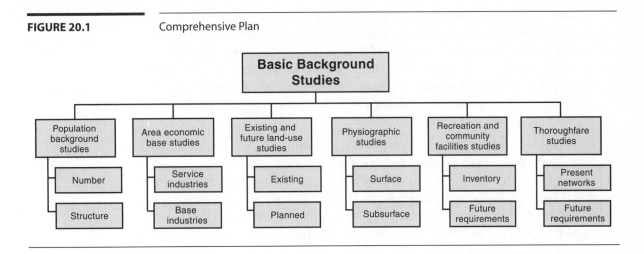

1 goals and provides residents with a number of feasible alternative plans
2 for achieving those goals. The job of collecting, sorting, analyzing, and
3 reporting is handled by the staff of the planning commission.

4   The planning commission support staff is composed of full-time city
5 or county employees. Staff members are normally college-trained or
6 university-trained planners. They have learned how to evaluate the
7 economic base of a city. They know the most productive sources of
8 information regarding population, proper land uses, and support
9 requirements for future growth. The planning support staff collects and
10 refines the raw data to produce the basic studies needed to develop a
11 flexible, comprehensive plan for future growth.

12 ## ■ THE PLANNING PROCESS

13 ### BASIC BACKGROUND STUDIES

14 Before the goals, objectives, and policies can be finalized, the planning
15 commission and its support staff must have a good idea of what has
16 happened in the past, what the present situation is, and what projections
17 indicate for the future. Six types of background studies (see Figure 20.1)
18 are used by planners:

19   1. Population background studies

20   2. Economic base studies

21   3. Existing land-use studies

22   4. Physiographic studies

23   5. Recreation and community facilities studies

24   6. Thoroughfare studies

25 **Population background studies.**   The population and its geographic
26 distribution are the basic determinants of comprehensive planning.
27 Population studies are the most basic and important of all planning
28 studies. These studies identify the following: the composition of the

1 population; the number of households and their approximate incomes;
2 and the numbers and locations of different ethnic groups, occupations of
3 residents, and educational levels. With this demographic information,
4 predictions can be made for the future. In Florida, predictions normally
5 are limited to periods of five years to ten years into the future. In states
6 where growth is slow, the planning predictions may be projected for
7 15 years to 20 years into the future.

8   Population studies give planners an indication of the number of new
9 households expected to move into an area. This information is of great
10 assistance in estimating the cost of social services for a larger, and in some
11 cases older, population. Planners can alert cities and counties to the
12 number of additional police officers, firefighters, teachers, medical
13 facilities, and the like that will be required to handle the new residents.

14 **Economic base studies.**   **Economic base studies** analyze the effect of
15 base-industry employment in the area. **Base industries** are those
16 industries that attract outside money to the area, such as film making,
17 fertilizer plants, and the citrus industry. **Service industries** are those such
18 as grocery stores, barber shops, and retail stores, whose customers are
19 primarily local residents. These industries keep money already in the area
20 circulating but attract little outside money to the area.

21   These studies also will reveal whether an area is principally tourist-
22 oriented, industrial, commercial, educational, or agricultural in character.
23 Perhaps the area can boast of several economic activities. The more
24 diversified the economic base, the more stable the area economy tends to
25 be. This contributes to growth and stable property values.

26 **Existing land-use studies.**   To plan for future land use, the planning
27 commission takes an inventory of all public and private land uses. The
28 commission does a complete survey of land uses, with detailed maps
29 plotting each separate land parcel. Individual lots and tracts can be
30 identified on land-use maps with colors or codes to indicate the present
31 use of the land. Once completed, existing land-use patterns dictate, to a
32 great degree, the location of future land uses. Generally, professional
33 planners use five basic land-use categories: (1) residential, (2) commercial,
34 (3) industrial, (4) agricultural, and (5) special use. Basic land-use
35 classifications are divided further into subcategories. For example, a
36 county might use:

37 • *residential:* single-family, one-family to four-family, multifamily;

38 • *commercial:* neighborhood shopping, community business,
39   professional offices, shopping center, central business district;

40 • *industrial:* component assembly, light manufacturing, heavy
41   industry, warehousing; and

42 • *special use:* public schools, churches, recreational areas (community
43   parks and national parks).

44   Unfortunately, there is no uniform standard of land-use classification
45 that applies to all parts of the state. Each planning commission or zoning

1   authority may establish any system desired to prevent encroachment of
2   incompatible uses.

3   Once the land-use studies are complete and all of the current uses of
4   individual parcels are accounted for, it is a relatively simple matter to
5   determine the number of acres being utilized for each classification. This
6   information can then be coordinated with results of the population
7   studies to develop a preliminary land-use plan for the future.

8   **Physiographic studies.**   Physiographic studies help avoid unexpected
9   problems with soil conditions: drainage, soil percolation, and load-
10 bearing capacity. They describe the physical structure of the land. All of
11 the various soil types are cataloged and then plotted on a map. Each soil
12 type is coded to indicate recommended usage. For example, some soil
13 types require floating foundations or special pilings. Areas where these
14 types of soil conditions are found are not suitable for high-rise buildings.
15 Some soils do not drain well, necessitating special storm drainage
16 systems. Physiographic studies with accompanying maps are a factor in
17 determining the highest and best use of specific tracts of land.

18 **Recreation and community facilities studies.**   These studies, which
19 should be coordinated with the population studies, plan for public and
20 private recreation areas. Parks, playgrounds, beaches, and municipal
21 facilities are identified and plotted on a map. A relationship then can be
22 established to indicate the population number and type to be served.

23 When the existing community facilities are located and plotted, plans
24 can be made for the location of appropriate similar facilities in those areas
25 marked for future growth. Projections can be made for the number and
26 location of additional parks, playgrounds, and community recreational
27 facilities needed to serve the planned residential areas.

28 **Thoroughfare studies.**   Thoroughfare studies are designed to identify
29 existing and projected traffic circulation systems. They are closely related
30 to population and economic studies. Federal and state laws require that
31 cities of 50,000 people or more do urban area thoroughfare studies to
32 reflect present and future transportation networks. Because cities of that
33 size have an effective market area much larger than that contained within
34 the city limits, these studies must include the surrounding urban areas,
35 which are considered part of the metropolitan market area.

36 Thoroughfare studies are normally a joint venture involving city,
37 county, and state transportation departments and regional planning
38 commissions. Such studies must anticipate requirements for ingress and
39 egress and traffic flow to future residential and commercial areas that may
40 be still in the planning stage. They also must anticipate increased amounts
41 of roadway and pedestrian traffic generated by new residents. In
42 addition, they must consider the transportation requirements of
43 neighboring cities and counties. Because most counties share
44 transportation problems with their neighbors, they share the need for
45 joint planning efforts.

GOALS FORMULATION

When the background studies are completed, the planning support staff will have provided the planning commission with the information needed to enter the next phase of city planning: formulating goals. Before the data from the background studies are converted into a single comprehensive plan for growth management, the planning commission attempts to find out what type of city the residents want. Some cities mail each resident a questionnaire, some use inserts in local newspapers, some hold public hearings, and some have members of the planning commission make presentations to social and civic clubs. The main purpose of this phase of city planning is to identify broad planning objectives that the community residents want to achieve.

Time and time again, experience has demonstrated that the desires of the population must be considered if a comprehensive plan is to be effective. This is one of the reasons a planning commission should include representatives from occupations not related to real estate or development.

■ ZONING LAWS AND CODE ENFORCEMENT

Zoning ordinances are enacted to ensure that property owners adhere to the planned types of land uses and to protect the integrity of the comprehensive plan. No other land-use controls affect all properties in a community to a greater degree than zoning ordinances. Used in conjunction with building codes, they are effective in protecting property values.

Zoning ordinances are local laws that implement the comprehensive plan. Local government exercises *police power* by regulating and controlling the use of land and structures within designated land-use districts or zones. Each zone is assigned a specific land-use classification. Unless an exception is granted, only the assigned land use is allowed in a particular zone to protect against uses that might reduce the value of neighboring properties. Zoning ordinances regulate the following:

- Permissible uses for each parcel of land

Police Power = Zoning

- Lot size

- Type of structures

- Building heights

- Setback requirements (the space between lot lines and building lines)

- Density (the ratio of land area to structure area also known as *floor area ratio*—determined by dividing the total floor area of a building by the total land area of the site)

Building codes protect the public health and safety from inferior construction practices. Building codes set minimum standards for materials and quality of workmanship, sanitary equipment, electrical wiring, fire prevention, and so forth. Florida has a statewide building

1 code called the *Florida Building Code.* Additionally, cities and counties may
2 enforce more stringent building code requirements.

 wwweb.link   *To learn more about the Florida unified building code on the Internet, visit* **http://www.FloridaBuilding.org.**

3 Local government enforces building codes. The process begins by
4 issuing a *building permit* after review of the architectural and engineering
5 drawings. Municipal inspectors visit each job site and conduct building
6 inspections at various phases of the construction. The inspections must
7 pass before the next phase of construction can proceed. A final **certificate**
8 **of occupancy** is issued once construction is completed and the municipal
9 building inspector agrees that the structure conforms to code.

10 **Health ordinances** control maintenance and sanitation of public
11 spaces. The local health department inspects and enforces sanitary
12 standards in a community's food and drinking establishments.

RESIDENTIAL

14 *Residential zoning* regulates *density,* meaning the number of units (homes)
15 per acre. Several subcategories establish different minimum sizes for lots.

16 *Example:* Imagine that residential zone R-1A requires that all lots in
17 that subcategory contain at least 9,000 square feet of land. This auto-
18 matically restricts the number of lots a developer can create from each
19 acre in a subdivision. Every acre of land contains 43,560 square feet. A
20 given developer is going to develop 100 acres. In the process of turning
21 raw land into a subdivision, between 20 percent and 25 percent of the
22 land is commonly used for streets and open space. Wider streets and
23 open green space add quality but reduce the amount of land available
24 for lots. Using 25 percent loss for streets, the developer can determine
25 the number of lots per acre (density) permitted by the R-1A zoning.

26 43,560 square feet per acre × .75 land available for lots =
27 32,670 square feet available per acre

28 32,670 ÷ 9,000 minimum square feet per lot =
29 3.63 lots per acre (density)

30 3.63 × 100 acres = 363 total subdivision lots

31 In the same county, residential zoning subcategory R-1AA may
32 require one-acre lots, and R-1B may require only a minimum of 8,000
33 square feet per lot. Zoning authorities may create as many zoning
34 subcategories as needed. They also fix the criteria for each subcategory.

COMMERCIAL

36 The purpose of *commercial zoning* is to regulate *intensity* of use. Intensity
37 is determined by the type and amount of pedestrian and vehicular traffic
38 generated by a commercial enterprise. Businesses that generate a great
39 deal of traffic, such as service stations, are normally less desirable next to
40 quiet residential areas. In contrast, a physician's office or an attorney's
41 office does not create the same degree of threat to residential values.
42 Zoning ordinances normally recognize these conditions by creating a

1 *buffer zone* between residential and commercial zones. A **buffer zone** is a
2 strip of land separating one land use from another. Frequently, the buffer
3 zone will allow multifamily zoning (for example, apartments) next to
4 single-family residential areas, then a professional business zone, then
5 higher intensity zones.

INDUSTRIAL

7 *Industrial zoning* also is intended to *regulate* intensity of use. In addition,
8 industrial zoning subcategories are used to control the amount and
9 location of industrial offshoots resulting from different kinds of
10 industrial activity. A wide industrial-base city may have many
11 subcategories of industrial zoning, whereas a city oriented toward
12 agriculture, tourism, or education may have only one or two industrial
13 subcategories. One innovation in industrial zoning has been industrial
14 subdivisions, or *industrial parks*. (See also Chapter 1.)

AGRICULTURAL

16 The *agricultural zoning* classification is an all-inclusive category; it is not
17 divided into subcategories. If the existing use of the property is for some
18 type of agriculture, no zoning controls will attempt to regulate the type
19 of agriculture permitted. If the use fails to qualify for an agricultural
20 classification, the property then can be rezoned into another zoning
21 category.

SPECIAL USE

23 Although the county property appraiser may be interested in knowing
24 exactly what level of government owns what property, most zoning
25 authorities consider all property owned by all levels of government as a
26 type of special-use property. Public zoning is a subcategory of special-use
27 zoning, which includes, for example, city parks, county courthouses, and
28 federal post office buildings. This zoning category is exempt from local
29 zoning regulation.

■ APPEALS AND EXCEPTIONS

ZONING BOARD OF ADJUSTMENT

32 Owners of real estate may appeal enforcement of zoning restrictions in
33 cases where strict compliance would cause undue hardship or reduce
34 property values. To handle appeals and requests for relief, most zoning
35 authorities have established a semijudicial body called the *Zoning Board
36 of Adjustment*, or simply *Board of Adjustment*. The primary function of the
37 Zoning Board of Adjustment is to provide property owners some degree
38 of relief from otherwise rigid zoning codes. The board must take all
39 possible precautions to render objective, unbiased decisions because its
40 quasi-judicial powers give it some of the characteristics of a court. Once
41 the Zoning Board of Adjustment renders a decision, most zoning laws

1 will allow a property owner only one additional avenue of appeal,
2 litigation in the courts.

Variances. A **variance** allows a property owner to *vary* from strict
4 compliance with all or part of a zoning code because to comply would
5 force an undue hardship on the property owner. Two conditions must be
6 met before a property owner may be granted a variance from existing
7 zoning requirements:

8 1. The property owner must show that a *hardship* exists or will be
9   created by strict compliance with zoning requirements and that he
10   or she did nothing to cause the hardship. This will prevent a
11   property owner or developer from taking some action designed for
12   private benefit with the expectation that the Zoning Board of
13   Adjustment will accept or approve the situation the property
14   owner or developer created.

15 2. The Zoning Board of Adjustment must use the same established
16   criteria to judge the validity of all requests for a variance. This
17   ensures fair and impartial treatment for each property owner
18   requesting a variance.

19 Many people have trouble with the word *hardship*. It has nothing to do
20 with economic or personal hardships. It involves land *use*, and the
21 hardship must relate to the use of the property. For example, suppose you
22 bought a nice lot on a river where zoning restrictions require "setback"
23 distances of 25 feet from the front of the lot and 30 feet from the river or
24 rear of the lot. Imagine you are about to start construction of a new house
25 designed to fit precisely the above setback requirements when a survey
26 reveals that erosion by the river over time has carried away 10 feet from
27 the river side of your lot. The maximum setback distance possible is now
28 only 20 feet. Because zoning restrictions require 30 feet, you will be in
29 violation if you go ahead with construction. Violation of zoning laws can
30 cause removal of the offending structure. To prevent potential trouble,
31 you request a variance. The hardship exists, and you did nothing to cause
32 the hardship. You would have met the hardship requirement for a
33 variance (the first condition in the preceding list).

Special exceptions. The Zoning Board of Adjustment is authorized to
35 issue **special exceptions** for controlling the location of particular land
36 uses. A dentist's office might be granted a special exception in an area
37 located near a large mobile home community. Another example is an
38 adult day-care facility in a residential area composed primarily of retirees.
39 A special exception grants a specific use of a particular parcel. Special
40 exceptions are a departure from the zoning ordinance, generally permitted
41 in cases where it is determined that the surrounding area would be better
42 served by allowing the special exception. Most communities require
43 public hearings before a special exception is granted so that property
44 owners of surrounding parcels have an opportunity to provide input in
45 the decision process.

Legally nonconforming uses. If a property's use was lawfully
47 established but no longer conforms to the use regulations of the zone in
48 which it is located because of the enactment of a new zoning ordinance,

---

TABLE 20.1 Government Land-Use Controls

Method	Function
Building code	Controls construction and materials
Zoning ordinance	Controls utilization
Health ordinance	Controls maintenance and sanitation
Variance	Permission to build or use to relieve a hardship *not* caused by owner
Special exception	Permission to build or use in apparent conflict with existing zoning ordinance
Nonconforming use	Permission to continue to use in spite of enacted zoning ordinance

---

1 the use is allowed to continue as **a nonconforming use.** For example, a
2 small neighborhood gas station might have located in an area that was
3 later zoned residential. The small gas station within the new residential
4 zone is *grandfathered* as a nonconforming use.

5   The U.S. Constitution prohibits depriving a person of property
6 without due process or fair compensation. Local governments may not
7 employ eminent domain powers to correct nonconforming uses unless
8 the property is taken for a public use. The methods used to correct a
9 nonconforming use vary around the state. Most zoning authorities
10 allow a time period long enough for nonconforming property owners to
11 recapture their investment in the property. After the expiration of this
12 designated period, the property owner must convert the use of the
13 property to that use for which the area is zoned. If, during the designated
14 period, the structure on the property is damaged or more than 50 percent
15 destroyed, the property must be converted to a use that conforms with
16 area zoning. Other communities allow a legal nonconforming use to
17 continue until ownership changes. Nonconforming-use properties usually
18 are not permitted to be increased in size or to undergo structural changes.
19 Most zoning authorities restrict repairs and maintenance of such properties
20 to those needed for sanitation and safety purposes. These procedures are
21 designed to result in all properties eventually becoming conforming-use
22 properties. (Government land-use controls are shown in Table 20.1.)

DEVELOPMENTS OF REGIONAL IMPACT   Meers in Gainsville – Holliday Inn.

24 As the state grows, planning assumes an ever-increasing importance and
25 responsibility. Regional planning groups are becoming more instrumental
26 in controlling growth. In fact, no planned development of sufficient size
27 to affect surrounding areas can be approved without regional planning
28 approval. Developments of Regional Impact (DRIs) have become the

subject of a separate statute in Florida to ensure better control of the environment, today and in the future.

The term *development of regional impact* means any development that, because of its character, size, or location, will have a substantial effect on the health, safety, or welfare of citizens of more than one county in the state. Statewide guidelines and standards, along with numerical "thresholds" (limits), are used to determine whether particular developments must undergo DRI review. The review process evaluates everything from air quality to roads and schools. DRIs include projects such as shopping centers and malls, industrial plants and parks, port facilities, and residential developments.

Regional planning commissions (or councils) are organized in much the same manner as county or city planning groups. The commission members are appointed, and a trained professional support staff assists with administrative and technical matters. Like their local counterparts, regional planning commissions are advisory in nature. This means that the appointing authority (city or county for the area in which a project is located) makes the decision to implement, reject, or modify recommendations submitted by the regional planning group.

 Planned unit development.   Both a legal and a development design concept, a **planned unit development (PUD)** permits a mix of land uses along with a high density of residential units. PUDs have specific characteristics that set them apart from the usual neighborhood and subdivision developments:

- The density of dwelling units is higher than that allowed for conventional, single-family developments.

- Typically, most dwelling units are either apartments or town houses (multifamily).

- Dwelling units are normally clustered, with planned green spaces between clusters.

- Most PUDs include residential areas, shopping areas, and professional offices.

Ordinances regulating PUDs usually allow higher population densities as a trade-off for complying with very strict requirements for development plan approval.

Environmental impact statement.   An *environmental impact statement* (EIS) is a required description of the probable cost-benefit impact that a proposed large development project will have on the environment during all phases of development. To ensure that environmental amenities are given the same consideration as economic and technical elements, the study must estimate the effects of the development project on waste-disposal systems, air quality, existing or proposed thoroughfare systems, and local employment, as well as any long-term effects on the earth's surface. DRIs, PUDs, and even regional shopping malls are required to submit an EIS, usually to a regional planning agency.

■ SUMMARY

The planning of community development in the United States has experienced highs and lows in acceptance. City planning is the effort to manage, coordinate, and regulate growth. Ideally, a planning board (commission) consists of appointed lay citizens. It serves as an advisory body to the elected city or county government. A professional planning support staff collects raw data, refines them, and produces the basic studies needed to develop a flexible, comprehensive plan for future growth. Zoning ordinances and building codes are important means for controlling land use in a community. Zoning boards of adjustment provide an avenue for appeal when property owners feel that existing zoning laws cause them undue hardship or a reduction in their property values.

■ REVIEW QUESTIONS

1. One of the major reasons for the lack of emphasis on city planning in the 1800s was the
   A. focus on identifying and locating rural tracts for farming using a new method of describing real property.
   B. philosophy of laissez-faire.
   C. reduction in university course offerings in real estate and urban development.
   D. exodus from the farms to the cities for jobs.

2. The subsection in Florida's Growth Management Act that requires that parks, roads, sewers, and drinking water be available before new development is allowed is referred to as the
   A. utilities provision.
   B. infrastructure provision.
   C. concurrency provision.
   D. level of service provision.

3. A planning commission is normally composed of
   A. trained professional planners.
   B. elected officials.
   C. appointed unpaid members.
   D. members of the primary legislative city or county body.

4. The best composition of a planning commission is generally thought to be one with representation from
   A. each licensed professional occupation.
   B. senior adult homeowners because of their experience.
   C. real estate and mortgage lending firms.
   D. a cross section of interests.

5. In municipalities with planning commissions, the final authority in planning matters is the
    A. planning commission chairperson.
    B. professional staff director.
    C. elected city government officials.
    D. planning commission support staff supervisor.

6. The primary function of a planning commission is to
    A. make policy recommendations to the elected government body.
    B. make policy recommendations to the trained professional staff.
    C. advise the next higher planning board (county, regional, etc.) of its recommendations and actions.
    D. collect, refine, and produce the basic studies needed to develop a comprehensive plan for future growth.

7. A strip of land that separates one land use from another is referred to as a(n)
    A. easement.
    B. egress.
    C. buffer zone.
    D. median.

8. The most basic of all the background planning studies is the
    A. economic base study.
    B. land-use study.
    C. community facilities study.
    D. population study.

9. A land-use study
    A. shows where future land uses should be.
    B. involves plotting each parcel on a land-use map.
    C. requires an inventory of public and private land uses.
    D. involves all of the above.

10. Population background studies include an estimate of
    A. the number of new households expected to move into the area.
    B. the best housing markets of the future.
    C. the future cost of social services.
    D. all of the above.

11. Base industries contribute to stability and growth; service industries are the businesses that
    A. do not attract much outside money to the area.
    B. attract outside money to the area.
    C. manufacture and export products.
    D. create and export service assistance.

12. Physiographic studies reveal the
    A. physical location of shopping centers and subdivisions.
    B. transportation network structure.
    C. surface and subsurface structure of land.
    D. density and intensity structure of population.

13. Thoroughfare studies are normally a
    A. city project.
    B. county project.
    C. state project.
    D. cooperative project.

14. To be granted a variance, a property owner must provide evidence that
    A. the same treatment has been afforded other owners.
    B. a hardship related to land use exists.
    C. the variance, if granted, will be for the owner's use only.
    D. the land use existed before passage of zoning laws.

15. Residential zoning is designed to regulate
    A. intensity.
    B. frequency.
    C. density.
    D. all of the above.

16. Commercial zoning is designed to regulate
    A. intensity.
    B. frequency.
    C. density.
    D. all of the above.

17. A small general store that existed before a change to residential zoning would be an example of a
    A. special exception.
    B. variance.
    C. PUD.
    D. nonconforming use.

18. The legal right to enact zoning laws is derived from
    A. police powers.
    B. public policy.
    C. property taxation.
    D. all of the above.

19. Zoning ordinances regulate
    A. the firewall rating of a wall located between the kitchen and dining areas of a restaurant.
    B. the setback requirements of a building from the property lines.
    C. the electrical rating of the wiring in a residential home.
    D. all of the above.

20. A parcel of land contains 75 acres. A developer has reserved 25 percent of the land for streets and green space. Applicable zoning regulations require a minimum of 9,500 square feet per residential lot. The number of permissible lots is
    A. 86.
    B. 232.
    C. 257.
    D. 260.

CHAPTER 21

Case Studies in Real Estate

repo Through.

■ INTRODUCTION

Among the numerous teaching-learning tools available, the case study is perhaps the best method for helping future licensees become aware of some of the problems and decisions they will face in the normal course of real estate activity. Experience has demonstrated that the best results are obtained by having students read and analyze case studies in advance of class, with the idea of participating actively in subsequent classroom discussion concerning the ethics and legalities involved.

The cases that follow provide prospective licensees with an opportunity to: (1) study the findings of facts in actual cases, (2) apply their understanding of the Florida Real Estate License Law to these facts, and (3) gain practical experience in recognizing violations of the law. If applicants understand the license law, can analyze common situations facing licensees, and can identify possible violations of the law, they will be more competent as licensees and also less likely to violate the law.

Selection of this group of case studies was based on frequency of violation, seriousness of the violation, and instructional value and ease. All these cases are a matter of public record, having been reported in the "Disciplinary Actions" section of the *Florida Real Estate Commission News & Report*. Fictitious names have been used to conceal the identities of the actual licensees (or former licensees). With the exception of minor editorial changes in format and content, the case material is intact from the original DBPR documents.

A synopsis of the facts in each case, the specific charges against each licensee (the violations), and the penalties assessed are to be explored in class. The synopsis, violations, and penalties in each case may also be found in the author's book, *Florida Real Estate Exam Manual*, current edition.

■ CASE STUDY #1

Department of Business and   vs.   Respondent
Professional Regulation, Florida
Real Estate Commission,
Petitioner

Administrative
Complaint:

The Petitioner seeks disciplinary action against the Respondent and against her license to practice real estate. In the aftermath of Hurricane Andrew, Jim Jones and Sandy Smith sought to rent a place to live until repairs could be made to their home. Jones responded to a newspaper advertisement placed by the Respondent and her brokerage firm on behalf of the owners, the Dows. The Respondent, a licensed real estate sales associate, showed Jones and Smith the house and they indicated they wished to rent it. Before finalizing the rental, the Respondent called the Dows to discuss the agreement. Ms. Dow proceeded to inquire of the Respondent regarding race and ethnic background of Jones and Smith. The conversation included, in part:

Ms. Dow:	Are they Hispanic?
Respondent:	No.
Ms. Dow:	Are they black?
Respondent:	Yes.
Ms. Dow:	No, I cannot rent the house to black people because I live in part of the house and because of what the neighbors will say about something like that.
Respondent:	We are not supposed to discriminate that way.
Ms. Dow:	Look for someone else.

The Respondent contacted Jones and Smith and told them that the owners did not want persons of color in their house. The Respondent recommended that Jones and Smith retain a lawyer. Ultimately, the Dows were found guilty of discrimination by HUD and ordered to pay a $10,000 fine and damages of $35,000 each to Jones and Smith. HUD also fined the Respondent (licensee) $100 and required her to attend fair housing training. The FREC voted, in its separate disciplinary case, to suspend the sales associate's license for two years and impose a $1,000 fine. This Ruling was, however, overturned on appeal on the grounds that the FREC did not have the disciplinary guidelines in place for the type of violation charged. Following this case, Rule 61J2-24.001, F.A.C., was amended.

Discussion Questions:

1. Which subsections of Chapter 475, F.S., were violated?

2. What was the violation that the Respondent committed?

3. How should the Respondent have handled the initial questioning by Ms. Dow regarding the racial or ethnic background of Jones and Smith?

Synopsis of Facts:

Violations:

Penalty:

■ CASE STUDY #2

Department of Business and   vs.   C. Jones, Respondent
Professional Regulation, Division
of Real Estate, Petitioner

*Administrative
Complaint:*

The Petitioner seeks disciplinary action against the Respondent and against her license to practice. The Respondent, a licensed real estate broker associate, was and is employed by XYZ Realty, Inc., Apopka. Respondent Jones listed a house owned by Lorenzo and Sophia Cannariato for $48,000 in June [year 1]. In August [year 1], potential buyer Julia Fay Spivey submitted an offer of $46,500 for the house.

The buyer was unable to qualify for a mortgage on property valued above $40,000. Respondent Jones then prepared two offers, one indicating a purchase price of $40,000 and the other showing a purchase price of $6,500. Both offers were submitted and accepted as a total purchase price of $46,500.

The buyer then used the $40,000 contract to obtain a first mortgage loan from First Federal of Apopka. First Federal was not made aware of the true purchase price of $46,500. The Uniform Settlement Statement used at the closing showed a purchase price of only $40,000. The transaction closed on October 28, [year 1].

Discussion Questions:

1. Which subsections of Chapter 475, F.S., did the Respondent violate, and what were the violations?

2. Did the Respondent's actions constitute fraud?

3. What are the essential elements of actionable fraud in a civil proceeding? Were the essential elements of fraud present in this case?

Synopsis of Facts:

Violations:

Penalty:

■ CASE STUDY #3

Department of Business and vs. A. Smith, Respondent
Professional Regulation, Florida
Real Estate Commission,
Petitioner

Recommended Order: Pursuant to notice, a hearing was held before Administrative Law Judge Arnold H. Pollack, Division of Administrative Hearings, on July 27, [year 2]. The issue: whether disciplinary action is called for due to violations alleged in the Administrative Complaint. Appearances were made by:

For Petitioner: Tina Hipple, Esquire
Gary Printly, Esquire, DBPR

For Respondent: Erik C. Larsen, Esquire

On December 29, [year 1], the Petitioner filed an Administrative Complaint alleging Respondent Smith was guilty of a number of violations of Florida statutes during April and May [year 1]. On February 2, [year 2], the Respondent executed an Election of Rights form disputing the allegations and requested a formal hearing.

Findings of Fact: At all times pertinent to the hearing, the Respondent was a licensed real estate sales associate in Florida employed by registered real estate broker B. Brown, Longwood. On April 3, [year 1], the Respondent's broker listed the seven-year-old house that he had managed for absentee owners William and Gloria Thomas for $42,500, through an exclusive listing. After informing the principals that a price of $40,000 was a fair price, the asking price of $42,500 was arrived at to give the Thomases some bargaining room.

On April 15, [year 1], the Respondent submitted an offer as buyer to purchase the house for $40,000, with closing set for June 30, [year 1]. On April 16, [year 1], Respondent Smith unilaterally changed the closing date to May 30, [year 1]. The Thomases telegraphed their acceptance of the offer the same day, with the exception that closing would be on or before May 15, [year 1].

On April 28, [year 1], Respondent Smith showed the house to Mr. and Mrs. Philip Fillman, recent arrivals in the area, and advised them that comparable homes were selling for between $55,000 and $61,000, representing the house as a good investment at $45,500.

The prospects asked if the owners would accept less, and the Respondent replied that they would not, having already refused a lesser offer. At no time did the Respondent indicate that he already had the house under contract for $40,000 or that he was representing himself. At no time was any offer for the property, other than that submitted by the Respondent for $40,000, which was accepted by the Thomases, ever submitted to them by the Respondent, Mr. Brown, the broker, or anyone else.

The Fillmans agreed to pay $45,500, and on April 28, [year 1], executed a contract to buy the property with a down payment of $6,000 payable to A. Smith, the Respondent. Smith deposited the check in his personal account. The Respondent named himself as seller on the contract and indicated without explanation to the buyers that he had "control" of the property. Closing was set for June 1, [year 1].

Both transactions were closed in Orlando on May 14, [year 1], in succession. At the first closing, which was not personally attended by the Thomases, they conveyed the property to Respondent Smith. At the second closing moments later, the Respondent conveyed the property to the Fillmans. The buyers signed an insurance form authorizing payment of $159.05 to the original absentee owners (the Thomases), which resulted in the first contact between the Thomases and the Fillmans. Thereafter, both parties learned the true sequence of events.

Respondent Smith contends that he had contracted to buy the property to live in, if his wife approved, or to otherwise lease it as an investment. However, the Respondent had just recently moved into a newly built house and had put the property in question up for sale within two weeks of contracting to buy it. Smith also indicated that he had been a real estate agent for a few months only, yet his Florida application for licensure shows approximately five years of experience as a real estate agent in Maryland.

Discussion Questions:

1. Which subsections of Chapter 475, F.S. were violated, and what were the violations?

2. Are the elements of fraud present in this case?

3. Can an administrative penalty be imposed on a licensee for dishonest acts when dealing for his own account?

Synopsis of Facts:

Violations:

Penalty:

■ CASE STUDY #4

Department of Business and   vs.   G. Green, Respondent
Professional Regulation, Division
of Real Estate, Petitioner

Administrative Complaint:

The Petitioner seeks disciplinary action against the Respondent and against his license to practice. Respondent Green was a licensed real estate sales associate, at all times alleged herein, in the employ of corporate broker XYZ Realty, Inc., Mt. Dora. On June 24, [year 1], the Respondent obtained a written listing for the sale of vacant land owned by Richard and Patricia Jungferman. The Respondent was advised by the owners that the existing mortgage was a ten-year partially amortized mortgage with a final balloon payment. Respondent Green failed, refused, or neglected to note on the listing agreement or in the multiple-listing service information or to advise cooperating agents, the purchaser, or the closing attorney that the assumable existing mortgage required a balloon payment.

A sale contract was signed on August 9, [year 1]. The closing was held September 8, [year 1]. The Respondent knew, or should have had reason to believe, that the purchaser, John A. Henns, thought the assumable mortgage was a conventional 20-year mortgage rather than a partially amortized mortgage. The purchaser put his faith in the acts and conduct of the Respondent out of trust in and reliance on the Respondent.

Discussion Questions:

1. What is a partially amortized mortgage and balloon payment?

2. Which subsection of Chapter 475, F.S., was violated, and what were the violations?

3. Does the Respondent salesperson have potential liability in a civil suit?

Synopsis of Facts:

Violations:

Penalty:

■ CASE STUDY #5

	Department of Business and vs. B. Brown, Respondent Professional Regulation, Florida Real Estate Commission, Petitioner
Recommended Order:	This case was heard in Orlando on September 30, [year 3], before Administrative Law Judge R. T. Carpenter, Division of Administrative Hearings. The parties were represented by:
For Petitioner:	Bruce D. Lamb, Esquire, DBPR
For Respondent:	B. Brown

For Respondent: continued —

This matter arose on Petitioner's Administrative Complaint against Respondents B. Brown, C. Jones, and XYZ Realty, Inc. Petitioner later dismissed its complaint against the latter two Respondents without notice to either the Administrative Law Judge or Respondent Brown.

Respondent Brown requested a 15-day extension to file posthearing proposed findings, but permitted the time allowed to file depositions and proposed findings to expire without filing either.

Findings of Fact: Respondent Brown is a licensed real estate sales associate. She has not been issued a broker's license.

Respondent did, on her own initiative, arrange for and collect lease monies for out-of-state owners after she left ABC Realty, Inc. While the lease arose out of an exclusive-right-of-sale listing with ABC Realty, the firm was not interested in handling the lease, and Respondent Brown undertook this transaction as a favor to the owners. The Respondent located a lessee in October of [year 1]. She forwarded a copy of the lease agreement to the owners along with a bill for her expenses and her personal check for the first month's rent plus security deposit. Thereafter, the check was not honored by the bank. Additional rent collected was not sent to the owners. In August of [year 2], Respondent Brown made full restitution to the owners.

In mitigation, the Respondent stated that her estranged husband had withdrawn the original funds intended to cover the returned check and that other divorce and related expenses led her to spend funds she later collected. She also stated that she did not seek a commission or charge a monthly fee, as is customary when handled through a brokerage, for obtaining the lease.

Discussion Questions: 1. Which subsections of Chapter 475, F.S., were violated, and what were the violations?

2. Did the Respondent violate her fiduciary relationship with her broker or her obligations to the principal?

3. What are the presumptions in Chapter 475.43, F.S.?

4. What course of action should the Respondent have followed?

Synopsis of Facts:

Violations:

Penalty:

Practice End-of-Course Exam

This practice exam consists of 100 multiple-choice questions. A student who achieves a score of at least 80 percent without using any reference material should be in a strong position relative to subsequent examinations. It is recommended that at least two hours or more of uninterrupted time be budgeted to take this exam. A tear-out answer sheet is provided at the end of the book for your convenience.

1. John is a licensed real estate broker. He has been hired by a lender to appraise a home for a buyer who has made application for an FHA loan. Which statement is TRUE regarding this situation?
   A. John's broker's license entitles him to appraise this property.
   B. John may not charge for this assignment.
   C. John is required to be a state-certified appraiser to perform this appraisal assignment.
   D. John may not accept this appraisal assignment because to do so would be a conflict of interest.

2. Leasehold estates do NOT include a(n)
   A. tenancy at will.
   B. holdover tenancy.
   C. estate for years.
   D. remainder estate.

3. The Florida Real Estate Commission must notify which agency when it takes disciplinary action against any of the agency's licensees?
   A. Division of Time Shares
   B. Division of Professions
   C. Division of Regulation
   D. Division of Florida Land Sales, Condominiums, and Mobile Homes

4. Failure to comply with the statute of frauds will result in a(n)
   A. charge of fraud.
   B. illegal contract.
   C. unenforceable contract.
   D. revocation of licensure.

5. The only broker for a firm had her license revoked. What action, if any, will be taken against the sales associates' licenses registered under the broker?
   A. The licenses will be placed in involuntary inactive status.
   B. The licenses will be unaffected.
   C. The licenses will be suspended until new employment is secured.
   D. The licenses will become null and void.

6. A broker received a $5,000 deposit from a buyer on Tuesday at 1 P.M. The seller will not be available until Monday. The broker's normal banking day is Monday. The broker is required to deposit the $5,000 before the end of
   A. the next business day.
   B. business on Wednesday.
   C. business on Thursday.
   D. business on Friday.

7. Which expense is subtracted to derive NOI?
   A. Vacancy and collection losses
   B. Mortgage payments
   C. Income taxes
   D. Depreciation

8. Mr. Brown wanted to build a motel. A broker showed him three choice sites zoned hotel-motel. Brown promised to decide on a site in three weeks, so the broker took a two-week vacation. When the broker returned, Mr. Brown bought one of these sites. The broker sold the site, not knowing that the zoning on that site had been changed to industrial. Which is correct?
   A. The broker is guilty of culpable negligence.
   B. The broker is not guilty of wrongdoing.
   C. The property owner is guilty of fraud.
   D. The broker is guilty of fraud.

9. The mortgage clause that requires the lender to waive the right to a deficiency judgment against the borrower, relieving the borrower of personal liability to repay the loan, is referred to as a(n)
   A. right to reinstate clause.
   B. indemnity clause.
   C. exculpatory clause.
   D. hold-harmless clause.

10. The broker is a single agent of the seller. The principal has disclosed to the broker that the roof leaks, although there is no visible evidence of a water problem. The broker has satisfied her legal obligation to both the principal and all prospective buyers if she discloses
    A. that the roof leaks.
    B. that the roof appears to be in good condition.
    C. nothing about the condition of the roof unless specifically asked about the roof's condition.
    D. that she is bound by confidentiality to her principal.

11. The seller instructs the listing broker not to show his home to members of a protected class. The broker informs the seller that this would be a violation of the Fair Housing Laws, but the seller is insistent. Which choice is the broker's best course of action under these circumstances?
    A. Report the incident to the Fair Housing Administration.
    B. Report the seller to the DBPR.
    C. Withdraw from the listing agreement.
    D. Follow the seller's instructions because to do otherwise would violate the broker's fiduciary duties to the seller.

12. A broker has a listing priced at $120,000. An uninformed buyer offers her $125,000. The broker buys the property for $120,000, then sells it for $125,000. Which is FALSE?
    A. The $5,000 profit is called an "overage."
    B. The $5,000 profit is called a "secret profit."
    C. The broker has violated her duties to the seller.
    D. This is legal as long as the broker withdraws from the listing first.

13. Lucille has homesteaded her residence. She is a nonveteran who is totally and permanently disabled due to a serious car accident. Lucille is also legally blind. What is her cumulative tax exemption on her homesteaded residence?
    A. $25,000
    B. $25,500
    C. $26,000
    D. $50,500

14. The duties of a real estate licensee, owed to a buyer or seller who engages the real estate licensee as a single agent, include all EXCEPT
    A. dealing honestly and fairly.
    B. limited confidentiality, unless waived in writing by a party.
    C. presenting all offers and counteroffers in a timely manner, unless previously directed otherwise in writing.
    D. loyalty.

15. Federal savings associations that are members of the Federal Home Loan Bank System are regulated by the
    A. Federal Home Loan Mortgage Corporation.
    B. Office of Thrift Supervision.
    C. Federal Reserve System.
    D. Resolution Trust Corporation.

16. A sales associate who is employed by an owner-developer who owns properties in the name of various entities may be issued
    A. multiple licenses.
    B. a group license.
    C. a commercial license.
    D. a branch office license.

17. Tenant Ted signed a lease for ten years requiring a monthly base rent of $1,900, plus 2 percent of all monthly gross sales volume over $95,000. Ted also must pay all property taxes, insurance, and other costs normally considered property owner's costs. This is a
    A. gross lease.
    B. fixed lease.
    C. variable sale lease.
    D. net lease.

18. A real estate license may be revoked or canceled without prejudice for which action?
    A. Culpable negligence
    B. Failure to account and deliver escrow funds
    C. Issuance of a license by mistake by the Commission
    D. Conversion

19. Broker Joan Sunville's license was in involuntary inactive status for two years and one month. To operate again as an active licensee, Joan must complete
    A. 60 hours of the broker's postlicensing education course, 28 hours of continuing education, and pass the broker's licensing exam.
    B. 42 hours of continuing education and pass the continuing education course exam.
    C. FREC Course I and pass the sales associate's licensing exam.
    D. FREC Course II and pass the broker's licensing exam.

20. Mitch successfully negotiated (and was handsomely paid for) the sale of a Federal Communications Commission license for a television station. Mitch is not a licensed real estate broker or sales associate. Mitch
    A. has violated SEC regulations.
    B. has not violated F.S. 475.
    C. has acted as an unlicensed real estate broker.
    D. must secure a communications license from the DBPR.

21. Which statement concerning characteristics of the real estate market is FALSE?
    A. Real estate is immobile.
    B. The market is slow to respond to changes in supply and demand.
    C. The real estate market is organized and controlled centrally.
    D. Land is indestructible.

22. A comparable property has one more bedroom ($8,000) and is on a slightly larger lot ($2,000) than the subject property. The comparative market analysis requires a net adjustment of
    A. minus $8,000 to the comparable property.
    B. plus $2,000 to the subject property.
    C. plus $10,000 to the subject property.
    D. minus $10,000 to the comparable property.

23. Which entity MAY NOT be registered as a real estate brokerage?
    A. Corporation for profit
    B. Corporation sole
    C. Partnership
    D. Sole proprietorship

24. The formula to calculate the overall capitalization rate is
    A. NOI ÷ Value (or price).
    B. NOI × Value (or price).
    C. Debt service × Value (or price).
    D. NOI ÷ Owner's equity.

25. Which is NOT a requirement under RESPA?
    A. Use of the HUD Form 1 by the closing agent
    B. A copy of the HUD information booklet to the mortgage applicant within three business days
    C. Give mortgage applicant a list of competing lenders so that the consumer can comparison shop for the best rate
    D. Give mortgage applicant an estimate of settlement costs within three business days

26. A transaction broker does NOT have which duty?
    A. Duty of using skill, care, and diligence in the transaction
    B. Duty of accounting for all funds
    C. Duty to disclose all known facts that materially affect the value of residential real property and are not readily observable to the buyer
    D. Full fiduciary duties to both the buyer and the seller

27. A license becomes ineffective when it is
    A. revoked.
    B. suspended.
    C. canceled.
    D. expired for more than two years.

28. Excel Realty is a transaction broker for buyer Andrew. Andrew wants to purchase a new home so the sales associate takes him to three model centers listed by three competing real estate companies. The sales associate must give the no brokerage relationship notice to
    A. Andrew.
    B. the model home employees at each model center.
    C. no one.
    D. the owner-developer of each new homes subdivision.

29. Title to real property is technically conveyed when the deed is
    A. recorded in the public records.
    B. voluntarily delivered and voluntarily accepted.
    C. signed and witnessed.
    D. acknowledged.

30. Which variable does NOT influence demand?
    A. Availability of mortgage credit
    B. Availability of construction loans
    C. Income of consumers
    D. Consumer tastes and preferences

31. A real estate licensee is obligated to communicate to the seller
    A. all offers, unless specifically instructed by the seller to accept on his or her behalf.
    B. only all written offers.
    C. all oral and written offers, regardless of how worthy they may be in the broker's opinion.
    D. all offers up until such time as there is a contract pending.

32. A single agent broker received an offer on a listed property at the seller's price and terms. Before informing the seller, the broker received a higher offer. She submitted only the first offer, and the seller, her principal, accepted it. The broker
    A. has violated her fiduciary duty to her principal.
    B. is guilty of conversion.
    C. has fulfilled her duty to the seller because the offer was for the seller's full price and terms.
    D. is not required to submit the second offer.

33. Mr. Doer earned a $7,500 commission by selling a coin-operated laundry business, which has six more years before the expiration of its present lease. Mr. Doer
    A. must be registered with the Florida Retail Commission as a business broker.
    B. must be registered with the Florida Real Estate Commission as a business broker.
    C. must be registered with the Florida Real Estate Commission as a real estate licensee.
    D. need not be registered with any state agency in the given situation.

34. Three claimants have come before the Commission requesting relief from the Real Estate Recovery Fund. All three claimants were involved in the same real estate transaction. Payment for their claims, in the aggregate, is limited to
    A. $150,000.
    B. $75,000.
    C. $50,000.
    D. $25,000.

35. The rate of interest that the Federal Reserve Bank charges member banks for borrowing from the Federal Reserve Bank is referred to as
    A. discount points.
    B. the discount rate.
    C. the prime rate.
    D. the reserve requirement.

36. Local government exercises its greatest effect on the real estate business by
    A. creating tax shelters for those developing low-income housing.
    B. using zoning, taxation, and the planning process.
    C. providing financing where justified.
    D. supervising contractors and their on-the-job performance.

37. Which information must be disclosed to all prospective buyers?
    A. The seller's brother was murdered in the residence.
    B. A previous occupant was infected with HIV.
    C. The home is situated in a flood-prone area.
    D. The neighborhood residents are Hispanic.

38. Which statement does NOT describe a planned unit development?
    A. Density of dwelling units is usually higher than is allowed for typical single-family subdivisions.
    B. Dwelling units are typically clustered, with planned green space areas between clusters.
    C. Industrial parks are a welcomed offshoot of the PUD concept.
    D. Most PUDs include a mixture of residential, shopping, and professional areas.

39. Insulation is rated by its ability to resist
    A. cold temperatures.
    B. heat flow.
    C. cold wind.
    D. severe temperatures.

40. A licensee makes a statement that is material to the transaction as if it were a fact when the licensee does not know if the statement is true or false, and the buyer relies on the statement. As a result of the statement made by the licensee, the buyer suffers damages. This situation constitutes
    A. culpable negligence.
    B. fraud.
    C. breach of trust.
    D. deceptive services.

41. The DBPR may issue which penalty for an initial offense of a minor violation by a licensee?
    A. Notice of noncompliance
    B. Subpoena to appear
    C. Notice of assignment
    D. Final order

42. Mort owns a farm in fee simple. He deeds the farm to Ned until Ned dies, at which time Opal will acquire a fee simple title to the farm. Opal's interest in the farm is a
    A. life estate.
    B. fee simple estate.
    C. reversion estate.
    D. remainder estate.

43. Business brokers appraise businesses using appraisal methods similar to real estate appraisal EXCEPT for the additional technique of
    A. stock, bond, and debenture analysis.
    B. asset appreciation analysis.
    C. working capital analysis.
    D. liquidation analysis.

44. What authority originates from the U.S. Constitution and relates to protection of health and welfare of citizens at local levels?
    A. Escheat
    B. Situs
    C. Police power
    D. Community protection power

45. Which element is NOT essential in a valid real estate sale contract?
    A. A legal objective or purpose
    B. Competent parties
    C. An earnest money deposit
    D. The vendor's signature

46. A provision in all mortgages that allows the delinquent mortgagor to avoid foreclosure by paying all of the back mortgage payments, late penalties, and costs of collection up until the time of foreclosure sale is the
    A. equity of redemption.
    B. due-on-sale clause.
    C. acceleration clause.
    D. defeasance clause.

47. The statute of limitations is the authority that outlines the
    A. requirement that real estate sale contracts be in writing.
    B. essential elements of a contract.
    C. remedies available in case of breach.
    D. period of time during which a contract may be enforced.

48. The statute of frauds applies to
    A. all legal contracts and other documents.
    B. the transfer of personal property.
    C. instruments of conveyance of real property.
    D. acts of fraud by licensees.

49. The documentary stamp tax on deeds is based on the
    A. "new" money involved in the transaction.
    B. amount of the mortgage loan.
    C. amount of the new mortgage.
    D. entire sale price of the property.

50. Which statement concerning tenancy by the entireties is FALSE?
    A. It is a form of concurrent ownership.
    B. The estate includes right of survivorship.
    C. The property must be owned by a wife and her husband.
    D. The deed must specifically state intent to create such a tenancy.

51. The financial term applied to the use of borrowed funds to finance the purchase of an office building is
    A. leverage.
    B. liquidity.
    C. intermediation.
    D. disintermediation.

52. A mortgage in which changes in the interest rate may cause changes in the monthly payment amount is called a(n)
    A. partially amortized mortgage.
    B. adjustable-rate mortgage.
    C. graduated-payment mortgage.
    D. escalator mortgage.

53. Depreciation (cost recovery)
    A. may be taken on a principal residence.
    B. includes the cost of land in the amount to be depreciated.
    C. is an allowable deduction that requires no current outlay of cash.
    D. does not include the mortgaged portion of an apartment building in the amount to be depreciated.

54. Constructive notice is
    A. information learned by reading, seeing, or hearing.
    B. information advertised in the newspaper.
    C. provided by recording in the public records.
    D. notarizing a conveyance.

55. In a deed, the warranty of quiet enjoyment pertains to
    A. peace and tranquility on and around the property.
    B. peaceful possession undisturbed by others' claims of title.
    C. guaranteed satisfaction with the property.
    D. property that is completely vacated.

56. The law that requires that the annual percentage rate be disclosed to consumers is the
    A. Real Estate Settlement Procedures Act.
    B. Equal Credit Opportunity Act.
    C. Truth-in-Lending Act.
    D. Florida "Little FTC Act."

57. The document that controls the title closing on the day of closing is the
    A. sale contract.
    B. listing contract.
    C. closing statement.
    D. broker's closing statement.

58. The government survey method of legal description
    A. is the most accurate method.
    B. was used in the 13 original colonies.
    C. has as a basis a principal meridian and a base line.
    D. features a critical reference called the *point of beginning*.

59. A buyer who obtains a mortgage loan that covers the purchase of a condominium plus furniture, appliances, and other personal property such as towels and kitchen utensils has a
    A. blanket mortgage.
    B. chattel mortgage.
    C. wraparound mortgage.
    D. package mortgage.

60. A type of roof style that slopes from the ridge to four opposite sides and allows continuous eave venting around the entire house perimeter is the
    A. gable.
    B. hip.
    C. mansard.
    D. salt box.

61. Which estate includes the right of survivorship?
    A. Joint tenancy
    B. Fee simple estate
    C. Tenancy in common
    D. Tenancy for years

62. A title theory state is one in which a mortgage
    A. transfers title to the lender or escrow agent until the loan is paid.
    B. creates only an encumbrance on title to a property.
    C. creates a tenancy in common until the loan is paid.
    D. creates a joint tenancy for the lender until the loan is paid.

63. Which term refers to a situation where during the early years of a loan the principal balance increases?
    A. Graduated payments
    B. Positive leverage
    C. Negative amortization
    D. Reverse annuity

64. Which statement is true regarding the monthly payments on a 30-year, fully amortized loan?
    A. Initially, interest is the smallest portion of the payment.
    B. Initially, principal and interest are approximately equal.
    C. Initially, interest is the larger portion of the payment.
    D. Level monthly payment means the same amount of principal is paid each month.

65. When the Fed wants to ease a tight money supply, it may
    A. increase the discount rate.
    B. issue new Treasury securities.
    C. raise the reserve requirement.
    D. buy Treasury securities.

66. How much personal money may a broker place in a property management escrow account?
    A. None
    B. $200
    C. $1,000
    D. $5,000

67. An example of an ad valorem tax is a(n)
    A. special assessment.
    B. property tax.
    C. income tax.
    D. zoning tax.

68. Which individual is NOT exempt from real estate licensure
    under F.S. 475?
    A. An individual who sells cemetery lots for compensation
    B. A mortgage broker who deals in personal property only
    C. A business broker who negotiates leases of business
       property only
    D. A court-appointed personal representative liquidating the real
       property of an estate

69. If a developer wants to develop a new subdivision, she must
    submit a(n)
    A. subdivision plat map to the planning commission.
    B. site plan to the Zoning Board of Adjustment.
    C. existing land-use study to the planning commission.
    D. thoroughfare study to the Department of Transportation.

70. You have been hired to appraise the local public library building.
    The approach that is likely to be the most relevant is the
    A. comparable sales approach.
    B. cost-depreciation approach.
    C. public land and property approach.
    D. income capitalization approach.

71. In the cost-depreciation approach, estimating accrued depreciation
    involves estimating
    A. the amount of allowable cost recovery.
    B. the value of allowable expenses.
    C. the loss in value of the improvements.
    D. effective gross income.

72. The purchase price of a business minus the value of the tangible
    assets of that business equals the intangible assets of the business,
    referred to as
    A. personal property.
    B. real property.
    C. common stock.
    D. goodwill.

73. Sales associate Sally received a $5,000 earnest money deposit from a buyer. She immediately delivered the deposit to her broker. The broker deposited the check on the third business day into his general operating account.
    A. This is the proper procedure for the handling of earnest money deposits.
    B. This is an example of commingling of escrow funds.
    C. The broker is guilty of dishonest dealing by trick, scheme, or devise.
    D. This is the proper procedure, provided the broker uses a title company that has trust powers.

74. Sales associate Terry Stoufer may have which information entered on her license, if applicable?
    A. Terry's Real Estate Services
    B. Terry Stoufer, LLC
    C. Terry Stoufer Enterprises, LLC
    D. Best Homes, Inc.

75. If all legislated requirements have previously been met, an active broker in Florida may hold an active license in
    A. Florida only.
    B. Florida and any other state whose licensing laws have not been violated; however, a licensee may hold only one active license at any one time.
    C. Florida and any other state or foreign country whose licensing laws have not been violated.
    D. any other state or foreign country whose licensing laws have not been violated, provided the Florida license was placed on inactive status.

76. Which statement is FALSE regarding a corporation for profit that is doing business as a real estate broker?
    A. The broker must file a charter with the Florida Department of State.
    B. There must be at least one officer who is an active real estate broker.
    C. The corporation must be registered with the FREC.
    D. All stockholders must be registered with the FREC as inactive brokers.

77. A broker who changes his or her business address must notify the Commission of the address change within how many days?
    A. 60
    B. 30
    C. 10
    D. 5

78. In relation to Section 1 of a township, Section 12 is due
    A. north.
    B. east.
    C. west.
    D. south.

79. Jack is a 72-year-old retired college professor. The local lender to whom Jack applied for a 30-year mortgage denied Jack's loan application, even though he has sufficient income from his pension plan and an excellent credit history.
    A. This is a violation of the Fair Housing Laws.
    B. The lender's actions are legal because it is unlikely that Jack will survive the term of the loan.
    C. This is an example of redlining.
    D. The lender's actions are a violation of the Equal Credit Opportunity Act.

80. Essential elements of a deed do NOT include
    A. voluntary delivery and acceptance.
    B. good or valuable consideration.
    C. signature of two witnesses.
    D. signature of a competent grantee.

81. A person must hold an active real estate license if, for express or for implied compensation, he or she
    A. advertises a list of available rental properties.
    B. manages an apartment building complex on site and for salary only.
    C. rents mobile home lots in a mobile home park.
    D. manages condominium rentals for single-unit owners.

82. Individuals who originate loans, often with their own funds, and who may serve as loan correspondents are referred to as
    A. mortgage brokers.
    B. mortgage bankers.
    C. mortgage finders.
    D. secondary lenders.

83. The Florida Real Estate Commission is empowered by law to
    A. levy fines up to, but not exceeding, $500.
    B. impose prison sentences up to 60 days.
    C. assess damages resulting from breach of contract suits.
    D. reprimand, fine, or otherwise discipline licensees.

84. If a seller refuses to pay a broker her sales commission after the residential property is sold, the broker may
    A. file a vendor's lien on the owner's property.
    B. file a suit in the courts for her commission.
    C. refuse to permit the closing to occur.
    D. keep the binder deposit as just compensation.

85. If you have located a township numbered T2S, R4E, the township due south of that township is
    A. T2N, R1E.
    B. T2S, R5E.
    C. T3S, R4E.
    D. T2S, R3E.

86. In Florida real property is assessed on January 1 of each year, and property taxes become a lien on the property on
    A. January 1, the same year.
    B. April 1, the next year.
    C. November 1, the same year.
    D. December 31, the same year.

87. Brokers should not accept the task of appraising a parcel
    A. unless they also hold an appraisal license or certification.
    B. unless the appraisal assignment is contingent on securing the listing on the property.
    C. if they have previously sold the property.
    D. if their fees are contingent on the appraised value.

88. Which information is confidential?
    A. Minutes of the meetings of the FREC
    B. Final disciplinary action taken against a licensee
    C. An examinee's grade on the state licensing examination
    D. The name and address of the principal broker for a particular brokerage entity

89. A prospective tenant purchased a rental list from a broker and then rented a duplex that the list said included all utilities. The tenant discovered that only water was included in the rent and notified the broker within the legislated time limit. The tenant is entitled to
    A. nothing unless the request for a refund is made in writing.
    B. 75 percent of the rental list fee.
    C. 100 percent of the fee paid.
    D. no refund because the tenant agreed to rent the property.

90. Victor represents a motel owner who wishes to list one of his motels for sale. The owner has told Victor that he does not want to sell the motel to any racial minorities.
    A. Because this is not a sale of a residential dwelling under the Fair Housing Act, Victor may honor the owner's instructions.
    B. Victor may not refuse to show or sell the motel to a minority buyer; however, the owner may refuse to sell to certain individuals if he sells the property "for sale by owner."
    C. It would be a violation of the Fair Housing Act to abide by the owner's wishes.
    D. To refuse to sell or lease any real property based on one's race is a violation of the federal Civil Rights Act of 1866.

91. A property has been appraised at $157,800. The sale price is $165,000. The buyers have pledged a $3,000 earnest money deposit. The lender has told them they will need to pay additional funds as down payment in the amount of $28,560. Calculate the loan-to-value ratio.
    A. 90 percent
    B. 80 percent
    C. 75 percent
    D. 70 percent

92. The following taxes were paid at the closing of a new home: $1,540 state documentary stamp tax on the deed, $693 state documentary stamp tax on the note, and $396 state intangible tax on the mortgage. What was the purchase price of the home?
    A. $198,000
    B. $220,000
    C. $346,500
    D. $440,000

93. What would be the total required taxes for the loans on a $47,500 tract that sold with $10,000 cash down, a new second mortgage of $15,500, and an assumed mortgage of $22,000 that was previously recorded?
    A. $332.50
    B. $206.25
    C. $162.25
    D. $131.25

94. You have a level-payment, amortized mortgage of $42,000 at 12½ percent for 30 years. The monthly payment is $448.25. What amount of interest will be paid from the second monthly payment?
    A. $432.83
    B. $432.94
    C. $437.39
    D. $437.50

95. Your seller owns a home appraised at $52,500. She still owes $32,760 on the first mortgage and $4,200 on a second mortgage. Your sales commission will be $3,640. What is your seller's equity in the home?
    A. $11,900
    B. $13,589
    C. $15,540
    D. $19,740

96. The city has decided to pave the streets of a recently incorporated community. Property owners are to be assessed 70 percent of the cost of paving, which is found to be $25 per foot. The 70 percent assessment tax is to be apportioned between owners on both sides of the streets. What will the special assessment be for a property with 80 feet of frontage?
    A. $350
    B. $700
    C. $1,400
    D. $2,000

97. A property has been assessed at $40,000. The city tax rate is 10 mills, the county tax rate is 9 mills, and the school board levy is 8 mills. The owner has qualified for and received homestead tax exemption. How much will the owner save from his county taxes as a result of the homestead tax exemption?
    A. $135
    B. $225
    C. $405
    D. $675

98. A developer purchased three oceanfront lots, each measuring 75 by 110 feet, for $20 per square foot. The developer later sold the lots for $200,000 each. What was the developer's percentage of profit on the sale of the three lots? (Round to nearest percent.)
    A. 18 percent
    B. 20 percent
    C. 21 percent
    D. 25 percent

99. A sales associate accepts employment with a broker at 45 percent of sales commissions earned as a result of his sales efforts. The broker lists a property for $48,000, with a 7 percent sales commission agreed to by the owner. The sales associate sells the property at the listed sale price. What is the broker's share of the commission?
    A. $1,512
    B. $1,848
    C. $1,884
    D. $3,360

100. Mr. Zee is a licensed real estate broker. He has a buyer who is interested in investing in income-producing property. Mr. Zee finds a property producing net income of $1,750 per month. Ms. Buyer informs Mr. Zee that she will buy the property if he can get it for a price that will return her 14 percent per year on her investment. If the desired 14 percent rate of return is regarded as a 14 percent capitalization rate, what will Mr. Zee's buyer be willing to pay for the property?
    A. $12,500
    B. $21,000
    C. $125,000
    D. $150,000

Acronym IRMA

Once upon A BAR SALE, IRMA took a walk and fell into a HOT CAN PITT. She met Mike PET, a handsome MALE, who invited her to dinner and to go CEDDING. They fell in love, drew the WILD CARD in a poker game, settled their CBS v. CIA suit, and were married in the DELL. They had a baby named IRV who got the COLIC. They took him to the doctor, who found the cause to be DUPE DUST. They saved for a down payment, bought a house through FHA, watched it increase in value faster than the CPI, and lived happily ever after!

The Closing

A BAR SALE	Real estate services (Chapter 2)
IRMA	Test for fixtures (Chapter 8)
HOT CAN	Conditions for alienation by adverse possession (Chapter 9)
PITT	Four unities of a joint tenancy (Chapter 8)
PET	Government restrictions (Chapter 9)
MALE	Conflicting demands settlement procedure (Chapter 5)
CEDDING	Elements of a deed (Chapter 9)
WILD CARD	Ways an offer is terminated (Chapter 11)
CBS vs. CIA	Appraisal adjustments (Chapter 15)
DELL	Private restrictions (Chapter 9)
IRV	Income capitalization formula (Chapter 15)
COLIC	Elements of a valid real estate contract (Chapter 11)
DUPE	Bundle of rights (Chapter 8)
DUST	Characteristics of value (Chapter 15)
FHA	Federal Housing Administration (Chapter 11)
SNI	State transfer taxes (Chapter 14)
CPI	Consumer Price Index (Chapter 15)

Know Your Ors and Ees

assignor: person who transfers a legal right to another
(e.g., mortgagee selling mortgages and notes; a buyer
transferring rights to another person in a sale contract)

assignee: person to whom a legal right is transferred (e.g., Fannie Mae
buying mortgages and notes in the second mortgage market)

grantor: party giving the deed that conveys title (e.g., seller in a sale
contract)

grantee: party receiving the deed and acquiring title (e.g., buyer in a
sale contract)

lessor: landlord who gives lease

lessee: tenant who receives lease

lienor: person who has a claim on another's property

lienee: person whose property is subject to a claim or charge by
another

mortgagor: borrower who gives note and mortgage to obtain a loan

mortgagee: lender who receives note and mortgage

offeror: buyer making an offer to purchase

offeree: seller receiving an offer to purchase, who accepts, counters,
or rejects the offer

optionor: owner who gives an option to a buyer

optionee: buyer who receives an option contract

vendor: seller in a sale contract

vendee: buyer in a sale contract

Glossary

Abandonment A surrender of rights; point when a broker makes no effort to service or sell listed property; failure to perform.

Absentee owner A property holder who does not reside on the property and who usually relies on a property manager to supervise the investment.

Abstract of title Condensed history of title to real property consisting of a summary of the links in the "chain of title" extracted from documents bearing on the title status.

Acceleration clause Stipulation in a mortgage that the entire unpaid balance of the debt may become due and payable if a default of expressed conditions should occur.

Acceptance Voluntary receipt of an item offered by another.

Accretion Gradual addition of land caused by natural forces, such as wind, tide, flood, or watercourse deposits.

Acknowledgment Formal declaration before an authorized official, by the person who executed the instrument, that it is a free act.

Actual notice Information a person has actually learned by reading, seeing, or hearing.

Adjudication A judicial or court decision.

Adjustable-rate mortgage (ARM) A financing technique in which the lender can raise or lower the interest rate according to a set index.

Adjusted basis The owner's original cost plus buying expenses plus capital improvements.

Administrative law judge An attorney employed by the Division of Administrative Hearings, Department of Administration, to hear complaints and issue recommended orders.

Ad valorem According to the value; in proportion to worth.

Advance fees Up-front money collected by a broker for the listing of real property.

Adversary Opponent; a person or group that opposes another.

Adverse interest A purpose in opposition to the interest of another party (as, for example, with a buyer and a seller).

Adverse possession A method of obtaining title to real property by occupying it in an open and hostile manner contrary to the interests of the owner.

Affidavit A sworn statement written down before a notary or public official.

After-tax cash flow (*See* Cash flow.)

Agency Express or implied authorization for one person to act for another.

Agent A representative; one who is authorized to act on behalf of another.

Agreement for deed (*See* Contract for deed.)

Agricultural Defined in Chapter 475, F.S., to mean property zoned as such, consisting of more than ten acres.

Air rights The freedom to use the open space above a property.

Alienation The act of transferring ownership, title, or an interest or estate in real property.

Allodial system A theory of land ownership that individuals may own land free of the rights of an overlord.

Alluvion (alluvium) The increase of land by the gradual and imperceptible action of natural forces (e.g., deposits of sand and mud on a riverbank).

Amortized mortgage A loan characterized by payment of a debt by regular installment payments.

Anniversary date Recurring each year; the date an insurance policy must be renewed to continue in effect.

Annual debt service The amount of money required each year for the payment of all mortgage interest and principal.

Annual percentage rate (APR) Total yearly cost of credit.

Appeal A request to some authority for a decision or judgment.

Applicant A person who applies for something; a candidate.

Appraisal Professional service provided by a registered, licensed, or certified appraiser or real estate licensee to produce an estimate of value.

Appraisal plant Copies of current statistics and publications kept by appraisers in their library or record room.

Appraised value Estimated worth of a property determined by someone qualified in valuation.

Appraiser, real estate One who is a registered, licensed, or certified by the DBPR and provides an estimate of value.

Appreciation An increase in value.

Arbitration The act of having a third party render a binding decision in a dispute between two parties.

Arrears The state of being behind in the discharge of an obligation; paid at the end of the period for which due (the opposite of in advance).

Assemblage The combining of two or more adjoining properties into one tract.

Assessed value Worth established for each unit of real property for tax purposes by a county property appraiser.

Assessment The imposition of a tax or charge according to a preset rate; the allocation of the proportionate individual share of a common expense in a condo or co-op building.

Asset Anything of value.

Assignee Person to whom a right or interest is transferred.

Assignment Written instrument that serves to transfer the rights or interests of one person to another.

Assignment of mortgage A legal instrument that states that the mortgagee assigns (transfers) the mortgage and promissory note to the purchaser.

Assignor Person who gives his or her legal rights or interests to another person.

Associate Person working for a broker.

Association An organization of persons having a common interest.

Assumption of mortgage The taking over of an existing mortgage by a buyer.

Attachment A legal writ obtained to prevent removal of property that is expected to be used to satisfy a judgment.

Attorney-in-fact One who is authorized to perform certain acts for another under a power of attorney.

Attorney, power of Designation of another person to act for a principal who may not be present.

Automated underwriting A service that enables lenders to obtain a credit risk classification using applications software in the loan underwriting process.

Balance sheet A financial report that shows the company's financial position at a stated moment in time.

Balloon payment A single, large payment made at maturity of a partially amortized mortgage to pay off the debt in full.

Bargain and sale deed A type of deed in which title is transferred and a limited number of warranties are made respecting title to or use of the property.

Base industries Businesses that attract outside money into the area; primary.

Base lines Imaginary lines running east and west and crossing a principal meridian at a definite point; used by surveyors for reference in locating and describing land under the government survey system.

Before-tax cash flow (BTCF; cash throwoff; gross spendable income) The resulting amount when annual debt service is subtracted from net operating income.

Biennium (biennial) A period of two years.

Bilateral contract An agreement wherein both parties are legally obligated to each other to perform.

Binder A memorandum given subject to the writing of a formal contract for sale, usually acknowledging receipt of a portion of the down payment for purchase of real property.

Blanket mortgage One debt instrument covering two or more parcels.

Blind advertisement An advertisement of a principal's property providing only a telephone number, a post office box, and/or an address without the licensed name of the brokerage firm.

Blockbusting The illegal practice of inducing homeowners to sell their property by making misrepresentations regarding the entry or prospective entry of minority persons in order to cause a turnover of properties in the neighborhood; discriminatory acts against sellers.

Bona fide Without deceit or fraud; genuine; in good faith.

Boot Money or other property that is not like-kind, which is given to make up any difference in value or equity between exchanged properties.

Borrower (debtor) The mortgagor; one who gives a mortgage as security for a debt.

Branch office A business location other than the real estate broker's principal place of business.

Breach Failure to do or perform what has been promised.

Broker A licensee who acts as an intermediary between two parties and negotiates contracts between them.

Broker associate An individual who is qualified to be issued a broker's license but who operates as a sales associate in the employ of another.

Buffer zone A strip of land separating one land use from another.

Building codes Government ordinances regulating construction practices and materials.

Business brokerage The sale, purchase, or lease of businesses that provide goods and/or services.

Business broker Real estate licensees who engage in the sale, purchase, or lease of businesses.

Business opportunity brokerage The real estate activity dealing in the sale, purchase, or lease of businesses.

Business trust (syndicate) A group of people who associate with each other for the purpose of purchasing shares or units at a specified amount per unit, with the money raised to be used to purchase the real property, often for subdividing and resale.

Buydown A financing technique in which points are paid to the lender by the seller or builder that lowers (buys down) the effective interest rate paid by the buyer/borrower, thus reducing the amount of the monthly payment for a set period of time.

Buyer brokerage agreement An employment contract with a purchaser.

Buyer's market The supply of available properties exceeds the demand.

Bylaws Rules that govern the administration of the condominium.

Canceled A license ceases to exist, effective as of the date approved by the Commission, and does not involve disciplinary action.

Capital The collective wealth (money and property) of a person or business; the investment in a property. (*See also* Equity.)

Capital asset Certain property held by a taxpayer, not including inventory for sale to customers.

Capital-deficit area A region where the total amount of local savings is not sufficient to finance economic development already under way in that area.

Capital gain The profit from the sale of an asset, including real property.

Capitalization rate The relationship between the net income from a real estate investment and the present value.

Cash flow (after-tax cash flow) The resulting amount when annual debt service, tax liability, and capital improvement costs are subtracted from net operating income.

Caveat emptor Let the buyer beware!

Cease and desist order An action by a government agency to require a person or business to stop an illegal or unfair practice.

Censure An official act of strong disapproval.

Certificate of occupancy An occupancy permit issued by the local government after construction is completed and the final inspection is approved.

Certificate of title opinion (opinion of title) A document signed by a title examiner (attorney or title company agent) stating the judgment that, based on an examination of the public records, the seller has good title to the property being conveyed to the buyer (not to be confused with title insurance).

Certified appraiser (*See* State-certified appraiser.)

Certiorari, writ of An order to bring from a lower court to an appellate court an action or record of proceedings in a case.

Chain of title A successive listing of all previous holders of title (owners) back to an acceptable starting point.

Chattel Any item of personal property. (*See also* Personal property.)

Check A square measuring 24 miles on each side and representing the largest unit of measure in the government survey system.

Circuit breakers Devices that will shut off the flow of electricity if more electrical current is flowing through the wire than the wire can handle.

Citations Statements of alleged violations and the penalties to be imposed.

Civil Rights Act of 1866 A federal act that prohibits any type of discrimination based on race in any real estate transaction (sale or rental) without exception.

Clause A distinct provision in a written document.

Closing Final settlement between the buyer and seller; the date on which title passes from the seller to the buyer.

Cloud on title Any defect, valid claim, or encumbrance that serves to impair the title or curtail an owner's rights.

Collateral Real or personal property pledged as security on a debt.

Collusion Two or more parties jointly attempting to defraud a third party.

Color of title A condition in which ownership of real property appears to be good but is not good because of a defect.

Commercial A classification of real estate that includes income-producing properties such as office buildings, gasoline stations, restaurants, shopping centers, hotels and motels, and parking lots. Commercial property usually must be zoned for business purposes.

Commingle To mix together money or a deposit with personal funds; combine; intermingle.

Commission Compensation paid to a broker or sales associate for successfully concluding a real estate transaction; short form for the Florida Real Estate Commission (FREC).

Common elements The parts of a multiple-ownership property not included in the units; those parts in which each unit owner holds an undivided interest.

Common law A system of law based on accepted customs and traditions.

Community property Real property acquired during a marriage. (Florida is not a community property state.)

Comparable property (comparable; comp) A recently sold property similar to one being evaluated.

Comparative market analysis (CMA) An informal estimate of market value performed by a real estate licensee for the seller to assist in arriving at an appropriate listing price, or if working with the buyer, an informal estimate of market value to assist the buyer in arriving at an appropriate offering price.

Compensation Anything of value or a valuable consideration, directly or indirectly paid, promised, or expected to be paid or received.

Competent A party to a contract who possesses the legal capacity to enter into a binding contract.

Complainant A person who makes an allegation or a charge against another (the respondent). (*See also* Plaintiff.)

Complaint Formal allegation or charge.

Comprehensive plan (master plan) A statement of policies for the future physical development of an area (e.g., city, county, region).

Concealment The act of keeping from sight or keeping secret.

Concurrency A provision in Florida's Growth Management Act that mandates that the infrastructure, such as roads and water and waste treatment facilities needed to support additional population, be in place before new development is allowed.

Concurrent ownership Ownership by two or more persons at the same time, such as joint tenants, tenants by the entirety, or tenants in common.

Condemnation The taking of private real property for a public purpose under the right of eminent domain for a fair price.

Condominium A multiunit project consisting of individual ownership of a dwelling unit and undivided ownership of common areas.

Conflicting demands When different parties each make claims that are inconsistent with one another.

Conforming loan A standardized conventional loan written on uniform documents that meets the purchase requirements of Fannie Mae and Freddie Mac.

Consideration Inducement offered to conclude a contract.

Construction lien A claim based on the principle of "unjust enrichment"; favors parties who have performed labor or delivered materials or supplies for the repair or building of an improvement to real property.

Constructive notice The recording of a document or an instrument in the public records designed to give adequate notice to all.

Consumer Price Index (CPI) A measurement of average price changes of goods and services using a base period.

Contract An agreement between two or more competent parties to do, or not do, some legal act for a legal consideration.

Contract for deed A financing technique wherein the seller agrees to deliver the deed at some future date and the buyer takes possession while paying the agreed amount (also called *land contract*, an *installment sale contract*, and an *agreement for deed*).

Conventional mortgage A real estate loan granted that is neither FHA-insured nor VA-guaranteed.

Conversion Unauthorized use or retention of money or property that rightfully belongs to another person.

Convertible mortgage A financing instrument allowing a change from an adjustable-rate to a fixed-rate mortgage.

Conveyance Written instrument that serves to transfer an interest in real property from one party to another.

Cooperative A multiunit project consisting of individual dwelling units owned by the corporation in which the individual apartment tenants own stock rather than owning their respective units.

Co-ownership (concurrent or multiple ownership) Title to real property held by two or more persons at the same time.

Corner lot A lot bounded with streets on two sides (intersecting).

Corporation An artificial or fictitious person formed to conduct specified types of business activities.

Corporation not for profit An artificial or fictitious person organized for business purposes and similar to a corporation for profit.

Corporation sole An artificial or fictitious person formed by an ecclesiastical body.

Cost The amount to produce or acquire something.

Cost-depreciation approach A method for estimating the market value of a property based on the cost to buy the site and to construct a new building on the site, less depreciation.

Counselors Professionals who analyze existing or potential real estate problems and recommend a course of action.

Counteroffer A rejection of the original offer by proposing a new offer, thereby terminating the original offer.

Covenant A warranty, guarantee, or promise formally given in a legal document.

Credit As a verb, to make an entry on the right or credit side of an account; as a noun, payment or value received.

Creditor A lender; person or business entity to whom a debt is owed.

Cul-de-sac lot A lot located where a street is open at one end only and the street has a circular turnaround at the other end.

Culpable negligence Inadequate attention to duties and obligations by one who knows, or should know, what is required of him or her.

Curable When the correction of a defect results in as much added value as the cost to correct the defect.

Curbstone operation Conducting business without maintaining an office.

Current mailing address Where a licensee receives letters and so forth through the U.S. Postal Service.

Customer One with whom the broker or sales associate hopes to be successful in accomplishing the purpose of employment. Per Section 475.01, F.S., a member of the public who is or may be a buyer or seller of real property and may or may not be represented by a real estate licensee in an authorized brokerage relationship.

Damages Losses incurred as a result of a breach of contract or some other cause. (*See also* Liquidated damages and Unliquidated damages.)

Debit As a verb, to make an entry on the left or charge side of an account; as a noun, a charge or expense.

Decedent A deceased person, usually one who has recently died.

Declaration The legal document that the developer of a condominium must file and record in order to create a condominium under state law.

Declaration of trust A formal instrument filed by a business trust with the Department of State as a prerequisite for creating the trust.

Declaratory judgment A course of action declaring rights claimed under a contract or statute intended to prevent loss or to guide performance by the party or parties affected.

Dedication An offer of land for some public use, by an owner, together with acceptance by or on behalf of the public.

Deed A type of conveyance; a written instrument to transfer title to real property from one party to another.

Deed in lieu of foreclosure A friendly foreclosure (nonjudicial procedure) in which the mortgagor gives title to the mortgagee.

Deed restrictions Provision placed in deeds to control future uses of the property.

Default Failure to comply with the terms of an agreement or to meet an obligation when due.

Defeasance clause A provision in a mortgage that specifies the terms and conditions to be met in order to avoid default and thereby defeat the mortgage.

Defect (*See* Cloud on title.)

Defendant The person or party being sued or charged.

Deficiency decree Judgment brought when a mortgage is foreclosed and the sale proceeds fail to cover the costs of the sale, taxes, and the unpaid mortgage balance.

Demand The quantity of goods or services wanted by consumers.

Demand deposits Checking accounts; payable on demand by holder.

Denial A refusal or rejection.

Density The number of homes or lots per acre.

Deposit Earnest money or some other valuable consideration given as evidence of good faith to accompany an offer to purchase or rent. (*See also* Binder and Earnest money.)

Deposition Written testimony of a witness under oath.

Depreciation A loss in value for any reason; a deduction for tax purposes.

Descent The passage of title to real property upon the death of the owner to his or her legal descendants.

Designated sales associates Two real estate licensees designated to represent the buyer and the seller as single agents in a nonresidential transaction. The buyer and seller must have assets of $1 million or more and sign disclosures stating their assets meet the required threshold.

Development of regional impact (DRI) A large project affecting more than one county.

Devise A gift of real property by a will.

Devisee One who receives real property under a will.

Devisor One who gives real property through a will.

Discount points A method for increasing a lender's yield. (*See also* Point, Mortgage discount.)

Discount rate The amount of interest the Federal Reserve charges to lend money to its eligible banks.

Disintermediation A disengagement process when depositors withdraw money from savings for direct investment in stocks, money market funds, and other securities.

Doc stamps An abbreviated term for documentary stamp tax.

Document Any written paper that provides information or evidence.

Documentary stamp tax on deeds, state Tax required on all deeds or other documents used as conveyances. The charge is based on the total purchase price.

Documentary stamp tax on notes, state Tax required on all promissory notes. The cost is based on the face value of the note.

Dormer A projection built out from the slope of a roof, used to house windows on the upper floor and to provide additional light and ventilation.

Double-hung A window consisting of two sashes that move up and down in a pair of channels and are held open by tension springs.

Down payment A portion of a purchase price paid prior to closing the transaction. Earnest money may be part of or the entire down payment.

Draw (installment) Disbursement made by a lender to a builder.

Dual agency Representing both principals in a transaction (not a legal agency relationship in Florida).

Dual agent A broker who represents both the buyer and the seller of a transaction in a fiduciary capacity.

Due-on-sale clause A provision in a conventional mortgage that entitles the lender to require the entire loan balance to be paid in full if the property is sold.

Dynamic risk The risk that arises from the continual change in the business environment and therefore dynamic risk cannot be transferred to an insurer.

Earnest money deposit A type of money that a broker may handle for others in the ordinary course of business; also referred to as good-faith deposit or binder deposit.

Easement A right, privilege, or interest in real property that one individual has in lands belonging to another; a legal right to trespass; right-of-way authorizing access to or over land.

Easement appurtenant An easement that runs with the land and benefits an adjacent parcel of land.

Easement by necessity An easement created by a court of law in cases where justice and necessity dictate it, such as when property is landlocked.

Easement by prescription A right acquired by an adverse user to use the land of other, created through a court of law after longtime uninterrupted use.

Easement in gross A type of easement that benefits an individual or business entity and is not related to a specific adjacent parcel, for example, utility easements.

Economic base studies An analysis of employment in the primary industries of a region.

Economic life The period of time a property may be expected to be profitable or productive; useful life.

Effect a sale A provision in a listing contract requiring the broker to obtain a signed contract from a ready, willing, and able buyer on the terms specified.

Effective gross income (EGI) The resulting amount when vacancy and collection losses are subtracted from potential gross income. (*See also* Vacancy and collection losses.)

Elective share An estate defined as consisting of 30 percent of the decedent's personal property and Florida real property, except homestead-exempt property and claims.

Eminent domain The constitutional right given to a unit of government to take private property involuntarily if taken for public use and a fair price is paid to the owner.

Employer The individual who hires the services of another.

Empty nester Older parents whose housing needs change after their children have moved away.

Encroachment Unauthorized use of another person's property.

Encumbrance Any lien, claim, or liability affecting the title or attaching to real property.

Encumbrance clause A provision in a deed to real property that warrants that no liens, claims, or liabilities exist on the property being conveyed, except as specified.

Equitable title The right of a vendee to obtain absolute ownership of property to which the vendor has legal title; the interest held by a vendee under a sale contract or contract for deed; beneficial interest.

Equity The market value of a property less any debt against it; in a business entity, assets minus liabilities equals capital (owner's equity); a system of legal rules administered by a court of chancery.

Equity of redemption The right of a mortgagor, before a foreclosure sale, to reclaim forfeited property by paying the entire indebtedness.

Erosion Gradual loss of land due to water or other natural causes.

Escalator clause A provision in a mortgage permitting the lender to increase the interest rate that is usually tied to an event or a contingency.

Escheat Reversion of property to the state when an owner dies without leaving a will or any known heirs.

Escrow account An account in a bank, title company, credit union, savings association, or trust company used solely for safekeeping customer funds and not for deposit of personal funds; impound account or trust account.

Escrow disbursement order (EDO) A course of action for determining the disposition of a contested deposit.

Estate Tenancy; the interest one holds in real property; the total of one's property and possessions.

Estate by the entireties A tenancy created by husband and wife jointly owning real property with instant and complete right of survivorship.

Estate for life (*See* Life estates.)

Estate for years A tenancy measured from a starting date to a termination date (may be for a few days or longer than any natural life; e.g., a leasehold is an estate for years).

Estate in fee (*See* Fee simple estate.)

Estate in reversion An estate that comes back to the original grantor.

Estate in severalty Ownership of property vested in one person alone, also known as sole ownership.

Estate in sole Real property owned by a corporation sole.

Estate of freehold (*See* Freehold estate.)

Estate of remainder An estate that can become effective only after another estate has terminated.

Estoppel A principle of law that prohibits (stops) a person from defending himself or herself against his or her own acts or lack of action.

Estoppel certificate A written statement that bars the signer from making a claim inconsistent with the instrument (commonly used with a mortgage assumption).

Ethics The moral obligations and duties that a member of a profession or craft owes to the public, to a client, or to other members of the profession or craft.

Evidence Any proof that may legally be admitted in settlement of an issue.

Exclusion The right of an owner to control entry onto the property.

Exclusive-agency listing Employment contract given to one real estate broker as the sole agent for the sale of an owner's property.

Exclusive-right-of-sale listing An employment contract given to one real estate broker as the sole agent for the sale of an owner's property, with the commission going to that broker regardless of who actually sells the property during the employment contract period.

Exculpatory clause A provision in a mortgage or note in which the lender waives the right to a deficiency judgment against the borrower and the borrower is relieved of personal liability to repay the loan.

Executed contract An agreement in which the terms have been fully performed by all parties; a signed document.

Executive power, FREC Duties related to the education of licensees, the regulating of professional practices, and the publishing of materials.

Executory contract An agreement containing some act or condition that remains to be completed.

Exempt property Property that has been decreed to be excluded from taxation or claim by others.

Express contract An agreement wherein the terms are specifically stated by the parties, either orally, in writing, or by a combination of the two.

Facsimile ("fax") An exact copy.

Factor market A resource pool representing the four major elements (factors) of production that are bought and sold.

Fair Housing Act An act contained in Title VIII of the Civil Rights Act of 1968 that created protected classes of people and prohibits discrimination when selling or renting residential property when based on race, color, religion, sex, national origin, familial status, or handicap status.

Familial status As defined in the Fair Housing Act, a situation in which one or more individuals younger than 18 live with a parent or legal guardian. Pregnant women are also specifically covered under the Act.

Fannie Mae A private institution in the secondary mortgage market that buys and sells mortgages.

Farm area A selected and limited geographical district to which a sales associate devotes special attention and study; to farm an area or neighborhood.

Federal Deposit Insurance Corporation (FDIC) A federal agency that insures deposits of member banks and savings associations.

Federal Housing Administration (FHA) Insures mortgage loans made by FHA-approved lenders on homes that meet FHA standards in order to make mortgages more desirable investments for lenders.

Federal Housing Finance Board (FHFB) Supervises regional Federal Home Loan Banks and oversees their mortgage lending.

Federal Reserve System (the Fed) A central banking authority that influences the cost, availability, and supply of money.

Federal Trade Commission (FTC) A federal agency that investigates and eliminates unfair and deceptive trade practices.

Federally related transaction Any sale transaction that ultimately involves a federal agency in either the primary or secondary mortgage market. Under FIRREA, state-certified or state-licensed appraisers must be used for certain loans in federally related transactions.

Fee simple estate The most comprehensive and complete interest one can hold in real property; freehold estate. Also known as fee or fee simple absolute.

Fictitious name (*See* Trade name.)

Fiduciary A person in a position of trust and confidence with respect to another person.

Fiduciary relationship An alliance of trust and confidence that creates a moral and legal obligation when extended by one person and accepted by another.

Final order A decision rendered by the FREC.

Find a purchaser A provision in a listing contract requiring a broker to produce a ready, willing, and able buyer or offer on the terms specified.

Fixture An object that was once considered to be personal property but has become real property because of attachment to, or use in, improvements to real property.

Flag lot A lot characterized by a long access road or driveway leading back to the main part of the lot.

Follow-up What a sales associate does after a sale to maintain customer contact and goodwill.

Foreclosure A court process to transfer title to real property used as security for debt as a means of paying the debt by involuntary sale of the property.

Formal complaint An outline of the charges against a licensee that must be answered within the statutory time limit.

Formal contract Any agreement that contains all the essentials of a contract, including that it is in writing and under seal; a contract dependent on a particular form.

Formal hearing (*See* Hearing.)

Fraud The intent to misrepresent a material fact or to deceive to gain an unfair advantage or to harm another person.

Freddie Mac Formerly called the Federal Home Loan Mortgage Corporation (FHLMC). A secondary mortgage market institution that buys and sells conventional, FHA, and VA loans.

Free and clear Title to real property that is absolute and unencumbered.

Freehold estate A tenancy in real property with no set termination date that can be measured by the lifetime of an individual or can be inherited by heirs.

Further assurance A provision in a deed containing a covenant or warranty to perform any further acts the grantee (buyer) might require to perfect title to the property.

Gable A roof design that peaks at the center ridge and extends downward on two opposite sides.

General agent A representative authorized by the principal to perform only acts related to a business or to employment of a particular nature.

General lien A claim that may affect all of the properties of a debtor.

General partnership An association of two or more persons for the purpose of jointly conducting a business, each being responsible for all the debts incurred in the conducting of that business.

General warranty deed An instrument of conveyance containing the strongest and most comprehensive promises of further assurance possible for a grantor (seller) to convey to a grantee (buyer).

Going concern value The worth of a business, including real estate, goodwill, and earning capacity.

Good consideration A promise that cannot be measured in terms of money, such as love and affection.

Good faith A party's honest intent to transact business, free from any intent to defraud the other party; each party's faithfulness to one's duty or obligations set forth by contract.

Good faith estimate A preliminary accounting of expected closing costs. The Real Estate Settlement Procedures Act requires lenders to give loan applicants a good faith estimate that lists the charges the buyer is likely to pay at closing.

Goodwill An intangible asset (value) of a business.

Government lot Fractional piece of land less than a quarter section resulting from geographical features (e.g., lakes, streams) interfering with land surveying.

Government National Mortgage Association (GNMA) ("Ginnie Mae") A federal agency that is part of the Department of Housing and Urban Development (HUD). Ginnie Mae plays an important role in achieving the HUD's goal of providing low-cost mortgage credit to traditionally underserved sectors of the housing market.

Government survey system A type of land description, developed by the federal government for subdividing lands utilizing surveying lines.

Grantee Party who receives a deed or grant; buyer.

Granting clause The provision in a deed that specifies the names of the parties involved, the words of conveyance, and a description of the property.

Grantor Party who signs and gives a deed; seller.

Green Belt Law, Florida Legislation that authorizes county property appraisers to assess land used for agricultural purposes according to its current value as agricultural land.

Gross income multiplier (GIM) A rule of thumb for estimating the market value of commercial and industrial properties; the ratio to convert annual income into market value.

Gross lease An agreement for the tenant to pay a fixed (base) rent and the landlord pays all of the expenses associated with the property.

Gross rent multiplier (GRM) A rule of thumb for estimating the market value of income-producing residential property; the ratio to convert rental income into market value.

Ground lease An agreement for the tenant to lease the land only and erect a building on the land.

Group license A right granted a sales associate or broker associate to work various properties owned by affiliated entities under one owner developer.

Habendum A provision in a deed to real property that stipulates the estate or interest the grantee is to receive and the type of title conveyed.

Handbook Published by the Florida Real Estate Commission for study and guidance of students, applicants, licensees, and members of the general public on Florida Statute 475 and other laws, acts, rules, and regulations. (Available on the DRE's Web site.)

Handicap status As defined in the Fair Housing Act, a physical or mental impairment that substantially limits one or more major life activities.

Hazard insurance Coverage by contract whereby one party undertakes to guarantee another party against loss resulting from physical damage to real property.

Health ordinances Local codes that regulate maintenance and sanitation of public spaces.

Hearing A session in which testimony and arguments are presented, especially before an official.

Highest and best use A principle of value that focuses on the most profitable legal use to which a property can be put.

Hip Pitched roof with sloping sides and ends.

Home equity loan A mortgage secured by a personal residence. It provides a line of credit available for draws when needed by the homeowner. It is sometimes used as a home improvement loan.

Homestead Term used to describe three separate but related situations: (1) a tax exemption, (2) a tract of land limited in size, and (3) a statutory condition designed to protect the interests of a spouse and lineal descendants.

Household One individual, or a group of individuals, living in one dwelling unit.

Hypothecation To pledge real or personal property as security for a debt or obligation without giving up possession of the property.

Immune Real property that is owned by a unit of government and is not subject to taxation.

Implied Expressed indirectly (e.g., an implied contract).

Implied contract An agreement wherein the terms are not stated but are inferred from the conduct of the parties.

Implied listing An employment contract that arises from the conduct of the broker and seller and may be enforceable even though not clearly spelled out in words.

Improvement Addition that increases the value of real property (not repairs).

Income Amount earned or gained, not return of capital.

Income capitalization approach A method for estimating the market value of a property based on the present and future income the property can be expected to generate.

Income statement A summary of all income and expenses of a business for a stated period of time.

Incurable When the cost to correct a defect is greater than the value added by the cure.

Ineffective Status of a license when it is inactive or has been suspended.

Industrial Properties that include (1) sites in industrial parks or subdivisions, (2) redeveloped industrial parcels in central areas, and (3) industrial acreage.

Informal hearing A respondent who does not dispute allegations of material fact in the administrative complaint may request an informal hearing before the FREC for final action on the complaint.

Injunction A writ or order by a court forbidding a party from doing something.

In-migration Movement into a community or region by new residents.

Instrument Any legal or formal writing, such as a will, option, lease, contract, or deed.

Insurance (*See* Hazard insurance.)

Insurance clause A provision in a mortgage that requires the mortgagor to obtain and keep current a hazard insurance policy.

Intangible asset Something of value lacking physical substance; existing only in connection with something else (e.g., the goodwill of a business).

Intangible tax on mortgages, state Tax required prior to a mortgage being recorded. The cost is based on the face value of the mortgage.

Intensity The concentration of activity (pedestrian and vehicular traffic) used as a means of designating land for commercial zones.

Interest The price paid for the use of borrowed money; estate.

Interest rate The percentage charged for the use of borrowed money.

Interior lot A lot that is bounded on either side by another lot (lots in the middle of the block—not on the corner).

Intermediation The process whereby financial middlemen consolidate many small savings accounts belonging to individual depositors and invest those funds in large, diversified projects.

Intermingle (*See* Commingle.)

Interpleader A course of action when two contesting parties cannot reach an arbitrated agreement; A legal proceeding whereby the broker, having no financial interest in the disputed funds, deposits with the court the disputed escrow deposit so that the court can determine who is the rightful claimant.

Interval ownership Fee simple possession, for the limited time purchased (one or more weeks), of a time-share unit, complete with deed, title, and equity.

Intestate Without a will.

Investment The outlay of money in anticipation of income or profit; the sum risked or the property purchased.

Investment contract A type of security using the sale of real property as the investment.

Investment value The worth of a property to a particular investor based on his or her desired rate of return, risk tolerance, etc.

Involuntary inactive The license status that results when a license is not renewed at the end of the license period.

Involuntary liens Claims imposed against real property without the consent of the owner (e.g., taxes, special assessments).

Joint tenancy An estate or interest owned by more than one person, each having equal rights to possession and enjoyment; the interest a deceased tenant conveys to surviving tenants by specific wording in the deed establishing the joint tenancy.

Joint venture (joint adventure) Two or more parties in an arrangement confined to only one or a limited number of business deals.

Judgment Decree of a court that not only declares that one party owes another party a debt but also fixes the debt amount.

Judicial review The power of a court to reexamine statutes or administrative acts and to determine their validity; a rehearing or appeal to a higher court.

Just value The fair market value.

Key lot A long skinny lot similar to the shaft of a key that is often bounded by as many as five or six lots (the term also refers to a lot that has added value because of its strategic location).

Kickback Payment of money from someone other than the buyer or seller associated with real estate business.

Laissez-faire Allow to act; noninterference by government in trade, industry, and individual action generally.

Land The surface of the earth and everything attached to it by nature.

Land contract (*See* Contract for deed.)

Land description (legal description) A definite and positive written identification of a specific parcel of land and its location without additional oral testimony.

Lay member One not belonging to or connected with a particular profession.

Lease An estate for years; an agreement that does not convey ownership but does convey possession and use for a period of time and for compensation.

Leasehold estate A tenancy in real property held under a lease arrangement for a definite number of years; nonfreehold.

Legal description A series of boundary lines on the earth's surface.

Legally sufficient A complaint that contains facts indicating that a violation has occurred of a Florida statute, a DBPR rule, or a FREC rule.

Lender's policy Title insurance issued for the unpaid mortgage amount to protect the lender against title defects.

Lessee A tenant or leaseholder; party given a lease.

Lessor The landlord or owner; party granting a lease.

Level-payment plan A method for amortizing a mortgage whereby the borrower pays the same amount each month.

Leverage The use of borrowed funds to finance the purchase of an asset; the use of another's money to make more money.

Liabilities Debts; financial obligations; drawbacks.

License A privilege granted by the state to operate as a real estate broker, broker associate, or sales associate; a type of time-share interest.

Licensee An individual who has qualified for, and been registered as, a real estate broker, broker associate, or sales associate.

Licensure Certification as a licensee; the granting by the state of a license to practice real estate.

Lien A claim on property for payment of some obligation or debt.

Lienee One whose property is subject to a claim or charge by another.

Lienor One who has a claim or charge on the property of another.

Lien theory Legal concept that regards a mortgage as a just claim on specific property pledged as security for a mortgage debt.

Life estates Tenancies whose durations are limited to the life of some person; freehold.

Limited liability company (LLC) An alternative, hybrid business entity with the combined characteristics and benefits of both limited partnerships and S corporations.

Limited liability partnership A business entity that features protection from personal liability but with fewer legal restrictions compared with other business entities.

Limited partnership A business entity consisting of one or more general partners and one or more limited partners.

Lineal Descended in a direct family line; relating to or derived from ancestors.

Liquidated damages The amount of valuable consideration specified in an agreement as a penalty for default. (*See also* Damages.)

Liquidation The process of determining liabilities and apportioning the assets in order to discharge the indebtedness of a business to be sold.

Liquidity The ability to convert noncash assets into cash quickly; refers to a firm's cash position and its ability to meet obligations.

Lis pendens A pending legal action.

Listing Oral or written employment agreement between a broker (or a sales associate employed by a broker) and the property owner; authorization to sell, rent, or exchange.

Litigation A lawsuit; the act of carrying on a lawsuit; a case before a court of law.

Littoral rights Legal rights related to land abutting an ocean, sea, or lake, usually extending to the high-water mark.

Loan correspondent Generally, a mortgage banker or company that provides services for lending institutions.

Loan-to-value (LTV) ratio Relationship between amount borrowed and appraised value (or sale price) of a property.

Lot and block A type of legal description of land.

Maintenance clause A provision in a mortgage agreement that requires mortgagors (borrowers) to maintain mortgaged property in good condition.

Majority A person having attained 18 years of age, or having married, or by court order; no longer a minor; a number greater than half the total.

Malfeasance The committing of an unlawful act, especially by a public official.

Mandamus, writ of An order of a superior court directing a lower court or body to do some specified act.

Mandate Directive from a higher authority to a lower body.

Marital assets Real and personal property acquired during marriage.

Marketable title (merchantable title) Rights to real property that are so clear that a buyer may have peaceful and quiet enjoyment of the property free of litigation.

Market value The most probable price a property will bring from a fully informed buyer, willing but not compelled to buy, and the lowest price a fully informed seller will accept if not compelled to sell.

Master in chancery An appointed assistant to a court.

Mechanic's lien (*See* Construction lien.)

Mediation The act of having a third party attempt to reconcile a dispute between two parties.

Meeting of the minds The point when two people, thinking of the same thing, reach an agreement through an offer and acceptance.

Meridian Any of the imaginary lines of longitude on the earth's surface; in land description, the vertical lines running in a north-south direction parallel to the principal (prime) meridian and separating the various ranges.

Metes-and-bounds description A method of legal description that identifies a property by specifying the shape and boundary dimensions of the parcel. A metes-and-bounds description starts at the point of beginning and follows the boundaries of the land by compass direction and linear measurements and returns to the point of beginning.

Middleman An intermediary who merely brings two parties together.

Mill A unit of money used to specify a property tax rate ($1 for each $1,000 of taxable value).

Millage A tax rate, expressed as the number of mills to be applied.

Misdemeanor Any crime punishable by fine or imprisonment other than in a penitentiary.

Misfeasance A lawful act done in a negligent or unlawful manner.

Misrepresentation A false or misleading statement of a material fact; concealment of a material fact.

Monetary policy The actions undertaken by the Fed to influence the availability and cost of money and credit.

Monument Man-made or natural object used to establish boundaries of land.

Moral turpitude An act of corruption, vileness, or moral depravity; a disgraceful action or deed.

Mortgage A written agreement that pledges property as security for payment of a debt.

Mortgage banker An individual (or company) who makes loans with the expectation of reselling them to institutional lenders. (*See also* Mortgage company.)

Mortgage broker One who finds a lender for a potential borrower, and vice versa.

Mortgage company A mortgage loan company that originates, services, and sells loans to investors.

Mortgagee A lender who holds a mortgage on specific property as security for the money loaned to the borrower.

Mortgage insurance premium (MIP) Fee paid by FHA borrowers to obtain a loan (up-front and annual).

Mortgagor A borrower who gives a mortgage on his or her property in order to obtain a loan from a lender.

Multiple licenses Licenses held by a broker in two or more real estate brokerage firms.

Multiple-listing service (MLS) An arrangement among members of a real estate board or exchange that allows each member broker to share listings with other members so that greater exposure is obtained and a greater chance of sale will result.

Negative amortization A financing arrangement whereby monthly mortgage payments are less than required to pay both interest and principal. The unpaid amount is added to the loan balance.

Net income Profit from property or business after expenses have been deducted; effective gross income less operating expenses.

Net lease An agreement for the tenant to pay fixed rent plus property costs such as taxes, insurance, and utilities.

Net listing An agreement or contract to sell or rent a property for a specified minimum net amount for the owner.

Net operating income (NOI) The resulting amount when all operating expenses are subtracted from effective gross income.

Nolo contendere A pleading of no contest by a defendant; a plea in a criminal action not admitting guilt but subjecting the defendant to punishment as if it were a guilty plea.

Nonconforming use Continuing land use that is not in compliance with zoning ordinances.

Nonfreehold estate (leasehold interest) An estate in real property in which ownership is for a determinable time period, as in a lease.

Note Legal evidence of a debt that must accompany a mortgage in Florida; a legally executed pledge to pay a stipulated sum of money. (*See also* Promissory note.)

Notice (*See* Actual notice and Constructive notice.)

Notice of noncompliance Issued by the DBPR in the case of a minor rule violation that does not endanger the public health, safety, and welfare.

Novation The substitution of a new party and/or new terms to an existing obligation.

Obligee A lender or mortgagee.

Obligor A borrower or mortgagor.

Obsolescence A cause of loss in value. (*See also* Depreciation.)

Offer An intentional proposal or promise made by one party to act or perform, provided the other party acts or performs in the manner requested.

Offeree One who receives an offer, usually the seller.

Offeror One who makes an offer, usually the buyer.

Office of Thrift Supervision (OTS) A branch of the U.S. Treasury Department that replaced the Federal Home Loan Bank Board as regulator of the thrift industry.

Open-end clause A provision in a mortgage allowing the borrower to increase the loan amount as long as the total debt does not exceed the original mortgage loan amount, with the lender often reserving the right to adjust the interest rate to current market rates; a mortgage for future advances.

Open listing An employment contract given to any number of brokers who work simultaneously to sell the owner's property.

Open market operations Purchase and sale of U.S. Treasury and federal agency securities.

Opinion of title A formal statement by an attorney regarding the status of a title after examination of the chain of title.

Opinion of value An estimate of a property's worth given by a licensee for the purpose of a prospective sale.

Option contract A right or privilege to purchase or lease real property at a specified price during a designated period based on a sufficient consideration.

Optionee The party who takes an option and pays a consideration.

Optionor The party who gives an option and receives a consideration.

Origination fee, loan A charge by a lender for taking a mortgage in exchange for a loan.

Ostensible partnership One or more parties cause a third party to be deceived into believing that a business relationship exists when no such arrangement exists.

Overage (secret profit; secret commission) Retaining more than the agreed amount of sales commission, without the express knowledge and consent of the parties involved; a form of fraud.

Overall capitalization rate (OAR) The relationship between annual net operating income and the value or sale price of a property.

Overimprovement An addition or change to property not in line with its highest and best use, or a betterment that exceeds that justified by local conditions.

Owner-developer An unlicensed entity that sells, exchanges, or leases its own property.

Owner's policy Title insurance issued for the total purchase price of the property to protect the new owner against unexpected risks.

Package mortgage A loan covering both real and personal property.

Parol contract An agreement that is not in writing.

Partially exempt Property subject to taxation, but the owner is partially relieved of the burden.

Partial release clause Stipulates the conditions under which the mortgagee will grant freeing building lots from a mortgage lien upon payment of a certain amount of money.

Partnership Two or more competent individuals each of whom agrees to share in the profits and losses of the business.

Pass-through securities Certificates pledging a group (pool) of existing government-backed mortgages used for the purpose of channeling funds into housing markets.

Patent The instrument that conveys real property from the state or federal government to an individual.

Penalty clause A provision in a mortgage that requires the borrower to pay a penalty in money if the mortgage payments are made in advance of the normal due date or if the mortgage is paid in full ahead of schedule.

Percentage lease An agreement for the tenant to pay rent based on the gross sales received by doing business on the leased property.

Per diem By the day; per day; an allowance for daily expenses.

Performance Point when a party or parties to a contract fulfill the promises or obligations in the contract.

Personal property Tangible and movable property (transferred by bill of sale); property not classified as real property. Also known as personalty or chattel.

Personal representative Administrator of a deceased person's estate.

Personalty (*See* Personal property.)

Petition for review A request to a court of appeal (appellate court) asking it to examine the record of the proceedings in a specific case. (*See also* Judicial review.)

Pier A type of building foundation that uses columns of masonry to support the structure.

Pitch The slope of a roof.

Plaintiff The person or party bringing suit or charges; the complaining party; complainant.

Planned unit development (PUD) A residential project with mixed land uses and high residential density.

Planning Devising ways and means for achieving desired goals.

Planning commission (board) An official agency, usually made up of appointed lay citizens, that directs and controls the use, design, and development of land in a city, county, or region.

Plat (plat map) (*See* Subdivision plat map.)

Plottage The added value as a result of combining two or more properties into one large parcel.

Point, mortgage discount A charge of 1 percent of the mortgage value; assessment by a lender to increase the interest yield to compete with the interest yield from other types of investments. (*See also* Discount points.)

Point of beginning (POB) The starting (and ending) place in a land survey using the metes-and-bounds method of property description.

Point of contact information Any means by which to contact the brokerage firm or individual licensee including mailing address(es), physical street address(es), e-mail address(es), telephone number(s), or facsimile telephone number(s).

Police power The authority of government to protect the property, life, health, and welfare of its citizens.

Policy manual The notebook of written rules and regulations that set desired standards and procedures in an office.

Potential gross income (PGI) The total annual income a property would produce with 100 percent occupancy and no collection or vacancy losses.

Power of attorney (*See* Attorney, power of.)

Premises section (*See* Granting clause.)

Prepayment clause A provision in a mortgage that allows the mortgagor to pay the mortgage debt ahead of schedule without penalty.

Prepayment penalty The amount set by the creditor that the debtor is charged for retiring the debt early.

Prescription, easement by A method of acquiring an interest in real property through long and continued use.

Present value The worth of all future benefits of an investment in terms of today's dollars.

Price The amount paid for something.

Prima facie evidence Requiring no further proof; acceptable on the face of.

Primary lender Financial institution that makes mortgage loans directly to borrowers (e.g., savings association, bank).

Primary market A source for the purchase of a mortgage loan by a borrower.

Principal The party employing the services of a real estate broker; amount of money borrowed in a mortgage loan, excluding interest and other charges.

Principal meridians Imaginary lines running north and south and crossing a base line at a definite point; used by surveyors for reference in locating and describing land under the government survey system.

Private mortgage insurance (PMI) Needed to insure all of the mortgage representing more than 80 percent of appraised value or purchase price.

Probable cause Reasonable grounds or justification for prosecuting.

Probation A suspended sentence during good behavior, usually under supervision.

Procuring cause The person whose efforts are the cause of an executed sale contract, regardless of who actually writes the contract.

Professional Association (PA) A business corporation consisting of one or more individuals engaged in a primary business that provides a professional service (e.g., lawyer, doctor).

Profit The amount one makes over and above one's cost.

Pro forma statement An estimate of the economic results of a proposed project; a projected income statement.

Progression The principle that states that the value of an inferior property is enhanced by its association with superior properties of the same type.

Promissory note A written promise to pay a specific amount. (*See also* Note.)

Promulgate The formal act of announcing a statute or an administrative rule. To publish and officially announce a new or amended rule or statute. The FREC may promulate rules and regulations.

Property A bundle of legal rights.

Property insurance (*See* Hazard insurance.)

Property management The leasing, managing, marketing, and overall maintenance of property for others.

Proprietary lease A written agreement between the owner-corporation and the tenant-stockholder in a cooperative apartment.

Prorate To divide or assess proportionate shares of charges and credits between the buyer and the seller according to their individual period of ownership.

Puffing Comments or opinions not made as representations of fact and thus not grounds for misrepresentation.

Purchase-money mortgage (PMM) Any new mortgage taken as part of the purchase price of real property by the seller.

Quadrant Quarter; any of the four quarters into which something is divided.

Qualification The process of reviewing prior to approval (of a buyer's housing needs and financial abilities, of a borrower's mortgage loan application, or of an application for licensure). (*See also* Underwriting.)

Quasi As if; of a similar nature; seemingly.

Quasi-legislative Powers delegated to the FREC to enact rules and regulations, decide questions of practice, and validate records (imprint with FREC's seal).

Quasi-judicial Powers delegated to the FREC to discipline real estate licensees for violations of real estate license law and FREC administrative rules.

Quasi partnership (*See* Ostensible partnership.)

Quiet enjoyment A provision in a deed guaranteeing that the buyer may enjoy possession of the property in peace and without disturbance by reason of other claims on the title by the seller or anyone else.

Quiet title A suit or action in a court to remove a defect, cloud, or claim against the title to real property.

Quitclaim deed A type of deed that will effectively convey any present interest, claim, or title to real property that the seller (grantor) may own.

Quorum The minimum number of persons who may lawfully transact the business of a meeting (51 percent or four of the members of the Florida Real Estate Commission).

Range In the government survey system of land description, a vertical strip of land six miles wide located between two consecutive submeridians or range lines.

Range lines (submeridians) The surveyed north-south lines running every six miles east and west of the principal meridian.

Ratio The relationship in quantity, size, or amount between two things; proportion.

Ready, willing, and able "Ready" indicates the buyer is in a position and of a mind to complete the transaction; "willing" implies that the buyer desires to do so at the price and terms agreed; "able" refers to the buyer's financial ability to produce the required money when necessary.

Real estate Land, including the air above and the earth below, plus any permanent improvements affecting the utility of the land; real property; property that is not personal property.

Real estate business A commercial activity in which the sale, purchase, leasing, rental, exchange, or management of real property is conducted by qualified and licensed parties acting either for themselves or for others for compensation.

Real estate profession A profession requiring knowledge of real estate values, experience in dealing with the public, plus exceptional personal integrity and character as qualifications to act as advisors and agents for members of the public.

Real estate services Real estate activities involving compensation for performing the activities for another.

Real property Any interest or estate in land, including leaseholds, subleaseholds, business opportunities and enterprises, and mineral rights; real estate.

REALTOR® A real estate broker who is a member of a local board of REALTORS® and is affiliated with the state association (Florida Association of REALTORS®) and the National Association of REALTORS® (not synonymous with "real estate agent").

Realty A synonym for real estate and real property.

Reasonable time A variable period of time, which may be affected by market conditions, desires of the owner, supply and demand, fluctuations of values, or an official decision.

Receiver An independent party appointed by a court to impartially preserve and manage property that is involved in litigation, pending final disposition of the matter before the court.

Receivership clause A provision in a mortgage, related to income-producing property, that is designed to require that income derived shall be used to make mortgage payments in the event the mortgagor (borrower) defaults.

Recommended order A determination by an administrative law judge that includes findings and conclusions as well as other information required by law or agency rule to be in a final order.

Reconciliation The process of weighting the estimates of value derived from the sales comparison, cost, and income approaches to arrive at a final estimate of market value.

Record To place any document or instrument affecting title or an interest in real property in the public records of the county in which the property is located.

Recovery fund (Real Estate Recovery Fund) A state-regulated account to cover claims of aggrieved parties who have suffered monetary losses from licensee's actions.

Recovery period The assigned time over which property is depreciated for tax purposes.

Rectangular method (*See* Government survey system.)

Redemption To repurchase, to buy back, to recover property used as security for a mortgage by paying the debt. (*See also* Equity of redemption.)

Redlining Discriminatory financing by a lending institution.

Registration Authorization by the state to place an applicant on the register (record) of officially recognized individuals and businesses.

Regression The principle that states that the value of a superior property is adversely affected by its association with an inferior property of the same type.

REIT A method of pooling investment money using the trust form of ownership.

Release clause A provision in a blanket mortgage covering more than one unit of real property that provides for the mortgagor to obtain freedom from the mortgage for each unit when a designated amount has been paid to the mortgagee for each unit.

Reliction Gradual receding of water and resulting permanent increase in land once covered.

Remainderman The party designated to receive an estate at the end of a life estate.

Renunciation To abandon an acquired right without transferring that right to another.

Replacement cost The expenditure of constructing a building with current materials and techniques that has the same functional utility as the structure being appraised.

Replacement reserves (reserve for replacements) A portion of the annual income set aside for covering the cost of major components (e.g., air-conditioning) that wear out faster than the building itself.

Reprimand An official act of oral and/or written criticism with a formal warning included.

Reproduction cost Amount required to duplicate the property exactly.

Rescind To annul, cancel, repeal, or terminate.

Reserve for replacements (*See* Replacement reserves.)

Reserve requirements The amount of funds that an institution must hold in reserve against deposit liabilities.

Residential sale The sale of improved residential property of four or fewer units, the sale of unimproved residential property intended for use as four or fewer units, or the sale of agricultural property of ten or fewer acres.

Respondent A person who answers to an informal complaint proceeding prior to being adjudged innocent or being named as a defendant.

Restriction Any device or action that controls or limits the use of real property.

Restrictive covenants Conditions placed by developers that affect how the land can be used in an entire subdivision.

Reversion That portion of the net proceeds from the sale of property that represents the return of the investor's capital.

Revocation To cancel, rescind, annul, or make void; the permanent cancellation of a person's license.

Right of survivorship A situation by which the remaining joint tenant succeeds to all right, title, and interest of the deceased joint tenant without the need for probate proceedings.

Right-to-use A leasehold interest in a time-share unit based on the limited time (one or more weeks) specified in the agreement.

Riparian rights Private ownership rights extending to the normal high-water mark along a river or stream and including access rights to water, boating, bathing, and dockage in accordance with state and federal statutes.

Risk The chance of loss of all or a part of an investment; the uncertainty of financial loss.

Rural Housing Services Administration An agency of the Department of Agriculture that offers assistance to rural residents and communities.

R-value A special rating or method of judging the insulating effectiveness of insulation products.

Sale and leaseback A financing arrangement in which an investor buys property owned and used by a business accompanied by a simultaneous leasing back of the property to the business by the buyer-investor.

Sale contract (deposit receipt contract; purchase agreement; contract for sale and purchase) An agreement whereby one party agrees to sell and the other party agrees to buy according to the terms set forth.

Sales associate A licensed individual who, for compensation, is employed by a broker or owner-developer.

Sales comparison approach A method for estimating the market value of a property by comparing similar properties to the subject property.

Satisfaction of mortgage A certificate issued by the lender when the debt obligation is paid in full.

Savings Association Insurance Fund (SAIF) A federal agency that insures deposits of member savings associations.

Seal A mark, emblem, or impression on a document used to authenticate the document or a signature.

Secondary lender Agency or financial institution that buys mortgage loans previously made by primary lenders.

Secondary market A source for the purchase and sale of existing mortgages.

Second mortgage (secondary financing) A loan that is junior or subordinate to a first mortgage, normally taken out when the borrower needs more money.

Secret profit or commission (*See* Overage.)

Section One of the primary units of measurement in the government survey system of land description. A section is one mile square and contains 640 acres.

Security Evidence of a debt or of ownership.

Seisin (seizin) A covenant in a deed that warrants that the grantor (seller) holds the property by virtue of a fee simple title and has a complete right to dispose of same. Also known as seizin clause.

Seller's market The demand for available properties exceeds the supply.

Separate property Real property owned by a husband or wife prior to the marriage with the spouse having no present rights in such property; property owned individually.

Service industries Businesses that attract local money (e.g., grocery stores, retail shops).

Servicing disclosure statement A disclosure statement given to borrowers that discloses whether the lender intends to service the loan or transfer it to another lender or servicing company.

Setback Restrictions established by zoning or deed on the space required between lot lines and building lines.

Severalty Sole ownership of real property ("severed" from all others).

Severance The act of removing something attached to the land (e.g., fruit, timber, fence).

Single agent Per Section 475.01, F.S., a broker who represents, as a fiduciary, either the buyer or seller but not both in the same transaction.

Single-hung A window characterized by a movable lower sash.

Site plan A document that indicates the improvement details for a project of greater-than-average size.

Situs Relationships and influences created by location of a property that affect value (e.g., accessibility, personal preference).

Slab-on-grade Concrete foundation poured directly on the ground.

Sole proprietorship Dealing as an individual in business.

Special agent One authorized by a principal to perform a particular act or transaction, without contemplation of continuity of service as with a general agent.

Special assessments Taxes levied against properties to pay for all, or part of, improvements that will benefit the properties being assessed.

Special exception An individual ruling in which a property owner is granted the right to a use otherwise contrary to law.

Special information booklet A booklet containing consumer information regarding closing costs the borrower may incure at closing. The Real Estate Settlement Procedures Act requires lenders to give the booklet to loan applicants.

Specific liens Claims that affect only the property designated in the lien instruments or agreements.

Specific performance A remedy for an injured party obtained through a court of equity, which requires specific accomplishment of the contract terms by a defendant.

State-certified appraiser A person verified by the DBPR as qualified to issue state-certified real property appraisals.

Static risk Risk that can be transferred to an insurer such as the risk of vandalism, fire, and so forth.

Statute An established rule or law passed by a legislative body.

Statute of frauds An act that requires that certain real estate instruments and contracts affecting title to real property be in writing in order to be enforceable.

Statute of limitations An act that prescribes specific time restrictions for enforcement of rights by action of law.

Stay Delay temporarily; stop for a limited time.

Steering Discriminatory acts against buyers.

Stock The ownership element in a corporation usually divided into shares and represented by transferable certificates (may be divided into two or more classes of differing rights and stated values).

Subbaselines (*See* Township lines.)

Subdivide To segment large, acquired tracts of real property in order to create small tracts for the purpose of resale.

Subdivision plat map A plan of a tract of land subdivided into lots and showing required or planned amenities.

Subject property The real property under discussion or appraisal.

Subject to the mortgage A buyer makes regular periodic payments on the mortgage but does not assume responsibility for the mortgage.

Sublease A lessee leasing a property to a third party for a period of time less than the original lease (also referred to as *subletting*).

Submeridians (*See* Range lines.)

Subordination Made subject to or subservient to; assignment to a lesser role or position.

Subordination clause A provision in a mortgage in which the lender voluntarily permits a prior or subsequent mortgage to take priority over the lender's otherwise superior mortgage; the act of yielding priority.

Subpoena A writ or order commanding the person named to appear and testify in a legal proceeding.

Subrogation (*See* Subordination.)

Substitution, principle of An economic law of value: no prudent buyer will pay more for a property than the cost of an equally desirable replacement property.

Suit An act of suing; an action in a court of law for the recovery of a right or claim.

Summary suspension Emergency or immediate action against a license to protect the public.

Supersedeas, writ of A stay of enforcement; temporary stop in a legal proceeding; restraining order.

Supply The quantity of goods or services offered for sale to consumers.

Survey The procedure used to measure and describe a specific tract of real property for the purpose of determining exact boundaries and the area contained therein.

Survivorship, right of A legal concept whereby the surviving owners of a joint interest in real property are entitled to the interest formerly owned by one or more deceased owners.

Suspension To cause to cease operating for a period of time; the temporary withholding of a person's license rendering it ineffective; a period of enforced inactivity.

Syndicate (*See* Business trust.)

Tangible asset Anything of substance; personal and real property (e.g., cash, building, equipment, land).

Tax Compulsory payment paid by a citizen to a unit of government.

Taxable income Gross income minus tax deductions; net operating income plus reserve for replacements minus financing costs and allowable depreciation.

Taxable value The assessed value less allowable exemptions resulting in an amount to which the tax rate is applied to determine property taxes due.

Tax certificate A document sold by a local tax authority granting the certificate buyer the right to receive delinquent taxes plus interest when paid by the legal property owner.

Tax clause A provision in a mortgage that requires the borrower to pay all legitimate property taxes.

Tax deed A type of deed used to convey title after real property is sold at auction by public authority for nonpayment of taxes.

Tax district An authority, such as a city, county, school board, or special levy area (e.g., water district), with the power to assess property owners annually in order to meet its expenditures for the public good.

Tax lien A claim against real property arising out of nonpayment of the property taxes.

Tax rate The percentage of value that is used to determine the amount of tax to be levied against each individual unit of property; ad valorem (according to the value).

Tax shelter An investment that shields items of income or gain from payment of income taxes; a term used to describe some tax advantages of owning real property (or other investments), including postponement or even elimination of certain taxes.

Telephone solicitation The initiation of a telephone call for the purpose of encouraging the purchase of, or investment in, property, goods, or services.

Tenancy The estate or rights of a tenant. (*See also* Estate.)

Tenancy at sufferance An estate lawfully acquired for a temporary period of time but retained after a period of lawful possession has expired; nonfreehold estate.

Tenancy at will An estate that may be terminated by either party at any time upon proper notice; nonfreehold estate.

Tenancy by the entireties An estate created by husband and wife jointly owning real property with instant and complete right of survivorship.

Tenancy in common A form of ownership by two or more persons each having an equal or unequal interest and passing the interest to heirs, not to surviving tenants.

Tenant A person or party with rights of occupancy or possession of real property.

Term mortgage A nonamortizing loan that normally calls for repayment of the principal in full at the end of the loan term.

Testate Having left a will.

Testator (testatrix) A person who makes a will.

Third party Generally, a member of the public; not the principal or agent in a transaction.

Tier An east-west row of townships (as used in the government survey method of land description).

Time is of the essence A phrase in a contract making failure to perform by a specified date a breach or violation of the agreement.

Time-share An individual interest in a real property unit together with a right of exclusive use for a specified number of days or weeks per year.

T-intersection lot An interior lot that suffers from its location at the end of a T-intersection (a street ends in front of the lot).

Title The group of rights that represent ownership of real property and the quality of the estate owned; evidence of ownership of property; legal title.

Title insurance A policy of insurance that protects the holder from any loss resulting from defects in the title.

Title plant Copies of recorded documents from the public records kept by title insurance companies; record room.

Title search An examination of all of the public records to determine whether any defects exist in the chain of title.

Title theory Legal concept that vests title to mortgaged property in the mortgagee (lender) or a third party.

Topography Surface features (natural and manufactured) of land (e.g., lakes, mountains, roads).

Township A square tract of land measuring six miles on each side and including 36 sections (formed by the crossing of range and township lines).

Township lines (subbaselines) The east-west survey lines located every six miles north and south of the primary base line.

Trade fixture An article that is attached by a commercial tenant as a necessary part of the tenant's business and is personal property.

Trade name Any adopted or fictitious name used to designate a business concern.

Transaction broker A broker who provides limited representation to a buyer, a seller, or both in a real estate transaction, but does not represent either in a fiduciary capacity or as a single agent.

Triggering terms The Truth-in-Lending Act requires creditors to disclose certain information if certain credit terms, called triggering terms, are included in the advertisement. Triggering terms include the amount or percentage of down payment, number of payments, period (term) of repayment, amount of any payment, and the amount of any finance charges.

Trust A right of property, either real or personal, held by one party for the benefit of another.

Trust account (*See* Escrow account.)

Trustee (escrow agent) A person or party, either appointed or required by law to administer or manage another's property.

Underwriting (loan qualification; risk analysis) The analysis of the extent of risk assumed by a lender in connection with a proposed mortgage loan.

Undivided interest An interest in the entire property, rather than ownership of a particular part of the property.

Unenforceable A contract that was valid when made but either cannot be proved or will not be upheld by a court.

Unilateral contract An agreement in which only one party promises to perform without receiving a reciprocal promise to perform from the other party.

Unincorporated association A group of people associated together for some common, noncommercial purpose.

Unities (four unities) Individual prerequisites required to constitute a single joint tenancy.

Universal agent A representative authorized by the principal to perform all acts that the principal can personally perform and that may be lawfully delegated to another.

Unliquidated damages The amount of valuable consideration awarded by a court to an injured party as a result of default. (*See also* Damages.)

Usury Charging a rate of interest greater than the legal one; unlawful interest.

Vacancy and collection losses A deduction from potential gross income for (1) current or expected future space not rented due to tenant turnover and (2) loss from uncollected rent due from delinquent tenants.

Vacancy rate The percentage of rental units that are not occupied.

Vacate To set aside, cancel, or annul; to leave empty.

Valid Sufficient to be legally binding; enforceable.

Valid contract An agreement binding on both parties and legally enforceable against all parties to the agreement.

Valuable consideration The money or a promise of something that can be measured in terms of money.

Value The worth of something.

Variable lease An agreement for the tenant to pay specified rent increases based on a predetermined index (CPI) at set future dates.

Variance An exception to zoning regulations or ordinances granted to relieve a hardship.

Vendee The buyer or purchaser of real property under an agreement of sale.

Vendor The seller of real property in an agreement of sale.

Vendor's lien A claim against property giving the seller the right to hold the property as security for any unpaid purchase money.

Veterans Affairs, Department of (VA) Guarantees mortgage loans to encourage private lending agencies to give liberal mortgages to veterans and their spouses.

Void Invalid; without force; no longer effective.

Voidable A contract that because of the manner or method in which it was brought about, one of the parties is allowed to avoid his or her contractual duties.

Voluntary inactive The license status that results when a licensee has met all of the requirements for licensure, yet the licensee chooses not to engage in the real estate business, and has requested his or her license be placed in this status.

Voluntary liens Claims imposed against real property with the consent of the owner.

Warrant A guarantee or covenant, as in a warranty deed.

Warranty deed (*See* General warranty deed.)

Warranty forever A provision in a deed guaranteeing that the seller will for all time defend the title and possession for the buyer.

Waste An improper use or abuse of property by one who holds less than the fee simple ownership of it.

Will A written document legally executed by which an individual disposes of his or her estate, effective after death.

Witness A person who gives testimony; one who observes and attests to the signing or executing of a document.

Wraparound mortgage A financing technique in which the payment of the existing mortgage is continued (by the seller) and a new, higher interest rate mortgage, which is larger than the existing mortgage, is paid by the buyer-borrower.

Writ A court order directing a party to do a specific act, usually to appear in, or report to, a court of law.

Writ of certiorari (*See* Certiorari, writ of.)

Writ of mandamus (*See* Mandamus, writ of.)

Writ of supersedeas (*See* Supersedeas, writ of.)

Yield The rate of return; the return on an investment or the amount of profit stated as a percentage of the amount invested; the ratio of the annual net income from a property to the cost or market value of the property.

Zoning ordinances Classification of real property for various purposes; the government power to control and supervise the utilization of privately owned real property (actually, the exercise of police powers).

Note Regarding Glossary of Terms: The authors have, out of necessity, had to limit the number of terms used and defined in this textbook (more than 600). Entire books exist with nothing but real estate terms and definitions. The authors recommend the latest edition of The Language of Real Estate, also published by Dearborn™ Real Estate Education, as an excellent reference to be used now and in your real estate future. More than 2,800 terms are carefully defined and explained.

Index

A

AARP, 267
A Bar Sale, 24
Absentee owners, 5
Abstract continuation, 307–8
Abstract of title, 172
Abstractor, 172
Acceleration clause, 253, 255
Acceptance, of offer, 216
Accessibility to public areas, 129
Accounting, 381–82
Accrued depreciation, 334
Acknowledgment, 171
Acronyms, 465
Active income, 403
Act of severance, 148
Actual notice, 170–71
Adjudication, 15
Adjustable-rate mortgage (ARM),
    265–67
Adjusted basis, 402
Adjustment grid, 329
Adjustment process, 329–30
Administrative complaint, 105
Administrative penalties, 110–11
Administrative Procedures Act, 14
Ad valorem tax, 390
Advance rents, 135
Adverse possession, 169–70
Advertising
    bait and switch, 130
    blind, 76
    by brokerage, 76–78, 95
    discriminatory statements prohib-
        ited, 127
    false advertising, 76
    by real estate schools, 42
    rental properties and, 85
    triggering terms in, 130
Affiliated business relationships (affili-
    ates), 131–33
Age 65 and older exemption, 395
Age-life method, 335–36
Agent, 48, 62
Aggravating circumstances, 113
Agreement for deed, 264
Agriculture
    agricultural specialization, 4
    agricultural zoning, 432
    Green Belt Law, 395–96
    real estate investment, 371
Air cooling, 361, 362
Air rights, 147
Alienation, 168
Allodial system, 146
Amendment 10, 396
American Association of Retired Persons
    (AARP), 267
American Land Title Association form,
    173

Americans with Disabilities Act of 1990,
    129
Amortized mortgage, 262, 300
Analyzing investment properties,
    372–76
    legal characteristics, 375–76
    location, 373
    physical characteristics, 373–75
    relationship to economy, 373
Annual percentage rate (APR), 130
Antitrust laws, 86–87
Appraisal(s), 6, 302
    of businesses, 382–83
    defined, 6
    graduate students in, 25
    regulation, 322
    report, 327
    terms, 345
Appraisal Foundation, 322
Appraiser Qualifications Board, 322
Arbitration, 82
Armed forces exemptions, 38
Arrears, 303
Assemblage, 345
Assessed value, 322, 391
Assessment fees, 157
Assessor's parcel number, 205
Asset, 378, 382
Asset depreciation, 381
Assignment, 218
    of lease, 182
    of mortgage, 249–50
Assignor/assignee, 218, 466
Assumption (of existing mortgage), 263
    FHA loans, 258
    mortgage interest and, 305
    VA loans, 260
Attachment, 148
Attest Statement (Form DBPR-0030), 16
Attorney(s), 25
    as escrow agent, 79, 81
Attorney-in-fact, 25, 219
Automated underwriting, 272
Awning windows, 363

B

Background studies (planning), 427–29
Bait and switch advertising, 130
Balance sheet analysis, 381
Balloon construction, 355
Balloon payment, 261
Bankruptcy, 60, 114, 115, 217
Banks
    commercial, 284–85
    mutual savings banks, 285
Bargain and sale deed, 176
Base industries, 428
Bilateral contract, 214, 223
Binder deposits, 78
Biweekly mortgage, 262
Blanket mortgages, 254

Blind advertising, 76
Blockbusting, 127
Board of Adjustment, 432
Boeckh Building Valuation Manual, 333
Bond, 248
Boot, 405
Borrower covenants and agreements,
    251–53
Branch offices, 74–75
Breach
    of contract, 217–18
    defined, 116
    of trust, 86, 88
Broker(s), 15
    brokerage office requirement, 74–76,
        95
    business brokers, 4
    death of, 60
    duties of, 2
    experience requirements, 22
    as expert, 85–86
    licensing requirements, 21–22
    personal interest in property, 54
    post-licensing education, 22–23, 36
    sales associate job change, 88–89
Brokerage fee, 221
Brokerage relationships, 47–61
    disclosure requirements, 56
    duties, 55
    in Florida, 49–60
    law of agency, 48–49
    no brokerage relationship, 55, 65, 66
    nonresidential transactions, 59, 66
    practical applications, 56–58
    record keeping, 60
    residential transactions, 50
    single agent, 52–55, 63
    terminating, 60
    transaction broker, 50–52, 63
    transition to another relationship,
        58–59, 67
Broker associate, 15
Broker's commission, 307
BTUs, 362
Budgeting, 381
Buffer zone, 431
Building assessment, 374–75
    exterior considerations, 374
    interior considerations, 374
    operating expenses, 375
Building codes, 178, 413, 430–31
    violation disclosure, 228
Building permit, 8, 431
Built-up roofs, 357
Bundle of rights, 146
Bureau of Labor Statistics, 324
Business appraisals, 382–83
Business brokerage, 378–82
Business brokers, 4

ANSWER SHEET
PRACTICE EXAM

Score: _____

Wrong Ways to mark answers:

RIGHT WAY to mark answers:

●

1 Ⓐ Ⓑ Ⓒ Ⓓ	21 Ⓐ Ⓑ Ⓒ Ⓓ	41 Ⓐ Ⓑ Ⓒ Ⓓ	61 Ⓐ Ⓑ Ⓒ Ⓓ	81 Ⓐ Ⓑ Ⓒ Ⓓ
2 Ⓐ Ⓑ Ⓒ Ⓓ	22 Ⓐ Ⓑ Ⓒ Ⓓ	42 Ⓐ Ⓑ Ⓒ Ⓓ	62 Ⓐ Ⓑ Ⓒ Ⓓ	82 Ⓐ Ⓑ Ⓒ Ⓓ
3 Ⓐ Ⓑ Ⓒ Ⓓ	23 Ⓐ Ⓑ Ⓒ Ⓓ	43 Ⓐ Ⓑ Ⓒ Ⓓ	63 Ⓐ Ⓑ Ⓒ Ⓓ	83 Ⓐ Ⓑ Ⓒ Ⓓ
4 Ⓐ Ⓑ Ⓒ Ⓓ	24 Ⓐ Ⓑ Ⓒ Ⓓ	44 Ⓐ Ⓑ Ⓒ Ⓓ	64 Ⓐ Ⓑ Ⓒ Ⓓ	84 Ⓐ Ⓑ Ⓒ Ⓓ
5 Ⓐ Ⓑ Ⓒ Ⓓ	25 Ⓐ Ⓑ Ⓒ Ⓓ	45 Ⓐ Ⓑ Ⓒ Ⓓ	65 Ⓐ Ⓑ Ⓒ Ⓓ	85 Ⓐ Ⓑ Ⓒ Ⓓ
6 Ⓐ Ⓑ Ⓒ Ⓓ	26 Ⓐ Ⓑ Ⓒ Ⓓ	46 Ⓐ Ⓑ Ⓒ Ⓓ	66 Ⓐ Ⓑ Ⓒ Ⓓ	86 Ⓐ Ⓑ Ⓒ Ⓓ
7 Ⓐ Ⓑ Ⓒ Ⓓ	27 Ⓐ Ⓑ Ⓒ Ⓓ	47 Ⓐ Ⓑ Ⓒ Ⓓ	67 Ⓐ Ⓑ Ⓒ Ⓓ	87 Ⓐ Ⓑ Ⓒ Ⓓ
8 Ⓐ Ⓑ Ⓒ Ⓓ	28 Ⓐ Ⓑ Ⓒ Ⓓ	48 Ⓐ Ⓑ Ⓒ Ⓓ	68 Ⓐ Ⓑ Ⓒ Ⓓ	88 Ⓐ Ⓑ Ⓒ Ⓓ
9 Ⓐ Ⓑ Ⓒ Ⓓ	29 Ⓐ Ⓑ Ⓒ Ⓓ	49 Ⓐ Ⓑ Ⓒ Ⓓ	69 Ⓐ Ⓑ Ⓒ Ⓓ	89 Ⓐ Ⓑ Ⓒ Ⓓ
10 Ⓐ Ⓑ Ⓒ Ⓓ	30 Ⓐ Ⓑ Ⓒ Ⓓ	50 Ⓐ Ⓑ Ⓒ Ⓓ	70 Ⓐ Ⓑ Ⓒ Ⓓ	90 Ⓐ Ⓑ Ⓒ Ⓓ
11 Ⓐ Ⓑ Ⓒ Ⓓ	31 Ⓐ Ⓑ Ⓒ Ⓓ	51 Ⓐ Ⓑ Ⓒ Ⓓ	71 Ⓐ Ⓑ Ⓒ Ⓓ	91 Ⓐ Ⓑ Ⓒ Ⓓ
12 Ⓐ Ⓑ Ⓒ Ⓓ	32 Ⓐ Ⓑ Ⓒ Ⓓ	52 Ⓐ Ⓑ Ⓒ Ⓓ	72 Ⓐ Ⓑ Ⓒ Ⓓ	92 Ⓐ Ⓑ Ⓒ Ⓓ
13 Ⓐ Ⓑ Ⓒ Ⓓ	33 Ⓐ Ⓑ Ⓒ Ⓓ	53 Ⓐ Ⓑ Ⓒ Ⓓ	73 Ⓐ Ⓑ Ⓒ Ⓓ	93 Ⓐ Ⓑ Ⓒ Ⓓ
14 Ⓐ Ⓑ Ⓒ Ⓓ	34 Ⓐ Ⓑ Ⓒ Ⓓ	54 Ⓐ Ⓑ Ⓒ Ⓓ	74 Ⓐ Ⓑ Ⓒ Ⓓ	94 Ⓐ Ⓑ Ⓒ Ⓓ
15 Ⓐ Ⓑ Ⓒ Ⓓ	35 Ⓐ Ⓑ Ⓒ Ⓓ	55 Ⓐ Ⓑ Ⓒ Ⓓ	75 Ⓐ Ⓑ Ⓒ Ⓓ	95 Ⓐ Ⓑ Ⓒ Ⓓ
16 Ⓐ Ⓑ Ⓒ Ⓓ	36 Ⓐ Ⓑ Ⓒ Ⓓ	56 Ⓐ Ⓑ Ⓒ Ⓓ	76 Ⓐ Ⓑ Ⓒ Ⓓ	96 Ⓐ Ⓑ Ⓒ Ⓓ
17 Ⓐ Ⓑ Ⓒ Ⓓ	37 Ⓐ Ⓑ Ⓒ Ⓓ	57 Ⓐ Ⓑ Ⓒ Ⓓ	77 Ⓐ Ⓑ Ⓒ Ⓓ	97 Ⓐ Ⓑ Ⓒ Ⓓ
18 Ⓐ Ⓑ Ⓒ Ⓓ	38 Ⓐ Ⓑ Ⓒ Ⓓ	58 Ⓐ Ⓑ Ⓒ Ⓓ	78 Ⓐ Ⓑ Ⓒ Ⓓ	98 Ⓐ Ⓑ Ⓒ Ⓓ
19 Ⓐ Ⓑ Ⓒ Ⓓ	39 Ⓐ Ⓑ Ⓒ Ⓓ	59 Ⓐ Ⓑ Ⓒ Ⓓ	79 Ⓐ Ⓑ Ⓒ Ⓓ	99 Ⓐ Ⓑ Ⓒ Ⓓ
20 Ⓐ Ⓑ Ⓒ Ⓓ	40 Ⓐ Ⓑ Ⓒ Ⓓ	60 Ⓐ Ⓑ Ⓒ Ⓓ	80 Ⓐ Ⓑ Ⓒ Ⓓ	100 Ⓐ Ⓑ Ⓒ Ⓓ

Please Help Us Help You!

_____
today's date

Mail or fax after you have received your State exam results

FEEDBACK SHEET

1. I took the real estate course at _____ .

2. I completed the course in _____ , _____ .
    month   year

3. My score on the 100-question Practice Exam in the book was _____ .

    My score on the Sales Associate's Course Examination was _____ .

    My score on the State Licensing Exam was _____ .

4. I found this book to be: ❑ excellent

                                ❑ really helpful

                                ❑ not so hot

5. My major suggestion for improving this book is:

6. I used the following to help me with the course and/or review:

    (check as many as apply)

	During the course	Preparing for course exam	Preparing for state exam
REAL ESTATE MATH	_____	_____	_____
KEY POINT REVIEW—AUDIO CDS	_____	_____	_____
FLORIDA REAL ESTATE EXAM MANUAL	_____	_____	_____

7. I plan to take the Post-Licensing Education course within _____ months of obtaining my sales associate's license. (We recommend *within six months*.)

8. Other comments:

**FLORIDA REAL ESTATE
PRINCIPLES, PRACTICES & LAW**
29th Edition

Fax#: (312) 577-2467

Thank you for completing and mailing or faxing this form.

NOTE: This page, when folded over and taped,
becomes a postage-free envelope that has been
approved by the United States Postal Service.
It has been provided for your convenience.

Important—Please Fold Over and Tape Before Mailing

Important—Please Fold Over and Tape Before Mailing

Return Address:

_____

_____

_____

BUSINESS REPLY MAIL

FIRST CLASS MAIL   PERMIT NO. 88176   CHICAGO, IL

POSTAGE WILL BE PAID BY ADDRESSEE:

Dearborn™
Real Estate Education
30 South Wacker Drive
Suite 2500
a division of Dearborn Financial Publishing, Inc.
Chicago, Illinois 60606-7481

Attn: Editorial Department